CHAPTER 10

Degrees of Freedom for an Independent-Samples t Test

$$df_{total} = df_X + df_Y$$

Pooled Variance

$$s^2_{pooled} = \left(\frac{df_X}{df_{total}}\right)s^2_X + \left(\frac{df_Y}{df_{total}}\right)s^2_Y$$

Variance for a Distribution of Means for an Independent-Samples t Test

$$s^2_{M_X} = \frac{s^2_{pooled}}{N_X} \qquad s^2_{M_Y} = \frac{s^2_{pooled}}{N_Y}$$

Variance for a Distribution of Differences Between Means

$$s^2_{difference} = s^2_{M_X} + s^2_{M_Y}$$

Standard Deviation of the Distribution of Differences Between Means

$$s_{difference} = \sqrt{s^2_{difference}}$$

t Statistic for an Independent-Samples t Test

$$t = \frac{(M_X - M_Y) - (\mu_X - \mu_Y)}{s_{difference}}$$

often abbreviated as:

$$t = \frac{(M_X - M_Y)}{s_{difference}}$$

Confidence Interval for an Independent-Samples t Test

$$(M_X - M_Y)_{lower} = -t\,(s_{difference}) + (M_X - M_Y)_{sample}$$

$$(M_X - M_Y)_{upper} = t\,(s_{difference}) + (M_X - M_Y)_{sample}$$

Effect Size for an Independent-Samples t Test

$$\text{Cohen's } d = \frac{(M_X - M_Y) - (\mu_X - \mu_Y)}{s_{pooled}}$$

for a t distribution for a difference between means

CHAPTER 11

One-Way Between-Groups ANOVA

$$df_{between} = N_{groups} - 1$$

$$df_{within} = df_1 + df_2 + \ldots + df_{last}$$

(in which df_1 etc. are the degrees of freedom, $N - 1$, for each sample)

$$df_{total} = df_{between} + df_{within}$$

$$\text{or } df_{total} = N_{total} - 1$$

$$GM = \frac{\Sigma(X)}{N_{total}}$$

$$SS_{total} = \Sigma(X - GM)^2 \text{ for each score}$$

$$SS_{within} = \Sigma(X - M)^2 \text{ for each score}$$

$$SS_{between} = \Sigma(M - GM)^2 \text{ for each score}$$

$$SS_{tota} = SS_{within} + SS_{between}$$

$$MS_{between} = \frac{SS_{between}}{df_{between}}$$

$$MS_{within} = \frac{SS_{within}}{df_{within}}$$

$$F = \frac{MS_{between}}{MS_{within}}$$

$$R^2 = \frac{SS_{between}}{SS_{total}}$$

Chapter 11 formulas continued on inside back cover

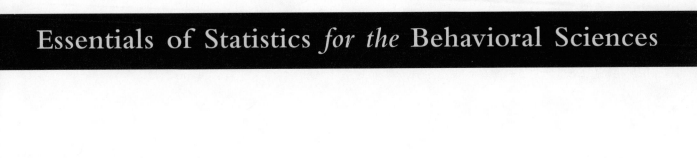

Essentials of Statistics *for the* Behavioral Sciences

Essentials of Statistics *for the* Behavioral Sciences

Susan A. Nolan • **Thomas E. Heinzen**

Seton Hall University   William Paterson University

Worth Publishers

Senior Publisher: Catherine Woods

Senior Acquisitions Editor: Charles Linsmeier

Development Editor: Michael Kimball

Marketing Manager: Amy Shefferd

Associate Director of Market Development: Carlise Stembridge

Media & Supplements Editor: Christine Burak

Photo Editor: Bianca Moscatelli

Photo Researcher: Julie Tesser

Interior & Cover Designer: Kevin Kall

Layout Design: Macmillan Publishing Services

Associate Managing Editor: Tracey Kuehn

Project Editor: Francine Almash

Production Manager: Sarah Segal

Illustrations: Northeastern Graphic, Inc.

Composition: Northeastern Graphic, Inc.

Printing & Binding: Worldcolor Versailles

Cover Painting: Josette Urso

Library of Congress Control Number: 2009940263

ISBN-13: 978-1-4292-2326-3
ISBN-10: 1-4292-2326-X

© 2011 by Worth Publishers
All rights reserved.

Printed in the United States of America

First Printing 2010

Worth Publishers
41 Madison Avenue
New York, NY 10010
www.worthpublishers.com

For Michael Kimball

Susan Nolan turned to psychology after suffering a career-ending accident on her second workday as a bicycle messenger. A native of Boston, she graduated from the College of Holy Cross and earned her PhD in clinical psychology from Northwestern University. Her research involves experimental investigations of the role of gender in the interpersonal consequences of depression, and studies on gender and mentoring in science and technology, funded in part by the National Science Foundation. Susan is the Chair of the Department of Psychology as well as Associate Professor of Psychology at Seton Hall University in New Jersey. She has served as a statistical consultant to researchers at several universities, medical schools, corporations, and nongovernmental organizations. Recently, she was appointed as a representative for the American Psychological Association at the United Nations in New York City.

Susan's academic schedule allows her to pursue one travel adventure per year, a tradition that she relishes. In recent years she has ridden her bicycle across the United States (despite her earlier crash), swapped apartments to live in Montreal, and explored the Adriatic coast in an intermittently roadworthy 1985 Volkswagen Scirocco. She writes much of the book on her annual trip to Bosnia-Herzegovina, where she and her husband, Ivan Bojanic, own a small house in the city of Banja Luka. They currently reside in Jersey City, New Jersey, where Susan roots feverishly, if quietly, for the Boston Red Sox.

Tom Heinzen was a 29-year-old college freshman, began graduate school days after the birth of his fourth daughter, and is still amazed that he and his wife, Donna, somehow managed to stay married. A magna cum laude graduate of Rockford College, he earned his PhD in social psychology at the State University of New York at Albany in just three years. He published his first book on frustration and creativity in government two years later, was a research associate in public policy until he was fired for arguing over the shape of a graph, consulted for the Johns Hopkins Center for Talented Youth, and then began a teaching career at William Paterson State University of New Jersey. He founded the psychology club, established an undergraduate research conference, and has been awarded various teaching honors while continuing to write journal articles, books, plays, and two novels that support the teaching of general psychology and statistics. He is also the editor of *Many Things to Tell You,* a volume of poetry by elderly writers.

His wife, Donna, is a physician's assistant who has volunteered her time in relief work following Hurricanes Mitch and Katrina. Their daughters are now scattered from Bangladesh to Mississippi to New Jersey and work in public health, teaching, and medicine. Tom is a mediocre French horn player, an enthusiastic but mediocre tennis player, and an ardent fan of both the New York Yankees and the Chicago Cubs.

BRIEF CONTENTS

C O N T E N T S

Essentials of Statistics for the Behavioral Sciences by Susan Nolan and Thomas Heinzen is a concise, readable text that covers key statistical concepts. Full of creative, step-by-step examples, *Essentials of Statistics* will enable students to learn how to choose the appropriate statistical test, understand its conceptual significance, and calculate each statistic. The text teaches students to apply concepts and formulas to statistical questions that they will encounter both in their academic lives and outside the classroom. The clear, accessible explanations highlight a conceptual understanding of statistics while minimizing the mathematical components. Nolan and Heinzen's *Essentials of Statistics* also provides numerous opportunities for students to evaluate their progress and practice what they're learning with three tiers of exercises—clarifying the concepts, calculating the statistics, and applying the concepts—integrated into the text after each major topic as well as at the end of each chapter.

A Conceptual Framework for Understanding Statistics

In every chapter, Nolan and Heinzen present each statistic in the way students will come to use them. Even though most students will never calculate a z score by hand or run a regression analysis without a computer, we do teach students how to calculate by hand. The authors stress the use of conceptual formulas and apply them to real statistical problems throughout the text. The authors also promote the use of statistical software packages, including featured coverage of SPSS®.

Pedagogy

Nolan and Heinzen have created a pedagogical framework for the textbook that supports student learning at each step of the learning process. In each chapter, the authors pair high-interest examples with explicit pedagogical elements to help retain student interest while advancing comprehension.

Illustrative, Step-by-Step Examples

The text is filled with real-world examples from a wide variety of sources in the behavioral sciences. Outlining procedures in a step-by-step fashion, the authors expertly guide students through each concept by applying the material creatively and effectively.

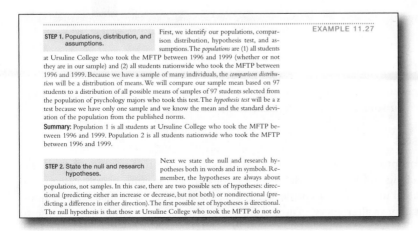

Mastering the Formulas and Mastering the Concepts

One of the most difficult tasks for students is bridging the role of formulas to the conceptual application of the data. The unique *Mastering the Formula* and *Mastering the Concept* marginal notes provide students with helpful tools that highlight each formula when it is first introduced and each important concept at its point of relevance.

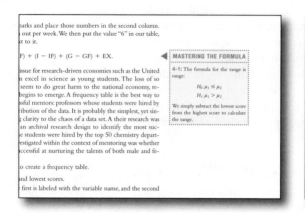

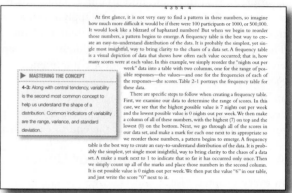

Before You Go On

Each chapter opens with a *Before You Go On* section that highlights the concepts students should have mastered before learning new material.

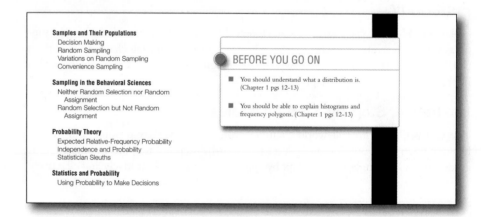

Practice

Experienced and novice instructors alike know the benefits of well-thought-out opportunities for students to practice what they're learning.

Exercises

The authors provide three tiers of exercises throughout the text to accommodate different teaching and learning styles. Each tier of exercises is conveniently categorized and identified in the end-of-chapter Exercises as well as the *Check Your Learning* questions that appear after every major section of a chapter. Instructors may choose to assign only those exercises that will benefit their students the most. The three tiers include:

- Clarifying the Concepts questions help students to master the general concept, the statistical terminology, and the conceptual assumptions of each topic.

- Calculating the Statistics exercises provide practice on the basic calculations for each formula and statistic.

- Applying the Concepts exercises apply statistical questions to real-world situations across the behavioral sciences.

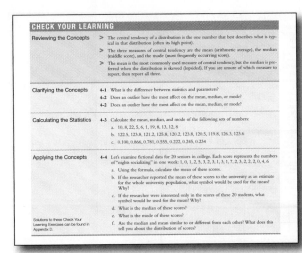

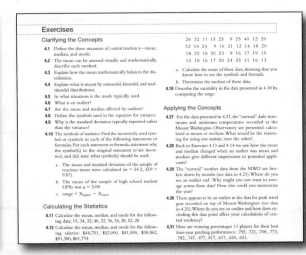

How It Works—Chapter-Specific Worked-Out Exercises

Many students have anxiety as they approach end-of-chapter exercises. To ease that anxiety, the *How It Works* section provides students with step-by-step worked-out exercises representative of those they will see at the end of the chapter. This section appears just before the end-of-chapter Exercises and acts as a model for the more challenging Applying the Concepts questions.

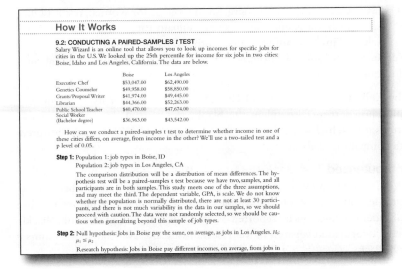

SPSS®

For those instructors who integrate SPSS into their course, we provide outlined instructions and screenshots of SPSS outputs to help students master use of this program with data from the text. For detailed coverage of SPSS, we offer a supplement textbook that can be ordered with the textbook: *SPSS: A User-Friendly Approach,* by Jeffery Aspelmeier and Thomas Pierce, Radford University.

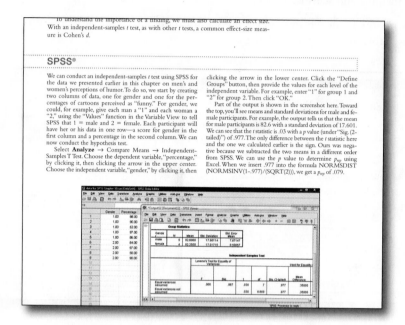

Supplements

We understand that one book alone cannot meet the education needs and teaching expectations of the modern classroom. Therefore, we have engaged colleagues to create a comprehensive supplements package that brings statistics to life for students and provides instructors with the resources necessary to effectively supplement their successful strategies in the classroom.

Instructor's Resources by Robin Freyberg, Stern College for Women, Yeshiva University, and special contributor Katherine Makarec, William Paterson University. Contents include Teaching Tips and sample course outlines. Each chapter includes a brief overview, discussion questions, classroom activities, handouts, additional reading suggestions, and online resources.

Test Bank by Kelly Goedert and Daniel Cruz, Seton Hall University. Contents include multiple-choice, true/false, fill-in-the-blank, and critical thinking/problem-solving questions for each chapter. The Test Bank also includes Web Quizzes featured on the book's companion Web site.

Diploma Computerized Test Bank (available for Windows or Macintosh on a single CD-ROM). The CD-ROM allows instructors to add an unlimited number of new questions; edit questions; format a test; scramble questions; and include figures, graphs, and pictures. Student grades can be reported to an accompanying gradebook. Blackboard and WebCT-formatted versions of the Test Bank are also available in the Course Cartridge and ePack.

iClicker Radio Frequency Classroom Response System. Offered by Worth Publishers, iClicker is Worth's new polling system, created by educators for educators. This radio frequency system is the hassle-free way to make class time more interactive. The system allows instructors to ask questions and instantly record responses, as well as take attendance, direct students through lectures, gauge student understanding of the material, and much more.

Worth Image and Lecture Gallery at www.worthpublishers.com/ilg. Using the Image and Lecture Gallery, instructors can browse or search and download text art, illustrations, outlines, and prebuilt PowerPoint slides for *all* Worth titles. Users can also create personal folders for easy organization of the materials.

Study Guide by Jennifer Coleman, Western New Mexico University. Contents include chapter outlines and learning objectives, chapter summaries and reviews, and multiple-choice study questions and answers.

SPSS®: A User-Friendly Approach by Jeffrey Aspelmeier and Thomas Pierce, Radford University. Using a proven teaching method, SPSS instruction is made accessible to students by building each section of the text around the storyline from a popular cartoon. Easing anxiety and giving students the necessary support to learn the material, *SPSS: A User-Friendly Approach* provides instructors and students with an informative guide to the basics of SPSS.

StatsPortal. This comprehensive learning system combines a fully customizable eBook, tutorials, applets, EESEE case studies, and homework management tools, all in one affordable and easy-to-use learning space. StatsPortal is available as a stand-alone product containing all the resources students need for the course or as a package with the physical textbook.

Acknowledgments

We would like to thank the many people who have contributed directly and indirectly to the writing of this text. We want to thank our students at Seton Hall University and William Paterson University for teaching us how to teach statistics in a way that makes sense.

Tom: The family members who know me on a daily basis and decide to love me anyway deserve more thanks than words can convey: Donna, Rebekah, Debbie, Amy, and Elizabeth. The close friends and colleagues who voiced encouragement and timely support also deserve my deep appreciation: Beth, Army, Culley, and Miran Schultz; Laura Cramer-Berness; Ariana DeSimone; J. Allen Suddeth; and Nancy Vail.

My students, in particular, have always provided a reality check on my teaching methods with the kind of candor that only students engaged in the learning process can bring.

Susan: I am grateful to my Northwestern University professors and classmates for convincing me that statistics can truly be fun. I am also eternally thankful to Beatrix Mellauner for bringing me and Tom Heinzen together as co-authors. I owe thanks, as well, to my Seton Hall colleagues—Kelly Goedert and Marianne Lloyd in particular—who are the source for an endless stream of engaging examples. Most importantly, I appreciate the insights of my students, who continually teach me how to teach statistics in a way that makes sense.

Much of the writing of this book took place during my sabbatical and ensuing summers in Bosnia and Herzegovina; I thank my Bosnian friends for their warmth and hospitality every time I visit. A special thank-you to the members of the Bojanic and Nolan clans—especially my parents, Diane and Jim, who have patiently endured the barrage of statistics I often inject into everyday conversation. Finally, I am most grateful to my husband, Ivan Bojanic, for the memorable adventures we've had (and the statistical observations that grew out of many of them); Ivan experienced the evolution of this book through countless road-trip conversations and late-night editorial sessions.

The contributions of the supplements authors are innumerable, and we would like to take a moment to highlight the impressive cast of instructors who have joined our team. Kelly Goedert, Katherine Makarec, Robert Weathersby, and Robin Freyberg are all professionals with a deep interest in creating successful classrooms and we appreciate the opportunity to work with people of such commitment.

Throughout the writing of the first edition, we relied on the criticism, corrections, encouragement, and thoughtful contributions from reviewers, focus group attendees, survey respondents, and class-testers. We thank them for their expertise and for the time they set aside to help us develop this textbook. Special thanks go to Jennifer Coleman at Western New Mexico University for her tireless work in developing the pedagogy with us, providing a responsible accuracy check, and contributing numerous ideas for us to consider as we continue to make these books even better.

Tsippa Ackerman
John Jay College

Danuta Bukatko
College of Holy Cross

Heidi Burross
Pima Community College

Jennifer Coleman
Western New Mexico University

Richard P. Conti
College of Saint Elizabeth

Nancy Dorr
The College of St. Rose

Nancy Gee
SUNY Fredonia

Marilyn Gibbons
Texas State University

Elizabeth Haines
William Paterson University

Roberto R. Heredia
Texas A&M International University

Cynthia O. Ingle
Bluegrass Community and Technical College

Jean Johnson
Governors State University

Min Ju
SUNY New Paltz

Karl Kelley
North Central College

Shelley Kilpatrick
Southwest Baptist University

Megan L. Knowles
University of Georgia

Jennifer Lancaster
St. Francis College

Christine MacDonald
Indiana State University

Suzanne Mannes
Widener University

Kelly Marin
Manhattan College

William Merriman
Kent State University

Chris Molnar
LaSalle University

Matthew Mulvaney
College at Brockport (SUNY)

Angela K Murray
University of Kansas

Aminda O'Hare
Kansas University

Sue Oliver
Glendale Community College

Stephen O'Rourke
The College of New Rochelle

Debra Oswald
Marquette University

Alison Papadakis
Loyola College in Maryland

Laura A. Rabin
CUNY Brooklyn

Ken Savitsky
Williams College

Heidi Shaw
Yakima Valley Community College

Ross B. Steinman
Widener University

Melanie Tabak
William Penn University

Mark Tengler
University of Houston-Clear Lake

Patricia Tomich
Kent State University

It has truly been a pleasure for us to work with everyone at Worth Publishers. From the moment we signed there, we have been impressed with the passionate commitment of everyone we encountered at Worth at every stage of the publishing process. Senior Publisher Catherine Woods fosters that commitment to quality in the Worth culture.

Michael Kimball, our development editor, is easy to work with but also is a brilliant writer and editor. His attention to every detail helped us to achieve our vision for this book and his impact can truly be seen on every page. Senior Acquisitions Editor Charles Linsmeier's impressive ability to assess ideas and face problems from multiple angles has contributed to a successful publication.

Associate Managing Editor Tracey Kuehn, Production Manager Sarah Segal, Project Editor Francine Almash, and Editorial Assistant Jaclyn Castaldo managed the production of the text and worked tirelessly to bring the book to fruition. Art Director Babs Reingold's commitment to artistic values in textbook publishing was inspiring. Kevin Kall, Designer, united beauty with clarity and content in the interior design. Photo Editor Bianca Moscatelli patiently trained us in the art of photo selection. Thanks to each of you for fulfilling Worth's promise to create a book whose aesthetics so beautifully support the specific pedagogical demands of teaching statistics.

Christine Burak, Media Editor, and Stacey Alexander, Production Manager, guided the development and creation of the supplements package, making life so much better for so many students and instructors. Amy Shefferd, Marketing Manager, and Carlise Stembridge, Associate Director of Market Development, quickly understood why we believe so deeply in this book, and each contributed tireless effort to advocate for this brief edition with our colleagues across the country.

An Introduction to Statistics and Research Design

BEFORE YOU GO ON

- You should be familiar with basic mathematics
  (Basic Mathematics Review Appendix A).

During the cholera epidemic of 1854, the first London victims all lived around Broad Street, very close to the Frith Street office of Dr. John Snow, who had spent years trying to determine how cholera was communicated from one person to another (Vinten-Johansen, Brody, Paneth, Rachman, & Rip, 2003). Fortunately, Snow had a specific idea he wanted to test. To do this, he identified each cholera victim and where that person lived. On a map of London, he marked with a dot the location of each cholera victim's home and placed X's to indicate where the water wells were. Almost all the deaths were near the Broad Street water well, the X circled in red on the map. The visual presentation of these data revealed that the closer a home was to the well, the more likely it was a death from cholera had occurred there.

Even after plotting his persuasive map, Snow still wanted to be sure that he was right about the Broad Street well. So he examined a sample of Broad Street well water under a microscope and discovered white particles floating in it. He took his findings to the Board of Guardians, who were startled by the odd theory that cholera was communicated in the water supply. They didn't know how to respond to Snow's bizarre suggestion that simply removing the handle to the water pump would stop the spread of the disease. The local government resisted, but Snow insisted. At last, the local authorities removed the pump handle and the rate of deaths from cholera declined dramatically.

▪ A **descriptive statistic** organizes, summarizes, and communicates a group of numerical observations.

▪ An **inferential statistic** uses sample data to make general estimates about the larger population.

▪ A **sample** is a set of observations drawn from the population of interest.

▪ The **population** includes all possible observations about which we'd like to know something.

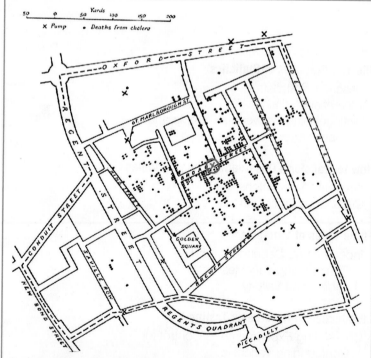

John Snow's Famous Map Dr. Snow mapped cholera deaths in relation to the Broad Street water well and, in doing so, solved the urgent mystery of how cholera could infect so many people so suddenly. The X's are all neighborhood wells. The X in the red circle is the Broad Street well. Each dot indicates that a person living at this address died of cholera, and a cluster of cases is clearly seen around the Broad Street well (but not around the other wells). Snow was careful to include the other X's to demonstrate that the deaths were closer to one specific source of water.

THE TWO BRANCHES OF STATISTICS

The cholera epidemic of 1854 claimed an estimated 19,000 lives across England (Creighton, 1894/1965). The number would have been much higher without the statistical genius of Dr. Snow. As we will see, his research anticipated the two main "branches" of modern statistics: descriptive statistics and inferential statistics.

Descriptive Statistics

Descriptive statistics organize, summarize, and communicate a group of numerical observations. Descriptive statistics describe large amounts of data in a single number or in just a few numbers. Let's illustrate descriptive statistics by using familiar numbers: body weights. The Centers for Disease Control and Prevention (CDC) (2004) reported that people in the United States weigh much more now than they did four decades ago. The average weight for women increased from 140.2 pounds in 1960 to 164.3 in 2002. For men, the average weight went from 166.3 to 191.0 pounds in the same time span. These averages are descriptive statistics because they *describe* the weights of many people in just one number. A single number reporting the average is far more useful than a long list of the weights of *every* person studied by the CDC.

Inferential Statistics

Inferential statistics use sample data to make general estimates about the larger population. Inferential statistics infer, or make an intelligent guess about, the population. For example, the CDC made inferences about weight even though it did not actually weigh *everyone* in the United States. Instead, the CDC studied a smaller, representative group of U.S. citizens to make an intelligent guess about the entire population.

> ◀ **MASTERING THE CONCEPT**
>
> **1.1:** Descriptive statistics summarize numerical information about a sample. Inferential statistics draw conclusions about the broader population based on numerical information from a sample.

Distinguishing Between a Sample and a Population

*A **sample** is a set of observations drawn from the population of interest.* When the CDC studied how much Americans weigh, the population of interest was everyone in the United States. Researchers usually study a sample, but they are really interested in the **population**, which *includes all possible observations about which we'd like to know something.* For example, the average weight of the CDC's sample of women and men is then used to estimate the average weight for the population of all women and men in the United States. We use the sample to estimate the population.

Samples are used most often because it is rare that we are able to study every person (or organization or laboratory rat) in a particular population. For one thing, it's far too expensive. In addition, it would take too long. Dr. Snow did not want to interview every family in the Broad Street neighborhood—people were dying too fast! Fortunately, what he learned from his sample also applied to the larger population.

Descriptive Statistics Summarize Information It is more useful to use a single number to summarize many people's weights than to provide a long, overwhelming list of each person's weight.

CHECK YOUR LEARNING

Reviewing the Concepts

> Descriptive statistics organize, summarize, and communicate large amounts of numerical information.

> Inferential statistics use sample data to draw conclusions about larger populations.

> Samples, or selected observations of a population, are intended to be representative of the larger population.

Clarifying the Concepts

1-1 Are data from samples or populations used in inferential statistics?

Calculating the Statistics

1-2 a. If your professor calculated the average grade for your statistics class, would that be considered a descriptive statistic or an inferential statistic?

b. If that same class "average" is being used to predict something about how future students might do in statistics, would that be considered a descriptive statistic or an inferential statistic?

Applying the Concepts

1-3 Imagine that the director of the counseling center at your university wants to examine the stress levels of students. From the student directory, she randomly chooses 100 of the 12,500 students and assesses their stress levels in a diagnostic interview. She reports that the average stress level is 18 on a scale of 1–50, a score she knows to be moderately high for college students. She concludes, and reports to the school newspaper, that the students at this institution have a moderately high stress level.

a. What is the sample?

b. What is the population?

Solutions to these Check Your Learning questions can be found in Appendix D.

c. What is the descriptive statistic?

d. What is the inferential statistic?

HOW TO TRANSFORM OBSERVATIONS INTO VARIABLES

- A **variable** is any observation of a physical, attitudinal, or behavioral characteristic that can take on different values.

- A **discrete observation** can take on only specific values (e.g., whole numbers); no other values can exist between these numbers.

- A **continuous observation** can take on a full range of values (e.g., numbers out to several decimal places); an infinite number of potential values exists.

We begin the research process by transforming observations about behavior into numbers. *Variables are observations of physical, attitudinal, and behavioral characteristics that can take on different values.* Behavioral scientists often study abstract variables such as motivation, self-esteem, and attitudes.

We use both discrete and continuous numerical observations to quantify variables. *Discrete observations can take on only specific values (e.g., whole numbers); no other values can exist between these numbers.* For example, if we measure the number of times we have to get up early in a particular week, the only possible values would be whole numbers. It is reasonable to assume that each participant in the study could have to get up early 0 to 7 times in any given week, but not 1.6 or 5.92 times.

Continuous observations can take on a full range of values (e.g., numbers out to several decimal places); an infinite number of potential values exists. For example, one person might complete a task in 12.839 seconds. Someone else might complete it in 14.870 seconds. The possible values are continuous, limited only by the number of decimal places we choose to use.

Discrete Observations

There are two types of observations that are always discrete: nominal variables and ordinal variables. *Nominal variables are used for observations that have categories, or names, as their values.* For example, when entering data into a statistics computer program, a researcher might code male participants with the number 1 and female participants with the number 2. But those numbers merely identify the gender category for each participant. The numbers do not imply that men are better than women because they get the first number, just as they do not suggest that women are twice as good as men because they happen to be coded as a 2. Nominal variables are always discrete (a whole number).

Ordinal variables are observations that have rankings (i.e., 1st, 2nd, 3rd, . . .) as their values. In team sports, for example, your team finishes the season in a particular "place," or rank. Whether your team goes to the playoffs is determined by its rank at the end of the season. It doesn't matter if your team won first place by one game or by many games. Like nominal observations, ordinal observations are always discrete. A team could be first or third or twelfth, but could not be ranked 1.563.

Nominal Variables Just Categorize If you wanted to compare the records of Republicans and Democrats, political party would be a nominal variable. Nominal observations merely name categories; the numbers don't have any meaning beyond a name.

Continuous Observations

The two types of observations that can be continuous are interval variables and ratio variables. *Interval variables are used for observations that have numbers as their values; the distance (or interval) between pairs of consecutive numbers is assumed to be equal.* For example, time is an interval variable because the interval from one second to the next is always the same. Some interval variables are also discrete variables, such as the number of times one has to get up early each week. This is an interval variable because the distance between numerical observations is assumed to be equal. The difference between 1 and 2 times is the same as the difference between 5 and 6 times. However, this observation is also discrete because, as noted earlier, the number of days in a week cannot be anything but whole numbers. Several social science measures are treated as interval measures but also are discrete, such as personality and attitude measures.

Studies that measure time and distance are continuous, interval observations. But they are also identified as *ratio* observations because zero has meaning for time and distance—such as time running out in a basketball game or crossing the finish line in a race. *Ratio variables are variables that meet the criteria for interval variables but also have meaningful zero points.* Sometimes ratio variables are discrete, however, as in the frequency of an event's occurrence. For example, the number of times a rat pushes a lever to receive food would be considered a ratio variable in that it has a true zero point—the rat might never push the bar (and go hungry).

Many cognitive studies use the ratio variable of reaction time to measure how quickly we process difficult information. For example, the Stroop test assesses how long it takes to read a list of color words printed in ink of the wrong color (see Figure 1-1). For example, the word *red* might be printed in blue or the word *blue* might be printed

■ A **nominal variable** is a variable used for observations that have categories, or names, as their values.

■ An **ordinal variable** is a variable used for observations that have rankings (i.e., 1st, 2nd, 3rd, . . .) as their values.

■ An **interval variable** is a variable used for observations that have numbers as their values, and the distance (or interval) between pairs of consecutive numbers is assumed to be equal.

■ A **ratio variable** is a variable that meets the criteria for an interval variable but also has a meaningful zero point.

FIGURE 1-1
Reaction Time and the Stroop Test

The Stroop test assesses how long it takes to read a list of color words printed in the wrong color, such as the word *red* printed in the color white. Try it and see how tricky (and frustrating) it can be: go to this book's Web site (www .worthpublishers.com/nolanessentials1e) and click on "Stroop Test."

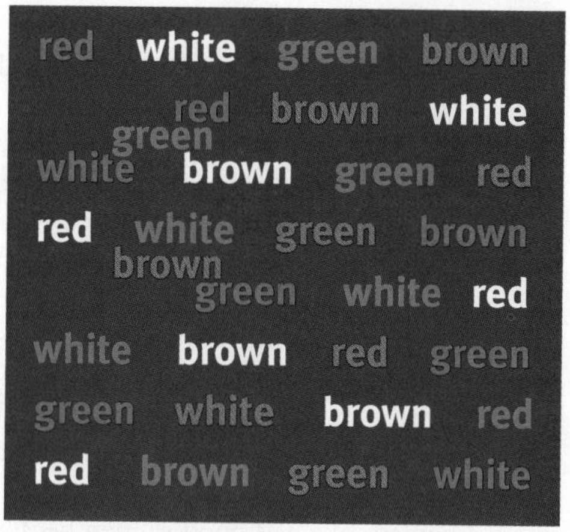

in green. If it takes you 1.264 seconds to press a computer key that accurately identifies that the word *red* printed in blue actually reads *red,* then your reaction time is a ratio variable; time always implies a meaningful zero.

You can experience for yourself how social scientists transform observations into numbers. Observe your own cognitive processes at work by taking the Stroop test, the short cognitive test presented in Figure 1-1 and available on the Web site that supports this textbook (www.worthpublishers.com/nolanessentials1e). This version of the Stroop test gives response times in whole numbers—for example, 12 seconds—although other versions are more specific and give response times to several decimal places, such as 12.1304 seconds.

Many statistical computer programs refer to both interval numbers and ratio numbers as scale observations because both interval observations and ratio observations are analyzed with the same statistical tests. Specifically, *a **scale variable** is a variable that meets the criteria for an interval variable or a ratio variable.* Computer programs such as the Statistical Package for the Social Sciences (SPSS) prompt us to identify whether the number we are entering into the computer is nominal, ordinal, or scale. Throughout this text, we use the term *scale variable* to refer to variables that are interval or ratio, but it is important to remember the distinction between interval variables and ratio variables. Table 1-1 summarizes the four types of variables.

> ▶ **MASTERING THE CONCEPT**
>
> **1.2:** The three main types of variables are nominal (or categorical), ordinal (or ranked), and scale. The third type (scale) includes both interval variables and ratio variables; the distances between numbers on the measure are meaningful.

TABLE 1-1. QUANTIFYING OUR OBSERVATIONS

There are four types of variables that we can use to quantify our observations. Two of them, nominal and ordinal, are always discrete variables. Interval variables can be discrete or continuous; ratio variables are almost always continuous.

	Discrete	Continuous
NOMINAL	Always	Never
ORDINAL	Always	Never
INTERVAL	Sometimes	Sometimes
RATIO	Seldom	Almost Always

CHECK YOUR LEARNING

Reviewing the Concepts	> Variables are quantified with discrete or continuous observations.
	> Depending on the study, statisticians select either nominal, ordinal, or scale (interval or ratio) variables.

Clarifying the Concepts 1-4 What is the difference between discrete observations and continuous observations?

Calculating the Statistics 1-5 Three female students complete a Stroop test. Lorna finishes in 12.67 seconds; Desiree finishes in 14.87 seconds; and Marianne finishes in 9.88 seconds.

   a. Are these data discrete or continuous?

   b. Is the variable an interval or ratio observation?

   c. On an ordinal scale, what is Lorna's score?

Applying the Concepts 1-6 Eleanor Stampone (1993) randomly distributed what appeared to be the same piece of paper to students in a large lecture center. Each paper contained one of three short paragraphs that described the interests and appearance of a female college student. The descriptions were identical in every way except for one adjective. The student was described as having either "short," "mid-length," or "very long" hair. At the bottom of each piece of paper, Stampone asked the participants (both female and male) to fill out a measure that indicated the probability that the student described in the scenario would be sexually harassed.

   a. What is the nominal variable used in Stampone's hair-length study? Why is this considered a nominal variable?

   b. What is the ordinal variable used in the study? Why is this considered an ordinal variable?

   c. What is the scale variable used in the study? Why is this considered a scale variable?

Solutions to these Check Your Learning questions can be found in Appendix D.

THREE TYPES OF VARIABLES

It is helpful to remember that variables vary. For example, when studying a discrete, nominal variable such as gender, we refer to gender as the variable because it can vary—either male or female. The term *level,* along with the terms *value* and *condition,* all refer to the same idea. ***Levels*** *are the discrete values or conditions that variables can take on.* For example, male is a level or value of the variable gender. Female is another level or value of the variable gender. In both cases, gender is the variable. Similarly, when studying a continuous, scale variable, such as how fast a runner completes a marathon, we refer to time as the variable. For example, 3 hours, 42 minutes, 27 seconds is one of an infinite number of possible times it would take to complete a marathon. The important thing to remember is this: variables vary.

Independent, Dependent, and Confounding Variables

There are three types of variables: independent, dependent, and confounding. Two of these variables are necessary for good research: independent variables and dependent variables. But a confounding variable is the enemy of good research. We usually conduct research to determine if one or more independent variables predicts a dependent variable. *An **independent variable** has at least two levels that we either manipulate or observe to determine its effects on the dependent variable.* For example, if we are

■ A **scale variable** is a variable that meets the criteria for an interval variable or a ratio variable.

■ A **level** is a discrete value or condition that a variable can take on.

■ An **independent variable** is a variable that we either manipulate or observe to determine its effects on the dependent variable.

Justin Sullivan/Getty Images

Was the Damage from Wind or Water? During Hurricane Katrina in 2005, high winds were confounded with high water so that often it was not possible to determine whether property damage was due to wind (insured) or to water (not insured).

studying whether gender predicts one's attitude about politics, then the independent variable is gender with two levels: female and male.

*The **dependent variable** is the outcome variable that we hypothesize to be related to, or caused by, changes in the independent variable.* For example, we hypothesize that the dependent variable (attitudes about politics) depends on the independent variable (gender). If you're in doubt as to which is the independent and which is the dependent variable, then ask yourself which one depends on the other; that one is the dependent variable.

*By contrast, a **confounding variable**, often simply called a confound, is any variable that systematically varies with the independent variable so that we cannot logically determine which variable is at work.* For example, prior to Hurricanes Katrina and Rita during the tragic summer of 2005, many insurance companies had insured people's homes against wind damage but not against flood damage. Hurricane winds bring water in many different ways: as rain, by causing higher tides and storm surge, and by creating structural damage that allows water into the home. Consequently, both wind and water contributed to the levees' breaking around New Orleans, as well as causing billions of dollars of additional damage all along the Gulf Coast. But logically, many insurance companies could argue that it was often unclear whether damage to a particular home was due to high winds or high water. Wind and water were confounded because no one could logically determine which of those two variables had caused damage to homes.

So how do we decide which is our independent variable and which might be a confounding variable? Well, it all comes down to what *you* decide to study. Let's use an example. Suppose you want to lose weight, so you start using a diet drug *and* begin exercising at the same time; the drug and the exercising are confounded because you cannot logically tell which one is responsible for any weight loss. If we hypothesize that a particular diet drug leads to weight loss, then whether someone uses the diet drug becomes the independent variable and exercise becomes the potentially confounding variable that we would try to control. On the other hand, if we hypothesize that exercise leads to weight loss, then the level of exercise becomes the independent variable and whether people use diet drugs along with it becomes the potentially confounding variable that we would try to control. In both of these cases, the dependent variable would be weight loss. But the researcher has to make some decisions about which variables to treat as independent variables, which variables need to be controlled, and which variables to treat as dependent variables. You, the experimenter, are in control of the experiment.

> ▶ **MASTERING THE CONCEPT**
>
> **1.3:** We conduct research to see if the independent variable predicts the dependent variable.

- A **dependent variable** is the outcome variable that we hypothesize to be related to, or caused by, changes in the independent variable.

- A **confounding variable** is any variable that systematically varies with the independent variable so that we cannot logically determine which variable is at work; also called a *confound*.

- **Reliability** refers to the consistency of a measure.

- **Validity** refers to the extent to which a test actually measures what it was intended to measure.

Reliability and Validity

One recently developed variable is particularly relevant for behavioral science majors trying to sort out their careers: the Consideration of Future Consequences (CFC) scale. You will want to evaluate yourself on this measure, shown in Figure 1-2, for three reasons. First, you will find it interesting to compare your CFC score to the scores of others in your class. Second, we use CFC scores in subsequent chapters to teach you about other aspects of statistics. Third, discovering your CFC score will help you gain a sense of why variables need to be reliable and valid.

For each of the statements below, please indicate whether the statement is characteristic of you on a scale of 1 to 5. If the statement is extremely uncharacteristic of you, write a 1 to the left of the question; if the statement is extremely characteristic of you, write a 5. Use the numbers in the middle if you fall between the extremes. Please keep the scale in mind as you rate each of the statements below.

Extremely Uncharacteristic				Extremely Characteristic
1	2	3	4	5

_____ 1. I consider how things might be in the future and try to influence those things with my day-to-day behavior.

_____ 2. Often I engage in a particular behavior to achieve outcomes that may not occur for many years.

_____ 3. I act only to satisfy immediate concerns, figuring the future will take care of itself.

_____ 4. My behavior is influenced only by the immediate (i.e., a matter of days or weeks) outcomes of my actions.

_____ 5. My convenience is a big factor in the decisions I make or the actions I take.

_____ 6. I am willing to sacrifice my immediate happiness or well-being to achieve future outcomes.

_____ 7. I think it is important to take warnings about negative outcomes seriously even if the negative outcome will not occur for many years.

_____ 8. I think it is more important to perform a behavior with important distant consequences than a behavior with less important immediate consequences.

_____ 9. I generally ignore warnings about possible future problems because I think the problems will be resolved before they reach crisis level.

_____ 10. I think that sacrificing now is usually unnecessary since future outcomes can be dealt with at a later time.

_____ 11. I act only to satisfy immediate concerns, figuring that I will take care of future problems that may occur at a later date.

_____ 12. Since my day-to-day work has specific outcomes, it is more important to me than behavior that has distant outcomes.

FIGURE 1-2
Consideration of Future Consequences (CFC) Scale

Fill out the CFC scale and calculate your personal score. When calculating your score, note that items 3, 4, 5, 9, 10, 11, and 12 are reverse scored (1 = 5, 2 = 4, 3 = 3, 4 = 2, 5 = 1). For example, if you had a 4 for item number 3, that 4 would become a 2. After reverse scoring these items, simply add up the scores for the individual items to get your total score. Your score will be easier to interpret if you then divide your total score by 12 (the number of items). A higher score indicates a greater degree of consideration about your future.

The CFC scale, is an example of a variable that has demonstrated both reliability and validity (Joireman, Sprott, & Spangenberg, 2005; Strathman, Gleicher, Boninger, & Edwards, 1994). *A **reliable** measure is one that is consistent.* If you were to weigh yourself on your bathroom scale now, and then again in an hour, you would expect your weight to be almost exactly the same. If your weight remains the same when you haven't done anything to change it, then your bathroom scale is reliable.

But a reliable measure is not necessarily a valid measure. *A **valid** measure is one that measures what it was intended to measure.* Your bathroom scale could be incorrect, but be consistently incorrect. In that case, your measure would be reliable, but not valid. A more extreme example is wanting to know your weight but using a ruler to determine it. We would get a number, and that number might be reliable, but it would not be a valid measure of your weight.

Any test with poor reliability cannot have high validity. It is not possible to measure what we intended to measure when the test itself produces varying results. The well-known Rorschach inkblot test is one example of a test whose reliability is questionable, so the validity of the information it produces is difficult to interpret (Wood, Nezworski, Lilienfeld, & Garb, 2003). For instance, two clinicians might analyze the identical set of responses to a Rorschach test and develop quite different interpretations of those responses—meaning it lacks reliability. Reliability can be increased with scoring guidelines, but that doesn't mean validity is increased. Just because two clinicians scoring a Rorschach test designate a person as psychotic, it doesn't necessarily mean that the person *is* psychotic. It might not be a valid measure of who is and isn't

◀ **MASTERING THE CONCEPT**

1.4: A good variable is both reliable and valid.

psychotic. Reliability is necessary, but not sufficient, to create a valid measure. Nevertheless, the idea that ambiguous images somehow invite revealing information remains attractive to many people; as a result, tests such as the Rorschach still are used frequently, even though there is much controversy about them (Wood et al., 2003).

CHECK YOUR LEARNING

Reviewing the Concepts

> Independent variables are manipulated by the experimenter.

> Dependent variables are outcomes in response to changes in the independent variable.

> Confounding variables systematically vary with the independent variable, so that we cannot logically tell which variable may have influenced the dependent variable.

> As the researcher, you can control factors that are not of interest to you, in order to explore the relation between independent and dependent variables.

> A variable is only useful if it is both reliable (consistent over time) and valid (assesses what it is intended to assess).

Clarifying the Concepts

1-7   The _____ variable predicts the _____ variable.

Calculating the Statistics

1-8   A researcher examines the effects of two variables on memory. One variable is beverage (caffeine or no caffeine) and the other variable is the subject to be remembered (numbers, word lists, aspects of a story).

　　a.   Identify the independent and dependent variables.

　　b.   How many levels do the variables of "beverage" and "subject to be remembered" have?

Applying the Concepts

1-9   Let's say you wanted to study the impact of declaring a major on school-related anxiety. You recruit 50 first-year university students who have not declared a major and 50 first-year university students who have declared a major. You have all 100 students complete an anxiety measure.

　　a.   What is the independent variable in this study?

　　b.   What are the levels of the independent variable?

　　c.   What is the dependent variable?

Solutions to these Check Your Learning questions can be found in Appendix D.

　　d.   What would it mean for the anxiety measure to be reliable?

　　e.   What would it mean for the anxiety measure to be valid?

INTRODUCTION TO HYPOTHESIS TESTING

When Dr. John Snow suggested that the pump handle be removed from the Broad Street well, he was testing his idea that the well water was contaminated. Social scientists use research to test their ideas through a specific statistics-based process called *hypothesis testing*. More formally, **hypothesis testing** *is the process of drawing conclusions about whether a particular relation between variables is supported by the evidence.* Typically, when we test a hypothesis, we examine data from a sample to draw conclusions about a population. There are many ways to conduct research. In this section, we discuss the process of determining our variables, two different ways to approach research, and two different experimental designs.

The following account is presented as a single-class experience; however, it actually represents a somewhat idealized process across many different statistics classes. We asked our students to develop a testable hypothesis about the value of taking a course in statistics. The research process developed along this line: "Maybe we could survey the alumni to find out if they are using statistics?"

Very soon, students developed a measure for an alumni survey that tested this hypothesis: "Learning statistics provides tangible financial benefits." They were proposing to ask alumni such questions as "How much money do you earn?" and "How often do you interpret or create statistical information?" The students also planned to ask the participants to rate how important a knowledge of statistics is to being promoted.

Then the students worked toward an operational definition of "the value of learning statistics." *An **operational definition** specifies the operations or procedures used to measure or manipulate a variable.* We could, for example, operationalize anxiety as a score on a self-report anxiety measure that a person completed on his or her own, as a clinician's rating of that person's anxiety following a diagnostic interview, or as a physiological measure such as heart rate that might be the product of anxiety. In the statistics class described above, the students proposed to measure the value of statistics in a very concrete way (income).

You already carry many hypotheses around in your head. You just haven't bothered to test them yet, at least not formally. For example, perhaps you believe that Americans use bank ATMs faster than Europeans or that smokers simply lack the willpower to stop. Maybe you are convinced that the parking problem on your campus is part of an uncaring conspiracy by administrators to make your life more difficult. In each of these cases, as shown in the accompanying Table 1-2, we can frame our hypothesis in terms of an independent variable and a dependent variable. Once again, the best way to learn about operationalizing a variable is to experience it for yourself. So propose a way to measure each of the variables identified in Table 1-2. We've given you a start with continent—North American versus European (an easy variable to operationalize)—and how bad the parking problem is (a more difficult variable to operationalize).

Conducting Experiments to Control for Confounding Variables

*A **correlation** is an association between two or more variables.* In Dr. Snow's cholera research, it was the idea of a systematic co-relation between two variables (the proximity to the Broad Street well and the number of deaths) that saved so many lives. Snow understood

- **Hypothesis testing** is the process of drawing conclusions about whether a particular relation between variables is supported by the evidence.

- An **operational definition** specifies the operations or procedures used to measure or manipulate a variable.

- A **correlation** is an association between two or more variables.

The Ethics of Experimental Design A disturbing pattern of psychological symptoms was called *shell shock* after World War I, *battle fatigue* or *war trauma* after World War II, and eventually *post-traumatic stress disorder* following the Vietnam War. Because we cannot randomly assign people either to participate in or be exempt from a war, we must use other research designs to isolate the effects and develop coping strategies.

GUO LEI/Xinhua/Landov

- An **experiment** is a study in which participants are randomly assigned to a condition or level of one or more independent variables.

- In **random assignment**, every participant in a study has an equal chance of being assigned to any of the groups, or experimental conditions, in the study.

- In a **between-groups research design**, participants experience one, and only one, level of the independent variable.

- In a **within-groups research design**, the different levels of the independent variable are experienced by all participants in the study; also called a *repeated-measures research design.*

TABLE 1-2. OPERATIONALIZED VARIABLES

The Independent Variable . . .	Predicts . . .	the Dependent Variable
Continent		who uses ATMs the fastest
Amount of willpower		level of cigarette smoking
Level of caring by administrators		how bad the parking problem is

Conceptual Variable	Operationalized Variable
Continent	North America or Europe
Who uses ATMs the fastest	
Amount of willpower	
Level of cigarette smoking	
Level of caring by administrators	
How bad the parking problem is	Ask students to rate the parking problem on a scale ranging from 1 (no problem) to 5 (the worst problem on campus)

the life-saving idea of a correlation many years before the mathematical formula for a correlation had been developed, so he tested his idea by displaying his data on a map rather than by testing with a formula. A correlation is just one way to test a hypothesis, but it is not the only way. In fact, when possible, researchers almost always prefer to conduct an experiment rather than a correlational study because it is easier to interpret the results.

*An **experiment** is a study in which participants are randomly assigned to a condition or level of one or more independent variables.* Random assignment means that neither the participants nor the researchers get to choose the condition. Experiments are the gold standard of hypothesis testing because they are the best way to control confounding variables. Controlling confounding variables allows researchers to infer a cause–effect relation between variables rather than merely a systematic association between variables. Even when researchers cannot conduct a true experiment, they include as many of the characteristics of an experiment as possible. The critical feature that makes a study worthy of the descriptor *experiment* is random assignment to groups.

Experiments create equality between groups by randomly assigning participants to different levels, or conditions, of the independent variable. *With **random assignment**, every participant in the study has an equal chance of being assigned to any condition.* Random assignment controls the effects of personality traits, life experiences, personal biases, or other potential confounds by distributing them across each condition of the experiment to an equivalent degree.

EXAMPLE 1.1

As you begin to understand how difficult it is to control confounding variables, you will gain a new respect for the power of randomness to wash out so many potential confounds. For example, a cognitive psychologist might want to study whether playing the video game Guitar Hero (the independent variable) improves reaction time (the dependent variable) as measured by a standard neuropsychological test. In such a study, it would not be ideal to ask people whether they play Guitar Hero and then measure their reaction times. Can you spot the confounding variable? People may choose to play Guitar Hero *because* they already have a fast reaction time and enjoy using their skill to get a high score on Guitar Hero. If that is the case, then of course those who play Guitar Hero will have faster reaction times—they already did before they took up the game!

It would be much more useful to set up an experiment that randomly assigns students to one of the two levels of the independent variable: play Guitar Hero or do not play Guitar Hero. Random assignment assures us that our two groups are roughly equal on all of the variables that might cause fast reaction times, such as hand-eye coordination, musical ability, and experience playing other video games. Random assignment attempts to diminish the effects of potential confounds. Specifically, random assignment to groups increases our confidence that the two groups are similar with regard to speed of reaction time *prior* to this experiment. (Figure 1-3 visually clarifies the difference between self-selection and random assignment. We explore more specifically how random assignment is implemented in Chapter 5.) If we use random assignment and the "play Guitar Hero" group has a faster average reaction time after the experiment, then we can conclude that playing Guitar Hero caused the faster reaction times.

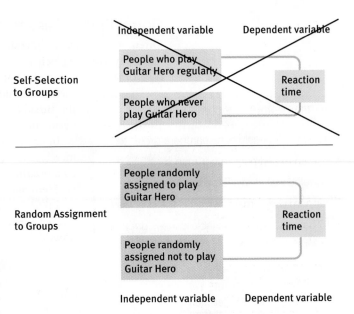

FIGURE 1-3
Self-Selected into or *Randomly Assigned* to One of Two Groups: Guitar Hero Players versus Non–Guitar Hero Players

This figure visually clarifies the difference between self-selection and random assignment. The design of the first study does not answer the question "Does playing Guitar Hero improve reaction time?"

Between-Groups Design versus Within-Groups Design

Experiments create meaningful comparison groups in several ways. However, most studies have either a *between-groups* research design or a *within-groups* (also called a *repeated-measures*) research design.

A **between-groups research design** *is an experiment in which participants experience one, and only one, level of the independent variable.* In some between-groups studies, the different levels of the independent variable serve as the only relevant distinction between two (or more) groups that otherwise have been made equivalent through random assignment. An experiment that compares a control group with an experimental group is an example of a between-groups design.

A **within-groups research design** *is a study in which the different levels of the independent variable are experienced by all participants in the study.* An experiment that compares the same group of people before and after they experience a level of an independent variable is an example of a within-groups design. The word *within* emphasizes that if you experience one condition of a study, then you remain within the study until you experience all conditions of the study. Many applied questions in the behavioral sciences are best studied using a within-groups design. This is particularly true of long-term (often called *longitudinal*) studies that examine how individuals and organizations change over time or of studies involving a naturally occurring event that cannot be duplicated in the laboratory. For example, we obviously cannot randomly assign people to either experience a hurricane or not experience a hurricane. However, we could use nature's predictability to anticipate hurricane season, collect "before" data, and then collect data once again "after" people experienced living through a hurricane. Such a before/after study is one version of a within-groups design.

Correlational Research

Often, we cannot conduct an experiment because it is unethical or impractical to randomly assign participants to conditions. In these cases, we must conduct another type of study. Dr. Snow's cholera research, for example, did not use random assignment; he could not randomly assign some people to drink water from the Broad Street well. His research design was correlational, not experimental.

In correlational studies, we do not manipulate either variable. We merely assess the two variables as they exist. For example, we might measure the interval variables of amount of time spent playing Guitar Hero and reaction time on a neuropsychological test. We might find that they are related (as is shown in Figure 1-4), but we would not have evidence that playing Guitar Hero causes a faster reaction time.

> ▶ **MASTERING THE CONCEPT**
>
> **1.5:** When possible, researchers prefer to use an experiment rather than a correlational study. Experiments use random assignment, which is the only way to determine if one variable causes another.

FIGURE 1-4
Correlation Between Reaction Time and Playing Guitar Hero

This graph depicts a relation between reaction time and hours spent playing Guitar Hero for a study of 10 fictional participants. The more one plays Guitar Hero, the faster one's reaction time tends to be.

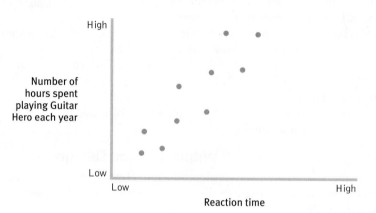

CHECK YOUR LEARNING

Reviewing the Concepts

> Hypothesis testing is the process of drawing conclusions about whether a particular relation between variables (your hypothesis) is supported by the evidence.

> All variables need to be operationalized–that is, you need to specify how they are to be measured or manipulated.

> Experiments attempt to explain a cause–effect relation between an independent variable and a dependent variable.

> Random assignment to groups, to control for confounding variables, is the hallmark of an experiment.

> Most studies have either a between-groups design or a within-groups design.

> Correlational studies can be used when it is not possible to conduct an experiment.

Clarifying the Concepts

1-10 How do the two types of research discussed in this chapter—experimental and correlational—differ?

1-11 How does random assignment help to address confounding variables?

continued on next page

Calculating the Statistics	**1-12** College admissions offices use several methods to operationalize the academic performance of high school students applying to college, including SAT scores. Can you think of other ways to operationalize this variable?

Applying the Concepts	**1-13** Expectations matter. Researchers examined how expectations based on stereotypes influence women's math performance (Spencer, Steele, & Quinn, 1999). Some women were told that a gender difference was found on a certain math test and that women tended to receive lower scores than men did. Other women were told that no gender differences were evident on the test. Women in the first group performed more poorly than men did, whereas women in the second group did not.

a. Briefly outline how researchers could conduct this research as a true experiment using a between-groups design.

b. Why would researchers want to use random assignment?

c. If researchers did not use random assignment but rather chose people who *already* were in those conditions (i.e., who already believed stereotypes or did not believe them), what might be the possible confounds? Name at least two.

d. How is math performance operationalized here?

e. Briefly outline how researchers could conduct this study using a within-groups design.

The solutions to these Check Your Learning questions can be found in Appendix D.

REVIEW OF CONCEPTS

The Two Branches of Statistics

Statistics is divided into two branches: *descriptive statistics* and *inferential statistics*. Descriptive statistics organize, summarize, and communicate large amounts of numerical information. Inferential statistics draw conclusions about larger *populations* based on smaller *samples* of that population. Samples are intended to be representative of the larger population.

How to Transform Observations into Variables

Observations may be described as either discrete or continuous. *Discrete observations* are those that can take on only certain numbers (e.g., whole numbers, such as 1), and *continuous observations* are those that can take on all possible numbers in a range (e.g., 1.68792). Two types of *variables* can only be discrete: nominal and ordinal. *Nominal variables* use numbers simply to give names to scores (e.g., 1 to stand for male on the nominal variable of gender). *Ordinal variables* are rank ordered (e.g., 1st place, 2nd place). Two types of variables can be continuous: interval and ratio. *Interval variables* are those in which the distances between numerical values are assumed to be equal; they include physical properties such as height as well as more abstract concepts such as personality traits. *Ratio variables* are those that meet the criteria for interval variables but also have a meaningful zero point. Time, for instance, is a variable for which a score of 0 has meaning. *Scale variable* is a term used for both interval and ratio variables, particularly within statistical computer software programs.

Three Types of Variables

Independent variables are manipulated by the experimenter. *Dependent variables* are outcomes in response to changes in the independent variable. If a variable is nominal, we refer to its categories as *levels*. *Confounding variables* systematically vary with the independent variable, so that we cannot logically determine which variable may have influenced the dependent variable. The independent and dependent variables allow researchers to test and explore the relations between variables. A variable is only useful if it is both *reliable* and *valid*. A reliable measure is one that is consistent, and a valid measure is one that assesses what it intends to assess.

An Introduction to Hypothesis Testing

Hypothesis testing is the process of drawing conclusions about whether a particular relation between variables is supported by the evidence. *Operational definitions* of the independent and dependent variables are necessary to test a hypothesis. *Experiments* attempt to identify a cause–effect relation between an independent variable and a dependent variable. *Random assignment* to groups, to control for confounding variables, is the hallmark of an experiment. Most studies have either a *between-groups design* or a *within-groups design*. *Correlational studies* can be used when it is not possible to conduct an experiment.

SPSS®

SPSS is divided into two main screens. The easiest way to move back and forth between these two screens is by using the two tabs located at the lower left labeled "Variable View" and "Data View."

To name the variables, go to "Variable View" and select:

Name. Write in a short version of the variable name, such as BDI for the Beck Depression Inventory, a common measure of depressive symptoms.

Type. For nominal variables, such as gender, change the type to "string" by clicking the cell in the column labeled "Type" then clicking the little gray box, choosing "string," and clicking "OK."

To tell SPSS what the variable name means, select:

Label. Write in the full name of the variable, such as Beck Depression Inventory.

To tell SPSS what the numbers assigned to any nominal variable actually mean, select:

Values. In the column labeled "Values," click on the cell next to the appropriate variable, then click on the little gray box on the right of that cell to access the tool that allows you to identify the values (or levels) of the variables. For example, if the nominal variable "gender" is part of the study, tell SPSS that 1 equals male and 2 equals female. The numbers are the values and the words are the labels.

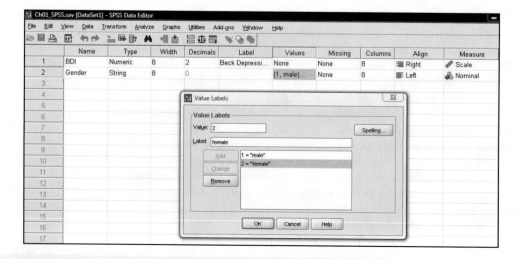

Now tell SPSS what kind of variables these are by selecting:

Measure. Highlight the type of variable by clicking on the cell in the column labeled "Measure" next to each variable, then clicking on the arrow to access the tool that allows you to identify whether the variable is scale, ordinal, or nominal. Notice that this is not necessary for nominal variables if the type is already listed as "string."

After describing all the variables in the study in "Variable View," switch over to "Data View" and notice that the information you entered was automatically transferred to that screen, but now the variables are displayed across the tops of the columns instead of along the left-hand side of the rows. You can now enter your data in "Data View" under the appropriate heading; each participant's data are entered across one row.

Exercises

Clarifying the Concepts

1.1 What is the difference between descriptive and inferential statistics?

1.2 What is the difference between a sample and a population?

1.3 Identify and define the four types of variables that researchers could use to quantify their observations.

1.4 Describe two ways that statisticians might use the word *scale.*

1.5 Distinguish discrete and continuous variables.

1.6 What is the relation between an independent variable and a dependent variable?

1.7 What are confounding variables (or simply confounds) and how are they controlled using random assignment?

1.8 What is the difference between reliability and validity, and how are they related?

1.9 To test a hypothesis, we need operational definitions of our independent and dependent variables. What is an operational definition?

1.10 In your own words, define the word *experiment*—first as you would use it in everyday conversation, and then as a researcher would use it.

1.11 What is the difference between experimental research and correlational research?

1.12 What is the difference between a between-groups research design and a within-groups research design?

1.13 In statistics, it is important to pay very close attention to language. The following statements are wrong but can be corrected by substituting one word or phrase. For example, the sentence "Only correlational studies can tell us something about causality" could be corrected by changing "correlational studies" to "experiments." Identify the incorrect word or phrase in each of the following statements, and supply the correct word.

  a. In a study on exam preparation, every participant had an equal chance of being told she had to study alone or being told she would study with a group. This was a correlational study.

  b. A psychologist was interested in studying the effects of the dependent variable of caffeine on hours of sleep, and he used a scale measure to assess sleep.

  c. A university assessed the reliability of a commonly used scale—a mathematics placement test—to determine if it were truly measuring math ability.

  d. In a within-groups experiment on calcium and osteoporosis, participants were assigned to one of two levels of the independent variable: no change in diet or calcium supplement.

  e. A researcher studied a population of 20 rats to determine whether changes in exposure to light would lead to changes in the dependent variable of amount of sleep.

Calculating the Statistics

1.14 A researcher studies the average distance that 130 people who are living in U.S. urban areas walk each week.

  a. What is the size of the sample?

  b. Identify the population.

1.15 Seventy-three people are stopped as they leave a popular grocery store, and the number of fruit and vegetable items they purchased is assessed.

  a. Calculate the size of the sample.

  b. Identify the population.

1.16 Is the "average" calculated in Exercise 1.14 a descriptive statistic or an inferential statistic if it is used to describe the 130 people studied?

1.17 Is the number of items counted in Exercise 1.15 a descriptive statistic or an inferential statistic if it is used to estimate the diets of all shoppers?

1.18 Referencing Exercise 1.14, how might you calculate the average distance walked in one week as a(n):

  a. ordinal measure?

  b. scale measure?

1.19 Referencing Exercise 1.15, how might you calculate the amount of fruit and vegetable items purchased on a trip to the store as a(n):

  a. nominal measure?

  b. ordinal measure?

  c. scale measure?

1.20 In the fall of 2008, the U.S. stock market plummeted several times, which meant grave consequences for the economy. A researcher might assess the economic effect this situation had by seeing how much money people saved in the year 2008. Those amounts could be compared to how much money people saved in more economically stable years. How might you calculate (or operationalize) economic implications at the national level?

1.21 A researcher might be interested in evaluating how the physical and emotional "distance" a person had from Manhattan at the time of the 9/11 terrorist attacks relates to the accuracy of memory for the event. Identify the independent variables and the dependent variable.

1.22 Referencing Exercise 1.21, imagine that physical distance is assessed as within 100 miles or 100 miles or farther; also, imagine that emotional distance is assessed as knowing no one who was affected, knowing people who were affected but lived, and knowing someone who died in the events. How many levels do the independent variables have?

1.23 How might you operationalize the dependent variable, accuracy of memory, for the event in Exercise 1.21?

1.24 A study of the effects of skin tone (light, medium, and dark) on the severity of facial wrinkles in middle age might be of interest to cosmetic surgeons.

   a. What is the independent variable in this study?

   b. What is the dependent variable in this study?

   c. How many levels does the independent variable have?

Applying the Concepts

1.25 The CDC reported very large weight increases for U.S. residents of both genders and of all age groups over the last four decades. Go to the Web site that reports these data (www.cdc.gov) and search for the article titled "Americans Slightly Taller, Much Heavier Than 40 Years Ago."

   a. What were the average weights of 10-year-old girls in 1963 and in 2002?

   b. Do you think the CDC weighed every girl in the United States to get these averages? Why would this not be feasible?

   c. How does the average weight of 10-year-old girls in 2002 represent both a descriptive and an inferential statistic?

1.26 The Health Study of Nord-Trøndelag County of Norway surveyed more than 60,000 people in a Norwegian county and reported that "people who have gastrointestinal symptoms, such as nausea, are more likely to have anxiety disorders or depression than people who do not have such symptoms."

   a. What is the sample used by these researchers?

   b. What is the population to which the researchers would like to extend their findings?

1.27 At the 2008 Beijing Summer Olympics, 23-year-old Michael Phelps won eight gold medals, a world record for the number of gold medals won in a single Olympic Games. One of his winning events was the 200-meter butterfly. For each of the following examples, identify the type of variable—nominal, ordinal, or scale.

   a. Phelps of the United States came in first, László Cseh of Hungary came in second, and Takeshi Matsuda of Japan came in third.

   b. Phelps finished in 1 minute and 52.03 seconds, a new world record. Cseh finished in 1:52.70, and Matsuda finished in 1:52.97.

   c. One might examine whether swimmers were impaired during the race or not. Phelps was blinded when his goggles filled with water. Neither Cseh nor Matsuda suffered any impairment.

1.28 The Kentucky Derby is perhaps the premier event in U.S. horse racing, and it provides many opportunities for identifying types of variables. For each of the following examples, identify the type of variable—nominal, ordinal, or scale.

   a. As racing fans, we would be very interested in the variable of finishing position. For example, a stunning upset took place in 2005 when Giacomo, a horse with 50-1 odds, won, followed by Closing Argument and then Afleet Alex.

   b. We also might be interested in the variable of finishing time. Giacomo won in 2 minutes, 2.75 seconds.

   c. If we were the betting type, we might examine the variable of payoffs. Giacomo was such a long shot that a $2.00 bet on him to win paid an incredibly high $102.60.

   d. We might be interested in the history of the Derby and the demographic variables of jockeys, such as gender or race. For example, in the first 28 runnings of the Kentucky Derby, 15 of the winning jockeys were African American.

   e. In the luxury boxes, high fashion reigns; we might be curious about the variable of hat wearing, observing how many women wear hats and how many do not.

1.29 For each of the following examples, state whether the interval variable is discrete or continuous.

   a. The capacity, in terms of songs, of an iPod

   b. The playing time of an individual song

   c. The cost in cents to download a song legally

   d. The number of posted reviews that a CD has on Amazon.com

   e. The weight of an MP3 player

1.30 The article "What's Wrong with the Rorschach: Science Confronts the Controversial Inkblot Test" (Wood et al., 2003) presents an overview of scientific evidence that suggests the Rorschach test performs poorly at diagnosing psychopathology, determining personality traits, and predicting future behavior. For example, the Rorschach tends to overdiagnose, labeling many people without psychopathology as sick.

a. Do these findings relate more to reliability or validity? Explain.

b. Explain how a test such as the Rorschach could be reliable, even if it was not valid.

1.31 You may have been in a wine store and wondered just how useful those posted wine ratings are (usually a scale with 100 as the top score). After all, aren't ratings subjective? Corsi and Ashenfelter (2001) studied whether wine experts are consistent. Knowing that the weather is the best predictor of price, the researchers wondered how well weather predicted experts' ratings. The variables used for weather included temperature and rainfall, and the variable used for wine experts' ratings was based on the numbers they assigned to each wine.

a. Name one independent variable. What type of variable is it? Is it discrete or continuous?

b. Name the dependent variable. What type of variable is it? Is it discrete or continuous?

c. How does this study reflect the concept of reliability?

d. Let's say that you frequently drink wine that's been rated highly by Robert Parker, one of the wine experts in this study. His ratings were determined to be reliable, and you find that you usually agree with Robert Parker. How does this observation reflect the concept of validity?

1.32 Go online and take the personality test found at www.outofservice.com/starwars. This test assesses your personality in terms of the characters from the original *Star Wars* series. (You may have to scroll down to get to the questions.)

a. What does it mean for a test to be reliable? Take the test a second time. Does it seem to be reliable?

b. What does it mean for a test to be valid? Does this test seem to be valid? Explain.

1.33 The *Star Wars* personality test from Exercise 1.32 asks a number of demographic questions at the end. For example, it asks "In what country did you spend most of your youth?"

a. Can you think of a hypothesis that might have led the developers of this Web site to ask this question?

b. For the hypothesis in part (a), identify the independent and dependent variables.

1.34 For each of the following hypotheses, identify the likely dependent variable and a likely way of operationalizing that dependent variable. Be specific.

a. Teenagers are better at video games than are adults in their 30s.

b. Spanking children leads them to be more violent.

c. Weight Watchers leads to more weight loss if you go to meetings than if you participate online.

d. Students do better in statistics if they study with other people than if they study alone.

e. Drinking caffeinated beverages with dinner makes it harder to get to sleep at night.

1.35 For each of the following hypotheses, identify the independent variable and the most likely levels of that independent variable.

a. Teenagers are better at video games than are adults in their 30s.

b. Spanking children leads them to be more violent.

c. Weight Watchers leads to more weight loss if you go to meetings than if you participate online.

d. Students do better in statistics if they study with other people than if they study alone.

e. Drinking caffeinated beverages with dinner makes it harder to get to sleep at night.

1.36 For each of the following variables—both described at some point in this chapter—state (i) how the researcher operationalized the variable and (ii) one other way in which the researcher could have operationalized the variable.

a. The distance between the well and the homes where people had died (in Dr. Snow's study)

b. The length of a woman's hair (in Eleanor Stampone's study)

1.37 Researchers at Washington State University (Joireman et al., 2005) reported that people with higher CFC scores tended to have less credit card debt and were less likely to buy on impulse.

a. Identify the independent and dependent variables in this study.

b. For the variable of impulse buying, give an example of an item that might have appeared on this survey instrument that would likely be valid.

1.38 Refer to the study described in the Exercise 1.37.

a. Is this study an experiment or a correlational study? Why?

b. Is it possible that a confounding variable might have affected these results? If yes, suggest at least one possible confounding variable.

c. Now that you know these results, suggest a related hypothesis about the CFC that might lead to a follow-up study.

1.39 Several studies have documented the susceptibility of people who are HIV-positive to cholera, likely because of weakened immune systems. Researchers in Mozambique (Lucas et al., 2005), a country where an estimated 20% to 30% of the population is HIV-positive, wondered whether an oral vaccine for cholera would work among people who are HIV-positive. Fourteen thousand people in Mozambique who tested positive for HIV were immunized against cholera. Soon thereafter, an epidemic of cholera spread through the region, giving the researchers an opportunity to test their hypothesis.

a. Describe a way in which the researchers could have conducted an experiment to examine the effectiveness of the cholera vaccine among people who are HIV-positive.

b. If the researchers did conduct an experiment, would this have been a between-groups or within-groups experiment? Explain.

c. The researchers did not randomly assign participants to vaccine or no-vaccine conditions; rather, they conducted a general mass immunization. Why does this limit their ability to draw causal conclusions? State at least one possible confounding variable.

1.40 Refer to the study on cholera and HIV described in Exercise 1.39. The researchers did not use random assignment when conducting this study.

a. List at least one practical reason that the researchers might not have used random assignment.

b. List at least one ethical reason that the researchers might not have used random assignment.

1.41 If we had been conducting the study described in Exercise 1.39 and were unconcerned with practicality and ethics, describe how we could have used random assignment.

1.42 Noting the marked increases in weight across the population, many researchers, nutritionists, and physicians have struggled to find ways to stem the tide of obesity in many Western countries. A number of exercise programs have been advocated by these clinicians and researchers, and there has been a flurry of research to determine their effectiveness. Pretend that you are in charge of a research program to examine the effects of an exercise program on weight loss in comparison with a no-exercise program.

a. Describe how you could study this exercise program using a between-groups research design.

b. Describe how you could study this exercise program using a within-groups design.

c. What is a potential confound of a within-groups design?

1.43 For decades, researchers, politicians, and tobacco company executives debated the relation between smoking and health problems, such as cancer.

a. Why was this research necessarily correlational in nature?

b. What confounding variables might make it difficult to isolate the effects of smoking tobacco on health?

c. How might the nature of this research and confounds "buy time" for the tobacco industry in acknowledging the hazardous effects of smoking?

d. All ethics aside, how could you study the relation between smoking and health problems using a between-groups experiment?

1.44 A researcher interested in the cultural values of individualistic and collectivistic societies collects data on the rate of relationship conflict experienced by 32 people who test high for individualism and 37 people who test high for collectivist values.

a. Is this research experimental or correlational? Explain.

b. What is the sample?

c. Write a possible hypothesis for this researcher.

d. How might we operationalize relationship conflict?

1.45 A researcher wants to know if people's concerns for the environment might vary as a function of incentives provided for recycling. Students living on a university campus are recruited to participate in a study. Some students are randomly assigned to a group in which they are rewarded financially for all of their recycling efforts for one month. The other students are randomly assigned to a group in which they are assessed a fee based on the amount of materials designated for recycling that they failed to recycle.

a. Is this research experimental or correlational? Explain.

b. Write a hypothesis for this researcher.

Terms

Frequency Distributions

Frequency Distributions

Frequency Tables
Grouped Frequency Tables
Histograms
Frequency Polygons
Applying Visual Depictions of Data

Shapes of Distributions

Normal Distributions
Skewed Distributions

BEFORE YOU GO ON

■ You should understand the different types of variables—nominal, ordinal, scale (Chapter 1).

■ You should understand the difference between a discrete variable and a continuous variable (Chapter 1).

It has been suggested that children who are exposed to fast-paced television programming—quick camera changes, lots of sound effects, multiple plots—have more difficulty with learning and tend to be less imaginative (Healy, 1990). More ominously, in 1997, more than 700 Japanese children were rushed to hospitals after viewing a particular scene from the cartoon show *Pokemon*. What the children saw that apparently triggered some seizures (Smillie, 1997) was a fast-paced scene with a strobe-like effect using red, white, and blue flashes that were combined with explosions of other colors (McCollum & Bryant, 2003). In the United States, the popular children's program *Sesame Street* has also been criticized for its fast pacing, which critics believe encourages children to love television but not to love learning (Postman, 1985).

To understand the effects of pacing, researchers created a simple list that reported the pacing scores for 85 different children's programs (McCollum & Bryant, 2003). In Table 2-1, you can see that *Mr. Rogers' Neighborhood* was the slowest-paced show (not surprising to those who have seen it) with a pacing score of 14.95. The fastest-paced show was *Bill Nye the Science Guy* with a pacing score of 50.60.

Of course, we can only understand the pattern of these numbers when they are ranked from the fastest-paced television show to the slowest-paced television show, or from the slowest to the fastest, and then organized in a way that makes sense. That is the main point of this chapter: the first thing to do when confronted with a data set is to order the list of numbers so that you can organize them and understand their overall pattern.

Do fast-paced programs harm children's ability to learn? The jury is still out. Even though *Sesame Street* is slow-paced relative to other shows, some researchers still regard it as too fast-paced to achieve its educational goals (Schmidt & Vandewater, 2008). However, the researchers who developed the pacing index discovered some other interesting information when they averaged the pacing of children's television shows across different networks. The rank-ordered list in Table 2-2 shows that commercial networks produced the fastest-paced shows and that educational televison produced the slowest-paced shows. Perhaps fast pacing helps commercial networks win the competition for viewers' eyes, while slow pacing wins the competition for viewers' minds.

■ A **raw score** is a data point that has not yet been transformed or analyzed.

■ A **frequency distribution** describes the pattern of a set of numbers by displaying a count or proportion for each possible value of a variable.

■ A **frequency table** is a visual depiction of data that shows how often each value occurred; that is, how many scores were at each value. Values are listed in one column, and the numbers of individuals with scores at that value are listed in the second column.

TABLE 2-1. The Pacing of Children's Television Shows

The fast pace of many children's television programs has been criticized for possibly lowering children's ability to concentrate. This table depicts a sample of the 85 television programs and a pacing index for each one. A higher index indicates a faster-paced program, and a lower index indicates a slower-paced program.

Television Show	Pacing Index
Bill Nye the Science Guy	50.60
Power Rangers	41.90
Tiny Toons	40.70
Charlie Brown	33.10
Scooby Doo	30.60
Simpsons	30.25
Batman	25.85
Sesame Street	24.80
Blue's Clues	21.85
Mr. Rogers' Neighborhood	14.95

In this chapter, we learn how to organize our individual data points in a table. Then, we go one step further and learn how to use two types of graphs—histograms and frequency polygons—to show the overall pattern of the data. Finally, we learn to use these graphs to understand the shape of the distribution of the data points. All of these tools are important steps for using statistics in the behavioral sciences.

Frequency Distributions

Researchers are usually most interested in the relations between two or more variables, such as the effect of a television show's pacing (the first variable) on children's learning (the second variable). But to understand the relation between variables, we must first understand each individual variable, the data points. The basic ingredients of a data set are called the ***raw scores***, *data that have not yet been transformed or analyzed*. In statistics, we organize our raw scores into a ***frequency distribution***, which *describes the pattern of a set of numbers by displaying a count or proportion for each possible value of a variable*. For example, a frequency distribution can display the pattern of the scores—the pacing indices—from the excerpted list of television shows, as in Table 2-2.

TABLE 2-2. The Pacing of Children's Shows by Network

When children's programs were categorized by network and then averaged, it was revealed that the fastest-paced programs were offered by commercial networks and the slowest-paced programs were offered by educational networks.

Network	Average Pacing Index
Commercial networks	34.29
Nickelodeon	33.03
Disney	32.55
PBS	27.26
The Learning Channel	25.35

There are several different ways to organize the data in terms of a frequency distribution. The first approach, the frequency table, is also the starting point for each of the three other ways that we will explore. A ***frequency table*** *is a visual depiction of data that shows how often each value occurred; that is, how many scores were at each value*. Once organized into a frequency table, the data can be displayed as a grouped frequency table, a frequency histogram, or a frequency polygon. These four methods of visually organizing data represent the basic tools in a statistician's toolbox. If one technique doesn't give us a clear picture of the data, another one might work better.

> ◀ **MASTERING THE CONCEPT**
>
> **2-1:** A frequency table shows the pattern of our data by indicating how many participants had each possible score. The data in a frequency table can be graphed in a frequency histogram or a frequency polygon.

Frequency Tables

EXAMPLE 2.1

A research team wondered why fewer women than men achieved high-prestige academic positions in the field of chemistry (Kuck, Buckner, Marzabadi, & Nolan, 2007). In the United States and many other countries, many women excel in science as

Does Mentoring Make a Difference? Data suggest that graduate school advisors make a difference in the field of chemistry. Some do much better than others in having their former students end up in prestigious academic positions.

young students but leave the field when they pursue higher levels of education. The focus of Kuck and colleagues' research (2007) was on mentoring, so they identified the most successful mentors: U.S. professors whose students were hired by the top 50 chemistry departments in the United States. They investigated whether these professors were equally successful at nurturing the talents of both male and female graduate students.

The participants in this archival study were all graduate school advisors who had at least three former PhD students go on to jobs as professors in one of the top 50 U.S. chemistry departments. Just 54 graduate advisors met this highly selective criterion. Each score represents the number of students successfully mentored by each different professor. Here are the data for the 54 top-producing graduate advisors:

3, 3, 3, 4, 5, 9, 5, 3, 3, 5, 6, 3, 4, 8, 6, 3, 3, 3, 4, 4, 4, 7, 6, 3, 5, 5, 7, 13, 3, 3, 3, 3, 3, 4, 4, 4, 5, 6, 7, 6, 7, 8, 8, 3, 3, 3, 5, 3, 3, 5, 3, 5, 3, 3

At first glance, it is not easy to find a pattern in these numbers. But when we reorder those numbers, a pattern begins to emerge. A frequency table is the best way to create an easy-to-understand distribution of the data. In this example, we simply organize the data into a table with two columns, one for the range of possible responses—the values—and one for the frequencies of each of the responses—the scores.

There are specific steps to follow when creating a frequency table. First, we examine our data to determine the range of scores. We know at a glance that the lowest score is 3. A quick glance also reveals that the highest score is 13; one professor successfully mentored 13 high-achieving students, a most impressive number. Simply noting that the scores range from 3 to 13 brings some clarity to the data set. But we can do even better.

After we identify the lowest and highest scores, we create the two columns that we see in Table 2-3 by counting how many graduate advisors fall at each value. This is done by going through the raw scores and determining how many fall at each value in the range. The appropriate number for each value is then recorded in the table. For example, there is only one advisor with 13 students, so a 1 is marked there. It is important to note that we include *all* numbers in the range; there are no advisors with 12, 11, or 10 students, so we put a 0 next to each one.

Here is a recap of the steps to create a frequency table:

1. Determine the highest score and the lowest score.
2. Create two columns: the first is labeled with the variable name, and the second is labeled "frequency."
3. List the full range of values that encompasses all the scores in the data set from highest to lowest. Include *all* values in the range, even those for which the frequency is 0.
4. Count the number of scores at each value, and write those numbers in the frequency column.

Creating a frequency table for the data gives us more insight into the set of numbers. As demonstrated in Table 2-4, we can also describe the number of advisors (who had a particular number of students now in top jobs) as percentages. To calculate a percentage, we divide the number of advisors in a category (categories based on numbers of students

TABLE 2-3. Frequency Tables and Graduate Advising

This frequency table depicts the number of students placed on the top 50 chemistry faculties by each top-producing graduate advisor. If you wanted a high-profile professorial job, which advisor would you want?

Former Students Now in Top Jobs	Frequency
13	1
12	0
11	0
10	0
9	1
8	3
7	4
6	5
5	9
4	8
3	23

Data from Kuck et al. (2007).

now in top jobs) by the total number of advisors, and then multiply by 100. As we observed earlier, one out of 54 advisors had 13 graduate students go on to top jobs.

$$\frac{1}{54}(100) = 1.85$$

So, for the score of 13 graduate students, the percentage for 1 of 54 advisors is 1.85%.

TABLE 2-4. Expansion of a Frequency Table

This frequency table is an expansion of Table 2-3, which depicts the numbers of students placed on the top 50 chemistry faculties by each top-producing graduate advisor. It now includes percentages, which are often more descriptive than the actual counts.

Former Students Now in Top Jobs	Frequency	Percentage
13	1	1.85
12	0	0.00
11	0	0.00
10	0	0.00
9	1	1.85
8	3	5.56
7	4	7.41
6	5	9.26
5	9	16.67
4	8	14.81
3	23	42.59

Data from Kuck et al. (2007).

Note that when we calculate statistics, we can come up with slightly different answers depending on how we round off at each step. If there are many steps, we can even come up with very different answers depending on our rounding decisions. In this book, we round off to three decimal places throughout our calculations, but we report our final answers to two decimal places, rounding up or down as appropriate. If you follow this guideline, then you should get the same answers that we get.

Grouped Frequency Tables

In the previous example, we used data that counted the numbers of people, which are whole numbers. In addition, the range was fairly limited—3 to 13. But often, data are not so easily understood. Consider these two situations:

1. When data can go to many decimal places, such as reaction times

2. When data cover a huge range, such as countries' populations

In both of these situations, the frequency table would go on for pages and pages—and nobody wants to read all those individual data. For example, if someone weighed only 0.0003 pound more than the next weight, that person would belong to a distinctive, unique category. Not only would we be creating an enormous amount of unnecessary work for ourselves, but we also wouldn't be able to see trends in the data. Fortunately, we have a technique to deal with these situations: *a **grouped frequency table** allows us to depict our data visually by reporting the frequencies within a given interval rather than the frequencies for a specific value.* The word *interval* is used in more than one way by statisticians. Here, it refers to a range of values (as opposed to an interval variable, the type of variable that we presume to have equal distances between values).

EXAMPLE 2.2

The following data exemplify the first of these two situations in which the data aren't easily conveyed in a standard frequency table. These are the pacing indices for the 85 television shows, some of which are listed in Table 2-1. The pacing index data are reported to two decimal places:

50.60 50.30 45.95 45.75 44.65 43.25 42.20 41.95 41.90 41.80

40.80 40.70 40.25 40.25 39.10 37.80 37.55 37.00 36.25 36.00

35.90 35.55 35.55 35.50 35.40 34.30 34.00 33.85 33.75 33.55

33.10 32.85 32.75 32.55 32.40 32.25 31.85 31.60 31.45 31.10

31.00 31.00 30.70 30.65 30.60 30.40 30.30 30.25 30.20 29.85

29.85 29.30 29.30 29.30 29.20 29.20 28.95 28.70 28.55 28.50

28.45 28.20 28.10 27.95 27.55 27.45 27.05 27.05 26.95 26.95

26.75 26.25 25.85 25.35 25.15 25.15 24.80 23.35 23.10 21.85

20.60 19.90 16.50 15.75 14.95

▪ A **grouped frequency table** is a visual depiction of data that reports the frequencies within a given interval rather than the frequencies for a specific value.

A quick glance at these data does not really tell us the pacing index of the typical television show. A frequency table wouldn't be very helpful either. The lowest score is 14.95 and the highest is 50.60. The top of a frequency table would look like Table 2-5. Such a table would be absurdly long and would not convey much more information that we could interpret than does the list of the original raw data.

TABLE 2-5. Unwieldy Frequency Table

A frequency table that lists every possible value is often not much more useful than a listing of every single score. Here we see the pacing indices of children's television shows, although it is only an excerpt of the possible indices. The full table would be ridiculously long.

Pacing Index	Frequency
50.60	1
50.59	0
50.58	0
50.57	0
50.56	0
50.55	0
50.54	0
50.53	0
.	.
.	.
.	.
14.96	0
14.95	1

Instead of reporting every single value in the range, we can report intervals, or ranges of values. Here are the five steps to generate a standard grouped frequency table:

STEP 1. Find the highest and lowest scores in the frequency distribution.

In our example, these scores are 14.95 and 50.60.

STEP 2. Determine the full range of data.

If there are decimal places, round both the highest and lowest scores down to the nearest whole numbers. If they already are whole numbers, use these. Subtract the lowest whole number from the highest whole number and add 1 to get the full range of the data. (Why do we add 1? Try it yourself. If we subtract 14 from 50, we get 36—but count the values from 14 through 50, including the numbers at either end. There are 37 numbers, and we want to know the full range of the data.)

In our example, 14.95 and 50.60 round down to 14 and 50, respectively; 50 − 14 = 36, and 36 + 1 = 37. Our scores fall within a range of 37.

STEP 3. Determine the number of intervals and the best interval size.

There is no consensus about the ideal number of intervals, but most researchers recommend between 5 and 10 intervals, depending on the data. If we have an enormous data set with a huge range, then we might have many more intervals than 10. To find the best interval range, we divide the range by the number of intervals we want, then round that answer to the nearest whole number. With wide ranges, it's a multiple of 10 or 100 or 1000; with smaller ranges, it could be as small as 2, 3, or 5, or even 1 (or less than 1 if the numbers go to many decimal places). Try several interval sizes to get the best whole number for the interval size.

In our example, we might choose to have about 8 intervals. If we choose 8, we'll have an interval size of 5.

STEP 4. Figure out the number that will be the bottom of the lowest interval.

We want the bottom of that interval to be a multiple of our interval size. For example, if we have 8 intervals of size 5, then we want the bottom interval to start at a multiple of 5. It could start at 0, 10, 55, or 105, depending on our data. We choose which one by selecting the multiple of 5 that is below our lowest score.

In our example, we have 8 intervals of size 5, so the bottom of our lowest interval should be a multiple of 5. Our lowest score is 14.95, so the bottom of our lowest interval would be 10. (If our lowest score were 7.22, we would choose 5. Note that this process might lead to one more interval than we planned for; this is perfectly fine. In our case, we have 9, rather than the 8 intervals we had estimated.)

STEP 5. Finish the table by listing the intervals from highest to lowest and then counting the numbers of scores in each.

This step is much like creating a frequency table (without intervals), which we discussed earlier. If we decide on intervals of size 5 and the first one begins at 10, then we count the five numbers that fall in this interval: 10, 11, 12, 13, and 14. The interval in this example runs from 10 to 14. (In reality, it runs from 10 to 14.9999, and the next one begins at 15, five digits higher than the bottom of the preceding interval.) A good rule of thumb is that the *bottom* of the intervals should jump by the chosen interval size, in this case 5.

In our example, the lowest interval would be 10 to 14, or 10.00 to 14.99. The next one would be 15.00 to 19.99, and so on.

The grouped frequency table in Table 2-6 gives us a much better sense of the pacing indices of the TV shows in this sample than either the list of raw data or a frequency table without intervals.

TABLE 2-6. Grouped Frequency Table

Grouped frequency tables make sense of data sets in which there are many possible values. This grouped frequency table depicts the frequencies for television show pacing indices. The table provides the number of TV programs with pacing indices within each interval of indices.

Interval	Frequency
50.00–54.99	2
45.00–49.99	2
40.00–44.99	10
35.00–39.99	11
30.00–34.99	24
25.00–29.99	27
20.00–24.99	5
15.00–19.99	3
10.00–14.99	1

Histograms

Even more than tables, graphs help us to see our data at a glance. The two most common methods for graphing scale data for one variable are the histogram and the frequency polygon. Here we learn to construct and interpret both the histogram (more common) and the frequency polygon (less common).

Histograms look like bar graphs but typically depict scale data with the values of the variable on the x-axis and the frequencies on the y-axis. Each bar reflects the frequency for each value or interval. The difference between histograms and bar graphs is that bar graphs typically provide scores for nominal data (e.g., frequencies of men and women); histograms typically provide frequencies for scale data (e.g., pacing indices). We can construct histograms from frequency tables or from grouped frequency tables. Histograms allow for the many intervals that typically occur with scale data. The bars are stacked one against the next, with the intervals meaningfully arranged from lower numbers (on the left) to higher numbers (on the right). With bar graphs, the categories do not need to be arranged in one particular order.

EXAMPLE 2.3

Let's start by constructing a histogram from a frequency table. Table 2-3 depicted the data on chemistry graduate advisors and the numbers of students they placed in top professorial positions. We construct a histogram by drawing the x-axis (horizontal) and y-axis (vertical) of a graph. We label the x-axis with the variable of interest—in our case, "number of students"—and we label the y-axis "frequency." As with most graphs, the lowest numbers start where the axes intersect and the numbers go up—as we go to the right on the x-axis and as we go up on the y-axis. Ideally, the lowest number on each axis is 0, so that the graphs are not misleading. However, if the range of numbers on either axis is far from 0, histograms sometimes use a number other than 0 as the lowest number. Further, if there are negative numbers among the scores (such as air temperature), the x-axis could have negative numbers.

Once we've created our graph, we draw bars for each value. Each bar is *centered on* the value for which it provides the frequency. The heights of the bars represent the numbers of scores that fell at each value—the frequencies. If no one had a score at a particular value, no bar is drawn. So, for the value of 7 on the x-axis, a bar centers on 7 with a height of 4 on the y-axis, indicating that four scores had a value of 7. See Figure 2-1 for the histogram for the "chemistry advisor" data.

Here is a recap of the steps to construct a histogram from a frequency table:

1. Draw the x-axis and label it with the variable of interest and the full range of values for this variable. (Include 0 unless all of the scores are so far from 0 that it's impractical.)

2. Draw the y-axis, label it "frequency," and include the full range of frequencies for this variable. (Include 0 unless it's impractical.)

3. Draw a bar for each value, centering the bar around that value on the x-axis and drawing the bar as high as the frequency for that value as represented on the y-axis.

Grouped frequency tables can also be depicted as histograms. Instead of listing values on the x-axis, we list the midpoints of intervals. Students commonly make mistakes in determining the midpoints of intervals. If three intervals range from 0 to 9, 10 to 19, and 20 to 29, what are the midpoints? If you said 4.5, 14.5, and 24.5, you're making a *very* common mistake. Remember, the intervals really go from

▪ A **histogram** looks like a bar graph but is typically used to depict scale data with the values of the variable on the x-axis and the frequencies on the y-axis.

FIGURE 2-1
Histogram for the Frequency
Table of Graduate Advisors

Histograms are graphic depictions of the
information in frequency tables or
grouped frequency tables. This
histogram shows us how many
graduate advisors placed different
numbers of students into top
professorial positions.

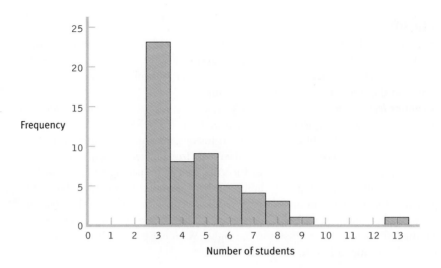

0.000000 to 9.999999, or as close as you can get to 10 without actually being 10. Given that there are 10 numbers in this range (0, 1, 2, 3, 4, 5, 6, 7, 8, and 9), the midpoint would be 5 from the bottom. So the midpoints for 0 to 9, 10 to 19, and 20 to 29 are 5, 15, and 25. A good rule: When determining a midpoint, look at the bottom of the interval that you're interested in and then the bottom of the next interval. What's the midpoint between the two interval minimums? Once you've determined your midpoints, check them; they should jump by the interval size. Here, the interval size is 10. Notice that the midpoints consistently jump by 10 (5, 15, and 25).

EXAMPLE 2.4

Let's look at the TV pacing index data in Table 2-1 for which we will construct a grouped frequency histogram. What are our midpoints? There are nine intervals: 10 to 14.99, 15.00 to 19.99, 20.00 to 24.99, and so on up to 50.00 to 54.99. Let's calculate the midpoint for the lowest interval. We should look at the bottom of this interval, 10.00, and the bottom of the next interval, 15.00. The midpoint of these numbers is 12.50; so that is the midpoint of this interval. The remaining intervals can be calculated the same way. We can then check to be sure they jump by exactly 5 each time. To calculate the midpoint of the highest interval, imagine that we had one more interval. If we did, it would start at 55.00. The midpoint of 50.00 and 55.00 is 52.50. Using these guidelines, we calculate our midpoints as 12.50, 17.50, 22.50, 27.50, 32.50, 37.50, 42.50, 47.50, and 52.50. We now can construct our histogram by placing these midpoints on the *x*-axis and then drawing bars that center on them and are as high as the frequency for each interval. The histogram for these data is shown in Figure 2-2.

Here is a recap of the steps to construct a histogram from a *grouped* frequency table:

1. Determine the midpoint for every interval.
2. Draw the *x*-axis and label it with the variable of interest and the midpoints for each interval of values on this variable. (Include 0 unless the values are so far from 0 that it's impractical.)

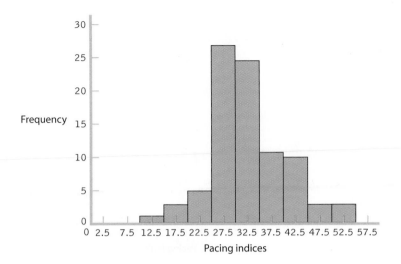

FIGURE 2-2
Histogram for the Grouped Frequency Table of TV Pacing Index Data

Histograms can also depict the data in a grouped frequency table. This histogram depicts the data seen in the grouped frequency table for TV pacing indices.

3. Draw the y-axis, label it "frequency," and include the full range of frequencies for this variable. (Include 0 unless it's impractical.)

4. Draw a bar for each midpoint, centering the bar on that midpoint on the x-axis and drawing the bar as high as the frequency for that interval as represented on the y-axis.

Frequency Polygons

Frequency polygons are constructed in a very similar way to histograms. As the name might imply, polygons are many-sided shapes. Histograms look like city skylines, but polygons look more like mountain landscapes. Specifically, a ***frequency polygon*** *is a line graph with the x-axis representing values (or midpoints of intervals) and the y-axis representing frequencies; a dot is placed at the frequency for each value (or midpoint), and the dots are connected.*

EXAMPLE 2.5

For the most part, we make frequency polygons exactly as we make histograms. Instead of constructing bars above each value or midpoint, however, we draw dots and connect them. The other difference is that we need to add an appropriate value (or midpoint) on either end of the graph so that we can draw lines down to 0, grounding our shape. Figure 2-3 shows the frequency polygon for the grouped frequency distribution of TV pacing indices that we constructed previously in Figure 2-2.

Here is a recap of the steps to construct a frequency polygon. When basing a frequency polygon on a frequency table, we place the specific values on the x-axis. When basing it on a grouped frequency table, we place the midpoints of intervals on the x-axis.

1. If based on a grouped frequency table, determine the midpoint for every interval. If based on a frequency table, skip this step.

2. Draw the x-axis and label it with the variable of interest and either the values or the midpoints. (Include 0 unless the values/midpoints are so far from 0 that it's impractical.)

- A **frequency polygon** is a line graph with the *x*-axis representing values (or midpoints of intervals) and the *y*-axis representing frequencies. A dot is placed at the frequency for each value (or midpoint), and the dots are connected.

FIGURE 2-3
**Frequency Polygon as Another
Graphing Option for the TV
Pacing Index Data**

Frequency polygons are an alternative to
histograms. This frequency polygon
depicts the same data that were
depicted in the histogram in Figure 2-2.
In either case, the graph provides an
easily interpreted "picture" of the
distribution.

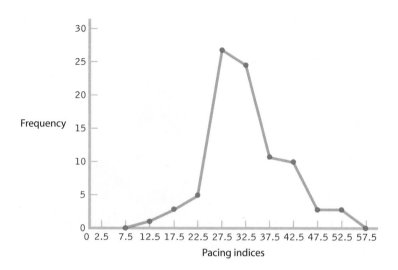

3. Draw the *y*-axis, label it "frequency," and include the full range of frequencies for this variable. (Include 0 unless it's impractical.)

4. Mark a dot above each value or midpoint depicting the frequency, as represented on the *y*-axis, for that value or midpoint, and connect the dots.

5. Add an appropriate hypothetical value or midpoint on both ends of the *x*-axis, and mark a dot for a frequency of 0 for each of these values or midpoints. Connect the existing line to these dots to create a shape rather than a "floating" line.

Applying Visual Depictions of Data

Frequency tables provide far more information than a jumble of raw data, and they lead to more specific research questions. Think back to the study of chemistry professors and the graduate students they advised (Kuck et al, 2007). From the frequency table, we can see that most of these professors trained just a few of these future top faculty members; only a few professors produced many top faculty members. Have you wondered why one advisor did so well, in comparison to his peers, in sending his students on to these prestigious jobs? The professor who trained 13 future top faculty members, Dr. Yuan T. Lee from the University of California at Berkeley, won a Nobel Prize. Did that have anything to do with his success in placing his students in these top jobs? Maybe. But maybe not. Many of Lee's students who went on to top professorships got their jobs *before* he won his Nobel Prize. There are other chemistry Nobel Prize winners in the United States who serve as graduate advisors, but no one else has Lee's record in placing students.

An Unusual Professor While at
the University of California at Berkeley,
Dr. Yuan T. Lee advised 13 chemistry
graduate students who went on to
become professors in one of the top
50 U.S. chemistry departments. A
frequency distribution demonstrates
that this number is far more than were
trained by any other professor, at
Berkeley or any other university, and
suggests research questions about what
specific qualities in an advisor lead to
student success.

CHECK YOUR LEARNING

Reviewing the Concepts

> The first step in organizing data for a single variable is to list all the values in order of magnitude and then count how many times each value occurs.

> There are four techniques for organizing information about a single variable: frequency tables, grouped frequency tables, histograms, and frequency polygons.

Clarifying the Concepts

2-1 Name four different ways to organize raw scores visually.

2-2 What is the difference between frequencies and grouped frequencies?

Calculating the Statistics

2-3 In 2005, *U.S. News & World Report* published a list of the best psychology departments in the United States for doctoral programs. The top 27 departments ranged from Stanford University at number 1 through a tie among the last six universities, which included Johns Hopkins and Northwestern Universities. Let's say you're interested in attending one of these schools, specifically one that has ethnic diversity. Seventeen of these schools reported the number of current students who are members of a racial or ethnic minority group. Here are those data:

17 17 8 12 3 59 41 3 32

4 10 59 20 1 9 3 27

a. Construct a grouped frequency table of these data.

b. Construct a histogram for this grouped frequency table.

c. Construct a frequency polygon for this grouped frequency table.

Applying the Concepts

2-4 Consider the data from Check Your Learning 2-3, as well as the table and graphs that you constructed.

a. What can we tell from the graphs and table that we cannot tell from the list of scores?

b. Why might percentages of students who are members of a minority group be more useful than these numbers? (*Hint:* The numbers of full-time psychology graduate students at these schools range from 19 to 258.)

Solutions to these Check Your Learning questions can be found in Appendix D.

c. Not all schools provided data. How might the schools that provided data on the number of minority students be different from schools that did not provide these data?

Shapes of Distributions

We begin a course in statistics by teaching you how to organize your data so that you can better understand the concept of a distribution, a major building block for statistical analysis. We can't get a sense of the overall pattern of data by looking at a list of numbers, but we *can* get a sense of the pattern by looking at a frequency table or grouped frequency table. We can get an even better sense by creating a graph, either a histogram or a frequency polygon. The two graphs allow us to see the overall pattern, or shape, of the distribution of data.

The shape of a distribution provides distinctive information. For example, when the U.S.-based General Social Survey (a large data set available to the public via the internet) asked people about the influence of children's programming—both network television and public television—their responses produced very different patterns for each type of children's programming (Figure 2-4). For example, the most common response for the network television shows was that they have a neutral influence, whereas the most common response for the public television shows was that they

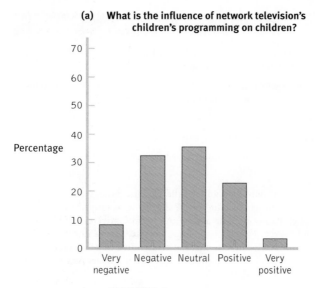

(a) **What is the influence of network television's children's programming on children?**

(b) **What is the influence of public television's children's programming on children?**

FIGURE 2-4
The Influence of Television Programming on Children

have a positive influence. In this section, we provide you with language that expresses the differences between these two patterns. Specifically, you'll learn to describe different shapes of distributions, including normal distributions and skewed distributions.

Normal Distributions

Many, but not all, descriptions of individual variables form a bell-shaped, or *normal*, curve. Statisticians use the word *normal* to describe distributions in a very particular way. *A **normal distribution** is a specific frequency distribution that is a bell-shaped, symmetric, unimodal curve* (Figure 2-5). People's attitudes toward the network programming of children's shows is an example of a distribution that approaches a normal distribution (Figure 2-4(a)). There are fewer scores at values that are farther from the center and even fewer scores at the most extreme values. Most scores cluster around the word "neutral" in the middle of the distribution, at the top of the bell.

Skewed Distributions

Reality is not always normally distributed, which means that the distributions describing those particular observations are not shaped normally. So we need a new term to help us describe such distributions—*skew*. **Skewed distributions** *are distributions in which one of the tails of the distribution is pulled away from the center.* Although the technical term for such data is *skewed*, a skewed distribution also may be described as lopsided, off-center, or simply asymmetric. Skewed data have an ever-thinning tail in one direction or the other. The distribution of people's attitudes toward the children's programming offered by public television is an example of a skewed distribution (Figure 2-5(b)). The scores cluster to the right side of the distribution around the word "positive," and the tail extends to the left.

When a distribution is ***positively skewed***, as in Figure 2-6a, *the tail of the distribution extends to the right, in a positive direction.* Positive skew sometimes occurs when there is a ***floor effect***, *a situation in which a constraint prevents a variable from taking on values below a certain point.* For example, the "chemistry advisor" data, with scores indicating how

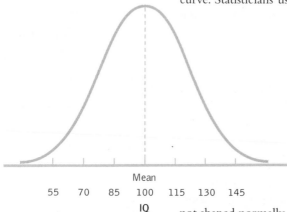

FIGURE 2-5
The Normal Distribution

The normal distribution, shown here for IQ scores, is a frequency distribution that is bell-shaped, symmetric, and unimodal. It is central to many calculations in statistics.

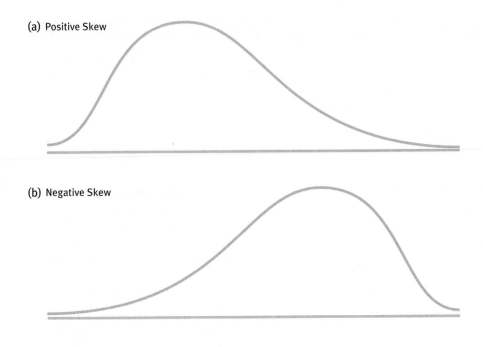

(a) Positive Skew

(b) Negative Skew

FIGURE 2-6
Two Kinds of Skew

The mnemonic "the tail tells the tale" means that the distribution with the long, thin tail to the right is positively skewed and the distribution with the long, thin tail to the left is negatively skewed.

- A **normal distribution** is a specific frequency distribution that is a bell-shaped, symmetric, unimodal curve.

- A **skewed distribution** is a distribution in which one of the tails of the distribution is pulled away from the center.

- With **positively skewed** data, the distribution's tail extends to the right, in a positive direction.

- A **floor effect** is a situation in which a constraint prevents a variable from taking on values below a certain point.

- **Negatively skewed** data have a distribution with a tail that extends to the left, in a negative direction.

- A **ceiling effect** is a situation in which a constraint prevents a variable from taking on values above a given number.

many former students went on to top jobs, is an example of a positively skewed distribution with a floor effect. The researchers considered only professors who had had at least three former students achieve this level of success, which means that the data were constrained at the lower end of the distribution.

The distribution in Figure 2-6b shows ***negatively skewed*** *data, which have a distribution with a tail that extends to the left, in a negative direction.* The distribution of people's attitudes toward children's programming by public television is favorable because it is clustered around the word "positive," but we describe the shape of that distribution as negatively skewed because the thin tail is to the left side of the distribution. Not surprisingly, negative skew is sometimes a result of a ***ceiling effect***, *a situation in which a constraint prevents a variable from taking on values above a given number.* If a professor gives an extremely easy quiz, a ceiling effect might result. A number of students would cluster around 100, the highest possible score, with a few stragglers down in the lower end. Some of the students with very high scores might have scored above 100 if the quiz had had extra credit, but they were limited by the ceiling of 100.

A handy mnemonic you can use to remember the difference between negatively skewed distributions and positively skewed distributions is "the tail tells the tale." Negative scores are to the left, so when the long, thin tail of a distribution is to the left of the distribution's center, we say that it is negatively skewed. When that long, thin tail of the distribution is to the right of the distribution's center, then we say that the distribution is positively skewed. We simply keep in mind that "the tail tells the tale" when we are trying to describe a skewed distribution as either negatively or positively skewed.

> ◀ **MASTERING THE CONCEPT**
>
> **2-2:** If a histogram indicates that our data are symmetric and bell-shaped, then the data are normally distributed. If the data are not symmetric and the tail extends to the right, the data are positively skewed; if the tail extends to the left, the data are negatively skewed.

CHECK YOUR LEARNING

Reviewing the Concepts

> A normal distribution is a specific distribution that is unimodal, symmetric, and bell-shaped.

> A skewed distribution "leans" either to the left or to the right. A tail to the left indicates negative skew, and a tail to the right indicates positive skew.

Clarifying the Concepts

2-5 Distinguish a normal distribution from a skewed distribution.

2-6 When the bulk of data cluster together but there is a trailing off of data to the left, there is _____ skew; when that trailing off of data extends to the right, there is _____ skew.

Calculating the Statistics

2-7 In Check Your Learning 2-3, you constructed three visual displays of the distribution of ethnic diversity in doctoral psychology programs. What kind of skew is evident in your graphs?

2-8 Alzheimer's disease is typically diagnosed in adults above the age of 70; however, we sometimes see cases diagnosed sooner that are labeled "early onset."

   a. Assuming that these early-onset cases represent unique trailing off of data on that one side, would this represent positive skew or negative skew?

   b. Do these data represent a floor effect or ceiling effect?

Applying the Concepts

Solutions to these Check Your Learning questions can be found in Appendix D.

2-9 Referring to Check Your Learning 2-8, what implication would identifying such skew have in the screening and treatment process for Alzheimer's disease?

REVIEW OF CONCEPTS

Frequency Distributions

The *raw scores* of our sample can be difficult to interpret just by glancing at them in their original form. Several techniques help us to understand our data visually; all are variants of *frequency distribution*. *Frequency tables* are composed of two columns, one with all possible values and one with a count of how often each value occurs among the scores in the data set. *Grouped frequency tables* allow us to work with more complicated data. Instead of containing values, the first column consists of intervals. *Histograms* display bars of different heights indicating the frequency of each value (or interval) that a variable can take on. *Frequency polygons* show frequencies with dots at different heights depicting the frequency of each value (or interval) that a variable can take on. The dots in a frequency polygon are connected to form the shape of the data.

Shapes of Distributions

The *normal distribution* is a specific distribution that is unimodal, symmetric, and bell-shaped. Data can also display *skewness*. A distribution that is *positively skewed* has a tail in a positive direction (to the right), indicating more extreme scores above the center. It sometimes results from a *floor effect* in which scores are constrained and cannot be below a certain number. A distribution that is *negatively skewed* has a tail in a negative direction (to the left), indicating more extreme scores below the center. It sometimes results from a *ceiling effect* in which scores are constrained and cannot be above a certain number.

SPSS®

The left-hand column in "Data View" is prenumbered, beginning with 1. Each column to the right of that number contains information about a particular variable; each row below that number represents a unique individual. Notice the choices at the top of the "Data View" screen. Enter the pacing index data from Table 2.1, then start following the menu by selecting **Analyze** → Descriptive Statistics → Frequencies. Then select the variables you want SPSS to de-

scribe, such as pacing indices, by highlighting them and clicking the arrow in the middle.

We also want to visualize each variable, so after selecing "Frequencies," select Charts → Histograms (click the box next to "with normal curve") → Continue → OK.

With all of the SPSS functions, an output screen automatically appears after clicking on OK. The screenshot shown here depicts the part of the SPSS output that includes the histogram.

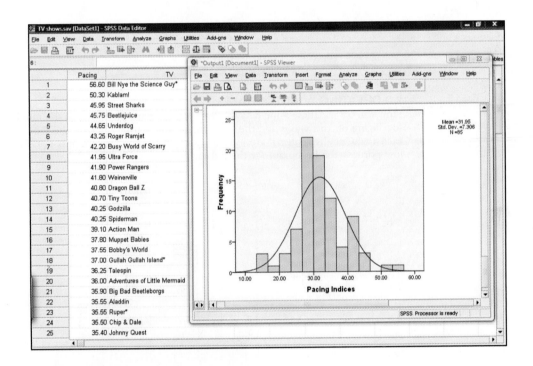

How It Works

2.1 CREATING A FREQUENCY TABLE

Imagine that you ask everyone in a class of 20 first-year college students how many nights they went out to socialize in the previous week. In this case, we might specify that *to socialize* means to leave your place of residence for at least three hours after 6:00 P.M. for any purpose unrelated to academic work. This observation allows only a very specific set of possible responses that range from not going out at all to going out every night: 0, 1, 2, 3, 4, 5, 6, or 7 nights. If we asked each of the 20 students how many nights a week they typically go out to socialize, we might get a data set of 20 numbers that looks like this:

```
1 2 7 6 1
2 6 5 4 4
0 3 2 2 3
4 3 5 4 4
```

How can we use these data to create a frequency table? First, we simply reorder the "nights socializing" data into a table with two columns, one for the range of possible responses—the values—and one for the frequencies of each of the responses—the scores. The frequency table for these data is given below.

Nights	Frequency
7	1
6	2
5	2
4	5
3	3
2	4
1	2
0	1

2.2 CREATING A HISTOGRAM

How can we use these same data to create a histogram? First, we put the number of nights socializing on the x-axis and the frequencies for each number on the y-axis. The bar for each frequency is centered around the appropriate number of nights out. The figure below portrays the histogram for these data.

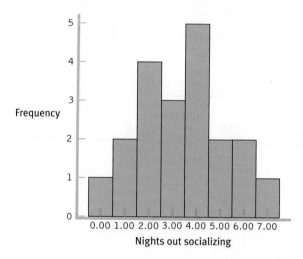

Exercises

Clarifying the Concepts

2.1 What are raw scores?

2.2 What are the steps to create a frequency table?

2.3 What is the difference between a frequency table and a grouped frequency table?

2.4 Describe two ways that statisticians might use the word *interval*.

2.5 What is the difference between a histogram and a frequency polygon?

2.6 What is the benefit of creating a visual distribution of data rather than simply looking at a list of the data?

2.7 In your own words, define the word *distribution*, first as you would use it in everyday conversation and then as a statistician would use it.

2.8 What is a normal distribution?

2.9 How do positively skewed distributions and negatively skewed distributions deviate from a normal distribution?

2.10 What are floor and ceiling effects?

Calculating the Statistics

2.11 Convert the following to percentages: 7 out of 39; 122 out of 300.

2.12 Counts are often converted to percentages. Convert 817 out of 22,140 into a percentage. Now convert 4009 out of 22,140 into a percentage. What type of variable (nominal, ordinal, or scale) are these data as counts? What kind of variable are they as percentages?

2.13 Throughout this book, final answers are reported to two decimal places. Report the following numbers this way: 0.0391, 198.2219, and 17.886.

2.14 On a test of marital satisfaction, scores could range from 0 to 27. What is the full range of data, according to the calculation procedure described in this chapter?

2.15 For the range referenced in Exercise 2.14, what would the interval size be if we wanted 6 intervals?

2.16 Referring to Exercise 2.15, list the 6 intervals.

2.17 If you have data that range from 2 to 68 and you want 7 intervals in a grouped frequency table, list your intervals.

2.18 A grouped frequency table has the following intervals: 30–44, 45–59, 60–74. If converted into a histogram, what would the midpoint of each interval be?

2.19 Referring to the grouped frequency table in Table 2-6, how many children's shows received pacing scores of 35 or higher?

2.20 Using the histogram in Figure 2-1, estimate how many graduate advisors had mentored between three and five students to top professorial positions.

2.21 If the average person convicted of murder killed only one person, serial killers would represent what kind of skew?

2.22 Would the data for number of murders by those convicted of the crime be an example of a floor or ceiling effect?

2.23 A researcher collects data on the ages of college students. As you have probably observed, the distribution of age clusters around 19 to 22 years, but there are extremes on both the low end (with youthful prodigies) and the high end (with nontraditional students returning to school).

a. What type of skew might you expect for such data?

b. Do the skewed data represent a floor or ceiling effect?

Applying the Concepts

2.24 The National Survey of Student Engagement (NSSE) surveys freshmen and seniors about their level of engagement in campus and classroom activities that enhance learning. Hundreds of thousands of students from over 1,200 schools have completed surveys since 1999, the first year that the NSSE was administered. Among the many questions on the NSSE, students were asked how often they were assigned a paper of 20 pages or more during the academic year. For a sample of 19 institutions classified as national universities that made their data publicly available through the *U.S. News & World Report* Web site, here are the percentages of students who said they were assigned between 5 and 10 20-page papers:

$$
\begin{array}{ccccccc}
0 & 5 & 3 & 3 & 4 & 10 & 2 \\
2 & 8 & 4 & 2 & 4 & 2 & 4 \\
4 & 4 & 4 & 3 & 5 & &
\end{array}
$$

a. Create a frequency table for these data. Include a third column for percentages.

b. For what percentage of these schools did exactly 4% of their students report that they wrote between 5 and 10 20-page papers that year?

2.25 The survey of earned doctorates regularly assesses the numbers and types of doctorates awarded at U.S. universities. Data for the length of time, in years, it takes to complete a doctorate can be found here. Below is a modified list of the completion data, truncated to whole numbers (8.7 became simply 8) and shortened to make your analysis easier. These data were collected every 5 years since 1982.

8	8	8	8	8	7	6
7	7	7	7	7	6	6
6	6	6	6	7	8	8
8	8	7	6	6	7	7
7	6	11	13	15	15	14
12	9	10	10	9	9	9

a. Create a frequency table for these data.

b. How many schools have an average completion time of 8 years or less?

c. Is a grouped frequency table necessary? Why or why not?

d. Describe how these data are distributed.

2.26 Refer to the data in Exercise 2.24.

a. Create a histogram of grouped data using 5 intervals.

b. How many schools had 6% or more of their students reporting that they wrote between 5 and 10 20-page papers that year?

c. How are the data distributed?

2.27 Refer to the data in Exercise 2.25.

a. Create a histogram for these data.

b. At how many universities did students take, on average, 10 or more years to complete their degree?

c. How are the data distributed?

2.28 A university's associate directors for whom a statistician was consulting were interested in alumni donations, as are many schools, not only because they want the money but also because it is one of the criteria by which *U.S. News & World Report* ranks U.S. institutions of higher learning. *U.S. News* includes this criterion because higher rates of alumni giving are seen as indicative of the satisfaction of former students. An increase in a school's overall ranking by this magazine has been demonstrated to translate into an increase in applications—and all schools want that—even though there is controversy about the validity of these rankings. One set of rankings is for the best national universities: institutions that offer undergraduate, master's, and doctoral degrees and have an emphasis on research. (Harvard tops the list that was published in 2005.) Here are the alumni giving rates that were reported in 2005; the rates are the percentages of alumni who donated to each of the top 70 national universities in the year prior to publication of these data.

```
48  61  45  39  46  37  38  34  33  47
29  38  38  34  29  29  36  48  27  25
15  25  14  26  33  16  33  32  25  34
26  32  11  15  25   9  25  40  12  20
32  10  24   9  16  21  12  14  18  20
18  25  18  20  23   9  16  17  19  15
14  18  16  17  20  24  25  11  16  13
```

a. How was the variable of alumni giving operationalized? What is another way that this variable could be operationalized?

b. Create a grouped frequency table for these data.

c. The data have quite a range, with the lowest scores belonging to Boston University, the University of California at Irvine, and the University of California at San Diego, and the highest belonging to Princeton University. What research hypotheses come to mind when you examine these data? State

at least one research question that these data suggest to you.

2.29 See the *U.S. News & World Report* data in Exercise 2.28.

a. Create a grouped histogram for these data. Be careful when determining the midpoints of your intervals!

b. Create a frequency polygon for these data.

c. Examine these graphs and give a brief description of the distribution. Are there unusual scores? Are the data skewed, and if so, in what direction?

2.30 Consider these three variables: finishing times in a marathon, number of university dining hall meals eaten in a semester on a three-meal-a-day plan, and scores on a scale of extroversion.

a. Which of these variables is most likely to have a normal distribution? Explain your answer.

b. Which of these variables is most likely to have a positively skewed distribution? Explain your answer, stating the possible contribution of a floor effect.

c. Which of these variables is most likely to have a negatively skewed distribution? Explain your answer, stating the possible contribution of a ceiling effect.

2.31 Here are the numbers of wins for the 30 NBA teams for the 2004–2005 NBA season.

```
45  43  42  33  33  54  47  44  42  30
59  45  36  18  13  52  49  44  27  26
62  50  37  34  34  59  58  51  45  18
```

a. Create a grouped frequency table for these data.

b. Create a histogram based on the grouped frequency table.

c. Write a summary describing the distribution of these data with respect to shape and direction of any skew.

d. State one research question that might arise from this data set.

2.32 The Centers for Disease Control and other organizations are interested in the health benefits of breast-feeding for infants. The National Immunization Survey includes questions about breast-feeding practices, including the question: "How long was [your child] breast-fed or fed breast milk?" The data for duration of breast-feeding in months for 20 hypothetical mothers are presented below.

```
0  7  0  12  9  3  2  0  6  10
3  0  2   1  3  0  3  1  1   4
```

a. Create a frequency table for these data. Include a third column for percentages.

b. Create a grouped frequency table for these data with three groups (create groupings around the midpoints of 2.5 months, 7.5 months, and 12.5 months).

2.33 Refer to the data in Exercise 2.32.

a. Create a histogram of the original data.

b. Create a histogram of the grouped data.

2.34 Refer to the data in Exercise 2.32.

a. Create a frequency polygon of the original data.

b. Create a frequency polygon of the grouped data.

2.35 Refer to the data and your work in Exercises 2.32 through 2.34.

a. Write a summary describing the distribution of these data with respect to shape and direction of any skew.

b. If you wanted the data to be normally distributed around 12 months, how would the data have to shift to fit that goal? How could you use knowledge about the current distribution to target certain women?

2.36 For each of the types of data described below, would you present individual data values or grouped data when creating a frequency distribution? Explain your answer clearly.

a. Eye color observed for 87 people

b. Minutes used on a cell phone by 240 teenagers

c. Time to complete the Boston Marathon for the nearly 22,000 runners who participate

d. Number of siblings for 64 college students

2.37 For each of the following types of data described below, what visual displays of data would be most appropriate to use? Explain your answer clearly.

a. Eye color observed for 87 people

b. Minutes used on a cell phone by 240 teenagers

c. Time to complete the Boston Marathon for the nearly 22,000 runners who participate

d. Number of siblings for 64 college students

2.38 The director of career services at a large university is offering training on résumé construction. In an effort to present up-to-date information, using 23 résumés he just reviewed for a receptionist position in his office, he counts the total number of words used. Here are the data:

226 339 220 295 180 214 257 201

224 237 223 301 267 284 238 251

278 294 266 227 281 312 332

a. Create a grouped frequency table with 4 intervals.

b. What does this information tell people who come to his training on résumé construction?

2.39 A college student is interested in how many friends the average person has. She decides to count the number of people who appear in photographs on display in dorm rooms and offices across her campus. She collects data on 84 students and 33 faculty members. The data are presented below.

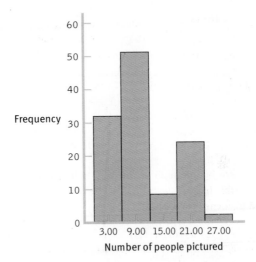

a. What kind of visual display is this?

b. Estimate how many people have fewer than six people pictured.

c. Estimate how many people have more than 18 people pictured.

2.40 Can you think of additional questions you might ask after reviewing the data displayed in Exercise 2.39?

2.41 Below is a subset of the data mentioned in Exercise 2.39.

1 5 3 9 13 0 18 15

3 3 5 7 7 7 11 3

12 20 16 4 17 15 16 10

6 8 8 7 3 17

a. Create a grouped frequency table for these data using 7 groupings.

b. Create a histogram of these grouped data.

2.42 Describe how the data in Exercises 2.39 and 2.41 are distributed.

2.43 Below are two displays of the friends data described in Exercise 2.39, one for the students and one for the faculty members studied. Describe how these two displays are different.

	Frequency	
Interval	Faculty	Students
0–3	21	0
4–7	11	26
8–11	1	24
12–15	0	2
16–19	0	27
20–23	0	3
24–27	0	2

Terms

raw score (p. 23)
frequency distribution (p. 23)
frequency table (p. 23)
grouped frequency table (p. 26)

histogram (p. 29)
frequency polygon (p. 31)
normal distribution (p. 35)
skewed distribution (p. 34)

positively skewed (p. 34)
floor effect (p. 34)
negatively skewed (p. 35)
ceiling effect (p. 35)

C H A P T E R   3

Visual Displays of Data

How to Mislead with Graphs

"The Most Misleading Graph
  Ever Published"
Techniques for Misleading with Graphs

Common Types of Graphs

Scatterplots
Line Graphs
Bar Graphs
Pictorial Graphs
Pie Charts

How to Build a Graph

Choosing the Type of Graph Based
  on Variables
How to Read a Graph
Guidelines for Creating the Perfect Graph
The Future of Graphs

BEFORE YOU GO ON

- You should know how to construct a
  histogram (Chapter 2).

- You should understand the difference between
  independent variables and dependent variables
  (Chapter 1).

43

It was so cold the morning of January 28, 1986, that icicles were hanging off the scaffolding surrounding the space shuttle *Challenger*. The night before, Morton Thiokol engineers and NASA officials had debated the data concerning the effect of cold temperatures on the giant rubber-like O-rings that sealed the separate sections of the rocket boosters. The engineers had even sent NASA officials 13 tables and graphs that documented increasing damage to the O-rings in colder weather, trying to make a case to delay the launch.

Figure 3-1 shows two of the graphs that obscure vital information in different ways. First, the viewer's attention is not directed to the critical variables of interest: temperature and damage to the O-rings (Tufte, 1997/2005). Instead, attention is directed to all those cute little rockets and only tangentially to the indicators of damage that appear to be randomly scattered among them. Second, the numbers revealing temperature have been turned sideways because the rockets are tall and narrow. Third, the second vital variable, indicating type of damage to the O-ring, is coded with arbitrary symbols—dots, diagonal bars, and vertical stripes—rather than something intuitive, such as progressively darker marks indicating progressively more damage. Tragically, the misleading tables and graphs were not persuasive, and NASA decided to go ahead with the shuttle launch. During the launch, a tiny gap in one of the *Challenger*'s O-rings started leaking. Later, cameras revealed that puffs of black smoke were visible on the launch pad. That O-ring leak grew into a flame and, then, 73 seconds after launch, the billion-dollar *Challenger* exploded as it tried to leave Earth's atmosphere, killing all seven of its astronauts.

In retrospect, the *Challenger* disaster could have been prevented by a graph, such as that shown in Figure 3-2, that described the systematic relation between two variables—temperature and damage to the O-ring material. Unfortunately, the graphs presented to NASA both before the *Challenger* exploded and during the investigation that followed were not created in a way that clearly demonstrated the relation between temperature and O-ring damage.

In this chapter, we explore the ways in which visual displays of data can both clarify and complicate data. We demonstrate how to recognize when others are lying with statistics and visual displays of these statistics. In the process, we introduce the most common types of graphs, when they should be used, and the guidelines for clear visual displays of data. We also introduce some graphing innovations and provide insights into the possible future of graphing.

FIGURE 3-1
Obscuring Vital Information

These two graphs contain the information that could have helped NASA delay the *Challenger* launch, but it was obscured in a few different ways (Tufte, 1997/2005): (1) the key, on the left, contains irrelevant symbols; (2) the graph, on the right, is organized by chronology rather than temperature, the key variable; and (3) the rocket images in both distract the viewer from vital information.

History of O-Ring Damage in Field Joints

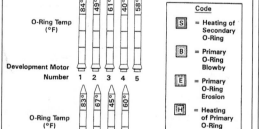

Reprinted by permission, Edward R. Tufte, *Visual Explanatios*, Graphics Press, Chesire, CT, 1997

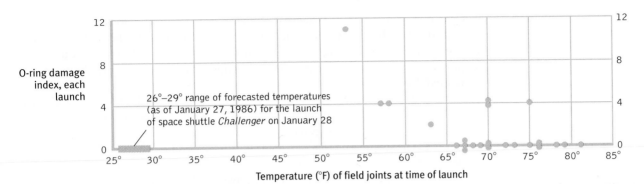

O-ring damage index, each launch

26°–29° range of forecasted temperatures (as of January 27, 1986) for the launch of space shuttle *Challenger* on January 28

Temperature (°F) of field joints at time of launch

FIGURE 3-2
Emphasizing Vital Information

Years after the Challenger disaster, Edward Tufte (1997) created a more conventional graph that succinctly portrayed the relation between temperature and damage to O-rings. Notice how this after-the-fact graph directs particular attention to information about the temperature on the morning of the launch.

How to Mislead with Graphs

The Morton Thiokol engineers who created graphs depicting the relation between temperature and O-ring damage didn't need fancier graphs; they needed clearer graphs. The purpose of a graph is to reveal and clarify relations between variables. One of the worst graphs ever created provides an opportunity to learn how to create, read, and interpret graphic information.

"The Most Misleading Graph Ever Published"

Learning how to lie with graphs allows you to spot those lies for yourself. We are indebted to Michael Friendly of York University for collecting and managing a Web site (Friendly, 2009) that humorously demonstrates the power of graphs both to deceive and to enlighten. Figure 3–3 was described as possibly "the most misleading graph ever published."

Before reading any further, look at Figure 3-3. Then write a short sentence about what the graph seems to communicate about the relation between the two variables of (1) cost of higher education and (2) quality of higher education at Cornell University.

At first glance, this graph appears to convey that _____
_____.

At least four lies can be found in this single graph. Some of them are subtle white lies that leave a false impression. Try to identify some of these lies before you read about them.

Lie 1: _____

Lie 2: _____

Lie 3: _____

Lie 4: _____

This graph from the *Ithaca Times* seems to tell a story of increasing cost and decreasing quality. The line representing tuition goes up and the line representing Cornell University's ranking goes down. But let's examine the variety of lies in this graph. Notice that the graph superimposes statistical information on a picture of Cornell University's campus, so the graph's underlying message gains credibility by being associated with this prestigious university.

The graph appears to answer the question in the headline: "Why does college have to cost so much?" That rising line represents rising tuition costs, as measured by the

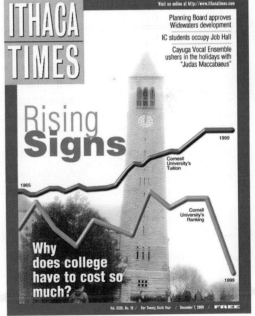

FIGURE 3-3
Graphs That Lie

Michael Friendly describes this graph as a "spectacular example of more graphic sins than I have ever seen in one image" and possibly "the most misleading graph ever published."

share of a student's family's median income, over *35 years*. Now look for the timeline that corresponds to the plummeting lower line. Can you find it? The apparently falling line represents the ranking of Cornell University over only *11 years*—but the graph does not clearly convey this critical information. The absence of critical information is a red flag.

Lie 1: The graph treats unequal scales as if they were equal. This lie uses identical distances (almost the width of the magazine cover) to represent very different time frames (11 years versus 35 years).

Lie 2: The graph unites incompatible measures. This lie compares an ordinal measure (university rank) to a scale measure (tuition as a proportion of income). The two ways of measuring a variable are incompatible, yet they are treated as if they were the same. This lie also helps to set up and anticipate the next lie.

Lie 3: The graph uses misleading starting points. This lie arbitrarily begins the line representing quality of education (Cornell's rank compared to other institutions) lower than the line representing tuition costs as a proportion of income, suggesting that an institution already failing to deliver what students are paying for has, over the last 11 or 35 years (!), become dramatically worse. There is no reason, except deception, to start one line higher or lower than the other. The scales are not comparable and should not even be placed in the same graph.

Lie 4: The graph *reverses* the implied meaning of up and down. Cornell University's ranking did indeed change over this 11-year period. It *improved* from 15th place nationally to 6th place! Cornell's ranking didn't get worse; it got better! Then why does the line representing Cornell's ranking go down? This astonishing graphic lie reversed the direction of the numbers. In the business of rankings, a low number is good, but the graphmaker made sure that the positive information about Cornell was portrayed by a line going down.

If this graph were true to its data, the line representing quality of education should be rising rather impressively, from 15th place to 6th place. Yet this line portrays Cornell's quality of education as falling dramatically! Taken at face value, the graph tells a negative story that might sell more newspapers, the most likely reason this misleading graph was created.

Techniques for Misleading with Graphs

A graph has a certain scientific aura, which makes us want to believe it. This makes us vulnerable to graphs that are actually misleading. Here are some of the most common ways to mislead viewers with graphic tricks.

1. The false face validity lie. Face validity refers to whether the method used to collect data seems (on the face of it) to represent what it says it represents. False face validity is when the method seems to represent what it says, but when you dig a little deeper, it does not. For example, someone might label a variable "aggression" even though what they actually measure is how many times people shout at each other. Some fairly happy families shout almost all the time, and many quiet families exchange polite comments with lethal intentions.

2. The biased scale lie. A biased scale slants information in a particular way. For example, some college courses use evaluation scales labeled "excellent," "very good," "good," "fair," and "poor." Three out of the five categories are very positive ratings; one is weaker but uses an ambiguous word ("fair"); only one category is actually negative ("poor"). People using this rating scale tend to give more positive ratings because most of the choices are positive. The scale is pulling for a certain response.

3. The sneaky sample lie. A sneaky sample occurs when the people who participate in a study are preselected so that the data turn out in a particular way. For example, some students like to peek at Web sites that rate professors, but the students most likely to participate in those rating sites are those who strongly dislike or strongly approve of a particular professor. It is not a representative sample of all students.

4. The extrapolation lie. This lie assumes knowledge of information outside the study. Extrapolation goes beyond the data by assuming that a pattern will continue indefinitely. For example, CB radios, a once-popular communication device now used mostly by long-distance truckers, have long since been replaced by mobile phones. Yet, in 1976, the *Complete CB Handbook* declared that the popularity of CB radios would only increase until CB instruction became part of the elementary school curriculum. Don't assume a pattern in your data will continue.

5. The inaccurate values lie. The inaccurate values lie can be subtly effective. Sometimes it involves telling the truth in one part of the data but visually distorting it in another place. Notice in Figure 3-4 how wide the "highway" is when the accelerating fuel-economy savings is coming at the viewer. The proportional change in distance between the beginning and the end of the highway is many times larger than the proportional change in the size of the data.

6. The outright lie. It is important for you to know that there are many examples of people making up data to lend an air of legitimacy to an otherwise weak argument. For example, Levitt and Dubner (2005) reported that Mitch Snyder, an advocate for the homeless, repeatedly cited a statistic in the early 1980s that there were 3 million homeless Americans, a number that would have meant that 1 in 75 Americans were homeless. Snyder eventually admitted he had lied because he had been pushed by reporters to provide a specific number.

> ◀ **MASTERING THE CONCEPT**
>
> **3-1:** Graphs are so persuasive that graph creators sometimes intentionally use them to mislead. When reading graphs, ask yourself about the sample, the variables, and the format of the graph.

FIGURE 3-4
The Inaccurate Values Lie

The visual lie told here is the result of a "highway" that spreads much farther apart than the data indicate. Michael Friendly (2005) asserts that "this graph, from the *New York Times,* purports to show the mandated fuel-economy standards set by the U.S. Department of Transportation. The standard required an increase in mileage from 18 to 27.5, an increase of 53%. The magnitude of increase shown in the graph is 783%, for a whopping lie factor = (783/53) = 14.8!"

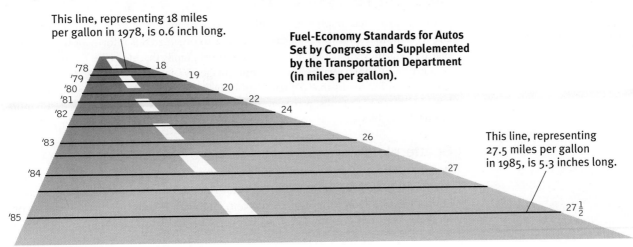

This line, representing 18 miles per gallon in 1978, is 0.6 inch long.

Fuel-Economy Standards for Autos Set by Congress and Supplemented by the Transportation Department (in miles per gallon).

This line, representing 27.5 miles per gallon in 1985, is 5.3 inches long.

'78 18
'79 19
'80 20
'81 22
'82 24
'83 26
'84 27
'85 27½

CHECK YOUR LEARNING

Reviewing the Concepts

> Graphing is a critical skill to have in our data-dependent society.

> Graphs can convey important information clearly or can obscure that information. Carefully examine visual displays of data and ask critical questions to be sure the graph creator wasn't exaggerating or misleading.

Clarifying the Concepts

3-1 What is the purpose of a graph?

Calculating the Statistics

3-2 Referring to Figure 3-4, the inaccurate values lie, calculate how much fuel-economy standards changed from 1981 to 1984 in miles per gallon and as a percentage change.

Applying the Concepts

3-3 Which of the two graphs below is misleading? Which seems to be an accurate depiction of the data? Explain your answer.

Connecticut Traffic Deaths, 1955–1956

Connecticut Traffic Deaths, 1951–1959

Solutions to these Check Your Learning questions can be found in Appendix D.

Common Types of Graphs

A well-constructed graph begins with raw data. As we know from the *Challenger* example, it is the responsibility of the researcher to organize this information in the way that best clarifies the data. This section discusses graphs that describe the relation between two or more variables in just one image. We learn how to create scatterplots and line graphs, graphs that depict relations between two scale variables. We also learn how to create bar graphs, pictorial graphs, and pie charts, graphs with one or more nominal variables along with a scale variable.

Scatterplots

*A **scatterplot** is a graph that depicts the relation between two scale variables.* The values of each variable are marked along the two axes. A mark is made to indicate the intersection of the two scores for each participant. The mark is above the participant's score on the *x*-axis and across from the score on the *y*-axis. A scatterplot is simple to construct either by hand or by computer. Consider sketching these graphs by hand first (although it may seem unnecessary) and then progress to the computer. If you have a solid foundation in written graphs, your computer-constructed graphs will be more accurate and more elegant.

EXAMPLE 3.1

In the example in Figure 3-5, a researcher might be interested in the effect that the amount of studying had on students' grades on a statistics exam. To study this, the researcher could gather two scores for each participant—the number of hours studied and the grade on the statistics exam. We must first decide which variable we believe is the independent variable (the variable doing the predicting) and which is the dependent variable (the variable being predicted). In this example, it is more likely that hours spent studying would predict the grade on the statistics exam. So, the independent variable (*x*) is the number of hours spent studying, and the dependent variable (*y*) is the grade on the statistics exam.

As seen in Figure 3-5, these data suggest that the more one studies, the better one performs on exams (please note that this isn't necessarily a causal relation). We now have a sense of our data and how the two variables are related. Note that the values on both axes go down to 0, reducing the likelihood of misinterpretation. In a situation in which the scores are all very high, however, it might be too unwieldy to include all the values. In such cases, it wastes space to have the axes go all the way down to 0. The data near the top would be compacted and more difficult to read. However, whenever practical, it's best to include 0.

Here is a recap of the steps to create a scatterplot:

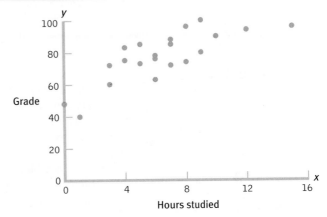

FIGURE 3-5
Scatterplot of Hours Studied and Statistics Grades
This scatterplot depicts the relation between hours spent studying and grades on a statistics exam. Each dot represents one student's score along the independent variable on the *x*-axis and along the dependent variable on the *y*-axis.

1. Organize the data by participant; each participant will have two scores, one on each scale variable.
2. Label the horizontal *x*-axis with the name of the independent variable and its possible values, starting with 0 if practical.
3. Label the vertical *y*-axis with the name of the dependent variable and its possible values, starting with 0 if practical.
4. Make a mark on the graph above each study participant's score on the *x*-axis and next to his or her score on the *y*-axis.

When we are interested in the relation between two variables, we first have to understand the different ways in which the two variables *might* be related—either linearly or nonlinearly (or not at all). *A **linear relation** between variables means that the relation between variables is best described by a straight line.* When the linear relation is positive, the pattern of data points flows upward and to the right. When the linear relation is negative, the pattern of data points flows downward and to the right. In both cases, the relation is best described by a straight line. For example, the data for hours studying and statistics grades shown in Figure 3-5 are related in a positive, linear way: on average, more hours of studying were associated with higher grades; on average, fewer hours of studying were associated with lower grades.

*A **nonlinear relation** between variables means that the relation between variables is best described by a line that breaks or curves in some way.* Because a scatterplot depicts every

■ A **scatterplot** is a graph that depicts the relation between two scale variables. The values of each variable are marked along the two axes, and a mark is made to indicate the intersection of the two scores for each participant. The mark is above the participant's score on the *x*-axis and across from the score on the *y*-axis.

■ A **linear relation** between variables means that the relation between variables is best described by a straight line.

■ A **nonlinear relation** between variables means that the relation between variables is best described by a line that breaks or curves in some way.

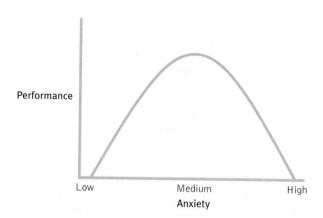

FIGURE 3-6
Nonlinear Relations

The Yerkes–Dodson law predicts that stress/anxiety improves test performance—but only to a point. Too much anxiety leads to an inability to perform at one's best. This inverted U-curve illustrates the concept, but a scatterplot would be a better clarification of the particular relation between these two variables.

observation, a visual inspection of a scatterplot shows if there is a linear or nonlinear relation between variables. (Note that two variables are not necessarily related in a nonlinear way if they are not related in a linear way. They might not be related at all!) It's important to remember that a nonlinear relation is still a relation. Because *nonlinear* simply means "not straight," there are several different kinds of nonlinear relations between variables.

Let's consider an example. According to some researchers, the Yerkes–Dodson law predicts the relation between level of anxiety and test performance. As professors, we don't want you so relaxed that you don't even show up for the test, but we don't want you so stressed out that you can't take the test because you're having a panic attack. We want you somewhere in the happy middle. For most of us, there seems to be a nonlinear relation (an upside-down U-curve) that describes the relation between arousal and test performance (Figure 3-6). And the best way to understand this relation between two variables is to see it in the line that summarizes the data from a scatterplot.

Line Graphs

A **line graph** *is used to illustrate the relation between two scale variables; sometimes the line represents the predicted y scores for each x value, and sometimes the line represents change in a variable over time.* One type of line graph is constructed using a scatterplot. The line of best fit is the line that minimizes the distances of the dots from that line. The line of best fit allows us to use the x value to predict the y value.

EXAMPLE 3.2

For example, we could use "time spent studying" scores (the x value) to predict "test scores" (the y value). If we know the general relation between hours studied and grades on the statistics exam, then we can predict the exam scores based on hours studied. The line of best fit allows us to make predictions when we know only one piece of information. Specifically, we can use the line of best fit in Figure 3-7 to predict that if a student studies for 2 hours, she will earn a test score of about 62; if she studies for 13 hours, she will earn about 100.

Here is a recap of the steps to create a scatterplot with a line of best fit:

1. Label the x-axis with the name of the independent variable and its possible values, starting with 0 if practical.

2. Label the y-axis with the name of the dependent variable and its possible values, starting with 0 if practical.

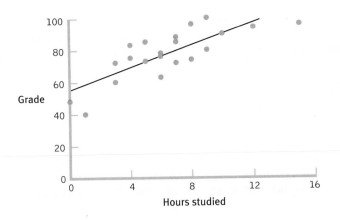

FIGURE 3-7
The Line of Best Fit

The line of best fit allows us to make predictions for a person's value on the *y* variable from his or her value on the *x* variable.

■ A **line graph** is used to illustrate the relation between two scale variables; sometimes the line represents the predicted *y* scores for each *x* value, and sometimes the line represents change in a variable over time.

■ A **time plot**, or **time series plot**, is a graph that plots a scale variable on the *y*-axis as it changes over an increment of time (e.g., second, day, century) labeled on the *x*-axis.

3. Make a mark above each study participant's score on the *x*-axis and next to his or her score on the *y*-axis.

4. In Chapter 14 you will learn how to use a regression equation to help you draw the line of best fit through the points on the scatterplot.

A second situation in which a line graph is more useful than just a scatterplot occurs with time-related data. *A **time plot**, or **time series plot**, is a graph that plots a scale variable on the y-axis as it changes over an increment of time (e.g., second, day, century) labeled on the x-axis.* As with a scatterplot, marks are placed above each value on the *x*-axis (e.g., at a given minute) at the value for that particular time on the *y*-axis (i.e., the score on the dependent variable). These marks are then connected with a line.

EXAMPLE 3.3

Notice how clearly the time plot in Figure 3-8 seems to tell the story of the numbers of homicides in Canada from 1961 through 1994 (Gimbarzevsky, 1995). Here we see a substantial increase in gun murders between the early 1960s and the mid-1970s; then

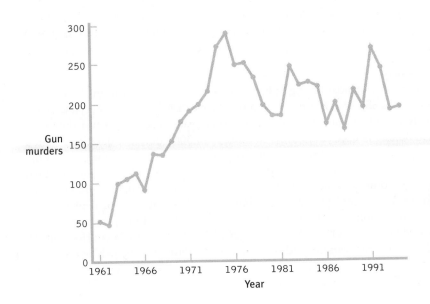

FIGURE 3-8
The Numbers of Gun Murders in Canada Between 1961 and 1994

Instead of answering a question about absolute numbers of gun murders, a better graph would answer the question about the numbers of deaths *per capita* to reflect possible changes in Canada's population over time.

the pattern becomes more erratic. This graph might lead us to even more interesting questions. Why was there an increase? Is there really an increase when we consider population growth during this time? An effective graph provokes more precise research questions.

Here is a recap of the steps to create a time plot:

1. Label the x-axis with the name of the independent variable and its possible values. The independent variable should be an increment of time (e.g., hour, month, year).

▶ **MASTERING THE CONCEPT**

3-2: Scatterplots and line graphs are used to depict relations between two scale variables.

2. Label the y-axis with the name of the dependent variable and its possible values, starting with 0 if practical.

3. Make a mark above each value on the x-axis at the value for that time on the y-axis.

4. Connect the dots.

Bar Graphs

Bar graphs are visual depictions of data when the independent variable is nominal and the dependent variable is scale. Each bar typically represents the average value of the dependent variable for each category. They are one of the most commonly used types of graphs. In a bar graph, the x-axis includes at least one nominal variable, such as gender (with separate bars for men and women); the y-axis describes a second variable, a scale variable, such as Consideration of Future Consequences (CFC) scores. Bar graphs allow us to compare the average CFC scores of men to the average CFC scores of women.

To recap the variables used to create a bar graph:

1. The x-axis of a bar graph indicates discrete levels of a nominal variable.

2. The y-axis of a bar graph may represent counts or percentages. But the y-axis of a bar graph can also indicate many other variables, such as scores on a personality scale, reaction time, or any other scale measure of a dependent variable.

- A **bar graph** is a visual depiction of data when the independent variable is nominal and the dependent variable is scale. Each bar typically represents the average value of the dependent variable for each category.

- A **Pareto chart** is a type of bar graph in which the categories along the x-axis are ordered from highest bar on the left to lowest bar on the right.

Bar graphs are flexible tools for the visual presentation of data. For example, if there are many categories to be displayed along the horizontal x-axis, researchers sometimes create a ***Pareto chart***, *a type of bar graph in which the categories along the x-axis are ordered from highest bar on the left to lowest bar on the right.* This ordering allows easier comparisons and easier identification of the most common and least common categories.

EXAMPLE 3.4

We can compare a standard bar graph to a Pareto chart for data from the General Social Survey (GSS). The National Opinion Research Center has interviewed approximately 2000 U.S. adults a year (almost every year) since 1972. Over the years, more than 38,000 people have answered more than 3000 different questions related to people's opinions, attitudes, and behaviors. Anyone can analyze their data. One question on the GSS asked respondents to consider an "admitted homosexual [who] wanted to make a speech in your community" and asked, "Should he be allowed to speak, or not?" Figure 3-9 includes two different ways of depicting the percentages of respondents in different U.S. regions who said the person should be "not allowed" to speak. One graph is a standard bar graph with categories ordered as the GSS orders the regions, and the other is a Pareto chart. Which one is easier to read?

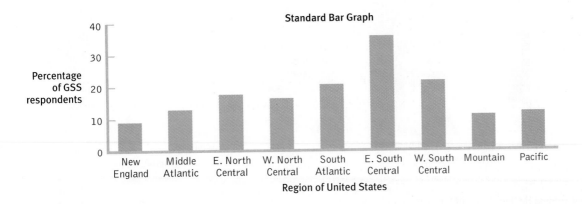

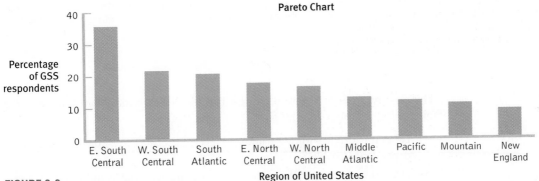

FIGURE 3-9
The Flexibility of the Bar Graph

The standard bar graph provides a comparison among nine nominal variables. The dependent variable is the percentage of respondents who said that an avowed homosexual should be "not allowed" to speak. The Pareto chart, a version of a bar graph, orders the categories from highest to lowest along the horizontal axis, which allows us to more easily pick out the highest and lowest bars. We can more easily know that respondents in the East South Central region had the highest percentage of respondents say that an avowed homosexual should be "not allowed" to speak and that New England had the lowest. We have to do more work to draw these conclusions from the original bar graph.

EXAMPLE 3.5

Bar graphs are often used in the applied behavioral sciences. For example, Newell, Rosenfeld, and Culbertson (1995) examined the effect of sexual harassment on the intention to remain in the Navy. We can see from Figure 3-10 that female Navy officers who reported that they had not been harassed had a somewhat higher intention of staying in the Navy for at least 20 years than did those who reported that they had been harassed.

But how dramatic is this difference? Manipulating the range of the y-axis can change the story that these data seem to be telling. Compare Figure 3-11 to Figure 3-10. Notice what happens when the values on the y-axis do not begin at 0, and when the intervals change from 0.5 to 0.05. The same data, presented with a different range displayed on the y-axis, leave a very different impression. Although a small difference seems apparent when we look at Figure 3-10, the difference appears very large in Figure 3-11. The key word here is *appears*. Regardless of where the y-axis begins, the data are the same! So pay close attention to the range of the y-axis. (*Note:* If the data are very far from zero, and it does not make sense to have the axis go down to zero, indicate this on the graph by including cut marks, or double slashes.)

Effect of Sexual Harassment Status on Female Navy Officers' Intentions to Stay in the Navy

FIGURE 3-10

Bar Graphs Highlight Differences Between Means

This bar graph depicts the mean ratings of intention to stay in the Navy for two groups of female Navy officers: those who reported having been harassed and those who reported not having been harassed. A bar graph can more vividly depict differences between means than just seeing the typed numbers themselves: 3.32 and 3.64.

Effect of Sexual Harassment Status on Female Navy Officers' Intentions to Stay in the Navy

FIGURE 3-11

Deceiving with the Scale

To exaggerate a difference between means, graphmakers sometimes compress the rating scale that they show on their graphs. When possible, label your axis beginning with 0.

Here is a recap of the steps to create a bar graph. The critical choice for you, the graph creator, is in step 2.

1. Label the *x*-axis with the name and levels (i.e., categories) of the nominal independent variable.

2. Label the *y*-axis with the name of the dependent variable and its possible values, starting with 0 if practical.

3. For every category, draw a bar with the height of that category's value on the dependent variable.

Pictorial Graphs

When only basic differences are being depicted—the difference between just two or three categories, for example—a pictorial graph is sometimes used. *A **pictorial graph** is a visual depiction of data typically used for an independent variable with very few levels (categories) and a scale dependent variable. Each category uses a picture or symbol to represent its value on the scale dependent variable.* Pictorial graphs are far more common in the popular media than in research journals, primarily because the pictures tend to confuse rather than clarify. For example, the pictures of little rockets in the *Challenger* data obscured a critical relation between variables.

Pictorial graphs often use pictures in place of bars. For example, the graphmaker might use stylistic drawings of people to indicate population size. If one city has double the population of another, the graphmaker might, as in Figure 3-12, make the drawing of the person twice as tall—but also twice as wide so that the taller person doesn't look stretched out. This has the misleading effect of making the taller drawing about four times as big in total area as the shorter one, when it is supposed to convey that the population is only twice as big. This is a very easy error to make, and for that reason many researchers avoid pictorial graphs.

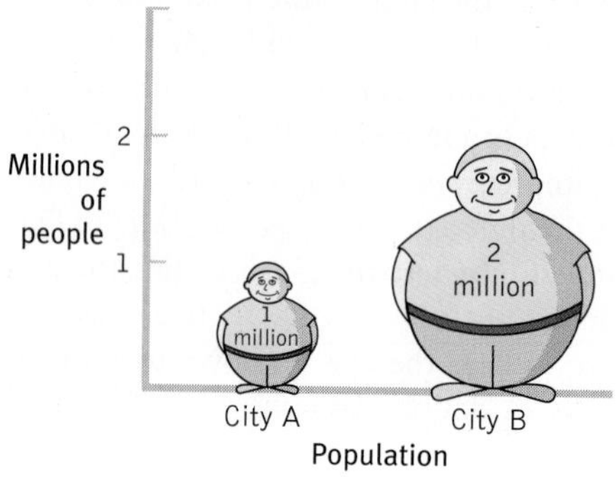

■ A **pictorial graph** is a visual depiction of data typically used for an independent variable with very few levels (categories) and a scale dependent variable. Each category uses a picture or symbol to represent its value on the scale dependent variable.

■ A **pie chart** is a graph in the shape of a circle with a slice for every category. The size of each slice represents the proportion (or percentage) of each category.

FIGURE 3-12

Distorting the Data with Pictures

With a pictorial graph, doubling the height of a picture is often coupled with doubling the width—you're multiplying by 2 twice. Instead of being twice as big, the picture is *four times* as big!

Pie Charts

*A **pie chart** is a graph in the shape of a circle with a slice for every category. The size of each slice represents the proportion (or percentage) of each category.* A pie chart's slices should *always* add up to 100% (or 1.00 if using proportions). Figure 3-13 includes a pie chart and a bar graph, both depicting the same data. As suggested by this comparison, data can almost always be presented more clearly in a table or bar graph than in a pie chart. Because of the profound limitations of pie charts and the ready alternatives, we do not outline the steps for creating a pie chart here.

◀ **MASTERING THE CONCEPT**

3-3: Bar graphs depict data for two or more categories. They are considered to depict data more clearly and accurately than either pictorial graphs or pie charts.

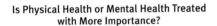

Is Physical Health or Mental Health Treated with More Importance?

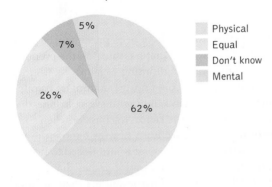

- Physical
- Equal
- Don't know
- Mental

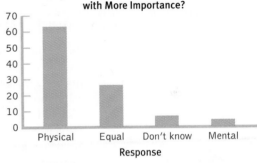

FIGURE 3-13
Pie Chart or Bar Graph?

A research firm hired by the Suicide Prevention Action Network (2004) asked participants, "Do you think that mental health and physical health are treated with equal importance in our current health care system?" We can see from the pie chart that most people (62%) believe that physical health is treated with more importance than is mental health; however, the bar graph is easier to interpret.

CHECK YOUR LEARNING

Reviewing the Concepts
> Scatterplots and line graphs allow us to see relations between two scale variables.
> When examining the relation between variables, it is important to consider linear and non-linear relations, as well as the possibility that no relation is present.
> Bar graphs, pictorial graphs, and pie charts depict the values on a scale variable for various levels of a nominal variable.
> Bar graphs are preferred; pictorial graphs and pie charts can be misleading.

Clarifying the Concepts
3-4 How are scatterplots and line graphs similar?
3-5 Why should we typically avoid using pictorial graphs or pie charts?

Calculating the Statistics
3-6 What type of visual display of data allows us to calculate or evaluate how a variable is changing over time?

continued on next page

Solutions to these Check Your Learning questions can be found in Appendix D.

Applying the Concepts

3-7 What is the best type of common graph to depict each of the following data sets and research questions? Explain your answers.

a. Depression severity and amount of stress for 150 university students. Is depression related to stress level?

b. Number of inpatient mental health facilities in Canada as measured every 10 years between 1890 and 2000. Has the number of facilities declined in recent years?

c. Number of siblings reported by 100 people. What size family is most common?

d. Mean years of education for six regions of the United States. Are education levels higher in some regions than in others?

e. Calories consumed in a day and hours slept that night for 85 people. Does the amount of food a person eats predict how long he or she sleeps at night?

How to Build a Graph

Part of the *Challenger* tragedy is not only that it could have been prevented, but that it came so close to being prevented. A clearly conceived graph created on the evening of January 27, 1986, could have changed history on the morning of January 28, 1986. A graph should provide information that an audience could not glean from text alone, or it should clarify an otherwise difficult-to-understand finding. If we conclude that a graph is appropriate to our needs, we want to know the factors to consider when choosing which kind of graph to create. In this section, we learn how to choose the most appropriate type of graph based on our data. A basic checklist is introduced to help you design a clear and compelling graph. We also discuss innovative graphs that highlight the exciting future of graphing that social scientists can harness to tell their stories.

Choosing the Type of Graph Based on Variables

When deciding what type of graph to use, first examine the variables. Decide which is the independent variable and which is the dependent variable. Also, identify what type of variable—nominal, ordinal, or scale (interval/ratio)—each of them is. Most of the time, the independent variable belongs on the horizontal *x*-axis and the dependent variable goes on the vertical *y*-axis.

Once we make a brief assessment of our variables, we can determine the appropriate graph:

1. If we have one scale variable (with frequencies), then we use a histogram or a frequency polygon (Chapter 2).
2. If we have one scale independent variable and one scale dependent variable, then we use a scatterplot or a line graph.
3. If we have one nominal independent variable and one scale dependent variable, then we use a bar graph or a Pareto chart.
4. If we have two or more nominal independent variables and one scale dependent variable, then we use a bar graph.

> ▶ **MASTERING THE CONCEPT**
>
> **3-4:** The best way to determine the type of graph to create is to identify your independent variable and dependent variable, along with the type of variable that each is—nominal, ordinal, or scale.

EXAMPLE 3.6

How to Read a Graph

Let's confirm your understanding of independent and dependent variables within the context of a graph by using the study of female Navy personnel's attitudes that we considered earlier. This time, the graph, shown in Figure 3-14, includes two independent variables: respondents' military rank and their harassment status. Try to answer the following questions *before* looking at the answers provided after the questions.

1. What variable are the researchers trying to predict? That is, what is the *dependent variable*?
2. Is the dependent variable nominal, ordinal, or scale?
3. What kinds of scores can participants get on the dependent variable? For example, if the dependent variable is gender, possible scores are male and female; if it's IQ as measured by the Wechsler Adult Intelligence Scale, then the possible scores are the IQ scores themselves, ranging from 0 to 145.
4. What variables did the researchers use to predict this dependent variable? That is, what are the *independent variables*?
5. Are these two independent variables nominal or scale?
6. What kinds of scores can participants get on each of these independent variables?

Now check your answers:

1. The dependent variable is the intention of staying in the Navy for 20 years.
2. Intention to stay in the Navy is a scale variable.
3. Intention scores represent an attitude scale with a range of 1 to 5.
4. The first independent variable is rank; the second independent variable is harassment status.
5. The two independent variables, rank and sexual harassment status, are both nominal variables.
6. The possible scores for rank are officer and enlisted. The possible scores for sexual harassment status are harassed and not harassed.

Because there are two independent variables—both of which are nominal—and one scale dependent variable, we used a bar graph to depict these data.

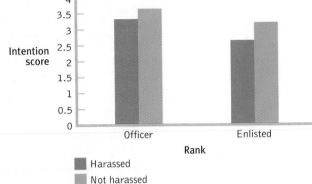

FIGURE 3-14
Two Independent Variables

Bar graphs can also include two independent variables. The dependent variable, intention score, goes on the *y*-axis and both independent variables go on the *x*-axis. One independent variable, rank, is indicated on the axis label and the other independent variable, harassment status, is indicated by a color-coded key. (Note that the graph creator could choose to reverse the placement of the two independent variables so that harassment status would be on the axis label and rank would be indicated by a color-coded key.)

Guidelines for Creating the Perfect Graph

To wrap up our discussion of graphing, here is a short checklist of questions to ask when you've created a graph or when you encounter a graph. Some we've mentioned previously, and all are wise to follow.

- Does the graph have a clear, specific title?
- Are both axes labeled with the names of the variables? Do all labels read left to right—even the one on the *y*-axis?
- Are all terms on the graph the same terms that are used in the text that the graph is to accompany? Have all abbreviations been eliminated?
- Are the units of measurement (e.g., minutes, percentages) included in the labels?
- Do the values on the axes either go down to 0 or have cut marks (double slashes) to indicate that they do not go down to 0?
- Are colors used in a simple, clear way—ideally, shades of gray instead of other colors?
- Has all chartjunk been eliminated?

The last of these guidelines involves a new term, the graph-corrupting fluff called *chartjunk,* a term coined by Tufte (2001/2006). According to Tufte, **chartjunk is any**

- **Chartjunk** is any unnecessary information or feature in a graph that detracts from a viewer's ability to understand the data.

Franck Fotos/Alamy

FIGURE 3-15
Chartjunk Run Amok

Moiré vibrations, such as those seen in the patterns on these bars, might be fun to use, but they detract from the viewer's ability to glean the story of the data. Moreover, the grid pattern behind the bars might appear scientific, but it serves only to distract. Ducks, like the 3-D shadow effect on the bars and the globe clip-art, add nothing to our data, and the colors are absurdly eye-straining. Don't laugh—we've had students submit carefully written research papers accompanied by graphs even more garish than this!

unnecessary information or feature in a graph that detracts from a viewer's ability to understand the data. Chartjunk can take the form of any of three unnecessary features, all demonstrated in the rather frightening graph in Figure 3-15.

1. ***Moiré vibrations*** *refer to any of the patterns that computers provide as options to fill in bars.* Tufte recommends using shades of gray instead of patterns.

2. ***Grids*** *refer to a background pattern, almost like graph paper, on which the data representations, such as bars, are superimposed.* Tufte recommends the use of grids only for hand-drawn drafts of graphs. They should never be in a final version of a graph.

3. ***Ducks*** *are features of the data that have been dressed up to be something other than merely data.* Think of ducks as data in costume. Named for the Big Duck, a store in Flanders, New York, that was built in the form of a very large duck, graphic ducks can be three-dimensional effects, cutesy pictures, fancy fonts, or any other flawed design features. All other things being equal, simpler graphs are easier to interpret. Avoid chartjunk!

> ▶ **MASTERING THE CONCEPT**
>
> **3-5:** Avoid chartjunk—any unnecessary aspect of a graph that detracts from its clarity.

The Future of Graphs

Once you learn to create clear graphs, you can create even more powerful graphs using new ideas and technology. Graphs are being used in many different and unexpected ways, so we predict an exciting future for visual displays of data.

Interactive Graphing   You have probably used interactive graphing tools already. For class, you may have used a CD-ROM, clicking a button to read more about Lawrence Kohlberg while viewing a moral development timeline. Outside of school, you may have used an interactive Web site to request an online comparison of two digital cameras.

However, few have taken advantage of interactive tools to create truly inspiring graphs. One informative and haunting example was published online in the *New York Times* on September 9, 2004, to commemorate the day on which the 1000th U.S. soldier died in Iraq. Titled "The Roster of the Dead," this beautifully designed tribute is formed by photos of each of the dead servicemen and -women. One can view these photographs by month of death, first letter of last name, home state, or age at death. Because the photos are the same size, the

Edward Tufte's Big Duck   The graphics theorist Edward Tufte named a type of chartjunk (graphic clutter) for the Big Duck, a Flanders, New York, store in the form of a duck.

stacking of the photos serves almost as a bar graph. By clicking on two or more months or on two or more ages, one can visually compare numbers of deaths among levels of a category.

Yet this interactive graph is even more nuanced than this, because it allows direct access to a part of the life stories of these soldiers. By holding the cursor over a photo that catches your eye, you can learn, for example, that Spencer T. Karol, regular duty in the U.S. Army, from Woodruff, Arizona, died on October 6, 2003, at the age of 20 from hostility-inflicted wounds. A thoughtfully designed interactive graph holds even more power than a traditional flat graph to educate, evoke emotion, and even make a political statement.

Clinical Applications Clinical psychology researchers have developed graphing techniques, illustrated in Figure 3-16, to help therapists predict when the therapy process appears to be leading to a poor outcome (Howard, Moras, Brill, Martinovich, & Lutz, 1996). They have developed a model that predicts an expected rate of recovery for a specific client. The independent variables include a number of pretherapy

■ **Moiré vibrations** are chartjunk that take the form of any of the patterns that computers provide as options to fill in bars.

■ **Grids** are chartjunk that take the form of a background pattern, almost like graph paper, on which the data representations, such as bars, are superimposed.

■ A **duck** is a form of chartjunk in which a feature of the data has been dressed up to be something other than merely data.

The Many Layers of Interactive Graphs Like the Roster of the Dead, the Murder Ink Map, published by Baltimore's City Paper, is an interactive graphic . At the macrolevel, this graph allows the viewer to see the number of people who have been murdered in the city of Baltimore in a given year, as well as where each murder took place. At the microlevel, the viewer can click on any of the numbered push-pins to read details about that particular murder—including the time, date, means, and whether the case has been solved.

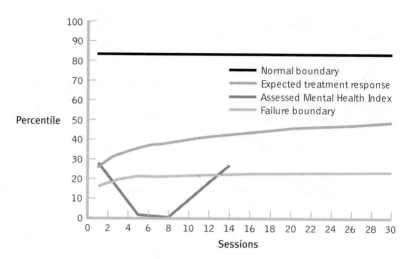

FIGURE 3-16
Graph as Therapy Tool

Some graphs allow therapists to compare the actual rate of a client's improvement with the expected rate given that client's characteristics. This client (Assessed Mental Health Index in gray) is doing worse than expected (expected treatment response in red) but has improved enough to be above the failure boundary (in yellow).

client characteristics, such as attitude toward therapy and the severity and pattern of psychopathology. The dependent variable is rate of improvement. The predicted rate of improvement is graphed as a line, somewhat like the line of best fit we saw earlier, but typically curved—perhaps an initial quick improvement, followed by steady improvement, and then a plateau. The therapist then adds points to the graph showing a client's actual status. This allows a therapist to determine how a client's *actual* rate of improvement compares to what would be expected for another client with similar characteristics. If therapy progresses more slowly than expected, then both the client and the therapist may be spurred to take action by the discrepancy in the graphs.

CHECK YOUR LEARNING

Reviewing the Concepts

> Graphs should be used when they add information to written text or help to clarify difficult material.

> To decide what kind of graph to use, we first determine whether the independent variable and the dependent variable are nominal, ordinal, or scale variables.

> A brief checklist of guidelines helps us develop a readily understandable graph. In particular, attention to the labeling of the graph and to the avoidance of chartjunk leads to a clearer graph.

> In the near future, online interactive graphs and graphs based on sophisticated prediction models such as those that forecast therapy outcomes, will become increasingly common.

Clarifying the Concepts

3-8 What is chartjunk?

Calculating the Statistics

3-9 Deciding what kind of graph to use depends largely on how variables are measured. Imagine a researcher is interested in how "quality of sleep" is related to typing performance (measured by the number of errors made). For each of the measures of sleep below, decide what kind of graph to use.

a. Total minutes slept

b. Sleep assessed as sufficient or insufficient

c. Using a scale from 1 (low quality sleep) to 7 (excellent sleep)

Applying the Concepts

Solutions to these Check Your Learning questions can be found in Appendix D.

3-10 Use Figure 3-15 to represent the data testing the hypothesis that exposure to the sun can impair IQ. Imagine that the researcher has recruited groups of people and randomly assigned them to different levels of exposure to the sun: 0, 1, 6, and 12 hours per day (enhanced, in all cases, by artificial sunlight when natural light is not available). The IQ scores are 142, 125, 88, and 80, respectively. Redesign this chartjunk graph, either by hand or using software, paying careful attention to the dos and don'ts outlined in this section.

REVIEW OF CONCEPTS

How to Mislead with Graphs

The ability to create and interpret graphs is becoming an essential skill if we wish to avoid misleading and being misled by others. Because visual displays of data are so easily manipulated, it is important to pay close attention to the details of graphs to be sure the graph creator isn't exaggerating or conveying false information.

Common Types of Graphs

When developing graphing skills, it is important to begin with the basics. Several types of graphs are commonly used by social scientists. *Scatterplots* depict the relation between two scale variables. They are useful when determining whether the relation between the variables is *linear* or *nonlinear*. Some *line graphs* expand on scatterplots by including a line of best fit. Others, called *time plots*, show the change in a scale variable over time.

Bar graphs are used to compare two or more categories of a nominal independent variable with respect to a scale dependent variable. A bar graph on which the categories are organized from the highest bar to the lowest bar, called a *Pareto chart*, allows for easy comparison of categories. Bar graphs can also be used with more than one nominal independent variable and one scale dependent variable. *Pictorial graphs* are like bar graphs except that pictures are used in place of bars. *Pie charts* are used to depict proportions or percentages on one nominal variable with just a few levels. Because both pictorial graphs and pie charts are frequently constructed in a misleading way or are misperceived, bar graphs are almost always preferred to pictorial graphs and pie charts.

How to Build a Graph

We first decide what type of graph to create by examining our independent and dependent variables, and identifying each as nominal, ordinal, or scale. We must then consider a number of guidelines to develop a clear, persuasive graph. It is important that all graphs be labeled thoroughly and appropriately and given a title that allows the graph to tell its story without additional text. For an unambiguous graph, it is imperative that graph creators avoid *chartjunk*, unnecessary information such as *moiré vibrations, grids,* and *ducks* that clutters a graph and makes it difficult to interpret. A checklist for the creation of clear graphs is included in this section.

Finally, keeping an eye to the future of graphing—including interactive graphs and the use of statistical models to predict therapy outcome—helps us stay at the forefront of graph-making in the social science fields.

SPSS®

SPSS allows us to create visual displays across several different menus; however, most graphing is done in SPSS using the Chart Builder, a very flexible graphing tool. This section walks you through the general steps to create a graph, using a scatterplot as an example. Before you start with these steps, enter the data below in the SPSS screenshot for hours studied and exam grades that were used to create the scatterplot in Figure 3-5.

Select **Graphs** → Chart Builder → Gallery. Under "Choose from:" select the type of graph by clicking on it. For example, to create a scatterplot, click on "Scatter/Dot." Then drag a sample graph from the right to the large box above. Usually, such as in the case of a scatterplot, you'll want the simplest graph, which tends to be the upper-left sample graph.

Finally, drag the appropriate variables from the "Variables:" box to the appropriate places on the sample graph (e.g., "x-axis"). For a scatterplot, drag "hours" to the x-axis

and "grade" to the y-axis. Chart Builder then looks like the screenshot shown here. Click OK and SPSS creates the graph.

Remember: you should not rely on the default choices of the software; you are the designer of the graph. Once the graph is created, you can change the graph's appearance by double-clicking on the graph to open the Chart Editor, the tool that allows you to make changes. Then click or double-click on the particular feature of the graph that you want to modify. Clicking once on part of the graph allows you to make some changes. For example, clicking the label of the y-axis allows you to retype the label; double-clicking allows you to make other changes, such as making the label horizontal (after double-clicking, select the orientation "Horizontal" under "Text Layout"). Play with the Chart Editor to learn the many aspects of the graph that you can tailor.

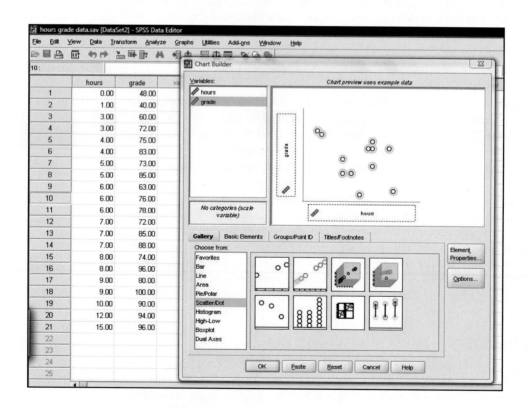

How It Works

3.1 CREATING A SCATTERPLOT

Gapminder.org is a wonderful Web site that allows the public to play with a graph and explore the relations between variables over time. Here are the scores for 10 countries on two variables.

Country	Children per woman (total fertility)	Life expectancy at birth (years)	Country	Children per woman (total fertility)	Life expectancy at birth (years)
Afghanistan	7.15	43.00	Bolivia	3.59	65.00
India	2.87	64.00	Ethiopia	5.39	53.00
China	1.72	73.00	Iraq	4.38	59.00
Hong Kong	0.96	82.00	Mali	6.55	54.00
France	1.89	80.00	Honduras	3.39	70.00

How can we create a scatterplot to help show the relation between these two variables? To create a scatterplot, we put total fertility on the *x*-axis and life expectancy in years on the *y*-axis. We then add a dot for each country at the intersection of its fertility rate and life expectancy. The scatterplot is shown in the figure below.

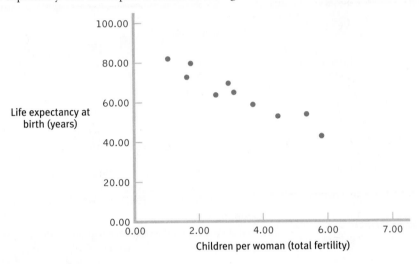

3.2 CREATING A BAR GRAPH

Here is the 2004 gross domestic product (GDP), in trillions of U.S. dollars, for each of the world economic powers that make up what is called the Group of Eight, or G8, nations.

Canada: 0.98   Italy: 1.67   United Kingdom: 2.14
France: 2.00   Japan: 4.62   United States: 11.67
Germany: 2.71   Russia: 0.58

How can we create a bar graph for these data? First, we put the countries on the *x*-axis. We might choose to put them in alphabetical order (or we might choose to create a Pareto chart in which the countries are ordered from highest to lowest GDP). Then, we draw a bar for each country with the height of its GDP. The figure below shows a bar graph with bars arranged in alphabetical order by country.

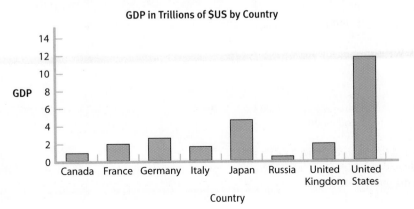

3.3 CREATING A PARETO CHART

How can we use the same G8 data as for the bar graph to create a Pareto chart? A Pareto chart is simply a bar graph in which the bars are arranged from highest value to lowest value. We would rearrange the countries so that they are ordered from the country with the highest GDP to the country with the lowest GDP. The Pareto chart is shown in the figure below.

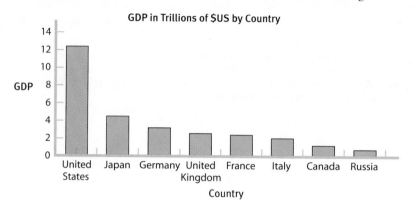

Exercises

Clarifying the Concepts

3.1 What are the six techniques discussed in this chapter for misleading with graphs?

3.2 What are the steps to create a scatterplot?

3.3 How can we tell whether two variables are linearly or nonlinearly related?

3.4 What is the difference between a line graph and a time plot?

3.5 What is the difference between a bar graph and a Pareto chart?

3.6 Bar graphs and histograms look very similar. In your own words, what is the difference between the two?

3.7 What are pictorial graphs and pie charts?

3.8 Why are bar graphs preferred over pictorial graphs and pie charts?

3.9 Why is it important to identify the independent variable and the dependent variable before creating a visual display?

3.10 Under what circumstances would your *x*-axis and *y*-axis not start at 0?

3.11 Chartjunk comes in many forms. What specifically are moiré vibrations, grids, and ducks?

Calculating the Statistics

3.12 Alumni giving rates calculated as the total dollars donated per year from 1999 to 2009 represent what kind of variable—nominal, ordinal, or scale? What would be an appropriate graph to depict these data?

3.13 Alumni giving rates calculated as the number of alumni who donated and the number who did not donate in a given year represent what kind of variable—nominal, ordinal, or scale? If you wanted to depict the mean age for each of these two groups, what would be an appropriate graph?

3.14 You are exploring the relation between gender and video game performance, as measured by final scores on a game.

   a. In this study, what are the independent and dependent variables?

   b. Is gender a nominal, ordinal, or scale variable?

   c. Is final score a nominal, ordinal, or scale variable?

   d. Which graph or graphs would be appropriate to depict the data? Explain why.

3.15 Would you describe these data as showing a linear or nonlinear relation? Explain.

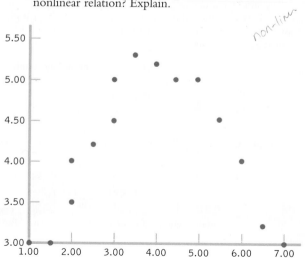

3.16 Would you describe these data as showing a linear or nonlinear relation? Explain.

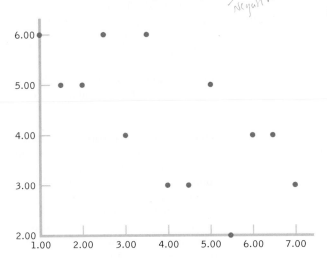

3.17 What elements are missing from the graphs in Exercises 3.15 and 3.16?

3.18 Below is a figure presenting the number of graduate students enrolled at a university, across six fall terms, as a percentage of the total student population.

a. What kind of visual display is this?

b. What other type of visual display could have been used?

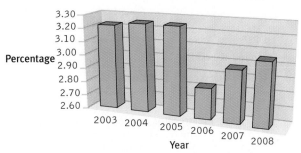

3.19 What is missing from the axes in the figure in Exercise 3.18?

3.20 What chartjunk is present in the figure in Exercise 3.18?

3.21 Using the figure in Exercise 3.18, estimate graduate student enrollment, as a percentage of the total student population, in the following fall terms:

a. 2003

b. 2004

c. 2006

3.22 How would the comparisons between bars in Exercise 3.18 change if the y-axis started at 0?

3.23 When creating a graph, we need to make a decision about the numbering of our axes. If you had the following range of data for one of your variables, how might you label the relevant axis?

337 280 279 311 294 301 342 273

3.24 If you had the following range of data for one of your variables, how might you label the relevant axis?

0.10 0.31 0.27 0.04 0.09 0.22 0.36 0.18

Applying the Concepts

3.25 A social psychologist studied the effect of height on perceived overall attractiveness. Students were recruited to come to a research laboratory in pairs. They were left to sit in the waiting room for several minutes and then were brought to separate rooms, where their heights were measured. They also filled out a questionnaire that asked, among other things, that they rate the attractiveness of the person who had been sitting with them in the waiting room on a scale of 1 to 10.

a. In this study, are the independent and dependent variables nominal, ordinal, or scale?

b. Which graph or graphs would be most appropriate to depict the data? Explain why.

c. If height ranged from 58 inches to 71 inches in this study, would your axis start at 0? Explain.

3.26 A social worker tracked the depression levels of clients being treated with cognitive-behavioral therapy for depression. For each client, depression was assessed at weeks 1 to 20 of therapy. She calculated a mean for all her clients at week 1, week 2, and so on, all the way through week 20.

a. What are the variables in this study?

b. Are the variables nominal, ordinal, or scale?

c. Which graph or graphs would be most appropriate to depict the data? Explain why.

3.27 An epidemiologist determined male suicide rates for 20 countries. For example, in 1996, the rate of male suicide in the United States was approximately 19.3 per 100,000 men, while in China that rate was approximately 15.9.

a. What are the variables in this study?

b. Are the variables nominal, ordinal, or scale?

c. What graph would be most appropriate to depict the data? Explain why.

d. If you wanted to track the suicide rates for three of these countries over 50 years, what type of graph might you use to show these data?

3.28 Every summer, the touring company America-by-Bicycle conducts its Cross-Country Challenge, a seven-week bicycle journey across the United States from San Francisco to Portsmouth, New Hampshire. At some point during the trip, the exhausted cyclists usually start to complain that the organizers are purposely planning for days with lots of hill and mountain climbing to coincide with longer distances. The staff who work on the tour counter that no relation exists between climbs and mileage and that the route is organized based on practicalities, such as the location of towns in which riders can stay. The organizers who planned the route (and who also own the company) say that they actually tried to reduce the mileage on the days with the worst climbs. Here are the approximate daily mileages and climbs (in vertical feet) as estimated from one rider's bicycle computer.

Mileage	Climb	Mileage	Climb	Mileage	Climb
83	600	69	2500	102	2600
57	600	63	5100	103	1000
51	2000	66	4200	80	1000
76	8500	96	900	72	900
51	4600	124	600	68	900
91	800	104	600	107	1900
73	1000	52	1300	105	4000
55	2000	85	600	90	1600
72	2500	64	300	87	1100
108	3900	65	300	94	4000
118	300	108	4200	64	1500
65	1800	97	3500	84	1500
76	4100	91	3500	70	1500
66	1200	82	4500	80	5200
97	3200	77	1000	63	5200
92	3900	53	2500		

a. Construct a scatterplot of the cycling data, putting mileage on the x-axis. Be sure to label everything and include a title.

b. We haven't learned to calculate inferential statistics on these data, so we can't really know what's going on, but do you think that the amount of vertical climb is related to a day's mileage? If yes, explain the relation in your own words. If no, explain why you think there is no relation.

No relation

c. It turns out that inferential statistics do not support the existence of a relation between these variables and that the staff seem to be the most accurate in their appraisal. Why do you think the cyclists and organizers are wrong in opposite directions? What does this say about people's biases and the need for data?

3.29 The Group of Eight (G8) consists of most of the major world economic powers. It meets annually to discuss pressing world problems. In 2005, for example, the agenda included global warming, poverty in Africa, and terrorism. Decisions made by G8 nations can have a global impact; in fact, the eight nations that make up the membership reportedly account for almost two-thirds of the world's economic output. Here are data for seven of the eight G8 nations for gross domestic product (GDP) in 2004 (according to the World Bank) and a measure of education. The measure of education is the percentage of the population between the ages of 25 and 64 that have at least one university degree (Sherman, Honegger, & McGivern, 2003). Russia is not included because no data point for education was available.

Country	GDP (in trillions of $US)	Percentage with University Degree
Canada	0.98	19
France	2.00	11
Germany	2.71	13
Italy	1.67	9
Japan	4.62	18
United Kingdom	2.14	17
United States	11.67	27

a. Create a scatterplot of these data with university degree on the x-axis, being sure to label everything and to give it a title. Later, we'll use statistical tools to determine the equation for the line of best fit. For now, draw a line of best fit that represents your best guess as to where it would go.

b. In your own words, describe the relation between these variables that you see in the scatterplot.

c. Education is on the x-axis, indicating that education is the independent variable. Explain why it is possible that education predicts GDP. Now reverse your explanation of the direction of prediction, explaining why it is possible that GDP predicts education.

3.30 The Canadian Institute for Health Information (CIHI) is a nonprofit organization that compiles data from a range of institutions—from governmental organizations to hospitals to universities. Among the many topics that interest public health specialists is the problem of low levels of organ donation. Medical advances have led to ever-increasing rates of transplantation, but organ donation has not kept up with medicine's ability to perform more sophisticated and more complicated surgeries. Recent data reported by CIHI (2005) provide Canadian transplantation and donation rates for 1994–2004. Here are the donor rates per million deaths.

Year	Donor Rate per Million Deaths	Year	Donor Rate per Million Deaths
1994	14.0	2000	15.3
1995	14.9	2001	13.5
1996	14.2	2002	12.9
1997	14.3	2003	13.5
1998	13.8	2004	13.1
1999	13.8		

a. Construct a time series plot from these data. Be sure to label and title your graph.

b. What story are these data telling?

c. If you worked in public health and were studying the likelihood that families would agree to donation, what research question might you ask about the possible reasons for the trend suggested by these data?

3.31 Universities are concerned with increasing the percentage of alumni who donate to the school because alumni donation rate is a factor in the *U.S. News & World Report* university rankings. What factors might play a role in alumni donation rates? Although we could test numerous variables, let's look at one: type of university. *U.S. News & World Report* lists the top-10 national universities (all of which are private), the top-10 public national universities, and the top-10 liberal arts colleges (also all private). National universities focus on graduate education and research, whereas liberal arts colleges focus on undergraduate education. To give you a sense of the type of institutions in each of these categories, the number-one schools for 2004 in the three categories were Harvard University, the University of California at Berkeley, and Williams College, respectively. Here are the 2004 alumni donation rates for the top-10 schools in each of these categories.

Top-10 Private National Schools	Top-10 Public National Schools	Top-10 Liberal Arts Schools
48%	15%	60%
61	14	63
45	26	52
39	16	53
46	25	66
37	26	52
38	15	55
34	9	55
33	12	53
47	32	48

a. What is the independent variable in this example? Is it nominal or scale? If nominal, what are the levels? If scale, what are the units and what are the minimum and maximum values?

b. What is the dependent variable in this example? Is it nominal or scale? If nominal, what are the levels? If scale, what are the units and what are the minimum and maximum values?

c. Construct a bar graph of these data using the default options in your computer software.

d. Construct a bar graph of these data, but change the defaults to satisfy the guidelines for graphs discussed in this chapter. Aim for simplicity and clarity.

e. What does the pattern of the data suggest?

f. Cite at least one research question that you might want to explore next if you worked for one of these universities—your research question should grow out of these data.

3.32 In How It Works 3.2 and 3.3, we created a bar graph and a Pareto chart for the 2004 GDP, in trillions of U.S. dollars, of each of the G8 nations.

a. Explain the difference between a Pareto chart and a bar graph.

b. What is the benefit of the Pareto chart over the bar graph?

3.33 Johnson, Koch, Fallow, and Huwe (2000) conducted a study of mentoring in two types of psychology doctoral programs: experimental and clinical. Students who graduated from the two types of programs were asked whether they had a faculty mentor while in graduate school. In response, 48.00% of clinical psychology students who graduated between 1945 and 1950 and 62.31% who graduated between 1996 and 1998 reported having had a mentor; 78.26% of experimental psychology students who graduated between 1945 and 1950 and 78.79% who graduated between 1996 and 1998 reported having had a mentor.

a. What are the two independent variables in this study, and what are their levels?

b. What is the dependent variable?

c. Create a bar graph that depicts the percentages for the two independent variables simultaneously.

d. What story is this graph telling us?

e. Was this a true experiment? Explain your answer.

3.34 Refer to the study described in Exercise 3.33.

a. Why would a time series plot be inappropriate for these data? What would a time series plot suggest about the mentoring trend for clinical psychology graduate students and for experimental psychology graduate students?

b. For four time points—1945–1950, 1965, 1985, and 1996–1998—the mentoring rates for clinical psychology graduate students were 48.00, 56.63, 47.50, and 62.31, respectively. For experimental psychology graduate students, the rates were 78.26, 57.14, 57.14, and 78.79, respectively. How does the story we see here conflict with the one that we developed based on just two time points?

3.35 Consider the data on alumni donations presented in Exercise 3.31.

a. Explain how these data could be presented as a pictorial graph. (Note that you do not have to construct such a graph.) What kind of picture could you use? What would it look like?

b. What are the potential pitfalls of a pictorial graph? Why is a bar chart usually a better choice?

3.36 The National Survey on Student Engagement (NSSE) has surveyed more than 400,000 students—freshmen and seniors—at 730 schools since 1999. Among the many questions on the NSSE, students were asked how often they "participated in a community-based project as part of a regular course." For the students at the 19 institutions classified as national universities that made their data publicly available through the *U.S. News & World Report* Web site, here are the data: never, 56%; sometimes, 31%; often, 9%; very often, 5%. (The percentages add up to 101% because of rounding.) Explain why a bar graph would be more suitable for these data than a pie chart.

3.37 The 2000 National Doctoral Program Survey asked 32,000 current and recent PhD students across all disciplines to respond to the statement "I am satisfied with my advisor." The researchers calculated the percentage of students who responded "agree" or "strongly agree": current students, 87%; recent grad-

uates, 86%; former students who left without completing the PhD, 48%.

a. Use a software program that produces graphs (e.g., Excel, SPSS, Minitab) and create a bar graph for these data.

b. Play with the options available to you. List aspects of the bar graph that you are able to change to make your graph meet the guidelines listed in this chapter. Be specific.

3.38 Give an example of a study—real or hypothetical—in the social sciences that might display its data using the following types of graphs. State your independent variable(s) and dependent variable, including levels for any nominal variables.

a. Frequency polygon

b. Line graph (line of best fit)

c. Bar graph (one independent variable)

d. Scatterplot

e. Time series plot

f. Pie chart

g. Bar graph (two independent variables)

3.39 What advice would you give to the creators of each of the following graphs? Consider the basic guidelines for a clear graph, chartjunk, and the six lies of statistics. Give three pieces of advice for each graph. Be specific—don't just say there's chartjunk; say exactly what you'd change.

a. The shrinking doctor:

b. Workforce participation:

How many of us work

40% — Women 25 years and over
50% — Women 15-24 years
60%
70% — Men 15-24 years
80% — Men 25 years and over

1.79 | 1.80 | 1.81 | 1.82 | 1.83

3.40 Find an article in the popular media (newspaper, magazine, Web site) that includes a graph in addition to the text.

a. Briefly summarize the main point of the article and graph.

b. What are the independent and dependent variables depicted in the graph? What kind of variables are they? If nominal, what are the levels?

c. What descriptive statistics are included in the article or on the graph?

d. In one or two sentences, what story is the graph (rather than the article) trying to tell?

e. How well do the text and graph match up? Are they telling the same story? Are they using the same terms? Explain.

f. Write a paragraph to the graph's creator with advice for improving it. Be specific, citing the guidelines from this chapter.

g. Redo the graph, either by hand or by computer, in line with your suggestions.

3.41 The Yerkes–Dodson graph demonstrates that graphs can be used to describe theoretical relations that can be tested. In a study that could be applied to the career decisions made during college, Gilovich and Medvec (1995) identified two types of regrets—regrets of action and regrets of inaction—and proposed that their intensity changes over time. You can think of these as Type I regrets—things you have done that you wish you had not done (regrets of action)—and Type II regrets—things you have not done that you wish you had (re-

grets of inaction). The researchers suggested a theoretical relation between the variables that might look something like the graph below.

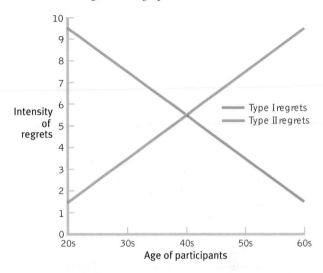

Intensity of regrets

Type I regrets
Type II regrets

Age of participants

a. Briefly summarize the theoretical relations proposed by the graph.

b. What are the independent and dependent variables depicted in the graph? What kind of variables are they? If nominal, what are the levels?

c. What descriptive statistics are included in the text or on the graph?

d. In one or two sentences, what story is the graph trying to tell?

3.42 The APA compiles many statistics about training and careers in the field of psychology. The accompanying graph tracks the numbers of bachelor's, master's, and doctoral degrees between the years 1970 and 2000.

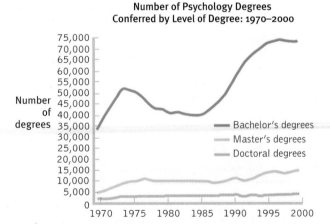

Number of Psychology Degrees Conferred by Level of Degree: 1970–2000

Number of degrees

Bachelor's degrees
Master's degrees
Doctoral degrees

1970 1975 1980 1985 1990 1995 2000

a. What kind of graph is this? Why did the researchers choose this type of graph?

b. Briefly summarize the overall story being told by this graph.

c. What are the independent and dependent variables depicted in the graph? What kind of variables are they? If nominal, what are the levels?

d. List at least three things that the graph creators did well (i.e., are in line with the guidelines for graph construction).

e. List at least one thing that the graph creators should have done differently (i.e., is not in line with the guidelines for graph construction).

f. Name at least one variable other than number that might be used to track the prevalence of psychology bachelor's, master's, and doctoral degrees over time.

g. The increase in bachelor's degrees over the years is not matched by an increase in doctoral degrees. List at least one research question that this finding suggests to you.

Terms

scatterplot (p. 48)

linear relation (p. 49)

nonlinear relation (p. 49)

line graph (p. 50)

time plot, or time series plot (p. 51)

bar graph (p. 52)

Pareto chart (p. 52)

pictorial graph (p. 54)

pie chart (p. 55)

chartjunk (p. 57)

moiré vibration (p. 58)

grid (p. 58)

duck (p. 58)

Central Tendency and Variability

Central Tendency

Mean, the Arithmetic Average
Median, the Middle Score
Mode, the Most Common Score
How Outliers Affect Measures of
  Central Tendency
Which Measure of Central Tendency
  Is Best?

Measures of Variability

Range
Variance
Standard Deviation

BEFORE YOU GO ON

■ You should understand what a distribution is (Chapter 2).

■ You should be able to explain histograms and frequency polygons (Chapter 2).

Nagasaki, Two Days Before the Atomic Bomb

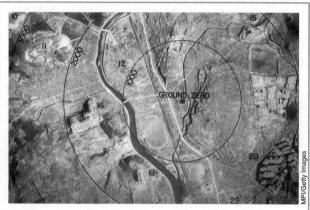

Nagasaki, Three Days After the Atomic Bomb

On August 9, 1945, chance variability in the cloud cover diverted a B-29 bomber from Kokura, Japan, to its secondary target, the city of Nagasaki. When the atomic bomb exploded a few hundred feet above a tennis court, all of the buildings and most of the people who lived in the city of Nagasaki simply disappeared; the people in Kokura survived. Chance variability matters.

How does any nation recover from such devastation? In 1950, an American statistician named W. Edwards Deming persuaded Japan's leading engineers and businesspeople that a statistical idea could re-create their entire industrial-based economy: variability. Deming's core statistical insight was that people were happy to pay for cars, kitchen appliances, and electronics with high reliability (low variability).

The Japanese industrial leadership embraced Deming, as well as his idea that it was management's job to reduce anything that contributes to product variability (an unreliable product). In manufacturing, variability might be due to using different suppliers because they submitted the lowest bid, using worn-out machinery to save money in the short term, or making working conditions unpleasant for employees.

Deming provided practical, statistical guidelines so that Japanese businesses could lower product variability. As Japan's industrial leaders applied Deming's statistical insight, they quickly discovered that controlling variability could be translated into thousands of different manufacturing solutions. The insight transformed the reputation of Japanese companies as manufacturers of cheap junk into one of manufacturers of high-quality products. To this day, the Japanese are specific about how they transformed their devastated nation from an economic disaster to an industrial leader: W. Edwards Deming.

Deming's statistical approach to manufacturing centered on variability, and in fact, variability is one of the basic building blocks of most statistical techniques. In this chapter, we learn about three common measures of variability in a distribution: range, variance, and standard deviation. But to fully understand variability, we first have to know how to identify the middle of a distribution. So before we learn about variability, we first introduce three measures of the middle of a distribution, or the central tendency: mean, median, and mode.

Central Tendency

▶ **MASTERING THE CONCEPT**

4-1: Central tendency is one of the most important ways to understand a distribution of data. We can use the mean, median, or mode as an indicator of central tendency.

Central tendency refers to the descriptive statistic that best represents the center of a data set, the particular value that all the other data seem to be gathering around. It's what we mean when we refer to the "typical" score. Simply creating a visual representation of the distribution, as we did in Chapter 2, often reveals its central tendency. The central tendency is usually at (or near) the highest point in the histogram or the polygon (Figure 4-1), but the specific way that data cluster around a distribution's central tendency can be measured three different ways: mean, median, and mode.

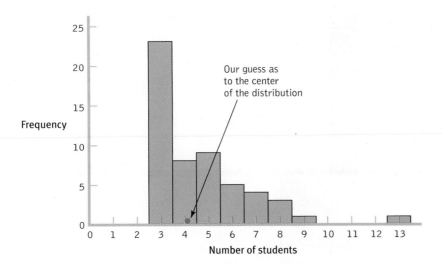

Frequency

Our guess as
to the center
of the distribution

Number of students

FIGURE 4-1
**Estimating Central Tendency
with Histograms**

Histograms and frequency polygons
allow us to see the likely center of our
sample's distribution. The arrow points
to our guess as to the center of the
distribution of numbers of students
mentored by chemistry professors.

Mean, the Arithmetic Average

The mean is simple to calculate and is the gateway to understanding statistical formulas. The mean is such an important concept in statistics that we provide you with four distinct ways to think about it: verbally, arithmetically, visually, and symbolically (using statistical notation).

The Mean in Plain English The most commonly reported measure of central tendency is *the **mean**, the arithmetic average of a group of scores.* The mean, often called the average, is used to represent the "typical" score in a distribution. This is different from the way we often use the word *average* in everyday conversation. We may refer to a person as average in a somewhat derogatory way, noting that someone is "just" average in athletic ability or a movie was "only" average. The word *average* connotes so many different shades of meaning that we need to define the mean arithmetically.

The Mean in Plain Arithmetic The mean is calculated by summing all the scores in a data set and then dividing this sum by the total number of scores. You likely have calculated means many times in your life.

....

For example, when we explore the numbers of students mentored by the 54 graduate advisors that we considered in Chapter 2, the mean would be calculated by first adding the number of students for each mentor, then dividing by the total number of mentors.

EXAMPLE 4.1

STEP 1. Add all of the scores together.

$3 + 3 + 3 + 4 + 5 + 9 + 5 + 3 + 3 + 5 + 6 + 3 + 4 + 8 + 6 + 3 + 3 + 3 + 4$
$+ 4 + 4 + 7 + 6 + 3 + 5 + 5 + 7 + 13 + 3 + 3 + 3 + 3 + 3 + 4 + 4 + 4 + 5$
$+ 6 + 7 + 6 + 7 + 8 + 8 + 3 + 3 + 3 + 5 + 3 + 3 + 5 + 3 + 5 + 3 + 3 = 250$

**STEP 2. Divide the sum of all scores
by the total number of scores.**

In this case, the sum of all scores is 250, which is then divided by 54, the number of scores in this sample:

$$250/54 = 4.63$$

- **Central tendency** refers to the descriptive statistic that best represents the center of a data set, the particular value that all the other data seem to be gathering around.

- The **mean** is the arithmetic average of a group of scores. It is calculated by summing all the scores and dividing by the total number of scores.

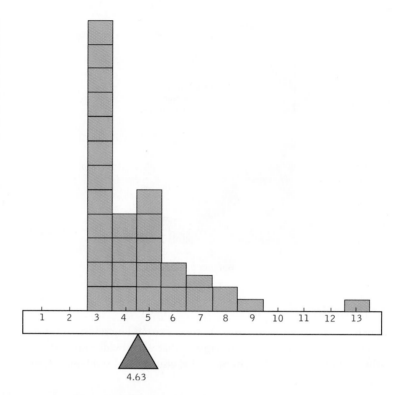

FIGURE 4-2
The Mean as the Fulcrum of Our Data

The mean, 4.63, is the balancing point for all the scores for "numbers of students mentored" for the advisors in our sample. Mathematically, the scores always balance around the mean for any sample.

4.63

Visual Representations of the Mean Think of the mean as the visual point that perfectly balances two sides of a distribution. For example, the mean of 4.63 "students mentored" is represented visually as the point that perfectly balances that distribution, shown in the histogram in Figure 4-2.

The Mean Expressed by Symbolic Notation Symbolic notation may sound far more difficult to understand than it really is. After all, you just calculated a mean without symbolic notation and without a formula. Fortunately, we only need to understand a handful of symbols to express the ideas necessary to understand statistics.

Here are the several symbols that represent the mean. For the mean of a sample, statisticians typically use M or $\overline{X}$. In this book, we use M; many other books also use M, but some use $\overline{X}$ (pronounced "X bar"). For a population, statisticians use the Greek letter μ (pronounced "mew") to symbolize the mean. (Although there are exceptions, Latin letters such as M tend to refer to numbers based on samples, and Greek letters such as μ tend to refer to numbers based on populations.) *The numbers based on samples are called* **statistics***;* M *is a statistic. The numbers based on populations are called* **parameters***;* μ *is a parameter.* Table 4-1 summarizes how these terms are used. As shown in

A **statistic** is a number based on a sample taken from a population; statistics are usually symbolized by Latin letters.

A **parameter** is a number based on the whole population; parameters are usually symbolized by Greek letters.

TABLE 4-1. The Mean in Symbols

The mean of a sample is an example of a statistic, whereas the mean of a population is an example of a parameter. The symbols we use depend on whether we are referring to the mean of a sample or a population.

Number	Used for	Symbol	Pronounced
Statistic	Sample	M or $\overline{X}$	"M" or "X bar"
Parameter	Population	μ	"mew"

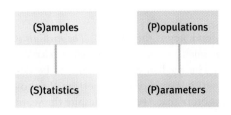

Figure 4–3, you can remember this distinction by the first letters of these words: *statistic* and *sample* both begin with *s*, and *parameter* and *population* both begin with *p*. These symbols are part of the language of statistics and help us to communicate with other statisticians.

A formula to calculate the mean of a sample would use the symbol *M* on the left side of the equation. The right side would provide information on the actual calculation of the mean. A single score is typically symbolized as *X*. We know that we're summing all the scores, all the *X*'s, so the first step is to use the summation sign, Σ (pronounced "sigma"), to indicate that we're summing a list of scores. As you might guess, the full expression for summing all the scores would be ΣX. This instructs us to add up all of the *X*'s in the sample.

Step 1: Add up all of the scores in the sample. In statistical notation, this is ΣX.

Step 2: Divide the sum of all of the scores by the total number of scores. The total number of scores in a sample is typically represented by *N*. (Note that the capital letter *N* is typically used when we refer to the number of scores in the entire data set; if we break the sample down into smaller parts, as we'll see in later chapters, we typically use the lowercase letter *n* for the number of scores in each part.) The full equation would be:

$$M = \frac{\Sigma X}{N}$$

> **MASTERING THE FORMULA**
>
> 4-1: The formula for the mean is: $M = \frac{\Sigma X}{N}$. To calculate the mean, we add up every score, then divide by the total number of scores.

EXAMPLE 4.2

Let's look at the mean for the mentoring data that we considered earlier in this section.

STEP 1. Add up every score.	The sum of all scores is 250.
STEP 2. Divide by the total number of scores.	The total number of scores is 54. So, if we divide 250 by 54, the result is 4.63. Here's how it would look as a formula:

$$M = \frac{\Sigma X}{N} = \frac{250}{54} = 4.63$$

Statisticians tend to be as specific with their symbols as they are with their words. For example, almost all symbols are italicized, whether in the formulas to calculate statistics or in the reporting of statistics. However, the actual numerical values of the statistics are not italicized. Furthermore, whether or not a symbol is capitalized usually has meaning. Changing a symbol from uppercase to lowercase often changes what it means. When you practice calculating means, use this formula, being sure to italicize the symbols and use capital letters for *M, X,* and *N*.

Median, the Middle Score

The second most common measure of central tendency is the median. *The **median** is the middle score of all the scores in a sample when the scores are arranged in ascending order.* We can think of the median as the 50th percentile. The median does not tend to be denoted by a symbol, although in APA style, the writing style of the American Psychological Association, it can be abbreviated as *mdn.* (Note that APA style, despite the word *psychological* in its name, is used across many of the social sciences; you are likely to use it in your courses regardless of your social science major.) To determine the median:

Step 1: Line up all the scores in ascending order.

Step 2: Find the middle score. With an odd number of scores, there will be an actual middle score. With an even number of scores, there will be no actual middle score. In this case, take the mean of the two middle scores.

Here are more specific instructions for finding the median. Keep in mind that with a distribution of only a few data points, we won't want to use the formula—just count how many numbers there are in the distribution and find the score that has the same number of scores above it and below it. Even with a distribution with many scores, the calculation is easy. All we do is divide the number of scores (*N*) by 2 and add ½— that is, 0.5. That number is the ordinal position (rank) of the median, or middle score. As illustrated below, simply count that many places over from the start of your scores and report that number.

Mean versus Median The median is the part of the roadway that divides the directions in which vehicles are permitted to drive. It can be dangerous to confuse the mean and the median, especially when you are calculating the "middle" of the roadway!

David De Lossy/Photodisc Green/Getty Images

EXAMPLE 4.3

Here is an example with an odd number of scores (representing numbers of students mentored for a sample of nine professors):

$$3, 4, 9, 4, 7, 7, 6, 3, 3$$

STEP 1. Line up the scores in ascending order:

$$3, 3, 3, 4, 4, 6, 7, 7, 9$$

| STEP 2. Find the middle score. | First we count the total number of scorces. There are 9 scores: 9/2 = 4.5. If we add 0.5 |

to this result, we get 5. Therefore, the median is the 5th score. We now count across to the 5th score. The median is 4.

EXAMPLE 4.4

Here is an example with an even number of scores. Using the same data as in the example with the odd number of scores, we add one more data point: 13.

| STEP 1. Line up the scores in ascending order. |

$$3, 3, 3, 4, 4, 6, 7, 7, 9, 13$$

| STEP 2. Find the middle score. | First we count the total number of scores. There are 10 scores. We then divide the |

number of scores by two: 10/2 = 5. If we add 0.5 to this result, we get 5.5; therefore, the median is the average of the 5th and 6th scores. The 5th and 6th scores are 4 and 6. The median is their mean, the mean of 4 and 6 = 5.

Mode, the Most Common Score

The *mode* is perhaps the easiest of the three measures of central tendency to calculate. *The **mode** is the most common score of all the scores in a sample.* It is readily picked out on a frequency table, histogram, or frequency polygon. Like the median, the mode does not tend to be represented by a symbol. It does not even have an APA abbreviation. When reporting modes, we use the word itself (e.g., the mode is . . .).

EXAMPLE 4.5

Determine the mode for the data for 54 graduate advisors from earlier in this chapter. Remember that each score represents the number of that graduate advisor's former students who went on to top jobs. The mode can be found either by searching the list of numbers for the most common score or by constructing a frequency table:

3, 3, 3, 4, 5, 9, 5, 3, 3, 5, 6, 3, 4, 8, 6, 3, 3, 3, 4, 4, 4, 7, 6, 3, 5, 5, 7, 13, 3, 3, 3, 3, 3, 4, 4, 4, 5, 6, 7, 6, 7, 8, 8, 3, 3, 3, 5, 3, 3, 5, 3, 5, 3, 3

Mode:_____

Did you get 3? If you didn't, you might have made a common mistake. The mode is the score that occurs most frequently, not the frequency of that score. So, in the data set above, the score 3 occurs 23 times. The mode is 3, *not* 23.

The mode in this example is particularly easy to determine because there is one most common score. Sometimes a data set has no specific mode. This is especially true when the scores are reported to several decimal places (and no number occurs twice). When there is no specific mode, we sometimes report the most common interval as the mode. Other data sets have more than one specific mode, where two or more different scores are the most common. When there is more than one mode, we report both, or all, of the most common scores. *When a distribution of scores has one mode, we refer to it as **unimodal**. When a distribution has two modes, we call it*

■ The **median** is the middle score of all the scores in a sample when the scores are arranged in ascending order. If there is no single middle score, the median is the mean of the two middle scores.

■ The **mode** is the most common score of all the scores in a sample.

■ A **unimodal** distribution has one mode, or most common score.

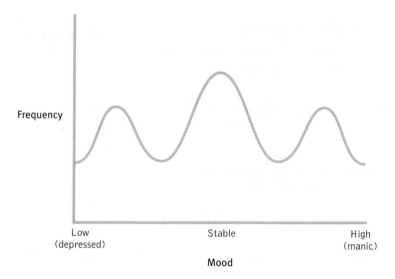

FIGURE 4-4
Bipolar Disorder and
the Modal Mood

Because people with bipolar disorder, especially those who are not receiving treatment, have three different mood states in their lives, it might be hard to determine a true center for their daily mood scores. The distribution might be multimodal, with one mode for depressive days, one for stable days, and one for manic days.

bimodal. *When a distribution has more than two modes, we call it* **multimodal**. *A histogram describing bipolar disease, for example, might be multimodal, as illustrated in Figure 4-4.*

As demonstrated in the example above, the mode can be used with scale data; however, it is more commonly used with nominal data. For example, Cancer Research UK (2003) reported that lung cancer was the most common cause of cancer death in the United Kingdom (22%). No other type of cancer came close. Colorectal cancer accounted for 10% of cancer deaths, breast cancer for 8%, and all other types for 7% or less. In this data set, the modal type of cancer death is lung cancer.

How Outliers Affect Measures of Central Tendency

The mean usually appears in journal articles and media reports. However, we use the median and mode when the data are skewed (lopsided). One common reason for skewed data is a statistical outlier. *An* **outlier** *is an extreme score that is either very high or very low in comparison with the rest of the scores in the sample.* To demonstrate the effect of outliers on the mean, as well as the median's resistance to the effect of outliers, let's use the statistical archives of America's national pastime, baseball.

Some baseball players have made a career out of their ability to steal bases. But one major league player eclipsed all others in terms of the total number of stolen bases: Rickey Henderson. Reported below are five top base-stealers in major league history and the number of bases stolen:

■ A **bimodal** distribution has two modes, or most common scores.

■ A **multimodal** distribution has more than two modes, or most common scores.

■ An **outlier** is an extreme score that is either very high or very low in comparison with the rest of the scores in a sample.

Rickey Henderson	1406
Lou Brock	938
Billy Hamilton	912
Ty Cobb	892
Tim Raines	808

EXAMPLE 4.6

To get a sense of the lifetime achievement of the best base-stealers, we might want to calculate the mean for these five players, using the formula to get a little more practice with the symbols of statistics.

$$M = \frac{\Sigma X}{N} = \frac{\Sigma(1406 + 938 + 912 + 892 + 808)}{5} = \frac{4956}{5} = 991.2$$

As often happens when there is an outlier, this mean is not the same as any of the scores in the sample. The mean of 991.2 is not typical for any of these five baseball players. An important feature of the mean, however, is that it is the point at which all the other scores would balance. Figure 4-5 demonstrates this using the analogy of a balance beam with the numbers of stolen bases from 808 to 1406 marked on it. Weights are placed to represent each of the scores in our sample. The seesaw is perfectly balanced if we put its fulcrum at the mean of 991.2.

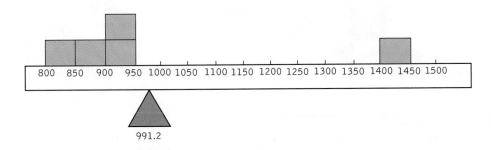

FIGURE 4-5
Outliers and the Mean

When there is an outlier, sometimes the mean is not representative of any one actual score. With the base-stealing data, the mean of 991.2 is above the lowest four scores and well below the highest. Rickey Henderson's score pulls the mean higher, even among the very best base-stealers ever.

When we look at the stolen base data, we notice that Rickey Henderson's score is very different from the others. Four of the scores are between 808 and 938, not a very wide range. But Rickey Henderson stole 1406 bases. When there is an outlier, like Rickey Henderson, it is important to consider what his score would do to the mean, especially if we have a small number of observations.

EXAMPLE 4.7

When we eliminate Rickey Henderson's score, the data are now 808, 892, 912, and 938, and the mean is now:

$$M = \frac{\Sigma X}{N} = \frac{\Sigma(808 + 892 + 912 + 938)}{4} = 887.5$$

The mean of these scores, 887.5, is a good deal lower than the mean of the scores that included Rickey Henderson's very high number of stolen bases. We see from Figure 4-6 that this mean, like the previous mean, marks the point at which all other scores are perfectly balanced around it. However, this mean is a little more representative of the scores—887.5 does seem to be a typical score for these four players.

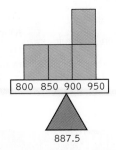

FIGURE 4-6
The Mean Without the Outlier

When the outlier—Rickey Henderson—is omitted from the base-stealing data, the mean is now more representative of the actual scores in the sample.

Which Measure of Central Tendency Is Best?

Different measures of central tendency can lead to very different conclusions. When a decision needs to be made about which measure to use, the choice is usually between the mean and the median. Typically, the mean is the measure of choice. However,

Celebrity Outliers Reports of the cost of a typical Manhattan apartment depend on whether the mean or the median is reported. Film star Gwyneth Paltrow and her husband, Coldplay lead singer Chris Martin, sold their Manhattan apartment in the spring of 2005 for around $7 million. Such a sale would be an outlier and would boost the mean; however, it would not affect the median. Of course, either way, the typical Manhattan apartment is not within the budget of the typical college graduate!

Mario Magnani/Getty Images

whenever the distribution is skewed by an outlier (or when the distribution of observations itself is skewed), the median is used to measure central tendency.

The mode is generally used in three situations: (1) when one particular score dominates a distribution; (2) to describe bimodal or multimodal distributions; and (3) when the data are nominal. When you are uncertain as to which measure is the best indicator of central tendency, report all three.

Central tendency communicates an enormous amount of information with a single number, so it is not surprising that measures of central tendency are among the most widely reported of descriptive statistics. Unfortunately, many people use them incorrectly. One particular statistical "lie" or trick that is used on consumers more than any other is reporting the mean instead of the median. To avoid being tricked when you see a report of central tendency, first notice whether it is reporting an average (mean) or a median. Second, if it is reporting a mean, think about whether that distribution is likely to be skewed by one extremely high number (as in the base-stealing example).

Here is another example in which the mean and median would lead to quite different conclusions: In an article on housing prices in Manhattan, the *New York Times* provided a model of responsible journalism by demonstrating that there is a story behind how central tendency is used to communicate real estate prices. Before the U.S. real estate bubble burst, William Neuman (2005) reported on record-high Manhattan housing prices of $750,000 (median) and $1,276,202 (mean). The mean was inflated by a few sales in the millions, outliers that would not affect the median. For example, the film star Gwyneth Paltrow and her husband, Chris Martin of the rock band Coldplay, sold their Manhattan apartment right around that time for about $7 million. This expensive price certainly would have inflated the mean, but it would not have affected the median.

> **MASTERING THE CONCEPT**
>
> **4-2:** The mean is the most common indicator of central tendency, but it is not always the best. When there is an outlier, it is usually better to use the median.

CHECK YOUR LEARNING

Reviewing the Concepts

> The central tendency of a distribution is the one number that best describes what is typical in that distribution (often its high point).

> The three measures of central tendency are the mean (arithmetic average), the median (middle score), and the mode (most frequently occurring score).

> The mean is the most commonly used measure of central tendency, but the median is preferred when the distribution is skewed (lopsided) or there is an outlier. If you are unsure of which measure to report, then report all three.

> The symbols used in statistics have very specific meanings; changing a symbol even slightly can change its meaning significantly.

Clarifying the Concepts	**4-1** What is the difference between statistics and parameters?
	4-2 Does an outlier have the greatest effect on the mean, median, or mode?
Calculating the Statistics	**4-3** Calculate the mean, median, and mode of the following sets of numbers.
	a. 10, 8, 22, 5, 6, 1, 19, 8, 13, 12, 8
	b. 122.5, 123.8, 121.2, 125.8, 120.2, 123.8, 120.5, 119.8, 126.3, 123.6
	c. 0.100, 0.866, 0.781, 0.555, 0.222, 0.245, 0.234
Applying the Concepts	**4-4** Let's examine fictional data for 20 seniors in college. Each score represents the number of nights a student spends socializing in one week: 1, 0, 1, 2, 5, 3, 2, 3, 1, 3, 1, 7, 2, 3, 2, 2, 2, 0, 4, 6
	a. Using the formula, calculate the mean of these scores.
	b. If the researcher reported the mean of these scores to the university as an estimate for the whole university population, what symbol would be used for the mean? Why?
	c. If the researcher were interested only in the scores of these 20 students, what symbol would be used for the mean? Why?
	d. What is the median of these scores?
Solutions to these Check Your Learning questions can be found in Appendix D.	e. What is the mode of these scores?
	f. Are the median and mean similar to or different from each other? What does this tell you about the distribution of scores?

Measures of Variability

After World War II, people often poked fun at the poor quality of Japanese transistor radios and other products. But it took just three years to transform Japanese manufacturing into an industry that made high-quality products through low variability. In statistics, *variability is a numerical way of describing how much spread there is in a distribution*. The measures of variability we learn about next provide new ways to describe the distribution of our data. One way to numerically describe the variability of a distribution is by computing its *range*. A second and more common way to describe variability is by computing *variance* and its square root, known as *standard deviation*.

Range

The range is the easiest measure of variability to calculate. *The **range** is a measure of variability calculated by subtracting the lowest score (the minimum) from the highest score (the maximum)*. *Maximum* and *minimum* are sometimes substituted in this formula to

---

◀ **MASTERING THE CONCEPT**

4-3: After central tendency, variability is the second most common concept to help us understand the shape of a distribution. Common indicators of variability are range, variance, and standard deviation.

▪ **Variability** is a numerical way of describing how much spread there is in a distribution.

▪ The **range** is a measure of variability calculated by subtracting the lowest score (the minimum) from the highest score (the maximum).

describe the highest and lowest scores, and some statistical computer programs abbreviate these as *max* and *min*. The range is represented in formula as:

$$\text{range} = X_{highest} - X_{lowest}$$

MASTERING THE FORMULA ▶

4-2: The formula for the range is: range $= X_{highest} - X_{lowest}$. We simply subtract the lowest score from the highest score to calculate the range.

Here are the scores for the chemistry professors we discussed earlier in the chapter. Each score represents the number of a professor's students who went on to obtain top academic jobs.

3, 3, 3, 4, 5, 9, 5, 3, 3, 5, 6, 3, 4, 8, 6, 3, 3, 3, 4, 4, 4, 7, 6, 3, 5, 5, 7, 13, 3, 3, 3, 3, 3, 4, 4, 4, 5, 6, 7, 6, 7, 8, 8, 3, 3, 3, 5, 3, 3, 5, 3, 5, 3, 3

EXAMPLE 4.8

We can determine the highest and lowest scores either by reading through the data or, more easily, by glancing at the frequency table for these data.

STEP 1. Determine the highest score.

In this case, the highest score is 13.

STEP 2. Determine the lowest score.

In this case, the lowest score is 3.

STEP 3. Calculate the range.

Subtract the lowest score from the highest score:

$$\text{range} = X_{highest} - X_{lowest} = 13 - 3 = 10.$$

The range can be a useful initial measure of variability, but what we learn from the range is limited. It is affected by our highest and lowest scores only. It does not take any other data points into account. The other scores could all be very close to the highest score or all huddled near the center. They could also be spread out evenly or have some other unexpected pattern. We can't know based only on the range.

Variance

Variance is the average of the squared deviations from the mean. It is a concept that we'll soon learn to calculate. Basically, however, variance refers to variability. When something varies, it must vary from, or be different from, some standard. That standard is the mean. So, when we compute variance, the number we arrive at is a number that describes the degree to which a distribution varies with respect to the mean. A small number indicates a small amount of spread or deviation around the mean, and a bigger number indicates a great deal of spread or deviation around the mean.

EXAMPLE 4.9

Students who seek therapy at university counseling centers often do not attend many sessions. For example, in one study, the median number of therapy sessions was 3 and the mean was 4.6 (Hatchett, 2003). Let's examine the spread of fictional scores for a sample of five students: 1, 2, 4, 4, and 10 numbers of therapy sessions, with a mean of 4.2 sessions. Next we find out how far each score deviates from the mean by subtracting the mean from every score. As you might expect, we label the column that lists our scores with an X. Here, our second column includes the results we get when we subtract the mean from each score, or $X - M$. We call each of these a ***deviation from the mean*** (or just a *deviation*)—*the amount that a score in a sample differs from the mean of the sample.*

X	X − M
1	−3.2
2	−2.2
4	−0.2
4	−0.2
10	5.8

But we can't just take the mean of the deviations. If we do (and if you try this, don't forget the signs—negative and positive), we get 0. In fact, every time we do this with any data set, the mean is 0. Are you surprised? Remember, the mean is the point at which all scores are perfectly balanced. Mathematically, the scores *have* to balance out. Yet we know that there *is* variability among these scores. The number representing the amount of variability is certainly not 0!

When we ask students for ways to eliminate the negative signs, two suggestions typically come up: (1) take the absolute value of the deviations, thus making them all positive, or (2) square all the scores, again making them all positive. It turns out that the latter, squaring all the deviations, is how statisticians solve this problem. Once we square our deviations, we can take their average and get a measure of variability.

To recap:

STEP 1. Subtract the mean from every score.	We call these deviations from the mean, or deviations.
STEP 2. Square every deviation from the mean.	We call these squared deviations.
STEP 3. Sum all of the squared deviations.	This is often called the sum of squared deviations, or the sum of squares for short.
STEP 4. Divide the sum of squares by the total number in the sample (*N*).	That is, we take the average of the squared deviations.

This number represents the mathematical definition of variance—the average of the squared deviations from the mean.

Let's calculate variance for our therapy session data. We add a third column to contain the squares of each of the deviations, then add all of these numbers up to compute the ***sum of squares*** (symbolized as *SS), the sum of each score's squared deviation from the mean.* In this case, the sum of the squared deviations is 48.80, so the average squared deviation is $48.80/5 = 9.76$. Thus, the variance equals 9.76.

■ **Variance** is the average of the squared deviations from the mean.

■ A **deviation from the mean** is the amount that a score in a sample differs from the mean of the sample; also called *deviation.*

■ The **sum of squares**, symbolized as *SS*, is the sum of the squared deviations from the mean for each score.

X	X − M	(X − M)²
1	−3.2	10.24
2	−2.2	4.84
4	−0.2	0.04
4	−0.2	0.04
10	5.8	33.64

[handwritten marginalia: 4.6; 180.6; 49.6; .576; .576; 775.0; 1006.352]

Now let's put this in equation form, which will make it look more complicated than it is but will continue to acclimate us to symbolic notation. We need a few new symbols at this point, because variance has several different symbols when it's calculated from a sample, including *SD²*, *s²*, and *MS*. *SD²* and *s²* come from the words *standard deviation squared*. *MS* comes from the words *mean square* (referring to the average of the squared deviations). We'll use *SD²* at this point, but we will alert you when we switch to other symbols for variance later. When variance is calculated from a population, it typically has just one symbol, σ^2 (pronounced "sigma squared"), and is a parameter. (Remember, Latin letters are used for statistics, which are calculated from samples, and Greek letters are used for parameters, which are calculated from or hypothesized for populations.)

We already know all the symbols needed to calculate variance: *X* to indicate the individual scores, *M* to indicate the mean, and *N* to indicate the sample size.

$$SD^2 = \frac{\Sigma(X - M)^2}{N}$$

As you can see, variance is really just a mean—the mean of squared deviations.

MASTERING THE FORMULA

4-3: The formula for variance is: $SD^2 = \frac{\Sigma(X - M)^2}{N}$. To calculate variance, subtract the mean (*M*) from every score (*X*) to calculate deviations from the mean; then square these deviations, sum them, and divide by the sample size (*N*). By summing the squared deviations and dividing by sample size, we are taking their mean.

Standard Deviation

EXAMPLE 4.10

Variance is useful, but not as useful as standard deviation. **Standard deviation** *is the square root of the average of the squared deviations from the mean, and is the typical amount that each score varies, or deviates, from the mean.* Standard deviation is perhaps better known as the square root of variance. The problem with variance—and the reason that we need standard deviation—is that it's not very easy to understand at a glance. Remember, the numbers of therapy sessions for the five students were 1, 2, 4, 4, and 10, with a mean of 4.2. The typical score does not vary from the mean by 9.76. The variance is based on *squared* deviations, not deviations, so it is too big. When we ask our students how to solve this problem, they invariably say "unsquare it," and that's just what we do. We take the square root of variance to come up with a much more useful number, the standard deviation. The square root of 9.76 is 3.12. Now we have a number that "makes sense" to us. We can now say that the typical number of therapy sessions for students in this sample is 4.2 and the typical amount a student varies from that is 3.12.

As you read journal articles, you often will see the mean and standard deviation reported as: (*M* = 4.2, *SD* = 3.12). A glance at our original data (1, 2, 4, 4, 10) tells us that these numbers make sense: 4.2 does seem to be approximately in the center; scores do seem to vary from 4.2 roughly by 3.12. The score of 10 is a bit of an outlier, but not so much that the mean and standard deviation are not somewhat representative of the typical score and typical deviation.

We didn't actually need a formula to get the standard deviation. We just took the square root of the variance. Perhaps you guessed the symbols for standard deviation

▪ **Standard deviation** is the square root of the average of the squared deviations from the mean, and is the typical amount that each score varies, or deviates, from the mean.

by just taking the square root of those for variance. With a sample, standard deviation is either *SD* or *s*. With a population, standard deviation is σ. Table 4-2 presents this information concisely. We can write the formula showing how standard deviation is calculated from variance:

$$SD = \sqrt{SD^2}$$

We also can write the formula showing how standard deviation is calculated from the original *X*'s, *M,* and *N*:

$$SD = \sqrt{\frac{\Sigma(X - M)^2}{N}}$$

◀ **MASTERING THE FORMULA**

4-4: The most basic formula for standard deviation is: $SD = \sqrt{SD^2}$. We simply take the square root of variance.

◀ **MASTERING THE FORMULA**

4-5: The full formula for standard deviation is: $SD = \sqrt{\frac{\Sigma(X - M)^2}{N}}$. To calculate standard deviation, subtract the mean from every score to calculate deviations from the mean. Then, square the deviations from the mean. Sum the squared deviations, then divide by the sample size. Finally, take the square root of the mean of the squared deviations.

TABLE 4-2. Variance and Standard Deviation in Symbols

The variance or standard deviation of a sample is an example of a statistic, whereas the variance or standard deviation of a population is an example of a parameter. The symbols we use depend on whether we are referring to the spread of a sample or a population.

Number	Used for . . .	Standard Deviation Symbol	Pronounced	Variance Symbol	Pronounced
Statistic	Sample	*SD* or *s*	As written	SD^2, s^2, or *MS*	Letters as written; if superscript 2, then followed by "squared" (e.g., "ess squared")
Parameter	Population	σ	"Sigma"	σ^2	"Sigma squared"

CHECK YOUR LEARNING

Reviewing the Concepts
> The simplest way to measure variability is the range, which is calculated by subtracting the lowest score from the highest score.
> Variance and standard deviation both measure the degree to which scores in a distribution vary from the mean. The standard deviation is simply the square root of the variance, it represents the typical deviation of a score from the mean.

Clarifying the Concepts
4-5 In your own words, what is variability?
4-6 Distinguish the range from the standard deviation. What does each tell us about the distribution?

Calculating the Statistics
4-7 Calculate the range, variance, and standard deviation for the following data sets (the same ones from the section on central tendency).
  a. 10, 8, 22, 5, 6, 1, 19, 8, 13, 12, 8
  b. 122.5, 123.8, 121.2, 125.8, 120.2, 123.8, 120.5, 119.8, 126.3, 123.6
  c. 0.100, 0.866, 0.781, 0.555, 0.222, 0.245, 0.234

Applying the Concepts
4-8 Final exam week is approaching and students are not eating as well as usual. Four students were asked how many calories of junk food they had consumed between

continued on next page

noon and 10:00 P.M. on the day before an exam. The estimated numbers of nutritionless calories, calculated with the help of a nutritional software program, were 450, 670, 1130, and 1460.

a. Using the formula, calculate the range for these scores.

b. What information can't you glean from the range?

c. Using the formula, calculate variance for these scores.

d. Using the formula, calculate standard deviation for these scores.

e. If a researcher were interested only in these four students, what symbols would she use for variance and standard deviation, respectively?

f. If another researcher hoped to generalize from these four students to all students at the university, what symbols would he use for variance and standard deviation?

Solutions to these Check Your Learning questions can be found in Appendix D.

REVIEW OF CONCEPTS

Central Tendency

Three measures of *central tendency* are commonly used in research. The *mean* is the arithmetic average of the data. The *median* is the midpoint of the data set; 50% of scores fall on either side of the median. The *mode* is the most common score in the data set. When there's one mode, the distribution is *unimodal;* when there are two modes, it's *bimodal;* and when there are three or more modes, it's *multimodal.* The mean is highly influenced by *outliers,* whereas the median and mode are resistant to outliers. It is important to consider whether outliers are present in our data set when deciding which measure of central tendency to use. Usually, however, the mean is the preferred measure. When the mean and other measures are used to describe samples, they're called *statistics* and symbolized by Latin letters; when they're used to describe populations, they're called *parameters* and symbolized by Greek letters.

Measures of Variability

The *range* is the simplest measure of *variability* to calculate. It is often used when the preferred measure of central tendency is the median. It is calculated by subtracting the minimum score in our data set from the maximum score. Variance and standard deviation are much more common measures of variability. They are used when the preferred measure of central tendency is the mean. *Variance* is the average of the squared deviations. It is calculated by subtracting the mean from every score to get *deviations from the mean,* then squaring each of the deviations and taking their mean. (The *sum of squares* of the deviations is used in many inferential statistics.) *Standard deviation* is the square root of variance. It is the typical amount that a score deviates from the mean.

SPSS®

The left-hand column in "Data View" is prenumbered, beginning with 1. Each column to the right of that number contains data for a particular variable; each row below that number represents a unique individual. Notice the choices at the top of the "Data View" screen. Enter the data for the numbers of students mentored by each professor that were used several times in this chapter, including in example 4.5.

To get a numerical description of a variable, select **Analyze** → Descriptive Statistic → Frequencies. Then, select the variable "students" by highlighting it and then clicking the arrow to move it from the left side to the right side. Then click: Statistics → Mean, Median, Mode, Std. deviation, Range → Continue → OK.

Your output will look like that in the screen shot shown here.

	students	va
1	3.00	
2	3.00	
3	3.00	
4	3.00	
5	3.00	
6	3.00	
7	3.00	
8	3.00	
9	3.00	
10	3.00	
11	3.00	
12	3.00	
13	3.00	
14	3.00	
15	3.00	
16	3.00	
17	3.00	
18	3.00	
19	3.00	
20	3.00	
21	3.00	
22	3.00	
23	3.00	
24	4.00	
25	4.00	

Statistics

numbers of students mentored

N	Valid	54.00
	Missing	.00
	Mean	4.63
	Median	4.00
	Mode	3.00
	Std. Deviation	2.04
	Range	10.00

numbers of students mentored

		Frequency	Percent	Valid Percent	Cumulative Percent
Valid	3	23	42.6	42.6	42.6
	4	8	14.8	14.8	57.4
	5	9	16.7	16.7	74.1
	6	5	9.3	9.3	83.3
	7	4	7.4	7.4	90.7
	8	3	5.6	5.6	96.3
	9	1	1.9	1.9	98.1
	13	1	1.9	1.9	100.0
	Total	54	100.0	100.0	

How It Works

4.1 CALCULATING THE MEAN

Here are data for the numbers of nights out socializing in a week for 20 students.

1, 2, 7, 6, 1, 2, 6, 5, 4, 4, 0, 3, 2, 2, 3, 4, 3, 5, 4, 4

How can we calculate the mean? First, we add up all of the scores:

$1 + 2 + 7 + 6 + 1 + 2 + 6 + 5 + 4 + 4 + 0 + 3 + 2 + 2 + 3 + 4 + 3 + 5 + 4 + 4 = 68$

Then we divide by 20, the number of scores:

$68/20 = 3.4$

With the formula $M = \frac{\Sigma X}{N}$, we'd calculate:

$$M = \frac{(1 + 2 + 7 + 6 + 1 + 2 + 6 + 5 + 4 + 4 + 0 + 3 + 2 + 2 + 3 + 4 + 3 + 5 + 4 + 4)}{20}$$

4.2 CALCULATING THE MEDIAN

Using the data for "nights out socializing," how can we calculate the median? The median is simply the middle score, or the average of the two middle scores. For these data, we first arrange the data from lowest score to highest score:

0 1 1 2 2 2 2 3 3 3 4 4 4 4 4 5 5 6 6 7

We divide the number of scores, 20, by 2 and add 1/2 to get 10.5. The mean of the 10th and 11th scores in the ordered list is the median—(3 + 4)/2 = 3.5. The median is 3.5.

4.3 CALCULATING THE MODE

How can we calculate the mode for the "nights out socializing" data? The mode is the most common score. We can determine this for these data by looking at the frequency distribution. Five people have a score of 4. The mode is 4.

4.4 CALCULATING VARIANCE

How can we calculate variance for the "nights out socializing" data? To calculate variance for these data, we first subtract the mean, 3.4, from every score to calculate a deviation. We then square the deviations. These calculations are shown in the table below.

X	(X − M)	(X − M)²
1	−2.4	5.76
2	−1.4	1.96
7	3.6	12.96
6	2.6	6.76
1	−2.4	5.76
2	−1.4	1.96
6	2.6	6.76
5	1.6	2.56
4	0.6	0.36
4	0.6	0.36
0	−3.4	11.56
3	−0.4	0.16
2	−1.4	1.96
2	−1.4	1.96
3	−0.4	0.16
4	0.6	0.36
3	−0.4	0.16
5	1.6	2.56
4	0.6	0.36
4	0.6	0.36

We then add all of the scores in the third column to get the sum of squared deviations, or the sum of squares. This sum is 64.8.

We can use the formula to complete our calculations:

$$SD^2 = \frac{\Sigma(X - M)^2}{N} = \frac{64.8}{20} = 3.24$$

The variance is 3.24.

4.5 CALCULATING STANDARD DEVIATION

How can we calculate standard deviation for the "nights out socializing" data? The standard deviation is the typical amount that the scores in a sample vary, or deviate, from the mean, and is the square root of the variance. For these data, we can calculate standard deviation directly from the variance we calculated above using this formula:

$$SD = \sqrt{SD^2} = \sqrt{3.24} = 1.80$$

The standard deviation is 1.80.

Exercises

Clarifying the Concepts

4.1 Define the three measures of central tendency: mean, median, and mode.

4.2 The mean can be assessed visually and arithmetically. Describe each method.

4.3 Explain how the mean mathematically balances the distribution.

4.4 Explain what is meant by unimodal, bimodal, and multimodal distributions.

4.5 In what situations is the mode typically used?

4.6 What is an outlier?

4.7 Are the mean and median affected by outliers?

4.8 Define the symbols used in the equation for variance:

$$SD^2 = \frac{\Sigma(X - M)^2}{N}$$

4.9 Why is the standard deviation typically reported rather than the variance?

4.10 Find the incorrectly used symbol or symbols in each of the following statements or formulas. For each statement or formula, (i) state which symbol(s) is/are used incorrectly, (ii) explain why the symbol(s) in the original statement is/are incorrect, and (iii) state what symbol(s) *should* be used.

  a. The mean and standard deviation of the sample of reaction times were calculated (m = 54.2, SD^2 = 9.87).

  b. The mean of the sample of high school student GPAs was μ = 3.08.

  c. Range = $X_{highest} - X_{lowest}$

Calculating the Statistics

4.11 Calculate the mean, median, and mode for the following data: 15, 34, 32, 46, 22, 36, 34, 28, 52, 28.

4.12 Calculate the mean, median, and mode for the following salaries: $44,751, $52,000, $41,500, $38,862, $51,380, $61,774.

4.13 Add another data point, 112, to the data presented in Exercise 4.11. Calculate the mean, median, and mode again. How does this new data point affect your calculations?

4.14 Add another salary, $97,582, to the data presented in Exercise 4.12. Calculate the mean, median, and mode again. How does this new salary affect your calculations?

4.15 Calculate the range, variance, and standard deviation for the data in Exercise 4.11.

4.16 Calculate the range, variance, and standard deviation for the salaries in Exercise 4.12.

4.17 How does the range change when you include the outlier salary, $97,582, with the data from Exercise 4.12?

4.18 Here are the *U.S. News & World Report* data again on alumni giving at the top 70 national universities.

48	61	45	39	46	37	38	34	33	47
29	38	38	34	29	29	36	48	27	25
15	25	14	26	33	16	33	32	25	34
26	32	11	15	25	9	25	40	12	20
32	10	24	9	16	21	12	14	18	20
18	25	18	20	23	9	16	17	19	15
14	18	16	17	20	24	25	11	16	13

  a. Calculate the mean of these data, showing that you know how to use the symbols and formula.

  b. Determine the median of these data.

4.19 Describe the variability in the data presented in Exercise 4.18 by computing the range.

4.20 The Mount Washington Observatory (MWO) in New Hampshire claims to have the world's worst weather. Below are some data on the weather extremes recorded at the MWO. Calculate the mean and median normal daily minimum temperature across the year.

	Normal Daily Maximum (°F)	Normal Daily Minimum (°F)	Record Low in °F (Year)	Peak Wind Gust in Miles per Hour (Year)
January	14.0	−3.7	−47 (1934)	173 (1985)
February	14.8	−1.7	−46 (1943)	166 (1972)
March	21.3	5.9	−38 (1950)	180 (1942)
April	29.4	16.4	−20 (1995)	231 (1934)
May	41.6	29.5	−2 (1966)	164 (1945)
June	50.3	38.5	8 (1945)	136 (1949)
July	54.1	43.3	24 (2001)	154 (1996)
August	53.0	42.1	20 (1986)	142 (1954)
September	46.1	34.6	9 (1992)	174 (1979)
October	36.4	24.0	−5 (1939)	161 (1943)
November	27.6	13.6	−20 (1958)	163 (1983)
December	18.5	1.7	−46 (1933)	178 (1980)

4.21 Calculate the mean, median, and mode for the record low temperatures recorded on top of Mount Washington presented in Exercise 4.20.

4.22 Calculate the mean, median, and mode for the peak wind gust data presented in Exercise 4.20.

4.23 When no mode appears in the raw data, we can compute a mode by breaking the data into intervals. How might you do this for the peak wind gust data presented in Exercise 4.20?

4.24 Calculate the range, variance, and standard deviation for normal daily minimum temperature across the years presented in Exercise 4.20.

4.25 Calculate the range, variance, and standard deviation for the record low temperatures recorded on top of Mount Washington presented in Exercise 4.20.

4.26 Calculate the range, variance, and standard deviation for the peak wind gust data presented in Exercise 4.20.

Applying the Concepts

4.27 For the data presented in Exercise 4.20, the "normal" daily maximum and minimum temperatures recorded at the Mount Washington Observatory are presented for each month. These are likely to be measures of central tendency for each month over time. Explain why these "normal" temperatures might be calculated as means or medians. What would be the reasoning for using one statistic over the other?

4.28 Back in Exercises 4.13 and 4.14 we saw how the mean and median changed when an outlier was included in the computations. If you were reporting the typical salary at a company, how might the mean and median give different impressions to potential applicants?

4.29 The "normal" weather data from the Mount Washington Observatory are broken down by months. Why might you not want to average across all months in a year? How else could you summarize the year?

4.30 There appears to be an outlier in the data for peak wind gust recorded on top of Mount Washington (see data in Exercise 4.20). Where do you see an outlier and how would excluding this data point affect the different calculations of central tendency?

4.31 Here are winning percentages for 11 players for their best four-year pitching performances: 0.755, 0.721, 0.708, 0.773, 0.782, 0.747, 0.477, 0.817, 0.617, 0.650, 0.651.

   a. What is the mean of these scores?

   b. What is the median of these scores?

   c. Compare the mean and median. Does the difference between them suggest that the data are skewed very much?

4.32 Briefly describe a real-life situation in which the median is preferable to the mean. Give hypothetical numbers for mean and median in your explanation. Be original! (Don't use home prices or another example from the chapter.)

4.33 Find an advertisement for a weight-loss product either online or in the print media—the more unbelievable the claims, the better!

   a. What does the ad promise that this product will do for the consumer?

   b. What data does it offer for its promised benefits? Does it offer any descriptive statistics or merely testimonials? If it offers descriptive statistics, what are the limitations of what they report?

   c. If you were considering this product, what measures of central tendency would you most like to see? Explain your answer, noting why not all measures of central tendency would be helpful.

   d. If a friend with no statistical background were considering this product, what would you tell him or her?

4.34 When you see an ad on TV for a body-shaping product (e.g., an abdominal muscle machine), often a person with a wonderful success story is featured in the ad. The statement "individual results may vary" hints at what kind of data the advertisement may be presenting.

   a. What kind of data is being presented in these ads?

   b. What statistics could be presented to help inform the public about how much "individual results might vary"?

4.35 The National Survey of Student Engagement asked students how often they asked questions in class or participated in classroom discussions. The options were "never," "sometimes," "often," and "very often." Here are the percentages, reported in 2005, of students who responded "very often" for the 31 institutions classified as liberal arts colleges that allowed their 2004 data to become public through the *U.S. News & World Report* Web site.

   58 45 53 45 65 41 50 46 54
   59 52 60 59 62 54 52 53 54
   83 60 32 62 50 50 43 32 53
   60 52 55 53

   a. What is the range of these data?

   b. The top college is Marlboro College in Vermont, and the two tied for lowest are Randolph-Macon Women's College in Virginia and Texas A&M University in Galveston. What research questions do these data suggest to you? State at least one research question generated by these data.

4.36 Here again are the data from the National Survey of Student Engagement for a sample of 19 national universities, as reported in 2005. These are the percentages of students who said they were assigned between 5 and 10 20-page papers.

   0 5 3 3 1 10 2
   2 3 1 2 4   2 1
   1 1 4 3 5

   a. Calculate the mean of these data using the symbols and formula.

   b. Calculate the variance of these data using the symbols and formula, but also using columns to show all calculations.

   c. Calculate the standard deviation using the symbols and formula.

   d. In your own words, describe what the mean and standard deviation of these data tell us about these scores.

4.37 For each of the following situations, state whether the mean would be a statistic or a parameter. Explain your answer.

a. According to 1991 Canadian census data, the mean income (from employment only) of French-speaking Canadians living in Ontario was $29,527, higher than the general population mean of $28,838.

b. In the 2004–2005 National Basketball Association season, the 30 teams won a mean 41.00 games.

c. The General Social Survey (GSS) includes a vocabulary test in which participants are given a series of words and asked to choose the appropriate synonym from a multiple-choice list of five words (e.g., *beast* with the choices *afraid, words, large, animal,* and *separate*). The mean vocabulary test score was 5.98.

d. The National Survey of Student Engagement (NSSE) asked students at participating institutions how often they discussed ideas or readings with their professors outside of class. Among the 19 national universities that made their data public, the mean percentage of students who responded "very often" was 8%.

4.38 Consider the many possible distributions of grades on a quiz in a statistics class; imagine that the grades could range from 0 to 100. For each of the following situations, give a hypothetical mean and median (that is, make up a mean and a median that might occur with a distribution that has this shape). Explain your answer.

a. Normal distribution

b. Positively skewed distribution

c. Negatively skewed distribution

4.39 For each of the following distributions, state whether it's more likely to be unimodal or bimodal. Explain your answer.

a. Age of patients in a hospital maternity ward

b. Depression scores on a Beck Depression Inventory

c. GRE scores of applicants to sociology graduate programs

d. The cost of an AIDS drug that is sold in developed countries in Europe, as well as in developing countries in Africa

4.40 Here are the numbers of wins for the 30 National Basketball Association teams in the 2004–2005 season.

45 43 42 33 33 54 47 44 42 30
59 45 36 18 13 52 49 44 27 26
62 50 37 34 34 59 58 51 45 18

a. Determine the mean, median, and mode of these data. Use symbols and the formula when showing your calculation of the mean.

b. Using software, calculate the range and standard deviation of these data.

c. Write a one- to two-paragraph summary describing the distribution of these data. Mention center,

variability, and shape. Be sure to discuss the number of modes (i.e., unimodal, bimodal, multimodal), any possible outliers, and the presence and direction of any skew.

4.41 The U.S. Census Bureau collects and analyzes data on numerous aspects of American life by state, including the percentage of people with high school degrees, bachelor's degrees, and advanced degrees. If you wanted to calculate the "average" percentage of people with advanced degrees across all states, would you report a mean, median, or mode? Explain your answer clearly.

4.42 According to a 2007 article on the Economist.com Web site, Americans are the international leaders in TV viewing, averaging 8 hours and 11 minutes a day. Below are approximate, daily average viewing times for 12 countries based on this source:

United States—8.2 hours

Turkey—5 hours

Italy—4.05 hours

Japan—3.75 hours

Spain—3.6 hours

Portugal—3.5 hours

Australia—3.2 hours

South Korea—3.16 hours

Canada—3.1 hours

Britain—3 hours

Denmark—3 hours

Finland—2.8 hours

a. Compute the mean and median across these 12 data points.

b. How are these statistics affected by including or excluding the United States?

4.43 Refer to the data from Exercise 4.42.

a. How do you think these daily "averages" were calculated—using means or medians?

b. Do you think TV viewing habits might vary by other personal or demographic characteristics? Could these represent confounds?

c. How might you collect samples to more specifically describe TV viewing habits as a function of other personal characteristics?

4.44 When the typical height or typical weight of children is plotted to create growth charts, do you think it would be appropriate to use the mean for these data? There are often outliers for height, but why might we not have to be concerned with their effect on these data?

4.45 Guinness World Records relies on what kind of data for its amazing claims?

Terms

central tendency (p. 72)

mean (p. 73)

statistic (p. 74)

parameter (p. 74)

median (p. 76)

mode (p. 77)

unimodal (p. 77)

bimodal (p. 78)

multimodal (p. 78)

outlier (p. 78)

variability (p. 81)

range (p. 81)

variance (p. 82)

deviation from the mean (p. 83)

sum of squares (p. 83)

standard deviation (p. 84)

Symbols

M	(p. 74)	mdn	(p. 76)	σ^2	(p. 84)
$\bar{X}$	(p. 74)	SS	(p. 83)	SD	(p. 85)
μ	(p. 74)	SD^2	(p. 84)	s	(p. 85)
X	(p. 75)	s^2	(p. 84)	σ	(p. 85)
N	(p. 75)	MS	(p. 84)		

Formulas

$M = \dfrac{\Sigma X}{N}$ (p. 75)

$\text{range} = X_{highest} - X_{lowest}$ (p. 82)

$SD^2 = \dfrac{\Sigma(X - M)^2}{N}$ (p. 84)

$SD = \sqrt{SD^2}$ (p. 85)

$SD = \sqrt{\dfrac{\Sigma(X - M)^2}{N}}$ (p. 85)

C H A P T E R   5

Sampling and Probability

Samples and Their Populations
Random Sampling
Convenience Sampling
The Problem with a Biased Sample
Random Assignment

Probability
Expected Relative-Frequency Probability
Independence and Probability

Inferential Statistics
Developing Hypotheses
Making a Decision

Type I and Type II Errors
Type I Errors
Type II Errors

 BEFORE YOU GO ON

■ You should understand the difference between a sample and a population (Chapter 1).

■ You should know what central tendency is, particularly the mean (Chapter 4).

Voter Sampling in the 2000 Presidential Election Sampling errors led to election-night confusion about the winner of the 2000 U.S. presidential election.

AP Photo/Michael Conroy

The 2000 U.S. presidential election was the closest election since 1986. As the television news organizations began to estimate the electoral college votes, it became clear that the election was extremely close. The winner in the pivotal state of Florida was destined to become the next president of the United States, and the networks were in keen competition to be the first to make the call. Based on sampling, Vice President Al Gore was declared the winner by ABC, CBS, CNN, Fox News, and NBC; but they were all forced to retract their reports when additional data challenged their earlier calls. Later, those same networks declared George Bush the winner in Florida (again, based on sampling). Then they retracted those reports, too. The eventual election result depended on a split decision made by the U.S. Supreme Court that overturned a split decision made by the Florida Supreme Court (Konner, Risser, & Wattenberg, 2001). Sampling errors were at the heart of the confusion.

Anytime we use a sample to draw conclusions about a population, we're relying on probability. We can't know for sure that our sample reflects the population. We can only say it is probable that it does. For example, exit polling samples a small number of voters to predict the winner of a particular political race. In 2000, the news organizations were eager to reach that larger conclusion because they all wanted to be first to declare either Al Gore or George Bush the winner in Florida, and therefore the next president of the United States. But just because something is probable doesn't mean it is certain. Unfortunately, three sampling errors led to the networks projecting the election for Gore and then for Bush when, in fact, the voting in Florida was too close to call for either candidate.

1. The sample size was too small (both the number of precincts sampled and the size of the samples within the precincts), which reduces our confidence that the sample represents the larger population.

2. The sample was biased; certain members of the population were less likely to be included in the sample. This occurred when pollsters decided ahead of time which Florida precincts were representative. The sample was also biased because some voters from the Republican-leaning Florida Panhandle, who are in a different time zone, weren't included in the early projections.

3. The samples were not independent. All five networks used the same source of information, the Voter News Service, even though the networks' on-air pronouncements were presented as independent research. Thus, it appeared as if five independent samples agreed on the outcome of the Florida vote, but it was really one error communicated across all five networks.

In this chapter, we learn more about the building blocks of inferential statistics. First, we learn ways to sample from populations, then how to assign members of our samples to groups. (In particular, we learn about random assignment, a procedure that was first introduced in Chapter 1 when we discussed experimental research.) An understanding of sampling is then improved with a basic understanding of probability. Finally, we combine these building blocks when we discuss inferential statistics and the process of developing a hypothesis about a population, which we will test using a sample.

Because conclusions drawn from inferential statistics are based on probability, we can never know for sure whether they are accurate. In the last section of the chapter, we learn about the two types of errors we can make when conducting inferential statistics. An understanding of probability, sampling, and inferential statistics will help you to avoid the mistakes made in the reporting of the 2000 presidential election, mistakes that are less likely to be repeated given the newfound caution of the once-burned networks.

Samples and Their Populations

Almost everything worth studying requires a sample, whether it is voting trends, a medical test for mononucleosis, or a test of memory following exposure to a chemical spill. As we know from the 2000 election, however, there are risks when we choose to sample from a population rather than study everyone in the population.

The goal of most researchers is to collect data from a sample that represents the population. There are two main types of samples: a random sample and a convenience sample. *A **random sample** is one in which every member of the population has an equal chance of being selected into the study. A **convenience sample** is one that uses participants who are readily available.* Random sampling remains the ideal and is far more likely to lead to a representative sample, as the Voter News Service certainly understood, but it is usually expensive and extremely difficult to achieve. By contrast, convenience sampling is usually both less expensive and much easier than random sampling; because of this, it is used most often, even though it might not lead to a representative sample.

Random Sampling

The safest way to collect a representative sample is by collecting a random sample. Let's consider how to generate a random sample by using a specific example.

Imagine that a town has recently experienced a traumatic mass murder and that there are exactly 80 police officers in the local department. You have been hired to determine whether peer counseling or professional counseling is the most effective way to treat officers suffering from post-traumatic stress disorder, whether or not they were directly involved in the incident. However, budget constraints dictate that the sample you can recruit must be very small, just 10 people. How do you maximize the probability that those 10 individuals will accurately represent the 80 officers?

Five officers are to be selected from the 80 and assigned to peer counseling, and another five are to be selected and assigned to counseling with a therapist. To accomplish this, each police officer is arbitrarily assigned a two-digit number from 01 to 80. Use the random numbers table on the next page to choose a sample of 10 police officers by arbitrarily selecting a point on the table and deciding to go across, back, up, or down to read through the numbers. Decide on your starting point and direction of counting and stick to it! For example, we could begin with the second number of the second row and count across. The first 10 numbers read: 97654 64501. (The spaces between sets of five numbers exist solely to make it easier to read the table.) The first pair of digits is 97, but we would ignore this number because we only have 80 people in our population. The next pair is 65. The 65th police officer in our list would be chosen for our sample. The next two pairs, 46 and 45, would also be in the sample, followed by 01. If we come across a number a second time—45, for example—we ignore it, just as we would ignore 00 and anything above 80.

> **MASTERING THE CONCEPT**
>
> There are two main types of samples in social science research. With the ideal type of sample, a random sample, every member of the population has an equal chance of being selected to participate in a study. With the less ideal but more common type of sample, a convenience sample, researchers use participants who are readily available.

■ A **random sample** is one in which every member of the population has an equal chance of being selected into the study.

■ A **convenience sample** is one that uses participants who are readily available.

Excerpt from a Random Numbers Table						
This is a small section from a random numbers table used to select participants from a population to be in a sample as well as to randomly assign participants to experimental conditions.						
04493	52494	75246	33824	45862	51025	61962
00549	97654	64501	88159	96119	63896	54692
35963	15307	26898	09354	33351	35462	77974
59808	08391	45427	26842	83609	49700	46058

Were you surprised that random sampling selected both the number 46 and the number 45? *Truly random numbers often have strings of numbers that do not seem to be random.* For example, notice the string of three 3's in the third row of the table.

In a large study, researchers rely on random numbers generated by a computer. You can find good random number generators online by Googling "random number generator." When we used an online random numbers generator to create a list of 10 unique numbers from the range 1–80, we were provided with the following output: 10, 23, 27, 34, 36, 67, 70, 74, 77, and 78. Of course, the list would be different each time we generate a random numbers list using these criteria. You might be surprised that 4 of the 10 numbers were in the 70s. Don't be. Random numbers are truly random, and sometimes randomness doesn't look random.

Random samples are almost never used in the social sciences because we almost never have access to the whole population from which to select our sample. If we were interested in studying the eating behavior of voles, we would never be able to list the whole population of voles so that we could select a random sample of voles. If we were interested in studying the effect of video games on the attention span of teenagers in the United States, we would not be able to identify all U.S. teenagers from which to choose a random sample. If we were interested in studying dyslexia in Canada, we could not test every Canadian for dyslexia. In the behavioral sciences, we are often unable to identify the entire population of interest.

The Whole Population of Voles? If we were interested in studying eating behavior in voles, we would not be able to access the entire worldwide population of voles so that we could select a sample randomly. We would probably use a convenience sample from an animal supply company.

Convenience Sampling

When you fill out an online poll asking you to vote for your favorite reality show contestant or college basketball team, you're part of a convenience sample. You're not being randomly selected from among all people who watch the reality show or among all college basketball fans. The polling organization is acquiring a sample in the most convenient way possible, by inviting those who visit its Web site to participate.

Because it is faster, easier, and cheaper, it is far more common to use a convenience sample than a random sample. We might use voles that we bought from an animal supply company, teenagers from the local high school, and Canadians with dyslexia identified through a university counseling center. A convenience sample limits our generalizability if it results in a sample that is not representative of the population. *Generalizability refers to researchers' ability to apply findings from one sample or in one context to other samples or contexts.* This principle is also called *external validity*. If we don't have sufficient generalizability, we never can be certain that results from our sample apply to the larger population of interest. Fortunately, one activity reduces the risks of a convenience sample more than any other: replication. ***Replication*** *refers to the duplication of scientific results, ideally in a different context or with a sample that has different characteristics.* In other words, do the study again. A study that is well designed and is replicated with different samples can provide reliable and valid information about a concept, despite reliance on convenience samples.

We must be even more cautious when we use a ***volunteer sample***, *a special kind of convenience sample in which participants actively choose to participate in a study.* Participants volunteer, or self-select (this is also called a *self-selected sample*), when they respond to recruitment flyers or choose to complete an online survey, such as in our examples of polls that recruit people to vote for a favorite reality show contestant or college basketball team. We should be very suspicious of volunteer samples, which may be very different from a randomly selected sample. For example, if money is offered for participation in a marketing study, the study may attract individuals who are unemployed or anxious about money. An online survey can only attract those with Internet access and those who visit the particular Web site that hosts the survey. Location, income, personality, and particular needs may all influence (bias) the outcomes of a study using a volunteer sample.

The Problem with a Biased Sample

An understanding of the importance of a representative sample can help you reduce your own biases when you encounter information in your own life. Consider the case of Lush. *Lush Times* is a colorful catalog of Lush's handmade cosmetics. The newspaper-style catalog clearly aims to entertain, but its ultimate goal is to sell cosmetics. Skin's Shangri La is one of the many face moisturizers that Lush offers, and a long description of its amazing moisturizing and skin-rejuvenating powers ends with two testimonials, one of which reads in part: "I'm nearly 60, but no one believes it, which proves Skin's Shangri La works!"

Knowing what you've now learned about the role of samples, let's examine the possible flaws of this "evidence"—a brief testimonial—for the supposed effectiveness of Skin's Shangri La.

Let's first consider the population and sample here. The population would be all women approaching age 60. The Lush marketers would like potential customers to think that they, too, could look years younger if they used this product. The sample would be the individual who wrote to Lush to share her experience. There are two major problems with this sample. First, and most important, one person can never constitute a representative sample. It would not even make sense to calculate statistics on data from one individual. Second, this is a special kind of convenience sample, a volunteer sample. The customer who had this experience chose to write to Lush. Was she likely to write to Lush if she did not feel very strongly about this product? Moreover, was Lush likely to publish her statement if it was not positive? So the sample is too small and is biased, just like the first and second errors we noted in the 2000 presidential election.

A second consideration—beyond the fact that this is a sample of one—is the type of person her age who would shop at Lush. Although Lush touts its products as meant for people of all ages, its marketing clearly seems targeted at young people. With colorful, cartoonlike drawings and catchy product names such as

- **Generalizability** refers to researchers' ability to apply findings from one sample or in one context to other samples or contexts; also called *external validity.*

- **Replication** refers to the duplication of scientific results, ideally in a different context or with a sample that has different characteristics.

- A **volunteer sample** is a special kind of convenience sample in which participants actively choose to participate in a study; also called a *self-selected sample.*

Testimonials as Evidence? Does one middle-aged woman's positive experience with Skin's Shangri La—"I'm nearly 60, but no one believes it"—provide evidence that this moisturizer causes younger-looking skin? Testimonials use a volunteer sample of one person, usually a biased individual; moreover, you can bet that the testimonial that a company uses in its advertising is the most flattering one.

Candy Fluff and Sonic Death Monkey, it seems likely that teens and 20-somethings are the intended consumers. What might you hypothesize about the type of 60-year-old woman who would shop at Lush in the first place? Might she have a more youthful mind-set than others her age?

A better way to approach the question of whether Skin's Shangri La works would be to conduct a true experiment, such as was described in Chapter 1. We could randomly assign a certain number of people to use this product and an equal number of people to use another product (or no product), and then see which group has better skin a certain number of weeks later. Which is more persuasive to you? A dubious testimonial or a well-designed study? If our honest answer is a dubious testimonial, then statistical reasoning once again leads us to ask a better question, albeit one that is more difficult to answer: What is it about us that is more responsive to an anecdote than a solid study? Statistical thinking can challenge us in unexpected ways, inspire introspection, and improve our daily decision making.

Random Assignment

We first introduced the concept of random assignment in Chapter 1 as one of the hallmarks of an experiment. Being randomly assigned into a particular experimental condition is very different from being randomly selected into a study in the first place. The distinction between random selection and random assignment is important: random selection refers to a method of creating a sample from a population; random assignment refers to a method we can use once we have a sample, whether or not the sample is randomly selected. Random *selection* is almost never used, but random *assignment* is frequently used. And random assignment can go a long way toward addressing the limitations of a convenience sample.

To randomly assign participants to groups, we use procedures very similar to those used for random selection. If a study has two levels of the independent variable, as in the study of police officers, then we would need to assign participants to one of two groups. We could decide, arbitrarily, to number the groups 0 and 1 for the "peer-counseling" group and the "therapist-counseling" group, respectively. We would select a place in the random numbers table to begin and then choose only the digits that were a 0 or 1, ignoring the others. If we began at the first number of the last row and read the numbers across, ignoring any number but 0 or 1, we would find 0010000. Hence, the first two participants would be in group 0, the third would be in group 1, and the next four would be in group 0. Again, notice the seemingly nonrandom pattern and remember that it *is* random.

▶ **MASTERING THE CONCEPT**

When possible, researchers use two main tools to make up for a lack of random selection. With random assignment, every participant has an equal chance of being assigned to any level of the independent variable. With replication, a study is repeated, ideally with diffferent participants or in a different context, to see whether the results are consistent.

If we used an online random numbers generator, we would instruct the computer to give us one set of 10 numbers that ranged from 0 to 1. We would instruct the program that the numbers should *not* remain unique because we want multiple 0's and multiple 1's. In addition, we would request that the numbers not be sorted because we want to assign participants in the order in which the numbers are generated. When we used an online random numbers generator, the 10 numbers were: 1110100001. In an experiment, we usually want equal numbers in our groups. If the numbers were not exactly half 1's and half 0's, as they are in this case, we could decide in advance to use only the first five 1's or the first five 0's.

It should be noted that even with random assignment we run the risk of an accidentally biased sample giving us bad (unrepresentative) information. Again, replication can rescue us from inaccurate conclusions. One study seldom convinces any scientist, but three or four studies that produce the same finding become pretty persuasive.

Twenty studies producing the same findings give us an extremely high level of confidence. Random assignment coupled with *replication* of research goes a long way toward making up for a lack of random selection. If we show results from a convenience sample, and then another independent convenience sample, generalization becomes more and more appropriate.

CHECK YOUR LEARNING

Reviewing the Concepts

> Data from a sample are used to draw conclusions about the larger population.

> In random sampling, every member of the population has an equal chance of being selected for the sample.

> Convenience samples are far more common than random samples in the behavioral sciences.

> In random assignment, every participant has an equal chance of being assigned to one of the experimental conditions.

> If a study that uses random assignment is replicated in several contexts, we can start to generalize the findings.

> Random numbers may not always appear to be all that random; there may seem to be patterns.

Clarifying the Concepts

5-1   What are the risks of sampling?

Calculating the Statistics

5-2   Use the random numbers table excerpt on page 96 to select six people out of a sample of 80. Start by assigning each individual a number, from 01 to 80. Then select six of these people by starting in the fourth row and going across. List the numbers of the six people who were selected.

5-3   Use the random numbers table excerpt to randomly assign these six people to one of two experimental conditions, numbered 0 and 1. This time, start at the top of the first column (with a 0 on top) and go down. When you get to the bottom of that column, start at the top of the second column (with a 4 on top). Using the numbers (0 and 1), list the order in which these people would be assigned to conditions.

Applying the Concepts

5-4   For each of the following scenarios, state whether random selection could have been used from a practical standpoint; explain your answer, including a description of the population to which the researcher likely wants to generalize. Then state whether random assignment could have been used; explain your answer.

a.   A health psychologist examined whether postoperative recovery time was less among patients who received counseling prior to surgery than among those who did not.

b.   The head of a school board asked a school psychologist to examine whether children in this school system would perform better in their history classes if they used an interactive textbook on CD-ROM as opposed to a traditional printed textbook.

c.   A clinical psychologist studied whether people with diagnosed personality disorders were more likely to miss therapy appointments than were people without diagnosed personality disorders.

Solutions to these Check Your Learning questions can be found in Appendix D.

Probability

When the results of voting exit polls are reported, we can never know for sure whether the estimated outcome, which is based on a sample, reflects the actual outcome (until, of course, the results are reported). This is because the actual outcome is based on the entire population. The news source usually tells us how likely—or

▶ **MASTERING THE CONCEPT**

In everyday life, we use the word probability very loosely—saying how likely a given outcome is in our subjective judgment. Statisticians are referring to something very particular when they refer to probability. For statisticians, probability is the actual likelihood of a given outcome in the long run.

how *probable*—it is that their estimate is accurate. In this section, we now turn our attention to this key statistical concept: probability. Probability is central to inferential statistics because we are basing a conclusion about a population on data collected from a sample. When calculating an inferential statistic, we are determining only that it is probable a given conclusion is true, not that it is certain.

Expected Relative-Frequency Probability

When we discuss probability in everyday conversation, we tend to think of what statisticians would call **personal probability**: *the likelihood of an event occurring based on an individual's opinion or judgment; also called subjective probability.* We might say something like "There's a 75% chance I'll finish my paper and go out tonight." We don't mean that the chance we'll go out is precisely 75%. Rather, this is our rating of our confidence that this event will occur. It's really just our best guess, a personal estimate.

Mathematicians and statisticians, however, use the word *probability* a bit differently than we do in everyday conversation. Statisticians are concerned with a different type of probability, one that is more objective. In a general sense, **probability** *is the likelihood that a certain outcome will occur out of all possible outcomes.* For example, we might talk about the likelihood of getting heads (a certain outcome) if we flip a coin 10 times (all possible outcomes). We use probability because we usually only have access to a sample (10 flips of a coin) when we want to know about an entire population (all possible flips of a coin).

In statistics, we are interested in an even more specific definition of probability—**expected relative-frequency probability**, *the likelihood of an event occurring based on the actual outcome of many, many trials.* When flipping a coin, the expected relative-frequency probability of heads, in the long run, is 0.50. Probability refers to the likelihood that something occurs, and frequency refers to how often a given outcome (e.g., heads or tails) occurs out of a certain number of trials (e.g., coin flips). *Relative* indicates that this number is relative to the overall number of trials, and *expected* indicates that it's what we would anticipate, which might be different from what actually occurs.

In reference to probability, the term **trial** *refers to each occasion that a given procedure is carried out.* For example, each time we flip a coin, it is a trial. **Outcome** *refers to the result of a trial.* For coin-flip trials, the outcome is either heads or tails. **Success** *refers to the outcome for which we're trying to determine the probability.* If we are testing for the probability of heads, then success is heads.

Determining Probabilities To determine the probability of heads, we would have to conduct many trials (coin flips), record the outcomes (either heads or tails), and determine the proportion of successes (in this case, heads).

Eyebyte/Alamy

EXAMPLE 5.1

The expected relative-frequency probability of getting heads on a coin flip is 0.50. If we flip that coin many, many times, we expect that half of those flips would be heads.

We can think of probability in terms of a formula. We calculate probability by dividing the total number of successes by the total number of trials. So, the formula would look like this:

$$probability = \frac{successes}{trials}$$

If we flip a coin 2000 times and get 1000 heads, then

$$\text{probability} = \frac{1000}{2000} = 0.50$$

To recap, to calculate probability:

STEP 1. Determine the total number of trials.

STEP 2. Determine the number of these trials that are considered successful outcomes.

STEP 3. Divide the number of successful outcomes by the number of trials.

People often confuse the terms *probability, proportion,* and *percentage.* Probability, the concept of most interest to us right now, is the proportion that we expect to see in the long run. The proportion is the number of successes divided by the number of trials. In the short run, in just a few trials, the proportion might not reflect the underlying probability. A coin flipped six times might have more or fewer than three heads, leading to a proportion of heads that does not parallel the underlying probability of heads. Both proportions and probabilities are written as decimals. A coin that comes up heads half the time in the long run has a 0.50 probability of heads.

Percentage is simply probability or proportion multiplied by 100. A flipped coin has a 0.50 probability of coming up heads and a 50% chance of coming up heads. The lowest possible probability or proportion is 0.0, and the lowest possible percentage is 0%. The highest possible probability or proportion is 1.0, and the highest possible percentage is 100%. Most people are already familiar with percentages, so simply keep in mind that probabilities are what we would expect in the long run, whereas proportions are what we observe.

One of the central characteristics of expected relative-frequency probability is that it only works in the long run. This is an important aspect of probability and is referred to as the *law of large numbers.* Think of the earlier discussion of random assignment in which we used a random numbers generator to create a series of 0's and 1's to assign participants to levels of the independent variable. In the short run, over just a few trials, we got strings of 0's and 1's and often did not end up with half 0's and half 1's, even though that is the underlying probability. With many trials, however, we're much more likely to get close to 0.50, or 50%, of each, although many strings of 0's or 1's would be generated along the way. In the long run, the results are quite predictable. Without many, many trials, we cannot determine expected relative-frequency probability.

Independence and Probability

A key factor in statistical probability is the fact that the individual trials must be independent. If they are not, then bias might be introduced in the same way that a sample can be biased by choosing too many people who are similar to one another. More specifically, if individual trials are not independent, then expected relative-frequency will not work out in the long run. This is yet another use of the word *independent,* one of the favorite words of statisticians. Here we use *independent* to mean that the outcome of each trial must not depend in any way on the outcome of

■ **Personal probability** refers to the likelihood of an event occurring based on an individual's opinion or judgment; also called *subjective probability.*

■ **Probability** is the likelihood that a certain outcome will occur out of all possible outcomes.

■ **Expected relative-frequency probability** is the likelihood of an event occurring based on the actual outcome of many, many trials.

■ In reference to probability, a **trial** refers to each occasion that a given procedure is carried out.

■ In reference to probability, **outcome** refers to the result of a trial.

■ In reference to probability, **success** refers to the outcome for which we're trying to determine the probability.

Gambling and Misperceptions of Probability Many people falsely believe that a slot machine that has not paid off in a long time is "due." A person may continue to feed coins into it in the expectation of an imminent payout. Of course, the slot machine itself, unless rigged, has no memory of its previous outcomes. Each trial is independent of the others.

previous trials. If we're flipping a coin, then each coin flip is independent of every other coin flip. Similarly, in research, each participant must be independent of every other participant, or our sample might be biased. If we're generating a random numbers list to select participants, each number must be generated without thought to the previous numbers. In fact, this is exactly why humans can't think randomly. We automatically glance at the previous numbers we have generated in order to best make the next one "random." If our next number depends on the previous one, it is not independent and it is not random. This is one reason we use a table or computer to generate a random numbers list. A computer does not have a memory for the previous numbers. Chance has no memory, and randomness is, therefore, the only way to assure that there is no bias.

CHECK YOUR LEARNING

Reviewing the Concepts

> Personal probability refers to the likelihood of an event occurring based on an individual's opinion or judgment.

> Expected relative-frequency probability is the the likelihood of an event occurring based on the actual outcome of many, many trials.

> The probability of an event occurring is the expected number of successes (the number of times the event occured) out of the total number of trials (or attempts) over the long run.

> Short-run proportions might have many different outcomes, whereas long-run proportions are more indicative of the underlying probabilities.

Clarifying the Concepts

5-5   Distinguish the personal probability assessments we perform on a daily basis from the objective probability statisticians use.

Calculating the Statistics

5-6   Calculate the probability for each of the following instances.
   a.   100 trials, 5 successes
   b.   50 trials, 8 successes
   c.   1044 trials, 130 successes

Applying the Concepts

5-7   Consider a scenario in which a student wonders whether men or women are more likely to use the ATM machine in the student center. He decides to observe those who use the ATM machine. (Assume that the university enrolls roughly equal numbers of women and men and that neither women nor men are more likely to use ATM machines.)

   a.   Define success as a woman using the ATM on a given trial. What proportion of successes *might* this student expect to observe in the short run?

Solutions to these Check Your Learning questions can be found in Appendix D.

   b.   What might this student expect to observe in the long run?

Inferential Statistics

In Chapter 1, we introduced the two main branches of statistics, descriptive statistics and inferential statistics. The link that connects the two branches is probability. Descriptive statistics allow us to summarize characteristics of the sample, but we must use probability to apply what we've learned from the sample to the larger population. As with exit polls, when we conduct social science research and use a sample to draw conclusions about a population, we're never certain that we know the truth about the population. We can only say that a certain conclusion is likely—or probable.

Developing Hypotheses

Probability theory can help us find answers for many of our research hypotheses. *New York Times* columnist John Tierney writes a blog called "TierneyLab" that reports on and conducts entertaining and relevant social science research. In one piece, titled "The Perils of Healthy Food," Tierney and his collaborators asked people to estimate the number of calories in a meal pictured in a photograph (Tierney, 2008a, 2008b). One group was shown a photo of an Applebee's Oriental Chicken Salad and a Pepsi. Another group was shown a photo of the same salad and Pepsi, but it also included a third item, Fortt's crackers with a label that clearly stated "Trans Fat Free." Tierney and his collaborators wondered if the addition of the "healthy" food item would affect people's calorie estimates. They tested a sample and used probability to apply their findings from the sample to the population.

Let's put this study in the language of research. The first step in hypothesis testing is to plan the collection of data from a sample, which includes identifying the population, recruiting a sample, and choosing the independent and dependent variables. The population would include all people living in the United States, a population chosen because of its increasing levels of obesity despite the increasing availability of healthy foods in the United States. The sample was people living in the Park Slope neighborhood of Brooklyn, an area that Tierney terms "nutritionally correct" for its abundance of organic food. This is not a representative sample of the entire United States, but it is an interesting choice. After all, if a healthy neighborhood is fooled by healthy food, this would suggest that less healthy neighborhoods would be fooled as well, perhaps even to a greater degree. The independent variable in this case is the presence or absence of the healthy crackers in the photo of the meal. The dependent variable is the number of calories estimated. The researchers used the number of calories estimated by this sample to make probability-based judgments about the numbers of calories that would be estimated by the population.

In this case, we might refer to the group that viewed the photo without the healthy crackers as the control group. *A control group is a level of the independent variable that does not receive the treatment of interest in a study.* It is designed to match the **experimental group**—*a level of the independent variable that receives the treatment or intervention of interest*—in all ways but the experimental manipulation itself. In this example, the experimental group would be those viewing the photo that included the healthy crackers.

A next step, one that ideally occurs before actually collecting data from our sample, and one that we'll see throughout this book, is the development of the hypotheses

- A **control group** is a level of the independent variable that does not receive the treatment of interest in a study. It is designed to match an experimental group in all ways but the experimental manipulation itself.

- An **experimental group** is a level of the independent variable that receives the treatment or intervention of interest in an experiment.

Using a Sample to Make Probability-Based Judgments About a Population Does the presence of a low-calorie item, such as a diet soda, make a higher-calorie item, such as french fries, seem healthier? Researchers use samples to test hypotheses such as this about a population.

to be tested in hypothesis testing. When we calculate inferential statistics, we're always comparing two hypotheses. One is *the **null hypothesis**—a statement that postulates that there is no difference between populations or that the difference is in a direction opposite from that anticipated by the researcher.* In most circumstances, we can think of the null hypothesis as the boring hypothesis because it proposes that nothing will happen. In many hypothesis tests, the difference being tested is a difference between means. In the healthy food study, the null hypothesis would be that the mean calorie estimate is the same for both populations, all people in the United States who view the photo without the healthy crackers and all people in the United States who view the photo with the healthy crackers. This hypothesis is boring because it proposes that nothing is going on, that there is no mean difference between the groups, and that the photo a participant sees makes absolutely no difference in calorie estimates.

By contrast, the research hypothesis, also called the *alternative hypothesis,* is usually the exciting and interesting one. *The **research hypothesis** is a statement that postulates that there is a difference between populations or sometimes, more specifically, that there is a difference in a certain direction, positive or negative.* This is usually the exciting hypothesis because it proposes a distinctive difference that is worthy of further investigation. Again, many hypothesis tests are exploring a difference between means. In the healthy food study, the research hypothesis would be that, on average, the calorie estimate is different for those viewing the photo with the healthy crackers than for those viewing the photo without the healthy crackers. It also could specify a direction—that the mean calorie estimate is higher (or lower) for those viewing the photo with the healthy crackers than for those viewing the photo with just the salad and Pepsi. Notice that, for all hypotheses, we are very careful to state the comparison group. We do not say merely that the group viewing the photo with the healthy crackers has a higher (or lower) average calorie estimate. We say that it has a higher (or lower) average calorie estimate *than* the group that views the photo without the healthy crackers.

We formulate our null hypothesis and research hypothesis to set them up against one another. We use statistics to determine the probability that there is a big enough difference between the means of our samples that we can conclude there's likely a difference between the means of the underlying populations. So, probability plays into the decision we make about our hypotheses.

Making a Decision

When we draw a conclusion at the end of a study, the data lead us to conclude one of two things:

1. We decide to *reject* the null hypothesis.
2. We decide to *fail to reject* the null hypothesis.

We always begin our reasoning about the outcome of an experiment by reminding ourselves that we are testing the (boring) null hypothesis. In terms of the healthy food study, the null hypothesis is that there is no mean difference between groups. More specifically, the null hypothesis is that the mean calorie estimate for the people who viewed the photo with just the salad and Pepsi is the same as the mean calorie estimate for the people who viewed the photo with the salad, Pepsi, and healthy crackers. In hypothesis testing, we determine the probability that we would see a difference between the means of our samples given that there is no actual difference between the underlying population means.

▪ The **null hypothesis** is a statement that postulates that there is no difference between populations or that the difference is in a direction opposite from that anticipated by the researcher.

▪ The **research hypothesis** (or *alternate hypothesis*) is a statement that postulates that there is a difference between populations or sometimes, more specifically, that there is a difference in a certain direction, positive or negative.

EXAMPLE 5.2

After we analyze the data, we are able to do one of two things:

1. *Reject the null hypothesis.* "I reject the idea that there is no mean difference between populations." Or more specifically, "I reject the idea that the mean calorie estimate is the same in the population from which we drew the control group that viewed the photo with the salad and Pepsi as it is in the population from which we drew the experimental group that viewed the photo with the salad, Pepsi, and healthy crackers." When we reject the null hypothesis that there is *no difference,* we can even assert what we believe the difference to be based on our actual findings. We can say that it seems that people who view a photo of a salad, Pepsi, and healthy crackers estimate a lower (or higher, depending on what we found in our study) number of calories, on average, than those who view a photo with only the salad and Pepsi.

2. *Fail to reject the null hypothesis.* "I do not reject the idea that there is no mean difference between populations." Or more specifically, "I do not reject the idea that the mean calorie estimate is the same in the population from which we drew the control group that viewed the photo with the salad and Pepsi as it is in the population from which we drew the experimental group that viewed the photo with the salad, Pepsi, and healthy crackers."

Let's take the first possible conclusion, to reject the null hypothesis. If the group that viewed the photo that included the healthy crackers has a mean calorie estimate that is a good deal higher (or lower) than the control group's mean calorie estimate, then we might be tempted to say that we *accept* our research hypothesis that there is such a mean difference in the populations—that the addition of the healthy crackers makes a difference. Probability plays a central role in determining that the mean difference is big enough that we're willing to say it's real. But rather than *accepting* the *research* hypothesis in this case, we *reject* the *null* hypothesis, the one that suggests there is nothing going on. We repeat: when the data suggest that there *is* a mean difference, we *reject* the idea that there is no mean difference.

The second possible conclusion is failing to reject the null hypothesis. There's a very good reason for thinking about this in terms of failing to reject the null hypothesis rather than accepting the null hypothesis. Let's say there's a small mean difference, and we conclude that we cannot reject the null hypothesis (remember, rejecting the null hypothesis is what you want to do!). We determine that it's just not likely enough—or probable enough—that the difference between means is real. It could be that a real difference between means didn't show up in this particular sample just by chance. There are many ways in which a real mean difference in the population might not get picked up by a sample. Again, we repeat: when the data do not suggest a difference, we *fail* to reject the null hypothesis, which is that there is no mean difference. The way we decide whether to reject the null hypothesis is based directly on probability. We calculate the probability that the data would produce a difference between means this large and in a sample of this size *if* there were nothing going on.

We will be giving you many more opportunities to get comfortable with the logic of formal hypothesis testing before we start applying numbers to it, but here are three easy rules and a table (Table 5-1) that will help keep you on track.

TABLE 5-1.

The null hypothesis posits no difference, on average, whereas the research hypothesis posits a difference of some kind. There are only two decisions we can make. We can fail to reject the null hypothesis if the research hypothesis is *not* supported, or we can reject the null hypothesis if the research hypothesis *is* supported.

	Hypothesis	Decision
Null Hypothesis	No mean change or difference	Fail to reject the null hypothesis (if research hypothesis is not supported)
Research Hypothesis	Mean change or difference	Reject the null hypothesis (if research hypothesis is supported)

1. Remember: the null hypothesis is that there is no difference between groups, and usually our hypotheses explore the possibility of a *mean* difference.

2. We either *reject* or *fail to reject* the null hypothesis. There are no other options.

3. We never use the word *accept* in reference to formal hypothesis testing.

Hypothesis testing is exciting when you care about the results. You may be wondering what happened in Tierney's study. Well, people who saw the photo with just the salad and Pepsi estimated, on average, that the 934-calorie meal was 1011 calories. When the 100-calorie crackers were added, the meal actually increased from 934 calories to 1034 calories; however, those who viewed this photo estimated, on average, that the meal was only 835 calories! So, even though the meal with the crackers was 100 calories *more,* the participants who viewed this photo estimated that it was 176 calories *fewer!* Tierney referred to this effect as "a health halo that magically subtracted calories from the rest of the meal." Interestingly, he did replicate this study with mostly foreign tourists in New York's Times Square, and he did not find this effect. He concluded that health-conscious people were more susceptible to bias.

CHECK YOUR LEARNING

Reviewing the Concepts

> In experiments, we often compare the average of the responses of those who receive our treatment or manipulation (the experimental group) with the average of the responses of similar people who do not receive the manipulation (the control group).

> Researchers develop two hypotheses: a null hypothesis, which theorizes no mean difference between levels of an independent variable in the population, and a research hypothesis, which theorizes a mean difference of some kind in the population.

> Researchers can draw two conclusions: they can reject the null hypothesis and conclude that they have supported the research hypothesis, or they can fail to reject the null hypothesis and conclude that they have not supported the research hypothesis.

Clarifying the Concepts

5-8   At the end of a study, what does it mean to reject the null hypothesis?

Calculating the Statistics

5-9   State the difference that might be expected based on the null hypothesis when studying the average test grades of students who attend review sessions versus those who do not.

Applying the Concepts

5-10 A university lowers the heat during the winter to save money, and professors wonder whether students will perform more poorly, on average, under cold conditions than under warm conditions. Several professors join forces to conduct a study in the hope of gathering data to encourage stingy administrators to restore full heat.

    a.   Cite the likely null hypothesis for this study.

    b.   Cite the likely research hypothesis.

    c.   If the cold temperature appears to decrease academic performance, on average, what will the researchers conclude in terms of formal hypothesis-testing language?

    d.   If the researchers do not gather sufficient evidence to conclude that the cold temperature leads to decreased academic performance, on average, what will they conclude in terms of formal hypothesis-testing language?

Solutions to these Check Your Learning questions can be found in Appendix D.

Type I and Type II Errors

Exit polling during the 2000 U.S. presidential election taught us that sampling errors can lead us to make a wrong decision. Even when sampling has been properly conducted, there are still two ways to make a wrong decision. We can reject the null hypothesis when we should not have rejected it, or we can fail to reject the null hypothesis when we should have rejected it. Similarly, if we examine jury decisions, it is important to be aware that there are two ways that a jury can come to a wrong decision. The jury doesn't want an innocent person to be found guilty, and the jury doesn't want a guilty person to be found innocent. Of course, we want to minimize the probability of making either kind of error. So, let's consider the two types of error using statistical language.

Type I Errors

If we reject the null hypothesis, but it was a mistake to do so, then we have committed a Type I error. Specifically, *a **Type I error** occurs when we reject the null hypothesis, but the null hypothesis is correct.* A Type I error is like a false-positive in a medical test. For example, if a woman believes she might be pregnant, then she might buy a home pregnancy test. In this case, the null hypothesis would be that she is not pregnant, and the research hypothesis would be that she is pregnant. If the test is positive, the woman rejects the null hypothesis—the one that theorizes that she is not pregnant. Based on the test, the woman believes she is pregnant. Pregnancy tests, however, are not perfect. If the woman receives a positive test and rejects the null hypothesis, it is possible that she is wrong and it is a false-positive. Based on the test, the woman believes she is pregnant even though she is not pregnant. A false-positive is equivalent to a Type I error.

As you might imagine, a Type I error typically leads to action, at least until we discover that it is an error. For example, the woman with a false-positive pregnancy test might announce the news to her family and start buying baby clothes. Or a person mistakenly diagnosed with a severe illness might begin expensive treatments. Many researchers consider the consequences of a Type I error to be particularly detrimental because people often take action based on a mistaken finding.

Type II Errors

If we fail to reject the null hypothesis but it was a mistake to do so, this is a Type II error. Specifically, *a **Type II error** occurs when we fail to reject the null hypothesis, but the null hypothesis is false.* A Type II error is like a false-negative in medical testing. In the pregnancy example above, the woman might get a negative result on the test and fail to reject the null hypothesis, the one that says she's not pregnant. In this case, she would conclude that she's not pregnant when she really is. A false-negative is equivalent to a Type II error.

A Type II error typically results in a failure to take action because a research intervention is not supported or, with respect to medical testing, a given diagnosis is not re-

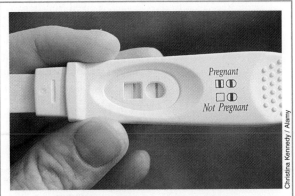

Type I and Type II Errors The results of a home pregnancy test are either positive (indicating pregnancy) or negative (indicating no pregnancy). If the test is positive, but the woman *is not* pregnant, this is equivalent to a Type I error in statistics. If the test is negative, but the woman *is* pregnant, this is equivalent to a Type II error in statistics. With pregnancy tests, as with hypothesis testing, people are more likely to act on a Type I error than on a Type II error. Although the line on the left is lighter than on the right, this particular pregnancy test seems to indicate that she is pregnant. If this is an error, it would be a Type I error.

◀ MASTERING THE CONCEPT

In hypothesis testing, there are two types of errors that we risk making. Type I errors, when we reject the null hypothesis when the null hypothesis is true, are like false positives on a medical test; we think someone *has* a disease, but they really don't. Type II errors, when we fail to reject the null hypothesis when the null hypothesis is not true, are like false negatives on a medical test; we think someone does *not* have a disease, but they really do.

■ A **Type I error** occurs when we reject the null hypothesis, but the null hypothesis is correct.

■ A **Type II error** occurs when we fail to reject the null hypothesis, but the null hypothesis is false.

ceived. Yet there are cases in which a Type II error can have serious consequences. For example, the pregnant woman who does not believe she is pregnant because of a Type II error may drink alcohol in a way that unintentionally harms her fetus. Similarly, a truly effective Alzheimer's drug might be kept from the market. The many thousands of people (and their families) who suffer from this terrible disease would continue to suffer. The answer is right under our noses, but we don't know it because of a Type II error.

CHECK YOUR LEARNING

Reviewing the Concepts
> When we draw a conclusion from inferential statistics, there is always a chance we are wrong.
> When we reject the null hypothesis, but the null hypothesis is true, we have committed a Type I error.
> When we fail to reject the null hypothesis, but the null hypothesis is not true, we have committed a Type II error.

Clarifying the Concepts
5-11 Explain how Type I and Type II errors both relate to the null hypothesis.

Calculating the Statistics
5-12 If out of every 280 innocent people on trial, 7 people are convicted of a crime, what is the rate of Type I errors?

5-13 If the court system fails to convict 11 out of every 35 guilty people, what is the rate of Type II errors?

Applying the Concepts
5-14 Researchers conduct a study on perception by having participants throw a ball at a target while wearing virtual-reality glasses and while wearing glasses that allow normal viewing. The null hypothesis is that there is no difference in performance when wearing the virtual-reality glasses or when wearing the glasses that allow normal viewing.

a. The researchers reject the null hypothesis, concluding that the virtual-reality glasses lead to a worse performance than the normal glasses. What error might the researchers have made? Explain.

Solutions to these Check Your Learning questions can be found in Appendix D.

b. The researchers fail to reject the null hypothesis, concluding that it is possible that the virtual-reality glasses have no effect on performance. What error might the researchers have made? Explain.

● ● ● ● ● ● ● REVIEW OF CONCEPTS

Samples and Their Populations

The gold standard of sample selection is *random sampling*, a procedure in which every member of the population has an equal chance of being chosen for study participation. A random numbers table or computer-based random numbers generator is used to ensure randomness. For practical reasons, random selection is uncommon in social science research. Many behavioral scientists use a *convenience sample*, a sample that is readily available to them. One kind of convenience sample is the *volunteer sample*, in which participants themselves actively choose to participate in the study. With random assignment, every participant in a study has an equal chance of being assigned to any of the experimental conditions. *Replication,* the duplication of scientific results, in conjunction with random assignment, can go a long way toward increasing our ability to *generalize* our findings beyond our samples.

Probability

When we think of probability, many of us think of *personal probability,* an individual's own judgment about the likelihood that an event will occur. Statisticians, however, are referring to *expected relative-frequency probability,* or the long-run expected outcome if an experiment or trial were repeated many, many times. A *trial* refers to each occasion that a procedure is carried out, and an *outcome* is the result of a trial. A *success* refers to the outcome for which we're trying to determine the probability. *Probability* is a basic building block of inferential statistics. When we draw a conclusion about a population based on a sample, we can only say that it is probable that our conclusion is accurate, not that it is certain.

Inferential Statistics

Inferential statistics, based on probability, start with a hypothesis. The *null hypothesis* is a statement that postulates that there is no average difference between populations. The *alternative* or *research hypothesis* is a statement that postulates that there is an average difference between populations. After conducting a hypothesis test, we have only two possible conclusions. We can either reject or fail to reject the null hypothesis. When we conduct inferential statistics, we often are comparing an *experimental group,* the group subjected to an intervention, with a *control group,* the group that is the same as the experimental group in every way except the intervention. We use probability to draw conclusions about a population by estimating the probability that we would find a given difference between sample means if there is no underlying difference between population means.

Type I and Type II Errors

Statisticians must always be aware that their conclusions may be wrong. If a researcher rejects the null hypothesis, but the null hypothesis is correct, the researcher is making a *Type I error.* If a researcher fails to reject the null hypothesis, but the null hypothesis is false, the researcher is making a *Type II error.*

SPSS®

There are many ways to look more closely at our independent and dependent variables.

We can request a variety of case summaries by selecting:

Analyze → Reports → Case Summaries

We then can highlight the variable of interest and click the arrow to move it under "Variables."

If we want to break it down by a second variable, we can highlight a second variable and click the bottom arrow to move it under "Grouping Variable(s)."

After making our choices, we click on "OK" to see the output screen.

For example, we could use the hours studied and exam grade data from the SPSS section of Chapter 3. We could select "grade" under "Variables" and "hours" under "Grouping Variable(s)." The output, part of which is shown in the screenshot here, tells us all the grades for students who studied a given number of hours. For example, this summary tells us that the two students who studied for three hours earned grades of 60 and 72 on the exam.

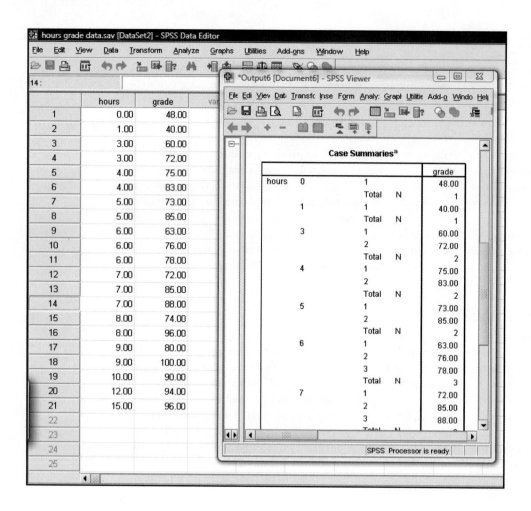

How It Works

5.1 USING RANDOM SELECTION

There are approximately 2000 school psychologists in Australia. A researcher has developed a new diagnostic tool to identify conduct disorder in children and wants to study ways to train school psychologists to administer it. How can she recruit a random sample of 30 school psychologists to participate in her study?

She could use an online random numbers generator to randomly select a sample of 30 school psychologists for this study from among the target population of 2000 Australian school psychologists. Let's try it. To do so, she would tell an online random numbers generator to produce one set of 30 numbers between 0001 and 2000. She would specify that she wants unique numbers, because no one can be in the study more than once. She can ask the program to sort the numbers, if she wishes, to more easily identify the participants who will comprise her sample.

When we generated a set of 30 random numbers, we got the following:

> 25, 48, 84, 113, 159, 165, 220, 312, 319, 330,
> 337, 452, 493, 562, 613, 734, 822, 860, 920, 924,
> 931, 960, 983, 1290, 1305, 1462, 1502, 1515, 1675, 1994

Of course, each time we generate a list of random numbers, it is different. Notice that the typical list of randomly generated numbers does not necessarily appear random. For example, in this list only 7 out of the 30 numbers are over 1000. It's weighted toward the lower numbers. There are also several cases in which numbers are close in value (e.g., 920 and 924). Based on these numbers, the 30 individuals would then be selected from a numbered list of the 2000 school psychologists.

5.2 USING RANDOM SELECTION
Imagine that the researcher described in How It Works 5.1 has developed two training modules. One is implemented in a classroom setting and requires that school psychologists travel to a nearby city for training. The other is a Web-based training module and is far more practical and cost-effective to use. She will administer a test to participants after training to determine how much they learned. Her hope is that the Web-based training will work as well as the classroom training, resulting in savings of both cost and time. How can she randomly assign half of the participants to classroom training and half to Web-based training?

In this case, the independent variable is type of training with two levels: classroom training and Web-based training. The dependent variable is amount of learning as determined by a test. This study is an experiment because participants are randomly assigned to conditions. To determine the condition to which each participant will be assigned, she could tell a random numbers generator to produce one set of 30 numbers between 0 and 1. She would not want the numbers to be unique because she wants more than one of each type. She would not want the numbers to be sorted. The 30 participants would be assigned based on the number associated with their position on the list of participants.

When we used an online random numbers generator, we got the following set of 30 numbers:

1, 1, 0, 0, 0, 0, 1, 1, 1, 0,
0, 1, 0, 0, 0, 0, 0, 0, 1, 1,
0, 1, 1, 1, 0, 0, 1, 1, 0, 0

This set contains 13 1's and 17 0's. If we wanted exactly 15 in each group, we could stop assigning people to the 0 condition when we reached 15 0's.

5.3 CALCULATING PROBABILITY
Let's say that a university provides every student with a laptop computer, but students complained that their computers "always" crashed when they were on the Internet and had at least three other programs open (e.g., word-processing program, music program, statistical software). One student thought this was an exaggeration and decided to calculate the probability that the campus computers would crash under these circumstances. How could he do this?

He could start by randomly selecting 100 different students to participate in his study. On the 100 students' computers, he could open three programs and then go online. He could then record whether each computer crashed under these conditions.

In this case, the trials would be the 100 instances (on 100 different laptops) in which the student opened three programs and then went online. The outcome would be whether or not the computer crashed. A success in this case would be a computer that crashed, and let's say that happened 55 times. (You might not consider a crashed computer a success, but in probability theory, a success refers to the outcome for which we want to determine the probability.) He could then take the number of successes (55) and divide by the number of trials:

55/100 = 0.55

So, the probability of a computer crashing when three programs are open and the student goes online is 0.55. Of course, to determine the true expected relative-frequency probability, he'd have to conduct many, many more trials.

Exercises

Clarifying the Concepts

5.1 Why do we study samples rather than populations?

5.2 What is the difference between a random sample and a convenience sample?

5.3 What is generalizability?

5.4 What is a volunteer sample, and what is the risk associated with it?

5.5 What is the difference between random sampling and random assignment?

5.6 What does it mean to replicate research, and how does this impact our confidence?

5.7 Ideally, an experiment would use random sampling so that the data would accurately reflect the larger population. For practical reasons, this is difficult to do. How does random assignment help make up for a lack of random selection?

5.8 Statisticians use terms like *trial, outcome,* and *success* in a particular way in reference to probability. What do each of these three terms mean in this context?

5.9 We distinguish between probabilities and proportions. How does each capture the likelihood of an outcome?

5.10 How is the term *independent* used by statisticians?

5.11 One step in hypothesis testing is to randomly assign members of the sample into the control group and the experimental group. What is the difference between these two groups?

5.12 What is the difference between a null hypothesis and a research hypothesis?

5.13 What are the two decisions or conclusions we can make about our hypotheses based on the data?

5.14 What is the difference between a Type I error and a Type II error?

Calculating the Statistics

5.15 Forty-three tractor-trailers are parked for the night in a rest stop along a major highway. You assign each truck a number from 1 to 43. Moving from left to right and using the second line in the random numbers table below, select four trucks to weigh as they leave the rest stop in the morning.

> 00190 27157 83208 79446 92987 61357
> 23798 55425 32454 34611 39605 39981
> 85306 57995 68222 39055 43890 36956
> 99719 36036 74274 53901 34643 06157

5.16 Airport security makes random checks of passenger bags every day. If one in every 10 passengers is checked, use the random numbers table in Exercise 5.15 to determine the first six people to be checked. Work from top to bottom, starting in the 4th column, and allow the number 0 to represent the 10th person.

5.17 Randomly assign nine people to three conditions of a study using the random numbers table in Exercise 5.15. Read from right to left starting in the top row. (*Note:* Assign people to conditions without concern for having an equal number of people in each condition.)

5.18 You are running a study with five conditions. Assign the first seven participants who arrive at your lab to conditions, not worrying about equal assignment across conditions. Use the random numbers table in Exercise

5.15, and read from left to right starting in the third row from the top.

5.19 What is the probability of hitting a target if, in the long run, 71 out of every 489 attempts actually hit the target?

5.20 On a game show, eight people have won the grand prize and a total of 266 people have competed. Estimate the probability of winning the grand prize.

5.21 Convert the following proportions to percentages:

   a. 0.0173

   b. 0.8

   c. 0.3719

5.22 Convert the following percentages to proportions:

   a. 62.7%

   b. 0.3%

   c. 4.2%

5.23 Using the random numbers table in Exercise 5.15, estimate the probability of the number 6 appearing in a random sequence of numbers. Base your answer on the numbers that appear in the first two rows.

5.24 Thirty-three skin samples are sent to a lab to test for the presence of irregular cells. Five results come back positive for irregular cells, when in fact nothing was wrong in any of the 33 samples. Estimate the probability of Type I errors.

5.25 Leaf samples are sent to a lab to check for a rare and deadly fungus. Of the 45 samples tested, the tests failed to show the presence of the fungus in six instances when in fact it was actually there in 16 instances. Estimate the probability of Type II errors.

5.26 Using the data from Exercise 5.24, if three results were negative for irregular cells when in fact they were present in all 33 examples, estimate the probability of Type II errors.

5.27 Using the data from Exercise 5.25, if one test result came back positive for the fungus when no fungus was present (out of 29 samples in which no fungus was present), estimate the Type I error rate.

Applying the Concepts

5.28 Was selection or assignment random? In France in the fall of 2005, many communities of immigrants from the Middle East and North Africa experienced a great deal of violence, particularly car burnings, committed by their young people. Social science research can help to diminish or avoid such violence. Consider the following hypothetical research on the French riots: Of the cities that shared this demographic, Marseilles was one of the few that saw relatively little violence. A researcher wants to compare Marseilles with Lyons, a city that saw a great deal of violence, to determine which characteristics may have moderated violence in Marseilles, specifically among high school students. Can she use random selection? Explain. Can she use random assignment? Explain.

5.29 Approximately 21,000 school psychologists are members of the U.S.-based National Association of School Psychologists. Of these, about 5000 have doctoral degrees. A researcher wants to randomly select 100 of the doctoral-level school psychologists for a survey study regarding aspects of their jobs, including the types of tasks in which they engage, settings in which they work, and attitudes about their careers. Use this excerpt from a random numbers table to answer the following questions:

```
04493  52494  75246  33824  45862  51025
00549  97654  64051  88159  96119  63896
35963  15307  26898  09354  33351  35462
59808  08391  45427  26842  83609  49700
```

a. What is the population targeted by this study? How large is it?

b. What is the sample desired by this researcher? How large is it?

c. Describe how the researcher would select his sample. Be sure to explain how the members of the population would be numbered and what sets of digits the researcher should ignore when using the random numbers table.

d. Beginning at the left-hand side of the top line and continuing with each succeeding line, list the first 10 participants that this researcher would select for his study.

5.30 Continuing with the study described in Exercise 5.29, once the researcher had randomly selected his sample of 100 school psychologists, he decided to randomly assign 50 of them to receive, as part of their survey materials, a newspaper article about the improving job market for school psychologists. He assigned the other 50 to receive a newspaper article about the declining job market for school psychologists. Unbeknownst to the participants (until the debriefing at the end of the survey), the articles were fictional. After reading the articles, the participants responded to questions about their attitudes toward their careers. The researcher wondered whether attitudes could be affected by external sources.

a. What is the independent variable in this experiment, and what are its levels?

b. What is the dependent variable in this experiment?

c. Write a null hypothesis and a research hypothesis for this study.

5.31 Refer to Exercises 5.29 and 5.30 when responding to the following questions:

a. Describe how the researcher would randomly assign the participants to the levels of the independent variable. Be sure to explain how the levels of the independent variable would be numbered and what sets of digits the researcher should ignore when using the random numbers table.

b. Beginning at the left-hand side of the bottom line of the random numbers table in Exercise 5.29, and continuing with the left-hand side of the line above it, list the levels of the independent variable to which the first 10 participants would be assigned.

c. Why do these numbers not appear to be random? Discuss the difference between short-run and long-run proportions.

5.32 Imagine that you have been hired by the Psychology Department at your school to administer a survey to psychology majors about their experiences in the department. You have been asked to randomly select 60 majors from the overall pool of 300. You are working on this project in your dorm room using a random numbers table because the server is down and you cannot use an online random numbers generator. Your roommate, who is patiently waiting for you to finish so you can go out, offers to write down a list of 60 random numbers between 001 and 300 for you so you can be done quickly. In about three to four sentences, explain to your roommate why she is not likely to create a list of random numbers.

5.33 For each of the following studies, state (i) whether random selection could have been used. Explain also to what population the researcher wanted to and could generalize, and state (ii) whether random assignment could have been used.

a. A researcher recruited 1000 U.S. physicians through the American Medical Association (AMA) to participate in a study of standards of confidentiality with respect to patient information. He wanted to compare perceptions of the standards among men versus women.

b. A developmental psychologist wondered whether children born preterm (premature) had different social skills at age five than children born full term.

c. A counseling center director wanted to compare the length of therapy in weeks for students who came in for treatment for depression versus students who came in for treatment for anxiety. She wanted to report these data to the university administrators to help develop the next year's budget.

d. An industrial/organizational psychologist wondered whether a new laptop design would affect people's response time when using the computer. He wanted to compare response times when using the new laptop with response times when using two standard versions of laptops, a Mac and a PC.

5.34 A volunteer sample is a kind of convenience sample in which participants select themselves to participate. On August 19, 2005, *USA Today* published an online poll on its Web site asking this question about U.S. college football: "Who is your pick to win the ACC conference this year?" Eight options—seven universities, including top vote-getters Virginia Tech and Miami, as well as "other"—were provided.

a. Describe the typical person who might volunteer to be in this sample. Why might this sample be biased, even with respect to the population of U.S. college football fans?

b. What is external validity? Why might external validity be limited in this sample?

c. What other problem can you identify with this poll?

5.35 *Cosmopolitan* magazine (*Cosmo* as it's known popularly) publishes many of its well-known quizzes on its Web site. One quiz is titled "Are You Obsessed with Appearances?" As if the fact that one reads *Cosmo* isn't enough to answer the question, the quiz poses 10 situations for which participants must choose how they'd act from among three limited options. A question about an invitation to a costume party for which one must dress as a musician offers these three choices: Lauryn Hill in "killer cargo pants," one of the Indigo Girls in a flannel shirt, and Madonna in her "ultra-glam Marilyn Monroe phase." Consider whether you want to use the quiz data to determine how obsessed women are with their appearance.

a. Describe the typical person who might respond to this quiz. How might data from such a sample be biased, even with respect to the overall *Cosmo* readership?

b. What is the danger of relying on volunteer samples in general?

c. What other problems do you see with this quiz? Comment on the types of questions and responses.

5.36 On its Web site, Advocates for Self-Government offers the "World's Smallest Internet Political Quiz," focusing on the U.S. political spectrum. Using just 10 questions, the quiz identifies an individual's political leanings. As of May 23, 2007, a total of 9,464,924 people had taken the quiz, and the breakdown into the five possible categories was: centrist, 33.49%; conservative, 8.88%; libertarian, 32.64%; liberal, 17.09%; and statist (big government), 7.89%.

a. Do you think these numbers are representative of the U.S. population? Why or why not?

b. Describe the people most likely to volunteer for this sample. Why might this group be biased in comparison to the overall U.S. population?

c. The Web site says, "Libertarians support maximum liberty in both personal and economic matters." Libertarians are not the predominant political group in the United States. Why, then, might libertarians form the largest category of quiz respondents?

d. This is a huge sample—9,464,924. Why is it not enough to have a large sample to conduct a study with high external validity? What would we need to change about this sample to increase external validity?

5.37 For each of the following hypothetical scenarios, state whether selection or assignment is being described. Is the method of selection or assignment random? Explain your answer.

a. A study of the services offered by counseling centers at Canadian universities studied 20 universities; every Canadian university had an equal chance of being in this study.

b. In a study of phobias, 30 rhesus monkeys were either exposed to fearful stimuli or not exposed to fearful stimuli. Every monkey had an equal chance of being placed in either of the exposure conditions.

c. A study of cell phone usage recruited participants by including an invitation to participate in their cell phone bills.

d. A study of visual perception recruited 120 Introduction to Psychology students to participate.

5.38 Short-run proportions are often quite different from long-run probabilities.

a. In your own words, explain why we would expect short-run proportions to fluctuate but why long-run probabilities are more predictable.

b. What is the expected long-run probability of heads if you flip a coin many, many times? Why?

c. Flip a coin 10 times in a row. What proportion are heads? Do this 5 times (and actually do it, don't just write down numbers!).

Proportion for first 10 flips:

Proportion for second 10 flips:

Proportion for third 10 flips:

Proportion for fourth 10 flips:

Proportion for fifth 10 flips:

d. Do the proportions in part (c) match the expected long-run probability in part (b)? Why or why not?

e. Imagine that a friend flipped a coin 10 times, got 9 out of 10 heads, and complained that the coin was biased. How would you explain to your friend the difference between short-term and long-term probability?

5.39 A deck of playing cards has 4 suits and 13 cards in each suit, for a total of 52 cards. Imagine you draw one card from the deck, record what the card is, and then put it back in the deck. Let's say you repeat this process 15 times, and 5 of the 15 cards are aces. Answer the following questions keeping this example in mind.

a. What does the term *probability* refer to? What is the probability of drawing an ace?

b. What does the term *proportion* refer to? What is the proportion of aces drawn?

c. What does the term *percentage* refer to? What is the percentage of aces drawn?

d. Based on these data (5 out of 15 cards were aces), do you have enough information to determine whether the deck is stacked (i.e., biased)? Why or why not? (*Note:* Four of the 52 cards should be aces.)

5.40 Gamblers often falsely predict the outcome of a future trial based on the outcome of previous trials. When trials are independent, we cannot predict the outcomes of a future trial based on the outcome of previous trials. For each of the following examples, (i) state whether the trials are independent or dependent and (ii) explain why. In addition, (iii) state whether it is possible that the quote is accurate or whether it is definitely fallacious, explaining how the independence or dependence of trials influences this.

a. You are playing Monopoly and have rolled a pair of sixes in 4 out of 10 of your last rolls of the dice. You say, "Cool. I'm on a roll. I'm likely to get sixes again on my next turn."

b. You are an Ohio State University football fan and are sad because they have lost two games in a row. You say, "That is really unusual; the Buckeyes are doomed this season. That's what happens with lots of early-season injuries."

c. You have a 20-year-old car that often has trouble starting. It has started every day this week, and now it's Friday. You say, "I'm doomed. It's been reliable all week, and even though I did get a tune-up last week, today is bound to be the day it fails me."

d. It's your first week at your corporate internship and you have to wear nylon stockings to the office if you're wearing a skirt. On the first and second days, you get a run in your stockings almost immediately, an indication of a defect. The third day, you put on yet another new pair of stockings and say, "OK, this pair has to be good. There's no way I'd have three bad pairs in a row. They're even from different stores!"

5.41 For each of the following studies, cite the likely null hypothesis and the likely research hypothesis.

a. A forensic cognitive psychologist wondered whether repetition of false information would increase the tendency to develop false memories, on average.

b. A clinical psychologist studied whether ongoing structured assessments of the therapy process would

lead to better outcome, on average, among outpatient therapy clients with depression.

c. A corporation recruited an industrial/organizational psychologist to explore the effects of cubicles (versus enclosed offices) on employee morale.

d. A team of developmental cognitive psychologists studied whether teaching a second language to children from birth affects children's ability to speak their native language.

5.42 For each of the following fictional outcomes, state whether you would reject or to fail to reject the null hypothesis (contingent, of course, on inferential statistics backing up the statement). Explain the rationale for your decision.

a. When false information is repeated several times, people seem to be more likely, on average, to develop false memories than when the information is not repeated.

b. Therapy clients with depression who have ongoing structured assessments of therapy seem to have lower depression levels post-therapy, on average, than do clients who do not have ongoing structured assessments.

c. Employee morale does not seem to be different, on average, whether employees work in cubicles or enclosed offices.

d. A child's native language does not seem to be different in strength, on average, based on whether the child is raised to be bilingual or not.

5.43 Examine the statements from Exercise 5.42, repeated here. If this conclusion is incorrect, what type of error have you made? Explain your answer.

a. When false information is repeated several times, people seem to be more likely, on average, to develop false memories than when the information is not repeated.

b. Therapy clients with depression who have ongoing structured assessments of therapy seem to have lower depression levels post-therapy, on average, than do clients who do not have ongoing structured assessments.

c. Employee morale does not seem to be different, on average, whether employees work in cubicles or enclosed offices.

d. A child's native language does not seem to be different in strength, on average, based on whether the child is raised to be bilingual or not.

5.44 Imagine you have made a new acquaintance in your statistics class with whom you study for tests. One day after hours of studying, your study partner asks you to go on a date. This invitation takes you by complete surprise and you have no idea what to say. You are not attracted to the person in a romantic way, but at the same time you do not want to hurt his or her feelings.

a. Create two possible responses to the person, one in which you *fail to reject the invitation* and another in which you *reject the invitation*.

b. How is your failure to reject the invitation different from rejecting or accepting the invitation?

5.45 Borsari and Carey (2005) randomly assigned 64 male students who had been ordered, after a violation of university alcohol rules, to meet with a school counselor to one of two conditions. Students were assigned to undergo either (1) a brief motivational interview (BMI), a recently developed intervention in which educational material is related to the students' own experiences, or (2) an alcohol education session (AE), a more established intervention in which educational material is simply presented with no link to students' experiences. Based on inferential statistics, the researchers concluded that those in the BMI group had, on average, fewer alcohol-related problems at follow-up than did those in the AE group.

a. What is the population of interest, and what is the sample in this study?

b. Was random selection used? Why or why not?

c. Was random assignment used? Why or why not?

d. What is the independent variable, and what are its levels? What is the dependent variable?

e. What is the null hypothesis, and what is the research hypothesis?

f. What decision did the researchers make? Use the language of inferential statistics.

g. If the researchers were incorrect in their decision, what kind of error did they make? Explain your answer. What are the consequences of this type of error, both in general and in this situation?

Terms

random sample (p. 95)

convenience sample (p. 95)

generalizability (p. 96)

replication (p. 97)

volunteer sample (p. 97)

personal probability (p. 100)

probability (p. 100)

expected relative-frequency probability (p. 100)

trial (p. 100)

outcome (p. 100)

success (p. 100)

control group (p. 103)

experimental group (p. 103)

null hypothesis (p. 104)

research hypothesis (p. 104)

Type I error (p. 107)

Type II error (p. 107)

The Normal Curve, Standardization, and z Scores

BEFORE YOU GO ON

- You should be able to create histograms and frequency polygons (Chapter 2).

- You should be able to describe distributions of scores in terms of central tendency, variability, and skewness (Chapters 2 and 4).

- You should understand that we can have distributions of scores based on samples, as well as distributions of scores based on entire populations (Chapter 5).

■ A **normal curve** is a specific bell-shaped curve that is unimodal, symmetric, and defined mathematically.

Abraham De Moivre was imprisoned in a French monastery for two years because of his religious beliefs. After his release, he fled France and ended up at Old Slaughter's Coffee House in London—the scene of a noisy explosion of intellectual freedom, political squabbles, and artists hustling for work. From his table there, De Moivre worked on a mathematical equation that he believed could predict random events, something that interested him and also allowed him to consult for a fee with the local gamblers and insurance brokers who also frequented Old Slaughter's Coffee House (Stigler, 1999). After all, they were betting men, and predicting the frequency of success and failure over the long run could create a financial edge. As we now know, De Moivre's significant contribution was expressed as a mathematical formula, but there is no record of him drawing the actual bell-shaped curve. Nevertheless, De Moivre's equation described what we now call the **_normal curve_**, *a specific bell-shaped curve that is unimodal, symmetric, and defined mathematically.*

De Moivre's powerful mathematical idea is far easier to understand as a picture, but drawing a sketch of the normal curve took about 200 years. In 1769, Daniel Bernoulli created a visual approximation of the normal curve. Then, 80 years later, in 1849, Augustus De Morgan made an informal sketch of the normal curve and mailed it to the astronomer George Airy (Stigler, 1999). (Both curves are shown in Figure 6-1.) The two men were stumbling toward a picture of the normal curve as they tried to manage patterns of errors in charting the stars.

Two critical features of the normal curve were apparent to these early astronomers. First, the pattern of errors was symmetric: the left side was a mirror image of the right. Second, the middle of the normal curve represented their best estimate of reality because it averaged the errors. The surrounding pattern of errors looked like a bell: only a few errors were way off by being extremely high or extremely low; most errors clustered tightly around the middle.

In this chapter, we learn several more building blocks of inferential statistics. First, we explore the characteristics of the normal curve. In particular, we learn how we can use it to standardize any variable using a tool called the *z* score so that we can make direct comparisons between scores on different measures. Finally, we learn about the central limit theorem. An understanding of the central limit theorem, coupled with a grasp of standardization, allows us to make comparisons between means in addition to scores.

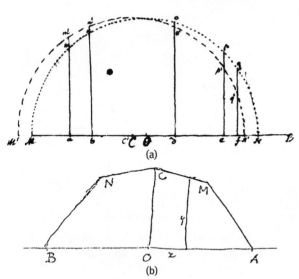

FIGURE 6-1
The Bell Curve Is Born

Daniel Bernoulli (a) created an approximation of the bell-shaped curve in this 1769 sketch "describing the frequency of errors." Augustus De Morgan (b) included this sketch in a letter to astronomer George Airy in 1849.

The Normal Curve

In this section, we learn more about the normal curve through a real-life example using heights.

EXAMPLE 6.1

Let's examine the heights, in inches, of a sample of 5 students taken from a larger sample that included several of the authors' statistics classes:

52 77 63 64 64

Figure 6–2 shows a histogram of those heights, with a normal curve superimposed upon the histogram. With so few scores, we can only begin to guess at the emerging shape of a normal distribution. Notice that three of the observations (63 inches, 64 inches, and 64 inches) are represented by the middle bar. This is why it is 3 times higher than the bars representing a single observation of 52 inches and another observation of 77 inches.

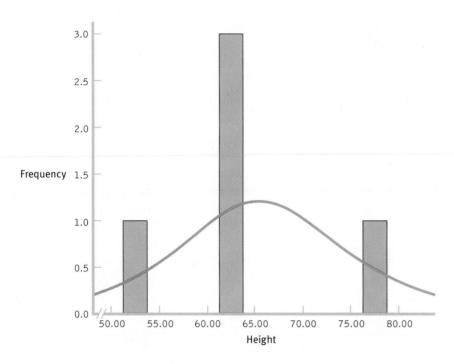

FIGURE 6-2
Sample of 5

Here is a histogram of the heights in inches of 5 students. With so few students, the data are unlikely to closely resemble the normal curve that we would see for an entire population of heights.

Now, here are the heights in inches from a random sample of 30 students:

52 77 63 64 64 62 63 64 67 52

67 66 66 63 63 64 62 62 64 65

67 68 74 74 69 71 61 61 66 66

Figure 6-3 shows the histogram for these data. Notice that the heights of 30 students resemble a normal curve more so than do the heights of just 5 students, although certainly not perfectly.

On the next page, Table 6-1 gives the heights in inches from a random sample of 140 students, and Figure 6-4 shows the histogram for these data.

More sample → Normal curve.
• Variables → Continuew.

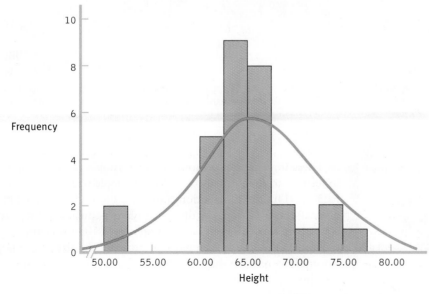

FIGURE 6-3
Sample of 30

Here is a histogram of the heights in inches of 30 students. With a larger sample, the data begin to resemble the normal curve of an entire population of heights.

TABLE 6-1. A Sample of Heights

These are the heights, in inches, of 140 students.

52	77	63	64	64	62	63	64	67	52
67	66	66	63	63	64	62	62	64	65
67	68	74	74	69	71	61	61	66	66
68	63	63	62	62	63	65	67	73	62
63	63	64	60	69	67	67	63	66	61
65	70	67	57	61	62	63	63	63	64
64	68	63	70	64	60	63	64	66	67
68	68	68	72	73	65	61	72	71	65
60	64	64	66	56	62	65	66	72	69
60	66	73	59	60	60	61	63	63	65
66	69	72	65	62	62	62	66	64	63
65	67	58	60	60	67	68	68	69	63
63	73	60	67	64	67	64	66	64	72
65	67	60	70	60	67	65	67	62	66

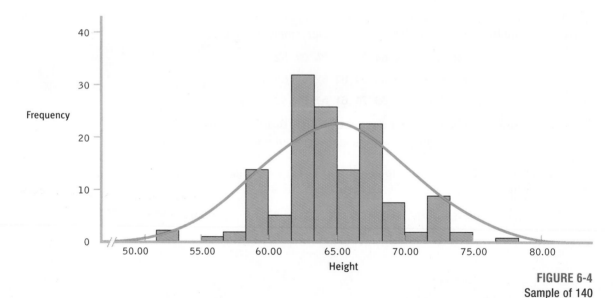

FIGURE 6-4
Sample of 140

Here is a histogram of the heights in inches of 140 students. As the sample increases, the shape of the distribution becomes more and more like the normal curve we would see for an entire population. Imagine the distribution of the data for a sample of 1000 students or of 1 million.

▶ **MASTERING THE CONCEPT**

6-1: The distributions of many variables approximate a normal curve, a mathematically defined, bell-shaped curve that is unimodal and symmetric.

These three images demonstrate why sample size is so important in relation to the normal curve. As the sample size increases from 5 to 30 to 140, the distribution more and more closely resembles a normal curve (as long as the underlying population distribution is normal). Imagine even larger samples—of 1000 students or of 1 million. As the size of the sample approaches the size of the population of interest, the shape of the distribution tends to be normally distributed.

CHECK YOUR LEARNING

Reviewing the Concepts

> The normal curve is a specific, mathematically defined curve that is bell-shaped and symmetric.

> The normal curve describes the distributions of many characteristics and measures that vary.

> As the size of a sample approaches the size of the population, the distribution resembles a normal curve (as long as the population is normally distributed).

Clarifying the Concepts   **6-1**   What does it mean to say that the normal curve is unimodal and symmetric?

Calculating the Statistics   **6-2**   In 2005, a sample of 225 students completed the Consideration of Future Consequences (CFC) scale, which you were able to take for yourself in Chapter 1. The scores are means of responses to the 12 items, with some responses reversed so that a high score indicates higher consideration of future consequences. Overall CFC scores, the mean of the item ratings for each participant, range from 1 to 5.

a. Here are CFC scores for five of those students, rounded to the nearest whole or half number to facilitate creation of a histogram: 3.5, 3.5, 3.0, 4.0, and 2.0. Create a histogram for these data, either by hand or using software.

b. Now create a histogram for the scores of 30 students. As before, the scores have been rounded to the nearest whole or half number.

3.5 3.5 3.0 4.0 2.0 4.0 2.0 4.0 3.5 4.5

4.5 4.0 3.5 2.5 3.5 3.5 4.0 3.0 3.0 2.5

3.0 3.5 4.0 3.5 3.5 2.0 3.5 3.0 3.0 2.5

Applying the Concepts   **6-3**   The histogram below uses the actual (not rounded) CFC scores for all 225 students. What do you notice about the shape of this distribution of scores as the size of the sample increases from 5 to 30 (in Check Your Learning 6-2 above) and then to 225?

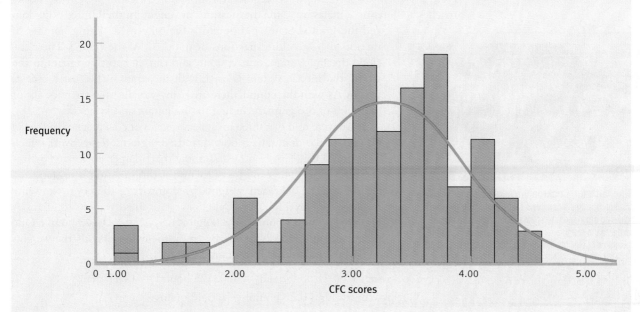

✳ Standardization, *z* Scores, and the Normal Curve

De Moivre's discovery of the normal curve meant that scientists could now make meaningful comparisons. When the data are normally distributed, we can compare a score on a variable to the entire distribution of scores. To do this, we convert a raw score to a standardized score (for which percentiles are already known). *The process of* ***standardization*** *converts individual scores to standard scores for which we know the percentiles (if the data are normally distributed). Standardization does this by converting individual scores from different normal distributions to a shared normal distribution with a known mean, standard deviation, and percentiles.*

In this section, we outline the reasons that statisticians need to be able to standardize, and then introduce the tool that helps us standardize, the *z* score. We show you how you can convert raw scores to *z* scores and *z* scores to raw scores. We also demonstrate how our knowledge of the distribution of *z* scores allows us to know what percentage of the population falls above or below a given *z* score.

The Need for Standardization — Compare 2 diff.

One of the first problems with making meaningful comparisons is that different variables are measured on different scales. For example, we measure height in inches but measure weight in pounds. In order to compare heights and weights, we need a way to put different variables on the same standardized scale. Fortunately, we can standardize different variables by using their means and standard deviations to convert any raw score into a *z* score. *A* ***z score*** *is the number of standard deviations a particular score is from the mean.* A *z* score is part of its own distribution, the *z* distribution, just as a raw score, such as a person's height, is part of its own distribution, a distribution of heights. (Note that as with all statistics, the *z* is italicized.) Any score on any measure can be converted to the *z* distribution.

> ▶ **MASTERING THE CONCEPT**
>
> **6-2:** *z* scores give us the ability to convert any variable to a standard distribution, allowing us to make comparisons among variables.

EXAMPLE 6.2

Here is a memorable example of standardization: comparing the weights of cockroaches. Different countries use different measures of weight. In the United Kingdom and the United States, the pound is typically used, with a number of variants that are either fractions or multiples of the pound. These include the mite, dram, ounce, stone, and ton. In most countries in the world, the metric system is used, with the gram as the basic unit of weight. As with the pound, there are many variants that are fractions or multiples of the gram, including the milligram and kilogram.

If we were told that three imaginary species of cockroaches had mean weights of 8.0 drams, 0.25 pound, and 98.0 grams, respectively, which one should we fear the most (assuming that a larger cockroach generates more fear)? The easiest way to answer this question is to standardize the three cockroach weights by comparing them on the same measure—for example, we could convert all these weights to grams. A dram is 1/256 of a pound, so 8.0 drams is 1/32 = 0.03125 pound. One pound equals 453.5924 grams. Based on these conversions, the weights could be standardized into grams as follows:

Standardizing Cockroach Weights Standardization creates meaningful comparisons by converting different scales to a common, or standardized, scale. We can compare the weights of these cockroaches using different measures of weights—including drams, pounds, and grams.

Michael Dick/Animals Animals-Earth Scenes

Cockroach 1 weighs 8.0 drams = 0.03125 pound = 14.17 grams

Cockroach 2 weighs 0.25 pound = 113.40 grams

Cockroach 3 weighs 98.0 grams

Standardizing by grams allows us to make meaningful comparisons. The second cockroach species tends to weigh the most: 113.40 grams. Fortunately, the biggest cockroach in the world weighs only about 35 grams and is about 80 millimeters (3.15 inches) long. Cockroaches 2 and 3 exist only in our imaginations. However, not all conversions are as easy as standardizing weights from different units into grams. That's why statisticians developed the z distribution.

Transforming Raw Scores into z Scores

Our desire to make meaningful comparisons forces us to convert raw scores into standardized scores, and we can always determine any score's distance from its mean in terms of standard deviations. For example, let's say you know that after taking the midterm examination, you are 1 standard deviation above the mean in your statistics class. Is this good news? What if you are 2 standard deviations above the mean? Are you even happier? What if you are 0.5 standard deviation below the mean? Understanding a score's relation to the mean of its distribution gives us important information about that score. For a statistics test, we know that being well above the mean is a good thing; in anxiety levels, we know that being well above the mean is usually a bad thing. z scores create an opportunity to make meaningful comparisons by putting different variables on a common scale.

The only information we need to convert any raw score to a z score is the mean and standard deviation of the population of interest. For instance, in the midterm example above, we are probably interested only in comparing our grade with the grades of others also taking this particular statistics course. In this case, the statistics class is the entire population of interest. Let's say that your particular score on the midterm is 2 standard deviations above the mean; so your z score is 2.0. Imagine that a friend's score is 1.6 standard deviations below the mean; your friend's z score is −1.6. What would your z score be if you fell exactly at the mean in your statistics class? If you guessed 0, you're correct. You would be 0 standard deviation from the mean.

Figure 6-5 illustrates two important features of the z distribution. First, the z distribution always has a mean of 0. So, if you are exactly at the mean, then you are 0 standard deviation from the mean. Second, the z distribution always has a standard deviation of 1. If your raw score is 1 standard deviation above the mean, you have a z score of 1.0. No matter what the mean and standard deviation of the original distribution, once we convert to the z distribution, the standard deviation is 1.0.

■ The process of **standardization** converts individual scores from different normal distributions to a shared normal distribution with a known mean, standard deviation, and percentiles.

■ A **z score** is the number of standard deviations a particular score is from the mean.

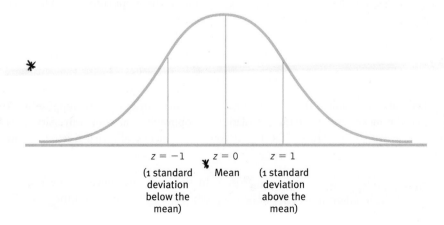

z = −1
(1 standard deviation below the mean)

z = 0
Mean

z = 1
(1 standard deviation above the mean)

FIGURE 6-5
The z Distribution

The z distribution always has a mean of 0 and a standard deviation of 1.

EXAMPLE 6.3

Let's calculate some z scores without a calculator or formula. Let's use the distribution of scores on a statistics exam, in which the students who took the exam make up the entire population of interest. (This example is illustrated in Figure 6-6.) If the mean on a statistics exam is 70, the standard deviation is 10, and your score is 80, what is your z score? In this case, you were exactly 10 points, or 1 standard deviation, above the mean, so your z score is 1.0. Now let's say your score is 50, which is 20 points, or 2 standard deviations, below the mean, so your z score is -2.0. What if your score were 85? Now you're 15 points, or 1.5 standard deviations, above the mean, so your z score is 1.5.

FIGURE 6-6
z Scores Intuitively

With a mean of 70 and a standard deviation of 10, we can calculate many z scores without a formula. A raw score of 50 has a z score of -2.0. A raw score of 60 has a z score of -1.0. A raw score of 70 has a z score of 0. A raw score of 80 has a z score of 1.0. A raw score of 85 has a z score of 1.5.

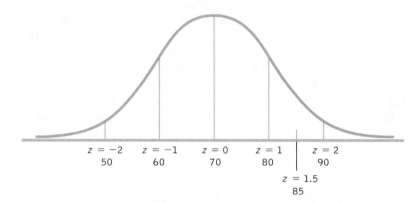

As you can see, we don't need a formula to calculate a z score when we're working with easy numbers. It is important, however, to learn the notation and language of statistics. So let's also convert z scores using a formula for when our numbers are not easy to work with. To calculate a particular z score, there are just two steps.

STEP 1. Determine the distance of a particular score from the population mean.

In this case, the score (X) and the population mean (μ) would be expressed in the equation:

$$X - \mu.$$

MASTERING THE FORMULA

6-1: The formula for a z score is $z = \dfrac{(X - \mu)}{\sigma}$. We calculate the difference between an individual score and the population mean, then divide by the population standard deviation.

STEP 2. Express this distance in terms of standard deviations.

Divide the distance by the standard deviation of the population, σ. The formula, therefore, is:

$$z = \frac{(X - \mu)}{\sigma}$$

EXAMPLE 6.4

 Let's take an example that is not so easy to calculate in our heads. Suppose we know that the mean height for the population of sophomores at your university is 64.886 with a standard deviation of 4.086. If you are 70 inches tall, what is your z score?

STEP 1. Subtract the mean of the population from your score.

In this case, the mean of the population, 64.886, is subtracted from the score, 70.

STEP 2. Divide by the standard deviation of the population.

The standard deviation of the population is 4.086. Here are those steps in the context of the formula:

$$z = \frac{(X - \mu)}{\sigma} = \frac{(70 - 64.886)}{4.086} = 1.25$$

You are 1.25 standard deviations above the mean.

We must be careful when we use a formula because it is easy to make a mistake when using a formula mindlessly. Always consider whether the answer makes sense. In this case, 1.25 is a positive *z* score, indicating that the height expressed as a *z* score is just over 1 standard deviation above the mean. This makes sense because the raw score of 70 is also just over 1 standard deviation above the mean of 64.886. If you do this quick check as you finish each problem on your homework or on a test, then you can correct mistakes before they cost you.

....

Let's take another example: What if you are 62 inches tall?

EXAMPLE 6.5

STEP 1. Subtract the mean of the population.

Subtract 64.886, the mean of the population, from your score, 62.

STEP 2. Divide by the standard deviation of the population.

The difference is divided by the standard deviation, 4.086. Here are those steps in the context of the formula:

$$z = \frac{(X - \mu)}{\sigma} = \frac{(62 - 64.886)}{4.086} = -0.71$$

You are 0.71 standard deviation *below* the mean.

Don't forget the sign of the *z* score. Changing a *z* score from negative 0.71 to positive 0.71 makes a big difference! Fortunately, even if you forgot to include the negative sign, then you could still catch your error if you considered whether the answer made sense. In this case, the height is lower than the mean, so the *z* score must be negative.

Estimating *z* Scores Would you guess that the person on the left has a positive or negative *z* score for height? What about the person on the right? A person who is very short has a below-average height and thus would have a negative *z* score. A person who is very tall has an above-average height and thus would have a positive *z* score.

Masterfile/Radius Images

EXAMPLE 6.6

Now let's demonstrate that the mean of the z distribution is always 0 and the standard deviation of the z distribution is always 1. We will continue to use the mean and standard deviation of heights from Examples 6.4 and 6.5 for this demonstration. (You can try it with any distribution for which you know the mean and standard deviation, though. The results will be the same every time.) The mean here is 64.886. Let's calculate what the z score would be at the mean.

| STEP 1. Subtract the mean of the population from a score right at the mean. | The mean of the population, 64.886, is subtracted from 64.886, a score right at the mean. |
| STEP 2. Divide by the standard deviation of the population. | We divide the difference by 4.086, as expressed in the following formula: |

$$z = \frac{(X - \mu)}{\sigma} = \frac{(64.886 - 64.886)}{4.086} = 0$$

The standard deviation is 4.086 inches. If someone is exactly 4.086 inches above the mean—that is, 1 standard deviation above the mean—his or her score would be $64.886 + 4.086 = 68.972$. Let's calculate what the z score would be for this person.

| STEP 1. Subtract the mean of the population from a score exactly one standard deviation above the mean. | The mean of the population, 64.886, is subtracted from 68.972, a score one standard deviation above the mean, 68.972. |
| STEP 2. Divide by the standard deviation of the population. | We divide the difference by 4.086, as expressed in the following formula: |

$$z = \frac{(X - \mu)}{\sigma} = \frac{(68.972 - 64.886)}{4.086} = 1$$

Transforming z Scores into Raw Scores

It's important also to realize that we can reverse the formula and convert a z score to a raw score, a calculation that will be useful in later chapters of this book. If we already know a z score, then we can reverse our calculations to determine the raw score. The formula is the same; we just plug in all the numbers instead of the X, then solve algebraically. Let's try it.

EXAMPLE 6.7

We'll use the same mean and standard deviation from our height example. The mean for the population is 64.886, with a standard deviation of 4.086. So, if you had a z score of 1.79, what is your height?

$$1.79 = \frac{(X - 64.886)}{4.086}$$

$$X = 1.79 (4.086) + 64.886 =$$

If we solve for *X*, we get 72.20. For those of you who prefer to minimize your use of algebra, we can do the algebra on the equation itself to derive a formula that gets the raw score directly. The formula is derived by multiplying both sides of the equation by σ, then adding μ to both sides of the equation. This isolates the *X*, as follows:

$$X = z(\sigma) + \mu$$

So there are two steps to converting a *z* score to a raw score:

> **MASTERING THE FORMULA**
>
> **6-2:** The formula to calculate the raw score from a *z* score is $X = z(\sigma) + \mu$. We multiply the *z* score by the standard deviation of the population, then add the mean of the population.

STEP 1. Multiply the *z* score by the standard deviation of the population.

STEP 2. Add the mean of the population to this product.

Let's try the same problem using this direct formula.

STEP 1. Multiply the *z* score by the standard deviation of the population.

The *z* score, 1.79, is multiplied by the standard deviation of the population, 4.086.

STEP 2. Add the mean of the population to this product.

The mean of the population, 64.886, is added to the product, 7.314, as expressed in the following formula:

$$X = 1.79(4.086) + 64.886 = \underline{72.20}$$

Regardless of whether we use the original formula or the direct formula, the height is 72.20 inches. As always, think about whether the answer seems accurate. In this case, the answer does make sense because the height is above the mean, and the *z* score is positive.

EXAMPLE 6.8

What if your *z* score is −0.44?

STEP 1. Multiply the *z* score by the standard deviation of the population.

The z score, −0.44, is multiplied by the standard deviation of the population, 4.086.

STEP 2. Add the mean of the population to this product.

The mean of the population, 64.886, is added to the product, −1.798, as expressed in the following formula:

$$X = -0.44(4.086) + 64.886 = 63.09$$

Your height is 63.09 inches. Don't forget the negative sign when doing this calculation. In this case, considering whether the answer makes sense would catch this. Here, we know the height is below the mean because the *z* score is negative.

Apples and Oranges
Standardization allows us to compare apples and oranges. If we can standardize the raw scores on two different scales, converting both scores to z scores, we can then compare the scores directly.

As long as we know the mean and standard deviation of the population, we can do two things: (1) calculate the raw score from its z score and (2) calculate the z score from its raw score.

As we'll soon learn z scores can be converted into percentages. So, another way to express standardization is to disprove the saying that "you can't compare apples and oranges." Well, yes we can. We can take any apple from a normal distribution of apples, find its particular z score using the mean and standard deviation for the distribution of apples, convert the z score to a percentile, and discover that a particular apple is, say, larger than 85% of all the other apples. Similarly, we can take any orange from a normal distribution of oranges, find its particular z score using the mean and standard deviation for the distribution of oranges, convert the z score to a percentile, and discover that this particular orange is, say, larger than 97% of all the other oranges. The orange (with respect to other oranges) is bigger than the apple (with respect to other apples), and yes, that is an honest comparison of apples and oranges. With standardization, we can compare anything, each relative to its own group.

The normal curve allows us to convert scores to percentiles because 100% of the population is represented under the bell-shaped curve. This means that the midpoint (which is the mean, the median, and the mode in a normal curve) is the 50th percentile. If your individual score on some test happens to be located to the right of the mean, you know that your score lies somewhere above the 50th percentile. A score to the left of the mean indicates that your score is somewhere below the 50th percentile. To make more specific comparisons, we convert raw scores to z scores and z scores to percentiles. As we just learned, a z score is the number of standard deviations a particular score is from the mean. The z score is part of a specific distribution. The ***z distribution*** *is a normal distribution of standardized scores—a distribution of z scores.* And the ***standard normal distribution*** *is a normal distribution of z scores.*

Most people are not content merely with knowing whether their own score is above or below the average score. After all, there is likely a big difference between scoring at the 51st and the 99th percentile in height, as shown in Figure 6-7. Both are above average, but the person whose height is at the 99th percentile is likely to be much, much taller than the person whose height is at the 51st percentile. The standardized z distribution allows us to do the following:

■ The ***z distribution*** is a normal distribution of standardized scores.

■ The **standard normal distribution** is a normal distribution of z scores.

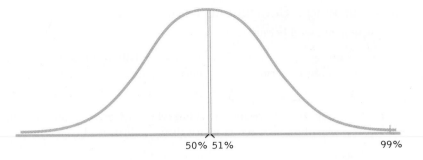

FIGURE 6-7
The All-Encompassing z Distribution

The z distribution theoretically includes all possible scores, so when it's based on a normal distribution, we know that 50% of the scores are above the mean and 50% are below the mean. But the 51st percentile and the 99th percentile are still far from each other, so two people making a comparison usually want more precise information than whether or not they are above average.

1. Transform raw scores into standardized scores called z scores
2. Transform z scores back into raw scores
3. Compare z scores to each other—even when the z scores represent raw scores on different scales
4. Transform z scores into percentiles that are more easily understood

Let's begin with an illustration that demonstrates how standardization makes meaningful comparisons possible, even when those comparisons belong to different distributions.

Using z Scores to Make Comparisons

Imagine that a friend is taking a course in statistics at the same time that you are, but with a different professor. Each professor has a different grading scheme, so each professor's class produces a different distribution of test scores that has meaning only within the context of that particular class. But now, thanks to standardization, we can convert each raw score to a z score and compare raw scores from *different* distributions.

EXAMPLE 6.9

For example, let's say that you both took a quiz this week. You got a 92 out of a possible 100; the distribution of your class had a mean of 78.1 and a standard deviation of 12.2. Your friend got an 8.1 out of a possible 10; the distribution of his class had a mean of 6.8 with a standard deviation of 0.74. Again, we're only interested in the classes that took the test, so these are populations rather than samples. Who did better?

If we standardize the two scores in terms of their respective distributions, then we can make a direct comparison of the two z scores:

Your score: $z = \dfrac{(X - \mu)}{\sigma} = \dfrac{(92 - 78.1)}{12.2} = 1.14$

Your friend's score: $z = \dfrac{(X - \mu)}{\sigma} = \dfrac{(8.1 - 6.8)}{0.74} = 1.76$

First, let's check our work. Do these answers make sense? Yes—both you and your friend scored above the mean, so you both have positive z scores. Second, we compare the z scores, the standardized versions of the two raw scores. Although you both scored well above the mean in terms of standard deviations, your friend did better with respect to his class than you did with respect to your class.

Making Comparisons z scores create a way to compare students taking different exams from different courses. If each exam score can be converted to a z score with respect to the mean and standard deviation for its particular exam, the two scores can then be compared directly.

Transforming z Scores into Percentiles

So z scores are useful because:

1. z scores give us a sense of where a score falls in relation to the mean of its population (in terms of the standard deviation of its population).
2. z scores allow us to compare scores from different distributions.

Yet we can be even more specific about where a score falls. So, an additional and particularly helpful use of z scores is that they also have this property:

3. z scores can be transformed into percentiles.

Because the shape of a normal curve is standard (unimodal and symmetric), we automatically know something about the percentage of any particular area under the curve. Think of the normal curve and the horizontal line below it as forming a shape. (In fact, it *is* a shape; it's essentially a frequency polygon that shows the frequencies for *every* score in the distribution.) Like any shape, the area below the normal curve can be measured. We quantify the space below a normal curve in terms of percentages. We can determine what percentage of the normal curve falls below or above any vertical line drawn through the curve.

Statisticians have determined the specific percentages that fall within each particular area of the normal curve. Remember that the normal curve is, by definition, symmetric. This means that exactly 50% of scores fall below the mean and 50% fall above the mean; that is, one side is a mirror image of the other. Figure 6-8 demonstrates that we can be even more specific than simply dividing the normal curve into two equal parts. Approximately 34% of scores fall between the mean and a z score of 1.0; and because of symmetry, 34% of scores also fall between the mean and a z score of −1.0. We also know that approximately 14% of scores fall between the z scores of 1.0 and 2.0, and, by symmetry, 14% of scores fall between the z scores of −1.0 and −2.0. Finally, we know that approximately 2% of scores fall between the z scores of 2.0 and 3.0, and 2% of scores fall between the z scores of −2.0 and −3.0.

By simple addition, we can determine that approximately 68% (34 + 34 = 68) of scores fall within 1 standard deviation—or one z score—of the mean; that approximately 96% (14 + 34 + 34 + 14 = 96) of scores fall within 2 standard deviations of the mean; and that all or nearly all (2 + 14 + 34 + 34 + 14 + 2 = 100) scores fall within 3 standard deviations of the mean. These percentages are useful guidelines for determining the percentage associated with a given z score. For example, if you know you are about 1 standard deviation above the mean on your statistics quiz, then you can add the 50% below the mean to the 34% between the mean and the z score of

FIGURE 6-8
The Normal Curve and Percentages

The standard shape of the normal curve allows us to know the approximate percentages under different parts of the curve. For example, about 34% of scores fall between the mean and a z score of 1.0.

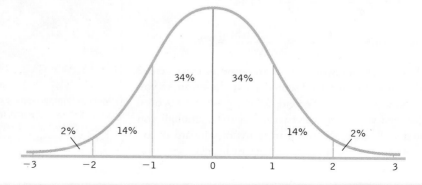

1.0 that you earned on your quiz, and know that your score corresponds to approximately the 84th percentile.

If you know that you are about 1 standard deviation below the mean, you know that you are in the lower 50% of scores and that 34% of scores fall between your score and the mean. By subtracting, you can calculate that $50 - 34 = 16\%$ of scores fall below you. Your score corresponds to approximately the 16th percentile. Scores on standardized tests, such as the SAT, are often expressed as percentiles.

For now, it's important to understand that the *z* distribution forms a normal curve with a unimodal, symmetric shape. Because the shape is known and 100% of the population falls beneath the normal curve, we can determine the percentage of any area under the normal curve. This is what we call "standardization." Through the normal curve and standardization, we can convert raw scores to *z* scores and *z* scores to percentiles.

CHECK YOUR LEARNING

Reviewing the Concepts
> Standardization is a way to create meaningful comparisons between observations from different distributions. It can be accomplished by transforming raw scores from different distributions into *z* scores, also known as standardized scores.

> A *z* score is the distance that a score is from the mean of its distribution in terms of standard deviations. *z* scores fall on the *z* distribution, and so when we convert raw scores to *z* scores, we can compare them.

> We also can transform *z* scores to raw scores by reversing the formula.

> *z* scores correspond to known percentiles that communicate how an individual compares with the larger distribution.

Clarifying the Concepts

6-4 Describe the process of standardization.

6-5 What do the numeric value and the sign (negative or positive) of a *z* score indicate?

Calculating the Statistics

6-6 If the mean of a population is 14 and the standard deviation is 2.5, calculate *z* scores for the following observations:

a. 11.5

b. 18

6-7 Using the same population parameters as in Check Your Learning 6-6, convert these *z* scores to raw scores:

a. 2

b. −1.4

Applying the Concepts

6-8 A study of Consideration of Future Consequences (CFC) found a mean CFC score of 3.51, with a standard deviation of 0.61, for the 664 students in the sample (Petrocelli, 2003). For this exercise, treat 3.51 and 0.61 as population parameters.

a. If a student has a CFC score of 2.3, what is her *z* score? Roughly, to what percentile does this *z* score correspond?

b. If a student has a CFC score of 4.7, what is his *z* score? Roughly, to what percentile does this *z* score correspond?

c. If a student has a CFC score at the 84th percentile, what is her *z* score?

d. What is the raw score of the student at the 84th percentile? Use symbolic notation and the formula. Explain why this answer makes sense.

continued on next page

6-9   Samantha has high blood pressure but exercises and has a health score of 84 on a scale with a mean of 93 and a standard deviation of 4.5 (a higher score indicates better health). Nicole is of normal weight but has high cholesterol, and she has a wellness score of 332 on a scale with a mean of 312 and a standard deviation of 20.

a.   Without using a formula, who would you say is in better health?

b.   Using standardization, who is in better health? Provide details using symbolic notation.

c.   Based on their *z* scores, what percentage of people are in better health than Samantha and Nicole, respectively?

Solutions to these Check Your Learning questions can be found in Appendix D.

The Central Limit Theorem

In the early 1900s, W. S. Gossett discovered how the predictability of the normal curve could improve quality control in the Guinness ale factory. One of the practical problems that Gossett faced was related to sampling yeast cultures in order to produce a more reliable-tasting ale. Too little yeast led to incomplete fermentation, whereas too much led to bitter-tasting beer. To sample both accurately and economically, Gossett averaged samples of four observations to see how well they represented a known population of 3000 (Gossett, 1908, 1942; Stigler, 1999). This small adjustment (taking the *average* of four samples rather than one sample) is possible because of the central limit theorem. The **central limit theorem** *asserts that a distribution of sample means approaches a normal curve as sample size increases.* More specifically, the central limit theorem demonstrates two important principles:

1. Repeated sampling of means approximates a normal curve, *even when the original population is not normally distributed*.

2. A distribution of means is less variable than a distribution of individual scores.

Instead of randomly sampling a single data point, Gossett randomly sampled four data points from the population of 3000 and computed the average of those four data points. He did this repeatedly, and then used those many arithmetic averages to create a new distribution of averages called a **distribution of means**, *a distribution composed of many means that are calculated from all possible samples of a given size, all taken from the same population.* Put another way, the numbers that make up the distribution of means are not individual scores; they are *means* of samples of individual scores. Gossett experimented with using the average of four data points as his sample, but there is nothing magical about the number four. A larger sample size is better, but Gossett could have used any number greater than one to create averaged samples that could be expressed as a distribution of means. The important outcome is that a distribution of means more consistently produces a normal distribution (although with less variance) *even when the population distribution is not normal.* The average of a sample is a more precise estimate of the population mean than an individual score. Repeated sampling of means produces a normal distribution even when the original distribution of scores is not normal.

In this section, we learn how to create a distribution of means, as well as to calculate a *z* score for a mean (more accurately called a *z statistic* when calculated for means rather than scores). We also learn why the central limit theorem indicates that a distribution of means is more useful than a distribution of scores when conducting hypothesis testing.

▶ **MASTERING THE CONCEPT**

6-3: The central limit theorem demonstrates that a distribution made up of the means of many samples (rather than individual scores) approximates a normal curve, even if the underlying population is not normally distributed.

▪ The **central limit theorem** refers to how a distribution of sample means is a more normal distribution than a distribution of scores, even when the population distribution is not normal.

▪ A **distribution of means** is a distribution composed of many means that are calculated from all possible samples of a given size, all taken from the same population.

Creating a Distribution of Means

The central limit theorem underlies many statistical processes. It is when we have a distribution of means that the central limit theorem becomes important. The distribution of means is more tightly clustered (has a smaller standard deviation) than a distribution of scores.

EXAMPLE 6.10

In an exercise that we conduct in class with our students, we write the numbers in Table 6-1 (on page 120) on 140 individual index cards that can be mixed together in a hat or bowl. The numbers represent the heights, in inches, of 140 college students from the authors' classes. As before, we assume that we are interested in only these 140 students—that they comprise our entire population.

1. First, we randomly pull one card at a time and record its score by marking it on a histogram chart above the appropriate value. After recording the score, we return the card to the container representing the population of scores and mix all the cards before pulling the next card. (Not surprisingly, this is known as *sampling with replacement*.) We continue until we have plotted at least 30 scores, drawing a square for each one above the appropriate value on the *x*-axis, so that bars emerge above each value. This creates the beginning of a *distribution of scores*. Using this method, we created the histogram in Figure 6-9 on the next page.

2. Now, we randomly pull three cards at a time, compute the mean of these three scores (rounding to the nearest whole number for the purposes of this exercise), and record this mean on a different histogram chart. As before, we draw a square for each mean above the appropriate value, with each stack of squares resembling a bar. Again, we return each set of three cards to the population and mix before pulling the next set of three. We continue until we have plotted at least 30 values. This is the beginning of a *distribution of means*. Using this method, we created the histogram in Figure 6-10 on the next page.

The distribution of scores in Figure 6-9, similar to those we create when we do this exercise in class, ranges from 52 to 74, with a peak in the middle. If we had a larger population, and if we pulled many more numbers, our distribution would become more and more normal. Notice that the distribution is centered roughly around the actual population mean, 64.89. Also notice that all, or nearly all, scores fall within 3 standard deviations of the mean. The population standard deviation of these scores is 4.09. So nearly all scores should fall within this range:

$$64.89 - 3(4.09) = 52.62 \text{ and } 64.89 + 3(4.09) = 77.16$$

In fact, the range of scores in this population of 140 heights is very close to this, 52 through 77 (even though the highest score we pulled was 74).

Is there anything different about the distribution of means in Figure 6-10 as compared to the distribution of scores in Figure 9-9? Yes, there are not as many means at the far tails of the distribution of means. We have a smaller range; we no longer have any values in the 50s or 70s. However, there are no changes in the center of the distribution as a result of shifting from scores to means. The distribution of means is still centered around the actual mean of 64.89. This makes sense. The means of three scores each come from the same set of scores, so the mean of the individual sample means should be exactly the same as the mean of the whole population of scores.

Why does the spread decrease when we create a distribution of means rather than a distribution of scores? When we plotted individual *scores,* an extreme score was plotted on the distribution. But when we plotted *means,* we averaged that extreme score with two other scores. It is unlikely that all three scores were that extreme in the same

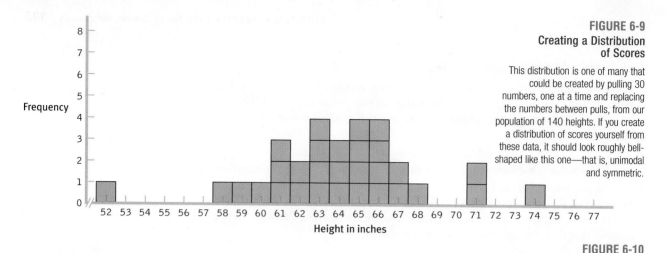

FIGURE 6-9
Creating a Distribution of Scores

This distribution is one of many that could be created by pulling 30 numbers, one at a time and replacing the numbers between pulls, from our population of 140 heights. If you create a distribution of scores yourself from these data, it should look roughly bell-shaped like this one—that is, unimodal and symmetric.

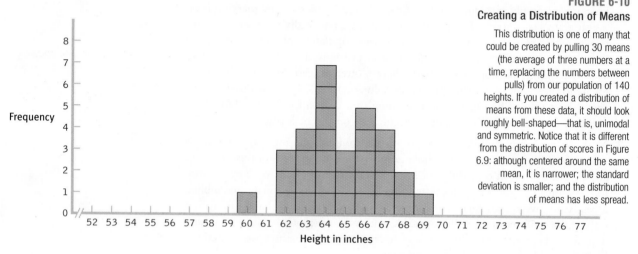

FIGURE 6-10
Creating a Distribution of Means

This distribution is one of many that could be created by pulling 30 means (the average of three numbers at a time, replacing the numbers between pulls) from our population of 140 heights. If you created a distribution of means from these data, it should look roughly bell-shaped—that is, unimodal and symmetric. Notice that it is different from the distribution of scores in Figure 6.9: although centered around the same mean, it is narrower; the standard deviation is smaller; and the distribution of means has less spread.

direction. So, each time we pulled a score in the 70s, we tended to pull two lower scores as well, and the mean was lower than the 70s. When we pulled a score in the 50s, we tended to pull two higher scores as well, and the mean was higher than the 50s.

What do you think would happen if we created a distribution of means of 10 scores rather than 3? As you might guess, the distribution would be even narrower, because there would be more scores to balance the occasional extreme score. The means of 10 scores are likely to be even closer to the actual mean of 64.89. What if we created a distribution of means of 100 scores or 10,000 scores? The larger the sample size, the smaller the spread of the distribution of means.

All the central limit theorem requires to work its magic is a distribution comprised of many sample means. In fact, distributions of means computed from samples of at least 30 usually produce an approximately normal curve. So even when the population distribution is extremely skewed, repeated sampling of means from that distribution produces a normal curve.

Characteristics of the Distribution of Means

▶ **MASTERING THE CONCEPT**

6-4: A distribution of means has the same mean as a distribution of scores from the same population, but a smaller standard deviation.

Because the distribution of means is less variable than the distribution of scores, the distribution of means needs its own standard deviation— a smaller standard deviation than the one we used for the distribution of individual scores (remember, the distribution of means is more tightly clustered around the mean). We need to use the standard deviation that is tailored to the distribution of means so we can calculate an appropriate z score for the distribution of means.

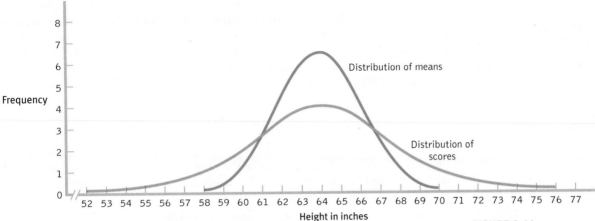

FIGURE 6-11
Using the Appropriate Measure of Spread

Because the distribution of means is narrower than the distribution of scores, it has a smaller standard deviation. This standard deviation has its own name: standard error.

We can use the data presented in Figure 6-11 to visually verify that the distribution of means needs its own (smaller) standard deviation (rather than the standard deviation that describes the population). Using the population mean of 64.886 and the population standard deviation of 4.086, the z scores for 60 and 69 are -1.20 and 1.01, respectively—not even close to 3 standard deviations. These z scores are wrong for this distribution. We need to use a standard deviation of the sample *means* rather than a standard deviation of the individual *scores*.

We use slightly modified language and symbols to distinguish this new standard deviation of the sampling distribution of means from the standard deviation of the population distribution of scores. The mean of the distribution of means is the same as the mean of the population of scores, but it has a different symbol. To indicate that this is the mean of a distribution of means, the symbol is μ_M (pronounced "mew sub em"). The μ indicates that it is the mean of a *population,* and the subscript M indicates that the population is composed of *sample means*—the means of all possible samples of a given size from a particular population of individual scores.

We also need a new symbol and a new name for the standard deviation of the distribution of means—the typical amount that a sample mean varies from the population mean. The symbol is σ_M (pronounced "sigma sub em"). The subscript M again stands for mean; this is the standard deviation of the population of means calculated for *all possible samples* of a given size. The symbol also has its own name to differentiate it from the standard deviation of a set of individual scores; ***standard error*** *is the name for the standard deviation of a distribution of means.* Table 6-2 summarizes the alternative names that describe these related ideas.

Fortunately, there is a simple calculation that lets us know exactly how much smaller the standard error, σ_M, is than the standard deviation, σ. As we've noted, the larger the

TABLE 6-2. PARAMETERS FOR DISTRIBUTIONS OF SCORES VERSUS MEANS

When we determine the parameters of a distribution, we must consider whether the distribution is composed of means or scores.

DISTRIBUTION	SYMBOL FOR MEAN	SYMBOL FOR SPREAD	NAME FOR SPREAD
Scores	μ	σ	Standard deviation
Means	μ_M	σ_M	Standard error

Standard error is the name for the standard deviation of a distribution of means.

╔══════════════════════════════════════╗
MASTERING THE FORMULA

6-3: The formula for standard error is: $\sigma_M = \dfrac{\sigma}{\sqrt{N}}$. We divide the standard deviation for the population by the square root of the sample size.
╚══════════════════════════════════════╝

sample size, the narrower the distribution of means. This also means that the larger the sample size, the smaller the standard deviation of the distribution of means—the standard error. We calculate the standard error by using the size of the sample that was used to calculate the many means that make up the distribution. The standard error is the standard deviation of the population divided by the square root of the sample size, N. The formula is:

$$\sigma_M = \frac{\sigma}{\sqrt{N}}$$

EXAMPLE 6.11

Imagine that the standard deviation of the distribution of individual scores is 5 and we have a sample of just 10 people. The standard error would be:

$$\sigma_M = \frac{\sigma}{\sqrt{N}} = \frac{5}{\sqrt{10}} = 1.58$$

The spread is smaller when we calculate a mean for 10 individuals because any extreme scores are balanced by less extreme scores. With a larger sample size of 200, the spread is even smaller because there are many more scores close to the mean to balance out any extreme scores. It would be rare to get a sample mean very far from the actual mean. The standard error would then be:

$$\sigma_M = \frac{\sigma}{\sqrt{N}} = \frac{5}{\sqrt{200}} = 0.35$$

As sample size increases, the spread decreases. The means that make up the distribution of means tend to be closer to the actual population mean.

A distribution of means faithfully obeys the central limit theorem. Even if the population of individual scores is *not* normally distributed, the distribution of means will approximate the normal curve if the samples are composed of at least 30 scores. The three graphs in Figure 6-12 depict: (a) a distribution of individual scores that is extremely skewed in the positive direction, (b) the less skewed distribution that results

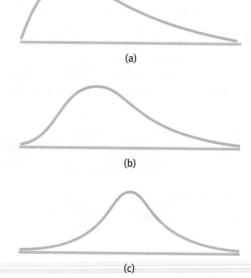

A severely skewed distribution of scores in a population

(a)

A less severely skewed distribution of means using samples of 2 from the same population

(b)

FIGURE 6-12
The Mathematical Magic of Large Samples

Even with a population of individual scores that are not normally distributed, the distribution of means approximates a normal curve as the sample gets larger.

A normal distribution of means using samples of 25 from the same population

(c)

when we create a distribution of means using samples of 2, and (c) the approximately normal curve that results when we create a distribution of means using samples of 25.

We have learned three important characteristics of the distribution of means:

1. Regardless of sample size, the mean of a distribution of means approaches the mean of the population of individual scores.
2. The standard deviation of a distribution of means (called the standard error) is smaller than the standard deviation of a distribution of scores. The standard error can be calculated by dividing the standard deviation of the population of individual scores by the square root of the sample size. As sample size increases, the standard error becomes ever smaller.
3. The shape of the distribution of means approximates the normal curve if the distribution of the population of individual scores has a normal shape or if the size of each sample that makes up the distribution is at least 30 (central limit theorem).

Using the Central Limit Theorem to Make Comparisons with z Scores

z scores are a standardized version of raw scores based on the population. But we seldom have the entire population to work with, so we typically calculate the mean of a sample and calculate a z score based on a distribution of means. When we calculate our z score, we simply use a distribution of means instead of a distribution of scores. The z formula changes only in the symbols it uses:

$$z = \frac{(M - \mu_M)}{\sigma_M}$$

Note that we now use M instead of X because we are calculating a z score for a sample mean rather than for an individual score. Because the z score now represents a mean, not an actual score, it is often referred to as a *z statistic*. Specifically, the z statistic tells us how many standard errors a sample mean is from the population mean.

> **MASTERING THE FORMULA**
>
> 6-4: The formula for z based on the mean of a sample is: $z = \frac{(M - \mu_M)}{\sigma_M}$.
> We subtract the mean of the distribution of means from the mean of our sample, then we divide by the standard error, the standard deviation of the distribution of means.

EXAMPLE 6.12

Let's consider a distribution for which we know the population mean and the population standard deviation. As you know, scores on most IQ measures are standardized to have a population mean of 100 and a standard deviation of 15. Imagine that we devise a set of brain exercises to increase IQ. We take a representative sample of 90 adults and enroll them in our brain boot camp. After they've performed three months of mental aerobics, we measure their IQ scores and find that the mean IQ score is 102. Is this an extreme sample mean given the population?

To find out, let's imagine the distribution of IQ scores collected after participants have performed their three months of mental aerobics. The distribution of means for samples of 90 IQ scores would be collected the same way we collected the means of three heights in our earlier example—just with far, far more means. It would have the same mean as the population, but the spread would be smaller. Any extreme IQ scores would likely be balanced by less extreme scores when each mean is calculated, so the distribution would be less variable. Before we calculate the z statistic, let's use proper symbolic notation to indicate the mean and the standard error of the sample of people in our brain boot camp:

$$\mu_M = \mu = 100$$

$$\sigma_M = \frac{\sigma}{\sqrt{N}} = \frac{15}{\sqrt{90}} = 1.581$$

At this point, we have all the information we need to calculate the z statistic:

$$z = \frac{(M - \mu_M)}{\sigma_M} = \frac{(102 - 100)}{1.581} = 1.27$$

From this z statistic, we could determine how extreme the mean IQ is in terms of a percentage. Then we could draw a conclusion about whether we would be likely to find a mean IQ of 102 in a sample of 90 people if the brain aerobics did *not* work. The useful combination of a distribution of means and a z statistic has led us to a point where we're prepared for inferential statistics and hypothesis testing.

CHECK YOUR LEARNING

Reviewing the Concepts

> According to the central limit theorem, a distribution of sample means based on 30 or more scores approximates the normal distribution, even if the original population is not normally distributed.

> A distribution of scores can have the same mean as a distribution of means. However, a distribution of scores contains more extreme scores, a bigger range, and a bigger standard deviation than a distribution of means; this is another principle of the central limit theorem.

> z scores may be calculated from a distribution of scores or from a distribution of means. The logic of the two calculations is identical, but they use slightly different symbols. When we calculate a z score for a mean, we usually call it a z statistic.

> For the measure of spread, the two calculations use different terms: *standard deviation* for a distribution of scores and *standard error* for a distribution of means.

> Just as with z scores, the z statistic tells us about the relative position of a mean within a distribution, and this can be expressed as a percentile.

Clarifying the Concepts

6-10 What are the main ideas behind the central limit theorem?

6-11 Explain what a distribution of means is.

Calculating the Statistics

6-12 The mean of a distribution of scores is 57 with a standard deviation of 11. Calculate the standard error for a distribution of means based on samples of 35 people.

Applying the Concepts

6-13 Let's return to the selection of 30 CFC scores that we considered in Check Your Learning 6-2(b):

3.5 3.5 3.0 4.0 2.0 4.0 2.0 4.0 3.5 4.5

4.5 4.0 3.5 2.5 3.5 3.5 4.0 3.0 3.0 2.5

3.0 3.5 4.0 3.5 3.5 2.0 3.5 3.0 3.0 2.5

a. What is the range of these scores?

b. Take three means of 10 scores each from this sample of scores, one for each row. What is the range of these means?

c. Why is the range smaller for the *means* of samples of 10 scores than for the individual *scores* themselves?

Solutions to these Check Your Learning questions can be found in Appendix D.

d. The mean of these 30 scores is 3.32. The standard deviation is 0.69. Using symbolic notation and formulas (where appropriate), determine the mean and standard error of the distribution of means computed from samples of 10.

REVIEW OF CONCEPTS

The Normal Curve

Three ideas about the normal curve help us to understand inferential statistics. First, the *normal curve* describes the variability of many physical, psychological, and behavioral characteristics. Second, the normal curve may be translated into percentages, allowing us to standardize variables and make direct comparisons of scores on different measures. Third, a distribution of means, rather than scores, produces a more normal curve. The last idea is based on the central limit theorem, by which we know that a distribution of means will be normally distributed as long as the samples from which the means are computed are of a sufficiently large size, usually at least 30.

Standardization, *z* Scores, and the Normal Curve

The process of *standardization* converts raw scores into *z scores*. Raw scores from any normal distribution—anything from heights to psychosis scores—can be converted to the *z distribution*. *z* scores tell us how far a given raw score falls from its mean in terms of standard deviation. We can convert raw scores to *z* scores and reverse the formula to convert *z* scores to raw scores. Standardization using *z* scores has two important applications. First, standardized scores—that is, *z* scores—can be looked up on a *z* table to determine the percentile rank of given raw scores. Second, we can directly compare *z* scores from different raw-score distributions. *z* scores work the other way around as well; if we know someone's percentile, we can look up the corresponding *z* score and then convert it to a raw score.

The Central Limit Theorem

The *z* distribution can be used with a *distribution of means* in addition to a distribution of scores. Distributions of means have three characteristics. First, they have the same mean as the population of individual scores from which they are calculated. Second, they have a smaller spread, which means we must adjust for sample size. The standard deviation of a distribution of means is called the *standard error*. The decreased variability is due to the fact that extreme scores are balanced by less extreme scores when means are calculated. Third, distributions of means are normally distributed in two situations: (1) the underlying population of scores is normal or (2) the means are computed from sufficiently large samples, usually at least 30 individual scores. This second situation is described by the *central limit theorem*, the principle that a distribution of sample means will be normally distributed even if the underlying distribution of scores is not normally distributed, as long as there are enough scores, usually at least 30, comprising each sample. The characteristics of the normal curve allow us to make inferences from small samples using standardized distributions, such as the *z* distribution. The *z* distribution can be used for means, as well as individual scores, if we determine the appropriate mean and standard deviation.

SPSS®

SPSS lets us understand each variable, identify its skewness, and explore how well it fits with a normal distribution. Enter the 140 heights from Table 6-1.

We can identify outliers that might skew the normal curve by selecting **Analyze** → Descriptive Statistics → Explore → Statistics → Outliers. Click "Continue," and then "OK." Be sure to choose the variable of interest, "Heights," by clicking it on the left and then using the arrow to move it to the right. The screenshot shown here depicts part of the output.

We encourage you to play with the data so you can explore the many features within SPSS. It is always helpful when we work with our own data. SPSS is probably easiest to learn when we know the source of every number and why we decided to include it in our study in the first place. It's also much more interesting to test our own ideas!

How It Works

6.1 CONVERTING RAW SCORES TO z SCORES

Georgiou and colleagues (1997) reported that college students had healthier eating habits, on average, than did those who were neither college students nor college graduates. The journal article reported means and standard deviations for students and nonstudents on a number of eating measures. For example, the 412 students in the study ate breakfast a mean of 4.1 times per week with a standard deviation of 2.4. Imagine that this is the entire population of interest; thus, these numbers can be treated as parameters. How can we use this transformation to calculate z scores?

Using symbolic notation and the formula, we can calculate the z score for a student who eats breakfast six times per week as follows:

$$z = \frac{(X - \mu)}{\sigma} = \frac{(6 - 4.1)}{2.4} = 0.792$$

Now, calculate the z score for a student who eats breakfast twice a week. We can calculate this z score as follows:

$$z = \frac{(X - \mu)}{\sigma} = \frac{(2 - 4.1)}{2.4} = -0.875$$

6.2 STANDARDIZATION WITH z SCORES AND PERCENTILES

Who is doing better financially—Maria Sharapova, with respect to the 10 tennis players with the highest incomes, or Tiger Woods, with respect to the 10 golfers with the highest incomes? In 2005, Forbes.com listed the 10 most powerful tennis players in terms of earnings and media exposure, regardless of gender. Sharapova, the first Russian (man or woman) to be ranked number one internationally in tennis, ranked second in earnings, with an income of $18.2 million, much of it from endorsements for companies such as Canon and Motorola. In 2005, Golfdigest.com listed the top-50 earners in golf, regardless of gender. Woods placed first, with $89.4 million (over one-fourth of it just from Nike endorsements!). But top golfers tend to make more than top tennis players. In comparison to his top-10 peers, did Woods really do better financially than Sharapova did in comparison to her top-10 peers?

For tennis, the mean for the top 10 was $11.58 million, with a standard deviation of $6.58 million. Based on this, Maria Sharapova's *z* score is:

$$z = \frac{(X - \mu)}{\sigma} = \frac{(18.2 - 11.58)}{6.58} = 1.01$$

We can also estimate her percentile rank. Fifty percent of scores fall below the mean and about 34% fall between the mean and a *z* score of 1.0: 50 + 34 = 84. Sharapova is at approximately the 84th percentile among the top-10 tennis players with the highest incomes.

For golf, the mean for the top 10 was $30.01 million, with a standard deviation of $28.86 million. Based on this, Tiger Woods's *z* score is:

$$z = \frac{(X - \mu)}{\sigma} = \frac{(89.4 - 30.01)}{28.86} = 2.06$$

We can also estimate his percentile rank. Fifty percent of scores fall below the mean; about 34% fall between the mean and 1 standard deviation above the mean; and about 14% fall between 1 and 2 standard deviations above the mean: 50 + 34 + 14 = 98. Woods is at approximately the 98th percentile among the top-10 golfers with the highest incomes.

In comparison to the top-10 earners in their respective sports, Woods outearned Sharapova.

Exercises

Clarifying the Concepts

6.1 Explain how the word *normal* is used in everyday conversation; then explain how statisticians use it.

6.2 What point on the normal curve represents the most commonly occurring observation?

6.3 How does the size of a sample of scores affect the distribution of data?

6.4 Explain how the word *standardize* is used in everyday conversation; then explain how statisticians use it.

6.5 What is a *z* score?

6.6 Give three reasons why *z* scores are useful.

6.7 What are the mean and standard deviation of the *z* distribution?

6.8 Why is the central limit theorem such an important idea for dealing with a population that is not normally distributed?

6.9 What does the symbol μ_M stand for?

6.10 Why does the standard error become smaller simply by increasing the sample size?

6.11 What does a *z* statistic—a *z* score based on a distribution of means—tell us about a sample mean?

6.12 Each of the following equations has an error. Identify and fix the error and explain your work.

a. $\sigma_M = \frac{\mu}{\sqrt{N}}$

b. $z = \frac{(\mu - \mu_M)}{\sigma_M}$

c. $z = \frac{(M - \mu_M)}{\sigma_M}$

d. $z = \frac{(X - \mu)}{\sigma}$

Calculating the Statistics

6.13 Create a histogram for these three sets of scores. Each set of scores represents a sample taken from the same population.

a. 6 4 11 7 7

b. 6 4 11 7 7 2 10 7 8 6 6 7 5 8

c. 6 4 11 7 7 2 10 7 8 6 6 7 5 8 7 8 9 7 6 9 3 9 5 6 8 11 8 3 8 4 10 8 5 5 8 9 9 7 8 7 10 7

d. What do you observe happening across these three distributions?

6.14 If a population has a mean of 250 and standard deviation of 47, calculate *z* scores for each of the following observations:

a. 391

b. 273

c. 199

d. 160

6.15 A population has a mean of 1179 and a standard deviation of 164. Calculate *z* scores for each of the following observations:

a. 1000

b. 721

c. 1531

d. 1184

6.16 Using the population described in Exercise 6.14, compute the *z* score for 250. Explain the meaning of the value you obtain.

6.17 Using the population described in Exercise 6.14, compute the *z* scores for 203 and 297. Explain the significance of these values.

6.18 For a population with a mean of 250 and a standard deviation of 47, return each of the following *z* scores to raw scores on this variable.

a. 0.54

b. −2.66

c. −1.0

d. 1.79

6.19 Another population has a mean of 1179 and a standard deviation of 164. Return each of the following *z* scores to original scores.

a. −0.23

b. 1.41

c. 2.06

d. 0.03

6.20 The verbal subtest of the GRE has a population mean of 500 and a population standard deviation of 100 by design. Convert the following *z* scores to raw scores *without* using a formula.

a. 1.5

b. −0.5

c. −2.0

6.21 Using what we know about the population of GRE scores from Exercise 6.20, convert the same *z* scores to raw scores using symbolic notation and the formula.

a. 1.5

b. −0.5

c. −2.0

6.22 A study of Consideration of Future Consequences (CFC) found a mean score of 3.51, with a standard deviation of 0.61, for the 664 students in the sample (Petrocelli, 2003). For the sake of this exercise, let's assume that this particular sample comprises the entire population of interest.

a. If your CFC score is 4.2, what is your *z* score? Use symbolic notation and the formula. Explain why this answer makes sense.

b. If your CFC score is 3.0, what is your *z* score? Use symbolic notation and the formula. Explain why this answer makes sense.

c. If your *z* score is 0, what is your CFC score? Explain.

6.23 Compare the following "apples and oranges": a score of 45 when the population mean is 51 and the standard deviation is 4 and a score of 732 when the population mean is 765 and the standard deviation is 23.

a. Convert these scores to standardized scores.

b. Using the standardized scores, what can you say about how these two scores compare to each other?

6.24 Compare the following scores:

a. A score of 811 when $\mu = 800$ and $\sigma = 29$ against a score of 4524 when $\mu = 3127$ and $\sigma = 951$

b. A score of 17 when $\mu = 30$ and $\sigma = 12$ against a score of 67 when $\mu = 88$ and $\sigma = 16$

6.25 Answer each of the following questions, assuming a normal distribution:

a. What percentage of scores fall below the mean?

b. What percentage of scores fall between 1 standard deviation below the mean and 2 standard deviations above the mean?

c. What percentage of scores lies beyond 2 standard deviations away from the mean (on both sides)?

d. What percentage of scores are between the mean and 2 standard deviations above the mean?

e. What percentage of scores falls under the normal curve?

6.26 Compute the standard error (σ_M) for each of the following, assuming the population has a mean of 100 and standard deviation of 20:

a. Samples of size 45

b. Samples of size 100

c. Samples of size 4500

6.27 A parent population has a mean of 55 and a standard deviation of 8. Compute μ_M and σ_M for each of the following samples:

a. $N = 30$

b. $N = 300$

c. $N = 3000$

6.28 Compute *z* statistics for each of the following, assuming the population has a mean of 100 and a standard deviation of 20:

a. A mean of 101 is observed based on a sample of 43 scores.

b. A mean of 96 is observed based on a sample of 60 scores.

c. A mean of 100 is observed based on a sample of 29 scores.

Applying the Concepts

6.29 We asked 150 students (in our statistics classes) how long, in minutes, they typically spent getting ready for a date. The scores range from 1 minute to 120 minutes, and the mean is 51.52 minutes. Here are the data for 40 of those students:

```
30  90  60  60   5  90   30  40  45  60
60  30  90  60  25  10   90  20  15  60
60  75  45  60  30  75   15  30  45   1
20  25  45  60  90  10  105  90  30  60
```

a. Construct a histogram for the 10 scores in the first row.

b. Construct a histogram for all 40 of these scores.

c. What happened to the shape of the distribution as you increased the number of scores from 10 to 40? What do you think would happen if the data for all 150 students were included? What if we included 10,000 scores? Explain this phenomenon.

d. Are these distributions of scores or distributions of means? Explain.

e. The data here are self-reported. That is, our students wrote down how many minutes they believe that they typically take to get ready for a date. This accounts for the fact that the data include many "pretty" numbers, such as 30, 60, or 90 minutes. What might have been a better way to operationalize this variable?

f. Do these data suggest any hypotheses that you might like to study? List at least one.

6.30 The verbal subtest of the GRE has a population mean of 500 and a population standard deviation of 100 by design (the quantitative subtest has the same mean and standard deviation).

a. Use symbolic notation to state the mean and standard deviation of the GRE verbal test.

b. Convert a GRE score of 700 to a *z* score *without* using a formula.

c. Convert a GRE score of 550 to a *z* score *without* using a formula.

d. Convert a GRE score of 400 to a *z* score *without* using a formula.

6.31 A sample of 150 statistics students reported the typical number of hours that they sleep on a weeknight. The mean number of hours was 6.65, and the standard deviation was 1.24. (For this exercise, treat this sample as the entire population of interest.)

a. What is *always* the mean of the *z* distribution?

b. Using the sleep data, demonstrate that your answer to part (a) is the mean of the *z* distribution. (*Hint:* Calculate the *z* score for a student who is exactly at the mean.)

c. What is *always* the standard deviation of the *z* distribution?

d. Using the sleep data, demonstrate that your answer to part (c) is the standard deviation of the *z* distribution. (*Hint:* Calculate the *z* score for a student who is exactly 1 standard deviation above or below the mean.)

e. How many hours of sleep do you typically get on a weeknight? What would your *z* score be compared with this population?

• **6.32** A sample of 148 of our statistics students rated their level of admiration for Hillary Rodham Clinton on a scale of 1 to 7. The mean rating was 4.06, and the standard deviation was 1.70. (For this exercise, treat this sample as the entire population of interest.)

a. Use these data to demonstrate that the mean of the *z* distribution is always 0.

b. Use these data to demonstrate that the standard deviation of the *z* distribution is always 1.

c. Calculate the *z* score for a student who rated his admiration of Hillary Rodham Clinton as 6.1.

d. A student had a *z* score of −0.55. What rating did she give for her admiration of Hillary Rodham Clinton?

6.33 We have already discussed summary parameters for CFC scores for the population of participants in a study by Petrocelli (2003). The mean CFC score was 3.51, with a standard deviation of 0.61. (Remember that even though this was a sample, we treated the sample of 664 participants as the entire population.) Imagine that you randomly selected 40 people from this population and had them watch a series of videos on financial planning after graduation. The mean CFC score after watching the video was 3.62. We want to know whether watching these videos might change CFC scores in the population.

a. Why would it not make sense to compare this sample with the distribution of scores? Be sure to discuss the spread of distributions in your answer.

b. Using symbolic notation and formulas, what are the appropriate measures of central tendency and variability for the distribution from which this sample comes?

c. Using symbolic notation and the formula, what is the *z* statistic for this sample mean?

d. Roughly, to what percentile does that *z* statistic correspond?

6.34 A CFC study found a mean CFC score of 3.51, with a standard deviation of 0.61, for the 664 students in the sample (Petrocelli, 2003).

   a. Imagine that your *z* score on the CFC score is −1.2. What is your raw score? Use symbolic notation and the formula. Explain why this answer makes sense.

   b. Imagine that your *z* score on the CFC score is 0.66. What is your raw score? Use symbolic notation and the formula. Explain why this answer makes sense.

6.35 For each of the following variables, would the distribution of scores likely approximate a normal curve? Explain your answer.

   a. Number of movies that college students watch in a year

   b. Number of full-page advertisements in magazines

   c. Human birth weight in Canada

6.36 Georgiou and colleagues (1997) reported that college students had healthier eating habits, on average, than did those who were neither college students nor college graduates. The 412 students in the study ate breakfast a mean of 4.1 times per week with a standard deviation of 2.4. For this exercise, imagine that this is the entire population of interest; thus, these numbers can be treated as parameters.

   a. Roughly, what is the percentile for a student who eats breakfast four times per week?

   b. Roughly, what is the percentile for a student who eats breakfast six times per week?

   c. Roughly, what is the percentile for a student who eats breakfast twice a week?

6.37 A common quandary faces sports fans who live in the same city but avidly follow different sports. How does one determine whose team did better with respect to its league division? In 2004, the Boston Red Sox won the World Series; just months later, their local football counterparts, the New England Patriots, won the Super Bowl. In 2005, both teams made the play-offs but lost early on. Which team was better in 2005? The question, then, is: Were the Red Sox better, as compared to other teams in the American League of Major League Baseball, than the Patriots, as compared to the other teams in the American Football Conference of the National Football League? Some of us could debate it for hours, but it's better to examine some statistics. Let's operationalize performance over the season as the number of wins during regular season play.

   a. In 2005, the mean number of wins for baseball teams in the American League was 81.71, with a standard deviation of 13.07. Because all teams were included, these are population parameters.

The Red Sox won 95 games. What is their *z* score?

   b. In 2005, the mean number of wins for football teams in the American Football Conference was 8.13, with a standard deviation of 3.70. The Patriots won 10 games. What is their *z* score?

   c. Which team did better, according to these data?

   d. How many games would the team with the lower *z* score have had to win to beat the team with the higher *z* score?

   e. List at least one other way we could have operationalized the outcome variable (i.e., team performance).

6.38 Our statistics students, as noted in Exercise 6.32, were asked to rate their admiration of Hillary Rodham Clinton on a scale of 1 to 7. They also were asked to rate their admiration of Jennifer Lopez and Venus Williams on a scale of 1 to 7. As noted earlier, the mean rating of Clinton was 4.06 with a standard deviation of 1.70. The mean rating of Lopez was 3.72 with a standard deviation of 1.90. The mean rating of Williams was 4.58 with a standard deviation of 1.46. One of our students rated her admiration of Clinton and Williams at 5 and her admiration of Lopez at 4.

   a. What is her *z* score for her admiration rating of Clinton?

   b. What is her *z* score for her admiration rating of Williams?

   c. What is her *z* score for her admiration rating of Lopez?

   d. Compared to the other statistics students in our sample, which celebrity does this student most admire? (We can tell by her raw scores that she prefers Clinton and Williams to Lopez, but when we take into account the general perception of these celebrities, how does this student feel about them?)

   e. How do *z* scores allow us to make comparisons that we cannot make with raw scores? That is, describe the benefits of standardization.

6.39 Let's look at baseball and football again, but this time we'll look at data for all of the teams in Major League Baseball (MLB) and the National Football League (NFL), respectively.

   a. In 2005, the mean number of wins for MLB teams was 81.00, with a standard deviation of 10.83. The perennial underdogs, the Chicago Cubs, had a *z* score of −0.18. How many games did they win?

   b. In 2005, the mean number of wins for all NFL teams was 8.00, with a standard deviation of 3.39. The New Orleans Saints had a *z* score of −1.475. How many games did they win?

   c. The Pittsburgh Steelers were just below the 84th percentile in terms of NFL wins. How many games did they win? Explain how you obtained your answer.

d. Explain how you can examine your answers in parts (a), (b), and (c) to determine if the numbers make sense.

6.40 Researchers have reported that the projected life expectancy for people diagnosed with human immunodeficiency virus (HIV) and receiving antiretroviral therapy (ART) is 24.2 years (Schackman et al, 2006). Imagine that the researchers determined this by following 250 people with HIV who were receiving ART and calculating the mean. (The 24.2 is actually a projected number rather than a mean for a sample.)

a. What is the variable of interest?

b. What is the population?

c. What is the sample?

d. For the population, describe what the distribution of *scores* would be.

e. For the population, describe what the distribution of *means* would be.

f. If the distribution of the population were skewed, would the distribution of scores likely be skewed or approximately normal? Explain your answer.

g. Would the distribution of means be skewed or approximately normal? Explain your answer.

6.41 The revised version of the Minnesota Multiphasic Personality Inventory (MMPI-2) is the most frequently administered self-report personality measure. Test-takers respond to more than 500 true/false statements, and their responses are scored, typically by a computer, on a number of scales (e.g., hypochondriasis, depression, psychopathic deviation). Respondents receive a *T* score on each scale that can be compared to norms. (It is important to note that *T* scores are different from the *t* statistic we will learn about in a few chapters; you're likely to encounter *T* scores if you take psychology classes, and it's good to be aware that they're different from the *t* statistic.) *T* scores are another way to standardize scores so that percentiles and cutoffs can be determined. The mean *T* score is always 50, and the standard deviation is always 10. Imagine that you administer the MMPI-2 to 95 respondents who have recently lost a parent; you wonder whether their scores on the depression scale will be, on average, higher than the norms. You find a mean score on the depression scale of 55 in your sample.

a. Using symbolic notation, report the mean and standard deviation of the population.

b. Using symbolic notation and formulas (where appropriate), report the mean and standard error for the distribution of means to which your sample will be compared.

c. In your own words, explain why it makes sense that the standard error is smaller than the standard deviation.

6.42 You may need to find an apartment to rent upon graduation. The Internet is a valuable source of data to aid you in your search. From neighborhood safety to available transportation to housing costs, recent data can steer you in the right direction. On a Web site, San Mateo County in California published extensive descriptive statistics from its 1998 Quality of Life Survey. The county reported that the mean house payment (mortgage or rent) was $1225.15, with a standard deviation of $777.50. It also reported that the mean cost of an apartment rental, rather than a house rental or a mortgage, was $868.86. For this exercise, treat the overall mean housing payment as a parameter, and treat the mean apartment rental cost as a statistic based on a sample of 100.

a. Using symbolic notation and formulas (where appropriate), determine the mean and the standard error for the distribution of means for the overall housing payment data.

b. Using symbolic notation and the formula, calculate the z statistic for the cost of an apartment rental.

c. Why is it likely that the z statistic is so large? (*Hint:* Is this distribution likely to be normal? Explain.)

d. Why is it permissible to use the normal curve percentages associated with the z distribution even though the data are not likely normally distributed?

6.43 The GSS is a survey of approximately 2000 adults conducted each year since 1972, for a total of more than 38,000 people. During several years of the GSS, participants were asked how many close friends they have. The mean for this variable is 7.44 friends, with a standard deviation of 10.98. The median is 5.00 and the mode is 4.00.

a. Are these data for a distribution of scores or a distribution of means? Explain.

b. What do the mean and standard deviation suggest about the shape of the distribution? (*Hint:* Compare the sizes of the mean and the standard deviation.)

c. What do the three measures of central tendency suggest about the shape of the distribution?

d. Let's say that these data represent the entire population. Pretend that you randomly selected a person from this population and asked how many close friends she or he had. Would you compare this person to a distribution of scores or a distribution of means? Explain your answer.

e. Now pretend that you randomly selected a sample of 80 people from this population. Would you compare this sample to a distribution of scores or a distribution of means? Explain your answer.

f. Using symbolic notation, calculate the mean and standard error of the distribution of means.

g. What is the likely shape of the distribution of means? Explain your answer.

6.44 Refer to Exercise 6.43. Again, pretend that the GSS sample is the entire population of interest.

a. Imagine that you randomly selected one person from this population who reported that he had 18 close friends. Would you compare his score to a distribution of scores or a distribution of means? Explain your answer.

b. What is his *z* score? Based on this *z* score, what is his approximate percentile?

c. Does it make sense to calculate a percentile for this person? Explain your answer. (*Hint:* Consider the shape of the distribution.)

6.45 Refer to Exercise 6.43. Again, pretend that the GSS sample is the entire population of interest.

a. Imagine that you randomly selected 80 people from this population who had a mean of 8.7. Would you compare this sample mean to a distribution of scores or a distribution of means? Explain your answer.

b. What is the *z* statistic for this mean? Based on this *z* statistic, what is the approximate percentile for this sample?

c. Does it make sense to calculate a percentile for this sample? Explain your answer. (*Hint:* Consider the shape of the distribution.)

6.46 Refer to Exercises 6.43 through 6.45. Let's say that you decide to use the GSS data to test whether people who live in rural areas have a different mean number of friends than does the overall GSS sample. Again, treat the overall GSS sample as the entire population of interest. Let's say that you select 40 people living in rural areas and find that they have an average of 3.9 friends.

a. What is the independent variable in this study? Is this variable nominal, ordinal, or scale?

b. What is the dependent variable in this study? Is this variable nominal, ordinal, or scale?

c. Would we compare our data to a distribution of scores or a distribution of means? Explain your answer.

d. Using symbolic notation and formulas, calculate the mean and standard error for the distribution of means.

e. Using symbolic notation and the formula, calculate the *z* statistic for this sample.

f. What is the approximate percentile for this sample?

Terms

Formulas

$$z = \frac{(X - \mu)}{\sigma} \quad \text{(p. 124)}$$

$$X = z(\sigma) + \mu \quad \text{(p. 127)}$$

$$\sigma_M = \frac{\sigma}{\sqrt{N}} \quad \text{(p. 136)}$$

$$z = \frac{(M - \mu_M)}{\sigma_M} \quad \text{(p. 137)}$$

Symbols

Hypothesis Testing with z Tests

BEFORE YOU GO ON

■ You should understand how to calculate a z statistic for a distribution of scores and for a distribution of means (Chapter 6).

■ You should understand that the z distribution allows us to determine the percentage of scores (or means) that fall below a particular z statistic (Chapter 6).

Copyright photograph A.C. Barrington Brown. Reproduced by permission of the Fisher Memorial Trust.

Experimental Design. R.A. Fisher was inspired by the "lady drinking tea" who claimed that she could distinguish the taste of a cup of tea that had been poured tea first versus one that had been poured milk first. His book, *The Design of Experiments*, demonstrated how statistics became meaningful within the context of an experimental design.

One of the turning points in the history of statistics occurred in the early 1920s. Statistician R. A. Fisher drew a cup of tea from a large urn and offered it to Dr. B. Muriel Bristol. She politely declined because she preferred the taste of tea when the milk had been poured into the cup first.

"Nonsense. Surely it makes no difference," Fisher replied.

Dr. Bristol insisted that she could tell the difference, and William Roach (who would later marry Bristol) suggested, "Let's test her." This was one of the first times that experimental design had been so directly wedded to inferential statistics.

Roach prepared a taste test by pouring cups of tea, some with tea first and others with milk first. Fisher's mind was suddenly awhirl with statistical concerns such as how many cups should be used, their order of presentation, and how to control chance variations in temperature or sweetness. The case of the lady drinking tea became the opening example for the first textbook linking statistics with experimental design, Fisher's 1935 classic *The Design of Experiments*.

This tea-first versus milk-first experiment demonstrated how probability could be used to test a hypothesis. For example, we know how many times Dr. Bristol should identify the milk-first cup of tea simply by chance—50%. Given that standard, we can establish a probability, somewhere above 50%, beyond which we can declare that Bristol's tea-tasting abilities are significantly different from what we would expect by chance—that is, whether she really could tell the difference between a milk-first cup of tea and a tea-first cup of tea. The important idea here is that probability could be used to test a hypothesis. The statistical results of this informal experiment were never recorded, but Roach reportedly said, "Miss Bristol divined correctly more than enough of those cups into which tea had been poured first to prove her case" (Box, 1978, p. 134).

This chapter introduces the basic logic and steps to conduct inferential statistics, or hypothesis testing. Hypothesis testing is a way of thinking that provides evidence either to support our commonsense observations or to debunk them. Hypothesis testing in the behavioral sciences tries to ask "yes or no" questions so that we can test our so-called common sense empirically. To apply hypothesis testing to problems such as the proper preparation of tea, we focus our discussion on the simplest hypothesis test, the *z* test. A **z test** *is a hypothesis test in which we compare data from one sample to a population for which we know the mean and standard deviation.* We learn how the *z* distribution and the *z* test make fair comparisons possible through standardization. Specifically, we learn the following:

1. How to use a *z* table
2. How to implement the basic steps of hypothesis testing
3. How to conduct a *z* test to compare a single sample to a known population

The *z* Table

In Chapter 6, we learned that the *z* distribution is mathematically defined, and we can know the specific percentage below any given point on the *z* distribution. However, percentages that accompanied the *z* statistic were only introduced for whole number *z* statistics. For example, we learned that 34% of the distribution falls between the mean and 1 standard deviation of the mean (above or below). In this section, we learn how to use the *z* table to be more exact and to calculate percentages for any *z* statistic, even if it's not a whole number. This is yet another tool that will allow us to conduct hypothesis testing.

■ A **z test** is a hypothesis test in which we compare data from one sample to a population for which we know the mean and the standard deviation.

Hypothesis testing allows us to draw conclusions about the data we have collected to test a hypothesis, such as whether or not Dr. Bristol could accurately detect whether tea or milk was poured into a cup first. Understanding its logic and when it can be used provides a foundation for the more commonly used hypothesis tests that you will learn about in later chapters. This chapter focuses on the z test, the simplest of the hypothesis tests. With the z test, as with all the other hypothesis tests, there are three different ways to identify the same point beneath the normal curve: raw score, z score, and percentile ranking. The z table is the tool that allows us to transition from one to another of these ways to identify a point, and it is a fundamental tool of hypothesis testing.

Raw Scores, z Scores, and Percentages

The z table is the key to standardization. It allows us to translate the standardized z distribution into percentages and individual z scores into percentile ranks. The ability to convert individual z scores to percentile ranks is key to one of the steps of hypothesis testing, and it builds on what we have already learned about normal distributions. Specifically, we learned that (1) about 68% of scores fall within one z score of the mean, (2) about 96% of scores fall within two z scores of the mean, and (3) nearly all scores fall within three z scores of the mean. These guidelines are useful, but the table of z scores and percentages is more specific. The z table is printed in its entirety in Appendix B, but an excerpt from it is reproduced in Table 7-1 for your convenience.

We can determine the percentage associated with a given z statistic by following two steps.

> Step 1: Convert a raw score into a z score.
>
> Step 2: Look up a given z score on the z table to find the percentage of scores *between the mean and that z score.*

TABLE 7-1. Excerpt from the z Table

The z table provides the percentage of scores between the mean and a given z value. The full table includes positive z statistics from 0.00 to 4.50. The negative z statistics are not included because all we have to do is change the sign from positive to negative. The percentage between the mean and a positive z statistic is identical to the percentage between the mean and the negative version of that z statistic. Remember, the normal curve is symmetric: one side always mirrors the other.

z	% Between Mean and z
.	.
.	.
.	.
0.97	33.40
0.98	33.65
0.99	33.89
1.00	34.13
1.01	34.38
1.02	34.61
.	.
.	.
.	.

FIGURE 7-1
The Standardized *z* Distribution

We can use a *z* table to determine the percentages below and above a particular *z* score. For example, 34% of scores fall between the mean and a *z* score of 1.

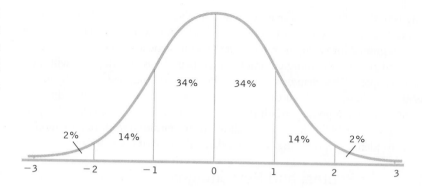

▶ **MASTERING THE CONCEPT**

7-1: We can use the *z* table to look up the percentage of scores between the mean of the distribution and a given *z* statistic.

Note that the *z* scores in a *z* table are all positive. Because the normal curve is symmetric, calculating the percentage between the mean and a given positive *z* score is identical to calculating the percentage between the mean and the negative version of that *z* score (see Figure 7-1). So including the negative *z* scores would be redundant.

Let's learn how to use the *z* table. To do so, we'll consider a study about the effect of height on peer relations and social adjustment among adolescents in grades 6 through 12 (Sandberg, Bukowski, Fung, & Noll, 2004). Researchers conducted the study to see whether very short children and adolescents tended to have poorer psychological adjustment than taller children and, therefore, should be treated with growth hormone.

To begin, researchers categorized children into one of three groups—short, average, or tall. Researchers decided to classify children as short if they were in the bottom 5% of heights, according to published norms for a given age and gender (Sandberg et al, 2004). They were classified as tall if they were in the top 5%. They were classified as average height if they were in the middle 90%. Growth charts developed by the Centers for Disease Control (CDC; National Center for Health Statistics, 2000) indicated that for 15-year-old boys the mean height was approximately 67.00 inches with a standard deviation of 3.19. For 15-year-old girls, the mean height was approximately 63.80 inches with a standard deviation of 2.66. Let's consider two fictional examples related to the CDC height data, one for a score above the mean and then one for a score below the mean.

EXAMPLE 7.1

Jessica, a 15-year-old girl in one of the recruited classes, is 66.41 inches tall (just over 5 feet, 6 inches).

STEP 1. Convert Jessica's raw score to a *z* score (as we learned in Chapter 6).

To convert the raw score to a *z* score, we use the mean ($\mu = 63.80$) and standard deviation ($\sigma = 2.66$) for the heights of girls:

$$z = \frac{(M - \mu)}{\sigma} = \frac{(66.41 - 63.80)}{2.66} = 0.98$$

STEP 2. Look up 0.98 on the *z* table to find the associated percentage between the mean and Jessica's *z* score.

Once we know that the associated percentage is 33.65%, we can determine a number of percentages related to her *z* score. Here are three.

1. *Jessica's percentile rank, the percentage of scores below her score:* We add the percentage between the mean and the positive z score to 50%, which is the percentage of scores below the mean (50% of scores are on each side of the mean).

Jessica's percentile is 50% + 33.65% = 83.65%

Figure 7-2 shows this visually. As with the calculation of z scores, we can run a quick mental check of the likely accuracy of our answer. We're interested in calculating the percentile of a *positive* z score. Because it is above the mean, we know that the answer must be higher than 50%. And it is. If it were not, we would know to work through our calculations again to catch our error.

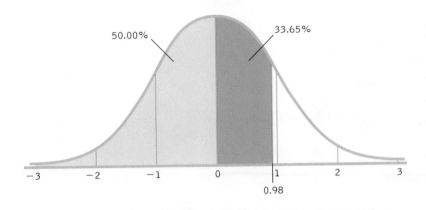

FIGURE 7-2

Calculating the Percentile for a Positive z Score

Drawing curves helps us to determine the appropriate percentage. For a positive z score, we add 50% to the percentage between the mean and that z score to get the total percentage below that z score, the percentile. Here, we add the 50% below the mean to the 33.65% between the mean and a z score of 0.98 to calculate the percentile, 83.65%.

2. *The percentage of scores above Jessica's score:* We subtract the percentage between the mean and the positive z score from 50%, which is the full percentage of scores above the mean:

50% − 33.65% = 16.35%

So 16.35% of 15-year-old girls' heights fall above Jessica's height. Figure 7-3 shows this visually. Here, it makes sense that the percentage would be smaller than 50%; because the z score is positive, we could not have more than 50% above it. An alternative approach may strike you as a simpler way to compute the percentage of scores above Jessica's score: subtract Jessica's percentile rank of 83.35% from 100%. This gives you the same 16.35%. Alternatively, you could look under the column in the z table labeled "in the tail."

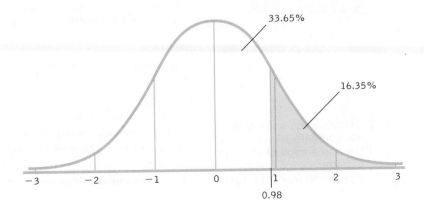

FIGURE 7-3

Calculating the Percentage Above a Positive z Score

For a positive z score, we subtract the percentage between the mean and that z score from 50% (the total percentage above the mean) to get the percentage above that z score. Here, we subtract the 33.65% between the mean and the z score of 0.98 from 50%, which yields 16.35%.

3. *The scores at least as extreme as Jessica's z score, in both directions:* When we begin hypothesis testing, it will be useful to know the percentage of scores that are at least as extreme as a given *z* score. In this case, 16.35% of heights are extreme enough to have *z* scores above Jessica's *z* score of 0.98. But remember that the curve is symmetric. This means that another 16.35% of the heights are extreme enough to be below a *z* score of −0.98. So we can double 16.35% to find the total percentage of heights that are as far as or farther from the mean than is Jessica's height:

$$16.35\% + 16.35\% = 32.70\%$$

So 32.7% of heights are at least as extreme as Jessica's height in either direction. Figure 7-4 shows this visually.

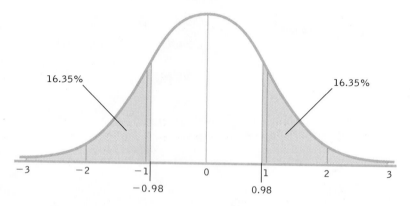

FIGURE 7-4
Calculating the Percentage at Least as Extreme as Our *z* Score

For a positive *z* score, we double the percentage above that *z* score to get the percentage of scores that are at least as extreme—that is, at least as far from the mean—as our *z* score is. Here, we double 16.35% to calculate the percentage at least this extreme: 32.70%.

What group would Jessica fall in? Because 16.35% of 15-year-old girls are taller than Jessica, she is not in the top 5%. So she would be classified as of average height according to the researchers' definition of *average.*

EXAMPLE 7.2

Now let's repeat this process for a score below the mean. Manuel, a 15-year-old boy in one of the recruited classes, is 61.20 inches tall (about 5 feet, 1 inch). Keeping in mind that the height norms for boys are different from the height norms for girls, we want to know if Manuel can be classified as short (using the researchers' criteria of 5%, 90%, and 5%). Remember, for boys the mean height is 67.00 inches, and the standard deviation for height is 3.19 inches.

STEP 1. Convert Manuel's raw score to a z score:

To convert the raw score to a *z* score, we use the mean ($\mu = 67.00$) and standard deviation ($\sigma = 3.19$) for the height of boys.

$$z = \frac{(X - \mu)}{\sigma} = \frac{(61.20 - 67.00)}{3.19} = -1.82$$

STEP 2. Calculate the percentile, the percentage above, and the percentage at least as extreme for the negative z score for Manuel's height.

We need to use the full table in Appendix B. The *z* table includes only positive *z* scores, so we look up 1.82 and find 46.56% between the mean score and the *z* score. Of course, percentages are always positive, so don't add a negative sign here!

1. *Manuel's percentile score, the percentage of scores below his score:* For a negative z score, we subtract the percentage between the mean and the z score from 50%, the total percentage below the mean:

Manuel's percentile is 50% − 46.56% = 3.44% (Figure 7-5)

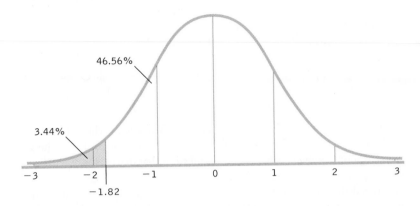

FIGURE 7-5
Calculating the Percentile for a Negative z Score

As with positive z scores, drawing curves helps us to determine the appropriate percentage for negative z scores. For a negative z score, we subtract the percentage between the mean and that z score from 50% (the percentage below the mean) to get the percentage below that negative z score, the percentile. Here we subtract the 46.56% between the mean and the z score of −1.82 from 50%, which yields 3.44%.

2. *The percentage of scores above Manuel's score:* We add the percentage between the mean and the negative z score to 50%, the percentage above the mean:

50% + 46.56% = 96.56%

So 96.56% of 15-year-old boys' heights fall above Manuel's height (Figure 7-6).

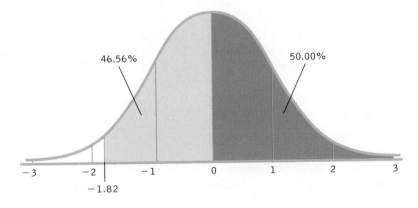

FIGURE 7-6
Calculating the Percentage Above a Negative z Score

For a negative z score, we add the percentage between the mean and that z score to 50% (the percentage above the mean) to get the percentage above that z score. Here we add the 46.56% between the mean and the z score of −1.82 to the 50% above the mean, which yields 96.56%.

3. *The scores at least as extreme as Manuel's z score, in both directions:* In this case, 3.44% of 15-year-old boys have heights that are extreme enough to have z scores below −1.82. And because the curve is symmetric, another 3.44% of heights are extreme enough to be above a z score of 1.82. So we can double 3.44% to find the total percentage of heights that are as far as or farther from the mean than is Manuel's height:

3.44% + 3.44% = 6.88%

So 6.88% of heights are at least as extreme as Manuel's in either direction (Figure 7-7).

FIGURE 7-7

Calculating the Percentage at Least as Extreme as Our *z* Score

FIGURE 7-7

Calculating the Percentage at Least as Extreme as Our *z* Score

With a negative *z* score, we double the percentage below that *z* score to get the percentage of scores that are at least as extreme—that is, at least as far from the mean—as our *z* score is. Here, we double 3.44% to calculate the percentage at least this extreme: 6.88%.

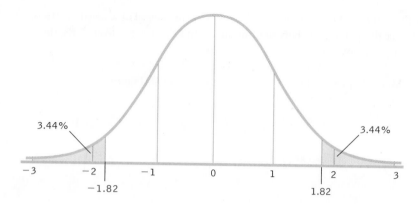

In what group would the researchers classify Manuel? Manuel has a percentile rank of 3.44%. He is in the lowest 5% for heights for boys of his age, so he would be classified as short. Now we can get to the question that drives this research. Does Manuel's short stature doom him to a life of few friends and poor social adjustment? Researchers compared the means of the three groups—short, average, and tall—on several measures of peer relations and social adjustment, but they did not find evidence of psychological differences among these three groups (Sandberg et al, 2004).

EXAMPLE 7.3

Here is an example demonstrating that we can seamlessly shift among raw scores, *z* scores, and percentile ranks. Many high school students in North America take the Scholastic Aptitude Test (SAT), a common university admissions requirement. The parameters for the SAT are meant to be a mean of 500 and a standard deviation of 100. So let's imagine that Jo, a high school student hoping to attend college, took the SAT and scored at the 63rd percentile. What was her raw score? First, we draw a curve, as in Figure 7-8. We add a line at the point below which approximately 63% of scores fall. We know that this score is above the mean because 50% of scores fall below the mean, and 63% is larger than 50%.

Using the drawing as a guideline, we see that we have to calculate the percentage between the mean and the *z* score of interest. We calculate this by subtracting the 50% below the mean from Jo's score, 63%:

$$63\% - 50\% = 13\%$$

We look up the closest percentage to 13% in the *z* table (which is 12.93%) and find an associated *z* score of 0.33. This is above the mean, so we do not need to label

FIGURE 7-8

Calculating a Score from a Percentile

We can convert a percentile to a raw score by calculating the percentage between the mean and the *z* score, and looking up that percentage on the *z* table to find the associated *z* score. We would then convert the *z* score to a raw score using the formula. Here, we look up 13.00% on our *z* table (12.93% is the closest percentage) and find a *z* score of 0.33, which we can then convert to a raw score.

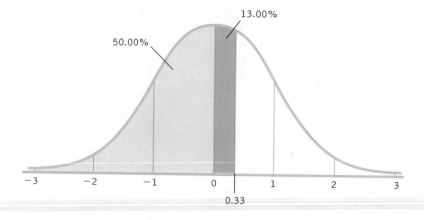

it with a negative sign. We can then convert the z score to a raw score using the formula that we learned in Chapter 6:

$$X = z(\sigma) + \mu = 0.33(100) + 500 = 533$$

Jo, whose SAT score was at the 63rd percentile, had a raw score of 533.

Let's do our quick mental check of the answer: this score is above the mean, just as we would expect given a percentage above 50%.

The *z* Table and Distributions of Means

In hypothesis testing, we use means rather than scores, because we would always study a sample rather than an individual. Fortunately, the z table can also be used to determine percentages and z statistics for distributions of means calculated from many people. The process is identical to that described for distributions of scores, but with the additional step that we first have to calculate the mean and the standard error for the distribution of means.

EXAMPLE 7.4

Many graduate programs select students based, in part, on their Graduate Record Exam (GRE) scores. For example, about half of the doctoral programs and one-third of the master's programs in psychology in the United States require that students take the GRE psychology test. Most of these subject tests have been used for many years, so we can know the actual population mean and population standard deviation; for example, the mean was 554 and the standard deviation was 99 for the years 1995 to 1998 (Matlin & Kalat, 2001).

Now, imagine that we want to figure out statistically how well psychology students at our institution perform on the GRE psychology test compared to all psychology students who have taken this test (assume that the mean and standard deviation have not changed greatly since 1998). We record the psychology test scores of a representative sample, 90 graduating seniors in our Psychology Department, and find that the mean score is 568. We want to know how much better (or worse) students in our department are doing in comparison to the mean score of the population. z statistics make that comparison possible.

The distribution of means has the same mean as the distribution of scores for the population (554), but the spread is smaller and must be calculated. Before we calculate the z statistic, let's use proper symbolic notation to indicate the mean and the standard error of this distribution of means:

$$\mu_M = \mu = 554$$

$$\sigma_M = \frac{\sigma}{\sqrt{N}} = \frac{99}{\sqrt{90}} = 10.436$$

At this point, we have all the information we need to calculate the percentage using the two steps we learned earlier.

STEP 1. Convert to a *z* statistic using the mean and standard error that we just calculated.

$$z = \frac{(M - \mu_M)}{\sigma_M} = \frac{(568 - 554)}{10.436} = 1.34$$

STEP 2. Determine the percentage below this *z* statistic.

To do this, we draw a curve that includes the mean of the *z* distribution, 0, and this *z* statistic, 1.34 (Figure 7-9). We shade the area in which we are interested, everything below 1.34. Then we look up the percentage between the mean and the *z* statistic of 1.34. The *z* table indicates that this percentage is 40.99, which we write in the section of the curve between the mean and 1.34. We write 50% in the half of the curve below the mean. We add 40.99% to the 50% below the mean to get the percentile rank, 90.99%. (Subtracting from 100%, only 9.01% of mean scores would be higher than our mean if they come from this population.) Based on this percentage, the mean GRE psychology test score of our sample is quite high. But it would take hypothesis testing to actually draw a conclusion about whether students at this school are doing better than the national average.

FIGURE 7-9
Percentile for the Mean of a Sample

We can use the *z* table with sample means, just as we can use it with sample scores. The only difference is that we must use the mean and the standard error of the distribution of means rather than of the distribution of the population of scores. Here, our *z* score of 1.34 is associated with a percentage of 40.99% between the mean and the *z* score. Added to the 50% below the mean, the percentile is 50% + 40.99% = 90.99%.

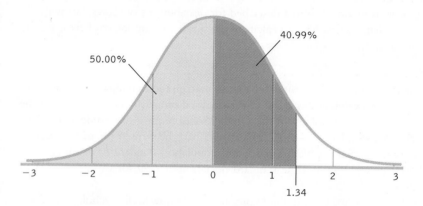

In the next section, we learn the assumptions that we must make when we conduct hypothesis testing. We then learn the six steps of hypothesis testing using the *z* distribution. We learn the steps to reject, or fail to reject, the null hypothesis (in our previous example, that the students in this department do *not* receive different scores on average than do students in the entire population). Only then can we draw a conclusion about what the data are saying. In the last section, we use a similar example to demonstrate a *z* test.

CHECK YOUR LEARNING

Reviewing the Concepts

> Raw scores, *z* scores, and percentile rankings are three ways to describe the same score within a normal distribution.

> If we know the mean and the standard deviation of a population, we can convert a raw score to a *z* score and then use the *z* table to determine percentages below, above, or at least as extreme as this *z* score.

> We can use the *z* table in reverse as well, taking a percentage and converting it into a *z* score and then a raw score.

> These same conversions can be conducted on a sample mean instead of a score. The procedures are identical, but we must use the mean and the standard error of the distribution of means, instead of the mean and the standard deviation of the distribution of scores.

Clarifying the Concepts

7-1 What information do we need to know about a population of interest in order to use the *z* table?

7-2 How do *z* scores relate to raw scores and percentile ranks?

| Calculating the Statistics | 7-3 | If the percentage of scores between a z score of 1.37 and the mean is 41.47%, what percentage of scores lies between −1.37 and the mean? |
| | 7-4 | If 12.93% of scores fall between the mean and a z score of 0.33, what percentage of scores falls below this z score? |

| Applying the Concepts | 7-5 | Every year, the Educational Testing Service (ETS) administers the Major Field Test in Psychology (MFTP) to graduating psychology majors. In 2003, Baylor University wondered how its students compared to the national average. On its Web site, Baylor reported that the mean and the standard deviation of the 18,073 U.S. students who took this exam were 156.8 and 14.6, respectively. Thirty-six students in the Psychology and Neuroscience Department at Baylor took the exam; these students had a mean score of 164.6. |

> a. What is the percentile rank for the sample of students at Baylor? Use symbolic notation and write out your calculations.

> b. What percentage of samples of this size scored higher than the students at Baylor?

Solutions to these Check Your Learning questions can be found in Appendix D.

> c. What can you say about how Baylor University psychology students compared to students across the nation?

The Assumptions and the Steps of Hypothesis Testing

The story of the lady tasting tea used an informal experiment to test a hypothesis. The formal process of hypothesis testing is based on particular assumptions about the data, and statisticians are careful to articulate those assumptions. Statisticians have also discovered when it is relatively safe to violate those assumptions. This next section focuses first on the assumptions connected with hypothesis testing. Then the six steps of formal hypothesis testing are introduced.

The Three Assumptions for Conducting Analyses

Before we introduce the steps of hypothesis testing, it is important to explore the ideal conditions under which hypothesis testing takes place. We call these conditions "assumptions." We all make assumptions in our everyday lives, and when conducting hypothesis testing, statisticians also make assumptions. In statistics, *assumptions are the characteristics that we ideally require the population from which we are sampling to have so that we can make accurate inferences.* So we want to analyze our data using the appropriate statistical test, and we would like to violate as few assumptions as possible. The assumptions introduced here hold for the hypothesis test that we will learn in this chapter, the z test.

In fact, these assumptions also hold for several other hypothesis tests that we'll learn about in the next few chapters—the hypothesis tests, like the z test, that we call parametric tests. *Parametric tests are statistical analyses based on a set of assumptions about the population.* By contrast, *nonparametric tests are statistical analyses that are not based on a set of assumptions about the population.* If we don't meet the assumptions, we have to consider which statistical analyses to use—parametric tests or nonparametric tests. Our goal is to match the appropriate statistical test with the characteristics of our data. To do that, we need to learn the three main assumptions for parametric tests, so we begin with those before outlining the steps of hypothesis testing.

First, we assume that the dependent variable is assessed using a scale measure. This simply means that there is an equal distance between numbers. For example, the difference between 30 and 31 seconds is the same as the difference between 109 and 110 seconds; time is a scale variable. If it's clear that the variable is nominal or ordinal, we should not make this assumption.

■ An **assumption** is a characteristic that we ideally require the population from which we are sampling to have so that we can make accurate inferences.

■ A **parametric test** is an inferential statistical analysis based on a set of assumptions about the population.

■ A **nonparametric test** is an inferential statistical analysis that is not based on a set of assumptions about the population.

Second, we assume that the participants are randomly selected. Ideally, for hypothesis tests to provide accurate results, the participants in the sample must have been selected randomly. Every member of the population of interest must have had an equal chance of being chosen for participation in the study, something that rarely occurs in research. It is more likely that participants are a convenience sample than that participants are randomly selected.

Third, the distribution of the population of interest must be approximately normal. Many distributions are approximately normal, but it is important to remember that there are important exceptions to this guideline (Micceri, 1989). Because hypothesis tests deal with sample means rather than individual scores, as long as the sample size is at least 30 (in most cases, based on the central limit theorem), it is likely that this assumption is met.

Inferential statistics are based on assumptions that aren't always met. However, many parametric hypothesis tests can be conducted even if the assumptions are not met (Table 7-2). Often, parametric inferential statistics are robust against violations of these assumptions. ***Robust hypothesis tests are those that produce fairly accurate results even when the data suggest that the population might not meet some of the assumptions.***

Why bother learning about the assumptions when we know that many hypothesis tests are robust to violations of these assumptions, and so it is often allowable to violate them? These three statistical assumptions represent the ideal conditions of most research. The researcher who is able to meet all three assumptions tends to produce more valid research. *Meeting the assumptions improves the quality of our research, but not meeting the assumptions doesn't necessarily invalidate our research.*

> ▶ **MASTERING THE CONCEPT**
>
> **7-2:** When we calculate a parametric statistic, ideally we have met assumptions regarding the population distribution. For a *z* test, the dependent variable should be on a scale measure, the sample should be randomly selected, and the underlying population should have an approximately normal distribution (or our samples should be at least 30).

TABLE 7-2. The Three Assumptions for Hypothesis Testing

We must be aware of the assumptions for the hypothesis test that we choose, and we must be cautious in choosing to proceed with a hypothesis test even though our data may not meet all of the assumptions. Note that in addition to these three assumptions, for many hypothesis tests, including the *z* test, the independent variable must be nominal.

The Three Assumptions	Breaking the Assumptions
1. Dependent variable is on a scale measure.	Usually OK if the data are not clearly nominal or ordinal.
2. Participants are randomly selected.	OK if we are cautious about generalizing.
3. Population distribution is approximately normal.	OK if the sample includes at least 30 scores.

The Six Steps of Hypothesis Testing

Hypothesis testing can be broken down into six standard steps. There are variations within the six steps based on each specific distribution and its appropriate hypothesis test, but the framework is always the same.

Step 1: Identify the populations, comparison distribution, and assumptions.

The first step of hypothesis testing is to identify the populations to be compared, the comparison distribution, the appropriate test, and its assumptions. The purpose of the first step is to make sure that it is OK to proceed with a particular hypothesis test. When we first approach hypothesis testing, we consider the characteristics of our data to determine the distribution to which we will compare our sample. First, we state the populations represented by the two groups to be compared. Then we identify the comparison distribution (e.g., distribution of means). Finally, we identify the hypothesis test that we would use for that distribution and check the assumptions for that hypothesis test.

Step 2: State the null and research hypotheses.

The second step is to state the null and research hypotheses. It is important to note that both hypotheses are about the populations, rather than the samples. The null hypothesis is usually the "boring" one, positing no change or no difference. The research hypothesis is the "exciting" one, the one positing that, for example, a given intervention will lead to a change or a difference. It is best to state the null and research hypotheses in both words and symbolic notation.

Step 3: Determine the characteristics of the comparison distribution.

The third step is to state the relevant characteristics of the comparison distribution, the distribution based on the null hypothesis. In all cases, in a later step we will compare the data from our sample (or samples) to a comparison distribution based on the null hypothesis to determine how extreme our sample data are. For now, for *z* tests, we will determine the mean and standard error of the comparison distribution. These numbers describe the distribution represented by the null hypothesis. The numbers that we determine in this step will be used in the actual calculations of our test statistic.

Step 4: Determine critical values, or cutoffs.

The fourth step is to determine the critical values, or cutoffs, on the comparison distribution indicating how extreme our data must be, in terms of the test statistic (e.g., z), to reject the null hypothesis. Often called simply *cutoffs,* these numbers are also called **critical values,** the test statistic values beyond which we reject the null hypothesis. In most cases, we determine two cutoffs, one for extreme samples below the mean and one for extreme samples above the mean. Typically, the critical values, or cutoffs, are based on a standard that statisticians have somewhat arbitrarily adopted—the most extreme 5% of the comparison distribution curve: 2.5% on either end. At times, cutoffs are based on a less conservative percentage, such as 10%, or a more conservative percentage, such as 1%. Regardless of the chosen cutoff, the area beyond the cutoff, or critical value, is often referred to as the critical region. Specifically, the **critical region** *refers to the area in the tails of the comparison distribution in which we reject the null hypothesis if our test statistic falls there.*

These percentages are typically written as probabilities; that is, 5% would be written as 0.05. *The probabilities used to determine the critical values, or cutoffs, in hypothesis testing are called **p levels.*** They are often also called *alphas.*

Step 5: Calculate the test statistic.

In the fifth step, we calculate our test statistic. To do this, we have to collect data from our sample if we haven't already. Hypothesis testing requires the calculation of a test statistic to determine whether the data from our sample really add up to a trustworthy scientific finding—that is, whether we can reject our null hypothesis. At this point, we use the information from step 3 to calculate our test statistic, such as a *z* statistic. As we noted earlier, the critical values, or cutoff values, are determined in terms of the test statistic. For example, in a *z* test the critical values are on the *z* distribution, and so the critical values are *z* statistics. Because of this, we can directly compare our test statistic to the critical values to determine if our sample is extreme enough to warrant a rejection of the null hypothesis.

Step 6: Make a decision.

In the final step, we decide whether to reject or fail to reject the null hypothesis. Based on the available evidence, we either reject the null hypothesis if our test statistic is beyond our cutoffs, or we fail to reject the null hypothesis if our test statistic is not beyond our cutoffs.

These six steps of hypothesis testing are summarized in Table 7-3.

■ A **robust** hypothesis test is one that produces fairly accurate results even when the data suggest that the population might not meet some of the assumptions.

■ A **critical value** is a test statistic value beyond which we reject the null hypothesis; often called a *cutoff.*

■ The **critical region** refers to the area in the tails of the distribution in which we reject the null hypothesis if our test statistic falls there.

■ The probability used to determine the critical values, or cutoffs, in hypothesis testing is called a ***p* level**; often called *alpha.*

■ A finding is **statistically significant** if the data differ from what we would expect by chance if there were, in fact, no actual difference.

> **TABLE 7-3.** The Six Steps of Hypothesis Testing
>
> We use the same six basic steps with each type of hypothesis test.
>
> 1. Identify the populations, distribution, and assumptions and then choose the appropriate hypothesis test.
> 2. State the null and research hypotheses in both words and symbolic notation.
> 3. Determine the characteristics of the comparison distribution.
> 4. Determine the critical values, or cutoffs, that indicate the points beyond which we will reject the null hypothesis.
> 5. Calculate the test statistic.
> 6. Decide whether to reject or fail to reject the null hypothesis.

When we are able to reject the null hypothesis, we often refer to our results as "statistically significant." A finding is ***statistically significant*** *if the data differ from what we would expect by chance if there were, in fact, no actual difference.* The word *significant* is another one of those statistical terms with a very particular meaning. The phrase *statistically significant* does not necessarily mean that the finding is important or meaningful. A small difference could be statistically significant without indicating anything important from a practical point of view.

CHECK YOUR LEARNING

Reviewing the Concepts

> When we conduct hypothesis testing, we have to consider the assumptions for that particular test.

> Parametric statistics are those that are based on assumptions about the population distribution; nonparametric statistics have no such assumptions about the population distribution. However, parametric statistics are often robust to violations of the assumptions.

> The three assumptions for a *z* test are that the dependent variable is on a scale measure, the sample is randomly selected, and the underlying population distribution is approximately normal.

> There are six standard steps for hypothesis testing. First, we identify our population, comparison distribution, hypothesis test, and assumptions. Second, we state our null and research hypotheses. Third, we determine the characteristics of the comparison distribution. Fourth, we determine the critical values, or cutoffs, on the comparison distribution. Fifth, we calculate our test statistic. Sixth, we decide whether to reject or fail to reject the null hypothesis.

> The standard practice of statisticians is to consider simple statistics that occur less than 5% of the time based on the null hypothesis as statistically significant, warranting rejection of that null hypothesis; observations that occur more often than 5% of the time do not support this decision, and thus we fail to reject the null hypothesis.

Clarifying the Concepts

7-6 Explain the three assumptions made for most parametric hypothesis tests.

7-7 How do critical values help us to make a decision about the hypothesis?

Calculating the Statistics

7-8 If a researcher always sets the critical region as 8% of the distribution, if the null hypothesis is true, how often will he reject the null hypothesis?

7-9 Rewrite each of these percentages as probabilities, or *p* levels.

   a. 15%

   b. 3%

   c. 5.5%

Applying the Concepts

7-10 For each of the following scenarios, state whether each of the three basic assumptions for parametric hypothesis tests is met. Explain your answers and label the three assumptions (1) through (3).

a. Researchers compared the ability of experienced clinical psychologists versus clinical psychology graduate students to diagnose a patient based on a one-hour interview. For two months, either a psychologist or a graduate student interviewed every outpatient at the local community mental health center who had already received diagnoses based on a number of criteria. The psychologists and graduate students were given a score of correct or incorrect for each diagnosis.

b. Behavioral scientists wondered whether animals raised in captivity would be healthier with diminished human contact. Twenty large cats (e.g., lions, tigers) were randomly selected from all the wild cats living in zoos in North America. Half were assigned to the control group—no change in human interaction. Half were assigned to the experimental group—no humans entered their cages except when the animals were not in them, one-way mirrors were used so that the animals could not see zoo visitors, and so on. The animals received a score for health over one year; points were given for various illnesses; a very few sickly animals had extremely high scores.

Solutions to these Check Your Learning questions can be found in Appendix D.

An Example of the *z* Test

The story of the lady tasting tea is a story about how statisticians use hypothesis testing to understand human behavior. In this next section, we apply what we've learned about hypothesis testing–including the six steps–to a specific example of a *z* test. We should note that *z* tests are rarely used in actual social science research. It's rare that we have one sample and that we know both the mean and the standard deviation of the population.

EXAMPLE 7.5

An individual psychology major can compare her or his knowledge of psychology to that of students nationwide, or a group of psychology majors at one university can compare their knowledge, on average, to students graduating from other colleges and universities. As discussed in Check Your Learning 7-5, the Major Field Test in Psychology (MFTP) allows individual students, as well as entire departments, to compare their scores to national norms.

Baylor University published the data on its 36 students but did not conduct hypothesis testing to determine whether its students' mean score was significantly different from the population mean score. However, researchers did use hypothesis testing

Graduation Psychology majors from different universities compete with one another for places in graduate programs, internships, and jobs. The MFTP provides an indication of how well a given university has prepared its students.

Peter Hvizdak/The Image Workszz

Louie Psihoyos/Corbis

to compare the MFTP scores of graduating psychology majors at Ursuline College in Ohio to those of the entire population (Frazier & Edmonds, 2002). The researchers reported that they used the national mean of 156.5, a bit different from that used by Baylor (probably because it was from an earlier year). They did not indicate the national standard deviation, but let's assume that it was the same as that used by Baylor, 14.6. The 97 students in the Ursuline College sample, who took the MFTP between 1996 and 1999, had a mean score of 156.11. Here's how to apply hypothesis testing when comparing a sample of psychology majors in one department to psychology majors nationwide.

We will use the six steps of hypothesis testing to analyze the MFTP data from the Ursuline College Psychology Department, just as we will use this six-step approach for many other statistical tests. In fact, we will use the six-step approach so often in this text that it won't be long before it becomes an automatic way of thinking for you. Below, each step is followed by a summary that models how to report hypothesis tests on practice exercises, test problems, and research projects.

STEP 1. Populations, distribution, and assumptions.

First, we identify our populations, comparison distribution, hypothesis test, and assumptions. The *populations* are (1) all students at Ursuline College who took the MFTP between 1996 and 1999 (whether or not they are in our sample) and (2) all students nationwide who took the MFTP between 1996 and 1999. Because we are studying a sample rather than an individual, the *comparison distribution* will be a distribution of means. We will compare our sample mean based on 97 students from the population at Ursuline College to a distribution of all possible means of samples of 97 students selected from the population of all psychology majors nationwide who took this test. The *hypothesis test* will be a *z* test because we have only one sample and we know the mean and the standard deviation of the national population from the published norms.

Let's examine the *assumptions* for a *z* test. (1) The data seem to be on a scale measure; study participants received scores from 120 to 200. (2) It was not reported whether sample participants were selected randomly from among all Ursuline psychology majors (Frazier & Edmonds, 2002). If they were not, this limits our ability to generalize beyond this sample to other Ursuline students. (3) The comparison distribution should be normal. In this case, we have a sample size of 97, which is greater than 30, so based on the central limit theorem, we know that our comparison distribution will be approximately normal.

Summary: Population 1: All students at Ursuline College who took the MFTP between 1996 and 1999. Population 2: All students nationwide who took the MFTP between 1996 and 1999.

The comparison distribution will be a distribution of means. The hypothesis test will be a *z* test because we have only one sample and we know the population mean and standard deviation. This study meets two of the three assumptions and may meet the third. The dependent variable is scale. In addition, there are more than 30 participants in the sample, indicating that the comparison distribution will be normal. We do not know whether the data were randomly selected, however, so we must be cautious when generalizing.

STEP 2. State the null and research hypotheses.

Next we state the null and research hypotheses both in words and in symbols. Remember, the hypotheses are always about populations, not samples. In most forms of hypothesis testing, there are two possible sets of hypotheses: directional (predicting either an increase or decrease, but not both) or nondirectional (predicting a difference in either direction).

The first possible set of hypotheses is directional. The null hypothesis is that those at Ursuline College who took the MFTP do *not* do better on average than those in the nationwide population who took the test; in other words, they could have the same or lower mean levels, but not higher. The research hypothesis is that students at Ursuline College who took the MFTP do better on average than those in the nationwide population who took the test. (Note that the direction could be reversed; the research hypothesis could posit that Ursuline College students do worse on average than the nationwide population.)

The symbol for the null hypothesis is H_0. The symbol for the research hypothesis is H_1. Throughout this text, we use μ for the mean because hypotheses are about populations and their parameters, not about samples and their statistics. So, in symbolic notation, the hypotheses are:

$$H_0: \mu_1 \leq \mu_2$$

$$H_1: \mu_1 > \mu_2$$

These express in symbols what was previously expressed in words. For the null hypothesis, the symbolic notation says that the mean MFPT score for those in population 1, the Ursuline College students, is not greater than the mean MFPT score of the nationwide students in population 2. For the research hypothesis, the symbolic notation says that the mean MFPT score in population 1 is greater than the mean MFPT score in population 2.

This hypothesis test is considered a one-tailed test. *A **one-tailed test** is a hypothesis test in which the research hypothesis is directional, positing either a mean decrease or a mean increase in the dependent variable, but not both, as a result of the independent variable.* One-tailed tests are rarely seen in the research literature; they are used only when the researcher is absolutely certain that the effect cannot go in the other direction or would not be interested in the result if it did.

The second set of hypotheses is nondirectional. The null hypothesis states that the Ursuline College students who took the MFTP (whether or not in our sample) have the same average score as do those in the nationwide population of students. The research hypothesis is that the Ursuline College students who took the MFTP have a different average score from those in the nationwide population. The means of the two populations are posited to be different, but neither mean is predicted to be lower or higher.

The hypotheses in symbols would be:

$$H_0: \mu_1 = \mu_2$$

$$H_1: \mu_1 \neq \mu_2$$

For the null hypothesis, the symbolic notation says that those in population 1, the Ursuline College students, perform the same, on average, as the students comprising population 2, the nationwide students. For the research hypothesis, the symbolic notation says that the mean MFTP score for the students in population 1 is not the same as the mean MFTP score for the students in population 2.

This hypothesis test is considered a two-tailed test. *A **two-tailed test** is a hypothesis test in which the research hypothesis does not indicate a direction of the mean difference or change*

■ A **one-tailed test** is a hypothesis test in which the research hypothesis is directional, positing either a mean decrease or a mean increase in the dependent variable, but not both, as a result of the independent variable.

■ A **two-tailed test** is a hypothesis test in which the research hypothesis does not indicate a direction of the mean difference or change in the dependent variable, but merely indicates that there will be a mean difference.

▶ **MASTERING THE CONCEPT**

7-3: We conduct a one-tailed test if we have a directional hypothesis, such as that our sample will have a higher (or lower) mean than the population. We use a two-tailed test if we have a nondirectional hypothesis, such as that our sample will have a different mean from the population.

in the dependent variable, but merely indicates that there will be a mean difference. Two-tailed tests are much more common than are one-tailed tests. If a researcher expects a difference in a certain direction, he or she might have a one-tailed hypothesis; however, if the results come out in the opposite direction, the researcher cannot then switch the direction of the hypothesis.

Summary: Null hypothesis: Ursuline College students who took the MFTP have the same mean scores as do those in the nationwide population of students—$H_0: \mu_1 = \mu_2$. Research hypothesis: Ursuline College students who took the MFTP have different mean scores from those in the nationwide population—$H_1: \mu_1 \neq \mu_2$.

STEP 3. Determine the characteristics of the comparison distribution.

Now we determine the characteristics that describe the distribution with which we will compare our sample. For z tests, we must know the mean and the standard error of the distribution of the means. Here, we have been informed that the population mean for the students who took the MFTP nationwide is 156.5 and the standard deviation for this population is 14.6. Because we usually use a sample mean in hypothesis testing, rather than a single score, we must use the standard error of the mean instead of the population standard deviation (of the scores). The characteristics of the comparison distribution are determined as follows:

$$\mu_M = \mu = 156.5$$
$$\sigma_M = \frac{14.6}{\sqrt{97}} = 1.482$$

Summary: $\mu_M = 156.5$; $\sigma_M = \frac{14.6}{\sqrt{97}} = 1.482$.

STEP 4. Determine critical values, or cutoffs.

Next we must determine critical values, or cutoffs, to which we can compare our test statistic. As stated previously, the research convention is to set the cutoffs to a p level of 0.05. For a two-tailed test, this indicates the most extreme 5%—that is, the 2.5% at the bottom of the comparison distribution and the 2.5% at the top. Because we will be calculating a test statistic for our sample—specifically a z statistic—we will report cutoffs in terms of z statistics. We will use the z table to determine the statistics for the top and bottom 2.5%.

We know that 50% of the curve falls above the mean, and we know 2.5% falls above the critical z statistic. By subtracting (50% − 2.5% = 47.5%), we determine that 47.5% of the curve falls between the mean and the critical z statistic. When we look up this percentage on the z table, we find a z statistic of 1.96. So the critical values are −1.96 and 1.96 (see Figure 7-10).

Summary: Our cutoff z statistics are −1.96 and 1.96.

STEP 5. Calculate the test statistic.

In step 5, we calculate our test statistic, in this case a z statistic, to find out what the data really say. We use the mean and standard error calculated in step 3:

$$z = \frac{(M - \mu_M)}{\sigma_M} = \frac{(156.11 - 156.5)}{1.482} = -0.26$$

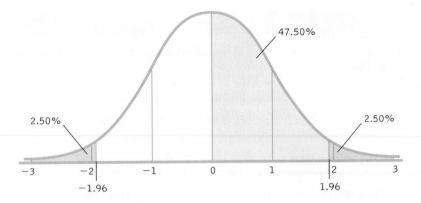

FIGURE 7-10
Determining Critical Values for a z Distribution

We typically determine critical values in terms of z statistics so that we can easily compare a test statistic to determine whether it is beyond the critical values. Here the z scores of −1.96 and 1.96 indicate the most extreme 5% of the distribution, 2.5% in each tail.

Summary: $z = \dfrac{(156.11 - 156.5)}{1.482} = -0.26$

STEP 6. Make a decision.

Finally, we compare our test statistic to our critical values so that we can make a decision about this finding. We first add the test statistic to the drawing of the curve that includes the critical z statistics (Figure 7-11). If the test statistic is beyond the cutoffs—that is, if it is in the critical region—we can reject the null hypothesis. In this example, if the test statistic were in the critical region, we would report whether the Ursuline College students are higher or lower on average than the nationwide population.

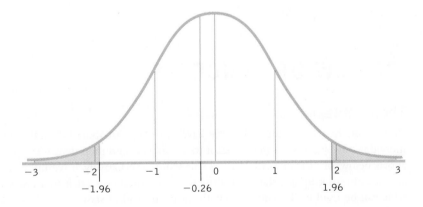

FIGURE 7-11
Making a Decision

To decide whether to reject the null hypothesis, we compare our test statistic to our critical values. In this instance, our z score of −0.26 is not beyond the critical value of −1.96, so we cannot reject the null hypothesis.

If the test statistic is not beyond the cutoffs, we fail to reject the null hypothesis. This means that we can only conclude that there is no evidence from this study to support the research hypothesis. There might be a real mean difference that is not extreme enough to be picked up by the hypothesis test. We just can't know. In the current example, the test statistic of −0.26 is not even near either critical value. So we must fail to reject the null hypothesis. We conclude that there is no evidence from this study to support the research hypothesis.

Summary: We fail to reject the null hypothesis; we conclude that there is no evidence from this study to support the research hypothesis.

CHECK YOUR LEARNING

Reviewing the Concepts

> *z* tests are conducted in cases in which we have one sample and we know both the mean and the standard deviation of the population.

> We must decide whether to use a *one-tailed test*, in which the hypothesis is directional, or a *two-tailed test*, in which the hypothesis is nondirectional.

> One-tailed tests are rare in the research literature.

Clarifying the Concepts

7-11 What does it mean to say a test is directional or nondirectional?

Calculating the Statistics

7-12 Calculate the characteristics (μ_M and σ_M) of a comparison distribution for a sample mean based on 53 participants, when the population has a mean of 1090 and a standard deviation of 87.

7-13 Calculate the *z* statistic for a mean of 1094 based on the above sample of 53 people when $\mu = 1090$ and $\sigma = 87$.

Applying the Concepts

7-14 According to the Web site for the Coffee Research Institute, the average coffee drinker in the United States consume 3.1 cups of coffee daily. Let's assume the population standard deviation is 0.9 cups. Jillian decides to study coffee consumption at her local coffee shop, Javalina, which also functions as a cybercafé. She wants to know if people sitting and working in a coffee shop will drink a different amount of coffee than what might be expected in the general U.S. population. Throughout the course of two weeks, she collects data on 34 people who spend most of the day at the coffee shop. The average number of cups consumed by this sample is 3.17 cups. Assess the significance of this sample mean by using the six steps of hypothesis testing.

Solutions to these Check Your Learning questions can be found in Appendix D.

● ● ● ● ● ● REVIEW OF CONCEPTS

The *z* Table

The *z* table has several uses when we have normally distributed data. If we know an individual raw score, we can convert it to a *z* statistic and then determine percentages above, below, or at least as extreme as this score. Alternatively, if we know a percentage, we can look up a *z* statistic on the table and then convert it to a raw score. The table can be used in the same way with means instead of scores.

The Assumptions and the Steps of Hypothesis Testing

Assumptions are the criteria that are met, ideally, before conducting a hypothesis test. *Parametric tests* are those that require assumptions about the population, whereas *nonparametric tests* are those that do not. Three basic assumptions apply to many hypothesis tests. First, the dependent variable should be on a scale measure. Second, the data should be from a randomly selected sample. Third, the population distribution should be normal (or there should be at least 30 scores in the sample). A *robust* hypothesis test is one that produces valid results even when all assumptions are not met.

There are six steps that apply to every hypothesis test. First, we determine the populations, comparison distribution, appropriate hypothesis test, and assumptions. Second, we state our null and research hypotheses. Third, we determine the characteristics of the comparison distribution that we will use to calculate the test statistic. Fourth, we determine our *critical values,* or *cutoffs,* usually based on a *p level,* or *alpha,* of 0.05, demarcating the 5% most extreme parts of the comparison distribution. In a two-tailed test, the area in the most extreme 5% (2.5% in each tail) is called the *critical region.* Fifth, we calculate our test statistic. Sixth, we use that test statistic to decide to reject or fail to reject the null hypothesis. A finding is deemed *statistically significant* when we have rejected the null hypothesis.

An Example of the *z* Test

z tests are conducted in the rare cases in which we have one sample and we know both the mean and the standard deviation of the population. We must decide whether to use a *one-tailed test,* in which the hypothesis is directional, or a *two-tailed test,* in which the hypothesis is nondirectional.

SPSS®

SPSS can transform raw data from different scales into standardized data on one scale that is based on the *z* distribution. SPSS gives us many opportunities to look at standardized scores instead of raw scores. We can try this using the numbers of mentored students who received top chemistry department jobs from Chapter 2.

We can standardize our variable by selecting: **Analyze** → Descriptive Statistics → Descriptives. We then select the relevant variable by clicking it on the left side, then clicking the arrow to move it to the right. Check the box identified as "Save standardized values as variables" and click "OK." We can see the new column of standardized variables in the screenshot here, under the heading "Zstudents."

We can also identify outliers that might skew the normal curve by selecting: **Analyze** → Descriptive Statistics → Explore → Statistics → Outliers. Be sure to select the variable of interest by clicking it on the left side, then clicking the arrow to move it to the right side. We can see the part of the output that shows the most extreme scores in the screenshot here.

Because raw scale data can be reexpressed as standardized data, SPSS gives us a variety of opportunities within different menus to listen to the story of our data in the language of *z* scores.

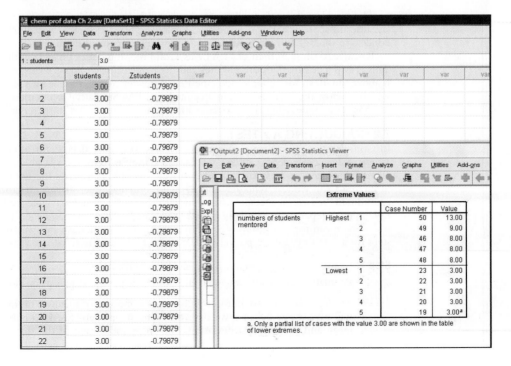

How It Works

7.1 TRANSITIONING FROM RAW SCORES TO *z* SCORES AND PERCENTILES

Physician assistants (PAs) are increasingly central to the health care system in North America. Students who graduated from PA programs in 2004 reported their income (American Academy of Physician Assistants, 2005). Those who chose to work in emergency medicine had a mean income of $76,553 with a standard deviation of $14,001. Their median income was $74,044. Those who chose to work in family/general medicine had a mean income of $63,521, with a standard deviation of $11,554. Their median income was $62,935. How can we compare the income of one PA, Gabrielle, who earns $75,500 a year in emergency medicine with that of another PA, Colin, who earns $64,300 a year in family/general medicine?

The *z* distribution should only be used with individual scores if the distribution is approximately normal. For both distributions of incomes, the medians are relatively close to the means of their own distributions. This suggests that the distributions are not skewed. Additionally, the standard deviations are not large relative to the size of the respective means, which suggests that the variability is not too great. In essence, these two distributions seem to be relatively normal and as such it is appropriate to use the *z* distribution to determine percentiles.

Gabrielle chose to work in emergency medicine and earned $75,500 in her first year out of her PA program. From the information we have, we can calculate her *z* score and her percentile on income—that is, the percentage of PAs working in emergency medicine who make less than she does. Her *z* score is:

$$z = \frac{(X - \mu)}{\sigma} = \frac{(75,500 - 76,553)}{14,001} = -0.075$$

The *z* table tells us that 3.19% of people fall between Gabrielle's income and the mean. Because her score is below the mean, we calculate 50% − 3.19% = 46.81%. Gabrielle's income is in the 46.81st percentile for PAs working in emergency medicine.

Colin chose to work in family/general medicine and earned $64,300 in his first year out of his PA program. His *z* score is:

$$z = \frac{(X - \mu)}{\sigma} = \frac{(64,300 - 63,521)}{11,554} = 0.067$$

The *z* table tells us that 2.79% of people fall between Colin's income and the mean. Because his score is above the mean, we calculate 50% + 2.79% = 52.79%. Colin's income is in the 52.79th percentile for PAs working in general medicine.

Relative to those in their chosen fields, Colin is doing better financially than Gabrielle. This is evidenced by both the *z* scores and the percentiles. Colin's *z* score of 0.067, which is above the mean for general medicine PAs, is greater than Gabrielle's *z* score of −0.075, which is below the mean for emergency medicine PAs. Similarly, Colin's income is at about the 53rd percentile, whereas Gabrielle's income is at about the 47th percentile.

7.2 CONDUCTING A *z* TEST

In Consideration of Future Consequences (CFC) summary data, Petrocelli (2003) found a mean CFC score of 3.51 with a standard deviation of 0.61 for a large sample. (For the sake of this example, let's assume that Petrocelli's sample comprises the entire population of interest.) You wonder whether students who joined a career discussion group have improved CFC scores, on average, compared with the population. Forty-five students in your Psychology Department regularly attend these discussion groups and then take the CFC scale. The mean for this group is 3.7. From this information, how can we conduct all six steps for a *z* testing using a *p* level of 0.05 and a two-tailed test?

Step 1: Population 1: All students in career discussion groups.

Population 2: All students who did not participate in career discussion groups.

The comparison distribution will be a distribution of means. The hypothesis test will be a *z* test because we have only one sample, and we know the population mean and the standard deviation. This study meets two of the three assumptions and does not seem to meet the third. The dependent variable is on a scale measure. In addition, there are more than 30 participants in the sample, indicating that the comparison distribution will be normal. The data were not randomly selected, however, so we must be cautious when generalizing.

Step 2: Null hypothesis: Students who participated in career discussion groups had the same CFC scores, on average, as students who did not participate ($H_0: \mu_1 = \mu_2$). Research hypothesis: Students who participated in career discussion groups had different CFC scores, on average, from students who did not participate ($H_0: \mu_1 \neq \mu_2$).

Step 3: $\mu_M = \mu = 3.51$; $\mu_M = \dfrac{\sigma}{\sqrt{N}} = \dfrac{0.61}{\sqrt{45}} = 0.091$

Step 4: Our critical z statistics are -1.96 and 1.96.

Step 5: $z = \dfrac{(M - \mu_M)}{\sigma_M} = \dfrac{(3.7 - 3.51)}{0.091} = 2.09$

Step 6: Reject the null hypothesis. It appears that students who participate in career discussions have higher CFC scores, on average, than do students who do not participate.

Exercises

Clarifying the Concepts

7.1 What is a percentile?

7.2 When we look up a z score on the z table, what information can we report?

7.3 How do we calculate the percentage of scores below a particular positive z score?

7.4 How is calculating a percentile for a mean from a distribution of means different from doing so for a score from a distribution of scores?

7.5 In statistics, what do we mean by assumptions?

7.6 What sample size is recommended in order to meet the assumption of a normal distribution, even when the population of interest is not normal? greater than 30

7.7 What is the difference between parametric tests and nonparametric tests?

7.8 What are the six steps of hypothesis testing?

7.9 What are critical values and the critical region?

7.10 What is the standard size of the critical region used by statisticians?

7.11 What does *statistically significant* mean to statisticians?

7.12 What do these formulas mean: $H_0: \mu_1 = \mu_2$ and $H_1: \mu_1 \neq \mu_2$?

7.13 Using everyday language, rather than statistical language, explain why the words *critical region* might have been chosen to define the area in which we reject the null hypothesis.

7.14 Using everyday language, rather than statistical language, explain why the word *cutoff* might have been chosen to define the point beyond which we reject the null hypothesis.

7.15 What is the difference between a one-tailed hypothesis test and a two-tailed hypothesis test in terms of critical regions?

Calculating the Statistics

7.16 Calculate the following for a z score of 0.74, with a tail of 22.96%:

a. What percentage of scores falls below this z score?

b. What percentage of scores falls between the mean and this z score?

c. What proportion of scores falls below a z score of -0.74?

7.17 Using the z table in Appendix B, calculate the following percentages for a z score of -0.08:

a. Above this z score

b. Below this z score

c. At least as extreme as this z score

7.18 Using the z table in Appendix B, calculate the following percentages for a z score of 1.71:

a. Above this z score

b. Below this z score

c. At least as extreme as this z score

7.19 Rewrite each of the following percentages as probabilities, or p levels:

(cont)

a. 5%

b. 83%

c. 51%

7.20 Rewrite each of the following probabilities, or *p* levels, as percentages:

a. 0.19

b. 0.04

c. 0.92

7.21 If the critical values for a hypothesis test occur where 2.5% of the distribution is in each tail, what are the cutoffs for *z*?

7.22 For each of the following *p* levels, what percentage of the data will be in each critical region for a two-tailed test?

a. 0.05 ×100 /2 ⎡ 2·5 in each tail ⎤

b. 0.10   ⎢ 5 in each tail ⎥

c. 0.01   ⎣ ·5 in each tail. ⎦

7.23 Calculate the percentage of scores in a one-tailed critical region for each of the following *p* levels:

a. 0.05

b. 0.10

c. 0.01

$\frac{100}{\sqrt{50}} = 14.1$

$500 - 542$

7.24 If you are performing a hypothesis test using a *z* statistic in which you sampled 50 people and found an average SAT verbal score of 542 (assume we know the population mean to be 500 and the standard deviation to be 100), calculate the mean and spread of the comparison distribution (μ_M and σ_M).

7.25 You are conducting a hypothesis test based on a sample of 132 people for whom you observed a mean SAT verbal score of 490. Using the information in Exercise 7.24, calculate the mean and spread of the comparison distribution (μ_M and σ_M).

7.26 If the critical values for a statistical test are -1.96 and 1.96, determine if you would reject or fail to reject the null hypothesis in each of the following cases:

a. $z = 1.06$

b. $z = -2.06$

c. A *z* score beyond which 7% of the data fall in each tail

7.27 If the critical values for a statistical test are -2.58 and 2.58, determine if you would reject or fail to reject the null hypothesis in each of the following cases:

a. $z = -0.94$

b. $z = 2.12$

c. A *z* score for which 49.6% of the data fall between *z* and the mean

7.28 Use the critical values for *z* of ± 1.65 and a *p* level of approximately 0.10, or 10%. For each of the following values, determine if you would reject or fail to reject the null hypothesis:

a. $z = 0.95$

b. $z = -1.77$

c. A *z* statistic that 2% of the scores fall above

Applying the Concepts

7.29 Elena, a 15-year-old girl, is 58 inches tall. Based on what we know, the average height for girls at this age is 63.80 inches with a standard deviation of 2.66 inches.

a. Calculate her *z* score.

b. What percentage of girls are taller than Elena?

c. What percentage of girls are shorter?

d. How much would she have to grow to be perfectly average?

e. If Sarah is in the 75th percentile for height at the age of 15 years, how tall is she?

f. How much would Elena have to grow in order to be at the 75th percentile with Sarah?

7.30 Kona, a 15-year-old boy, is 72 inches tall. According to the CDC, the average height at this age is 67.00 inches with a standard deviation of 3.19 inches.

a. Calculate Kona's *z* score.

b. What is Kona's percentile score for height?

c. What percentage of boys this age are shorter than Kona?

d. What percentage of heights are at least as extreme as Kona's, in each direction?

e. If Ian is in the 30th percentile for height as a 15-year-old male, how tall is he? How does he compare to Kona?

7.31 Imagine a class of thirty-three 15-year-old girls with an average height of 62.6 inches. Remember, $\mu = 63.8$ inches and $\sigma = 2.66$ inches.

a. Calculate the *z* statistic.

b. How does this sample of girls compare to the distribution of sample means?

c. What is the percentile rank for this sample?

7.32 Imagine a basketball team comprised of thirteen 15-year-old boys. The average height of the team is 69.5 inches. Remember, $\mu = 67$ inches and $\sigma = 3.19$ inches.

a. Calculate the *z* statistic.

b. How does this sample of boys compare to the distribution of sample means?

c. What is the percentile rank for this sample?

7.33 Imagine your statistics professor lost all records of students' raw scores on a recent test. However, she did record students' z scores for the test, as well as the class average at 41 out of 50 points and the standard deviation of 3 points (treat these as population parameters). She informs you that your z score was 1.10.

   a. What was your percentile score on this test?

   b. Using what you know about z scores and percentiles, how did you do on this test?

   c. What was your original test grade?

7.34 Using what we know about the height of 15-year-old girls (again, $\mu = 63.8$ inches and $\sigma = 2.66$ inches), imagine a teacher finds the average height of 14 female students in one of her classes to be 62.4 inches.

   a. Calculate the mean and standard error of the distribution of mean heights.

   b. Calculate the z statistic for this group.

   c. What percentage of mean heights, based on samples of this size, would we expect to be shorter than this group?

   d. How often do mean heights as extreme or more extreme than this size occur in this population?

   e. If statisticians define sample means that occur less than 5% of the time as "special" or rare, what would you say about this result?

7.35 Another teacher decides to average the height of all male students in all of his classes throughout the day. By the end of the day, he has measured the heights of 57 boys and calculated an average of 68.1 inches ($\mu = 67$ inches and $\sigma = 3.19$ inches).

   a. Calculate the mean and standard error of the distribution of mean heights.

   b. Calculate the z statistic for this group.

   c. What percentage of mean heights, based on samples of this size, would we expect to be taller than this group?

   d. How often do mean heights as extreme or more extreme than this size occur in this population?

   e. How does this result compare to the statistical significance cutoff of 5%?

7.36 For each of the following examples, state the null hypothesis and the research hypothesis, both in words and symbolic notation:

   a. A researcher is interested in studying the use of antibacterial products and the dryness of people's skin. He thinks these products might alter the moisture in skin compared to non-antibacterial products.

   b. A student wonders if grades in a class are in any way related to where a student sits in the classroom; in particular, do students who sit in the front row get better grades, on average, than the general population of students?

   c. Cell phones are everywhere and we are now available by phone almost all of the time. Does this translate into a change in the nature or closeness of our long-distance relationships?

7.37 For each of the following examples (the same as in Exercise 7.36), identify whether the research has expressed a directional or nondirectional hypothesis:

   a. A researcher is interested in studying the use of antibacterial products and the dryness of people's skin. He thinks these products might alter the moisture in skin compared to non-antibacterial products.

   b. A student wonders if grades in a class are in any way related to where a student sits in the classroom; in particular, do students who sit in the front row get better grades, on average than the general population of students?

   c. Cell phones are everywhere and we are now available by phone almost all of the time. Does this translate into a change in the nature or closeness of our long-distance relationships?

7.38 Hurricane Katrina hit New Orleans on August 29, 2005. The National Weather Service Forecast Office maintains online archives of climate data for all U.S. cities and areas. These archives allow us to find out, for example, how the rainfall in New Orleans that August compared to the other months of 2005. The table below shows the National Weather Service data (rainfall in inches) for New Orleans in 2005.

January	4.41
February	8.24
March	4.69
April	3.31
May	4.07
June	2.52
July	10.65
August	3.77
September	4.07
October	0.04
November	0.75
December	3.32

   a. Calculate the z score for August. (*Note:* These are raw data for the population, rather than summaries, so you have to calculate the mean and the standard deviation first.)

b. What is the percentile for the rainfall in August? Does this surprise you? Explain.

c. When our results surprise us, it is worthwhile to examine the individual data more closely, or even to go beyond the data we have. The daily climate data, as listed by this source, for August 2005 show the code "M" next to August 29, 30, and 31 for all climate statistics. The code indicates that "[RE-MARKS] ALL DATA MISSING AUGUST 29, 30, AND 31 DUE TO HURRICANE KATRINA." Pretend it was your consulting job to determine the percentile for that August. Write a brief paragraph for your report, explaining why the data you generated are likely to be inaccurate.

d. What raw scores would mark the cutoff for the top and bottom 10% for these data? Based on these scores, what months had extreme data for 2005? Why should we not trust these data?

7.39 IQ scores are designed to have a mean of 100 and a standard deviation of 15. IQ testing is one way in which individuals are categorized as having different levels of mental disabilities; there are four levels of mental disability between the IQ scores of 0 and 70.

a. People with IQ scores of 20–35 are said to have a severe mental disability and can learn only basic skills (e.g., how to talk, basic self-care). What percentage of people fall in this range?

b. People with IQ scores of 50–70 are in the topmost category of IQ scores that qualify as impairment. They are said to have a mild mental disability. They can attain as high as a sixth-grade education and are often self-sufficient. What percentage of people fall in this range?

c. A person has an IQ score of 66. What is her percentile?

d. A person falls at the 3rd percentile. What is his IQ score? Would he be classified as having a mental disability?

7.40 Boone (1992) examined scores on the Wechsler Adult Intelligence Scale—Revised (WAIS-R) for 150 adult psychiatric inpatients. He determined the "intrasubtest scatter" score for each inpatient. Intrasubtest scatter refers to patterns of responses in which respondents are almost as likely to get easy questions wrong as hard ones. High levels of intrasubtest scatter indicate unusual patterns of responses; because the questions start at low levels of difficulty and get increasingly more difficult, we would expect more wrong answers near the end. Boone wondered if psychiatric patients would have different response patterns from nonpatients. He compared the intrasubtest scatter for his sample of 150 patients to population data from the WAIS-R standardization group. Assume that he had access to both means and standard deviations for this population. Boone reported

that "the standardization group's intrasubtest scatter was significantly greater than those reported for the psychiatric inpatients" and concluded that such scatter is normal.

a. What are the two populations?

b. What would the comparison distribution be? Explain.

c. What hypothesis test would you use? Explain.

d. Check the assumptions for this hypothesis test and label your answer (1) through (3).

e. What does Boone mean when he says *significantly*?

7.41 Refer to the scenario described in Exercise 7.40.

a. State the null and research hypotheses for a two-tailed test in both words and symbols.

b. Imagine that, based on these findings, you wanted to replicate this study. Based on the findings described in Exercise 7.40, state the null and research hypotheses for a one-tailed test in both words and symbols.

7.42 Let's consider whether college football teams are more likely or less likely to be mismatched in the upper National Collegiate Athletic Association (NCAA) divisions. The highest division, Division I (technically, Division I-A), includes such vaunted teams as the Ohio State University Buckeyes and the University of Michigan Wolverines. During week 11 of the fall 2006 college football season, Ohio State beat Illinois by 7 points and Michigan beat Ball State by 8. Overall, however, the 53 Division I games had a mean spread (winning score minus losing score) of 16.189 that week, with a standard deviation of 12.128. We took a sample of four games that were played that week in the next-highest league, Division I-AA, to see if the spread was different; one of the many leagues within Division I-AA, the Patriot League, played four games that weekend.

a. List the independent variable and dependent variable in this example.

b. Did we use random selection? Explain.

c. Identify the populations of interest in this example.

d. State the comparison distribution.

e. Check the assumptions for this test.

7.43 Refer to Exercise 7.42.

a. State the null hypothesis and the research hypothesis for a two-tailed test in both words and symbols.

b. One of our students hypothesized that the spread would be bigger among the Division I-AA teams because "some of them are really bad and would get trounced." State the one-tailed null hypothesis and research hypothesis based on our student's prediction in both words and symbols.

7.44 Refer to Exercise 7.42. The results for the four Patriot League games are as follows:

Holy Cross, 27/Bucknell, 10

Lehigh, 23/Colgate, 15

Lafayette, 31/Fordham, 24

Georgetown, 24/Marist, 21

a. Conduct steps 3 through 6 of hypothesis testing. (You already conducted steps 1 and 2 in Exercises 7.42 and 7.43, respectively.)

b. Would you be willing to generalize these findings beyond our sample? Explain.

7.45 *z* tests are often used when a researcher wants to compare his or her sample to known population norms. The Graded Naming Test (GNT) asks respondents to name objects in a set of 30 black-and-white drawings. The test, often used to detect brain damage, starts with easy words like *kangaroo* and gets progressively more difficult, ending with words like *sextant*. The GNT population norm for adults in England is 20.4. Roberts (2003) wondered whether a sample of Canadian adults had different scores from adults in England. If they were different, the English norms would not be valid for use in Canada. The mean for 30 Canadian adults was 17.5. For the purposes of this exercise, assume that the standard deviation of the adults in England is 3.2.

a. Conduct all six steps of a *z* test. Be sure to label all six steps.

b. Some words on the GNT are more commonly used in England. For example, a *mitre,* the headpiece worn by bishops, is worn by the Archbishop of Canterbury in public ceremonies in England. No Canadian participant correctly responded to this item, whereas 55% of English adults correctly responded. Explain why we should be cautious about applying norms to people different from those on whom the test was normed.

7.46 When we conduct a one-tailed test instead of a two-tailed test, there are small changes in steps 2 and 4 of hypothesis testing. Let's consider Exercise 7.45 on the Graded Naming Test. (*Note:* For this example, assume that those from populations other than the one on which it was normed will score lower, on average. That is, hypothesize that the Canadians will have a lower score.)

a. Conduct step 2 of hypothesis testing for a one-tailed test—stating the null and research hypotheses in words and in symbols.

b. Conduct step 4 of hypothesis testing for a one-tailed test—determining the cutoff.

c. Conduct step 6 of hypothesis testing for a one-tailed test—making a decision.

d. Under which circumstance—a one-tailed or a two-tailed test—is it easier to reject the null hypothesis? Explain.

e. If it becomes easier to reject the null hypothesis under one type of test (one-tailed versus two-tailed), does this mean that there is now a bigger difference between the samples? Explain.

7.47 When we change the *p* level that we use as a cutoff, there is a small change in step 4 of hypothesis testing. Although 0.05 is the most commonly used *p* level, other values, such as 0.01, are often used. Let's consider Exercise 7.45 on the Graded Naming Test.

a. Conduct step 4 of hypothesis testing for a *p* level of 0.01—determining the cutoff.

b. Conduct step 6 of hypothesis testing for a *p* level of 0.01—making a decision.

c. With which *p* level—0.05 or 0.01—is it easier to reject the null hypothesis? Explain.

d. If it is easier to reject the null hypothesis with certain *p* levels, does this mean that there is now a bigger difference between the samples? Explain.

7.48 A recent research report (Behenam & Pooya, 2006) began, "There is probably no other area of health care that requires a cooperation to the extent that orthodontics does," and explored factors that affected the number of hours per day that patients wore their orthodontic appliances. The patients in the study reported that they used their appliances, on average, 14.78 hours per day, with a standard deviation of 5.31. We'll treat this group as the population for the purposes of this example. Let's say a researcher wanted to study whether a DVD with information about orthodontics led to an increase in the amount of time patients wear their appliances but decided to use a two-tailed test to be conservative. Let's say he studied the next 15 patients at his clinic, asked them to watch the DVD, and then found that they wore their appliances, on average, 17 hours per day.

a. What is the independent variable? What is the dependent variable?

b. Did the researcher use random selection to choose his sample? Explain your answer.

c. Conduct all six steps of hypothesis testing. Be sure to label all six steps.

d. If the researcher's decision in step 6 was wrong, what type of error would he have made? Explain your answer.

Terms

z test (p. 148)
assumption (p. 157)
parametric test (p. 157)
nonparametric test (p. 157)

robust (p. 158)
critical value (p. 159)
critical region (p. 159)
p level (p. 159)

statistically significant (p. 160)
one-tailed test (p. 163)
two-tailed test (p. 163)

Symbols

H_0 (p. 163)
H_1 (p. 163)

Confidence Intervals, Effect Size, and Statistical Power

> ### ● BEFORE YOU GO ON
>
> ■ You should know how to conduct a *z* test
> (Chapter 7).
>
> ■ You should understand the concept of
> statistical significance (Chapter 7).

"Math Class Is Tough" Teen Talk Barbie, with her negative proclamation about math class, was a lightning rod for discussions about gender stereotypes and the evidence for actual gender differences. Some of Barbie's negative press related not to the fact that girls *can* do math well, but rather that Barbie's message might doom them to even poorer performance. The media tend to play up gender differences instead of the less interesting (and more frequent) realities of gender similarities.

"Want to go shopping? OK, meet me at the mall."

"Math class is tough."

With these and 268 other phrases, Teen Talk Barbie was introduced to the market in July 1992. By September, it was being publicly criticized for its negative message about girls and math. At first, Mattel, the doll's maker, refused to pull it from store shelves, citing other more positive phrases in Barbie's repertoire, such as "I'm studying to be a doctor." But the bad press escalated, and Mattel backed down by October. The controversy took a while to subside, however, even showing up as a parody on a 1994 *Simpsons* episode when Lisa Simpson boycotted the fictional Malibu Stacy doll, which said things like "Thinking too much gives you wrinkles."

The controversy over gender differences in mathematical reasoning ability began shortly after publication of a study in the prestigious journal *Science*. Researchers reported results from a sample of about 10,000 male and female students in grades 7 through 10 who were in the top 2% to 3% on standardized tests of mathematics (Benbow & Stanley, 1980). In this sample, the boys' average score on the mathematics portion of the SAT test was 32 points higher than the girls' average score. This result is why researchers were able to reject the null hypothesis that there was no mean difference between boys and girls with respect to SAT math scores.

Based on this gender difference, the study gained an enormous amount of media attention (Jacob & Eccles, 1982). But the danger of reporting a statistically significant difference between two group means is that such a difference can falsely imply that all or most of the members of one group are different from all or most of the members of the other group. As we can see in Figure 8-1, such an assertion about gender differences in mathematical reasoning ability would be far from the truth. Part of this misunderstanding is caused by the language of statistics: "statistically significant" does *not* mean "very important."

It took a meta-analysis, a study of all the studies about a particular topic, to clarify the research on gender differences in mathematical reasoning ability. Different researchers compiled the results from 259 differences between means representing data from 1,968,846 male participants and 2,016,836 female participants (Hyde, Fennema, & Lamon, 1990). Here's what they discovered:

1. Mean gender differences in overall mathematical reasoning ability were very small.
2. When the extreme tails of the distribution were eliminated (such as remedial programs, gifted programs, or the population studied by Benbow and Stanley), the size of the mean gender difference was even smaller *and* reversed direction, now favoring women and girls rather than men and boys.
3. The superiority of one gender over another depended on the mathematical task. For example, women and girls tended to perform slightly better, on average, than men and boys on mathematical computation; men and boys tended to perform slightly better, on average, than women and girls on mathematical problem solving.

The authors of this meta-analysis included a graph of two normal distributions that represent the small mean difference in favor of male participants that they found in their overall examination of studies (see Figure 8-1). Are you surprised that a small (but statistically significant) gender difference is almost completely overlapping? This is a case in which hypothesis testing alone inadvertently encouraged a profound misunderstanding (Jacob & Eccles, 1986).

Fortunately, statisticians have figured out ways to move beyond the flaws in hypothesis testing. In this chapter, we

FIGURE 8-1
A Gender Difference in Mathematics Performance

This graph represents the amount of overlap that would be expected if the distributions for males and females differed, on average, by the amount that Hyde and colleagues (1990) reported in their meta-analysis of gender differences in mathematics performance.

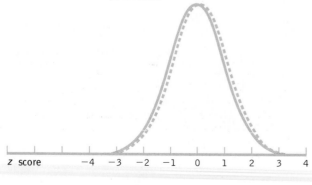

z score   −4   −3   −2   −1   0   1   2   3   4

learn how to compute confidence intervals. Rather than presenting just the mean difference between our samples, we'll be presenting a range of plausible mean differences for the population. Then, we learn to calculate effect sizes, so we can report whether mean differences are small, medium, or large (just as researchers did in the meta-analysis). We also introduce p_{rep}, an alternate to a p value. Finally, with an understanding of statistical power, we can make sure we have a sufficient sample size to detect any real difference that exists in the population.

- A **point estimate** is a summary statistic from a sample that is just one number used as an estimate of the population parameter.

- An **interval estimate** is based on a sample statistic and provides a range of plausible values for the population parameter.

Confidence Intervals

The study that determined the average SAT mathematics score for boys was 32 points higher than the average SAT mathematics score for girls sounded convincing, but the presentation was misleading. Researchers calculated a difference between means by subtracting the mean score for girls from the mean score for boys. All three summary statistics—the mean for boys, the mean for girls, and the difference between them—are point estimates. *A **point estimate** is a summary statistic from a sample that is just one number used as an estimate of the population parameter.* Instead, research should be presented with interval estimates when possible.

Interval Estimates

*An **interval estimate** is based on a sample statistic and provides a range of plausible values for the population parameter.* Interval estimates are frequently used in media reports, particularly when reporting political polls, and are usually constructed by adding and subtracting a margin of error from a point estimate. For example, a December 2008 Gallup poll found that Americans rated then President-Elect Barack Obama as their most admired man in the world (Saad, 2008). Obama was chosen by 32% of respondents, and the margin of error was 3%. So, the interval estimate around the point estimate of 32% is 29% to 35%.

> ◀ **MASTERING THE CONCEPT**
>
> **8-1:** We can use a sample to calculate a point estimate—one plausible number, such as a mean—for our population. We also can use a sample to calculate an interval estimate—a range of plausible numbers, such as a range of means—for our population.

EXAMPLE 8.1

Let's look at one example more closely. A survey asked 800 adult respondents to select one out of six celebrity couples that they'd most like to meet (the polling company, inc., 2006). Film legends Joanne Woodward and the since-deceased Paul Newman came out on top, chosen by 29% of respondents, ahead of more in-the-news couples like Katie Holmes and Tom Cruise. The margin of error was reported to be ±3.5%.

Because $29 - 3.5 = 25.5$ and $29 + 3.5 = 32.5$, the interval estimate for Newman and Woodward is 25.5% to 32.5%. Interval estimates provide a range of plausible values, not just one statistic.

What's particularly useful about margins of error is that we can figure out more than one interval estimate for the same poll to see if they overlap. Angelina Jolie and Brad Pitt came in second with 18%, giving an interval estimate of 14.5% to 21.5%. There's no overlap with the first-place couple, a strong indication that Newman/Woodward really were the most popular couple among those in the entire population, as well as those in this sample. However, if Jolie/Pitt had received 23% of the vote,

Popularity Contest Joanne Woodward and Paul Newman beat out the second-place couple, Angelina Jolie and Brad Pitt, as the celebrity couple that Americans most want to meet. The globe-trotting darlings of the tabloids, Angelina and Brad, were chosen by 18% of the 800 respondents, 11 percentage points behind Woodward and Newman. This 18% is a point estimate. There was a margin of error of ±3.5%, giving an interval estimate of 14.5–21.5%.

AP Photo/Matt Sayles

■ A **confidence interval** is an interval estimate, based on the sample statistic, that includes the population mean a certain percentage of the time, were we to sample from the same population repeatedly.

that would have placed them only 5% behind Newman/Woodward, and they'd have had an interval estimate of 19.5% to 26.5%. This range would have overlapped with the one for Newman/Woodward, an indication that both couples could plausibly have had the same percentage of popularity in the general population.

In research, the idea of a margin of error is expressed as an interval estimate, usually a confidence interval. A confidence interval is a calculated range of values that surrounds the point estimate. More specifically, *a **confidence interval** is an interval estimate, based on the sample statistic, that includes the population mean a certain percentage of the time, were we to sample from the same population repeatedly.* (*Note:* We are not saying that we are confident that the population mean falls in the interval; we are merely saying that we expect to find the population mean within a certain interval a certain percentage of the time [usually 95%] when we conduct this same study.)

The confidence interval is centered around the mean of the sample. For a confidence interval, the 95% confidence level is most commonly used, which indicates the 95% that falls *between* the two tails (i.e., $100\% - 5\% = 95\%$). Note the terms used here: the confidence *level* is 95%, but the confidence *interval* is the range between the two values that surround the sample mean.

In the following section, we establish a 95% confidence interval using the z distribution.

Calculating Confidence Intervals with *z* Distributions

The symmetry of the z distribution makes it easy to calculate confidence intervals. Remember, we use a z distribution when we know the population mean and population standard deviation. And we conduct a z test by collecting data from a sample and then comparing its mean to that of the population.

EXAMPLE 8.2

We already conducted hypothesis testing for an example of the Major Field Test in Psychology (MFTP)—comparing the average score of students at Ursuline College to the population mean for all students who took the MFTP nationwide (Frazier & Edmonds, 2002). Now we will use the same data to calculate a confidence interval. The population mean was 156.5, and the population standard deviation was assumed to be 14.6. The 97 students in the Ursuline College sample had a mean MFTP score of 156.11. When we conducted hypothesis testing, we centered our curve around the mean according to the null hypothesis, the population mean of 156.5. We determined critical values based on this mean and compared our sample mean to these cutoffs. These two means are very close together, so it is not surprising that we were not able to reject the null hypothesis that there was no mean difference between the two groups. The test statistic was not beyond the cutoff z statistic.

There are several steps to calculating a confidence interval.

STEP 1. Draw a picture of a distribution that will include the confidence interval.

We draw a normal curve (see Figure 8-2) that has the *sample* mean, 156.11, at its center instead of the *population* mean, 156.5.

STEP 2. Indicate the bounds of the confidence interval on the drawing.

We draw a vertical line from the mean to the top of the curve. For a 95% confidence interval, we also draw two small vertical lines to indicate the middle 95% of the normal curve (2.5% in each tail, for a total of 5%).

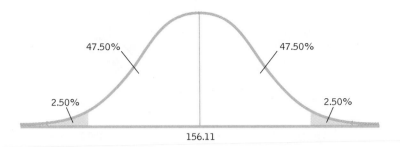

FIGURE 8-2
A 95% Confidence Interval, Part I

To begin calculating a confidence interval for a *z* distribution, we draw a normal curve, place the sample mean at its center, and indicate the percentages within and beyond the confidence interval.

We then write the appropriate percentages under the segments of the curve. The curve is symmetric, so half of the 95% falls above and half falls below the mean. Half of 95 is 47.5, so we write 47.5% in the segments on either side of the mean. In the tails beyond the two lines that indicate the end of the middle 95%, we also write the appropriate percentages. Because 50% falls on each side of the mean and 47.5% falls between the mean and each end of the confidence interval, we know that 50% − 47.5% = 2.5% falls beyond each end of the confidence interval.

STEP 3. Determine the *z* statistics that fall at each line marking the middle 95%.

To do this, we turn back to our versatile *z* table in Appendix B. The percentage between the mean and each of our *z* scores is 47.5%. When we look up this percentage in the *z* table, we find a *z* statistic of 1.96. (Note that this is identical to the cutoffs for the *z* test; this will always be the case because the *p* level of 0.05 corresponds to a confidence level of 95%.) We can now add the *z* statistics of −1.96 and 1.96 to our curve, as seen in Figure 8-3.

STEP 4. Turn the *z* statistics back into raw means.

We use the formula for this conversion, but first we must identify the appropriate mean and standard deviation. There are two important points to remember. First, we center our interval around the *sample* mean (not the *population* mean). So we use the sample mean of 156.11 in our calculations. Second, because we have a sample *mean* (rather than an individual *score*), we use a distribution of means. So we have to calculate standard error as our measure of spread:

$$\sigma_M = \frac{\sigma}{\sqrt{N}} = \frac{14.6}{\sqrt{97}} = 1.482$$

Notice that this is the same standard error that we calculated previously when we conducted a hypothesis test.

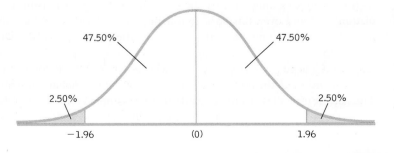

FIGURE 8-3
A 95% Confidence Interval, Part II

The next step in calculating a confidence interval is identifying the *z* statistics that indicate each end of the interval. Because the curve is symmetric, the *z* statistics will have the same magnitude—one will be negative and one will be positive (−1.96 and 1.96).

FIGURE 8-4
A 95% Confidence Interval,
Part III

The final step in calculating a
confidence interval is converting the *z*
statistics that indicate each end of the
interval into raw means.

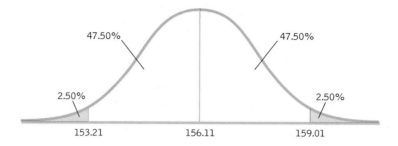

Using this mean and standard error, we can calculate the raw mean at each end of the confidence interval, the lower end and the upper end, and add them to our curve as in Figure 8–4:

$$M_{lower} = -z(\sigma_M) + M_{sample} = -1.96(1.482) + 156.11 = 153.21$$

$$M_{upper} = z(\sigma_M) + M_{sample} = 1.96(1.482) + 156.11 = 159.01$$

Our 95% confidence interval, reported in brackets as is typical, is [153.21, 159.01].

MASTERING THE FORMULA

8-1: The formula for the lower bound of a confidence interval using a *z* distribution is $M_{lower} = -z(\sigma_M) + M_{sample}$, and the formula for the upper bound is $M_{upper} = z(\sigma_M) + M_{sample}$. The first symbol in each formula refers to the mean at that end of the confidence interval. To calculate each bound, we multiply the *z* statistic by the standard error, then add the sample mean. The *z* statistic for the lower bound is negative, and the *z* statistic for the upper bound is positive.

STEP 5. Check that the confidence interval makes sense.

The sample mean should fall exactly in the middle of the two ends of the interval.

$$153.21 - 156.11 = -2.9 \text{ and } 159.01 - 156.11 = 2.9$$

We have a match. The confidence interval ranges from 2.9 below the sample mean to 2.9 above the sample mean. You can think of this number, 2.9, as the margin of error. The confidence interval, then, can be thought of as the range comprised by the sample mean plus and minus the margin of error [153.21, 159.01].

To recap the steps for creation of a confidence interval for a *z* statistic:

1. *Draw* a normal curve with the *sample* mean in the center.
2. *Indicate* the bounds of the confidence interval on either end, and write the percentages under each segment of the curve.
3. *Look up* the *z* statistics for the lower and upper ends of the confidence interval in the *z* table. These are always −1.96 and 1.96 for a 95% confidence interval.
4. *Convert* the *z* statistics to raw means for the lower and upper ends of the confidence interval.
5. *Check* your answer; each end of the confidence interval should be exactly the same distance from the sample mean.

If we were to sample 97 Ursuline College psychology majors from the same population over and over, this 95% confidence interval would include the population mean 95% of the time. Note that the population mean for all students taking the MFTP, 156.5, falls within this interval. This means it is plausible that the sample of Ursuline College psychology students who took the MFTP comes from the population according to the null hypothesis—all psychology students who took the MFTP. The data do not allow us to conclude that the sample comes from a different population; that is, we cannot conclude that Ursuline College students performed any better or worse than the national population on the MFTP. The conclusions from both the z test and the confidence interval are the same, but the confidence interval gives us more information—an interval estimate, not just a point estimate.

CHECK YOUR LEARNING

Reviewing the Concepts

> A point estimate is just a single number, such as a mean, that provides a plausible value for the population parameter. An interval estimate is based on our sample statistic and provides a range of plausible values for the population parameter.

> A confidence interval is one kind of interval estimate and can be created around a sample mean using a z distribution.

> We can also think of the confidence interval as the range formed when we add and subtract a margin of error from the sample mean.

> The confidence interval confirms the results of the hypothesis test while adding more detail.

Clarifying the Concepts

8-1 Why are interval estimates better than point estimates?

Calculating the Statistics

8-2 If 21% of voters want to raise taxes, with a margin of error of 4%, what is your interval estimate? What is the point estimate?

Applying the Concepts

8-3 In How It Works 7.2, we calculated a z test based on the following information adapted from a study by Petrocelli (2003) that used the Consideration of Future Consequences (CFC) scale as the dependent variable. The population mean CFC score was 3.51, with a standard deviation of 0.61. The sample of interest was composed of 45 students who joined a career discussion group, and the study examined whether this might have changed CFC scores. The mean for this group is 3.7.

a. Calculate a 95% confidence interval for this study.

b. Explain what this confidence interval tells us.

Solutions to these Check Your Learning questions can be found in Appendix D.

c. Why is this confidence interval superior to the hypothesis test that we conducted in Chapter 7?

Effect Size and p_{rep}

Researchers tend to be interested in big effects, but hypothesis testing by itself can create an illusion of exaggerated importance. As we learned with the research on gender differences in mathematical reasoning ability, "statistically significant" does *not* mean that the findings from a study are necessarily consequential or important. Statistically significant only means that those findings are unlikely to occur if in fact the null hypothesis is true.

The Effect of Sample Size on Statistical Significance

A very small difference found using a very large sample can be statistically significant because sample size strongly influences the outcomes of hypothesis

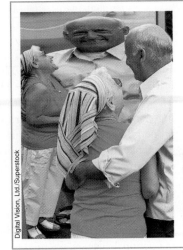

Digital Vision, Ltd./Superstock

Misinterpreting Statistical Significance Statistical significance that is achieved by merely collecting a very large sample can make a research finding appear to be far more important than it really is, just as a curved mirror can exaggerate a person's size.

testing. Specifically, increasing our sample size increases our test statistic for every hypothesis test, including the z test. Let's look at an example. Researchers reported data for GRE psychology test scores over several years in the 1990s: $\mu = 554, \sigma = 99$ (Matlin & Kalat, 2001). In a fictional example in Chapter 7, we reported that 90 graduating seniors had a mean of 568. Based on the sample size of 90, we reported the mean and standard error for the distribution of means as:

$$\mu_M = 554; \sigma_M = \frac{\sigma}{\sqrt{N}} = \frac{99}{\sqrt{90}} = 10.436$$

The test statistic calculated from these numbers was:

$$z = \frac{(M - \mu_M)}{\sigma_M} = \frac{(568 - 554)}{10.436} = 1.34$$

What would happen if we increased our sample size to 200? We'd have to recalculate our standard error to reflect the larger sample, and then recalculate our test statistic to reflect the smaller standard error.

$$\mu_M = 554; \sigma_M = \frac{\sigma}{\sqrt{N}} = \frac{99}{\sqrt{200}} = 7.000$$

$$z = \frac{(M - \mu_M)}{\sigma_M} = \frac{(568 - 554)}{7.000} = 2.00$$

What if we increased the sample size to 1000?

$$\mu_M = 554; \sigma_M = \frac{\sigma}{\sqrt{N}} = \frac{99}{\sqrt{1000}} = 3.131$$

$$z = \frac{(M - \mu_M)}{\sigma_M} = \frac{(568 - 554)}{3.131} = 4.47$$

What if we increased it to 100,000?

$$\mu_M = 554; \sigma_M = \frac{\sigma}{\sqrt{N}} = \frac{99}{\sqrt{100,000}} = 0.313$$

$$z = \frac{(M - \mu_M)}{\sigma_M} = \frac{(568 - 554)}{0.313} = 44.73$$

Notice that each time we increased our sample size, our standard error decreased and our test statistic increased. The original test statistic, 1.34, was not beyond the critical values of 1.96 and −1.96. However, the remaining test statistics (2.00, 4.47, and 44.73) were all more extreme than the positive critical value, 1.96, with each succeeding test statistic beating the critical value by a larger and larger amount. When used properly, a large sample size makes a statistic more powerful. In their study of gender differences in mathematics performance, researchers studied 10,000 participants, a very large sample (Benbow & Stanley, 1980). It is not surprising, then, that a small difference would be a statistically significant difference.

Let's consider, logically, why it makes sense that a large sample should allow us to reject the null hypothesis more readily than a small sample. If we randomly selected 5 people among all those who had taken the GRE and they had GRE scores well above the national average, we might say, "Well, it's possible that we just happened to choose

5 people with high scores." But if we selected 1000 people with GRE scores well above the national average, it seems very unlikely that this would have occurred by chance—that we just happened to choose 1000 people with high scores. This is the reason we can be more confident that a difference occuring with a large sample is a real difference.

But just because a real difference exists does not mean it is a large, or meaningful, difference. The difference we found with 5 people might be exactly the same as the difference we found with 1000 people. As we demonstrated with multiple z tests with different sample sizes, we might fail to reject the null hypothesis with a small sample but then reject the null hypothesis for the same-size difference between two means with a large sample. Our conclusions can be different simply because of a difference in the size of our sample. Conversely, a finding that is statistically significant might not be of practical importance.

> ◀ **MASTERING THE CONCEPT**
>
> **8-2:** As sample size increases, so does the test statistic (if all else stays the same). Because of this, a small difference might not be statistically significant with a small sample, but might be statistically significant with a large sample.

To demonstrate the difference between statistical significance and practical importance, Cohen (1990) offered the example of a "definite" correlation between height and IQ observed in a sample of 14,000 children. This finding was reported by the popular media to be a statistically significant but small effect. Based on the reported correlation, Cohen calculated that a person would have to grow by 3.5 feet to increase IQ by 30 points (2 standard deviations). Height may have been significantly related to IQ, but there was only a very small effect with no practical real-world application.

We demonstrated how increasing the sample size can lead to an increased test statistic during hypothesis testing. In other words, it becomes progressively easier to declare statistical significance as we increase our sample size, the N. A small difference between a sample mean and a population mean *might not* be statistically significant with a small sample, but it *could* be statistically significant with a somewhat larger sample, and *would almost certainly* be statistically significant with an extremely large sample. A larger sample size should influence our level of confidence that the story is true, but it shouldn't increase our confidence that the story is important. *Statistical significance does not indicate practical importance.*

What Effect Size Is

A statistically significant finding, particularly one from a study using a large sample, may indicate a genuine difference between groups, but a trivial one. This is where effect size comes in. ***Effect size*** *indicates the size of a difference and is unaffected by sample size.* Effect size tells us how much two populations *do not* overlap. Simply put, the less overlap, the bigger the effect size. The amount of overlap between two distributions can be decreased in two ways:

1. If their means are farther apart
2. If the variation within each population is smaller

Figure 8-5 shows that overlap decreases and effect size increases when means are farther apart. Figure 8-6 shows that overlap decreases and effect size increases when the variability within each distribution becomes smaller. Effect size takes into account both ways in which the overlap of two distributions is affected: (1) the mean difference, and (2) the variability of the population distributions based on individual scores (not the sampling distribution of means).

When we investigated the story of gender differences in mathematical reasoning ability, you may have noticed that we described the size of the findings as "small" (Hyde,

■ **Effect size** indicates the size of a difference and is unaffected by sample size

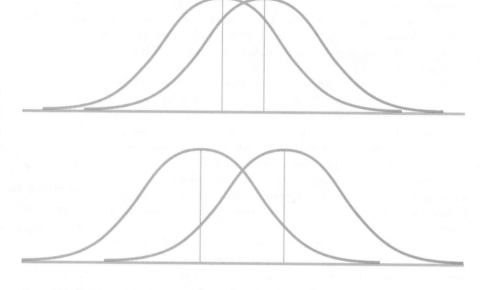

FIGURE 8-5
Effect Size and Mean Differences

When two population means are farther apart, as in the bottom pair of curves, the overlap of the distributions is less and the effect size is bigger.

FIGURE 8-6
Effect Size and Standard Deviation

When two population distributions decrease their spread, as in the bottom pair of curves, the overlap of the distributions is less and the effect size is bigger.

2005). Because effect size is a standardized measure based on scores rather than means, we can compare the effect sizes of different studies with one another. A study based on large sample sizes that shows statistical significance might have a smaller effect size than a study based on small sample sizes that is not statistically significant.

EXAMPLE 8.3

To see why we use the distribution of scores instead of the distribution of means, let's examine Figure 8-7. First of all, assume that each of these distributions is based on the same underlying population. Second, notice that all means represented by the vertical

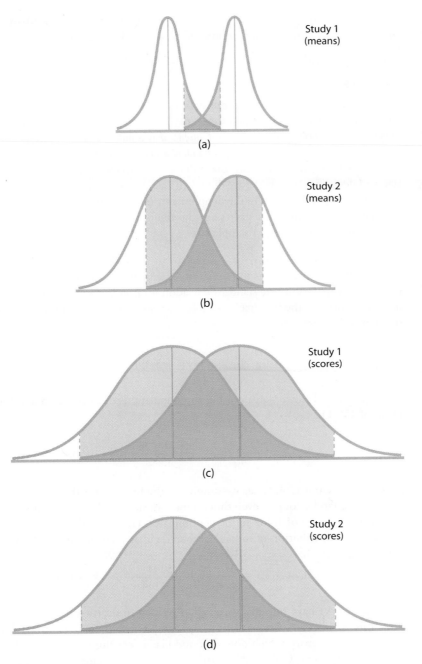

(a)

Study 1
(means)

(b)

Study 2
(means)

(c)

Study 1
(scores)

(d)

Study 2
(scores)

FIGURE 8-7
Making Fair Comparisons

The top two pairs of curves (a and b) depict two studies, study 1 and study 2. The first study (a) compared two samples with very large sample sizes, so each curve was very narrow. The second study (b) compared two samples with much smaller sample sizes, so each curve was wider. The first study has less overlap, but that doesn't mean it has a bigger effect than study 2; we just can't compare the effects. The bottom two pairs (c and d) depict the same two studies, but using standard deviation for individual scores. Now they are comparable and we see that they have the same amount of overlap—the same effect sizes.

lines are identical. The only differences are those due to the spread of the distributions. The small degree of overlap in the tall, skinny distributions of means in Figure 8-7a is the result of a very large sample size. The greater degree of overlap in the somewhat wider distributions of means in Figure 8-7b is the result of a smaller sample size. By contrast, the distributions of scores represented in Figures 8-7c and 8-7d are the result of actual scores rather than sample means for these two studies. Because these flatter, wider distributions include actual scores, sample size is not an issue in making comparisons.

In this case, the amounts of real overlap in Figures 8-7c and 8-7d are identical. We can directly compare the amount of overlap and see that they have the same effect size.

Cohen's d

There are many different effect-size statistics, but they all neutralize the influence of sample size. When we conduct a z test, the effect-size statistic is typically Cohen's d, developed by Jacob Cohen (1988). ***Cohen's d** is a measure of effect size that assesses the difference between two means in terms of standard deviation, not standard error.* In other words, Cohen's d allows us to measure the difference between means using the number of standard deviations, much like we did when calculating a z statistic. We accomplish this by using standard deviation in the denominator (rather than standard error). Why? Remember that standard error makes an adjustment for sample size, and effect size aims to disregard the influence of sample size.

EXAMPLE 8.4

Let's calculate Cohen's d for the situation for which we constructed a confidence interval. We simply substitute standard deviation for standard error. When we calculated the test statistic for the 97 Ursuline College students on the MFTP, we first calculated the standard error:

$$\sigma_M = \frac{\sigma}{\sqrt{N}} = \frac{14.6}{\sqrt{97}} = 1.482$$

We calculated the z statistic using the population mean of 156.5 and the sample mean of 156.11:

$$z = \frac{(M - \mu_M)}{\sigma_M} = \frac{(156.11 - 156.5)}{1.482} = -0.26$$

To calculate our Cohen's d, we simply use the formula for the z statistic, substituting σ for σ_M (and μ for μ_M, even though these means are always the same). This means we use 14.6 instead of 1.482 in the denominator. The Cohen's d is now based on the spread of the distribution of individual scores, rather than the distribution of means.

$$\text{Cohen's } d = \frac{(M - \mu)}{\sigma} = \frac{(156.11 - 156.5)}{14.6} = -0.03$$

> **MASTERING THE FORMULA**
>
> **8-2:** The formula for Cohen's d for a z statistic is: Cohen's $d = \frac{(M - \mu)}{\sigma}$. It is the same formula as for the z statistic, except we divide by the population standard deviation, rather than standard error.

Now that we have our effect size, often written in shorthand as $d = -0.03$, what does it mean? First, we know that the two sample means are 0.03 standard deviation apart, which doesn't sound like a very big difference, and it isn't. Jacob Cohen, the guru of effect sizes, developed guidelines for what constitutes a small effect (0.2), a medium effect (0.5), or a large effect (0.8). Table 8-1 displays these guidelines, along with the amount of overlap between two curves that is indicated by an effect of that size. No sign is provided because it is the magnitude of an effect size that matters; an effect size of -0.5 is the same size as one of 0.5.

Based on these numbers, the effect size for our study of Ursuline College students, -0.03, is not even at the level of a small effect. It's practically 0. This makes sense., because the average score of the Ursuline College students was almost identical to that of the general population of psychology students.

> ▶ **MASTERING THE CONCEPT**
>
> **8-3:** Because a statistically significant effect might not be an important one, we should calculate effect size in addition to conducting a hypothesis test. We can then report whether a statistically significant effect is small, medium, or large.

TABLE 8-1. Cohen's Conventions for Effect Sizes: *d*

Jacob Cohen has published guidelines (or conventions), based on the overlap between two distributions, to help researchers determine whether an effect is small, medium, or large. These numbers are not cutoffs, merely rough guidelines to aid researchers in their interpretation of results.

Effect Size	Convention	Overlap
Small	0.2	85%
Medium	0.5	67%
Large	0.8	53%

▪ **Cohen's *d*** is a measure of effect size that assesses the difference between two means in terms of standard deviation, not standard error.

▪ ***p*rep** is the probability of replicating an effect given a particular population and sample size.

p_{rep}

Like Jacob Cohen, Peter Killeen has explored methods to understand the findings of hypothesis testing in ways that are more accurate and useful. Killeen (2005) developed p_{rep}, *the probability of replicating an effect given a particular population and sample size.* One can interpret p_{rep} as "This effect will replicate $100(p_{rep})$% of the time" (Killeen, 2005, p. 349). So a p_{rep} of 0.99 indicates that the effect would replicate, given the same population and sample size, 99% of the time.

Killeen and others promote the use of p_{rep} because it is easier to understand than p and, consequently, is more difficult to misinterpret. The editors of the Association for Psychological Science prefer p_{rep} to p and strongly recommend its use in the journals that they publish. p_{rep} is most easily calculated using computer software, but first we have to know our specific p value, not just whether or not our test statistic is beyond our critical value. We calculate p_{rep} in two steps.

Step 1: Calculate the specific p value associated with our test statistic.

To do this, we look up our test statistic on the table in Appendix B. In the Ursuline College example, our z statistic was -0.26. If we look up this number in the z table, we find a percentage of 39.74% falling beyond our z statistic. Because we conducted a two-tailed test and the table only provides the percentage in one tail, we have to double the percentage to get the total p value in percentage form, 79.48%. We would divide by 100 to get the p value in terms of proportion rather than percentage, 0.7948.

Step 2: Using Microsoft Excel, calculate p_{rep}.

Input the following into one cell of a spreadsheet: =NORMSDIST(NORMSINV(1-P)/(SQRT(2))) (Killeen, 2005). We substitute the actual p value for the letter P, so we'd enter: =NORMSDIST(NORMSINV(1-.7948)/(SQRT(2))). When we press "enter," Excel calculates p_{rep}. In this case, it is 0.2803, which indicates that we would expect this effect to replicate, given the same population and sample size, 28.03% of the time.

CHECK YOUR LEARNING

Reviewing the Concepts

> As sample size increases, the test statistic becomes more extreme and it becomes easier to reject the null hypothesis.

> A statistically significant result is not necessarily one with practical importance.

> Effect sizes are calculated with respect to scores, rather than means, so are not contingent on sample size.

continued on next page

> The size of an effect is based on the difference between two group means and the amount of variability within each group.

> Effect size for a *z* test is measured with Cohen's *d*, which is calculated much like a *z* statistic.

> Cohen has published conventions so that a statistician can get a sense of whether an effect is small, medium, or large.

> We can also calculate p_{rep}, the probability of replicating an effect given a particular population and sample size.

Clarifying the Concepts	**8-4** Distinguish statistical significance and practical importance.
	8-5 What is effect size?
	8-6 What is p_{rep}?
Calculating the Statistics	**8-7** Using IQ as a variable, where we know the mean is 100 and the standard deviation is 15, calculate Cohen's *d* for an observed mean of 105.
	8-8 A researcher calculated a *p* value of 0.22 for her *z* statistic. Using Microsoft Excel, determine p_{rep}.
Applying the Concepts	**8-9** In Check Your Learning 8-3, we calculated a confidence interval based on CFC data. The population mean CFC score was 3.51, with a standard deviation of 0.61. The sample was composed of 45 students who joined a career discussion group, and the study examined whether this might have changed CFC scores. The mean for this group is 3.7.
	a. Calculate the appropriate effect size for this study.
	b. Citing Cohen's conventions, explain what this effect size tells us.
Solutions to these Check Your Learning questions can be found in Appendix D.	c. Now consider the effect of the effect size. Does this finding have any consequences or implications for anyone's life?

Statistical Power

The effect-size statistic tells us that the public controversy over gender differences in mathematical ability was justified: the observed gender differences had no practical importance. Calculating statistical power (along with effect size and confidence intervals) is another way to limit such controversies from developing in the first place.

Power is a word that statisticians use in a very specific way. **Statistical power** *is a measure of our ability to reject the null hypothesis given that the null hypothesis is false.* In other words, statistical power is the probability that we will reject the null hypothesis when we *should* reject the null hypothesis—the probability that we will not make a Type II error.

Statistical Power Statistical power, like the progressive powers of a microscope used to show the fine details of a butterfly's wing, refers to our ability to detect differences that really exist.

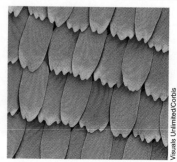

© Reuters/Corbis

Visuals Unlimited/Corbis

The calculation of statistical power ranges from a probability of 0.00 to a probability of 1.00 (or from 0% to 100%). It indicates the probability that we will be able to reject the null hypothesis—given a specific sample size and a specific effect size—if the null hypothesis should be rejected. Statisticians have historically considered a probability of 0.80 as the minimum for conducting a study. If we have an 80% chance of correctly rejecting the null hypothesis, then it is appropriate to conduct the study. Let's look at statistical power for a one-tailed z test.

The Importance of Statistical Power

To understand statistical power, we need to consider several characteristics of the two populations of interest: the population to which we're comparing our sample (population 1) and the population that we believe our sample represents (population 2). We represent these two populations visually as two overlapping curves. Let's consider a visual example for a variation on a study we used as an example in Chapter 4—a study aimed at determining whether an intervention changes the mean number of sessions attended at university counseling centers.

> ◀ **MASTERING THE CONCEPT**
>
> **8-4:** Statistical power is the likelihood of rejecting the null hypothesis when we should reject the null hypothesis. Researchers consider a probability of 0.80—an 80% chance of rejecting the null hypothesis if we should reject it—to be the minimum for conducting a study.

EXAMPLE 8.5

STEP 1. Determine the information needed to calculate statistical power—the population mean, the population standard deviation, the hypothesized mean for the sample, the sample size, and standard error based on this sample size.

In this example, the population mean number of sessions attended is 4.6, with a population standard deviation of 3.12. Let's say that we plan to have students sign contracts to attend a certain number of sessions, in the hope that this will improve attendance. More specifically, we hypothesize that a sample of 9 counseling center clients will have a mean number of sessions of 6.2, an increase in the mean of 1.6 and the equivalent of a Cohen's d of about 0.5, a medium effect. Because we have a sample of 9, we need to convert our standard deviation to standard error; to do this, we divide the standard deviation by the square root of the sample size and find that the standard error is 1.04. The numbers needed to calculate statistical power are summarized in Table 8-2.

You might wonder how we came up with the hypothesized sample mean, 6.2, above. We can never know, particularly prior to a study, what the actual effect will be. Population 2, therefore, is hypothetical; that is, we can't actually see it or know its

TABLE 8-2. The Ingredients for the Calculation of Statistical Power *not a w Test.*

To calculate statistical power for a z test, we must know the original population means and population standard deviation. We must calculate the standard error using the planned sample size. We must also have an estimate of the mean of population 2, our expectation of what the sample mean will be. It is useful to determine all these numbers before beginning.

Ingredients for Calculating Power	Counseling Center Study
Mean of population 1	$\mu_{M_1} = \mu = 4.6$
Standard deviation of the population	$\sigma = 3.12$
Standard error (using the planned sample size)	$\sigma_M = \dfrac{\sigma}{\sqrt{N}} = \dfrac{3.12}{\sqrt{9}} = 1.04$
Planned sample size	$N = 9$
Mean of population 2 (expected sample mean)	$M = 6.2;\ \mu_{M_2} = 6.2$

▪ **Statistical power** is a measure of our ability to reject the null hypothesis given that the null hypothesis is false.

summary parameters, so, ultimately, we're making an educated guess. Researchers typically estimate the mean of population 2 by examining the existing research literature or by deciding how large an effect size would make the study worthwhile (Murphy & Myors, 2004). In this case, we hypothesized a medium effect of a Cohen's d of 0.5, which translated to an increase in the mean of 1.6, from 4.6 to 6.2.

STEP 2. Determine a critical value in terms of the z distribution and in terms of the raw mean so that statistical power can be calculated.

For our example, the distribution of means for population 1, centered around 4.6, and the distribution of means for population 2, centered around 6.2, are shown in Figure 8-8. This figure also shows the critical value for a one-tailed test with a p level of 0.05. The critical value in terms of the z statistic is 1.64, which can be converted to a raw mean of 6.306.

$$M = 1.64(1.04) + 4.6 = 6.306$$

The p level is shaded in dark purple and marked as 5.0% (α). The critical value of 6.306 marks off the upper 5% of the distribution based on the null hypothesis, that for population 1.

This critical value, 6.306, has the same meaning as it did in hypothesis testing. If the test statistic for a sample falls above this cutoff, then we can reject the null hypothesis. Notice that the mean we estimated for population 2 does *not* fall above the cutoff. If the actual difference between the two populations—counseling center clients who do not sign a contract and counseling center clients who do sign a contract—is what we expect, then we can already see that there is a good chance we will not reject the null hypothesis. This indicates that we might not have enough statistical power.

STEP 3. Calculate the statistical power—the percentage of the distribution of means for population 2 (the distribution centered around the hypothesized sample mean) that falls above the critical value.

The proportion of the curve above the critical value, shaded in light purple in Figure 8-8, is statistical power, which can be calculated with the use of your z table. Remember, statistical power is the chance that we will reject the null hypothesis if we *should* reject the null hypothesis. If in fact population 2 exists, then the intervention really helps; it raises the mean number of sessions from 4.6 to 6.2, and as we know from our earlier calculations, this is a medium effect.

Statistical power in this case is the percentage of the distribution of means for population 2 (the distribution centered around 6.2) that falls above the critical value of 6.306. We'll convert this critical value to a z statistic based on the hypothesized mean of 6.2.

FIGURE 8-8
Statistical Power:
The Whole Picture

Now we can visualize statistical power in the context of two populations. Statistical power is the percentage of the distribution of means for population 2 that is above the cutoff, 46.02%. Alpha is the percentage of the distribution of means for population 1 that is above the cutoff; alpha is set by the researcher and is usually 0.05, or 5%.

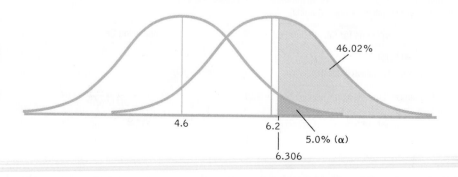

$$z = \frac{(6.306 - 6.2)}{1.04} = 0.102$$

We can look up this z statistic on the z table to determine the percentage above a z statistic of 0.102. That percentage, the area shaded in light purple in Figure 8-8, is 46.02%.

From Figure 8-8, we can see the cutoff, or critical value, as determined in reference to population 1; in raw-score form, it is 6.306. We can see that the percentage of the distribution of means for population 1 that falls above 6.306 is 0.05, or 5%, the usual p level, or alpha (sometimes written as a symbol, a), that was introduced in Chapter 7. The p level, or alpha, is the chance of making a Type I error. When we turn to the distribution of means for population 2, the percentage above that same cutoff is the statistical power. Given that population 2 exists, 46.02% of the time that we select a sample of size 9 from this population, we will be able to reject the null hypothesis. This is far below the 80% considered adequate when conducting a study. We would be wise to increase the size of our sample in this particular study.

On a practical level, statistical power calculations tell researchers how many participants are needed to conduct a study whose finding we can trust. Remember, however, that statistical power is based, to some degree, on hypothetical information. It is helpful guidance, but it is an estimate, not an exact number. We turn next to several factors that affect statistical power.

Three Factors That Affect Statistical Power

We've already discussed the effect of increasing sample size on the likelihood of rejecting the null hypothesis, but there are multiple ways to increase the power of a statistical test. Here are three, listed in order from what is usually the easiest to the most difficult when you first design your study:

(1) Increase alpha. In Figure 8-9, we see how statistical power increases when we take a p level of 0.05 and increase it to 0.10. This has the side effect of increasing the probability of a Type I error from 5% to 10%, however, so researchers choose to increase their statistical power in this manner only under particular circumstances.

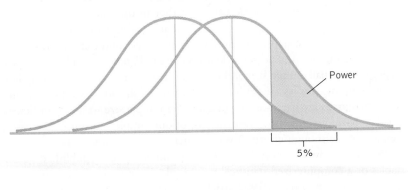

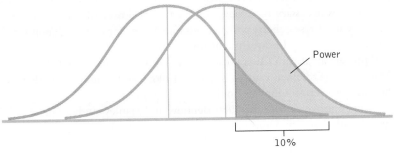

FIGURE 8-9
Increasing Alpha

As we increase our alpha from the standard of 0.05 to a larger level, such as 0.10, our statistical power increases. Because this also increases the probability of a Type I error, this is not usually a good method for increasing statistical power.

FIGURE 8-10
**Two-Tailed Versus
One-Tailed Tests**

A two-tailed test divides alpha into two
tails. When we use a one-tailed test,
putting our entire alpha into just one
tail, we increase our chances of
rejecting the null hypothesis, which
translates into an increase in statistical
power.

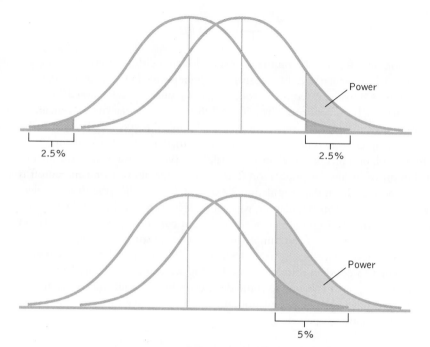

FIGURE 8-10
Two-Tailed Versus One-Tailed Tests

A two-tailed test divides alpha into two tails. When we use a one-tailed test, putting our entire alpha into just one tail, we increase our chances of rejecting the null hypothesis, which translates into an increase in statistical power.

(2) Turn a two-tailed hypothesis into a one-tailed hypothesis. We have been using a simpler one-tailed test, which provides more statistical power; however, researchers usually begin with the more conservative two-tailed test. In Figure 8-10, we see the difference between the less powerful two-tailed test (top pair of curves) and the more powerful one-tailed test (bottom pair of curves). The top pair of curves, with a two-tailed test, shows statistical power of less than 50%; the bottom pair of curves, with a one-tailed test, shows statistical power closer to 50%. If we are interested *only* in an outcome in one direction, we may consider a one-tailed test; however, it is usually best to be conservative and use a two-tailed test.

(3) Increase N. As we demonstrated earlier in this chapter, increasing sample size leads to an increase in the test statistic, making it easier to reject the null hypothesis because a larger test statistic is more likely to fall beyond our cutoff. The influence of sample size on statistical power is demonstrated in Figure 8-11. The upper pair of curves represents a small sample size, and the lower pair represents a larger sample size. In the upper pair, the curves are fairly wide because of the small sample size. In the lower pair, the curves are narrower because a larger sample size means a smaller standard error. We have direct control over the size of our samples, so simply increasing N is often an easy (although effortful) way to increase statistical power.

Statistical power is most frequently determined by using published statistical power tables or a computerized statistical power calculator. One of the best published tables is by Jacob Cohen in his 1992 article "A Power Primer." Cohen provides a table of sample sizes necessary to achieve 0.80 statistical power (the amount considered adequate by most researchers) with various effect sizes for eight different hypothesis tests. Also, many statistical power calculators can be found by conducing an online search for "power calculator." Or you can download the free software G★Power, available for Mac or PC (Erdfelder, Faul, & Buchner, 1996; search online for G★Power or find the link on the Web site for this book).

The controversy over the 1980 Benbow and Stanley study of gender differences in mathematical ability demonstrates why it is important to go beyond hypothesis test-

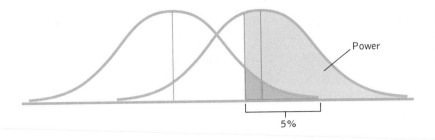

FIGURE 8-11
Increasing Sample Size

As sample size increases (from the top set to the bottom set of curves), the distributions of means become more narrow and there is less overlap. Less overlap means more statistical power.

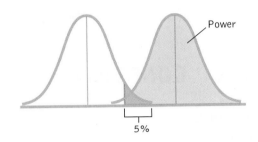

ing. A graph informed us that the two distributions of male and female scores were almost identical—the two distributions overlapped almost completely. However, the study used 10,000 participants, so it had plenty of statistical power, and we can trust that the statistically significant difference they found was real. But the effect size informed us that this statistically significant difference was trivial—it had no practical importance. Combining all four ways of analyzing the data (hypothesis testing, confidence intervals, effect size, and power analysis) provides a more complete, precise description of data.

CHECK YOUR LEARNING

Reviewing the Concepts

> Statistical power is the probability that we will reject the null hypothesis if we should reject it.

> Ideally, a study is not conducted unless the researcher has 80% statistical power; that is, at least 80% of the time we will correctly reject the null hypothesis.

> Statistical power is affected by several factors, but most directly by sample size.

> Before conducting a study, researchers often use a statistical power table or online statistical power calculator to determine the number of participants they will need to ensure statistical power of 0.80.

> To get the most complete story about our data, it is best to combine the results of a hypothesis test with the information gained from computing confidence intervals, effect size, p_{rep}, and power.

Clarifying the Concepts

8-10 What are three ways to increase the power of a statistical test?

Calculating the Statistics

8-11 Check Your Learning 8-3 and 8-9 discussed a study aimed at changing CFC scores through a career discussion group. Imagine that those in the career discussion group of 45 students have a mean CFC score of 3.7. Let's say that you know that the population mean CFC score is 3.51, with a standard deviation of 0.61. Calculate statistical power for this as a one-tailed test.

continued on next page

Applying the Concepts

Solutions to these Check Your Learning questions can be found in Appendix D.

8-12 Refer to Check Your Learning 8-11.

a. Explain what the number obtained in your statistical power calculation means.

b. Describe how the researchers might increase statistical power.

REVIEW OF CONCEPTS

Confidence Intervals

A summary statistic, such as a mean, is a *point estimate* of the population mean. A more useful estimate is an *interval estimate,* a range of plausible numbers for the population mean. The most commonly used interval estimate in the social sciences is the *confidence interval,* which can be created around a mean using a z distribution. The confidence interval is created by subtracting and adding a margin of error from a mean or difference between means. The confidence interval provides the same information as a hypothesis test but also gives us a range of values; thus, it is more useful than a hypothesis test.

Effect Size and p_{rep}

Knowing that a difference is statistically significant does not provide information about the size of the effect, particularly because of the effect of sample size on the size of the test statistic. A study with a large sample size might find a small effect to be statistically significant, whereas a study with a small sample might fail to detect a large effect. To understand the importance of a finding, we must calculate an *effect size.* Effect sizes are independent of sample size because they are based on distributions of scores rather than distributions of means. One common effect-size measure is *Cohen's d,* which can be used when a z test has been conducted. We can compare effect sizes with guidelines developed by Cohen to get a sense of how large they are.

When we conduct hypothesis testing, we can also calculate p_{rep} in addition, or as an alternative, to p. Developed as a more easily interpretable and less easily misunderstood indicator of the outcome of a hypothesis testing, p_{rep} is the probability of replicating an effect given a particular population and sample size.

Statistical Power

Statistical power is a measure of our ability to correctly reject the null hypothesis; that is, it is the chance that we will not commit a Type II error when the research hypothesis is true. Statistical power is affected most directly by sample size, but it is also affected by the choice of alpha (cutoff p level) and the decision to use a one-tailed or two-tailed test. Researchers often use a computerized statistical power calculator to determine the appropriate sample size to achieve 0.80, or 80%, statistical power, given certain considerations (e.g., expected effect size, alpha).

How It Works

8.1 CALCULATING CONFIDENCE INTERVALS

The Graded Naming Test (GNT) asks respondents to name objects in a set of 30 black-and-white drawings in order to detect brain damage. The GNT population norm for adults in England is 20.4. Researchers wondered whether a sample of Canadian adults had different scores from adults in England (Roberts, 2003). If the scores were different, the English norms would not be valid for use in Canada. The mean for 30 Canadian adults was 17.5. Assume that the standard deviation of the adults in England is 3.2. How can we calculate a 95% confidence interval for these data?

Given $\mu = 20.4$ and $\sigma = 3.2$, we can start by calculating standard error:

$$\sigma_M = \frac{\sigma}{\sqrt{N}} = \frac{3.2}{\sqrt{30}} = 0.584$$

We then find the z values that mark off the most extreme 0.025 in each tail, which are -1.96 and 1.96. We calculate the lower end of the interval as:

$$M_{lower} = -z(\sigma_M) + M_{sample} = -1.96(0.584) + 17.5 = 16.36$$

We calculate the upper end of the interval as:

$$M_{upper} = z(\sigma_M) + M_{sample} = -1.96(0.584) + 17.5 = 16.36$$

The 95% confidence interval around the mean of 17.5 is [16.36, 18.64].

How can we calculate the 90% confidence interval for the same data? In this case, we find the z values that mark off the most extreme 0.05 in each tail, which are -1.645 and 1.645. We calculate the lower end of the interval as:

$$M_{lower} = -z(\sigma_M) + M_{sample} = -1.645(0.584) + 17.5 = 16.54$$

We calculate the upper end of the interval as:

$$M_{upper} = z(\sigma_M) + M_{sample} = 1.645(0.584) + 17.5 = 18.46$$

The 90% confidence interval around the mean of 17.5 is [16.54, 18.46].

What can we say about these two confidence intervals in comparison to each other? The range of the 95% confidence interval is larger than that of the 90% confidence interval. When calculating the 95% confidence interval, we are describing where we think a larger portion of our sample means will fall if we repeatedly select samples of this size from the same population (95% as opposed to 90%), so we have a larger range within which those means are likely to fall.

8.2 CALCULATING EFFECT SIZE

The Graded Naming Test (GNT) study has a population norm for adults in England of 20.4. Researchers found a mean for 30 Canadian adults of 17.5, and we assumed a standard deviation of adults in England of 3.2 (Roberts, 2003). How can we calculate an effect size for these data?

The appropriate measure of effect size for a z statistic is Cohen's d, which is calculated as:

$$d = \frac{M - \mu}{\sigma} = \frac{20.4 - 17.5}{3.2} = 0.91$$

Based on Cohen's conventions, this is a large effect size.

Exercises

Clarifying the Concepts

8.1 What specific danger exists when reporting a statistically significant difference between two group means?

8.2 In your own words, define the word *confidence*—first as you would use it in everyday conversation and then as

a statistician would use it in the context of a confidence interval.

8.3 Why do we calculate confidence intervals?

8.4 What are the five steps to create a confidence interval for a z distribution?

8.5 In your own words, define the word *effect*—first as you would use it in everyday conversation and then as a statistician would use it.

8.6 What effect does increasing the sample size have on the standard error and the test statistic for every hypothesis test?

8.7 Relate effect size to the concept of overlap between comparison distributions.

8.8 What does it mean to say the effect-size statistic, such as Cohen's *d,* neutralizes the influence of sample size?

8.9 What are Cohen's guidelines for small, medium, and large effects?

8.10 Why is it useful to calculate p_{rep} in addition to, or instead of, a *p* value?

8.11 In your own words, define the word *power*—first as you would use it in everyday conversation and then as a statistician would use it.

8.12 How does power relate to Type II errors?

8.13 Traditionally, what minimum percentage chance of correctly rejecting the null hypothesis do we need in order to proceed with our experiment?

8.14 Explain how increasing alpha increases power.

8.15 How are power and effect size different but related?

Calculating the Statistics

8.16 In statistics, concepts are often expressed in symbols and equations. For each of the following, (i) identify the incorrect symbol, (ii) state what the correct symbol should be, and (iii) explain why the initial symbol was incorrect.

  a. $M_{lower} = -z(\sigma) + M_{sample}$

  b. $d = \dfrac{M - \mu}{\sigma_M}$

8.17 In 2008, the Gallup poll asked people whether or not they were suspicious of steroid use among Olympic athletes. Thirty-five percent of respondents indicated suspicion when they saw an athlete break a track-and-field record, with a 4% margin of error. Calculate an interval estimate.

8.18 Twenty-two percent of Gallup respondents indicated suspicion of steroid use by athletes who broke world records in swimming. Calculate an interval estimate using a margin of error at 3.5%.

8.19 In 2006, approximately 47% of Americans, when surveyed by a Gallup poll, felt that having a gun in the home made them safer than having no gun. The margin of error reported was 3%. Construct an interval estimate.

8.20 For each of the following confidence intervals, indicate how much of the distribution would be placed in the cutoff region for a two-tailed test.

  a. 80%

  b. 85%

  c. 99%

8.21 For each of the following confidence intervals, look up the critical cutoff *z* value for a two-tailed test.

  a. 80%

  b. 85%

  c. 99%

8.22 Calculate the 95% confidence interval for the following fictional data regarding daily TV viewing habits: $\mu = 4.7$ hours; $\sigma = 1.3$ hours; sample of 78 people with a mean of 4.1 hours.

8.23 Calculate the 80% confidence interval for the same fictional data regarding daily TV viewing habits: $\mu = 4.7$ hours; $\sigma = 1.3$ hours; sample of 78 people with mean of 4.1 hours.

8.24 Calculate the 99% confidence interval for the same fictional data regarding daily TV viewing habits: $\mu = 4.7$ hours; $\sigma = 1.3$ hours; sample of 78 people with mean of 4.1 hours.

8.25 Calculate the standard error for each of the following sample sizes when $\mu = 1014$ and $\sigma = 136$:

  a. 12

  b. 39

  c. 188

8.26 For a given variable, imagine we know that the population mean is 1014 and the standard deviation is 136. A mean of 1057 is obtained based on sampling. Calculate the *z* test statistic for this mean, assuming it was found using each of the following sample sizes:

  a. 12

  b. 39

  c. 188

8.27 Calculate the effect size for the mean of 1057 observed in Exercise 8.26 where $\mu = 1014$ and $\sigma = 136$.

8.28 Calculate the effect size for each of the following average SAT math scores. Remember, SAT math is standardized such that $\mu = 500$ and $\sigma = 100$.

  a. 61 people sampled have a mean of 480

  b. 82 people sampled have a mean of 520

  c. 6 people sampled have a mean of 610

8.29 For each of the effect-size calculations in Exercise 8.28, identify the size of the effect using Cohen's guidelines. Remember, for SAT math, $\mu = 500$ and $\sigma = 100$.

  a. 61 people sampled have a mean of 480

  b. 82 people sampled have a mean of 520

  c. 6 people sampled have a mean of 610

8.30 For each of the following d values, identify the size of the effect using Cohen's guidelines.

   a. $d = 0.79$

   b. $d = -0.43$

   c. $d = 0.22$

   d. $d = -0.04$

8.31 The first step in calculating p_{rep} is knowing the actual p value of your test statistic. For each of the following z statistics, calculate the p value for a one-tailed test.

   a. 2.23

   b. -1.82

   c. 0.33

8.32 For each of the following z statistics, calculate the p value for a two-tailed test.

   a. 2.23

   b. -1.82

   c. 0.33

8.33 The second step in calculating p_{rep} is conducted using software such as Microsoft Excel. For each of the three z statistics you considered in Exercise 8.31 as a one-tailed test, determine p_{rep}. Be sure to use the appropriate p values.

   a. 2.23

   b. -1.82

   c. 0.33

8.34 For each of the three z statistics you considered in Exercise 8.32 as a two-tailed test, determine p_{rep}.

   a. 2.23

   b. -1.82

   c. 0.33

8.35 Using the table of numbers provided below, calculate statistical power for a one-tailed test ($a = 0.05$, or 5%) aimed at determining if those in the sample sleep fewer hours, on average, than those the population.

Mean of population 1	16 hours of sleep
Standard deviation of the population	1.7 hours of sleep
Standard error	$\sigma_M = \dfrac{\sigma}{\sqrt{N}} = \dfrac{1.7}{\sqrt{37}} = 0.279$
Sample size	37 infants
Mean of population 2	14.9 hours of sleep

Applying the Concepts

8.36 A friend reads in her *Introduction to Psychology* textbook about a minority group in Japan, the Buraku- min, who are racially the same as other Japanese people but are viewed as outcasts because their ancestors were employed in positions that involved the handling of dead animals (e.g., butchers). In Japan, the text reported, mean IQ scores of Burakumin were 10 to 15 points below mean IQ scores of other Japanese. In the United States, where Burakumin experienced no discrimination, there was no mean difference (from Ogbu, 1986, as reported in Hockenbury & Hockenbury, 2003). Your friend says to you: "Wow—when I taught English in Japan last summer, I had a Burakumin student. He seemed smart; perhaps I was fooled." What should your friend consider about the two distributions, the one for Burakumin people and the one for other Japanese people?

8.37 Here are summary data from a z test regarding scores on the Consideration of Future Consequences scale (Petrocelli, 2003): the population mean (μ) is 3.51, and the population standard deviation (σ) is 0.61. Imagine that a sample of students had a mean of 3.7.

   a. Calculate the test statistic for a sample of 5 students.

   b. Calculate the test statistic for a sample of 1000 students.

   c. Calculate the test statistic for a sample of 1,000,000 students.

   d. Explain why the test statistic varies so much even though the population mean, population standard deviation, and sample mean do not change.

   e. Why might sample size pose a problem for hypothesis testing and the conclusions we are able to draw?

8.38 In an exercise in Chapter 7, we asked you to conduct a z test to ascertain whether the Graded Naming Test (GNT) scores for Canadian participants differed from the GNT norms based on adults in England. The mean for a sample of 30 adults in Canada was 17.5. The normative mean for adults in England is 20.4, and we assume a population standard deviation of 3.2. With 30 participants, the z statistic was -4.97 and we were able to reject the null hypothesis.

   a. Calculate the test statistic for 3 participants. How does the test statistic change compared to when N of 30 was used? Conduct step 6 of hypothesis testing. Does your conclusion change? If so, does this mean that the actual difference between groups changed? Explain.

   b. Calculate the test statistic for 100 participants. How does the test statistic change?

   c. Calculate the test statistic for 20,000 participants. How does the test statistic change?

   d. What is the effect of sample size on the test statistic?

   e. As the test statistic changes, has the underlying difference between groups changed? Why might this present a problem for hypothesis testing?

8.39 Unsavory researchers know that one can cheat with hypothesis testing. That is, they know that a researcher can stack the deck in her or his favor, making it easier to reject the null hypothesis.

    a. If you wanted to make it easier to reject the null hypothesis, what are three specific things you could do?

    b. Would it change the actual difference between your samples? Why is this a potential problem with hypothesis testing?

8.40 A midwestern university reported that its social science majors tended to outperform its humanities majors on the LSATs (which gives them an edge at getting into law school). Sadie, an English major, and Kofi, a sociology major, both just took the LSAT.

    a. Can we tell which student will do better on the LSAT? Explain your answer.

    b. Draw a picture that represents what the two distributions, that for social science majors and that for humanities majors at this institution, might look like with respect to one another.

8.41 Your roommate is reading *Fantasyland: A Season on Baseball's Lunatic Fringe* (Walker, 2006) and is intrigued by the statistical methods used by competitors in fantasy baseball leagues (in which competitors select their own team of baseball players from across all major league teams, and win the fantasy league if their eclectic roster of players outperforms the chosen mixes of other fantasy competitors). Among the many statistics reported in the book is a finding that major league baseball players who recently had a third child show more of a decline in performance than players who recently had a first child or a second child. Your friend remembers that Johnny Damon had a third child within the last few years and drops him from consideration for his fantasy team.

    a. Explain to your friend why a difference between means doesn't provide information about any specific individual player. Include a drawing of overlapping curves as part of your answer. On the drawing, mark places on the *x*-axis that might represent a player from the distribution of those who recently had a third child (mark with an *X*) scoring *above* a player from the distribution of those who recently had a first or second child (mark with a *Y*).

    b. Explain to your friend that a statistically significant difference doesn't necessarily indicate a large effect size. How might a measure of effect size, such as Cohen's *d,* help us understand the importance of these findings and compare them to other predictors of performance that might have larger effects?

    c. Given that the reported association is true, can we conclude that having a third child *causes* a decline

in performance? Explain your answer. What confounds might lead to the difference observed in this study?

    d. Given the relatively limited numbers of major league baseball players (and the relatively limited numbers of those who recently had a child—whether first, second, or third), what general guess would you make about the likely statistical power of this analysis?

8.42 In an exercise in Chapter 7, we asked whether college football teams tend to be more likely or less likely to be mismatched in the upper National Collegiate Athletic Association (NCAA) divisions. During week 11 of the fall 2006 college football season, the population of 53 Division I-A games had a mean spread (winning score minus losing score) of 16.189, with a standard deviation of 12.128. We took a sample of four games that were played that week in the next-highest league, Division I-AA, to see if the spread was different; one of the many leagues within Division I-AA, the Patriot League, played four games that weekend. Their mean was 8.75.

    a. Calculate the 95% confidence interval for this sample.

    b. State in your own words what we learn from this confidence interval.

    c. What information does the confidence interval give us that we also get from a hypothesis test?

    d. What additional information does the confidence interval give us that we do not get from a hypothesis test?

8.43 Using the football data presented in Exercise 8.42, practice evaluating data using confidence intervals.

    a. Compute the 80% confidence interval.

    b. How does your conclusion and the confidence interval change as you move from 95% confidence to 80% confidence?

    c. Why don't we talk about having 100% confidence?

8.44 In Exercises 8.42 and 8.43, we considered the study of week 11 of the fall 2006 college football season, during which the population of 53 Division I-A games had a mean spread (winning score minus losing score) of 16.189, with a standard deviation of 12.128. The sample of four games that were played that week in the next-highest league, Division I-AA, had a mean of 8.75.

    a. Calculate the appropriate measure of effect size for this sample.

    b. Based on Cohen's conventions, is this a small, medium, or large effect size?

    c. Why is it useful to have this information in addition to the results of a hypothesis test?

8.45 In Exercises 8.42 and 8.43, we considered the study of week 11 of the fall 2006 college football season. In an exercise in Chapter 7, we conducted a two-tailed hypothesis test and calculated a z statistic of -1.23.

   a. Determine p_{rep} for this example.

   b. Explain in your own words what this means.

8.46 According to the Nielsen Company, Americans spend $345 million on chocolate during the week of Valentine's Day. Let's assume that we know the average married person spends $45 with a population standard deviation of $16. In February 2009, the U.S. economy was in the throes of a recession and threat of depression. Comparing data for Valentine's Day spending in 2009 with what is generally expected might give us some indication of the attitudes of American citizens.

   a. We obtain a sample of 18 married people and find that they spent $38 on average. Compute the 95% confidence interval.

   b. How does the 95% confidence interval change if our sample mean was based on 180 people?

   c. If you were testing a hypothesis that things had changed under the financial circumstances of 2009, what conclusion would you draw in part (a) versus part (b)?

   d. Compute the effect size based on these data and describe the size of the effect.

8.47 Let's assume the average speed of a serve in men's tennis is around 135 mph with a standard deviation of 6.5 mph. Because these statistics are calculated over many years and many players, we will treat them as population parameters. We develop a new training method that will increase arm strength, the force of the tennis swing, and the speed of the serve, we hope. We recruit 9 professional tennis players to use our method. After six months, we test the speed of their serve and compute an average of 138 mph.

   a. Using a 95% confidence interval, test the hypothesis that our method makes a difference.

   b. Compute the effect size and describe its strength.

8.48 Let's assume the average speed of a serve in women's tennis is around 118 mph with a standard deviation of 12 mph. We recruit 26 amateur tennis players to use our method this time, and after six months we calculate a group mean of 123 mph.

   a. Using a 95% confidence interval, test the hypothesis that our method makes a difference.

   b. Compute the effect size and describe its strength.

8.49 In Exercise 8.38, we explored a study of the Graded Naming Test.

   a. In Chapter 7, we calculated a z statistic of -4.97 for 30 participants. Determine p_{rep} for this example. (*Note:* Excel won't work with a proportion of 0.0000, so use a proportion of 0.000001, a number very close to 0, instead.)

   b. In one part of the question, you were asked to calculate the z statistic for a sample of just 3 participants. Based on the z statistic you calculated, what is p_{rep}?

   c. Keeping all else the same, what happens to p_{rep} as sample size increases?

8.50 Calculate power for the test performed in Exercise 8.47 using the following alpha levels in a one-tailed test:

   a. alpha of 0.05, or 5%

   b. alpha of 0.10, or 10%

   c. Explain how power is affected by alpha in these calculations.

8.51 We can witness the importance of alpha by recomputing power for the data presented in Exercise 8.35.

   a. For this new computation, use alpha of 0.01, or 1%, for the one-tailed test.

   b. Explain why changing alpha affects power.

   c. If using a smaller alpha reduces power, why not use a larger alpha?

8.52 Use the data presented in Exercise 8.35 to answer these questions.

   a. Without performing any computations, describe how power is affected by performing a two-tailed test.

   b. Why are two-tailed tests recommended over one-tailed tests?

8.53 The easiest way to affect a hypothesis test is to increase our sample size. Similarly, true results may sometimes be missed because a sufficient sample was not used in the research.

   a. Perform steps 5 and 6 of the hypothesis test on the data in Exercise 8.35 with a sample of 37.

   b. Perform the same steps of the hypothesis test but assume our mean was based on only 4 infants.

8.54 The easiest way to increase statistical power is to increase our sample size. Similarly, statistical power decreases with a smaller sample size. Use the data in Exercises 8.35 and 8.53 to answer the following questions.

   a. Compute the statistical power of the one-tailed statistical test with alpha of 0.05 when N is 4.

   b. How does that value compare to when N was 37 in Exercise 8.35?

8.55 In several exercises in this chapter, we considered the study of week 11 of the fall 2006 college football season, during which the population of 53 Division I-A games had a mean spread (winning score minus losing score) of 16.189, with a standard deviation of 12.128. The sample of four games that were played that week in the next-highest league, Division I-AA, had a mean of 8.75.

a. Calculate statistical power for this study using a one-tailed test.

b. What does the statistical power suggest about how we should view the findings of this study?

c. Using G★Power or an online power calculator, calculate statistical power for this study for a one-tailed test with a p level of 0.05.

Terms

point estimate (p. 177)
interval estimate (p. 177)
confidence interval (p. 178)

effect size (p. 183)
Cohen's d (p. 186)

p_{rep} (p. 187)
statistical power (p. 188)

Formulas

$M_{lower} = -z(\sigma_M) + M_{sample}$ (p. 180)

$M_{upper} = z(\sigma_M) + M_{sample}$ (p. 180)

Cohen's $d = \dfrac{(M - \mu)}{\sigma}$ for a z distribution (p. 186)

p_{rep} =NORMSDIST (NORMSINV(1 -P)/ (SQRT(2))) [used in Microsoft Excel] (p. 187)

Symbols

Cohen's d (or just d) (p. 186)
p_{rep} (p. 187)
α (p. 190)

The Single-Sample *t* Test and the Paired-Samples *t* Test

BEFORE YOU GO ON

- You should know the six steps of hypothesis testing (Chapter 7).

- You should know how to determine a confidence interval for a *z* statistic (Chapter 8).

- You should understand the concept of effect size and know how to calculate Cohen's *d* for a *z* test (Chapter 8).

Holiday Weight Gain and Two-Group Studies Two-group studies indicate that the average holiday weight gain by college students is less than many people believe, only about 1 pound.

Upon arriving at college, many undergraduate students are faced with what might seem like incessant warnings about weight gain, including the dreaded "freshman 15," the waistline expansions resulting from spring break excess, and the pounds put on over the annual winter holidays. In North America, as in many other parts of the world, the winter holiday season is a time when family food traditions take center stage. These holiday foods usually are readily available, beautifully presented, and high in calories. Popular wisdom suggests that many Americans add 5 to 7 pounds to their body weight over the holiday season. But before/after studies suggest a far more modest increase: a weight gain of just over 1 pound (Hull, Radley, Dinger, & Fields, 2006; Roberts & Mayer, 2000; Yanovski et al, 2000).

A 1-pound weight gain over the holidays might not seem so bad, but weight gained over the holidays tends to stay (Yanovski et al, 2000). The data provide other insights about holiday weight gain. For example, female students at the University of Oklahoma gained a little less than 1 pound, male students a little more than 1 pound, and students who were already overweight gained an average of 2.2 pounds (Hull et al, 2006).

The fact that researchers used two groups in their study—students before the holidays and students after the holidays—is significant for this chapter.

The versatility of the *t* distributions allows us to compare two groups. We can compare one sample to a population when we don't know all of the details about the parameters, and we can compare two samples to each other. There are two ways to compare two samples: we can use a within-groups design (as when the same people are weighed before and after the holidays) or a between-groups design (as when different people are in the pre-holiday sample and the post-holiday sample). Whether we use a within-groups design or a between-groups design to collect the data for two groups, we use a *t* test. For a within-groups design, we use a paired-samples *t* test. Because the steps for a paired-samples *t* test are similar to those for a single-sample *t* test, we learn about these two tests in this chapter. For a between-groups design, we use an independent-samples *t* test. Because the calculations for an independent-samples *t* test are a bit different from the first two types of *t* tests, we learn about that test in Chapter 10.

> ▶ **MASTERING THE CONCEPT**
>
> **9-1:** There are three types of *t* tests. We use a single-sample *t* test when we are comparing a sample mean to a population mean but do not know the population standard deviation. We use a paired-samples *t* test when we are comparing two samples and every participant is in both samples—a within-groups design. We use an independent-samples *t* test when we are comparing two samples and every participant is in only one sample—a between-groups design.

The *t* Distributions

When we compare the average weight of a sample of people before the holidays to the average weight of a sample of people after the holidays, we are concerned about whether the samples are fair representations of the larger populations. The *t* test, based on the *t* distributions, tells us how confident we can be that what we have learned from our samples generalizes to the larger populations.

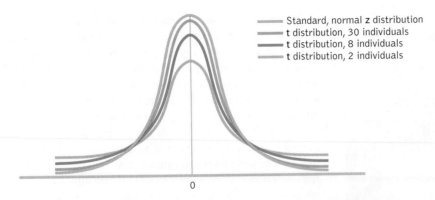

Standard, normal **z** distribution
t distribution, 30 individuals
t distribution, 8 individuals
t distribution, 2 individuals

0

FIGURE 9-1
The Wider and Flatter
***t* Distributions**

For smaller samples, the *t* distributions are wider and flatter than the *z* distribution. As the sample size increases, however, the *t* distributions approach the shape of the *z* distribution. In this figure, the *t* distribution most similar to the *z* distribution is that for a sample of approximately 30 individuals. This makes sense because a distribution derived from a larger sample size would be more likely to be similar to that of the entire population than one derived from a smaller sample size.

The *t* distributions are used when we don't have enough information to use the *z* distribution. Specifically, we have to use a *t* distribution when we don't know the population standard deviation or when we compare two samples to one another. As Figure 9-1 demonstrates, there are many *t* distributions—one for each possible sample size. As the sample size gets smaller, we become less certain about what the population distribution really looks like, and they distributions become flatter and more spread out. However, as the sample size gets bigger, the *t* distributions begin to merge with the *z* distribution because we gain confidence as more and more participants are added to our study.

> ◀ **MASTERING THE CONCEPT**
>
> **9-2:** We use a *t* distribution instead of a *z* distribution when sampling requires us to estimate the population standard deviation from the sample standard deviation or when we compare two samples to one another.

Estimating Population Standard Deviation from the Sample

Before we can conduct a *t* test, we have to estimate the standard deviation. To do this, we use the standard deviation of the sample data to estimate the standard deviation of the entire population. Estimating the standard deviation is the only practical difference between conducting a *z* test with the *z* distribution and conducting a *t* test with a *t* distribution. Here is the standard deviation formula that we have used up until now with a sample:

$$SD = \sqrt{\frac{\Sigma(X - M)^2}{N}}$$

We need to make a correction to this formula to account for the fact that there is likely to be some level of error when we're estimating the population standard deviation from a sample. Specifically, any given sample is likely to have somewhat less spread than is the entire population. One tiny alteration of this formula leads to the slightly larger standard deviation of the population that we estimate from the standard deviation of the sample. Instead of dividing by *N*, we divide by $(N - 1)$ to get the mean of the squared deviations. Subtraction is the key. Dividing by a slightly smaller number, $(N - 1)$, instead of by *N* increases the value of the standard deviation. For example, if the numerator was 90 and the denominator (*N*) was 10, the answer is 9; if we divide by $(N - 1) = (10 - 1) = 9$, the answer is 10, a slightly larger value. So the formula for estimating the standard deviation of the population from the standard deviation of the sample is:

$$s = \sqrt{\frac{\Sigma(X - M)^2}{(N - 1)}}$$

> **MASTERING THE FORMULA**
>
> **9-1:** The formula for standard deviation when estimating from a sample is: $s = \sqrt{\frac{\Sigma(X - M)^2}{(N - 1)}}$. We subtract 1 from the sample size in the denominator to correct for the probability that the sample standard deviation slightly underestimates the actual standard deviation in the population. ◀

Multitasking If multitasking reduces productivity in a sample, we can statistically determine the likelihood that multitasking reduces productivity among a much larger population.

Notice that we call this standard deviation *s* instead of *SD*. It still uses Latin rather than Greek letters because it is a statistic (from a sample) rather than a parameter (from a population). From now on, we will calculate the standard deviation in this way (because we will be using the sample standard deviation to estimate the population standard deviation), and we will be calling our standard deviation *s*.

Let's apply the new formula for standard deviation to an everyday situation that many of us can relate to: multitasking. This formula marks an important step in conducting a *t* test. Researchers conducted a study in which employees were observed at one of two high-tech companies for over 1000 hours (Mark, Gonzalez, & Harris, 2005). The employees spent just 11 minutes, on average, on one project before an interruption. Moreover, after each interruption, they needed an average of 25 minutes to get back to the original project! So even though a person who is busy multitasking appears to be productive, maybe the underlying reality is that multitasking actually *reduces* overall productivity. How can we use a *t* test to determine the effects of multitasking on productivity?

Suppose you were a manager at one of these firms and decided to reserve a period from 1:00 to 3:00 each afternoon during which employees could not interrupt one another, but they might still be interrupted by phone calls or e-mails from people outside the company. To test your intervention, you observe five employees during these periods and develop a score for each—the time he or she spent on a selected task before being interrupted. Here are your fictional data: 8, 12, 16, 12, and 14 minutes. In this case, we are treating 11 minutes as the population mean, but we do not know the population standard deviation. As a key step in conducting a *t* test, we need to estimate the standard deviation of the population from the sample.

EXAMPLE 9.1

To calculate our estimated standard deviation for the population, there are two steps.

STEP 1. Calculate the sample mean.

Even though we are given a population mean (i.e., 11), we use the *sample* mean to calculate the corrected standard deviation for the *sample*. The mean for these 5 sample scores is:

$$M = \frac{(8 + 12 + 16 + 12 + 14)}{5} = 12.4$$

STEP 2. Use this sample mean in the corrected formula for the standard deviation.

$$s = \sqrt{\frac{\Sigma(X - M)^2}{(N - 1)}}$$

Remember, the easiest way to calculate the numerator under the square root sign is by first organizing our data into columns, as shown here:

X	X − M	(X − M)²
8	−4.4	19.36
12	−0.4	0.16
16	3.6	12.96
12	−0.4	0.16
14	1.6	2.56

Thus, the numerator is:

$$\Sigma(X - M)^2 = \Sigma(19.36 + 0.16 + 12.96 + 0.16 + 2.56) = 35.2$$

And given a sample size of 5, the corrected standard deviation is:

$$s = \sqrt{\frac{\Sigma(X - M)^2}{(N - 1)}} = \sqrt{\frac{35.2}{(5 - 1)}} = \sqrt{8.8} = 2.97$$

A Simple Correction: *N* − 1 When estimating variability, subtracting one person from a sample of four makes a big difference. Subtracting one person from a sample of thousands makes only a small difference.

Calculating Standard Error for the *t* Statistic

After we make the correction, we have an estimate of the standard deviation of the distribution of scores but not an estimate of the spread of a distribution of means, the standard error. As we did with the *z* distribution, we need to make our spread smaller to reflect the fact that a distribution of means is less variable than a distribution of scores. We do this in exactly the same way that we adjusted for the *z* distribution. We divide *s* by $\sqrt{N}$. The formula for the standard error as estimated from a sample, therefore, is:

$$s_M = \frac{s}{\sqrt{N}}$$

MASTERING THE FORMULA

9-2: The formula for standard error when we're estimating from a sample is: $s_M = \frac{s}{\sqrt{N}}$. It only differs from the formula for standard error we learned previously in that we're using *s* instead of σ because we're working from a sample instead of a population.

Notice that we have replaced σ with s because we are using the corrected standard deviation from the sample rather than the actual standard deviation from the population.

EXAMPLE 9.2

Here's how we would convert our corrected standard deviation of 2.97 (from the data above on minutes before an interruption) to a standard error. Our sample size was 5, so we divide by the square root of 5:

$$s_M = \frac{s}{\sqrt{N}} = \frac{2.97}{\sqrt{5}} = 1.33$$

So the appropriate standard deviation for the distribution of means—that is, its standard error—is 1.33. Just as the central limit theorem predicts, the standard error for the distribution of sample means is smaller than the standard deviation of sample scores (1.33 < 2.97).

(*Note:* This step leads to one of the most common mistakes that we see among our students. Because we have implemented a correction when calculating *s*, students want to implement an extra correction here by dividing by $\sqrt{(N-1)}$. Do not do this! We still divide by $\sqrt{N}$ in this step. We are making our standard deviation smaller to reflect the size of the sample; there is no need for a further correction to the standard error.)

Using Standard Error to Calculate the *t* Statistic

Once we know how to estimate the population standard deviation from our sample and then use that to calculate standard error, we have all the tools necessary to conduct a *t* test. The simplest type of *t* test is the single-sample *t* test. We introduce the formula for that *t* statistic here, and in the next section we go through all six steps for a single-sample *t* test. The formula to calculate the *t* statistic for a single-sample *t* test is identical to that for the *z* statistic, except that it uses the *estimated* standard error rather than the *actual* standard error of the population of means. So, *the **t** statistic indicates the distance of a sample mean from a population mean in terms of the standard error.* That distance is expressed numerically as the estimated number of standard errors between the two means. Here is the formula for the *t* statistic for a distribution of means:

$$t = \frac{(M - \mu_M)}{s_M}$$

MASTERING THE FORMULA

9-3: The formula for the *t* statistic is: $t = \frac{(M - \mu_M)}{s_M}$. It only differs from the formula for the *z* statistic in that we use s_M instead of σ_M, because we're using the sample to estimate standard error rather than using the actual population standard error.

Note that the denominator is the only difference between this formula for the *t* statistic and the formula used to compute the *z* statistic for a sample mean. The corrected denominator makes the *t* statistic smaller and thereby reduces the probability of observing an extreme *t* statistic. That is, a *t* statistic is not as extreme as a *z* statistic; in scientific terms, it's more conservative.

EXAMPLE 9.3

The *t* statistic for our sample of 5 scores representing minutes until interruptions is:

$$t = \frac{(M - \mu_M)}{s_M} = \frac{(12.4 - 11)}{1.33} = 1.05$$

As part of the six steps of hypothesis testing, this *t* statistic, 1.05, can help us make an inference about whether the communication ban from 1:00 to 3:00 affected the average number of minutes until an interruption.

As with the z distribution, statisticians have developed t tables that include probabilities under any area of the t curve. We provide you with a t table for many different sample sizes in Appendix B. The t table includes only the percentages of most interest to researchers—those indicating the extreme scores that suggest large differences between groups.

CHECK YOUR LEARNING

Reviewing the Concepts

> The t distributions are used when we do not know the population standard deviation or are comparing only two groups.

> The two groups may be a sample and a population, or the two groups may be two samples as part of a within-groups design or a between-groups design.

> Because we do not know the population standard deviation, we must estimate it, and estimating invites the possibility of more error.

> The formula for the t statistic for a single-sample t test is the same as the formula for the z statistic for a distribution of means, except that we use estimated standard error in the denominator rather than the actual standard error for the population.

Clarifying the Concepts

9-1 What is the t statistic?

9-2 Briefly describe the three different t tests.

Calculating the Statistics

9-3 Calculate the standard deviation for a sample (SD) and as an estimate of the population (s) using the following data: 6, 3, 7, 6, 4, 5.

9-4 Calculate the standard error for t for the data given in Check Your Learning 9-3.

Applying the Statistics

9-5 In our discussion of a study on multitasking (Mark et al, 2005), we imagined a follow-up study in which five employees were observed following a communication ban from 1:00 to 3:00. For each of the five employees, one task was selected. Let's now examine the time until work on that task was resumed. The fictional data for the 5 employees were 20, 19, 27, 24, and 18 minutes until work on the given task was resumed. Remember that the original research showed it took 25 minutes on average for an employee to return to a task after being interrupted.

   a. What distribution will be used in this situation? Explain your answer.

   b. Determine the appropriate mean and standard deviation (or standard error) for this distribution. Show all your work; use symbolic notation and formulas where appropriate.

   c. Calculate the t statistic.

Solutions to these Check Your Learning questions can be found in Appendix D.

The Single-Sample *t* Test

A before/after comparison of weight change over the holidays is only one of the interesting comparisons we can make using the t statistic. There might also be regional differences in how much people weigh. For example, the t statistic can be used to compare the average weight from a sample of people in a particular region with the national average. To answer that kind of question, we now demonstrate how to conduct a single-sample t test that uses a distribution of means.

*A **single-sample t test** is a hypothesis test in which we compare data from one sample to a population for which we know the mean but not the standard deviation.* The only thing we

■ The ***t* statistic** indicates the distance of a sample mean from a population mean in terms of the standard error.

■ A **single-sample *t* test** is a hypothesis test in which we compare data from one sample to a population for which we know the mean but not the standard deviation.

need to know to use a single-sample *t* test is the population mean. We begin with the single-sample *t* test because understanding it will help us when using the more sophisticated *t* tests that let us compare two samples.

The *t* Table and Degrees of Freedom

When we use the *t* distributions, we use the *t* table. There are different *t* distributions for every sample size, so we must take sample size into account when using the *t* table. However, we do not look up our actual sample size on the table. Rather, we look up **degrees of freedom**, *the number of scores that are free to vary when estimating a population parameter from a sample.* The phrase *free to vary* refers to the number of scores that can take on different values if we know a given parameter.

EXAMPLE 9.4

For example, the manager of a baseball team needs to assign nine players to particular spots in the batting order but only has to make eight decisions ($N - 1$). Why? Because only one option remains after making the first eight decisions. So before the manager makes any decisions, there are $N - 1$, or $9 - 1 = 8$, degrees of freedom. After the second decision, there are $N - 1$, or $8 - 1 = 7$, degrees of freedom, and so on.

As in the baseball example, there is always one score that cannot vary once all of the others have been determined. For example, if we know the mean of four scores is 6 and we know that three of the scores are 2, 4, and 8, then the last score *must* be 10. So the degrees of freedom is the number of scores in the sample minus 1; there is always one score that cannot vary. Degrees of freedom is written in symbolic notation as *df*, which is always italicized. The formula for degrees of freedom for a single-sample *t* test, therefore, is:

$$df = N - 1$$

> **MASTERING THE FORMULA**
>
> **9-4:** The formula for degrees of freedom for a single-sample *t* test is: $df = N - 1$. To calculate degrees of freedom, we subtract 1 from the sample size.

This is one key piece of information to keep in mind as we work with the *t* table. In the behavioral sciences, the degrees of freedom usually correspond to how many people are in the study or how many observations we make.

Table 9-1 is an excerpt from a *t* table, but an expanded table is included in Appendix B. Consider the relation between degrees of freedom and the cutoff, or critical value, needed to declare statistical significance. In the column corresponding to a one-tailed test at a *p* level of 0.05 with only 1 degree of freedom, the critical *t* value is

■ **Degrees of freedom** is the number of scores that are free to vary when estimating a population parameter from a sample.

TABLE 9-1. Excerpt from the *t* Table

When conducting hypothesis testing, we use the *t* table to determine critical values for a given *p* level, based on the degrees of freedom and whether the test is one- or two-tailed.

	One-Tailed Tests			Two-Tailed Tests		
df	0.10	0.05	0.01	0.10	0.05	0.01
1	3.078	6.314	31.821	6.314	12.706	63.657
2	1.886	2.920	6.965	2.920	4.303	9.925
3	1.638	2.353	4.541	2.353	3.182	5.841
4	1.533	2.132	3.747	2.132	2.776	4.604
5	1.476	2.015	3.365	2.015	2.571	4.032

6.314. With only 1 degree of freedom, the two means have to be extremely far apart and the standard deviation has to be very small in order to declare that a statistically significant difference exists. But with 2 degrees of freedom (two observations), the critical *t* value drops to 2.920. With 2 degrees of freedom, the two means don't have to be quite so far apart or the standard deviation so small. That is, it is easier to reach the critical value of 2.920 needed to declare that there is a statistically significant difference. We're more confident with two observations than with just one.

Now notice what happens when we increase the number of observations once again from two observations to three observations. The critical *t* value needed to declare statistical significance once again *decreases*, from 2.920 to 2.353. Our level of confidence in our observation increases with each additional observation; at the same time, the critical value decreases, becoming closer and closer to the related cutoff on the *z* distribution.

The *t* distributions become closer to the *z* distribution as sample size increases. When the sample size is large enough, the standard deviation of a sample is more likely to be equal to the standard deviation of the population. At large enough sample sizes, in fact, the *t* distribution is identical to the *z* distribution. Most *t* tables include a sample size of infinity (∞) to indicate a very large sample size (a sample size of infinity itself is, of course, impossible). The *t* statistics at extreme percentages for very large sample sizes are identical to the *z* statistics at the very same percentages. Check it out for yourself by comparing the *z* and *t* tables in Appendix B. For example, the *z* statistic for the 95th percentile—a percentage between the mean and the *z* statistic of 45%—is between 1.64 and 1.65; at a sample size of infinity, the *t* statistic for the 95th percentile is 1.645.

Let's remind ourselves why the *t* statistic merges with the *z* statistic as sample size increases. The underlying principle is easy to understand: more observations lead to greater confidence. Thus, more participants in a study—if they are a representative sample—correspond to increased confidence that we are making an accurate observation. So don't think of the *t* distributions as completely separate from the *z* distribution. Rather, think of the *z* statistic as a single-blade Swiss Army knife and the *t* statistic as a multiblade Swiss Army knife that still includes the single blade that is the *z* statistic.

Let's determine the cutoffs, or critical *t* value(s), for two research studies. For the first study, you may use the excerpt in Table 9-1. The second study requires the full *t* table in Appendix B.

> ◀ **MASTERING THE CONCEPT**
>
> **9-3:** As sample size increases, the *t* distributions more and more closely approximate the *z* distribution. You can think of the *z* statistic as a single-blade Swiss Army knife and the *t* statistic as a multiblade Swiss Army knife that includes the single blade that is the *z* statistic.

EXAMPLE 9.5

The study: A researcher collects Stroop reaction times for five participants who have had reduced sleep for three nights. She wants to compare this sample to the known population mean. Her research hypothesis is that the lack of sleep will slow participants down, leading to an increased reaction time. She will use a *p* level of 0.05 to determine her critical value.

The cutoff(s): This is a one-tailed test because the research hypothesis posits a change in only one direction—an increase in reaction time. There will be only a positive critical *t* value because we are hypothesizing an increase. There are five participants, so the degrees of freedom is:

$$df = N - 1 = 5 - 1 = 4$$

Her stated *p* level is 0.05. When we look in the *t* table under one-tailed tests, in the column labeled 0.05 and in the row for a *df* of 4, we see a critical value of 2.132. This is our critical *t* value.

EXAMPLE 9.6

The study: A researcher knows the mean number of calories a rat will consume in half an hour if unlimited food is available. He wonders whether a new food will lead rats to consume a different number of calories—either more or fewer. He studies 38 rats and uses a conservative critical value based on a *p* level of 0.01.

The cutoff(s): This is a two-tailed test because the research hypothesis allows for change in either direction. There will be both negative and positive critical *t* values. There are 38 rats, so the degrees of freedom is:

$$df = N - 1 = 38 - 1 = 37$$

His stated *p* level is 0.01. We want to look in the *t* table under two-tailed tests, in the column for 0.01 and in the row for a *df* of 37; however, there is no *df* of 37. In this case, we err on the side of being more conservative and choose the more extreme (i.e., larger) of the two possible critical *t* values, which is always the smaller *df*. Here, we look next to 35, where we see a value of 2.724. Because this is a two-tailed test, we will have critical values of −2.724 and 2.724. Be sure to list both values.

The Six Steps of the Single-Sample *t* Test

Now we have all the tools necessary to conduct a single-sample *t* test. So let's consider a hypothetical study and conduct all six steps of hypothesis testing.

EXAMPLE 9.7

Chapter 4 presented data that included the mean number of sessions attended by clients at a university counseling center. We noted that one study reported a mean of 4.6 sessions (Hatchett, 2003). Let's imagine that the counseling center hoped to increase participation rates by having students sign a contract to attend at least 10 sessions. Five students sign the contract, and these students attend 6, 6, 12, 7, and 8 sessions, respectively. The researchers are interested only in their university, so they treat the mean of 4.6 sessions as a population mean.

Nonparticipation in Therapy Clients missing appointments can be a problem for their therapists. A *t* test can compare the consequences between those who do and those who do not commit themselves to participating in therapy for a set period.

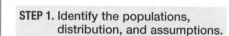

STEP 1. Identify the populations, distribution, and assumptions.

Population 1: All clients at this counseling center who sign a contract to attend at least 10 sessions. Population 2: All clients at this counseling center who do not sign a contract to attend at least 10 sessions.

The comparison distribution will be a distribution of means. The hypothesis test will be a single-sample *t* test because we have only one sample and we know the population mean but not the population standard deviation.

This study meets one of the three assumptions and may meet the other two: (1) The dependent variable is scale. (2) We do not know whether the data were randomly selected, however, so we must be cautious with respect to generalizing to other clients at this university who might sign the contract. (3) We do not know whether the population is normally distributed, and there are not at least 30 participants. However, the data from our sample do not suggest a skewed distribution.

STEP 2. State the null and research hypotheses.

Null hypothesis: Clients at this university who sign a contract to attend at least 10 sessions attend the same number of sessions, on average, as clients who do not sign such a contract—$H_0: \mu_1 = \mu_2$.

Zigy Kaluzny/Getty Images

Research hypothesis: Clients at this university who sign a contract to attend at least 10 sessions attend a different number of sessions, on average, from clients who do not sign such a contract—$H_1: \mu_1 \neq \mu_2$.

STEP 3. Determine the characteristics of the comparison distribution.

$$\mu_M = 4.6; s_M = 1.114$$

Calculations:

$$\mu_M = \mu = 4.6$$

$$M = \frac{\Sigma X}{N} = \frac{(6 + 6 + 12 + 7 + 8)}{5} = 7.8$$

X	X − M	(X − M)²
6	−1.8	3.24
6	−1.8	3.24
12	4.2	17.64
7	−0.8	0.64
8	0.2	0.04

The numerator is the sum of the squares:

$$\Sigma(X - M)^2 = \Sigma(3.24 + 3.24 + 17.64 + 0.64 + 0.04) = 24.8$$

$$s = \sqrt{\frac{\Sigma(X - M)^2}{(N - 1)}} = \sqrt{\frac{24.8}{(5 - 1)}} = \sqrt{6.2} = 2.490$$

$$s_M = \frac{s}{\sqrt{N}} = \frac{2.490}{\sqrt{5}} = 1.114$$

STEP 4. Determine the critical values, or cutoffs.

$$df = N - 1 = 5 - 1 = 4$$

For a two-tailed test with a *p* level of 0.05 and a *df* of 4, the critical values are −2.776 and 2.776 (as seen in the curve in Figure 9–2).

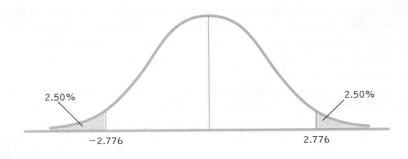

2.50%   2.50%

−2.776   2.776

FIGURE 9-2
Determining Cutoffs for a *t* Distribution

As with the *z* distribution, we typically determine critical values in terms of *t* statistics rather than means of raw scores so that we can easily compare a test statistic to them to determine whether the test statistic is beyond the cutoffs. Here, the cutoffs are −2.776 and 2.776, and they mark off the most extreme 5%, with 2.5% in each tail.

STEP 5. Calculate the test statistic.

$$t = \frac{(M - \mu_M)}{s_M} = \frac{(7.8 - 4.6)}{1.114} = 2.873$$

STEP 6. Make a decision.

Reject the null hypothesis; it appears that counseling center clients who sign a contract to attend at least 10 sessions do attend more sessions, on average, than do clients who do not sign such a contract (see Figure 9-3).

FIGURE 9-3
Making a Decision

To decide whether to reject the null hypothesis, we compare our test statistic to our critical *t* values. In this figure, the test statistic, 2.873, is beyond the cutoff of 2.776, so we can reject the null hypothesis.

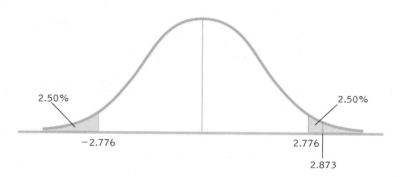

After completing our hypothesis test, we want to present the primary statistical information in a report. There is a standard American Psychological Association (APA) format for the presentation of statistics across the behavioral sciences so that the results are easily understood by the reader. You'll notice this format in almost every journal article that reports results of a social science study:

1. Write the symbol for the test statistic (e.g., *t*).
2. Write the degrees of freedom, in parentheses.
3. Write an equal sign and then the value of the test statistic, typically to two decimal places.
4. Write a comma and then the exact *p* value associated with the test statistic. (Note that we must use software to get the exact *p* value. For now, we can just say whether our *p* value is less than the *p* level of 0.05.)

In our example, then we reject the null hypothesis and the statistics would read:

$$t(4) = 2.87, p < 0.05$$

The statistic typically follows a statement about the finding, after a comma or in parentheses: for example, "It appears that counseling center clients who sign a contract to attend at least 10 sessions, on average, do attend more sessions than do clients who do not sign such a contract." The report would also include the sample mean and the standard deviation (not the standard error) to two decimal points. The descriptive statistics, typically in parentheses, would read, for our example: ($M = 7.80, SD = 2.49$). Notice that, due to convention, we use *SD* instead of *s* to symbolize the standard deviation.

As with a *z* test, we could present p_{rep} as an alternative to the *p* value, a change that has been encouraged by the Association for Psychological Science (APS). The *t* table in Appendix B only includes the *p* values of .10, .05, and .01, so we cannot use it to determine the actual *p* value for our test statistic. In the SPSS section of this chapter, we show you how you can use SPSS to determine the specific *p* value for the test statistic. Then we can insert the *p* value into the Excel formula introduced in Chapter 8 to determine p_{rep}: =NORMSDIST(NORMSINV(1-P)/(SQRT(2))). This procedure is the same for all three kinds of *t* tests—single-sample, paired-samples, and independent-samples *t* tests.

Calculating a Confidence Interval for a Single-Sample *t* Test

As with a *z* test, the APA recommends that researchers report confidence intervals and effect sizes, in addition to the results of hypothesis tests, whenever possible. We can calculate a confidence interval with the single-sample *t* test data. The population mean was 4.6, and we used the sample to estimate the population standard deviation to be 2.490 and the population standard error to be 1.114. The five students in the sample attended a mean of 7.8 sessions.

When we conducted hypothesis testing, we centered our curve around the mean according to the null hypothesis—the population mean of 4.6. We determined critical values based on this mean and compared our sample mean to these cutoffs. We were able to reject the null hypothesis that there was no mean difference between the two groups. The test statistic was beyond the cutoff *z* statistic. Now we can use the same information to calculate the 95% confidence interval around the sample mean of 7.8.

Step 1: Draw a picture of a *t* distribution that includes the confidence interval. We draw a normal curve (see Figure 9-4) that has the *sample* mean, 7.8, at its center (instead of the *population* mean, 4.6).

Step 2: Indicate the bounds of the confidence interval on the drawing. We draw a vertical line from the mean to the top of the curve. For a 95% confidence interval, we also draw two much smaller vertical lines indicating the middle 95% of the *t* distribution (2.5% in each tail for a total of 5%).

We then write the appropriate percentages under the segments of the curve. The curve is symmetric, so half of the 95% falls above and half falls below the mean. Thus, 47.5% falls on each side of the mean between the mean and the cutoff, and 2.5% falls in each tail.

Step 3: Look up the *t* statistics that fall at each line marking the middle 95%. For a two-tailed test with a *p* level of 0.05 and *df* of 4, the critical values are −2.776 and 2.776. We can now add these *t* statistics to our curve, as seen in Figure 9-5.

Step 4: Convert the *t* statistics back into raw means. As we did with the *z* test, we can use formulas for this conversion, but first we must identify the appropriate mean

> **◄ MASTERING THE CONCEPT**
>
> **9-4:** Whenever researchers conduct a hypothesis test, the APA encourages that, if possible, they also calculate a confidence interval and an effect size.

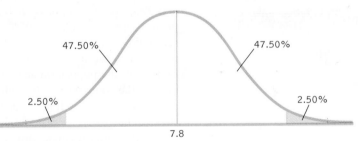

FIGURE 9-4
A 95% Confidence Interval for a Single-Sample *t* Test, Part I

To begin calculating a confidence interval for a single-sample *t* test, we place the sample mean, 7.8, at the center of a curve and indicate the percentages within and beyond the confidence interval.

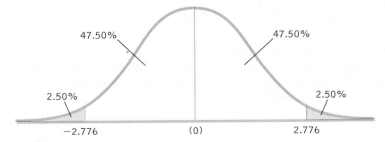

FIGURE 9-5
A 95% Confidence Interval for a Single-Sample *t* Test, Part II

The next step in calculating a confidence interval for a single-sample *t* test is to identify the *t* statistics that indicate each end of the interval. Because the curve is symmetric, the *t* statistics have the same magnitude—one is negative, −2.776, and one is positive, 2.776. The *t* statistic at the mean is always 0.

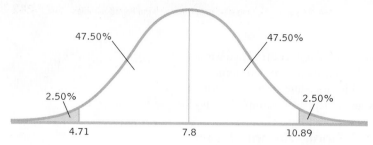

FIGURE 9-6

A 95% Confidence Interval for a Single-Sample *t* Test, Part III

The final step in calculating a confidence interval for a single-sample *t* test is to convert the *t* statistics that indicate each end of the interval into raw means, 4.71 and 10.89.

and standard deviation. There are two important points to remember. First, we center our interval around the *sample* mean (not the *population* mean). So we use the sample mean of 7.8 in our calculations. Second, because we have a sample *mean* (rather than an individual *score*), we use a distribution of means. So we use the standard error of 1.114 as our measure of spread.

Using this mean and standard error, we can calculate the raw mean at each end of the confidence interval, the lower end and the upper end, and add them to our curve as in Figure 9-6. The formulas are exactly the same as for the *z* test except that *z* is replaced by *t* and σ_M is replaced by s_M.

$$M_{lower} = -t(s_M) + M_{sample} = -2.776(1.114) + 7.8 = 4.71$$

$$M_{upper} = t(s_M) + M_{sample} = 2.776(1.114) + 7.8 = 10.89$$

Our 95% confidence interval, reported in brackets as is typical, is [4.71, 10.89].

Step 5: Check that the confidence interval makes sense. The sample mean should fall exactly in the middle of the two ends of the interval.

$$4.71 - 7.8 = -3.09 \text{ and } 10.89 - 7.8 = 3.09$$

We have a match. The confidence interval ranges from 3.09 below the sample mean to 3.09 above the sample mean. If we were to sample five students from the same population over and over, the 95% confidence interval would include the population mean 95% of the time. Note that the population mean, 4.6, does not fall within this interval. This means it is not plausible that this sample of students who signed contracts came from the population according to the null hypothesis—students seeking treatment at the counseling center who did not sign a contract. We can conclude that the sample comes from a different population; that is, we can conclude that these students attended more sessions than did the general population. As with the *z* test, the conclusions from both the single-sample *t* test and the confidence interval are the same, but the confidence interval gives us more information—an interval estimate, not just a point estimate.

Calculating Effect Size for a Single-Sample *t* Test

As with a *z* test, we can calculate the effect size (Cohen's *d*) for a single-sample *t* test. Let's calculate it for the counseling center study. Similar to what we did with the *z* test, we simply use the formula for the *t* statistic, substituting *s* for s_M (and μ for μ_M, even though these means are always the same). This means we use 2.490 instead of 1.114 in the denominator. The Cohen's *d* is now based on the spread of the distribution of individual scores, rather than the distribution of means.

$$\text{Cohen's } d = \frac{(M - \mu)}{s} = \frac{(7.8 - 4.6)}{2.490} = 1.29$$

Our effect size, *d* = 1.29, tells us that our sample mean and the population mean are 1.29 standard deviations apart. According to the conventions we learned in Chapter 8 (0.2 is a small effect; 0.5 is a medium effect; 0.8 is a large effect), this is a large effect. We can add the effect size when we report the statistics as follows: $t(4) = 2.87$, $p < 0.05$, $d = 1.29$.

MASTERING THE FORMULA

9-5: The formula for the lower bound of a confidence interval for a single-sample *t* test is $M_{lower} = -t(s_M) + M_{sample}$. The formula for the upper bound of a confidence interval for a single-sample *t* test is $M_{upper} = t(s_M) + M_{sample}$. The only differences from those for a *z* test are that in each formula *z* is replaced by *t* and σ_M is replaced by s_M.

MASTERING THE FORMULA

9-6: The formula for Cohen's *d* for a *t* statistic for a single sample is: Cohen's $d = \frac{(M - \mu)}{s}$. It is the same formula as for the *z* statistic, except that we divide by the estimated population standard deviation (*s*) rather than the estimated population standard error (s_M).

CHECK YOUR LEARNING

Reviewing the Concepts

> A single-sample *t* test is a hypothesis test in which we compare data from one sample to a population for which we know the mean but not the standard deviation.

> We consider degrees of freedom, or the number of scores that are free to vary, instead of *N* when we assess estimated test statistics against distributions.

> As sample size increases, our confidence in our estimates improves, degrees of freedom increase, and the critical value for *t* drops, making it easier to reach statistical significance. In fact, as sample size grows, the *t* distributions approach the *z* distribution.

> As with any hypothesis test, we identify the populations and comparison distribution and check the assumptions. We then state the null and research hypotheses. We next determine the characteristics of the comparison distribution, a distribution of means based on the null hypothesis. We must first estimate the standard deviation from our sample; then we must calculate the standard error. We then determine critical values, usually for a two-tailed test with a *p* level of 0.05. The test statistic is then calculated and compared to these critical values, or cutoffs, to determine whether to reject or fail to reject the null hypothesis.

> We can determine p_{rep} for our test statistic as an alternative to *p* value.

> We can calculate a confidence interval and an effect size, Cohen's *d*, for a single-sample *t* test.

Clarifying the Concepts

9-6   Explain the term *degrees of freedom*.

9-7   Why does a single-sample *t* test have more uses than a *z* test?

Calculating the Statistics

9-8   Compute degrees of freedom for each of the following:

a. An experimenter times how long it takes 35 rats to run through a maze with 8 pathways.

b. Test scores for 14 students are collected and averaged over 4 semesters.

9-9   Identify the critical *t* value for each of the following tests:

a. A two-tailed test with alpha of 0.05 and 11 degrees of freedom

b. A one-tailed test with alpha of 0.01 and *N* of 17

Applying the Concepts

Solutions to these Check Your Learning questions can be found in Appendix D.

9-10   Let's assume that according to university summary statistics, the average student misses 3.7 classes during a semester. Imagine the data you have been working with (6, 3, 7, 6, 4, 5) are the number of classes missed by a group of students. Conduct all six steps of hypothesis testing, assuming a two-tailed test with a *p* level of 0.05. (*Note:* The work for step 3 has already been completed in Check Your Learning exercises 9-3 and 9-4.)

The Paired-Samples *t* Test

Researchers found that weight gain over the holidays was far less than once thought. The dreaded "freshman 15" also appears to be an exaggerated myth. It's really less than 4 pounds, on average. One study sampled college students at a northeastern university and compared their weight at the beginning of the fall semester with how much they weighed by November (Holm-Denoma, Joiner, Vohs, & Heatherton, 2008). Male students gained an average of 3.5 pounds and female students gained an average of 4.0 pounds. These types of before/after comparisons can be tested by using the paired-samples *t* test.

■ The **paired-samples *t* test** is used to compare two means for a within-groups design, a situation in which every participant is in both samples; also called a *dependent-samples t test*.

The ***paired–samples t test*** (also called *dependent-samples t test*) *is used to compare two means for a within-groups design, a situation in which every participant is in both samples.* Although both terms—*paired* and *dependent*—are used frequently, we use the term *paired* in this book because it matches the language of some of the most-used statistical software packages. If an individual in the study participates in both conditions (such as a memory task after ingesting a caffeinated beverage and again after ingesting a noncaffeinated beverage), then her score in one depends on her score in the other. That's when we use the *dependent*-samples, or *paired*-samples, *t* test. Once you understand the single-sample *t* test, the paired-samples *t* test is simple. The major difference in the paired-samples *t* test is that we must create difference scores for every individual.

Distributions of Mean Differences

We already have learned about a distribution of scores and a distribution of means. Now we need to develop a distribution of mean *differences* so that we can establish a distribution that specifies the null hypothesis. Let's use pre- and post-holiday weight data to demonstrate how to create a distribution of mean differences, the distribution that accompanies a within-groups design.

Imagine that many college students' weights were measured before and after the winter holidays to determine if they changed, and you planned to gather data on a sample of three people. Imagine that you have two cards for each person on which weights are listed—one before the holidays and one after the holidays. So you have many pairs of cards, one for each student. First, you would randomly choose three pairs of cards. For each pair, you'd subtract the first weight from the second weight to calculate a difference score, and then you would calculate the mean of the differences in weights for these three people. Then you would randomly choose another three people from the population of many college students and calculate the mean of their three difference scores. And then you'd do it again, and again, and again. That's really all there is to it, except that we do this procedure many more times (although we are simplifying a bit here; we would actually replace every pair of cards before selecting the next). So there are two samples—college students before the holidays and college students after the holidays—but we're building just *one* curve of mean differences.

Let's say the first student weighed 140 pounds before the holidays and 144 pounds after the holidays; the difference between weights would be 144 − 140 = 4. Next, we put all the cards back and repeat the process. Let's say that this time we have weights of 126 pounds before the holidays and 124 pounds after the holidays; now the difference between means would be 124 − 126 = −2. A third student might weigh 168 both before and after the holidays for a difference between means of 0. We would take the mean of these three different scores, 0.667. We would then choose three more students and calculate the mean of their difference scores. Eventually, we would have many mean differences—some positive, some negative, and some right at 0— and could plot them on a curve. But this would only be the beginning of what this distribution would look like. If we were to calculate the whole distribution, then we would do this an uncountable number of times. When the authors calculated 30 mean differences for pairs of weights, we got the distribution in Figure 9-7

FIGURE 9-7
Creating a Distribution of Mean Differences

This distribution is one of many that could be created by pulling 30 mean differences, the average of three differences between pairs of weights, pulled one a time from a population of pairs of weights—one pre-holiday and one post-holiday. The population used here was one based on the null hypothesis, that there is no average difference in weight from before the holidays to after the holidays.

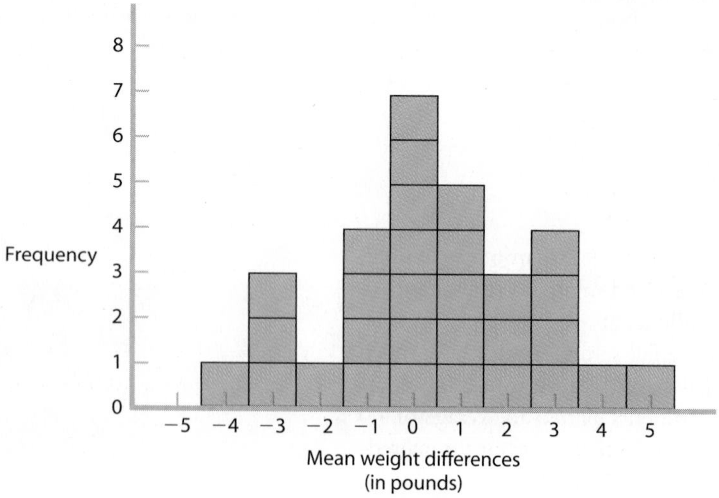

(we plotted means rounded to whole numbers). If no mean difference is found when comparing weights from before and after the holidays, as with the data we used to create Figure 9-7, the distribution would center around 0. According to the null hypothesis, we would expect no difference in average weight from before the holidays to after the holidays.

The Six Steps of the Paired-Samples *t* Test

In a paired-samples *t* test, each participant has two scores—one in each condition. When we conduct a paired-samples *t* test, we write the pairs of scores in two columns, side by side next to the same individual. We then subtract each score in one column from its paired score in the other column to create difference scores. Ideally, a positive difference score indicates an increase, and a negative difference score indicates a decrease. Typically, we subtract the first score from the second so that our difference scores match this logic. Now we implement the steps of the single-sample *t* test with only minor changes, as discussed in the steps below.

Large Monitors and Productivity Microsoft researchers and cognitive psychologists (Czerwinski et al, 2003) reported a 9% increase in productivity when research volunteers used an extremely large 42-inch display versus a more typical 15-inch display. Every participant used both displays and thus was in both samples. A paired-samples *t* test is the appropriate hypothesis test for this within-groups design.

Courtesy of Microsoft Research

EXAMPLE 9.8

Let's try an example from the social sciences. Computers and software companies often employ social scientists to research ways their products can better benefit users. For example, Microsoft researchers studied how 15 volunteers performed on a set of tasks under two conditions. The researchers compared the volunteers' performance on the tasks while using a 15-inch computer monitor and while using a 42-inch monitor (Czerwinski et al, 2003). The 42-inch monitor, far larger than most of us have ever used, allows the user to have multiple programs in view at the same time.

Here are five participants' fictional data, which reflect the actual means reported by researchers. Note that a smaller number is good—it indicates a faster time. The first person completed the tasks on the small monitor in 122 seconds and on the large monitor in 111 seconds; the second person in 131 and 116; the third in 127 and 113; the fourth in 123 and 119; and the fifth in 132 and 121.

STEP 1. Identify the populations, distribution, and assumptions.

The paired-samples *t* test is like the single-sample *t* test in that we analyze a single sample of scores. For the single-sample *t* test, we use individual scores; for the paired-samples *t* test, we use difference scores. For the paired-samples *t* test, one population is reflected by each condition, but the comparison distribution is a *distribution of mean difference scores* (rather than a distribution of means). The comparison distribution is the same as with the single-sample *t* test; it is based on the null hypothesis that posits no difference. So the mean of the comparison distribution is 0; this indicates a mean difference score of 0. The assumptions are the same as for the single-sample *t* test.

Summary: Population 1: People performing tasks using a 15-inch monitor. Population 2: People performing tasks using a 42-inch monitor.

The comparison distribution will be a distribution of mean difference scores based on the null hypothesis. The hypothesis test will be a paired-samples *t* test because we have two samples of scores, and every individual contributes a score to each sample.

◀ **MASTERING THE CONCEPT**

9-5: The steps for the paired-samples *t* test are very similar to those for the single-sample *t* test. The main difference is that we are comparing the sample mean difference between scores to that for the mean difference for the population according to the null hypothesis, rather than comparing the sample mean of individual scores to the population mean.

This study meets one of the three assumptions and may meet the other two: (1) The dependent variable is time, which is scale. (2) The participants were not randomly selected, however, so we must be cautious with respect to generalizing our findings. (3) We do not know whether the population is normally distributed, and there are not at least 30 participants. However, the data from our sample do not suggest a skewed distribution.

| STEP 2. State the null and research hypotheses. | This step is identical to that for the single-sample *t* test. Remember, hypotheses are always about populations, not about our spe- |

cific samples.

Summary: Null hypothesis: People who use a 15-inch screen will complete a set of tasks in the same amount of time, on average, as people who use a 42-inch screen—$H_0: \mu_1 = \mu_2$. Research hypothesis: People who use a 15-inch screen will complete a set of tasks in a different amount of time, on average, from people who use a 42-inch screen—$H_1: \mu_1 \neq \mu_2$.

| STEP 3. Determine the characteristics of the comparison distribution. | This step is similar to that for the single-sample *t* test in that we determine the appro- |

priate mean and standard error of the comparison distribution—the distribution based on the null hypothesis. In the single-sample *t* test, there was a comparison mean, and the null hypothesis posited that the sample mean would be the same as that of the comparison distribution. With the paired-samples *t* test, we have a sample of difference scores. According to the null hypothesis, there is no difference; that is, the mean difference score is 0. So the mean of the comparison distribution is always 0, as long as the null hypothesis posits no difference.

The standard error is calculated exactly as it is calculated for the single-sample *t* test, only we use the difference scores rather than the scores in each condition. To get the difference scores in the current example, we want to know what happens when we go from the control condition (small screen) to the experimental condition (large screen), so we subtract the first score from the second score. This means that a negative difference indicates a decrease in time when the screen goes from small to large and a positive difference indicates an increase in time. (The test statistic will be the same if we reverse the order in which we subtract, but the sign will change. In some cases, you can think about it as subtracting the "before" score from the "after" score.)

Another helpful strategy is to cross out the original scores once we've created the difference scores so that we remember to use only the difference scores from that point on. If we don't cross out the original scores, it is very easy to use them in our calculations and end up with an incorrect standard error.

Summary: $\mu_M = 0; s_M = 1.923$

Calculations: (Notice that we crossed out the original scores once we created our column of difference scores. We did this to remind ourselves that all remaining calculations involve the differences scores, not the original scores.)

X	Y	Difference	Difference − mean difference	Squared deviation
122	117	−11	0	0
131	116	−15	−4	16
127	113	−14	−3	9
123	119	−4	7	49
132	121	−11	0	0

The mean of the difference scores is:

$$M_{difference} = -11$$

The numerator is the sum of squares, *SS*:

$$0 + 16 + 9 + 49 + 0 = 74$$

$$s = \sqrt{\frac{74}{(5-1)}} = \sqrt{18.5} = 4.301$$

$$s_M = \frac{4.301}{\sqrt{5}} = 1.923$$

STEP 4. Determine the critical values, or cutoffs.

This step is the same as that for the single-sample *t* test. The degrees of freedom is the number of *participants* (not the number of scores) minus 1.

Summary: $df = N - 1 = 5 - 1 = 4$

Our critical values, based on a two-tailed test and a *p* level of 0.05, are −2.776 and 2.776, as seen in the curve in Figure 9-8.

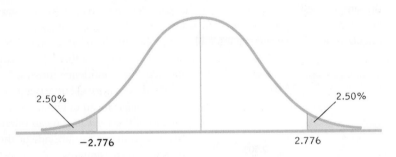

2.50%   2.50%

−2.776   2.776

FIGURE 9-8
Determining Cutoffs for a Paired-Samples *t* Test

We typically determine critical values in terms of *t* statistics rather than means of raw scores so that we can easily compare a test statistic to them to determine whether the test statistic is beyond the cutoffs.

STEP 5. Calculate the test statistic.

This step is identical to that for the single-sample *t* test.

Summary: $t = \frac{(-11 - 0)}{1.923} = -5.72$

STEP 6. Make a decision.

This step is identical to that for the single-sample *t* test. If we reject the null hypothesis, we need to examine the means of the two conditions (in this case, $M_X = 127; M_Y = 116$) so that we know the direction of the effect. Remember, even though the hypotheses are two-tailed, we report the direction of the effect.

Summary: Reject the null hypothesis. It appears that, on average, people perform faster when using a 42-inch monitor than when using a 15-inch monitor (as shown by the curve in Figure 9-9).

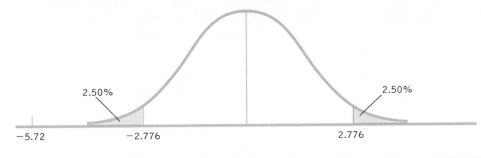

2.50%   2.50%

−5.72   −2.776   2.776

FIGURE 9-9
Making a Decision

To decide whether to reject the null hypothesis, we compare our test statistic to our critical values. In this figure, the test statistic, −5.72, is beyond the cutoff of −2.776, so we can reject the null hypothesis.

The statistics, as reported in a journal article, follow the same APA format as for a single-sample *t* test. We report the degrees of freedom, the value of the test statistic, and the *p* value associated with the test statistic (unless we use software, we can only indicate whether the *p* value is less than or greater than 0.05). In the current example, the statistics would read: $t(4) = -5.72, p < 0.05$.

(We would also include the means and the standard deviations for the two samples. We calculated the means in step 6 of hypothesis testing, but we would also have to calculate the standard deviations for the two samples to report them. In addition, we could report p_{rep} instead the *p* value. See the SPSS section of this chapter for details.)

Researchers note that the faster time with the large display might not *seem* much faster but that, in their research, they have had great difficulty identifying *any* factors that lead to faster times (Czerwinski et al., 2003). Based on their previous research, therefore, this is an impressive difference.

Calculating a Confidence Interval for a Paired-Samples *t* Test

As with most hypothesis testing, the APA also encourages the use of confidence intervals and effect sizes when conducting a paired-samples *t* test. Let's start by determining the confidence interval for the example we've been using. First, let's recap the information we need. The population mean difference according to the null hypothesis was 0, and we used the sample to estimate the population standard deviation to be 4.301 and standard error to be 1.923. The five participants in the study sample had a mean difference of −11. We will calculate the 95% confidence interval around the sample mean difference of −11.

Step 1: Draw a picture of a *t* distribution that includes the confidence interval.

We draw a normal curve (see Figure 9-10) that has the *sample* mean difference, −11, at its center instead of the *population* mean difference, 0.

Step 2: Indicate the bounds of the confidence interval on the drawing.

As before, 47.5% would fall on each side of the mean between the mean and the cutoff, and 2.5% would fall in each tail.

Step 3: Add the *t* statistics to the curve, as seen in Figure 9-11.

For a two–tailed test with a *p* level of 0.05 and 4 *df*, the critical values are −2.776 and 2.776.

Step 4: Convert the *t* statistics back into raw mean differences.

As we did with the other confidence intervals, we use the sample mean difference (−11) in our calculations and the standard error (1.923) as our measure of spread. We use the same formulas as for the single-sample *t* test, recalling that these means and standard errors are calculated from differences between two scores for each participant in the study, rather than an individual score for each participant. We have added these raw mean differences to our curve in Figure 9-12.

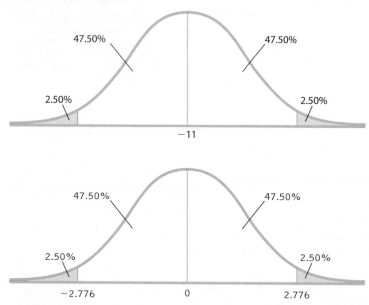

FIGURE 9-10

A 95% Confidence Interval for a Paired-Samples *t* Test, Part I

We start the confidence interval for a distribution of mean differences by drawing a curve with the sample mean difference, −11, in the center.

FIGURE 9-11

A 95% Confidence Interval for a Paired-Samples *t* Test, Part II

The next step in calculating a confidence interval for mean differences is identifying the *t* statistics that indicate each end of the interval. Because the curve is symmetric, the *t* statistics have the same magnitude—one is negative, −2.776, and one is positive, 2.776.

$$M_{lower} = -t(s_M) + M_{sample} = -2.776(1.923) + (-11) = -16.34$$

$$M_{upper} = t(s_M) + M_{sample} = 2.776(1.923) + (-11) = -5.66$$

Our 95% confidence interval, reported in brackets as is typical, is [−5.66, −16.34].

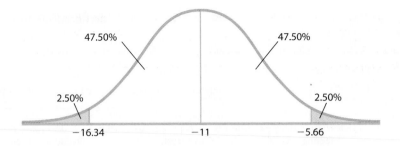

FIGURE 9-12
A 95% Confidence Interval for a Paired-Samples *t* Test, Part III

The final step in calculating a confidence interval for mean differences is converting the *t* statistics that indicate each end of the interval to raw mean differences, −16.34 and −5.66.

Step 5: Check that the confidence interval makes sense. The sample mean difference should fall exactly in the middle of the two ends of the interval.

$$-11 - (-5.66) = -5.34 \text{ and } -11 - (-16.34) = 5.34$$

We have a match. The confidence interval ranges from 5.34 below the sample mean difference to 5.34 above the sample mean difference. If we were to sample five people from the same population over and over, the 95% confidence interval would include the population mean 95% of the time. Note that the population mean difference according to the null hypothesis, 0, does not fall within this interval. This means it is not plausible that the difference between those using the 15-inch monitor and those using the 42-inch monitor is 0. We can conclude that, on average, people perform faster when using a 42-inch monitor than when using a 15-inch monitor. As with other hypothesis tests, the conclusions from both the paired-samples *t* test and the confidence interval are the same, but the confidence interval gives us more information—an interval estimate, not just a point estimate.

> **MASTERING THE FORMULA**
>
> **9-7:** The formula for the lower bound of a confidence interval for a paired-samples *t* test is $M_{lower} = -t(s_M) + M_{sample}$. The formula for the upper bound of a confidence interval for a paired-samples *t* test is $M_{upper} = t(s_M) + M_{sample}$. These are the same as for a single-sample *t* test, but remember that the means and standard errors are calculated from differences between pairs of scores, not individual scores.

Calculating Effect Size for a Paired-Samples *t* Test

As with a *z* test, we can calculate the effect size (Cohen's *d*) for a paired-samples *t* test. Let's calculate it for the computer monitor study. Again, we simply use the formula for the *t* statistic, substituting *s* for s_M (and μ for μ_M, even though these means are always the same). This means we use 4.301 instead of 1.923 in the denominator. Cohen's *d* is now based on the spread of the distribution of individual differences between scores, rather than the distribution of mean differences.

$$\text{Cohen's } d = \frac{(M - \mu)}{s} = \frac{(-11 - 0)}{4.301} = -2.56$$

Our effect size, *d* = −2.56, tells us that our sample mean difference and the population mean difference are 2.56 standard deviations apart. This is a large effect. Recall that the sign has no effect on the size of an effect: −2.56 and 2.56 are equivalent effect sizes. We can add the effect size when we report the statistics as follows: $t(4) = -5.72, p < 0.05, d = -2.56$.

> **MASTERING THE FORMULA**
>
> **9-8:** The formula for Cohen's *d* for a paired-samples *t* statistic is: Cohen's $d = \frac{(M - \mu)}{s}$. It is the same formula as for the single-sample *t* statistic, except that the mean and standard error are for difference scores rather than individual scores.

CHECK YOUR LEARNING

Reviewing the Concepts

> The paired-samples *t* test is used when we have data for all participants under two conditions—a within-groups design.

> In the paired-samples *t* test, we calculate a difference score for every individual. The statistic is calculated on those difference scores.

> We use the same six steps of hypothesis testing that we used with the *z* test and with the single-sample *t* test.

continued on next page

> We can calculate p_{rep}, a confidence interval, and an effect size (Cohen's *d*), for a paired-samples *t* test.

Clarifying the Concepts	
	9-11 How do we conduct a paired-samples *t* test?
	9-12 Explain what an individual difference score is, as it is used in a paired-samples *t* test.

Calculating the Statistics

9-13 Below are energy-level data (on a scale of 1 to 7, where 1 = feeling of no energy and 7 = feeling of high energy) for five students before and after lunch. Calculate the mean difference for these people so that loss of energy is a negative value. Assume you are testing the hypothesis that students go into what we call "food comas" after eating, versus lunch giving them added energy.

Before lunch	After lunch
6	3
5	2
4	6
5	4
7	5

Applying the Concepts

9-14 Using the energy-level data presented in Check Your Learning 9-13, let's test the hypothesis that students have different energy levels before and after lunch.

a. Perform the six steps of hypothesis testing.

b. Calculate the 95% confidence interval and describe how it results in the same conclusion as the hypothesis test.

Solutions to these Check Your Learning questions can be found in Appendix D.

c. Calculate and interpret Cohen's *d*.

REVIEW OF CONCEPTS

The *t* Distributions

The *t* distributions are similar to the *z* distribution, except that we must estimate the standard deviation from the sample. When estimating the standard deviation, we must make a mathematical correction to adjust for the increased likelihood of error. After estimating the standard deviation, the *t statistic* is calculated like the *z* statistic for distributions of means. The *t* distributions can be used to compare the mean of a sample to a population mean when we don't know the population standard deviation (single-sample *t* test), to compare two samples with a within–groups design (paired-samples *t* test), and to compare two samples with a between-groups design (independent-samples *t* test). We learned about the first two *t* tests in this chapter; the third *t* test is described in Chapter 10.

The Single-Sample *t* Test

Like *z* tests, *single-sample t tests* are conducted in the rare cases in which we have one sample that we're comparing to a known population. The difference is that we must know the mean and the standard deviation of the population to conduct a *z* test, whereas we only have to know the mean of the population to conduct a single-sample *t* test. There are many *t* distributions, one for every possible sample size. We look up the appropriate critical values on the *t* table based on *degrees of freedom,* a number calculated from the sample size. In addition to the hypothesis test we can calculate p_{rep}, a confidence interval, and an effect size (Cohen's *d*) for a single-sample *t* test.

The Paired-Samples *t* Test

A *paired-samples t test* is used when we have two samples and the same participants are in both samples; to conduct the test, we calculate a difference score for every individual. The comparison distribution is a distribution of mean difference scores. We can calculate p_{rep}, a confidence interval, and an effect size (Cohen's *d*) for a paired-samples *t* test.

SPSS®

The *t* test is used to compare only two groups. First, let's conduct a single-sample *t* test using the data on number of counseling sessions attended that we tested earlier in this chapter. The five scores were: 6, 6, 12, 7, and 8.

Select **Analyze** → Compare Means → One-Sample T Test. Then highlight the dependent variable (sessions) and click the arrow in the center to choose it. Type the population mean to which we're comparing our sample, 4.6, next to "Test Value" and click "OK." The screenshot here shows the data and output. You'll notice that the *t* statistic, 2.874, is almost identical to the one we calculated, 2.873. The difference is only due to our rounding decisions. Notice that the confidence interval is different from the one we calculated. This is an interval around the difference between the two means, rather than around the mean of our sample.

The *p* value is under "Sig (2-tailed)." The *p* value of .045 is less than the chosen *p* level of .05, an indication that this is

a statistically significant finding. We can use this *p* value in Excel to calculate our p_{rep}. When we replace P with .045 in the Excel formula, =NORMSDIST(NORMSINV(1-P)/ (SQRT(2))), we get a p_{rep} of .8847. If we were to replicate this study with the same sample size drawn from the same population, we could expect an effect in the same direction 88.47% of the time.

For a paired-samples *t* test, let's use the data from this chapter on performance using a small monitor versus a large monitor. Enter the data in two columns, with each participant having one score in the first column for his or her performance on the small monitor and one score in the second column for his or her performance on the large monitor.

Select **Analyze** → Compare Means → Paired-Samples T Test. Choose the dependent variable under the first condition (Small) by clicking it, then clicking the center arrow. Choose the dependent variable under the second condition (large) by

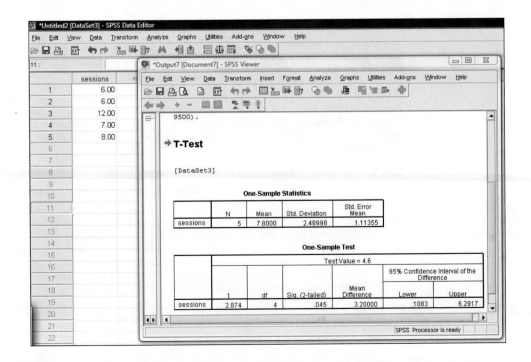

clicking it, then clicking the center arrow. Then click "OK." The data and output are shown in the screenshot. Notice that the *t* statistic and confidence interval match ours (5.72) and [−16.34, −5.66] except that the signs are different. This occurs because of the order in which one score was subtracted from the other score—that is, whether the score on the large monitor was subtracted from the score on the small monitor, or vice versa. The outcome is the same in either case. The *p* value is under "Sig. (2-tailed)" and is .005. We can use this number in Excel to determine the value for p_{rep}, .9657.

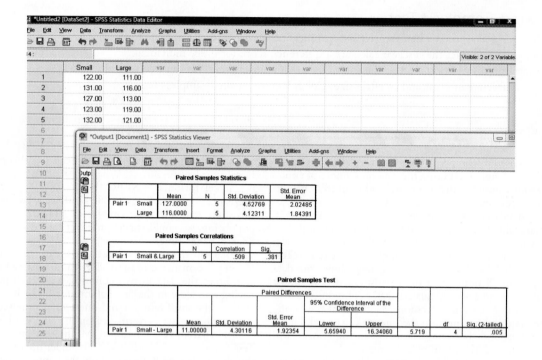

How It Works

9.1 CONDUCTING A SINGLE-SAMPLE *t* TEST

In How It Works 7.2, we conducted a *z* test for data from the Consideration of Future Consequences (CFC) scale (Petrocelli, 2003). How can we conduct all six steps for a single-sample *t* test for the same data using a *p* level of 0.05 and a two-tailed test? To start, we'll use the population mean CFC score of 3.51, but we'll pretend that we no longer know the population standard deviation. As before, we wonder whether students who joined a career discussion group might have improved CFC scores, on average, compared with the population. Forty-five students in the social sciences regularly attended these discussion groups and then took the CFC scale. The mean for this group is 3.7. The standard deviation for this sample is 0.52.

Step 1: Population 1: All students in career discussion groups

Population 2: All students who did not participate in career discussion groups

The comparison distribution will be a distribution of means. The hypothesis test will be a single-sample *t* test because we have only one sample, and we know the population mean but do not know the population standard deviation. This study meets two of the three assumptions and may meet the third. The dependent variable is scale. In addition, there are more than 30 participants in the sample, indicating that the comparison distribution will be normal. The data were not randomly selected, however, so we must be cautious when generalizing.

Step 2: Null hypothesis: Students who participated in career discussion groups had the same CFC scores, on average, as students who did not participate $H_0: \mu_1 = \mu_2$.

Research hypothesis: Students who participated in career discussion groups had different CFC scores, on average, from students who did not participate—$H_1: \mu_1 \neq \mu_2$.

Step 3: $\mu_M = \mu = 3.51; s_M = \dfrac{s}{\sqrt{N}} = \dfrac{0.52}{\sqrt{45}} = 0.078$

Step 4: $df = N - 1 = 45 - 1 = 44$

Our critical values, based on 44 degrees of freedom (because 44 is not in the table, we look up the more conservative degrees of freedom of 30), a *p* level of 0.05, and a two-tailed test, are -2.021 and 2.021.

Step 5: $t = \dfrac{(M - \mu_M)}{s_M} = \dfrac{(3.7 - 3.51)}{0.078} = 2.44$

Step 6: Reject the null hypothesis. It appears that students who participate in career discussion groups have higher CFC scores, on average, than do students who do not participate.

The statistics, as presented in a journal article, would read:

$t(44) = 2.44, p < 0.05$

9.2 CONDUCTING A PAIRED-SAMPLES *t* TEST

Salary Wizard is an online tool that allows you to look up incomes for specific jobs for cities in the United States. We looked up the 25th percentile for income for six jobs in two cities: Boise, Idaho, and Los Angeles, California. The data are below.

	Boise	Los Angeles
Executive chef	$53,047.00	$62,490.00
Genetics counselor	$49,958.00	$58,850.00
Grants/proposal writer	$41,974.00	$49,445.00
Librarian	$44,366.00	$52,263.00
Public schoolteacher	$40,470.00	$47,674.00
Social worker (with bachelor's degree)	$36,963.00	$43,542.00

How can we conduct a paired-samples *t* test to determine whether income in one of these cities differs, on average, from income in the other? We'll use a two-tailed test and a *p* level of 0.05.

Step 1: Population 1: Job types in Boise, Idaho

Population 2: Job types in Los Angeles, California

The comparison distribution will be a distribution of mean differences. The hypothesis test will be a paired-samples *t* test because we have two samples, and all participants are in both samples.

This study meets one of the three assumptions and may meet the third. The dependent variable, GPA, is scale. We do not know whether the population is normally distributed, there are not at least 30 participants, and there is not much variability in the data in our samples, so we should proceed with caution. The data were not randomly selected, so we should be cautious when generalizing beyond this sample of job types.

Step 2: Null hypothesis: Jobs in Boise pay the same, on average, as jobs in Los Angeles—$H_0: \mu_1 = \mu_2$. Research hypothesis: Jobs in Boise pay different incomes, on average, from jobs in Los Angeles—$H_1: \mu_1 \neq \mu_2$.

Step 3: $\mu_M = \mu = 0; S_M = 438.830$

Boise	Los Angeles	Difference (D)	$(D - M_{difference})$	$(D - M_{difference})^2$
$53,047.00	$62,490.00	9443	1528.667	2336821.797
$49,958.00	$58,850.00	8892	977.667	955832.763
$41,974.00	$49,445.00	7471	−443.333	196544.149
$44,366.00	$52,263.00	7897	−17.333	300.433
$40,470.00	$47,674.00	7204	−710.333	504572.971
$36,963.00	$43,542.00	6579	−1335.333	1783114.221

$$M_{difference} = 7914.333$$

$$SS = \Sigma(D - M_{difference})^2 = 5{,}777{,}187.333$$

$$s = \sqrt{\frac{\Sigma(D - M_{difference})^2}{(N-1)}} = \sqrt{\frac{5{,}777{,}186.334}{(6-1)}} = 1074.913$$

$$s_M = \frac{s}{\sqrt{N}} = \frac{1074.913}{\sqrt{6}} = 438.830$$

Step 4: $df = N - 1 = 6 - 1 = 5$

Our critical values, based on 5 degrees of freedom, a *p* level of 0.05, and a two-tailed test, are -2.571 and 2.571.

Step 5: $t = \frac{(M_{difference} - \mu_{difference})}{s_M} = \frac{7914.333 - 0}{438.830} = 18.04$

Step 6: Reject the null hypothesis. It appears that jobs in Los Angeles pay more, on average, than do jobs in Boise.

The statistics, as they would be presented in a journal article, are: $t(5) = 18.04$, $p < 0.05$

Exercises

Clarifying the Concepts

9.1 When should we use a *t* distribution?

9.2 Why do we modify the formula for calculating standard deviation when using *t* tests (and divide by $N - 1$)?

9.3 How is the calculation of standard error different for a *t* test than for a *z* test?

9.4 Explain why the standard error for the distribution of sample means is smaller than the standard deviation of sample scores.

9.5 Define the symbols in the formula for the *t* statistic: $t = \frac{(M - \mu_M)}{s_M}$.

9.6 Distinguish between within-group designs and between-group designs.

9.7 What do we mean when we say we have a distribution of mean differences?

9.8 Why is a two-tailed *t* test considered more conservative than a one-tailed *t* test?

9.9 What does the phrase *free to vary*, referring to a number of scores in a given sample, mean for statisticians?

9.10 How is the *t* critical value affected by sample size and degrees of freedom?

9.11 Why does the *t* distribution merge with the *z* distribution as sample size increases?

9.12 Explain what each part of the following statistic means, as it would be reported in the American Psychological Association (APA) format: $t(4) = 2.87$, $p = 0.032$.

9.13 What could you report instead of the *p* value in Exercise 9.12?

9.14 When do we use a paired-samples *t* test?

9.15 Explain the distinction between the terms *independent-samples* and *paired-samples* as they relate to *t* tests.

Calculating the Statistics

9.16 We use formulas to describe calculations. Find the error in symbolic notation in each of the following formulas. Explain why it is incorrect and provide the correct symbolic notation.

  a. $z = \frac{(X - M)}{\sigma}$

  b. $X = z(\sigma) - \mu_M$

  c. $\sigma_M = \frac{\sigma}{\sqrt{N-1}}$

  d. $t = \frac{(M - \mu_M)}{\sigma_M}$

9.17 For the following data (93, 97, 91, 88, 103, 94, 97), calculate the standard deviation under both of these conditions:

  a. For the sample

  b. As an estimate of the population

9.18 For the following data (1.01, 0.99, 1.12, 1.27, 0.82, 1.04), calculate the standard deviation under both of these conditions. (*Note:* You will have to carry some calculations out to the third decimal place to see the difference in calculations.)

  a. For the sample

  b. As an estimate of the population

9.19 Calculate the standard error for *t* for the sample used in Exercise 9.17 using symbolic notation: 93, 97, 91, 88, 103, 94, 97.

9.20 Calculate the standard error for *t* for the sample used in Exercise 9.18 using symbolic notation: 1.01, 0.99, 1.12, 1.27, 0.82, 1.04.

9.21 Calculate the *t* statistic for the data presented in Exercise 9.17, assuming $\mu = 96$. Again, the data are 93, 97, 91, 88, 103, 94, 97.

9.22 Calculate the *t* statistic for the data presented in Exercise 9.18, assuming $\mu = 0.96$. Again, the data are 1.01, 0.99, 1.12, 1.27, 0.82, 1.04.

9.23 Identify the critical *t* value in each of the following circumstances:

   a. A one-tailed test with 73 degrees of freedom at a *p* level of 0.10

   b. A two-tailed test with 108 degrees of freedom at a *p* level of 0.05

   c. A one-tailed test with 38 degrees of freedom at a *p* level of 0.01

9.24 Calculate degrees of freedom and identify the critical *t* value in each of the following circumstances:

   a. A two-tailed test based on 8 observations at a *p* level of 0.10

   b. A one-tailed test based on 42 observations at a *p* level of 0.05

   c. A two-tailed test based on 89 observations at a *p* level of 0.01

9.25 Identify *t* critical values for each of the following tests:

   a. A single-sample *t* test examining scores for 26 participants to see if there is any difference compared to the population, using a *p* level of 0.05

   b. A one-tailed, paired-samples *t* test performed on scores on the Marital Satisfaction Inventory for 18 couples who went through marriage counseling, using a *p* level of 0.01

   c. A two-tailed, single-sample *t* test, using a *p* level of 0.05, with 34 degrees of freedom

9.26 Assume we know the following for a two-tailed, single-sample *t* test, at a *p* level of 0.05: $\mu = 44.3$, $N = 114$, $M = 43$, $s = 5.9$.

   a. Calculate the *t* statistic.

   b. Calculate a 95% confidence interval.

   c. Calculate effect size using Cohen's *d*.

9.27 Assume we know the following for a two-tailed, single-sample *t* test: $\mu = 7$, $N = 41$, $M = 8.5$, $s = 2.1$.

   a. Calculate the *t* statistic.

   b. Calculate a 99% confidence interval.

   c. Calculate effect size using Cohen's *d*.

9.28 Assume we know the following for a paired-samples *t* test: $N = 32$, $M_{difference} = 1.75$, $s = 4.0$.

   a. Calculate the *t* statistic.

   b. Calculate a 95% confidence interval for a two-tailed test.

   c. Calculate effect size using Cohen's *d*.

9.29 Assume we know the following for a paired-samples *t* test: $N = 13$, $M_{difference} = -0.77$, $s = 1.42$.

   a. Calculate the *t* statistic.

   b. Calculate a 95% confidence interval for a two-tailed test.

   c. Calculate effect size using Cohen's *d*.

9.30 Each of the following is a *p* value for a specific *t* statistic. For each, use Excel to determine p_{rep}.

   a. 0.022

   b. 0.37

   c. 0.004

Applying the Concepts

9.31 For each of the problems described below, which are the same as those described in Exercise 9.25, identify what the *z* critical value would have been if there had been just one sample and we knew the mean and standard deviation of the population:

   a. A single-sample *t* test examining scores for 26 participants to see if there is any difference compared to the population, using a *p* level of 0.05

   b. A one-tailed, single-sample *t* test performed on scores on the Marital Satisfaction Inventory for 18 people who went through marriage counseling, using a *p* level of 0.01

   c. A two-tailed, single-sample *t* test, using a *p* level of 0.05, with 34 degrees of freedom

   d. Comparing the *t* critical values with the *z* critical values, explain how and why these are different.

9.32 On its Web site, the *Princeton Review* claims that students who have taken its course improve their GRE scores, on average, by 210 points. (No other information is provided about this statistic.) Treating this average gain as a population mean, a researcher wonders whether the far cheaper technique of practicing for the GRE on one's own using books and CD-ROMs would lead to a different average gain. She randomly selects five students from the pool of students at her university who plan to take the GRE. The students take a practice test before and after two months of self-study. They reported (fictional) gains of 160, 240, 340, 70, and 250 points. (Note that many experts suggest that the results from self-study are similar to those from a structured course if you have the self-discipline to go solo. Regardless of the format, preparation has been convincingly demonstrated to lead to increased scores.)

a. Using symbolic notation and formulas (where appropriate), determine the appropriate mean and standard error for the distribution to which we will compare this sample. Show all steps of your calculations.

b. Using symbolic notation and the formula, calculate the *t* statistic for this sample.

c. As an interested consumer, what critical questions would you want to ask about the statistic reported by the *Princeton Review*? List at least three questions.

9.33 The Florida Department of Corrections publishes an online death row fact sheet. It reports the average time on death row prior to execution as 11.72 years but provides no standard deviation. This mean is a parameter, as it is calculated from the entire population of executed prisoners in Florida. Has the time spent on death row changed in recent years? According to the execution list linked to the same Web site, the six prisoners executed in Florida during the years 2003, 2004, and 2005 spent 25.62, 13.09, 8.74, 17.63, 2.80, and 4.42 years on death row, respectively. (All were men, although Aileen Wuornos, the serial killer portrayed by Charlize Theron in the 2003 film *Monster,* was among the three prisoners executed by the state of Florida in 2002; Wuornos spent 10.69 years on death row.)

a. Using symbolic notation and formulas (where appropriate), determine the appropriate mean and standard error for the distribution of means. Show all steps of your calculations.

b. Using symbolic notation and the formula, calculate the *t* statistic for time spent on death row for the sample of recently executed prisoners.

c. The specific *p* value for the *t* statistic you just calculated is 0.929. Use Excel to determine p_{rep}. What does p_{rep} tell you about this study?

d. The execution list provides data on all prisoners executed since the death penalty was reinstated in Florida in 1976. Included for each prisoner are the name, race, gender, date of birth, date of offense, date sentenced, date arrived on death row, data of execution, number of warrants, and years on death row. State at least one hypothesis, other than year of execution, that could be examined using a *t* distribution and the comparison mean of 11.72 years on death row. Be specific about your hypothesis (and if you are truly interested, you can search for the data online).

e. What additional information would you need to calculate a *z* score for the length of time Aileen Wuornos spent on death row?

9.34 Refer to the information provided in Exercise 9.33 when answering the following:

a. Write hypotheses to address the question "Has the time spent on death row changed in recent years?"

b. Using these data as "recent years" and the mean of 11.72 years as the comparison, answer the question based on your *t* statistic, using alpha of 0.05.

9.35 Refer to the information provided in Exercise 9.33 when answering the following:

a. Calculate the confidence interval for this statistic based on the data presented.

b. What conclusion would you make about your hypotheses based on this confidence interval? What can you say about the size of this confidence interval?

9.36 Refer to the information provided in Exercise 9.33 and the work you have done through Exercise 9.35 when answering the following:

a. Calculate the effect size using Cohen's *d*.

b. Evaluate the size of this effect.

9.37 Many communities worldwide are lamenting the effects of so-called big box retailers (e.g., Wal-Mart) on their local economies, particularly on small, independently owned shops. Do these large stores affect the bottom lines of locally owned retailers? Imagine that you decide to test this premise. You assess earnings at 20 local stores for the month of October, a few months before a big box store opens. You then assess earnings the following October, correcting for inflation.

a. What are the two populations?

b. What would the comparison distribution be? Explain.

c. What hypothesis test would you use? Explain.

d. Check the assumptions for this hypothesis test.

e. What is one flaw in drawing conclusions from this comparison over time?

9.38 For the scenario described in Exercise 9.37 (big box stores and their effect on local retailers), state the null and research hypotheses in both words and symbols.

9.39 Bardwell, Ensign, and Mills (2005) assessed the moods of 60 male U.S. Marines following a month-long training exercise conducted in cold temperatures and at high altitudes. Negative moods, including fatigue and anger, increased substantially during the training and lasted up to three months after the training ended. Mean mood scores were compared to population norms for three groups: college men, adult men, and male psychiatric outpatients. Let's examine anger scores for six men at the end of training; these scores are fictional, but their mean and standard deviation are very close to the actual descriptive statistics for the sample: 14, 12, 13, 12, 14, 15.

a. The population mean anger score for college men is 8.90. Conduct all six steps of a single-sample *t* test. Be sure to label all six steps. Report the statistics as you would in a journal article.

b. Now calculate the test statistic to compare this sample mean to the population mean anger score for adult men ($M = 9.20$). You do not have to repeat all the steps from part (a), but conduct step 6 of hypothesis testing and report the statistics as you would in a journal article.

c. Now calculate the test statistic to compare this sample mean to the population mean anger score for male psychiatric outpatients ($M = 13.5$). Do not repeat all the steps from part (a), but conduct step 6 of hypothesis testing and report the statistics as you would in a journal article.

d. What can we conclude overall about Marines' moods following high-altitude, cold-weather training? Remember, if we fail to reject the null hypothesis, we can only conclude that there is no evidence from this study to support the research hypothesis. We cannot conclude that we have supported the null hypothesis.

9.40 The number of paid days off (i.e., vacation, sick leave) taken by eight employees at a local small business is compared to the national average. You are hired by the business owner, who has been in business for just 18 months, to help her determine what to expect for paid days off. In general, she wants to set some standard for her employees and for herself. Let's assume your search on the Internet for data on paid days off leaves you with the impression that the national average is 15 days. The data for the eight local employees during the last fiscal year are: 10, 11, 8, 14, 13, 12, 12, and 27 days.

a. Write hypotheses for your research.

b. Which type of test would be appropriate to analyze these data in order to answer your question?

c. Before doing any computations, do you have any concerns about this research? Are there any questions you might like to ask about the data you have been given?

9.41 Use the data presented in Exercise 9.40 to help this business owner understand her employees' experience with paid days off in greater detail.

a. Calculate the appropriate *t* statistic. Show all of your work in detail.

b. Draw a statistical conclusion for this business owner.

c. The *p* level for the test statistic you calculated in part (a) is 0.454. Using Excel, determine p_{rep}.

d. Calculate the confidence interval.

e. Calculate and interpret the effect size.

9.42 Consider all the results you calculated in Exercise 9.41. How would you summarize the situation for this business owner? Identify the limitations of your analyses, and discuss the difficulties of making comparisons between populations and samples. Make reference to the assumptions of the statistical test in your answer.

9.43 After further investigation, you discover that one of the data points, 27 days, was actually the owner's number of paid days off. Redo some of the work for Exercise 9.41 adapting for this new information by deleting that value.

a. Calculate the appropriate *t* statistic. Show all of your work in detail.

b. Draw a statistical conclusion for this business owner.

c. The *p* level for the test statistic you calculated in part (a) is now 0.003. Using Excel, determine p_{rep}.

d. Calculate and interpret the effect size.

e. Explain what changed in these analyses.

9.44 Is it harder to get into graduate programs in psychology or history? We randomly selected five institutions from among all U.S. institutions with graduate programs. The first number for each is the minimum GPA for applicants to the psychology doctoral program, and the second is for applicants to the history doctoral program. These GPAs were posted on the Web site of the well-known college guide company Peterson's.

Wayne State University: 3.0, 2.75

University of Iowa: 3.0, 3.0

University of Nevada–Reno: 3.0, 2.75

George Washington University: 3.0, 3.0

University of Wyoming: 3.0, 3.0

a. The participants are not people; explain why it is appropriate to use a paired-samples *t* test for this situation.

b. Conduct all six steps of a paired-samples *t* test. Be sure to label all six steps.

c. Report the statistics as you would in a journal article.

9.45 Using the data provided in Exercise 9.44, calculate the effect size and explain what this adds to your analysis.

9.46 In Chapter 1, you were given an opportunity to complete the Stroop task in which color words are printed in the wrong color; for example, the word *red* might be printed in the color blue. The conflict that arises when we try to read the words, but are distracted by the colors, increases our reaction time and decreases our accuracy. Several researchers have suggested that the Stroop effect can be decreased by hypnosis. Raz (2005) used brain-imaging techniques [i.e., functional magnetic resonance imaging (fMRI)] to demonstrate that posthypnotic suggestion led highly hypnotizable individuals to see Stroop words as nonsense words. Imagine that you are working with Raz and your assignment is to determine if reaction times decrease (remember, a decrease is a good thing; it indicates that participants are faster) when highly hypnotizable individuals receive a posthypnotic suggestion to view the words as nonsensical. You conduct the experiment on six individuals, once in each condition, and receive the following data; the first number is reaction time in seconds without the posthypnotic suggestion, and the second number is reaction time with the posthypnotic suggestion:

Participant 1: (12.6, 8.5)
Participant 2: (13.8, 9.6)
Participant 3: (11.6, 10.0)
Participant 4: (12.2, 9.2)
Participant 5: (12.1, 8.9)
Participant 6: (13.0, 10.8)

a. What is the independent variable and what are its levels? What is the dependent variable?

b. Conduct all six steps of a paired-samples *t* test. Be sure to label all six steps.

c. Report the statistics as you would in a journal article.

9.47 Let's consider Exercise 9.46 on the Stroop task and posthypnotic suggestion. When we conduct a one-tailed test instead of a two-tailed test, there are small changes in steps 2 and 4 of hypothesis testing.

a. Conduct step 2 of hypothesis testing—stating the null and research hypotheses in words and in symbols—for a one-tailed test.

b. Conduct step 4 of hypothesis testing—determining the critical value and drawing the curve—for a one-tailed test.

c. Conduct step 6 of hypothesis testing—making a decision—for a one-tailed test.

d. Under which circumstance—a one-tailed or a two-tailed test—is it easier to reject the null hypothesis? Explain.

e. If it becomes easier to reject the null hypothesis under one type of test (one-tailed versus two-tailed), does this mean that there is a bigger mean difference between the samples? Explain.

9.48 When we change the *p* level that we use as a cutoff, it causes a small change in step 4 of hypothesis testing. Although 0.05 is the most commonly used *p* level, other levels, such as 0.01, are also often used. Let's consider Exercise 9.46 on the Stroop task and posthypnotic suggestion.

a. Conduct step 4 of hypothesis testing—determining the critical value and drawing the curve—for a *p* level of 0.01.

b. Conduct step 6 of hypothesis testing—making a decision—for a *p* level of 0.01.

c. With which *p* level—0.05 or 0.01—is it easiest to reject the null hypothesis? Explain.

d. If it is easier to reject the null hypothesis with certain *p* levels, does this mean that there is a bigger mean difference between the samples? Explain.

9.49 Changing the sample size can have an effect on the outcome of a hypothesis test. Consider Exercise 9.46 on the Stroop task and posthypnotic suggestion.

a. Calculate the test statistic using only participants 1–3.

b. Is this test statistic closer to or farther from the cutoff? Does reducing the sample size make it easier or more difficult to reject the null hypothesis? Explain.

Terms

t statistic (p. 206)
single-sample *t* test (p. 207)

degrees of freedom (p. 208)
paired-samples *t* test (p. 216)

Formulas

$$s = \sqrt{\frac{\Sigma(X - M)^2}{(N - 1)}} \quad \text{(p. 202)}$$

$$s_M = \frac{s}{\sqrt{N}} \quad \text{(p. 205)}$$

$$t = \frac{(M - \mu_M)}{s_M} \quad \text{(p. 206)}$$

$$df = N - 1 \quad \text{(p. 208)}$$

$$M_{lower} = -t(s_M) + M_{sample} \quad \text{(p. 214)}$$

$$M_{upper} = t(s_M) + M_{sample} \quad \text{(p. 214)}$$

$$\text{Cohen's } d = \frac{(M - \mu)}{s} \quad \text{(p. 214)}$$

Symbols

s_M (p. 205)
t (p. 206)
df (p. 208)

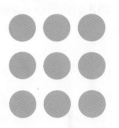

The Independent–Samples *t* Test

BEFORE YOU GO ON

- You should understand the differences between a distribution of scores, distribution of means, and distribution of mean differences (Chapters 7 and 9).

- You should know how to conduct a single-sample *t* test and a paired-samples *t* test, including the calculations for the corrected versions of standard deviation and variance (Chapter 9).

- You should understand the basics of determining confidence intervals (Chapter 8).

- You should understand the concept of effect size and know the basics of calculating Cohen's *d* (Chapter 8).

Stella Cunliffe Stella Cunliffe created a remarkable career through her statistical reasoning and became the first female president of the Royal Statistical Society. As a statistician, she used hypothesis testing to improve quality control at the Guinness Brewing Company and to shape public policy in the criminology division at the British Home Office.

Stella Cunliffe was the first woman elected president of the Royal Statistical Society. In her inaugural address, Cunliffe described her "exciting life" as a statistician. She talked about her research at the Guinness Brewing Company and what she had learned by applying statistics to human behavior: humans are full of "delightful idiosyncrasies" (Cunliffe, 1976; see Salsburg, 2001).

For example, Cunliffe devised an experiment to pinpoint the temperature at which people preferred to drink Guinness but ended up discovering that people do not like beer labeled with yellow seals, regardless of its temperature (colored seals were used to conceal the beer's temperature from the tasting panel). Cunliffe concluded that all observations of human behavior are contaminated because we "all have prejudices about certain numbers, letters, or colours, and all of us are very superstitious. We all behave irrationally" (p. 262, Cunliffe, 1976; see Salsburg, 2001).

Human irrationality is not the only way in which findings can be contaminated. For example, Cunliffe noticed that the woman who inspected the quality of handmade beer barrels had to divide them into two groups: accept or reject. However, the worker's decision was contaminated by the arrangement of her workstation. To accept a barrel, the worker just had to kick it downhill—a fairly easy task. To reject a barrel, however, she had to roll it uphill—a fairly difficult task. The difficulty of the task biased the worker so that she sometimes failed to reject deficient barrels that should have been rejected.

Fortunately, Cunliffe knew that she could decontaminate the worker's judgments by creating two fair comparison groups. Cunliffe redesigned the woman's workstation so that it was just as easy to reject a barrel as it was to accept a barrel—a change that represented a significant advance in quality control for the Guinness Brewing Company. In the behavioral sciences, the most common way to control human idiosyncrasies is by using random assignment to create independent groups; therefore, this chapter discusses

1. when to use an independent-samples *t* test;
2. how to interpret differences between two independent groups;
3. how to calculate a confidence interval and effect size for a between-groups study with two samples.

In Chapter 9, we learned how to conduct a single-sample *t* test (used when comparing one sample to a population for which we know the mean but not the standard deviation). We also learned how to conduct a paired-samples *t* test for a two-group study in which every participant was in both conditions of the study. In this chapter, we learn how to conduct a *t* test in a third situation: a two-group study in which each participant is in only one of the two conditions of the study. This hypothesis test is called an *independent-samples t test* because the scores for each group of participants are independent of what happens in the other group. We also demonstrate how to determine a confidence interval and calculate an effect size for situations in which we have two independent groups.

Conducting an Independent-Samples *t* Test

When Stella Cunliffe observed the woman making decisions about which barrels to accept and which to reject, she recognized that the two conditions were *not* independent of each other. The difficulty of rolling a barrel uphill made it more likely that the worker would accept the barrel and kick it downhill. However, when those conditions were made independent of each other—by redesigning the workstation—the worker was able to make independent, unbiased, fair judgments about the quality of beer barrels.

Creating independent groups is a common research strategy because often we do not—or cannot—have the same participants in both samples. When we test for differences between two independent groups, we use an ***independent-samples t test***, *which compares two means for a between-groups design, a situation in which each participant is assigned to only one condition.* This test uses a distribution of differences between means. This affects our *t* test in a few minor ways. As we will see, the biggest difference is that it takes more work to estimate the appropriate standard error. It's not difficult—just a bit time-consuming. After we discuss some of the differences, including the appropriate distribution, we look at an example from the area of gender differences and similarities. We introduce the specifics of the independent-samples *t* test in each step below.

> ◀ **MASTERING THE CONCEPT**
>
> **10-1:** An independent-samples *t* test is used when we have two groups and a between-groups research design—that is, every participant is in only one of the two groups.

A Distribution of Differences Between Means

Because we have different people in each condition of our study, we cannot create a difference score for each person. We're looking at overall differences between two independent groups. For this research design, we need to develop a new type of distribution, a distribution of *differences* between means, so that we can establish a distribution that specifies the null hypothesis.

Let's use the Chapter 6 data about heights to demonstrate how to create a distribution of differences between means, the distribution that accompanies a between-groups design. Let's say that we were planning to collect data on two groups of three people each and wanted to determine the comparison distribution for this research scenario. Remember that in Chapter 6, we used the example of a population of 140 college students from the authors' classes. We described writing the height of each student on a card and putting the 140 cards in a bowl. Let's use that example to create a distribution of differences between means. First, we would choose three cards and calculate the mean of the heights listed on them. This is the first group. Then, we would choose three other cards and calculate their mean. This is the second group. Then, we would subtract the second mean from the first. That's really all there is to it—except we do this procedure many more times. So, there are two samples and two sample means, but we're building just *one* curve of differences between means.

Here's an example. Let's say the first mean was 66 and the second was 64; the difference between means would be $66 - 64 = 2$. (Note that it's fine to subtract the first from the second, as long as we're consistent in our arithmetic.) Next, we put all of the cards back and repeat the process. Let's say that, this time, we calculate means of 65 and 68 for our two samples; now the difference between means would be $65 - 68 = -3$. We might do it a third time and find means of 63 and 63 for a difference of 0. Eventually, we would have many differences between means—some positive, some negative, and some right at 0—and could plot them on a curve. But this would only be the beginning of what this distribution would look like. If we were to calculate the whole distribution, then we would do this many, many more times. When creating the beginnings of a distribution of differences between means, the authors calculated 30 differences between means as seen in Figure 10-1.

> ■ An **independent-samples *t* test** is used to compare two means for a between-groups design, a situation in which each participant is assigned to only one condition.

FIGURE 10-1
Distribution of Differences Between Means

This curve represents the beginning of the development of a distribution of differences between means. It includes only 30 differences, whereas the actual distribution would include all possible differences.

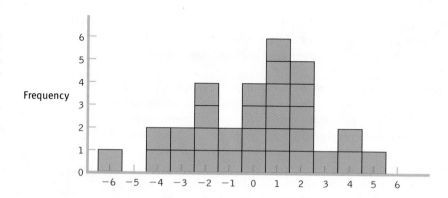

The Six Steps of an Independent-Samples *t* Test

EXAMPLE 10.1

Who do you think has a better sense of humor—women or men? Researchers at Stanford University examined brain activity in women and men during exposure to humorous cartoons (Azim, Mobbs, Jo, Menon, & Reiss, 2005). Using a brain-scanning technique called *functional magnetic resonance imaging,* researchers observed many similarities between the genders in their responses to humor. However, these brain scans indicated that women tended to use more language and more executive functioning (such as verbal abstraction and screening for irrelevant features) when processing humor than did men. Also, more activity was seen in the reward centers of women's brains than men's, the same reward centers that respond when receiving money, feeling happy, or ingesting cocaine. The researchers suggested that this might be because women have lower expectations of humor than do men, so find it more rewarding when something is actually funny.

However, the researchers were aware of other possible explanations for these findings. For example, they considered whether one gender is more likely to find humorous stimuli funny to begin with. They asked the 10 men and 10 women in their study to categorize 30 cartoons as either "funny" or "unfunny." Each participant received a score that represented her or his percentage of cartoons found to be "funny." The researchers conducted an independent-samples *t* test. Below are fictional data for nine people (four women and five men); these fictional data have approximately the same means as were reported in the original study. Notice that we do not need to have the same number of participants in each sample, although it is best if the sample sizes are fairly close.

Better Sense of Humor: Men or Women? We can use an independent-samples *t* test for a two-group design that explores whether men or women have a better sense of humor. The null hypothesis is that, on average, there is no difference between men and women.

Percentage of cartoons labeled as "funny"

Women: 84, 97, 58, 90

Men: 88, 90, 52, 97, 86

TABLE 10-1. Hypothesis Tests and Their Distributions

We must consider the appropriate comparison distribution when we choose which hypothesis test to use.

Hypothesis Test	Number of Samples	Comparison Distribution
z test	one	Distribution of means
Single-sample *t* test	one	Distribution of means
Paired-samples *t* test	two (same participants)	Distribution of mean difference scores
Independent-samples *t* test	two (different participants)	Distribution of differences between means

STEP 1. Identify the populations, distribution, and assumptions.

For the populations, this step is similar to that for the paired-samples *t* test: there are two populations—men and women. The comparison distribution, however, will be a distribution of differences between means (rather than a distribution of mean difference scores). Table 10-1 summarizes the distributions we have encountered with the hypothesis tests we have learned so far.

As usual, the comparison distribution is based on the null hypothesis. As with the paired-samples *t* test, the null hypothesis for the independent-samples *t* test posits no difference between means. So the mean of the comparison distribution would be 0; this reflects a mean difference between means of 0. We compare the difference between our sample means to a difference of 0, which is what would occur if there were no difference between groups. The assumptions are the same as for the single-sample *t* test and the paired-samples *t* test.

Summary: Population 1: Women exposed to humorous cartoons. Population 2: Men exposed to humorous cartoons.

The comparison distribution will be a distribution of differences between means based on the null hypothesis. The hypothesis test will be an independent-samples *t* test because we have two samples composed of different groups of participants. This study meets one of the three assumptions. (1) The dependent variable is a percentage of cartoons categorized as "funny," which is a scale variable. (2) We do not know whether the population is normally distributed, and there are not at least 30 participants. Moreover, the data suggest some negative skew; although this test is robust with respect to this assumption, we must be cautious. (3) The men and women in this study were not randomly selected from among all men and women, so we must be cautious with respect to generalizing our findings.

STEP 2. State the null and research hypotheses.

This step is identical to that for the previous *t* tests.

Summary: Null hypothesis: On average, women categorize the same percentage of cartoons as "funny" as men do—$H_0: \mu_1 = \mu_2$. Research hypothesis: On average, women categorize a different percentage of cartoons as "funny" as compared with men—$H_1: \mu_1 \neq \mu_2$.

STEP 3. Determine the characteristics of the comparison distribution.

This step is similar to that for previous *t* tests: We determine the appropriate mean and the appropriate standard error of the comparison distribution—the distribution based on the null hypothesis. According to the null hypothesis, no mean difference exists between the populations; that is, the difference between means is 0. So the mean of the comparison distribution is always 0, as long as the null hypothesis posits no mean difference. Because we have two samples, however, it is more complicated to calculate the appropriate measure of spread. There are five stages to this process. First, let's consider them in words; then we'll learn the calculations. These instructions are basic, and you'll understand them better when you do the calculations, but they'll help you to keep the overall framework in mind. (These verbal descriptions are keyed by letter to the calculation stages below.)

(a) Calculate the corrected variance for each sample. (Notice that we're working with variance, not standard deviation.)

(b) Pool the variances. Pooling involves taking an average of the two sample variances, while accounting for any differences in the sizes of the two samples. Pooled variance is an estimate of the common population variance.

(c) Convert the pooled variance from squared standard deviation (i.e., variance) to squared standard error (another version of variance) by dividing the pooled variance by the sample size, first for one sample and then again for the second sample. These are the estimated variances for each sample's distribution of means.

(d) Add the two variances (*squared* standard errors), one for each distribution of sample means, to calculate the estimated variance of the distribution of the mean differences.

(e) Calculate the square root of this form of variance (*squared* standard error) to get the estimated standard error of the distribution of mean differences.

Notice that stages (a) and (b) are an expanded version of the usual first calculation for a *t* test. Instead of calculating one corrected estimate of standard deviation, we're calculating two—one for each sample; and we're using variances instead of standard deviations. Because there are two calculations of variance, we have to combine them (i.e., the pooled variance). Stages (c) and (d) are an expanded version of the usual second calculation for a *t* test. Once again, we are converting to the standard error (only this time it is squared because we are working with variances). Once again, we combine the variances from each sample. In stage (e), we use the square root so that we have the standard error. Let's examine the calculations.

(a) We calculate the corrected variance for each sample (the corrected variance is the one we learned in Chapter 9 that uses $N - 1$ in the denominator). First, we calculate variance for X, the sample of women. Be sure to use the mean for the women's scores only, which is 82.25. Notice that the symbol for this variance uses s^2, instead of SD^2, just as the standard deviation uses s instead of SD in the previous *t* tests. Also, we have included the subscript X to indicate that this is the variance for the first sample, whose scores are arbitrarily called X. (Remember, don't take the square root. We want variance, not standard deviation.)

X	$X - M$	$(X - M)^2$
84	1.75	3.063
97	14.75	217.563
58	−24.25	588.063
90	7.75	60.063

Pooled variance is a weighted average of the two estimates of variance—one from each sample—that are calculated when conducting an independent-samples *t* test.

$$s_X^2 = \frac{\Sigma(X - M)^2}{N - 1} = \frac{(3.063 + 217.563 + 588.063 + 60.063)}{4 - 1} = 289.584$$

Now we do the same for *Y*, the men. Remember to use the mean for *Y*; it's easy to forget and use the mean we calculated earlier for *X*. The mean for *Y* is 82.6. The subscript *Y* indicates that this is the variance for the second sample, whose scores are arbitrarily called *Y*. (We could call these scores by any letter, but statisticians tend to call the scores in the first two samples *X* and *Y*.)

Y	Y − M	(Y − M)²
88	5.4	29.16
90	7.4	54.76
52	−30.6	936.36
97	14.4	207.36
86	3.4	11.56

$$s_Y^2 = \frac{\Sigma(Y-M)^2}{N-1} = \frac{(29.16 + 54.76 + 936.36 + 207.36 + 11.56)}{5-1} = 309.800$$

(b) We must pool the two estimates of variance. Because there are often different numbers of people in each sample, we cannot simply take their mean. We mentioned earlier in this book that estimates of spread taken from smaller samples tend to be less accurate. So we need to weight the estimate from the smaller sample a bit less and weight the estimate from the larger sample a bit more. We do this by calculating the proportion of degrees of freedom represented by each sample. Each sample has degrees of freedom of *N* − 1. We also calculate a total degrees of freedom that sums the degrees of freedom for the two samples. Here are the calculations for degrees of freedom for this independent-samples *t* test:

$$df_X = N - 1 = 4 - 1 = 3$$
$$df_Y = N - 1 = 5 - 1 = 4$$
$$df_{total} = df_X + df_Y = 3 + 4 = 7$$

Using these degrees of freedom, we can calculate a sort of average variance called a *pooled variance*. **Pooled variance** *is a weighted average of the two estimates of variance—one from each sample—that are calculated when conducting an independent-samples t test.* The estimate of variance from the larger sample counts for more in the pooled variance than does the estimate from the smaller sample because larger samples tend to lead to somewhat more accurate estimates than do smaller samples. Here's the formula for pooled variance and the calculations for this particular example:

$$s_{pooled}^2 = \left(\frac{df_X}{df_{total}}\right)s_X^2 + \left(\frac{df_Y}{df_{total}}\right)s_Y^2 = \left(\frac{3}{7}\right)289.584 + \left(\frac{4}{7}\right)309.800$$
$$= 124.107 + 177.029 = 301.136$$

(*Note:* If we had exactly the same number of participants in each sample, this would be an unweighted average—that is, we could compute the average in the usual way by summing the two sample variances and dividing by 2. Let's say we had 5 participants in each sample, and so each sample had 4 degrees of freedom. There would be 8 total degrees of freedom. So each sample's estimate of variance would account for

MASTERING THE FORMULA

10-1: There are three degrees of freedom calculations for an independent-samples *t* test. First, we calculate the degrees of freedom for the first sample by subtracting 1 from the number of participants in that sample: $df_X = N - 1$. Then we calculate the degrees of freedom for the second sample by subtracting 1 from the number of participants in that sample: $df_Y = N - 1$. Finally, we sum the degrees of freedom from the two samples to calculate the total degrees of freedom: $df_{total} = df_X + df_Y$.

MASTERING THE FORMULA

10-2: We use all three degrees of freedom calculations, along with our variance estimates for each sample, to calculate pooled variance: $s_{pooled}^2 = \left(\frac{df_X}{df_{total}}\right)s_X^2 + \left(\frac{df_Y}{df_{total}}\right)s_Y^2$. This formula takes into account the size of each sample. A larger sample has a larger degrees of freedom in the numerator, and that variance therefore has more weight in the pooled variance that is calculated.

4/8—which reduces to 1/2—of the pooled variance. Taking half of each is the same as adding them together and dividing them by 2.)

(c) Now that we have pooled the two variances, we have an estimate of spread; this is similar to the estimate of the standard deviation in the previous *t* tests, but now it's based on two samples (and it's an estimate of the variance rather than the standard deviation). The next calculation in the previous *t* tests was dividing standard deviation by $\sqrt{N}$ to get the standard error. In this case, we divide by N instead of $\sqrt{N}$. Why? Because we are dealing with variances, not standard deviations. Variance is the square of standard deviation, so we divide by the square of $\sqrt{N}$, which is simply N. We do this once for each sample, using the pooled variance as the estimate of spread. We use the pooled variance because an estimate based on two samples is likely better than an estimate based on one. The key here is to divide by the appropriate N; that is, when we do the calculations for the first sample, we divide by its N, 4. And when we do the calculations for the second sample, we divide by its N, 5.

$$s^2_{M_X} = \frac{s^2_{pooled}}{N_X} = \frac{301.136}{4} = 75.284$$
$$s^2_{M_Y} = \frac{s^2_{pooled}}{N_Y} = \frac{301.136}{5} = 60.227$$

(d) In stage (c), we calculated the variance versions of standard error for each sample, but we want only one such measure of spread when we calculate the test statistic. We must combine the two variances, similar to the way in which we combined the two estimates of variance in stage (b). This stage is even simpler, however. We merely add the two variances together. When we sum them, we get the variance of the distribution of differences between means, symbolized as $s^2_{difference}$. Here are the formula and the calculations for this example:

$$s^2_{difference} = s^2_{M_X} + s^2_{M_Y} = 75.284 + 60.227 = 135.511$$

(e) We now have paralleled the two calculations of the previous *t* tests by doing two things: (1) we calculated an estimate of spread (we made two calculations using a formula we learned in Chapter 9, one for each sample, then combined them), and (2) we then adjusted our estimate for the sample size (again, we made two calculations, one for each sample, then combined them). The main difference is that we have kept all calculations as variances rather than standard deviations. At this final stage, we must convert from variance form to standard deviation form. Because standard deviation is the square root of variance, we do this by simply taking the square root:

$$s_{difference} = \sqrt{s^2_{difference}} = \sqrt{135.511} = 11.641$$

Summary: The mean of the distribution of differences between means is: $\mu_X - \mu_Y = 0$. The standard error of the distribution of differences between means is: $s_{difference} = 11.641$.

STEP 4. Determine critical values, or cutoffs.

This step is similar to those for previous *t* tests, but we use the total degrees of freedom, df_{total}.

Summary: Our critical values, based on a two-tailed test, a *p* level of 0.05, and a df_{total} of 7, are -2.365 and 2.365 (as seen in the curve in Figure 10-2).

MASTERING THE FORMULA

10-3: The next step in calculating the *t* statistic for a two-sample, between-groups design is to calculate the variance version of standard error for each sample by dividing variance by sample size. We use the pooled version of variance for both calculations because it's more likely to be accurate than the individual variance estimate for each sample. For the first sample, the formula is: $s^2_{M_X} = \frac{s^2_{pooled}}{N_X}$. For the second sample, the formula is: $s^2_{M_Y} = \frac{s^2_{pooled}}{N_Y}$. Note that because we're dealing with variance, the square of standard deviation, we divide by N, the square of $\sqrt{N}$—the denominator for standard error.

MASTERING THE FORMULA

10-4: To calculate the variance of the distribution of differences between means, we sum the variance versions of standard error that we calculated in the previous step: $s^2_{difference} = s^2_{M_X} + s^2_{M_Y}$.

MASTERING THE FORMULA

10-5: To calculate the standard deviation of the distribution of differences between means, we take the square root of the previous calculation, the variance of the distribution of differences between means. The formula is: $s_{difference} = \sqrt{s^2_{difference}}$.

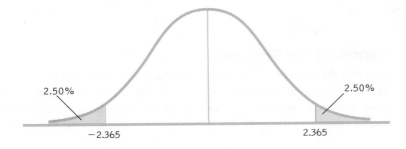

2.50%

2.50%

−2.365

2.365

FIGURE 10-2
Determining Cutoffs for an Independent-Samples *t* Test

To determine the critical values for an independent-samples *t* test, we use the total degrees of freedom, df_{total}. This is the sum of the degrees of freedom for each sample, which is $N − 1$ for each sample.

STEP 5. Calculate the test statistic.

This step is very similar to those for the previous *t* tests. Here we subtract the population difference between means based on the null hypothesis from the difference between means for our samples. The formula is:

$$t = \frac{(M_X − M_Y) − (\mu_X − \mu_Y)}{s_{difference}}$$

As in previous *t* tests, the test statistic is calculated by subtracting a number based on the populations from a number based on the samples, and then dividing by a version of standard error. Because the population difference between means (according to the null hypothesis) is almost always 0, many statisticians choose to eliminate the latter part of the formula. So the formula for the test statistic for an independent-samples *t* test is often abbreviated as:

$$t = \frac{M_X − M_Y}{s_{difference}}$$

You might find it easier to use the first formula, however, as it reminds us that we are subtracting the population difference between means according to the null hypothesis (0) from the actual difference between the sample means. This format more closely parallels the formulas of the test statistics we calculated in Chapter 9.

Summary: $t = \frac{(82.25 − 82.6) − (0)}{11.641} = −0.03$

◄ **MASTERING THE FORMULA**

10-6: We calculate the test statistic for an independent-samples *t* test using the following formula: $t = \frac{(M_X − M_Y) − (\mu_X − \mu_Y)}{s_{difference}}$. We subtract the difference between means according to the null hypothesis, usually 0, from the difference between means in our sample. We then divide this by the standard deviation of the differences between means. Because the difference between means according to the null hypothesis is usually 0, the formula for the test statistic is often abbreviated as: $t = \frac{M_X − M_Y}{s_{difference}}$.

STEP 6. Make a decision.

This step is identical to that for the previous *t* tests. If we reject the null hypothesis, we need to examine the means of the two conditions so that we know the direction of the effect.

Summary: Fail to reject the null hypothesis. We conclude that there is no evidence from this study to support the research hypothesis that either men or women are more likely than the opposite gender, on average, to find cartoons funny (as shown by the curve in Figure 10-3).

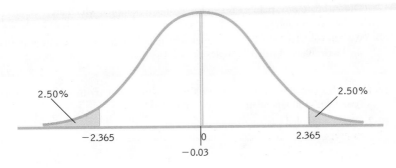

2.50%

2.50%

−2.365

0

2.365

−0.03

FIGURE 10-3
Making a Decision

As in previous *t* tests, in order to decide whether or not to reject the null hypothesis, we compare our test statistic to our critical values. In this figure, the test statistic, −0.03, is not beyond either −2.365 or 2.365. We fail to reject the null hypothesis and can only conclude that there is no evidence from this study to support the research hypothesis.

Reporting the Statistics

To report the statistics as they would appear in a journal article, follow the standard APA format, including the degrees of freedom, the value of the test statistic, and the actual p value associated with the test statistic if you used software. In the current example, the statistics would read:

$$t(7) = -0.03, p > 0.05$$

Because we didn't use software, we can only state that the p value is listed as greater than the cutoff of 0.05 an indication that we failed to reject the null hypothesis. The difference between men and women was *not* large enough that we could conclude that it was unlikely to have happened by chance.

As we noted in Chapter 9, we could present p_{rep} as an alternative to providing information about where the p value falls. Because the t table in Appendix B only includes the p values of .10, .05, and .01, we cannot use it to determine the actual p value for our test statistic. As we did in the previous chapter, we can use SPSS to determine the actual p value, and then use Excel to calculate p_{rep}. We demonstrate how to calculate p_{rep} for an independent-samples t test in the SPSS section of this chapter.

Regardless of whether we report p or p_{rep}, we would also include the means and standard deviations for the two samples. We calculated the means in step 3 of hypothesis testing, and we also calculated the variances (289.584 for women and 309.800 for men). We can calculate the standard deviations by taking the square roots of the variances. The descriptive statistics can be reported in parentheses as:

(Women: $M = 82.25$, $SD = 17.02$; Men: $M = 82.60$, $SD = 17.60$)

Always include the means and the standard deviations, as these are often the first statistics a reader turns to after noting the result of the hypothesis test.

CHECK YOUR LEARNING

Reviewing the Concepts

> In the independent-samples t test, we cannot calculate individual difference scores. That is why we compare the mean of one sample with the mean of the other sample.

> The comparison distribution is a distribution of differences between means. We are testing whether the difference we observe between the means of our two samples is a common difference or an unusual difference.

> We use the same six steps of hypothesis testing that we used with the z test and with the single-sample and paired-samples t tests.

> Conceptually, the t test for independent samples makes the same comparisons as the other t tests. However, the calculations are different, and critical values are based on degrees of freedom from two samples.

> Our estimate of variability is also based on two samples, which are weighted as a function of the size of each sample and then combined to create what is called *pooled variance*.

> We can calculate p_{rep} for an independent-samples t test in the same way that we did for single-sample and paired-samples t tests.

Clarifying the Concepts

10-1   In what situation do we conduct a paired-samples t test? In what situation do we conduct an independent-samples t test?

10-2   What is pooled variance?

Calculating the Statistics

10-3   Imagine you have the following data from two independent groups:

Group 1: 3, 2, 4, 6, 1, 2
Group 2: 5, 4, 6, 2, 6

Compute each of the following calculations needed to complete your final calculation of the independent-samples *t* test.

a. Calculate the corrected variance for each group.

b. Calculate degrees of freedom and pooled variance, s^2_{pooled}.

c. Calculate the variance version of standard error for each group.

d. Calculate the variance of the distribution of differences between means, then convert this number to standard deviations.

e. Calculate the test statistic.

Applying the Concepts   **10-4**   In Check Your Learning 10-3, you calculated several statistics; now let's consider a context for those numbers. Steele and Pinto (2006) examined whether people's level of trust in their direct supervisor was related to their level of agreement with a policy supported by that leader. They found that the extent to which subordinates agreed with their supervisor was statistically significantly related to trust and showed no relation to gender, age, time on the job, or length of time working with the supervisor. We have presented fictional data to re-create these findings, where group 1 represents employees with low trust in their supervisor and group 2 represents the high-trust employees. The scores presented are the level of agreement with a decision made by a leader, from 1 (strongly disagree) to 7 (strongly agree).

Group 1 (low trust in leader): 3, 2, 4, 6, 1, 2
Group 2 (high trust in leader): 5, 4, 6, 2, 6

a. State the null and research hypotheses.

b. Identify the critical values and make a decision.

c. Write your conclusion in a formal sentence that includes presentation of the statistic in APA format.

Solutions to these Check Your Learning questions can be found in Appendix D.

d. Explain why your results are different from those in the original research, despite having a similar mean difference.

Beyond Hypothesis Testing

After working at Guinness, Stella Cunliffe was hired by the British government's criminology department. While working with data there, Cunliffe noticed that adult male prisoners who had short prison sentences returned to prison at a very high rate. The relation between these two variables seemed to justify longer prison sentences to keep such habitual criminals off the streets, but Cunliffe looked more closely at the data. She noticed that the returning prisoners were almost all older people with mental health problems who had been sent to prison because the mental hospitals would not take them. Because of observations like this, researchers need ways to evaluate and interpret data that go beyond hypothesis testing.

Two ways that researchers can evaluate the findings of a hypothesis test are by calculating a confidence interval and an effect size. Both statistics provide detailed information that can help prevent misleading interpretations of the data.

Confidence Interval

Confidence intervals for the independent-samples *t* tests are calculated using the same logic we used for the *z* test and single-sample and paired sample *t* tests. Here, we'll create a confidence interval for the *difference between means* (rather than for the means themselves or for the mean differences). So we will use the difference between means for our samples and the standard error for the difference

> ◀ **MASTERING THE CONCEPT**
>
> **10-2:** As with the *z* test, the single-sample *t* test, and the paired-samples *t* test, we can determine a confidence interval and calculate a measure of effect size—Cohen's *d*—when we conduct an independent-samples *t* test.

between means, $s_{difference}$, that we calculate in an identical manner to the one used in hypothesis testing. But we're still creating an interval around a number (now a difference between means) based on some measure of variability (now the standard error for the difference between means).

We must also use the formula for the appropriate *t* statistic when calculating our raw differences between means. To do this, we use algebra on our original formula for an independent-samples *t* test to isolate the upper and lower mean differences, just as we used algebra in Chapter 6 to change our *z*-score formula to a raw-score formula. Here is the original *t* statistic formula:

$$t = \frac{(M_X - M_Y) - (\mu_X - \mu_Y)}{s_{difference}}$$

We now replace the population mean difference, $(\mu_X - \mu_Y)$, with the sample mean difference, $(M_X - M_Y)_{sample}$, because this is what the confidence interval is centered around. We also indicate that the first mean difference in the numerator refers to the bounds of the confidence intervals, the upper bound in this case:

$$t_{upper} = \frac{(M_X - M_Y)_{upper} - (M_X - M_Y)_{sample}}{s_{difference}}$$

With algebra, we can isolate the upper bound of the confidence interval to create the following formula for the upper bound of the confidence interval:

$$(M_X - M_Y)_{upper} = t(s_{difference}) + (M_X - M_Y)_{sample}$$

We create the formula for the lower bound of the confidence interval in exactly the same way, using the negative version of the *t* statistic:

$$(M_X - M_Y)_{lower} = -t(s_{difference}) + (M_X - M_Y)_{sample}$$

MASTERING THE FORMULA

10-7: The formulas for the upper and lower bounds of the confidence interval are $(M_X - M_Y)_{upper} = t(s_{difference}) + (M_X - M_Y)_{sample}$ and $(M_X - M_Y)_{lower} = -t(s_{difference}) + (M_X - M_Y)_{sample}$, respectively. In each case, we multiply the *t* statistic that marks off the tail by the standard deviation for the differences between means and add it to the difference between means in the sample. Remember that one of the *t* statistics is negative.

EXAMPLE 10.2

The steps for the confidence interval for a *t* statistic are the same as the steps for the confidence interval for a *z* statistic. Let's calculate the confidence interval that parallels the hypothesis test we conducted earlier comparing men's and women's perceptions of humorous cartoons (Azim et al., 2005). Previously, we calculated the difference between the means of these samples to be $82.25 - 82.6 = -0.35$; the standard error for the differences between means, $s_{difference}$, to be 11.641; and the degrees of freedom to be 7. (Note that the order of subtraction in calculating the difference between means is irrelevant; we could just as easily have subtracted 82.25 from 82.6 and gotten a positive result, 0.35.) If we had not already calculated these three values for the hypothesis test, we would, of course, have to calculate them for the confidence interval. Here are the five steps for determining a confidence interval for a difference between means:

STEP 1. Draw a normal curve with the sample difference between means in the center.

(See Figure 10-4.)

STEP 2. Indicate the bounds of the confidence interval on either end, and write the percentages under each segment of the curve.

(See Figure 10-4.)

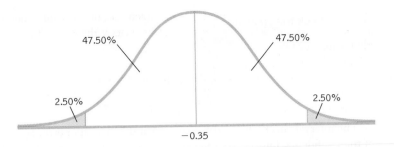

FIGURE 10-4
A 95% Confidence Interval for Differences Between Means, Part I

As with a confidence interval for a single-sample mean, we start the confidence interval for a difference between means by drawing a curve with the sample difference between means in the center.

STEP 3. Look up the *t* statistics for the lower and upper ends of the confidence interval in the *t* table.

Use a two-tailed test and a *p* level of 0.05 (which corresponds to a 95% confidence interval). Use the degrees of freedom—7—that we calculated earlier. The table indicates a *t* statistic of 2.365. Because the normal curve is symmetric, the bounds of our confidence interval fall at *t* statistics of -2.365 and 2.365. (Note that these cutoffs are identical to those used for the independent-samples *t* test. This is always the case for a given sample size because the *p* level of 0.05 corresponds to a confidence level of 95%.) We add those *t* statistics to our normal curve, as in Figure 10-5.

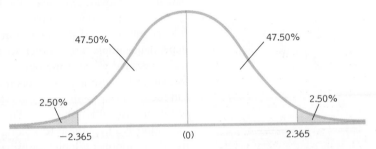

FIGURE 10-5
A 95% Confidence Interval for Differences Between Means, Part II

The next step in calculating a confidence interval is identifying the *t* statistics that indicate each end of the interval. Because the curve is symmetric, the *t* statistics have the same magnitude—one is negative and one is positive. (The *t* statistic at the center of the curve is always zero.)

STEP 4. Convert the *t* statistics to raw differences between means for the lower and upper ends of the confidence interval.

Be sure to pay attention to the negative signs in your calculations. For the lower end, the formula is:

$$(M_X - M_Y)_{lower} = -t(s_{difference}) + (M_X - M_Y)_{sample}$$
$$= -2.365(11.641) + (-0.35) = -27.88$$

For the upper end, the formula is:

$$(M_X - M_Y)_{upper} = t(s_{difference}) + (M_X - M_Y)_{sample}$$
$$= 2.365(11.641) + (-0.35) = 27.18$$

The confidence interval is $[-27.88, 27.18]$, as shown in Figure 10-6.

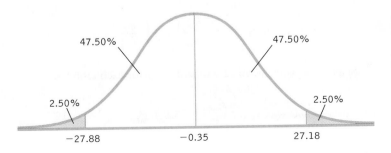

FIGURE 10-6
A 95% Confidence Interval for Differences Between Means, Part III

The final step in calculating a confidence interval is converting the *t* statistics that indicate each end of the interval into raw differences between means.

STEP 5. Check the answer.
Each end of the confidence interval should be exactly the same distance from the sample mean.

$$-27.88 - (-0.35) = -27.53$$
$$27.18 - (-0.35) = 27.53$$

The interval checks out, and we know that the margin of error is 27.53. The bounds of the confidence interval are calculated as the difference between sample means plus or minus 27.53.

The confidence interval is quite wide, indicating many plausible values for the difference between means. If we were to conduct this study many times, 95% of the time the population mean would be in our confidence interval. In this case, we have not pinpointed our estimate very closely. In addition, 0 falls within the interval, an indication that the two distributions could actually be identical. (Whenever 0 falls within the interval, it is plausible that there is no difference.) We can only conclude that these data do not provide evidence of a difference between sample means.

As in the previous example, we can compare the conclusion drawn from our confidence interval to that drawn from our hypothesis test. When we conducted the independent-samples *t* test earlier, we failed to reject the null hypothesis. Both statistical techniques led to the same outcome, but the confidence interval provided more information because it is an interval estimate rather than a point estimate. In fact, we can see from our confidence interval that we have a range of possible differences between means that is quite wide. The fact that confidence intervals give us the same information as a hypothesis test, along with even more information, is the major reason that their proponents lobby for using them routinely (e.g., Cohen, 1994) and that some call for an outright boycott of hypothesis tests altogether (e.g., Schmidt, 1996).

Effect Size

EXAMPLE 10.3

As with all hypothesis tests, it is recommended that the results be supplemented with an effect size that provides information about the importance of the results. For an independent-samples *t* test, we can use Cohen's *d* as our measure of effect size. We'll calculate Cohen's *d* using the data for men's and women's perceptions of humorous cartoons. Our fictional data provided means of 82.25 for women and 82.6 for men (Azim et al., 2005). Previously, we calculated a standard error for the difference between means, $s_{difference}$, of 11.641. Here are the calculations we performed:

Stage 1 (variance for each sample):

$$s_X^2 = \frac{\Sigma(X - M)^2}{N - 1} = 289.584; \; s_Y^2 = \frac{\Sigma(Y - M)^2}{N - 1} = 309.800$$

Stage 2 (combining variances):

$$s_{pooled}^2 = \left(\frac{df_X}{df_{total}}\right)s_X^2 + \left(\frac{df_Y}{df_{total}}\right)s_Y^2 = 301.136$$

Stage 3 (variance form of standard error for each sample):

$$s_{M_X}^2 = \frac{s_{pooled}^2}{N_X} = 75.284; \; s_{M_Y}^2 = \frac{s_{pooled}^2}{N_Y} = 60.227$$

Stage 4 (combining variance forms of standard error):

$$s^2_{difference} = s^2_{M_X} + s^2_{M_Y} = 135.511$$

Stage 5 (converting the variance form of standard error to the standard deviation form of standard error):

$$s_{difference} = \sqrt{s^2_{difference}} = 11.641$$

Because our goal is to disregard the influence of sample size in order to calculate Cohen's *d,* we want to use the standard deviation in the denominator, not the standard error. So we can ignore the last three stages, all of which contribute to the calculation of standard error. That leaves stages 1 and 2. It makes more sense to use the one that includes information from both samples, so we'll focus our attention on stage 2. Here is where many students make a mistake. What we have calculated in stage 2 is pooled *variance,* not pooled *standard deviation.* We must take the square root of the pooled variance to get the pooled standard deviation, the appropriate value for the denominator of our Cohen's *d.*

$$s_{pooled} = \sqrt{s^2_{pooled}} = \sqrt{301.136} = 17.353$$

The test statistic that we calculated for this study was:

$$t = \frac{(M_X - M_Y) - (\mu_X - \mu_Y)}{s_{difference}} = \frac{(82.25 - 82.6) - (0)}{11.641} = -0.03$$

For Cohen's *d,* we simply replace the denominator with standard deviation, s_{pooled}, instead of standard error, $s_{difference}$.

$$\text{Cohen's } d = \frac{(M_X - M_Y) - (\mu_X - \mu_Y)}{s_{pooled}} = \frac{(82.25 - 82.6) - (0)}{17.353} = -0.02$$

For this study, the effect size can be reported as: $d = -0.02$. The two sample means are only 0.02 standard deviation apart. The conventions for how large an effect is, shown again in Table 10-2, are the same as for Cohen's *d* for other hypothesis tests. According to Cohen's conventions, this is not even near the level of a small effect.

> **MASTERING THE FORMULA**
>
> **10-8:** We use pooled standard deviation to calculate Cohen's *d* for a two-sample, between-groups design. We calculate pooled standard deviation by taking the square root of the pooled variance that we calculated as part of the independent-samples *t* test: $s_{pooled} = \sqrt{s^2_{pooled}}$.

> **MASTERING THE FORMULA**
>
> **10-9:** For a two-sample, between-groups design, we calculate Cohen's *d* using the following formula: Cohen's $d = \frac{(M_X - M_Y) - (\mu_X - \mu_Y)}{s_{pooled}}$. The formula is similar to that for the test statistic in an independent-samples *t* test, except that we divide by pooled standard deviation, rather than standard error, because we want a measure of variability not altered by sample size.

TABLE 10-2. Cohen's Conventions for Effect Sizes: *d*

Jacob Cohen has published guidelines (or conventions), based on the overlap between two distributions, to help researchers determine whether an effect is small, medium, or large. These numbers are not cutoffs, merely rough guidelines to aid researchers in their interpretation of results.

Effect Size	Convention	Overlap
Small	0.2	85%
Medium	0.5	67%
Large	0.8	53%

CHECK YOUR LEARNING

Reviewing the Concepts

> A confidence interval can be created with a *t* distribution around a difference between means. In fact, the confidence interval alone allows you to test your hypothesis and provides additional, valuable information.

> An independent-samples *t* test should be supplemented with a measure of effect size. A commonly used measure of effect size is Cohen's *d*.

> The confidence interval and effect size help us evaluate the finding of our hypothesis test.

Clarifying the Concepts

10-5 Why do we calculate confidence intervals?

10-6 How does considering our conclusions in terms of effect size help to prevent incorrect interpretations of our findings?

Calculating the Statistics

10-7 Use the hypothetical data on level of agreement with a supervisor, as listed here and in Exercises 10.3 and 10.4, to calculate the following:

Group 1 (low trust in leader): 3, 2, 4, 6, 1, 2

Group 2 (high trust in leader): 5, 4, 6, 2, 6

a. Calculate the 95% confidence interval.

b. Calculate effect size using Cohen's *d*.

Applying the Concepts

Solutions to these Check Your Learning questions can be found in Appendix D.

10-8 Explain what the confidence interval calculated in Check Your Learning 10-7 tells us. Why is this confidence interval superior to the hypothesis test that we conducted?

10-9 Interpret the meaning of the effect size calculated in Check Your Learning 10-7. What does this add to the confidence interval and hypothesis test?

● ● ● ● ● ● ● REVIEW OF CONCEPTS

Conducting an Independent-Samples *t* Test

We use *independent-samples t tests* when we have two samples and different participants are in each sample. Because the samples are composed of different individuals, we cannot calculate difference scores, so the comparison distribution is a distribution of differences between means. Because we are working with two separate samples of scores (rather than one set of difference scores) when we conduct an independent-samples *t* test, we need additional steps to calculate an estimate of spread. We calculate two variances, then take a weighted average to calculate *pooled variance*. We convert the pooled variance to a version of variance for a distribution of means, one for each sample, then add them to combine them. Finally, we take the square root to get an estimate of standard error. We can present the statistics in APA style as we did with other hypothesis tests, and we can also calculate p_{rep}.

Beyond Hypothesis Testing

As with other forms of hypothesis testing, it is useful to replace or supplement the independent-samples *t* test with a confidence interval. A confidence interval can be created around a difference between means using a *t* distribution. It is created by subtracting and adding a margin of error from the difference between means. As with other confidence intervals, it provides the same information as a hypothesis test but also gives us a range of values.

To understand the importance of a finding, we must also calculate an effect size. With an independent-samples *t* test, as with other *t* tests, a common effect-size measure is Cohen's *d*.

SPSS®

We can conduct an independent-samples *t* test using SPSS for the data we presented earlier in this chapter on men's and women's perceptions of humor. To do so, we start by creating two columns of data, one for gender and one for the percentages of cartoons perceived as "funny." For gender, we could, for example, give each man a "1" and each woman a "2," using the "Values" function in the Variable View to tell SPSS that 1 = male and 2 = female. Each participant will have her or his data in one row—a score for gender in the first column and a percentage in the second column. We can now conduct the hypothesis test.

Select **Analyze** → Compare Means → Independent-Samples T Test. Choose the dependent variable, "percentage," by clicking it, then clicking the arrow in the upper center. Choose the independent variable, "gender," by clicking it, then clicking the arrow in the lower center. Click the "Define Groups" button, then provide the values for each level of the independent variable. For example, enter "1" for group 1 and "2" for group 2. Then click "OK."

Part of the output is shown in the screenshot here. Toward the top, you'll see means and standard deviations for male and female participants. For example, the output tells us that the mean for male participants is 82.6 with a standard deviation of 17.601. We can see that the *t* statistic is .03 with a *p* value (under "Sig. (2-tailed)") of .977. The only difference between the *t* statistic here and the one we calculated earlier is the sign. Ours was negative because we subtracted the two means in a different order from SPSS. We can use the *p* value to determine p_{rep} using Excel. When we insert .977 into the formula NORMSDIST (NORMSINV(1-.977)/(SQRT(2))), we get a p_{rep} of .079.

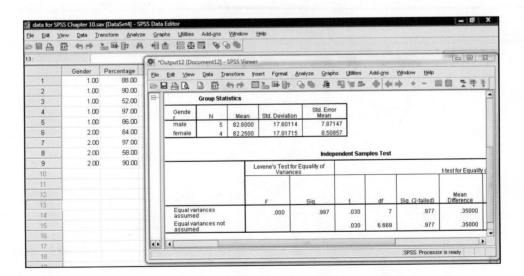

How It Works

10.1 INDEPENDENT-SAMPLES *t* TEST

Many different cell phone plans are available, including monthly plans and prepaid plans. In a given month, do people use more cell phone minutes if they have a monthly plan, for which they pay in advance for a certain number of minutes? Or do they use more minutes if they have a prepaid plan, for which they pay per minute used? Four people with a monthly plan and three with a prepaid plan were randomly selected from a directory of cell phone numbers. The minutes used over the previous month were recorded. Here are the data:

Monthly plan: 955, 1067, 1121, 1258

Prepaid plan: 856, 1000, 732

How can we conduct all six steps of hypothesis testing for an independent-samples t test for this scenario, using a two-tailed test with critical values based on a p level of 0.05? Here are the steps:

Step 1: Population 1: People with a monthly cell phone plan.

Population 2: People with a prepaid cell phone plan.

The comparison distribution will be a distribution of differences between means based on the null hypothesis. The hypothesis test will be an independent-samples t test because we have two samples composed of different groups of participants. This study meets two of the three assumptions and may meet the third. The dependent variable is minutes, which is scale. We do not know whether the population is normally distributed, and there are fewer than 30 participants, but the sample data do not indicate skew. Finally, the data were randomly selected.

Step 2: Null hypothesis: On average, people with a monthly cell phone plan use the same number of minutes as people with a prepaid plan—$H_0: \mu_1 = \mu_2$.

Research hypothesis: On average, people with a monthly cell phone plan use a different number of minutes from the people with a prepaid plan—$H_1: \mu_1 \neq \mu_2$.

Step 3: $(\mu_1 - \mu_2) = 0$; $s_{difference} = \sqrt{s^2_{difference}} = \sqrt{9741.373} = 98.698$

Calculations: $M_X = 1100.25$

X	X − M	(X − M)²
955	−145.25	21,097.563
1067	−33.25	1,105.563
1121	20.75	430.625
1258	157.75	24,885.063

$$s^2_X = \frac{\Sigma(X-M)^2}{N-1} = \frac{(21{,}097.563 + 1{,}105.563 + 430.625 + 24{,}885.063)}{4-1} = 15{,}839.605$$

$M_Y = 862.667$

Y	Y − M	(Y − M)²
856	−6.667	44.449
1000	137.333	18,860.353
732	−130.667	17,073.863

$$s^2_Y = \frac{\Sigma(Y-M)^2}{N-1} = \frac{(44.449 + 18{,}860.353 + 17{,}073.865)}{3-1} = 17{,}989.334$$

$df_X = N - 1 = 4 - 1 = 3$

$df_Y = N - 1 = 3 - 1 = 2$

$df_{total} = df_X + df_Y = 3 + 2 = 5$

$$s^2_{pooled} = \left(\frac{df_X}{df_{total}}\right)s^2_X + \left(\frac{df_Y}{df_{total}}\right)s^2_Y = \left(\frac{3}{5}\right)15{,}839.584 + \left(\frac{2}{5}\right)17{,}989.750 = 9503.763 + 7195.734 = 16{,}699.484$$

$$s^2_{M_X} = \frac{s^2_{pooled}}{N_X} = \frac{16{,}699.484}{4} = 4174.871$$

$$s^2_{M_Y} = \frac{s^2_{pooled}}{N_Y} = \frac{16{,}699.484}{3} = 5566.495$$

$$s^2_{difference} = s^2_{M_X} + s^2_{M_Y} = 4174.871 + 5566.495 = 9741.366$$

$$s_{difference} = \sqrt{s^2_{difference}} = \sqrt{9741.366} = 98.698$$

Step 4: Our critical values, based on a two-tailed test, a p of 0.05, and a df_{total} of 5, are −2.571 and 2.571.

Step 5: $t = \dfrac{(1100.25 - 862.667) - (0)}{98.698} = 2.41$

Step 6: Fail to reject the null hypothesis; we conclude that there is no evidence from this study to support the research hypothesis. The results would be reported in a journal article as:

$t(5) = 2.41, p > 0.05$

Exercises

Clarifying the Concepts

10.1 When is it appropriate to use an independent-samples *t* test?

10.2 Explain random assignment and what it controls.

10.3 What are independent events?

10.4 Explain how the paired-samples *t* test evaluates individual differences and the independent-samples *t* test evaluates group differences.

10.5 As they relate to comparison distributions, what is the difference between *mean differences* and *differences between means*?

10.6 As measures of variability, what is the difference between standard deviation and variance?

10.7 What is the difference between s_X^2 and s_Y^2?

10.8 What is pooled variance?

10.9 Why would we want the variability estimate based on a larger sample to count more (to be more heavily weighted) than one based on a smaller sample?

10.10 Define the symbols in the following formula: $s_{difference}^2 = s_{M_X}^2 + s_{M_Y}^2$

10.11 How do confidence intervals relate to margin of error?

10.12 What is the difference between pooled variance and pooled standard deviation?

10.13 How does the size of the confidence interval relate to the precision of our prediction?

10.14 Why does the effect-size calculation use standard deviation rather than standard error?

10.15 How do we interpret effect size using Cohen's *d*?

Calculating the Statistics

10.16 Below are several pairs of sample means. Calculate the differences between the means for students who sit in the front versus the back of a classroom for each of these four classes.

Mean Test Grades	Students in the Front	Students in the Back
Class 1	82	78
Class 2	79.5	77.41
Class 3	71.5	76
Class 4	72	71.3

10.17 Calculate s^2 for the following data:

Group 1: 97, 83, 105, 102, 92

Group 2: 111, 103, 96, 106

10.18 Calculate s^2 for the following data:

Liberals: 2, 1, 3, 2

Conservatives: 4, 3, 3, 5, 2, 4

10.19 Assuming these data are from two independent groups, calculate df_X, df_Y, and df_{total} for the data presented in Exercise 10.17.

10.20 Assuming these data are from two independent groups, calculate df_X, df_Y, and df_{total} for the data presented in Exercise 10.18.

10.21 Determine the critical values for *t* based on the *df* you calculated in Exercise 10.19, assuming a two-tailed test with a *p* level of 0.05.

10.22 Determine the critical values for *t* based on the *df* you calculated in Exercise 10.20, assuming a two-tailed test with a *p* level of 0.05.

10.23 Calculate the pooled variance, s_{pooled}^2, for groups 1 and 2 shown in Exercise 10.17.

10.24 Calculate the pooled variance, s_{pooled}^2, for the data from liberals and conservatives shown in Exercise 10.18.

10.25 Calculate the variance version of standard error for each sample in Exercise 10.17—for group 1 (97, 83, 105, 102, 92) and then again for group 2 (111, 103, 96, 106).

10.26 Calculate the variance version of standard error for each sample in Exercise 10.18—for the liberals (2, 1, 3, 2) and then for the conservatives (4, 3, 3, 5, 2, 4).

10.27 Using your work in Exercise 10.25, calculate the variance and the standard deviation of the distribution of differences between means for the data in groups 1 and 2.

10.28 Using your work in Exercise 10.26, calculate the variance and the standard deviation of the distribution of differences between means for the data from liberals and conservatives.

10.29 Calculate the *t* statistic for the data presented in Exercise 10.17.

10.30 Calculate the *t* statistic for the data presented in Exercise 10.18.

10.31 Calculate the 95% confidence interval for the data presented in Exercise 10.17.

10.32 Calculate the 95% confidence interval for the data presented in Exercise 10.18.

10.33 Calculate the effect size using Cohen's *d* for the data presented in Exercise 10.17.

10.34 Calculate the effect size using Cohen's *d* for the data presented in Exercise 10.18.

10.35 Find the critical *t* values for the following data sets:

  a. Group 1 has 21 participants and group 2 has 16 participants. You are performing a two-tailed test with a *p* level of 0.05.

  b. You studied 3-year-old children and 6-year-old children, with samples of 12 and 16, respectively. You are performing a two-tailed test with a *p* level of 0.01.

  c. You have a total of 17 degrees of freedom for a two-tailed test and a *p* level of 0.10.

Applying the Concepts

10.36 Numeric results for several independent-samples *t* tests are presented here. Decide whether each test is statistically significant, and report each result in the standard APA format.

  a. A total of 73 people were studied, 40 in one group and 33 in the other group. The test statistic was calculated as 2.126 for a two-tailed test with a *p* level of 0.05.

  b. One group of 23 people was compared to another group of 18 people. The *t* statistic obtained for their data was 1.77. Assume you were performing a two-tailed test with a *p* level of 0.05.

  c. One group of 9 mice was compared to another group of 6 mice, using a two-tailed test at a *p* level of 0.01. The test statistic was calculated as 3.02.

10.37 Using data from Exercise 9.46 on the effects of post-hypnotic suggestion on the Stroop effect, let's conduct an independent-samples *t* test. For this test, we will pretend that two sets of people participated in the study, when in truth data were collected from the same participants in a within-groups design. The first score obtained for each participant will be in the first sample—those not receiving a posthypnotic suggestion. The second score for each participant will be in the second sample—those receiving a posthypnotic suggestion. So, we have used the data to create two artificial groups:

  Sample 1: 12.6, 13.8, 11.6, 12.2, 12.1, 13.0
  Sample 2: 8.5, 9.6, 10.0, 9.2, 8.9, 10.8

  a. Conduct all six steps of an independent-samples *t* test. Be sure to label all six steps.

  b. Report the statistics as you would in a journal article.

10.38 In an example we sometimes use in our statistics classes, several semesters' worth of male and female students were asked how long, in minutes, they spend getting ready for a date. The data reported below reflect the actual means and the approximate standard deviations for the actual data from 142 students.

  Men: 28, 35, 52, 14
  Women: 30, 82, 53, 61

  a. Conduct all six steps of an independent-samples *t* test. Be sure to label all six steps.

  b. Report the statistics as you would in a journal article.

10.39 New garbage bags on the market have an "odor shield" designed to trap smells in the trashcan so your home is not filled with the smell of garbage. You speculate that an additional advantage to these garbage bags may be to reduce the number of flies attracted to the garbage at your home. You collect data on the number of fly larvae (flies in the worm stage; i.e., maggots) in the bottom of garbage cans after a two-week period at several different homes using bags with or without the odor shield. Here are your data:

  Odor-shield bags: 23, 19, 14
  Standard bags: 10, 15, 8, 4

  a. Conduct all six steps of an independent-samples *t* test. Be sure to label all six steps.

  b. Report the statistics as you would in a journal article.

  c. What variables might you control in this research, other than those mentioned (time frame and use of garbage cans)?

  d. According to SPSS, the actual *p* value for the test statistic is 0.042. Use Excel to determine p_{rep}.

10.40 At some vacation destinations, "all-inclusive" resorts allow you to pay a flat rate and then eat and drink as much as you want. There has been concern about whether these deals might lead to excessive consumption of alcohol by young adults on spring break trips. You decide to spend your spring break collecting data on this issue. Of course, you need to take all of your friends on this funded research trip, because you need a lot of research assistants! You collect data on the number of drinks consumed in a day by people staying at all-inclusive resorts and by those staying at noninclusive resorts. Your data include the following:

  All-inclusive resort guests: 10, 8, 13
  Noninclusive resort guests: 3, 15, 7

  a. Conduct all six steps of an independent-samples *t* test. Be sure to label all six steps.

  b. Report the statistics as you would in a journal article.

c. Was there a shortcut you could or did use to compute your hypothesis test?

d. According to SPSS, the actual *p* value for the test statistic is .687. Use Excel to determine p_{rep}.

10.41 Some people claim that women can experience "mother hearing," an increased sensitivity and awareness to noises, in particular those of children. This special ability is often associated with being a mother, rather than simply being female. Using hypothetical data, let's put this idea to the test. Imagine we recruit women to come to a sleep experiment where they think they are evaluating the comfort of different mattresses. While they are asleep, we introduce noises to test the minimum volume needed for the women to be awakened by the noise. Here are our data in decibels (dB):

Mothers: 33, 55, 39, 41, 67

Nonmothers: 56, 48, 71

a. Conduct all six steps of an independent-samples *t* test. Be sure to label all six steps.

b. Report the statistics as you would in a journal article.

c. According to SPSS, the actual *p* value for the test statistic is 0.282. Use Excel to determine p_{rep}.

10.42 In Exercise 10.37, we considered a study by Raz, Fan, and Posner (2005) that used brain-imaging techniques (i.e., functional magnetic resonance imaging) to explore whether posthypnotic suggestion led highly hypnotizable individuals to see Stroop words as nonsense words. You conducted an independent-samples *t* test on two samples—one consisting of those who received no posthypnotic suggestion (X) and one consisting of people who received a posthypnotic suggestion (Y). Here are some of the calculations we made while conducting the independent-samples *t* test:

$$M_X = 12.55; s_X^2 = \frac{\Sigma(Y-M)^2}{N-1} = 0.608$$

$$M_Y = 9.5; s_Y^2 = \frac{\Sigma(Y-M)^2}{N-1} = 0.680$$

$$df_X = N-1 = 6-1 = 5; df_Y = N-1 = 6-1 = 5;$$
$$df_{total} = df_X + df_Y = 5+5 = 10$$

$$s_{pooled}^2 = \left(\frac{df_X}{df_{total}}\right)s_X^2 + \left(\frac{df_Y}{df_{total}}\right)s_Y^2 = 0.300 + 0.340 = 0.640$$

a. Calculate the 95% confidence interval for these data.

b. State in your own words what we learn from this confidence interval.

c. What information does the confidence interval give us that we also get from the hypothesis test we conducted in Exercise 10.37?

d. What additional information does the confidence interval give us that we do not get from the hypothesis test we conducted in Exercise 10.37?

10.43 In Exercise 10.38, we reported data from our statistics classes in which male and female students were asked how long, in minutes, they typically spend getting ready for a date. Here are the data:

Men: 28, 35, 52, 14

Women: 30, 82, 53, 61

And here are some of the calculations needed to conduct an independent-samples *t* test:

$$M_X = 32.25; s_X^2 = \frac{\Sigma(X-M)^2}{N-1} = 249.584;$$

$$M_Y = 56.50; s_Y^2 = \frac{\Sigma(Y-M)^2}{N-1} = 461.667$$

$$df_X = N-1 = 4-1 = 3; df_Y = N-1 = 4-1 = 3;$$
$$df_{total} = df_X + df_Y = 3+3 = 6$$

$$s_{pooled}^2 = \left(\frac{df_X}{df_{total}}\right)s_X^2 + \left(\frac{df_Y}{df_{total}}\right)s_Y^2 = 124.792 + 230.834 = 355.626$$

$$s_{M_X}^2 = \frac{s_{pooled}^2}{N_X} = \frac{355.626}{4} = 88.907$$

$$s_{M_Y}^2 = \frac{s_{pooled}^2}{N_Y} = \frac{355.626}{4} = 88.907$$

$$s_{difference}^2 = s_{M_X}^2 + s_{M_Y}^2 = 88.907 + 88.907 = 177.814$$

$$s_{difference} = \sqrt{s_{difference}^2} = \sqrt{177.814} = 13.335$$

a. Calculate the 95% confidence interval for these data.

b. Calculate the 90% confidence interval for these data.

c. How are the confidence intervals different from each other? Explain why they are different.

10.44 Using the work you performed in Exercise 10.39, let's add a confidence interval to the hypothesis test.

a. Calculate the 95% confidence interval for these data.

b. Express the confidence interval in writing, according to the format discussed in the chapter.

c. State in your own words what we learn from this confidence interval.

10.45 As a follow-up to your hypothesis test in Exercise 10.40, add the following:

a. Calculate the 95% confidence interval for these data.

b. State in your own words what we learn from this confidence interval.

c. Express the confidence interval, in a sentence, as margin of error.

10.46 Following up on your work in Exercise 10.41, add the following:

    a. Calculate the 95% confidence interval for these data.

    b. State in your own words what we learn from this confidence interval.

    c. Explain why interval estimates are better than point estimates.

10.47 In Exercises 10.37 and 10.42, we considered a study by Raz and colleagues (2005) for which we conducted an independent-samples *t* test. En route to calculating our test statistic, we made the following calculations:

$$M_X = 12.55; \; s_X^2 = \frac{\Sigma(X - M)^2}{N - 1} = 0.600$$

$$M_Y = 9.5; \; s_Y^2 = \frac{\Sigma(Y - M)^2}{N - 1} = 0.680$$

$$df_X = N - 1 = 6 - 1 = 5; \; df_Y = N - 1 = 6 - 1 = 5;$$
$$df_{total} = df_X + df_Y = 5 + 5 = 10$$

$$s_{pooled}^2 = \left(\frac{df_X}{df_{total}}\right) s_X^2 + \left(\frac{df_Y}{df_{total}}\right) s_Y^2 = 0.300 + 0.340 = 0.640$$

    a. Calculate the appropriate measure of effect size for this sample.

    b. Based on Cohen's conventions, is this a small, medium, or large effect size?

    c. Why is it useful to have this information in addition to the results of a hypothesis test?

10.48 In an example we used in Exercises 10.38 and 10.43, we reported data from our statistics classes in which male and female students were asked how long, in minutes, they typically spend getting ready for a date. Here are some of the calculations we needed to conduct the independent-samples *t* test:

$$M_X = 32.25; \; s_X^2 = \frac{\Sigma(X - M)^2}{N - 1} = 249.584$$

$$M_Y = 56.50; \; s_Y^2 = \frac{\Sigma(Y - M)^2}{N - 1} = 461.667$$

$$df_X = N - 1 = 4 - 1 = 3; \; df_Y = N - 1 = 4 - 1 = 3;$$
$$df_{total} = df_X + df_Y = 3 + 3 = 6$$

$$s_{pooled}^2 = \left(\frac{df_X}{df_{total}}\right) s_X^2 + \left(\frac{df_Y}{df_{total}}\right) s_Y^2 = 124.792 + 230.834 = 355.626$$

$$s_{M_X}^2 = \frac{s_{pooled}^2}{N_X} = \frac{355.626}{4} = 88.907$$

$$s_{M_Y}^2 = \frac{s_{pooled}^2}{N_Y} = \frac{355.626}{4} = 88.907$$

$$s_{difference}^2 = s_{M_X}^2 + s_{M_Y}^2 = 88.907 + 88.907 = 177.814$$

$$s_{difference} = \sqrt{s_{difference}^2} = \sqrt{177.814} = 13.335$$

    a. Calculate the appropriate measure of effect size for this sample.

    b. Based on Cohen's conventions, is this a small, medium, or large effect size?

    c. Why is it useful to have this information in addition to the results of a hypothesis test?

10.49 Add to your work from Exercises 10.39 and 10.44 by completing the following:

    a. Calculate the appropriate measure of effect size for this sample.

    b. Based on Cohen's conventions, is this a small, medium, or large effect size?

    c. Why is it useful to have this information in addition to the results of a hypothesis test?

10.50 Add to your work from Exercises 10.40 and 10.45 by completing the following:

    a. Calculate the appropriate measure of effect size for this sample.

    b. Based on Cohen's conventions, is this a small, medium, or large effect size?

    c. Why is it useful to have this information in addition to the results of a hypothesis test?

10.51 Add to your work from Exercises 10.41 and 10.46 by completing the following:

    a. Calculate the appropriate measure of effect size for this sample.

    b. Based on Cohen's conventions, is this a small, medium, or large effect size?

    c. Why is it useful to have this information in addition to the results of a hypothesis test?

10.52 For each of the following three scenarios, state which hypothesis test you would use from among the four introduced so far: the *z* test, the single-sample *t* test, the paired-samples *t* test, and the independent-samples *t* test. (*Note:* In the actual studies described, the researchers did not always use one of these tests, often because the actual experiment had additional variables.) Explain your answer.

    a. A study of children who had survived a brain tumor revealed that they were more likely to have behavioral and emotional difficulties than were children who had not experienced such a trauma (Upton & Eiser, 2006). Forty families participated in the study. Parents rated children's difficulties, and the ratings data were compared with known means from published population norms.

    b. Talarico and Rubin (2003) recorded the memories of 54 students just after the terrorist attacks in the United States on September 11, 2001—some memories related to the terrorist attacks on that day (called *flashbulb memories* for their vividness and emotional content) and some everyday memories. They found that flashbulb memories were no more consistent over time than everyday memories, even though they were perceived to be more accurate.

c. The HOPE VI Panel Study (Popkin & Woodley, 2002) was initiated to test a U.S. program aimed at improving troubled public housing developments. Residents of five HOPE VI developments were examined at the beginning of the study so researchers could later ascertain whether their quality of life had improved. Means at the beginning of the study were compared to known national data sources (e.g., the U.S. Census, the American Housing Survey) that had summary statistics, including means and standard deviations.

10.53 For each of the following three scenarios, state which hypothesis test you would use from among the four introduced so far: the *z* test, the single-sample *t* test, the paired-samples *t* test, and the independent-samples *t* test. (*Note:* In the actual studies described, the researchers did not always use one of these tests, often because the actual experiment had additional variables.) Explain your answer.

a. Taylor and Ste. Marie (2001) studied eating disorders in 41 Canadian female figure skaters. They compared the figure skaters' data on the Eating Disorder Inventory to the means of known populations, including women with eating disorders. On average, the figure skaters were more similar to the population of women with eating disorders than to those without eating disorders.

b. In an article titled "A Fair and Balanced Look at the News: What Affects Memory for Controversial Arguments," Wiley (2005) found that people with a high level of previous knowledge about a given controversial topic (e.g., abortion, military intervention) had better average recall for arguments on both sides of that issue than did those with lower levels of knowledge.

c. Engle-Friedman and colleagues (2003) studied the effects of sleep deprivation. Fifty students were assigned to one night of sleep loss (students were required to call the laboratory every half-hour all night) and then one night of no sleep loss (normal sleep). The next day, students were offered a choice of math problems with differing levels of difficulty. Following sleep loss, students tended to choose less challenging problems.

10.54 Using the research studies described here (from Exercise 10.53), create null hypotheses and research hypotheses appropriate for the chosen statistical test:

a. Taylor and Ste-Marie (2001) studied eating disorders in 41 Canadian female figure skaters. They compared the figure skaters' data on the Eating Disorder Inventory to the means of known populations, including women with eating disorders. On average, the figure skaters were more similar to the population of women with eating disorders than to those without eating disorders.

b. In article titled "A Fair and Balanced Look at the News: What Affects Memory for Controversial Arguments," Wiley (2005) found that people with a

high level of previous knowledge about a given controversial topic (e.g., abortion, military intervention) had better average recall for arguments on both sides of that issue than did those with lower levels of knowledge.

c. Engle-Friedman and colleagues (2003) studied the effects of sleep deprivation. Fifty students were assigned to one night of sleep loss (students were required to call the laboratory every half-hour all night) and then one night of no sleep loss (normal sleep). The next day, students were offered a choice of math problems with differing levels of difficulty. Following sleep loss, students tended to choose less challenging problems.

10.55 Alice Waters, owner of the Berkeley, California, restaurant Chez Panisse, has long been an advocate for the use of simple, fresh, organic ingredients in both home and restaurant cooking. More recently, she has turned her considerable expertise to school cafeterias and their fare. Waters (2006) praises recent changes in school lunch menus that have expanded nutritious offerings, but she hypothesizes that students are likely to circumvent healthy lunches by avoiding vegetables and smuggling in banned junk food unless they receive accompanying nutrition education and hands-on involvement in their meals. She has spearheaded an Edible Schoolyard program in Berkeley, which involves public school students in the cultivation and preparation of fresh foods, and states that such interactive education is necessary to combat growing levels of childhood obesity. "Nothing less," Waters writes, "will change their behavior."

a. In your own words, what is Waters predicting? Citing the confirmation bias, explain why Waters's program, although intuitively appealing, should not be instituted nationwide without further study.

b. Describe a simple between-groups experiment with a nominal independent variable with two levels and a scale dependent variable to test Waters's hypothesis. Specifically identify the independent variable, its levels, and the dependent variable. State how you will operationalize the dependent variable.

c. Which hypothesis test would be used to analyze this experiment? Explain your answer.

d. Conduct step 1 of hypothesis testing.

e. Conduct step 2 of hypothesis testing.

f. State at least one other way you could operationalize the dependent variable.

g. Let's say, hypothetically, that Waters discounted the need for the research you propose by citing her own data that the Berkeley school in which she instituted the program has lower rates of obesity than other California schools. Describe the flaw in this argument by discussing the importance of random selection and random assignment.

10.56 Researchers at the Cornell University Food and Brand Lab conducted an experiment at a fitness camp for adolescents (Wansink & van Ittersum, 2003). Campers were given either a 22-ounce glass that was tall and thin or a 22-ounce glass that was short and wide. Campers with the short glasses tended to pour more soda, milk, or juice than campers with the tall glasses.

a. Is it likely that the researchers used random selection? Explain.

b. Is it likely that the researchers used random assignment? Explain.

c. What is the independent variable, and what are its levels?

d. What is the dependent variable?

e. What hypothesis test would the researchers use?

f. Conduct step 1 of hypothesis testing.

g. Conduct step 2 of hypothesis testing.

h. How could the researchers redesign this study so that they could use a paired-samples *t* test?

Terms

independent–samples *t* test (p. 233)
pooled variance (p. 237)

Formulas

$df_{total} = df_X + df_Y$ (p. 237)

$s^2_{pooled} = \left(\dfrac{df_X}{df_{total}}\right)s^2_X + \left(\dfrac{df_Y}{df_{total}}\right)s^2_Y$ (p. 237)

$s^2_{M_X} = \dfrac{s^2_{pooled}}{N_X}$ (p. 238)

$s^2_{M_Y} = \dfrac{s^2_{pooled}}{N_Y}$ (p. 238)

$s^2_{difference} = s^2_{M_X} + s^2_{M_Y}$ (p. 238)

$s_{difference} = \sqrt{s^2_{difference}}$ (p. 238)

$t = \dfrac{(M_X - M_Y) - (\mu_X - \mu_Y)}{s_{difference}}$, often (p. 238)

abbreviated as: $t = \dfrac{M_X - M_Y}{s_{difference}}$ (p. 238)

$(M_X - M_Y)_{upper} = t(s_{difference}) + (M_X - M_Y)_{sample}$ (p. 242)

$(M_X - M_Y)_{lower} = -t(s_{difference}) + (M_X - M_Y)_{sample}$ (p. 242)

$s_{pooled} = \sqrt{s^2_{pooled}}$ (p. 245)

Cohen's $d = \dfrac{(M_X - M_Y) - (\mu_X - \mu_Y)}{s_{pooled}}$

for a *t* distribution for a difference between means (p. 245)

Symbols

s^2_{pooled} (p. 237)

$s^2_{difference}$ (p. 238)

$s_{difference}$ (p. 238)

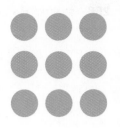

Between-Groups and Within-Groups ANOVA

BEFORE YOU GO ON

- You should understand the z distribution and the t distributions. You also should be able to differentiate among distributions of scores, means, and differences between means (Chapters 6, 7, 9, and 10).

- You should be able to differentiate among distributions of scores, means, mean differences, and differences between means (Chapter 4).

- You should be able to differentiate between between-groups designs and within-groups designs (Chapter 1).

- You should understand the concept of effect size (Chapter 8).

In 1986, California created a task force to promote self-esteem. The idea was that higher self-esteem could help to solve social problems such as drug abuse and teenage pregnancy. But California is not alone in its enthusiasm for promoting self-esteem. Within the education industry, the self-esteem movement has spread so effectively that a Google search found the words "elementary school mission statement self-esteem" on 308,000 Web pages (Twenge, 2006). For example, the mission statement of the Stephens Elementary School in Bartow, Florida (home of the Soaring Eagles), is "to provide educational opportunities in an environment that promotes learning, self-esteem, and confidence."

There are many reasons to believe that self-esteem could be the magic key to solving social problems. People with high self-esteem tend to be more satisfied with their lives and to experience more positive feelings; they are also less likely to be anxious or depressed (Myers & Diener, 1995; Twenge & Campbell, 2001). The downside to self-esteem, however, only comes into focus when we conduct experiments.

For example, in one experiment, researchers randomly assigned students who earned D's and F's on a midterm exam to one of three groups. Group 1 (the control group) received regular e-mails with review questions. Group 2 received review questions plus self-esteem-bolstering messages. Group 3 received review questions plus encouragement to take responsibility for their learning (Forsyth, Lawrence, Burnette, & Baumeister, 2007). As with self-esteem, encouraging students to take responsibility also is associated with academic achievement (Noel, Forsyth, & Kelley, 1987). More important for our purposes, group 3 adds another comparison group to this experiment that can help us better understand self-esteem.

These researchers could have conducted three separate experiments to compare group 1 with group 2, group 1 with group 3, and then group 2 with group 3, but putting all three groups in a single experiment is far more efficient (see Figure 11-1). Scores on the final exam for group 1 (the control group) and group 3 (the take-responsibility group) were about the same, on average, as their midterm grades (57% to 62%). However, the average scores on the final exam for group 2 (the self-esteem group) sank to a dismal 38%!

Encouraging students to take responsibility and building their self-esteem are both motivational interventions, but the findings indicated that neither group was motivated in a positive way. The control group and the take-responsibility group performed at about the same level, on average, but the self-esteem intervention actually had negative results. Adding group 3 to the study taught us that trying to motivate students by building their self-esteem is potentially dangerous.

In this chapter, we will be working with three or more groups as we learn about analysis of variance (ANOVA) and the F statistic. First, we learn about the distributions used with ANOVA, the F distributions. Then, we learn how to conduct an ANOVA when we have a between-groups design—a between-groups ANOVA. A new effect-size statistic used with ANOVA is introduced, and we learn how to conduct a post-hoc test to determine exactly which groups are different from one another. Finally, we learn how to conduct an ANOVA when we have a within-groups design—a within-groups ANOVA—as well as to calculate effect size and conduct a post-hoc test for this situation.

FIGURE 11-1
Comparing Three Groups

Researchers compared three groups in this one study, which allowed them to discover that a self-esteem intervention can backfire. To compare three or more groups in a single study is the main reason we use ANOVA.

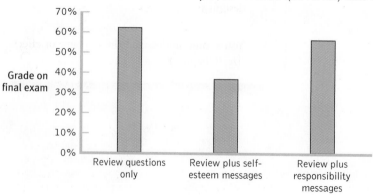

Using the *F* Distribution with Three or More Samples

A critical insight about self-esteem only revealed itself because the researchers used a three-group design. They were able to compare two different ways of motivating students, and then to compare both of those approaches to a control group. The particular comparison between the self-esteem group and the take-responsibility group clarified that building self-esteem was an intervention that backfired. However, a three-group comparison is more complicated than a two-group comparison, so it requires a distribution that can accommodate that complexity.

The *F* distributions are more complex than the *z* distribution or the *t* distributions. Just as the *z* distribution is still part of the *t* distributions, the *t* distributions are also part of the *F* distributions. The hypothesis tests based on all three types of distributions are based on the characteristics of the normal bell-shaped curve. In fact, these three distributions are like progressively more complex versions of the Swiss Army knife. Think of the *F* distributions as an elaborate Swiss Army knife that includes the single-bladed knife that represents the *z* distribution, the multi-bladed knife that represents the *t* distributions, as well as additional tools to make it much more versatile.

The hypothesis tests that we have learned so far—the *z* test and the three types of *t* test—are calculated in similar ways. In all cases, the statistics are calculated by dividing a numerator by a denominator. The numerator describes how far apart comparison groups are from each other by measuring some kind of difference (between scores, between means, between mean differences, or between differences between means). And the denominator represents some measure of variability, that is, some variation on a standard deviation. To summarize this pattern, the statistic is calculated simply by dividing a numerator that represents the difference between groups by a denominator that represents the variability within the groups—between-groups variability divided by within-groups variability.

For example, men are, on average, a little taller than women, on average. This is between-groups variability. Yet not all men are the same height and not all women are the same height. This is within-groups variability. As you have noticed, there is considerable overlap between the two distributions. Even though men are, on average, taller than women, on average, many women are taller than many men. As you'll soon learn, the calculation of the *F* statistic follows this same pattern.

We need the added versatility of the *F* statistic if we want to compare *three or more* different samples. The *F* statistic is based on the *F* distributions and is calculated when we conduct the hypothesis test called *analysis of variance* (ANOVA; pronounced "ah-**noe**-vah," with the emphasis on the second syllable). ***ANOVA** is a hypothesis test typically used with one or more nominal independent variables (with at least three groups overall) and a scale dependent variable.*

The *F* Distribution for Analyzing Variability to Compare Means

Like other test statistics, the *F* is a ratio of two measures of variability. Specifically, *the **F statistic** is a ratio of two measures of variance: (1) between-groups variance, which indicates differences among sample means, and (2) within-groups variance, which is essentially an average of the sample variances.*

z, t, and F Distributions The z, t, and F distributions are three increasingly complex variations on one great idea: the normal curve.

◀ **MASTERING THE CONCEPT**

11-1: The *F* statistic is used when we're comparing means for more than two groups. Like the *z* statistic and the *t* statistic, it's calculated by dividing some measure of variability among means by some measure of variability within groups.

■ **ANOVA** is a hypothesis test typically used with one or more nominal independent variables (with at least three groups overall) and a scale dependent variable.

$$F = \frac{\text{between-groups variance}}{\text{within-groups variance}}$$

So let's think through the basic logic of the calculation of an F statistic. For now, the description of the calculations is simplified to emphasize the logic of the F distributions.

First, let's consider how we calculate the numerator in the F ratio, the part of the formula that specifies differences between groups, when we have several means (so we cannot subtract one mean from another). To calculate the numerator, we determine the variability (the spread) among the three (or more) means. If there is a great deal of spread among several means, this suggests a difference exists among them. But if there is very little spread among the means, this suggests no reliable difference exists among them. So, to determine the numerator, we calculate the variance among the means of the samples of interest. We call this variance *the **between-groups variance** because it is an estimate of the population variance based on the differences among the means.*

For example, if we wanted to compare how fast people talk in Philadelphia, Memphis, Chicago, and San Diego, then the between-groups variance (in this case, the between-cities variance) is an estimate of the variability among the average number of words per minute spoken by the people representing each of those four cities.

To calculate the denominator of the F statistic, we calculate a version of variance. This variance is called *the **within-groups variance**, an estimate of the population variance based on the differences within each of the three (or more) sample distributions.* For example, not everyone living in Philadelphia speaks at the same pace. Neither does everyone living in Memphis, Chicago, or San Diego. There are within-city differences in talking speeds, so within-groups variance refers to the average of the amounts of variability within each city. Within-groups variance is essentially an average of the four variances, one for each city.

To calculate the F statistic, we simply divide the between-groups variance by the within-groups variance. If the between-groups variance (the numerator) is much larger than the within-groups variance (the denominator), then we can infer that the sample means are different from one another. However, if the between-groups variance is similar to the within-groups variance, then we cannot infer that the sample means are different from one another. We use the F table to determine whether the ratio of the differences among our groups to the differences within each of our groups is extreme enough to reject the null hypothesis and conclude that a difference exists. The variability used to calculate F is simply a way of measuring whether more than two groups vary from one another.

To summarize, we can think of within-groups variance as reflecting the difference between means that we'd expect just by chance. Variability exists within any population, so we would expect some difference among means just by chance. Between-groups variance reflects the difference between means that we found in our data. If this difference is much larger than the within-groups variance, what we'd expect by chance, then we can reject the null hypothesis and conclude that there is some difference between means.

The *F* Table

Many F distributions are represented in the F table, which includes several extreme probabilities and the range of sample sizes, represented by a type of degrees of freedom. The F table also includes a third factor, the number of samples. There is an F distribution for every possible combination of sample size, represented by one type of degrees of freedom, and number of samples, represented by another type of degrees of freedom.

> **TABLE 11-1.** Connections Among Distributions
>
> The z distribution is subsumed under the t distributions in certain specific circumstances, and both the z and t distributions are subsumed under the F distributions in certain specific circumstances.

	When Used	Links Among the Distributions
z	One sample; μ and σ are known	Subsumed under the t and F distributions
t	(1) One sample; only μ is known (2) Two samples	Same as z distribution if there is a sample size of ∞ (or just very large)
F	Three or more samples (but can be used with two samples)	Square of z distribution if there are only two samples and a sample size of ∞ (or just very large); square of t distribution if there are only two samples

For example, if we look in the F table under two samples for a sample size of infinity for the equivalent of the 95th percentile, we see 2.71. If we take the square root of this, we get 1.646. We can find 1.645 on the z table for the 95th percentile and on the t table for the 95th percentile with a sample size of infinity. (The slight differences are due only to rounding decisions.) These connections are summarized in Table 11-1.

The Language and Assumptions for ANOVA

Before we go on, let's discuss the language that statisticians use to describe ANOVAs (Landrum, 2005). The word *ANOVA* is almost always preceded by two adjectives, one indicating the number of independent variables and one indicating whether the participants are in one condition (between-groups) or all conditions (within-groups). For example, let's say we want to conduct an ANOVA with year in school as the one independent variable and Consideration of Future Consequences (CFC) scores as the dependent variable. An ANOVA that analyzes a study with just one independent variable is called a ***one-way ANOVA***, *a hypothesis test that includes one nominal independent variable with more than two levels and a scale dependent variable.*

A one-way ANOVA can have one of two research designs, within groups or between groups. When participants are in all levels, we are using a within-groups design. *A **within-groups ANOVA** is a hypothesis test in which there are more than two samples, and each sample is composed of the same participants.* This test is also called a *repeated-measures ANOVA*.

When participants are in only one level of the independent variable, we are using a between-groups design. *A **between-groups ANOVA** is a hypothesis test in which there are more than two samples, and each sample is composed of different participants.* For a comparison of CFC scores across years in school, participants can be in only one level of the independent variable. In this chapter, we focus on the between-groups ANOVA. As mentioned earlier, though, ANOVAs are always described by two adjectives. The ANOVA used to analyze the study that compares CFC scores across years in school would have two adjectives: *one-way* and *between-groups*. It would be a one-way between-groups ANOVA.

Regardless of the type of ANOVA, they all share the same assumptions. The assumptions for ANOVA represent the optimal conditions for a valid analysis of the data. If the conclusions of a study might be jeopardized by a huge deviation from the assumptions, then researchers either report and justify their decision to violate those assumptions in the write-up of their results or choose to conduct a more conservative nonparametric test (see Chapter 15). Let's consider each of the three assumptions.

The **F statistic** is a ratio of two measures of variance: (1) between-groups variance, which indicates differences among sample means, and (2) within-groups variance, which is essentially an average of the sample variances.

Between-groups variance is an estimate of the population variance based on the differences among the means.

Within-groups variance is an estimate of the population variance based on the differences within each of the three (or more) sample distributions.

A **one-way ANOVA** is a hypothesis test that includes one nominal independent variable with more than two levels and a scale dependent variable.

A **within-groups ANOVA** is a hypothesis test in which there are more than two samples, and each sample is composed of the same participants; also called a *repeated-measures ANOVA*.

A **between-groups ANOVA** is a hypothesis test in which there are more than two samples, and each sample is composed of different participants.

■ **Homoscedastic** populations are those that have the same variance; homoscedasticity is also called *homogeneity of variance.*

■ **Heteroscedastic** populations are those that have different variances.

The first assumption, that our samples are selected randomly, is necessary if we want to generalize beyond our sample. As with all hypothesis tests, if the study participants are not selected randomly, then our external validity—our ability to generalize beyond our sample—is limited. Because it is often impossible from a practical standpoint to use random selection, most researchers use ANOVA even when this assumption is violated.

The second assumption is that the population distribution is normal. As with the hypothesis tests we learned previously, we can examine the distributions of our samples to get a sense of what the underlying population distribution might look like. Moreover, adherence to a normal curve becomes less important as the sizes of our samples increase.

The third assumption is that the samples all come from populations with the same variances, an assumption called homoscedasticity. **Homoscedastic** *populations are those that have the same variance.* **Heteroscedastic** *populations are those that have different variances.* (Note that homoscedasticity is also often called *homogeneity of variance.*) We hope that the sample variances are quite similar (homoscedastic), but in real-life research we often find that the variances are quite different (heteroscedastic), particularly with smaller samples.

CHECK YOUR LEARNING

Reviewing the Concepts

> The F statistic, used in an analysis of variance (ANOVA), is essentially an expansion of the z statistic and the t statistic that can be used to compare more than two samples. Under certain conditions, we observe related values on all three tables.

> Like the z statistic and the t statistic, the F statistic is a ratio of a difference between group means (in this case, using a measure of variability) to a measure of variability within samples.

> We expect variability to occur within groups naturally. ANOVA tests whether the differences between groups are unexpectedly large relative to the variability we expect and observe within groups.

> One-way between-groups ANOVA is an analysis in which there is one independent variable with at least three levels and in which different participants are in each level of the independent variable. A within-groups ANOVA differs in that all participants experience all levels of the independent variable.

> The assumptions for ANOVA are that participants are randomly selected, the populations from which the samples are drawn are normally distributed, and those populations have the same variance (an assumption known as homoscedasticity).

Clarifying the Concepts

11-1 The F statistic is a ratio of what two kinds of variance?

11-2 What are the two types of research design for a one-way ANOVA?

Calculating the Statistics

11-3 Calculate the F statistic, writing the ratio accurately, for each of the following cases:

a. Between-groups variance is 8.6 and within-groups variance is 3.7.

b. Within-groups variance is 123.77 and between-groups variance is 102.4.

c. Between-groups variance is 45.2 and within-groups variance is 32.1.

Applying the Concepts

11-4 Consider the research on multitasking that we explored in Chapter 9 (Mark, Gonzalez, & Harris, 2005). Let's say we compared three conditions to see which one would lead to the quickest resumption of a task following an interruption. In one condition, the control group, no changes were made to the working environment. In the second condition, a communication ban was instituted from 1:00 to 3:00 P.M. In the third condition, a communication ban was instituted from 11:00 A.M. to 3:00 P.M. We recorded the time, in minutes, until work on an interrupted task was resumed.

a. What type of distribution would be used in this situation? Explain your answer.

b. In your own words, explain how we would calculate between-groups variance. Focus on the logic rather than the calculations.

Solutions to these Check Your Learning questions can be found in Appendix D.

c. In your own words, explain how we would calculate within-groups variance. Focus on the logic rather than the calculations.

One-Way Between-Groups ANOVA

The self-esteem study (Forsyth et al., 2007) provided an interesting finding—that a self-esteem intervention can backfire—because researchers compared three groups to each other. In fact, this is the main reason we use ANOVA, to compare three or more groups in a single study. In this section, we apply the principles of the ANOVA to hypothesis testing with a between-groups design.

Everything About ANOVA but the Calculations

To introduce the steps of hypothesis testing for a one-way between-groups ANOVA, we use a study about how foreign graduate students decide which U.S. institutions to attend.

EXAMPLE 11.1

Catherine Ruby (2006), a doctoral student in the education program at New York University, wondered what factors influenced foreign students' decisions to study at a particular U.S. university.

Ruby developed a survey asking current U.S. graduate students who were originally from foreign countries to rate factors that influenced their decision to attend their current graduate programs. As one aspect of her study, Ruby asked them to use a 1 to 5 rating of the importance of various financial aspects (e.g., availability of scholarships, amount of financial aid) in their decision to attend their universities. Ruby then separated their responses according to the four types of academic programs students were pursuing: arts and sciences, education, law, and business.

This survey design would be analyzed with a one-way between-groups ANOVA that uses the importance of financial aspects as the dependent variable. There is one independent variable (type of academic program) and it has four levels (arts and sciences, education, law, and business). It is a between-groups design because each student was earning a degree from one and only one of those programs. It is an ANOVA because it analyzes variance by estimating the variability among the types of programs and dividing it by the variability within the types of programs. The importance scores below are from 17 fictional foreign graduate students, but they have almost the same mean importance ratings of financial aspects as Ruby observed in her actual (much larger) data set.

Cindy Charles/Photo Edit

Criteria in Graduate School Selection and ANOVA What criteria do foreign students consider when choosing a graduate program in the United States? A doctoral student examined this topic in her dissertation, exploring the effects of a number of factors, including characteristics of both the students and the programs, on the decision-making process. With more than two samples in most analyses, ANOVA was the hypothesis test of choice.

Arts and sciences:	4, 5, 4, 3, 4
Education:	4, 3, 4, 4
Law:	3, 3, 2, 3
Business:	4, 4, 4, 3

Let's consider the six steps of hypothesis testing in the context of this particular one-way between-groups ANOVA. At this point, we will not calculate the test statistic. We will go through the framework of the test and then learn the calculations in the next section.

STEP 1. Identify the populations, distribution, and assumptions.

The first step of hypothesis testing is the identification of the populations to be compared, the comparison distribution, the appropriate test, and its assumptions. Let's summarize Ruby's study with respect to this first step of hypothesis testing.

Summary: *Identification of populations to be compared:* Population 1: All foreign graduate students enrolled in arts and sciences programs in the United States. Population 2: All foreign graduate students enrolled in education programs in the United States. Population 3: All foreign graduate students enrolled in law schools in the United States. Population 4: All foreign graduate students enrolled in business schools in the United States.

The comparison distribution and hypothesis test: The comparison distribution will be an *F* distribution. The hypothesis test will be a one-way between-groups ANOVA.

Assumptions: (1) The data are not selected randomly, so we must generalize only with caution. (2) We do not know if the underlying population distributions are normal, but the sample data do not indicate severe skew. (3) To see if we meet the homoscedasticity assumption, we will check to see if the variances are similar (typically, when the largest variance is not more than twice the smallest) when we calculate the test statistic. (*Note:* When calculating an ANOVA, be sure to return to this step to indicate whether we meet the assumption of equal variances.)

STEP 2. State the null and research hypotheses.

The second step is to state the null and research hypotheses. As usual, the hypotheses are about population means. The null hypothesis, as in previous hypothesis tests, posits no difference among the population means. The symbols are the same as before, but with more populations. The research hypothesis, however, is a bit different. We can reject the null hypothesis in an ANOVA even if only one group is different, on average, from the others. A statistically significant ANOVA can indicate that one group has a different mean from all other groups, that two groups have different means from two others, or that all groups have different means from each other. Any combination of differences between means is possible when we reject the null hypothesis, so the research hypothesis is that at least one population mean is different from at least one other population mean. Because there are several populations, we will not use symbols to express the research hypothesis. Only one group needs to be different, so $\mu_1 \neq \mu_2 \neq \mu_3 \neq \mu_4$ does not include all possible outcomes, just that in which all four population means are not equal to one another.

Summary: Null hypothesis: Foreign graduate students in arts and sciences, education, law, and business programs all rate financial factors the same, on average—$H_0: \mu_1 = \mu_2 = \mu_3 = \mu_4$. Research hypothesis: Foreign graduate students in arts and sciences, education, law, and business programs do not all rate financial factors the same, on average.

STEP 3. Determine the characteristics of the comparison distribution.

The third step is to explicitly state the relevant characteristics of the comparison distribution. This step is an easy one in ANOVA because most calculations for ANOVA are in step 5. Here we merely state that the comparison distribution is an *F* distribution and provide the appropriate degrees of freedom. As we discussed, the F statistic is a ratio of two independent estimates of the population variance, between-groups variance and within-groups variance (both of which we calculate in step 5). Each variance estimate has its own degrees of freedom. The sample between-groups variance estimates the population variance through the difference among the means of the samples, four in this case. The degrees of freedom for the between-groups variance estimate is the number of samples minus 1:

$$df_{between} = N_{groups} - 1 = 4 - 1 = 3$$

The between-groups degrees of freedom for this example is 3.

The sample within-groups variance estimates the variance of the population by averaging the variances of the samples, without regard to differences among the sample means. We first must calculate a degrees of freedom for each sample. For the first sample, we would calculate:

$$df_1 = n_1 - 1 = 5 - 1 = 4$$

n represents the number of participants in the particular sample. We would then do this for the remaining samples. For this example, there are four samples, so the formula would be:

$$df_{within} = df_1 + df_2 + df_3 + df_4$$

For this example, the calculations would be:

$$df_1 = 5 - 1 = 4$$
$$df_2 = 4 - 1 = 3$$
$$df_3 = 4 - 1 = 3$$
$$df_4 = 4 - 1 = 3$$
$$df_{within} = 4 + 3 + 3 + 3 = 13$$

Summary: We would use the F distribution with 3 and 13 degrees of freedom.

> ◀ **MASTERING THE FORMULA**
>
> **11-1:** The formula for the between-groups degrees of freedom is $df_{between} = N_{groups} - 1$. We subtract 1 from the number of groups in the study.

> ◀ **MASTERING THE FORMULA**
>
> **11-2:** The formula for the within-groups degrees of freedom for a one-way between-groups ANOVA conducted with group samples is $df_{within} = df_1 + df_2 + df_3 + df_4$. We sum the degrees of freedom for each of the four groups. We calculate degrees of freedom for each group by subtracting 1 from the number of people in that sample. For example, for the first group, the formula is $df_1 = n_1 - 1$.

STEP 4. Determine the critical value, or cutoff.

The fourth step is to determine a critical value, or cutoff, indicating how extreme our data must be to reject the null hypothesis. For ANOVA, we use an F statistic, which means that our critical value must be on an F distribution. For an F distribution, there is just one critical value. Moreover, the F statistic is always positive. (There is no negative F cutoff because the F is based on estimates of variance instead of standard deviation or standard error in both the numerator and denominator, and because variances are always positive.)

To determine the critical value, we examine the F table in Appendix B, a portion of which we have excerpted in Table 11-2. The between-groups degrees of freedom are found in a row across the top of the table. Notice that, in the full table, this row only goes up to 6, as it is quite rare to have more than seven conditions, or groups, in a study. The within-groups degrees of freedom are in a column along the left-hand side of the table. Because the number of participants in a study can range from few to many, the column continues for several pages with the same range of values of between-groups degrees of freedom on the top of each page.

When using the F table, first find the appropriate within-groups degrees of freedom along the left-hand side of the page, in this case 13. Then find the appropriate

TABLE 11-2. Excerpt from the *F* Table

We use the *F* table to determine critical values for a given *p* level, based on the degrees of freedom in the numerator (between-groups degrees of freedom) and the degrees of freedom in the denominator (within-groups degrees of freedom). Note that critical values are in italics for 0.10, regular type for 0.05, and boldface for 0.01.

Within-Groups Degrees of Freedom: Denominator	*p* level	Between-Groups Degrees of Freedom: Numerator			
		1	2	3	4 ...
.					
.					
.					
	0.01	**9.33**	**6.93**	**5.95**	**5.41**
12	0.05	4.75	3.88	3.49	3.26
	0.10	*3.18*	*2.81*	*2.61*	*2.48*
	0.01	**9.07**	**6.70**	**5.74**	**5.20**
13	0.05	4.67	3.80	3.41	3.18
	0.10	*3.14*	*2.76*	*2.56*	*2.43*
	0.01	**8.86**	**6.51**	**5.56**	**5.03**
14	0.05	4.60	3.74	3.34	3.11
	0.10	*3.10*	*2.73*	*2.52*	*2.39*
.					
.					
.					

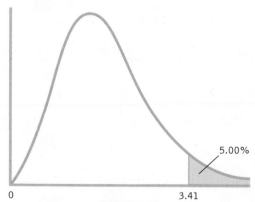

5.00%

0   3.41

FIGURE 11-2
Determining Cutoffs for an
***F* Distribution**

We determine a single critical value on an *F* distribution. Because *F* is a squared version of a *z* or *t* in some circumstances, we have only one cutoff for a two-tailed test.

between-groups degrees of freedom along the top, in this case 3. The place in the table where this row and this column intersect contains three numbers. Again, if you look to the left-hand side of the page, you'll see three possible *p* levels next to every value of within-groups degrees of freedom. From top to bottom, the table provides cutoffs for *p* levels of 0.01, 0.05, and 0.10. Researchers usually use the middle one, 0.05. For our test, we will choose the critical value, or cutoff, for a *p* level of 0.05: 3.41. We will reject the null hypothesis if the test statistic is greater than or equal to 3.41, as shown in the curve in Figure 11-2.

Summary: Our cutoff, or critical value, for the *F* statistic for a *p* level of 0.05 is 3.41, as displayed in the curve in Figure 11-2.

STEP 5. Calculate the test statistic.

In the fifth step, we calculate our test statistic. At this point, we calculate two estimates of the population variance. One, between-groups variance, is based on the differences among the sample means. The other, within-groups variance, is based on the variances of the samples without regard to how spread out the sample means are. We use the two estimates to calculate the *F* statistic. We directly compare this statistic to our cutoff to determine whether to reject the null hypothesis. We will learn to do these calculations in the next section.

Summary: To be calculated in the next section.

STEP 6. Make a decision.

In the final step, we decide whether to reject or fail to reject the null hypothesis. If the F statistic is beyond the critical value, then we know that it is in the most extreme 5% of possible test statistics *if* the null hypothesis is true. We can then reject the null hypothesis. If we are able to reject the null hypothesis, then we can draw a specific conclusion, such as "It seems that foreign graduate students studying in the United States rate financial factors differently, on average, depending on the type of program in which they are enrolled." Notice that we do not say *which* programs are different. ANOVA does not tell us where differences lie. ANOVA only tells us that at least one mean is significantly different from another.

If the test statistic is not beyond the critical value, then we must fail to reject the null hypothesis. The test statistic would not be very rare if the null hypothesis were true. In this circumstance, we report only that there is no evidence from the present study to support the research hypothesis.

Summary: We will be making an evidence-based decision, so we cannot make that decision until we complete step 5, in which we calculate the probabilities associated with that evidence. We will complete step 5 in the Making a Decision section below.

The Logic and Calculations of the *F* Statistic

We now know all the steps of hypothesis testing except how to calculate the F statistic. In this section, we learn the logic of ANOVA, the logic of calculating the between-groups variance and the within-groups variance, and the actual calculations necessary to compute the F statistic. Then we return to the steps of hypothesis testing to learn how to use data to make a decision for the specific example we have been considering. Fortunately, both the concept and the calculation of the F statistic use ideas that we are already familiar with.

Let's demonstrate how to use the statistical reasoning associated with the F statistic. You already have observed that grown men, on average, are slightly taller than grown women, on average. The language of statistics calls that kind of variability "between-groups variability." You also know that not all women are the same height and not all men are the same height. The language of statistics calls that kind of variability "within-groups variability." The F statistic is simply an estimate of between-groups variability divided by an estimate of within-groups variability.

$$F = \frac{\text{between–groups variability}}{\text{within–groups variability}}$$

Quantifying Overlap with ANOVA The F statistic is a ratio of two estimates of the population variance: between-groups variance and within-groups variance. The estimate of the between-groups variability appears in the numerator. The estimate of the within-groups variability appears in the denominator. Because the F statistic is a ratio of between-groups variability to within-groups variability, its value is large whenever the numerator is large and the denominator is small, and its value is small whenever the numerator is small and the denominator is large.

Figure 11-3 demonstrates that the amount of overlap is the result of only two influences: how far apart the means are (between-groups variance) and how spread out

> ◀ **MASTERING THE CONCEPT**
>
> **11-2:** When conducting an ANOVA, we use the same six steps of hypothesis testing that we've already learned. One of the differences from what we've learned is that we calculate an F statistic, the ratio of between-groups variance to within-groups variance.

Gender Differences in Height Men, on average, are slightly taller than women (between-groups variance). However, neither men nor women are all the same height within their groups (within-groups variance). F is between-groups variability divided by within-groups variability.

FIGURE 11-3
The Logic of ANOVA

Compare the top (a) and middle (b) sets of sample distributions. As the variability between means increases, the *F* statistic is larger. Compare the middle (b) and bottom (c) sets of sample distributions. As the variability within the samples themselves decreases, the *F* statistic is larger. The *F* statistic is larger as the curves overlap less. Both the increased spread among the sample means and the decreased spread within each sample contribute to this increase in the *F* statistic.

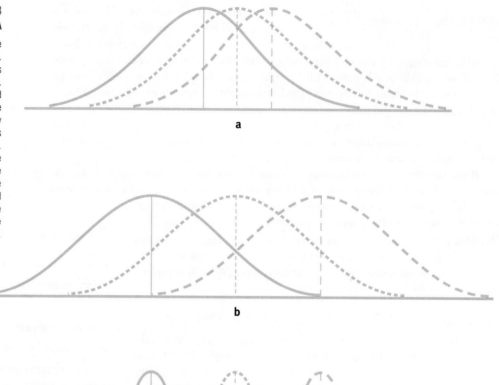

a

b

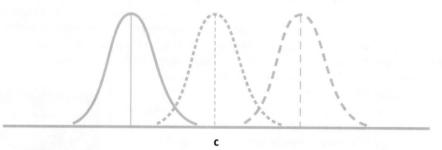

c

each distribution is (within-groups variance). Each set of three curves represents a different study. In the top set of three curves (a), there is a great deal of overlap among the sample distributions. This occurs both because the means are fairly close together and because there is so much variability within each of the samples. Three overlapping distributions like these could easily result from the same population just by chance.

In the second set of distributions (b), the three sample means are more widely separated but the variability among the scores in each group remains the same. There is much less overlap, but only because the means are farther apart. This increase in the difference between means increases the between-groups variance even though the within-groups variance is unchanged. Said another way, the *F* statistic is larger because the numerator is larger; the denominator has not changed. Overall, there is less overlap than in the top set of three curves. It would be somewhat surprising to draw these three samples from the same population just by chance.

The third set of distributions (c) represents what would occur if we kept the increased variability between the three means but decreased the variability within each of the samples. Compared to the top set of three curves (a), we have increased our between-groups variance (the numerator) *and* decreased our within-groups variance (the denominator). Both changes lead to a larger *F* statistic. But this change also leads to less overlap. Just from this graph (before calculating any numbers), it would be difficult to convince someone that these three samples were drawn by chance from the very same population.

These three sets of curves demonstrate how the F statistic captures the amount of overlap among samples by including two measures: (1) between-groups variance, a measure of how variable the means are with respect to one another, and (2) within-groups variance, a measure of how variable the scores are within each sample.

Two Ways to Estimate Population Variance Between-groups variability and within-groups variability are both estimates of population variance. Mathematically, if we calculate two estimates of variance and both are identical, then the F statistic, which is a ratio of the two estimates, will be 1.0. For example, if the estimate of the between-groups variance is 32 and the estimate of the within-groups variance is also 32, then the F statistic is $32/32 = 1.0$. Notice that this is a bit different from the z and t tests in which a z or t of 0 would mean no difference at all. Here, an F of 1 means no difference at all. As the sample means get farther apart, the between-groups variance (the numerator) increases, which means that the F statistic also increases.

Calculating the F Statistic with a Source Table Our goal in performing the calculations of ANOVA is to understand the *sources* of all the variability in a study. The measurement of variance is built on the idea of squared deviations from the mean. This is how we calculate most of the numbers that we use to calculate variance in ANOVA: squared deviations.

To conduct an ANOVA, we calculate many squared deviations and three sums of squares. We use a source table to help us to keep track of all the sources of variability that we discover in our study. *A **source table** presents the important calculations and final results of an ANOVA in a consistent and easy-to-read format.* A source table is shown in Table 11-3; the symbols in this table would be replaced by numbers in an actual source table.

We're going to explain the source table by discussing the meaning of each of the five columns in the source table shown in Table 11-3. For teaching purposes, we're going to explain column 1 first and then work backward from column 5 to column 4 to column 3 and finally to column 2.

Column 1: The first column, labeled "source," lists the sources, or origins, of the two estimates of population variance. One source of variability comes from the spread *between* means, and another source of variability comes from the spread among the scores *within* each sample. In this chapter, the main function of the row labeled "total" is to check our sum of squares (SS) and degrees of freedom (df) calculations. Now

TABLE 11-3. The Source Table Organizes Our ANOVA Calculations

A source table helps researchers organize the most important calculations necessary to conduct an ANOVA as well as the final results. The numbers 1–5 in the first row are used in this particular table only to help you understand the format of source tables; they would not be included in an actual source table.

1 Source	2 SS	3 df	4 MS	5 F
Between	$SS_{between}$	$df_{between}$	$MS_{between}$	F
Within	SS_{within}	df_{within}	MS_{within}	
Total	SS_{total}	df_{total}		

■ A **source table** presents the important calculations and final results of an ANOVA in a consistent and easy-to-read format.

let's work backward through the source table to learn how it describes the different sources of variability.

Column 5: The fifth column is labeled "*F.*" As you may remember, we need only simple division to calculate the *F* statistic: we divide the estimate of the between-groups variance by the estimate of the within-groups variance.

Column 4: The fourth column, labeled "*MS,*" describes how we arrived at the numerical estimate for *F. MS* is the conventional symbol for variance in ANOVA. It stands for "mean square" because variance is the arithmetic mean of the squared deviations. $MS_{between}$ and MS_{within}, therefore, refer to between-groups variance and within-groups variance, respectively. As already noted, we divide $MS_{between}$ by MS_{within} to calculate *F.*

Column 3: The third column is labeled "*df.*" This column shows the degrees of freedom, and we already have learned to calculate the $df_{between}$ and df_{within}. It's so easy to calculate the df_{total} that we'll just do it now. Any guesses on how to calculate the df_{total}? If you said "add up the other two," you're right:

MASTERING THE FORMULA

11-3: One formula for the total degrees of freedom for a one-way between-groups ANOVA is $df_{total} = df_{between} + df_{within}$. We sum the between-groups degrees of freedom and the within-groups degrees of freedom. An alternate formula is $df_{total} = N_{total} - 1$. We subtract 1 from the total number of people in the study—that is, from the number of people in all groups.

$$df_{total} = df_{between} + df_{within}$$

In our version of Ruby's study, $df_{total} = 3 + 13 = 16$. A second way to calculate df_{total} is:

$$df_{total} = N_{total} - 1$$

N_{total} refers to the total number of people in the entire study. In our abbreviated version of Ruby's study, there were four groups with 5, 4, 4, and 4 participants in the groups, and $5 + 4 + 4 + 4 = 17$. We calculate total degrees of freedom for this study as $df_{total} = 17 - 1 = 16$. If we calculate degrees of freedom both ways and the answers don't match up, then we know we have to go back and check our calculations.

Column 2: The all-important second column is labeled "*SS.*" This column includes the sums of squares, *SS*. We calculate three sums of squares: one for between-groups variability ($SS_{between}$), one for within-groups variability (SS_{within}), and one for total variability (SS_{total}). As with degrees of freedom, the first two sums of squares add up to the third. We should always calculate all three, however, to be sure they match.

The source table simply collects many of the things that we have already learned to do into one table. More specifically, it describes everything that we have learned about the sources of numerical variability in a particular study. Once we calculate our sums of squares for between-groups variance and within-groups variance, there are just two steps.

Step 1: Divide each sum of squares by the appropriate degrees of freedom—the appropriate version of $(N - 1)$.

We divide the $SS_{between}$ by the $df_{between}$ and the SS_{within} by the df_{within}. We then have the two variance estimates ($MS_{between}$ and MS_{within}).

Step 2: Calculate the ratio of $MS_{between}$ and MS_{within} to get the *F* statistic.

Once we have our sums of squared deviations, the rest of the calculation is simple division.

Sums of Squared Deviations Statistics defines deviance as variations from particular statistical norms. For ANOVA, there are three different types of statistical deviations because we are measuring deviations from three different means: (1) to calculate deviations between groups, (2) to calculate deviations within groups, and (3) to calculate total deviations. Calculating the amount of deviance is the first step needed to calculate each sum of squares: between, within, and total.

■ The **grand mean** is the mean of every score in a study, regardless of which sample the score came from.

TABLE 11-4. Calculating the Total Sum of Squares
....
The total sum of squares is calculated by subtracting the overall mean, called the *grand mean,* from every score to create deviations, then squaring the deviations and summing the squared deviations.

Sample	X	(X − GM)	(X − GM)²
Arts and sciences	4	0.412	0.170
	5	1.412	1.994
$M_{a\&s} = 4.0$	4	0.412	0.170
	3	−0.588	0.346
	4	0.412	0.170
Education	4	0.412	0.170
	3	−0.588	0.346
$M_{ed} = 3.75$	4	0.412	0.170
	4	0.412	0.170
Law	3	−0.588	0.346
	3	−0.588	0.346
$M_{law} = 2.75$	2	−1.588	2.522
	3	−0.588	0.346
Business	4	0.412	0.170
	4	0.412	0.170
$M_{bus} = 3.75$	4	0.412	0.170
	3	−0.588	0.346
	$GM = 3.588$		$SS_{total} = $ **8.122**

Let's start with the total sum of squares, SS_{total}. The best way to start is to organize all the scores, placing them in a single column with a horizontal line dividing each sample from the next. You can use the data (from our version of Ruby's study) in the column labeled "*X*" of Table 11-4 as your model, especially when calculating practice problems that have only a few data points in each group. The symbol *X* stands for individual scores, which is why there are 17 individual scores listed under that symbol in the table. Each set of scores is next to its sample. The means of each sample are included underneath the names of each sample. (We have included subscripts on each mean in the first column—e.g., *A&S* for arts and sciences—to indicate its sample.)

In this case, we want to know the total sum of squares, so we subtract the overall mean from each score, including everyone in the study, regardless of sample. The mean of all the scores is called the *grand mean,* and its symbol is *GM. The **grand mean** is the mean of every score in a study, regardless of which sample the score came from:*

$$GM = \frac{\Sigma(X)}{N_{total}}$$

The grand mean of these scores is 3.588. (As we have been doing so far, we will write each number to three decimal places until we get to the final answer, *F.* As we have done throughout this book, we will report the final answer to two decimal places.)

MASTERING THE FORMULA

11-4: The grand mean is the mean score of all people in a study, regardless of which group they're in. The formula is: $GM = \frac{\Sigma(X)}{N_{total}}$. We add up everyone's score, then divide by the total number of people in the study.

The third column in Table 11-4 shows the deviation of each score from the grand mean. The fourth column shows the squares of these deviations. For example, for the first score, 4, we subtract the grand mean:

$$4 - 3.588 = 0.412$$

Then we square the deviation:

$$(0.412)^2 = 0.170$$

Below the fourth column, we have summed the squared deviations: 8.122. This is the total sum of squares, SS_{total}. The formula for total sum of squares is:

$$SS_{total} = \Sigma(X - GM)^2$$

To calculate the total sum of squares, notice that we used the grand mean (GM) as the standard against which we measured all our deviations. This will change in the next step, when we calculate within-groups variance.

The model for calculating the within-groups sum of squares is shown in Table 11-5. This time the deviations are around the mean of each particular group. For the five

MASTERING THE FORMULA

11-5: The total sum of squares in an ANOVA is calculated using the following formula: $SS_{total} = \Sigma(X - GM)^2$. We subtract the grand mean from every score, then square these deviations. We then sum all the squared deviations.

TABLE 11-5. Calculating the Within-Groups Sum of Squares

The within-groups sum of squares is calculated by taking each score and subtracting the mean of the sample from which it comes—not the grand mean—to create deviations, then squaring the deviations and summing the squared deviations.

Sample	X	$(X - M)$	$(X - M)^2$
Arts and sciences	4	0	0
	5	1	1
$M_{a\&s} = 4.0$	4	0	0
	3	−1	1
	4	0	0
Education	4	0.25	0.063
	3	−0.75	0.563
$M_{ed} = 3.75$	4	0.25	0.063
	4	0.25	0.063
Law	3	0.25	0.063
	3	0.25	0.063
$M_{law} = 2.75$	2	−0.75	0.563
	3	0.25	0.063
Business	4	0.25	0.063
	4	0.25	0.063
$M_{bus} = 3.75$	4	0.25	0.063
	3	−0.75	0.563
$GM = 3.588$			$SS_{within} = \mathbf{4.256}$

scores in the first sample, we subtract their sample mean, 4.0. For the example, the calculation for the first score is:

$$(4 - 4)^2 = 0$$

For the four scores in the second sample, we subtract their sample mean, 3.75. And so on for all four samples. (*Note:* As a practical matter, a horizontal line between samples serves as a reminder to start using a new mean when calculating these within-groups deviations. Don't forget to switch means when you get to each new sample!)

Once we have all our deviations, we square them and sum them to calculate our within-groups sum of squares, 4.256, the number below the fourth column. Because we subtract the sample mean, rather than the grand mean, from each score, the formula is:

$$SS_{within} = \Sigma(X - M)^2$$

Notice that the weighting for sample size is built into the calculation. The first sample has five scores and contributes five squared deviations to the total. The other samples have only four scores, so they only contribute four squared deviations.

Finally, we calculate the between-groups sum of squares. Remember, our goal for this step is to estimate how much each *group* deviates from the overall grand mean, not each *individual participant,* so we use means rather than individual scores in our calculations. This step uses the same format as the other two sums of squares and almost the same calculations. For each of the 17 people in this study, we subtract the grand mean from the mean of the group to which that individual belongs.

For example, the first person has a score of 4 and belongs to the group labeled "arts and sciences," which has a mean that also happens to be 4. However, the grand mean is 3.588. We ignore this person's individual score and subtract 3.588 (the grand mean) from 4 (the group mean) to get the deviation score 0.412. The next person, also in the group labeled "arts and sciences," has a score of 5. The group mean of that sample is 4, and the grand mean is 3.588. Once again, we ignore that person's individual score and subtract 3.588 (the grand mean) from 4 (the group mean) to get the deviation score, also 0.412.

In fact, we subtract 3.588 from 4 for all five scores. We conduct the same calculation for every score in that group, as you can see in Table 11-6. When we get to the horizontal line between samples, we look for our next sample mean. For all four scores in the next sample, we subtract the grand mean, 3.588, from the sample mean, 3.75, and so on.

To summarize the calculation of the between-groups sum of squares, each deviation score within each group is computed by subtracting the grand mean from the mean of that group. To expedite the calculations, this subtraction can be performed just once for each group, and the squared deviation score can be multiplied by the number of participants in the group. Notice that the individual scores are *never* involved in our calculations, just their sample means and the grand mean! Also notice that the first group (arts and sciences) will have a little bit more weight in the calculation because it has five participants while the other three groups have only four. The third column of Table 11-6 includes the deviations and the fourth includes the squared deviations. The between-groups sum of squares, in

◀ **MASTERING THE FORMULA**

11-6: The within-groups sum of squares in a one-way between-groups ANOVA is calculated using the following formula: $SS_{within} = \Sigma(X - M)^2$. From each score, we subtract its group mean. We then square these deviations. We sum all the squared deviations for everyone in all groups.

TABLE 11-6. Calculating the Between-Groups Sum of Squares

The between-groups sum of squares is calculated by subtracting the grand mean from the sample mean for every score to create deviations, then squaring the deviations and summing the squared deviations. The individual scores themselves are not involved in any calculations.

Sample	X	$(M - GM)$	$(M - GM)^2$
Arts and sciences	4	0.412	0.170
	5	0.412	0.170
$M_{a\&s} = 4.0$	4	0.412	0.170
	3	0.412	0.170
	4	0.412	0.170
Education	4	0.162	0.026
	3	0.162	0.026
$M_{ed} = 3.75$	4	0.162	0.026
	4	0.162	0.026
Law	3	−0.838	0.702
	3	−0.838	0.702
$M_{law} = 2.75$	2	−0.838	0.702
	3	−0.838	0.702
Business	4	0.162	0.026
	4	0.162	0.026
$M_{bus} = 3.75$	4	0.162	0.026
	3	0.162	0.026
	$GM = 3.588$		$SS_{between} = $ **3.866**

MASTERING THE FORMULA

11-7: The between-groups sum of squares in an ANOVA is calculated using the following formula: $SS_{between} = \Sigma(M - GM)^2$. For each score, we subtract the grand mean from that score's group mean and square this deviation. Note that we do not use the scores in any of these calculations. We sum all the squared deviations.

bold under the fourth column, is 3.866. The formula for the between-groups sum of squares is:

$$SS_{between} = \Sigma(M - GM)^2$$

Now is the moment of arithmetic truth. Were our calculations correct? To find out, we add our within-groups sum of squares (4.256) to our between-groups sum of squares (3.866) to see if they equal the total sum of squares (8.122). Here's the formula:

MASTERING THE FORMULA

11-8: We can also calculate the total sum of squares for a one-way between-groups ANOVA by adding the within-groups sum of squares and the between-groups sum of squares: $SS_{total} = SS_{within} + SS_{between}$. This is a useful check on our calculations.

$$SS_{total} = SS_{within} + SS_{between}$$
$$8.122 = 4.256 + 3.866$$

Indeed, the total sum of squares, 8.122, does equal the sum of the other two sums of squares, 4.256 and 3.866. Our calculations were correct.

To recap (see Table 11-7), for the total sum of squares, we subtract the *grand mean* from each individual *score* to get the deviations. For the within-groups sum of squares, we subtract the appropriate *sample mean* from every *score*. And then, for the between-groups sum of squares, we subtract the *grand mean* from the appropriate *sample mean,* once for each score; for the between-groups sum of squares, the actual scores are never involved in any calculations.

TABLE 11-7. The Three Sums of Squares of ANOVA

The calculations in ANOVA are built on the foundation we learned in Chapter 4, sums of squared deviations. We calculate three types of sums of squares, one for between-groups variance, one for within-groups variance, and one for total variance. Once we have our three sums of squares, most of the remaining calculations involve simple division.

Sum of Squares	To calculate the deviations, subtract the . . .	Formula
Between-groups	Grand mean from the sample mean (for each score)	$SS_{between} = \Sigma(M - GM)^2$
Within-groups	Sample mean from each score	$SS_{within} = \Sigma(X - M)^2$
Total	Grand mean from each score	$SS_{total} = \Sigma(X - GM)^2$

Now we insert these numbers into our source table to calculate our F statistic. See Table 11–8 for the source table that lists all the formulas and Table 11–9 for the completed source table. We divide the between-groups sum of squares and the within-groups sum of squares by their associated degrees of freedom to get the between–groups variance and the within–groups variance. The formulas are:

$$MS_{between} = \frac{SS_{between}}{df_{between}} = \frac{3.866}{3} = 1.289$$

$$MS_{within} = \frac{SS_{within}}{df_{within}} = \frac{4.256}{13} = 0.327$$

MASTERING THE FORMULA

11-9: We calculate the mean squares from their associated sums of squares and degrees of freedom. For the between-groups mean square, we divide the between-groups sum of squares by the between-groups degrees of freedom: $MS_{between} = \frac{SS_{between}}{df_{between}}$. For the within-groups mean square, we divide the within-groups sum of squares by the within-groups degrees of freedom: $MS_{within} = \frac{SS_{within}}{df_{within}}$

TABLE 11-8. A Source Table with Formulas

This table summarizes the formulas for calculating an F statistic.

Source	SS	df	MS	F
Between	$\Sigma(M - GM)^2$	$N_{groups} - 1$	$\dfrac{SS_{between}}{df_{between}}$	$\dfrac{MS_{between}}{MS_{within}}$
Within	$\Sigma(X - M)^2$	$df_1 + df_2 + \ldots + df_{last}$	$\dfrac{SS_{within}}{df_{within}}$	
Total	$\Sigma(X - GM)^2$	$N_{total} - 1$		
[Expanded formula: $df_{within} = (N_1 - 1) + (N_2 - 1) + \ldots + (N_{last} - 1)$]				

TABLE 11-9. A Completed Source Table

Once we've calculated the sums of squares and the degrees of freedom, the rest is just simple division. We use the first two columns of numbers to calculate the variances and the F statistic. We divide the between-groups sum of squares and within-groups sum of squares by their associated degrees of freedom to get the between-groups variance and within-groups variance. Then we divide between-groups variance by within-groups variance to get the F statistic, 3.94.

Source	SS	df	MS	F
Between	3.866	3	1.289	**3.94**
Within	4.256	13	0.327	
Total	8.122	16		

MASTERING THE FORMULA

11-10: The formula for the F statistic is: $F = \dfrac{MS_{between}}{MS_{within}}$. We divide the between-groups mean square by the within-groups mean square.

We then divide the between-groups variance by the within-groups variance to calculate the F statistic. The formula, in bold in Table 11-8, is:

$$F = \frac{MS_{between}}{MS_{within}} = \frac{1.289}{0.327} = 3.94$$

Making a Decision

Now we have to come back to the six steps of hypothesis testing for ANOVA to fill in the gaps in steps 1 and 6. We finished step 5 in the previous section.

Step 1: We have to be sure that our variances were roughly equal in our four groups; researchers use statistical software such as SPSS to test whether the groups were selected from populations with equal variances. For now, we can use our within-groups variance column to determine this. Variance is computed by dividing the sum of squares by the sample size minus 1. We can add the squared deviations for each sample, then divide by the sample size minus 1. Table 11-10 shows the calculations for variance within each of the four samples. Because the largest variance, 0.500, is not more than twice the smallest variance, 0.251, we have met the assumption of equal variances for ANOVA.

Step 6: Now that we have our test statistic, we can compare it with our critical value. Previously, in step 4, we determined that the cutoff F statistic for the foreign graduate student example, per the table in Appendix B, was 3.41. The F statistic we calculated for these data was 3.94. As seen in Figure 11-4, the F statistic for this study is beyond the cutoff; therefore, we can reject the null hypothesis. It appears that foreign graduate students applying to some types of programs rate financial factors as more important, on average, than do foreign graduate students applying to other types of programs. The ANOVA, however, does not allow us to say more than this. We only know that at least one mean is different from at least one other mean. We do not know exactly where the difference or differences lie. We must conduct a follow-up analysis (described below) to determine what the differences might be.

Summary: We can reject the null hypothesis. It appears that the importance placed on financial factors differs, on average, based on type of program to which foreign graduate students are applying, as seen in the curve in Figure 11-4.

TABLE 11-10. Calculating Sample Variances

We calculate the variances of the samples by dividing each sum of squares by the sample size minus 1 to check one of the assumptions of ANOVA. For unequal sample sizes, as we have here, we want our largest variance (0.500 in this case) to be no more than twice our smallest (0.251 in this case). Two times 0.251 is 0.502, and so we meet this assumption.

Sample	Arts and Sciences	Education	Law	Business
	0	0.063	0.063	0.063
	1	0.563	0.063	0.063
Squared deviations:	0	0.063	0.563	0.063
	1	0.063	0.063	0.563
	0			
Sum of squares:	2	0.752	0.752	0.752
$N - 1$:	4	3	3	3
Variance:	**0.500**	**0.251**	**0.251**	**0.251**

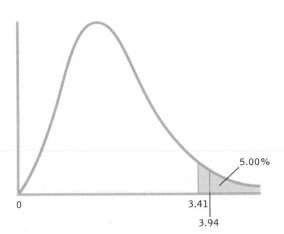

FIGURE 11-4
Making a Decision with an F Distribution

We compare the F statistic that we calculated for our samples to a single cutoff, or critical value, on the appropriate F distribution. We can reject the null hypothesis if the test statistic is beyond—more to the right than—the cutoff. Here, our F statistic of 3.94 is beyond the cutoff of 3.41, so we can reject the null hypothesis.

Note that we could choose to calculate p_{rep} instead of p for our F statistic. We would use the procedure introduced in earlier chapters in which we use statistical software such as SPSS to determine the specific p values for this F statistic, and then use Microsoft Excel to determine p_{rep}.

R^2, the Effect Size for ANOVA

In Chapter 8, we learned to calculate one measure of effect size, Cohen's d. Because this measure is calculated based on a difference between means, however, we can only use it in situations in which we have two means—the same situations in which we use a z test or a t test. When we calculate Cohen's d, we calculate a difference by subtracting one mean from another. When we have more than two means, we can't subtract one from another to calculate a difference. With ANOVA, we calculate a statistic called R^2 instead (pronounced "r squared"). R^2 is the proportion of variance in the dependent variable that is accounted for by the independent variable. Sometimes researchers use a very similar measure of effect size, η^2 (pronounced "eta squared"). We can interpret η^2 exactly as we interpret R^2.

Because R^2 is the proportion of variance accounted for by the independent variable, out of all possible variance, we calculate it by constructing a ratio, much as we did when we calculated an F statistic. For R^2, we use sums of squares as indicators of variability. The numerator is a measure of the variability that takes into account just the differences among means; we use the between-groups sum of squares, $SS_{between}$, for this because it assesses only the variability among the means, without regard to the variability within each sample. The denominator is a measure of the total variability. For this, we use the total sum of squares, SS_{total}, because it takes both between-groups variance and within-groups variance into account. The formula is:

$$R^2 = \frac{SS_{between}}{SS_{total}}$$

> ◀ **MASTERING THE CONCEPT**
>
> **11-3:** As with other hypothesis tests, it is recommended that we calculate an effect size in addition to conducting the hypothesis test. The most commonly reported effect size for ANOVA is R^2.

> **MASTERING THE FORMULA**
>
> **11-11:** The formula for the effect size we use with one-way between-groups ANOVA is $R^2 = \frac{SS_{between}}{SS_{total}}$. The calculation is a ratio, similar to the calculation for the F statistic. For R^2, we divide the between-groups sum of squares by the total sum of squares. ◀

EXAMPLE 11.2

Let's apply this to the ANOVA we just conducted. We can use the statistics in the source table shown in Table 11-11 to calculate R^2:

$$R^2 = \frac{SS_{between}}{SS_{total}} = \frac{3.866}{8.122} = 0.48$$

■ A **post-hoc test** is a statistical procedure frequently carried out after we reject the null hypothesis in an analysis of variance; it allows us to make multiple comparisons among several means; often referred to as a *follow-up* test.

■ The **Tukey** *HSD* **test** is a widely used post-hoc test that determines the differences between means in terms of standard error; the *HSD* is compared to a critical value; sometimes called the *q test.*

TABLE 11-11. Calculating R^2 from a Source Table

We can calculate R^2 directly from a completed source table. We simply divide the between-groups sum of squares by the total sum of squares to figure out the proportion of variance in the dependent variable accounted for by the independent variable.

Source	SS	df	MS	F
Between	3.866	3	1.289	3.94
Within	4.256	13	0.327	
Total	8.122	16		

TABLE 11-12. Cohen's Conventions for Effect Sizes: R^2

The following guidelines, called *conventions* by statisticians, are meant to help researchers decide how important an effect is. These numbers are not cutoffs, merely rough guidelines to aid researchers in their interpretation of results.

Effect Size	Convention
Small	0.01
Medium	0.06
Large	0.14

As with Cohen's *d,* there are conventions for R^2 that let us know whether our effect size is approximately small, medium, or large. Table 11-12 displays the conventions for R^2. From this table, we can see that our R^2 of 0.48 is very large. This is not surprising. With such small sample sizes, an effect would have to be quite large for the test statistic to be large enough that we could reject the null hypothesis. We can also turn our proportion into the more familiar language of percentages by multiplying by 100. We can then say that a specific percentage of the variance in the dependent variable was accounted for by the independent variable. In this case, we could say that 48% of the variability in ratings of the importance of financial factors is due to the type of program in which graduate students are enrolled.

Post-Hoc Tests

A statistically significant *F* calculated when conducting an ANOVA asserts that some difference exists somewhere in the study, and R^2 tells us how large that difference is, but neither statistic specifies which specific pairs of means are responsible for a statistically significant difference between groups. To determine where statistically significant differences probably are, we can start by looking at a graph of the data to figure out which means are farthest apart. We can't know for sure, however, until we conduct an additional test, called a *post-hoc test.*

A **post-hoc test** *is a statistical procedure frequently carried out after we reject the null hypothesis in an analysis of variance; it allows us to make multiple comparisons among several means.* The name of the test, post-hoc, means "after this" in Latin. This is why post-hoc tests are often referred to as *follow-up tests.* (Post-hoc tests are not conducted if we fail to reject the null hypothesis. In such a case, we would know that there are no statistically significant differences among means, so it would not make sense to ask precisely where those differences are.)

For example, Ruby's study of foreign graduate students led to a statistically significant result from the ANOVA. The means of financial factor ratings of students in the

> ▶ **MASTERING THE CONCEPT**
>
> **11-4:** ANOVA only tells us that there is a difference between at least two of the means in the study, but it doesn't tell us which means are different from each other. We must conduct a post-hoc test to determine exactly which pairs of means are statistically significantly different from each other.

different types of graduate programs (as seen in our example) are depicted in Figure 11-5. The means are: arts and sciences, 4.00; education, 3.75; law, 2.75; and business, 3.75. Notice that the graph is a Pareto chart because it organizes the bars from highest to lowest means. We conducted an ANOVA and were able to reject the null hypothesis. So we can say that an overall difference exists between the means. But where?

First, look at the graph and then consider the possibilities. Arts and sciences graduate students might rate financial factors higher, on average, than only the law students, with no other significant differences among means. Or arts and sciences graduate students might rate financial factors higher, on average, than graduate students in all three other programs. Or law students might rate financial factors as less important, on average, than graduate students in the other three programs. There are several possibilities, and we cannot state our conclusion until we examine each of them statistically using a post-hoc test.

A number of post-hoc tests are used, and most are named for their founders, almost exclusively people with fabulous names—for example, Bonferroni, Scheffé (pronounced "sheff-ay"), and Tukey (pronounced "too-kee"). These tests allow us to determine which means are statistically significantly different from one another once we determine that there is a difference somewhere.

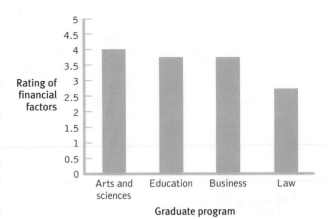

FIGURE 11-5
Which Graduate Programs Are Different?

This figure depicts the mean ratings of the influence of financial factors in decisions to attend graduate school among foreign graduate students in four different types of programs in the United States. When we conduct an ANOVA and reject the null hypothesis, we only know that there is a difference somewhere; we do not know where the difference lies. We can see several possible combinations of differences by examining the means on this graph. Further testing will let us know which specific pairs of means are different from one another.

Tukey *HSD*

The **Tukey** *HSD* **test** is a widely used post-hoc test that determines the differences between means in terms of standard error; the HSD is compared to a critical value. (It is sometimes called the *q test* because of the statistic on which it is based). *HSD* stands for "honestly significant difference" and indicates that we adjusted for the fact that we are making multiple comparisons. We only want to find differences that are "honestly" there.

The Tukey *HSD* test involves (1) the calculation of differences between each pair of means and (2) the division of each difference by the standard error. As with the *z* and *t* tests, we compare the *HSD* for each pair of means to a critical value (a *q* value found in the table for the *q* statistic in Appendix B) to determine if the means are different enough to reject the null hypothesis. The Tukey *HSD* test, therefore, is basically a variant of the *z* test and *t* tests; the parallel is easily seen in its formula for any two sample means:

$$HSD = \frac{(M_1 - M_2)}{s_M}$$

The formula for the standard error is:

$$s_M = \sqrt{\frac{MS_{within}}{N}}$$

MASTERING THE FORMULA

11-12: To conduct a Tukey *HSD* test, we first calculate standard error: $s_M = \sqrt{\frac{MS_{within}}{N}}$. We divide the MS_{within} by the sample size within each group and take the square root. We can then calculate the *HSD* for each pair of means: $HSD = \frac{(M_1 - M_2)}{s_M}$. For each pair of means, we subtract one from the other and divide by the standard error we calculated earlier.

MASTERING THE FORMULA

11-13: When we conduct an ANOVA with different-size samples, we have to calculate a harmonic mean, N': $N' = \dfrac{N_{groups}}{\Sigma(1/N)}$. To do that, we divide the number of groups in the study by the sum of 1 divided by the sample size for every group.

N in this case is the sample size within each group, with the assumption that all samples have the same number of participants.

The above calculations are easily done if all samples are the same size. However, when samples are different sizes, as in our example of foreign graduate students, we have to add one additional step: we must calculate a weighted sample size, also known as a *harmonic mean*. N' (pronounced "N prime") is weighted sample size, the harmonic mean. Its formula is:

$$N' = \frac{N_{groups}}{\Sigma(1/N)}$$

EXAMPLE 11.3

We calculate N' by dividing the number of groups (the numerator) by the sum of 1 divided by the sample size for every group (the denominator). For the example in which there were five students in arts and sciences programs and four in each of the other three programs, the formula is:

$$N' = \frac{4}{\left(\dfrac{1}{5} + \dfrac{1}{4} + \dfrac{1}{4} + \dfrac{1}{4}\right)} = \frac{4}{(0.20 + 0.25 + 0.25 + 0.25)} = \frac{4}{0.95} = 4.211$$

When sample sizes are not equal, we use a formula for s_M based on N' instead of N:

$$s_M = \sqrt{\frac{MS_{within}}{N'}} = \sqrt{\frac{0.327}{4.211}} = 0.279$$

MASTERING THE FORMULA

11-14: When we conduct an ANOVA with different-size samples, we have to calculate standard error using N': $s_M = \sqrt{\dfrac{MS_{within}}{N'}}$. To do that, we divide MS_{within} by N' and take the square root.

Now we calculate *HSD* for each pair of means. It does not matter in which order we decide to subtract our means. For example, we could subtract the mean for business from the mean for law, or the mean for law from the mean for business. Because of this, we ignore the sign of the answer; it is contingent on the arbitrary decision of which mean to subtract from the other.

Arts and sciences (4.00) versus education (3.75):

$$HSD = \frac{(4.00 - 3.75)}{0.279} = 0.896$$

Arts and sciences (4.00) versus business (3.75):

$$HSD = \frac{(4.00 - 3.75)}{0.279} = 0.896$$

Arts and sciences (4.00) versus law (2.75):

$$HSD = \frac{(4.00 - 2.75)}{0.279} = 4.480$$

Education (3.75) versus business (3.75):

$$HSD = \frac{(3.75 - 3.75)}{0.279} = 0$$

Education (3.75) versus law (2.75):

$$HSD = \frac{(3.75 - 2.75)}{0.279} = 3.584$$

Business (3.75) versus law (2.75):

$$HSD = \frac{(3.75 - 2.75)}{0.279} = 3.584$$

Now all we need is a critical value to which we can compare our *HSD*s. Then we can determine which pairs of means are significantly different from one another. Appendix B lists the cutoffs for the *HSD* in a *q* table because the *HSD* cutoffs are values of the *q* statistic; we have excerpted a portion of the *q* table in Table 11-13. The numbers of means being compared (levels of the independent variable) are in a row along the top of the *q* table, and the within-groups degrees of freedom are in a column along the left-hand side. We first look up the within-groups degrees of freedom for our test, 13, along the left column. We then go across from 13 to the numbers below the number of means being compared, 4. For a *p* level of 0.05, the cutoff *q* is 4.15. Again, the sign of our *HSD* does not matter because the order in which we subtract means is arbitrary. This is a two-tailed test, and any *HSD* above 4.15 or below −4.15 would be considered statistically significant.

By comparing the *HSD*s that we calculated above to the critical value of 4.15, we can see that there is only one statistically significant difference between means in this ANOVA (4.48). It appears that foreign graduate students in arts and sciences programs in the United States rate the importance of financial factors higher, on average, than do foreign graduate students in law programs in the United States. Because we

TABLE 11-13. Excerpt from the *q* Table

Like the *F* table, we use the *q* table to determine critical values for a given *p* level, based on the number of means being compared and the within-groups degrees of freedom. Note that critical values are in regular type for 0.05 and boldface for 0.01.

Within-Groups Degrees of Freedom	*p* level	... 3	*k* = Number of Treatments (levels) 4	5 ...
. . .				
12	.05	3.77	4.20	4.51
	.01	**5.05**	**5.50**	**5.84**
13	.05	3.73	4.15	4.45
	.01	**4.96**	**5.40**	**5.73**
14	.05	3.70	4.11	4.41
	.01	**4.89**	**5.32**	**5.63**
. . .				

have not rejected the null hypothesis for any other pairs, we can only conclude that there is not enough evidence to determine that these pairs of means are different.

What are some of the possible explanations for the graduate school findings? Perhaps law students expect to make a great deal of money upon graduation, so they don't tend to mind racking up large loans. Perhaps students who come from families with a lot of money tend to be more likely than those from families with less money to choose law than a master's or PhD in a field within arts and sciences. Or, perhaps Ruby happened to recruit a group of law students, just by chance, who did not tend to concern themselves with the cost of graduate school. Either way, the next step is replication.

CHECK YOUR LEARNING

Reviewing the Concepts

> One-way between-groups ANOVA uses the same six steps of hypothesis testing that we learned in Chapter 7, but with a few changes in steps 3 and 5.

> In step 3, we merely state the comparison distribution and provide two different types of degrees of freedom, df for the between-groups variance and df for the within-groups variance.

> In step 5, we complete the calculations, using a source table to organize the results. First, we estimate population variance by considering the differences among means (between-groups variance). Second, we estimate population variance by calculating a weighted average of the variances within each sample (within-groups variance).

> The calculation of variability requires several means, including sample means and the grand mean, which is the mean of all scores regardless of sample of origin.

> We divide between-groups variance by within-groups variance to calculate our F statistic. A higher F statistic indicates less overlap among the sample distributions, evidence that the samples come from different populations.

> Before making a decision based on the F statistic, we check to see that the assumption of equal sample variances is met. This assumption is met when the largest sample variance is not more than twice the amount of the smallest variance.

> As with other hypothesis tests, it is recommended that we calculate a measure of effect size when we have conducted an ANOVA. The most commonly reported effect size for ANOVA is R^2.

> If we are able to reject the null hypothesis in ANOVA, we're not finished. We must conduct a post-hoc test, such as a Tukey HSD test, to determine exactly which pairs of means are significantly different from one another.

> When computing our post-hoc Tukey HSD test on samples with unequal N's, we need to calculate a weighted sample size, called N'.

Clarifying the Concepts

11-5 If the F statistic is beyond the cutoff, what does that tell us? What doesn't that tell us?

11-6 When do we conduct a post-hoc test, such as a Tukey HSD test, and what does it tell us?

Calculating the Statistics

11-7 Calculate each type of degrees of freedom for the following data, assuming a between-groups design:

Group 1: 37, 30, 22, 29
Group 2: 49, 52, 41, 39
Group 3: 36, 49, 42

a. $df_{between} = N_{groups} - 1$
b. $df_{within} = df_1 + df_2 + \ldots + df_{last}$
c. $df_{total} = df_{between} + df_{within}$, or $df_{total} = N_{total} - 1$

11-8 Using the data in Check Your Learning 11-7, compute the grand mean.

11-9 Using the data in Check Your Learning 11-7, compute each type of sum of squares.

a. Total sum of squares

b. Within-groups sum of squares

c. Between-groups sum of squares

11-10 Using all of your calculations in Check Your Learning 11-7 to 11-9, perform the simple division to complete an entire between-groups ANOVA source table for these data.

Applying the Concepts

11-11 Let's create a context for the data provided above. Hollon, Thase, and Markowitz (2002) reviewed the efficacy of different treatments for depression, including medications, electroconvulsive therapy, psychotherapy, and placebo treatments. These data re-create some of the basic findings they present regarding psychotherapy. Each group is meant to represent people who received a different psychotherapy-based treatment, including psychodynamic therapy in group 1, interpersonal therapy in group 2, and cognitive-behavioral therapy in group 3. The scores presented here represent the extent to which someone responded to the treatment, with higher numbers indicating greater efficacy of treatment.

Group 1 (psychodynamic therapy): 37, 30, 22, 29

Group 2 (interpersonal therapy): 49, 52, 41, 39

Group 3 (cognitive-behavioral therapy): 36, 49, 42

a. Write hypotheses, in words, for this research.

b. Check the assumptions of ANOVA.

c. Determine the critical value for F for a p level of .05. Using your calculations from Check Your Learning 11-10, make a decision about these treatment options.

d. What follow-ups are needed, if any? If any are needed, perform the appropriate calculations and summarize your findings.

Solutions to these Check Your Learning questions can be found in Appendix D.

e. Calculate effect size for these data and interpret its meaning.

One-Way Within-Groups ANOVA

In Chapters 9 and 10, we learned about different kinds of t tests for two groups. Independent-samples t tests are used when the two groups have a between-groups design—participants are in only one group, or condition, within the study. Paired-samples t tests are used when the two groups have a within-groups design—partici-pants are in both groups or conditions. As explained earlier, when we have three groups, we have the same two options—between-groups and within-groups designs. We already saw how to conduct a one-way between-groups ANOVA. In this section, we learn how to conduct a one-way within-groups ANOVA (also called a *repeated-measures ANOVA*). Let's walk through the six steps of hypothesis testing and the calculation of effect size for an example.

Have you ever participated in a taste test? If you did, you were a participant in a within-groups experiment—a common technique among marketers and food lovers. Soft drink companies set up booths outside grocery stores and ask customers to taste-test Coke and Pepsi blind, and then pick their favorite. College students have argued about the best local pizza, then ordered one from each restaurant and conducted a taste challenge. And about a decade ago, when

Taste Tests Are Within-Groups Experiments In a taste test, every person tries every flavor to determine a favorite. So it is an experiment in which every participant is in every group, or condition.

pricier microbrew beers were becoming popular in North America, James Fallows found himself spending increasingly more on a bottle of beer and said to himself, "I love beer, but lately I've been wondering: Am I getting full value for my beer dollar?" He recruited 12 colleagues, all self-professed beer snobs, to see whether they really could tell if a beer was expensive or cheap (Fallows, 1999; http://www.slate.com/id/33771/).

Fallows wanted to know whether his recruits could distinguish among widely available beers that were categorized into three groups based on price—"high-end" beers like Sam Adams, "mid-range" beers like Budweiser, and "cheap" beers like Busch. All of these beers are lagers, the type of beer most commonly consumed in North America. Fallows chose lagers because they can be found at every price level, something not true of fancier beers such as stouts or pale ales. Here are data—mean scores on a scale of 0–100 for each category of beer—for five of the participants. (*Note:* The means for these participants are a little different from the overall sample but exhibit the same pattern. In addition, they have been rounded to the nearest whole number for the purposes of this example.)

Participant	Cheap	Mid-Range	High-End
1	40	30	53
2	42	45	65
3	30	38	64
4	37	32	43
5	23	28	38

The Benefits of Within-Groups ANOVA

Fallows reported his findings but did not conduct hypothesis testing. If he had, he would have used a one-way within-groups ANOVA to analyze these data. We use a one-way within-groups ANOVA when there's just one nominal independent variable (type of beer), the independent variable has more than two levels (cheap, mid-range, and high-end), the dependent variable is scale (ratings of beers), and every participant is in every group (each participant tastes the beers in every category).

In a within-groups design, we reduce error due to differences between our groups. Because each group includes exactly the same participants, we know that our groups are identical on all of the relevant variables. In the beer taste-test study, we know that each group is the same, on average, in taste preferences, amount of alcohol typically consumed, tendency to be critical or lenient when rating, and so on. This enables us to reduce within-groups variability due to differences among the people in our study. (As we'll soon see, we do this by calculating a fourth sum of squares to represent the variability for the individual participants in our study.) Our lower within-groups variability means a smaller denominator for our F statistic; a smaller denominator means a larger F statistic; and a larger F statistic means that it is easier to reject our null hypothesis. For this reason, we want to use a within-groups hypothesis test when we can.

> ▶ **MASTERING THE CONCEPT**
>
> **11-5:** A one-way within-groups ANOVA is used when we have one independent variable with at least three levels, a scale dependent variable, and participants who are in every group.

> ▶ **MASTERING THE CONCEPT**
>
> **11-6:** The calculations for a one-way within-groups ANOVA are similar to those for a one-way between-groups ANOVA, but we now calculate a subjects sum of squares in addition to the between-groups, within-groups, and total sums of squares. The subjects sum of squares reduces the within-groups sums of squares by removing variability associated with participants' differences.

The Six Steps of Hypothesis Testing

Now that we have an understanding of the benefits of within-groups ANOVA, we'll use the data from the beer taste test to walk through the steps of hypothesis testing. The ways in which a one-way within-groups ANOVA differs from a one-way between-groups ANOVA are pointed out as we come to them.

EXAMPLE 11.4

STEP 1. Identify the populations, distribution, and assumptions.

Most of this step is identical to that for a one-way between-groups ANOVA; however, there's one additional assumption for a within-groups ANOVA. We must be careful to avoid order effects. This does not seem to have occurred in this experiment. For all participants, beers were in cups with the same labels. For example, Budweiser was always in a cup labeled F. In addition, it appears that all participants tasted the beers in the same order: a mid-range beer, followed by a high-end beer, followed by a cheap beer, followed by another cheap beer, and so on. (Ideally, Fallows would have used counterbalancing, so that participants tasted the beers in different orders, and would have labeled cups on the bottom so that labels were not visible to participants.)

Summary: Population 1: People who drink cheap beer. Population 2: People who drink mid-range beer. Population 3: People who drink high-end beer.

The comparison distribution and hypothesis test: The comparison distribution will be an F distribution. The hypothesis test will be a one-way within-groups ANOVA.

Assumptions: (1) The participants were not selected randomly, so we must generalize with caution. (2) We do not know if the underlying population distributions are normal, but the sample data do not indicate severe skew. (3) To see if we meet the homoscedasticity assumption, we will check to see if the variances are similar (typically, when the largest variance is not more than twice the smallest) when we calculate the test statistic. (4) The experimenter did not counterbalance, so order effects might be present.

STEP 2. State the null and research hypotheses.

This step is identical to that for a one-way between-groups ANOVA.

Summary: Null hypothesis: People who drink cheap, mid-range, and high-end beer rate their beverages the same, on average—$H_0: \mu_1 = \mu_2 = \mu_3 = \mu_4$. Research hypothesis: People who drink cheap, mid-range, and high-end beer do not rate their beverages the same, on average.

STEP 3. Determine the characteristics of the comparison distribution.

As we did with a one-way between-groups ANOVA, we state that the comparison distribution is an F distribution and provide the appropriate degrees of freedom. The one difference with a one-way within-groups ANOVA is that we now calculate four degrees of freedom—between-groups, subjects, within-groups, and total. We noted earlier that we would have a fourth sum of squares, one for differences across participants. We call this the *subjects sum of squares,* or $SS_{subjects}$, which has its own degrees of freedom. When we conduct a one-way within-groups ANOVA, we calculate between-groups degrees of freedom and subjects degrees of freedom first because we multiply these two together to calculate the within-groups degrees of freedom.

So, we calculate the between-groups degrees of freedom exactly as before:

$$df_{between} = N_{groups} - 1 = 3 - 1 = 2$$

MASTERING THE FORMULA

11-15: The formula for the subjects degrees of freedom is $df_{subjects} = n - 1$. We subtract 1 from the number of participants in the study. We use the lowercase n to indicate that this is the number of data points in a single sample, even though we know that every participant is in all three groups.

MASTERING THE FORMULA

11-16: The formula for the within-groups degrees of freedom for a one-way within-groups ANOVA is $df_{within} = (df_{between})(df_{subjects})$. We multiply the between-groups degrees of freedom by the subjects degrees of freedom. This gives a lower number than we calculated for a one-way between-groups ANOVA because we want to exclude individual differences across groups from our within-groups sum of squares, and the degrees of freedom must reflect that.

MASTERING THE FORMULA

11-17: We can calculate the total degrees of freedom for a one-way within-groups ANOVA in two ways. We can sum all of the other degrees of freedom: $df_{total} = df_{between} + df_{subjects} + df_{within}$. Or we can subtract 1 from the total number of observations in the study: $df_{total} = N_{total} - 1$.

We next calculate the degrees of freedom that pairs with $SS_{subjects}$. Called $df_{subjects}$, it is calculated by subtracting 1 from the actual number of subjects, not data points. We use the lowercase n to represent that this is the number of participants in a single sample (even though they're all in every sample). The formula is:

$$df_{subjects} = n - 1 = 5 - 1 = 4$$

Once we know our between-groups degrees of freedom and our subjects degrees of freedom, we can calculate the within-groups degrees of freedom by multiplying the first two:

$$df_{within} = (df_{between})(df_{subjects}) = (2)(4) = 8$$

Note that the within-groups degrees of freedom is smaller than we would have calculated for a one-way between-groups ANOVA. For a one-way between-groups ANOVA, we would have subtracted 1 from each sample ($5 - 1 = 4$) and summed them to get 12. The within-groups degrees of freedom is smaller because we're excluding variability related to differences among the participants from the within-groups sum of squares, and the degrees of freedom must reflect that.

Lastly, we calculate total degrees of freedom using either method we learned earlier. We can sum the other degrees of freedom:

$$df_{total} = df_{between} + df_{subjects} + df_{within} = 2 + 4 + 8 = 14$$

Alternatively, we can use the second formula we learned before, treating the total number of participants as every data point, rather than every person. We know, of course, that there are just five participants and that they participate in all three levels of the independent variable, but for this step, we count the 15 total data points:

$$df_{total} = N_{total} - 1 = 15 - 1 = 14$$

We have calculated the four degrees of freedom that we will include in our source table. However, we only report the between-groups and within-groups degrees of freedom at this step.

Summary: We would use the F distribution with 2 and 8 degrees of freedom.

STEP 4. Determine the critical values, or cutoffs.

The fourth step is identical to that for a one-way between-groups ANOVA. We use our between-groups degrees of freedom and within-groups degrees of freedom to look up a critical value on the F table in Appendix B just as we did previously.

Summary: Our cutoff, or critical value, for the F statistic for a p level of 0.05 and 2 and 8 degrees of freedom is 4.46.

STEP 5. Calculate the test statistic.

As before, we calculate our test statistic in the fifth step. To start, we have to calculate four sums of squares—one each for between-groups, subjects, within-groups, and total. As before, for each sum of squares, we calculate deviations between two different types of means, square the deviations, and then sum the squared differences. We calculate a squared deviation for *every* score, so for each sum of squares in this example, we'll be summing 15 squared deviations.

As we did with the one-way between-groups ANOVA, let's start with the total sum of squares, SS_{total}. This can be calculated exactly as we calculated it previously:

$$SS_{total} = \Sigma(X - GM)^2 = 2117.732$$

Type of Beer	Rating (X)	($X - GM$)	($X - GM)^2$
Cheap	40	−0.533	0.284
Cheap	42	1.467	2.152
Cheap	30	−10.533	110.944
Cheap	37	−3.533	12.482
Cheap	23	−17.533	307.406
Mid-range	30	−10.533	110.944
Mid-range	45	4.467	19.954
Mid-range	38	−2.533	6.416
Mid-range	32	−8.533	72.812
Mid-range	28	−12.533	157.076
High-end	53	12.467	155.426
High-end	65	24.467	598.634
High-end	64	23.467	550.7
High-end	43	2.467	6.086
High-end	38	−2.533	6.416
$GM = 40.533$			$\Sigma(X - GM)^2 = 2117.732$

Next we calculate the between-groups sum of squares. It also is the same as for a one-way between-groups ANOVA:

$$SS_{between} = \Sigma(M - GM)^2 = 1092.135$$

Type of Beer	Rating (X)	Group Mean	($M - GM$)	($M - GM)^2$
Cheap	40	34.4	−6.133	37.614
Cheap	42	34.4	−6.133	37.614
Cheap	30	34.4	−6.133	37.614
Cheap	37	34.4	−6.133	37.614
Cheap	23	34.4	−6.133	37.614
Mid-range	30	34.6	−5.933	35.200
Mid-range	45	34.6	−5.933	35.200
Mid-range	38	34.6	−5.933	35.200
Mid-range	32	34.6	−5.933	35.200
Mid-range	28	34.6	−5.933	35.200
High-end	53	52.6	12.067	145.613
High-end	65	52.6	12.067	145.613
High-end	64	52.6	12.067	145.613
High-end	43	52.6	12.067	145.613
High-end	38	52.6	12.067	145.613
$GM = 40.533$				$\Sigma(M - GM)^2 = 1092.135$

So far, the calculations of our sums of squares for a one-way within-groups ANOVA have been the same as they were for a one-way between-groups ANOVA. We left the subjects sum of squares and within-groups sum of squares for last. Here is where we see some changes. We want to remove the variability due to participant differences from our estimate of variability. So we're going to calculate the subjects sum of squares separately from the within-groups sum of squares. To do that, we subtract the grand mean from each participant's mean *for all of his scores.* We first have to calculate a mean for each participant across the three conditions. For example, the first participant had ratings of 40 for cheap beers, 30 for mid-range beers, and 53 for high-end beers. This participant's mean is 41.

So, the formula for the subjects sum of squares is:

MASTERING THE FORMULA

11-18: The subjects sum of squares in a one-way within-groups ANOVA is calculated using the following formula: $SS_{subjects} = \Sigma(M_{participant} - GM)^2$. For each score, we subtract the grand mean from that participant's mean for all of his or her scores and square this deviation. (Note that we do not use the scores in any of these calculations. We sum all the squared deviations.)

$$SS_{subjects} = \Sigma(M_{participant} - GM)^2 = 729.738$$

Participant	Type of Beer	Rating (X)	Participant Mean	$(M_{participant} - GM)$	$(M_{participant} - GM)^2$
1	Cheap	40	41	0.467	0.218
2	Cheap	42	50.667	10.134	102.698
3	Cheap	30	44	3.467	12.02
4	Cheap	37	37.333	−3.2	10.24
5	Cheap	23	29.667	−10.866	118.07
1	Mid-range	30	41	0.467	0.218
2	Mid-range	45	50.667	10.134	102.698
3	Mid-range	38	44	3.467	12.02
4	Mid-range	32	37.333	−3.2	10.24
5	Mid-range	28	29.667	−10.866	118.07
1	High-end	53	41	0.467	0.218
2	High-end	65	50.667	10.134	102.698
3	High-end	64	44	3.467	12.02
4	High-end	43	37.333	−3.2	10.24
5	High-end	38	29.667	−10.866	118.07
	GM = 40.533				$\Sigma(M_{participant} - GM)^2 = 729.738$

We only have one sum of squares left to go. To calculate the within-group sum of squares from which we've removed the subjects sum of squares, we take the total sum of squares and subtract the two others that we've calculated so far—the between-groups sum of squares and the subjects sum of squares. The formula is:

MASTERING THE FORMULA

11-19: The within-groups sum of squares for a one-way within-groups ANOVA is calculated using the following formula: $SS_{within} = SS_{total} - SS_{between} - SS_{subjects}$. We subtract the between-groups sum of squares and subjects sum of squares from the total sum of squares.

$$SS_{within} = SS_{total} - SS_{between} - SS_{subjects}$$
$$= 2117.732 - 1092.135 - 729.738 = 295.859$$

We now have enough information to fill in the first three columns of our source table—the source, *SS,* and *df* columns. We'll calculate the rest of the source table as we did for a one-way between-groups ANOVA. For the three sources—between-groups, subjects, and within-groups—we divide the sum of squares by the degrees of freedom to get its variance, *MS.*

$$MS_{between} = \frac{SS_{between}}{df_{between}} = \frac{1092.135}{2} = 546.068$$

$$MS_{subjects} = \frac{SS_{subjects}}{df_{subjects}} = \frac{729.738}{4} = 182.435$$

$$MS_{within} = \frac{SS_{within}}{df_{within}} = \frac{295.859}{8} = 36.982$$

MASTERING THE FORMULA

11-20: We calculate the subjects mean square by dividing its associated sum of squares by its associated degrees of freedom: $MS_{subjects} = \frac{SS_{subjects}}{df_{subjects}}$.

We then calculate two F statistics—one for between-groups and one for subjects. For the between-groups F statistic, we divide its MS by the within-groups MS. For the subjects F statistic, we divide its MS by the within-groups MS.

$$F_{between} = \frac{MS_{between}}{MS_{within}} = \frac{546.068}{36.982} = 14.766$$

$$F_{subjects} = \frac{MS_{subjects}}{MS_{within}} = \frac{182.435}{36.982} = 4.933$$

MASTERING THE FORMULA

11-21: The formula for the subjects F statistic is: $F_{subjects} = \frac{MS_{subjects}}{MS_{within}}$. We divide the subjects mean square by the within-groups mean square.

The completed source table is:

Source	SS	df	MS	F
Between-groups	1092.135	2	546.068	14.766
Subjects	729.738	4	182.435	4.933
Within-groups	295.859	8	36.982	
Total	2117.732	14		

Here is a recap of the formulas used to calculate a one-way within-groups ANOVA.

Source	SS	df	MS	F
Between-groups	$\Sigma(M - GM)^2$	$N_{groups} - 1$	$\frac{SS_{between}}{df_{between}}$	$\frac{MS_{between}}{MS_{within}}$
Subjects	$\Sigma(M_{participant} - GM)^2$	$df_{subjects} = n - 1$	$\frac{SS_{subjects}}{df_{subjects}}$	$\frac{MS_{subjects}}{MS_{within}}$
Within-groups	$SS_{total} - SS_{between} - SS_{subjects}$	$(df_{between})(df_{subjects})$	$\frac{SS_{within}}{df_{within}}$	
Total	$\Sigma(M - GM)^2$	$N_{total} - 1$		

We have calculated two F statistics, but we're really only interested in one. We want to know if there's a statistically significant difference between groups, so we'll look at our between-groups F statistic, 14.766.

Summary: The F statistic associated with the between-groups difference is 14.77.

STEP 6. Make a decision.

This step is identical to that for the one-way between-groups ANOVA. If the F statistic is beyond the critical value, then we can reject the null hypothesis. We cannot, however, know where the difference lies. We can only know that at least two means are different from each other.

Summary: Our F statistic, 14.77, is beyond our critical value, 4.46. We can reject the null hypothesis. It appears that mean ratings of beers differ based on the type of beer in terms of price category—cheap, mid-range, or high-end.

Note that we could choose to calculate p_{rep} for this F statistic. We would use the procedure introduced in earlier chapters in which we use statistical software such as SPSS to determine the specific p values for the F statistic, and then use Microsoft Excel to determine p_{rep}.

MASTERING THE FORMULA

11-22: The formula for effect size for a one-way within-groups ANOVA is $R^2 = \dfrac{SS_{between}}{(SS_{total} - SS_{subjects})}$. We divide the between-groups sum of squares by the difference between the total sum of squares and the subjects sum of squares. We remove the subjects sum of squares so we can determine the variability explained only by between-groups differences.

R^2, the Effect Size for ANOVA

The calculations for R^2 for a one-way within-groups ANOVA and a one-way between-groups ANOVA are similar. As before, the numerator is a measure of the variability that takes into account just the differences among means, $SS_{between}$. The denominator is a bit different. It takes into account the total variability, SS_{total}, but removes the variability due to participant differences across groups, $SS_{subjects}$. This enables us to determine the variability explained only by between-groups differences. The formula is:

$$R^2 = \frac{SS_{between}}{(SS_{total} - SS_{subjects})}$$

EXAMPLE 11.5

Let's apply this to the ANOVA we just conducted. We can use the statistics in the source table shown in the first table on page 287 to calculate R^2:

$$R^2 = \frac{SS_{between}}{(SS_{total} - SS_{subject})} = \frac{1092.135}{(2117.732 - 729.738)} = 0.787$$

The conventions for R^2 are the same as those shown earlier in Table 11-12. This effect size of 0.787 is a large effect indicating that 78.7% of the variability in ratings of beer is explained by price.

Tukey HSD

We noted earlier that we have to conduct a post-hoc test to determine where differences lie. We'll use the same procedure that we used for a one-way between-groups ANOVA, the Tukey HSD test. We need to calculate an HSD for each pair of means, but first, we have to calculate the standard error:

$$s_M = \sqrt{\frac{MS_{within}}{N}} = \sqrt{\frac{36.982}{5}} = 2.720$$

Now that we have standard error, we can calculate HSD for each pair of means.

Cheap beer (34.4) versus mid-range beer (34.6):

$$HSD = \frac{(34.4 - 34.6)}{2.720} = -0.074$$

Cheap beer (34.4) versus high-end beer (52.6):

$$HSD = \frac{(34.4 - 52.6)}{2.720} = -6.691$$

Mid-range beer (34.6) versus high-end beer (52.6):

$$HSD = \frac{(34.6 - 52.6)}{2.720} = -6.618$$

Now we look up our critical value in the q table in Appendix B The numbers of means being compared (levels of the independent variable) are in a row along the top of the q table, in this case 3; and the within-groups degrees of freedom are in a column along the left-hand side, in this case 8. For a p level of 0.05, the cutoff q is 3.73. The sign of our HSD does not matter because the order in which we subtract means is arbitrary. This is a two-tailed test, and any HSD above 3.73 or below -3.73 would be considered statistically significant.

By comparing the HSDs that we calculated above to the critical values, we can see two statistically significant differences between means in this ANOVA, -6.691 and -6.618. It appears that high-end beers elicit higher average ratings than cheap beers and also elicit higher average ratings than mid-range beers. No statistically significant difference is found between cheap beers and mid-range beers.

It's not all that surprising that the expensive beers would come out ahead of the cheap and mid-range beers, but Fallows and his taste-testers were surprised that no observable average difference was found between the cheap beers and the mid-range beers. Fallows's advice to his beer-drinking colleagues? Buy high-end beer "when they want an individual glass of lager to be as good as it can be," but buy cheap beer "at all other times, since it gives the maximum taste and social influence per dollar invested." The mid-range beers? Not worth the money.

As social scientists, however, we should critically examine the research design and, regardless of its merits, call for a replication. In this case, did the darker color of Sam Adams (the beer that received the highest average ratings) give it away as a high-end beer? Did the fact that beers were labeled with letters lead to differences in ratings? For example, because of academic grading systems, A has a positive connotation and F has a negative one. Did the consistent order have an effect? The total amount of alcohol consumed was equivalent to more than two beers over about two hours. Did the later beers suffer in comparison to the earlier ones? Did the testers get more lenient? And the panel of tasters was all male and included mostly Microsoft employees. Would we get different results for female participants or for participants other than tech employees? There's always another study to be done.

CHECK YOUR LEARNING

Reviewing the Concepts
> We use a one-way within-groups ANOVA when we have a nominal independent variable with at least three levels, a scale dependent variable, and participants who experience all levels of the independent variable. It is also called a *repeated-measures ANOVA* because multiple measures are taken on the same participants.

> Because all participants experience all levels of the independent variable, we reduce our within-groups variability by reducing individual differences; each person serves as a control for him- or herself. A possible concern with this design is order effects.

> A one-way within-groups ANOVA uses the same six steps of hypothesis testing that we used for a one-way between-groups ANOVA—with one major exception. We calculate statistics for four sources, rather than three. In addition to between-groups, within-groups, and total, the fourth source is typically called "subjects."

continued on next page

> Although we calculate two F statistics, one for between-groups variability and one for subjects variability, it is usually the between-groups F that we compare to a critical value and about which we draw a conclusion.

> As with other hypothesis tests, it is recommended that we calculate a measure of effect size, R^2.

> As with a one-way between-groups ANOVA, if we are able to reject the null hypothesis in an ANOVA, we're not finished. We must conduct a post-hoc test, such as a Tukey HSD test, to determine exactly which pairs of means are significantly different from one another.

Clarifying the Concepts

11-12 Why is the within-groups variability, or sum of squares, smaller for the within-groups ANOVA compared to the between-groups ANOVA?

Calculating the Statistics

11-13 Calculate the four degrees of freedom for the following groups, assuming a within-groups design:

	Participant 1	Participant 2	Participant 3
Group 1	7	9	8
Group 2	5	8	9
Group 3	6	4	6

a. $df_{between} = N_{groups} - 1$

b. $df_{subjects} = n - 1$

c. $df_{within} = (df_{between})(df_{subjects})$

d. $df_{total} = df_{between} + df_{subjects} + df_{within}$; or $df_{total} = N_{total} - 1$

11-14 Calculate the four sums of squares for the data listed in Check Your Learning 11-13:

a. $SS_{total} = \Sigma(X - GM)^2$

b. $SS_{between} = \Sigma(M - GM)^2$

c. $SS_{subjects} = \Sigma(M_{participant} - GM)^2$

d. $SS_{within} = SS_{total} - SS_{between} - SS_{subjects}$

11-15 Using all of your calculations in Check Your Learning 11-13 and 11-14, perform the simple division to complete an ANOVA source table for these data.

Applying the Concepts

11-16 Let's create a context for the data presented in Check Your Learning 11-13. Suppose a car dealer wants to sell a car by having people test drive it and two other cars in the same class (e.g., midsize sedans). The data from these three groups might represent driving-experience ratings (from 1 = low quality to 10 = high quality) given by drivers after the test drives. Using the F values you calculated above, complete the following:

a. Write hypotheses, in words, for this research.

b. How might you conduct this research such that you would satisfy the fourth assumption of the within-groups ANOVA?

c. Determine the critical value for F and make a decision about the outcome of this research.

d. What follow-up tests are needed, if any?

Solutions to these Check Your Learning questions can be found in Appendix D.

REVIEW OF CONCEPTS

Using the F Distribution with Three or More Samples

The *F statistic* is used when we want to compare more than two means. As with the z and t statistics, the F statistic is calculated by dividing a measure of the differences among sample means (*between-groups variance*) by a measure of variability within the samples (*within–groups variance*). The hypothesis test based on the F statistic is called *analysis of variance (ANOVA)*.

ANOVA offers a solution to the problem of having to run multiple t tests because it allows for multiple comparisons in just one statistical analysis. There are several different types of ANOVA, and each has two descriptors. One indicates the number of independent variables, such as *one-way ANOVA* for one independent variable. The other indicates whether participants are in only one condition (*between-groups ANOVA*) or in every condition (*within-groups ANOVA*). The major assumptions for ANOVA are random selection of participants, normally distributed underlying populations, and *homoscedasticity,* which means that all populations have the same variance. (When the populations do not have the same variance it is called *heteroscedasticity*.) As with previous statistical tests, most real-life analyses do not meet all of these assumptions.

One-Way Between-Groups ANOVA

The one-way between-groups ANOVA uses the six steps of hypothesis testing that we have already learned, but with some modifications, particularly to steps 3 and 5. Step 3 is simpler than with t tests; we only have to state that the comparison distribution is an F distribution and provide the degrees of freedom. In step 5, we calculate the F statistic; a *source table* helps us to keep track of our calculations. The F statistic is a ratio of two different estimates of population variance, both of distributions of scores rather than distributions of means. The denominator, within-groups variance, is similar to the pooled variance of the independent-samples t test; it's basically a weighted average of the variance within each sample. The numerator, between-groups variance, is an estimate based on the difference between the sample means, but it is then inflated to represent a distribution of scores rather than a distribution of means. To perform the calculations for the F statistic we need to calculate the *grand mean*, the mean of every participant in our study, in addition to the means of samples.

A large between-groups variance and a small within-groups variance indicate a small degree of overlap among samples and likely a small degree of overlap among populations. A large between-groups variance divided by a small within-groups variance produces a large F statistic. If the F statistic is beyond a prescribed cutoff, or critical value, then we can reject our null hypothesis. As with other hypothesis tests, it also is recommended that we calculate an effect size—usually R^2—when we conduct an ANOVA.

When we reject the null hypothesis in an ANOVA, we only know that at least one of the means is different from at least one other mean. But we do not know exactly where the differences lie. We must conduct follow-up analyses called *post-hoc tests* to determine where differences lie. The *Tukey HSD test* is one of the most commonly used post-hoc tests.

One-Way Within-Groups ANOVA

We use a one-way within-groups ANOVA (also called a *repeated-measures ANOVA*) when we have one nominal variable with at least three levels and a scale dependent variable, and every participant experiences every level of the independent variable. The one-way within-groups ANOVA uses the same six steps of hypothesis testing that we used for a one-way between-groups ANOVA, except that we calculate statistics for four sources instead of three. We still calculate statistics for the between-groups, within-groups, and total sources, but we also calculate statistics for a fourth source, "subjects." Although we calculate two F statistics, one for our between-groups variability and one for our subjects variability, we compare the between-groups F statistic to a critical value and either reject or fail to reject the null hypothesis.

As with the one-way between-groups ANOVA, we should calculate a measure of effect size, usually R^2, and we should conduct a post-hoc test, such as the Tukey HSD test, if we rejected the null hypothesis.

SPSS®

The one-way ANOVA is used when we wish to make a comparison between three or more groups that all represent different levels of one nominal independent variable. For example, in this chapter, we compared international students in four different academic programs in terms of the importance they placed on the financial aspects of their program when making decisions about whether to enroll. The type of program was a nominal independent variable, and the rating of the financial aspects was a scale dependent variable. To conduct a one-way between-groups ANOVA on SPSS, we have to enter the data so that each participant has one row with all of her or his data. For example, one student would have a score in the first column indicating the type of program, perhaps a 1 for arts and sciences or a 3 for law school, and would have a score in the second column indicating the rating of the importance of financial aspects. The data as they should be entered are visible behind the output on the screenshot shown here.

Then we can instruct SPSS to conduct the ANOVA by selecting **Analyze** → Compare Means → One-Way ANOVA. Now select the variables. The independent variable, Type of

Program, goes in the box marked "Factor," and the dependent variable, Importance of Financial Aspects, goes in the box labeled "Dependent List." To request a post-hoc test to compare the means of the four groups, select "Post Hoc," then "Tukey," and then click "Continue." Click "OK" to run the ANOVA.

On the screenshot, we can see the source table near the top. Notice that the sums of squares, degrees of freedom, mean squares, and F statistic match the ones we calculated earlier. Any slight differences are due to differences in rounding decisions. The last column, titled "Sig.," says .033. This number indicates that the actual p value of this test statistic is just 0.033, which is less than the 0.05 p level typically used in hypothesis testing and an indication that we can reject the null hypothesis. If we wanted, we could use this p value to determine p_{rep}. Below the source table, we can see the output for the post-hoc test. Mean differences with an asterisk are statistically significant at a p level of 0.05. The output here matches the post-hoc test we conducted earlier. There is only one statistically significant difference—the one between the means for the arts and sciences program and the law program.

How It Works

11.1 CONDUCTING AN ANOVA

Irwin and colleagues (2004) are among a growing body of behavioral health researchers who are interested in adherence to medical regimens. These researchers studied adherence to an exercise regimen over one year in post-menopausal women, a time when women are increasingly at risk for medical problems that may be reduced by exercise. Among the many factors that the research team examined was attendance at a monthly group education program that taught tactics to change exercise behavior; the researchers kept attendance and divided participants into three categories based on the number of sessions they attended. (*Note:* The researchers could have kept the data as numbers of sessions, a scale variable, rather than dividing them into categories, a nominal variable.)

Here is an abbreviated version of this study with fictional data points; the means of these data points, however, are the actual means of the study.

<5 sessions: 155, 120, 130

5–8 sessions: 199, 160, 184

9–12 sessions: 230, 214, 195, 209

In this study, the independent variable was attendance, with three levels: <5 sessions, 5–8 sessions, and 9–12 sessions. The dependent variable was number of minutes of exercise per week. How can we analyze these data to determine if there are mean differences? Because we have one nominal independent variable with three between-groups levels and one scale dependent variable, we can conduct a one-way between-groups ANOVA.

Summary of Step 1

Population 1: Post-menopausal women who attended fewer than 5 sessions of a group exercise education program. Population 2: Post-menopausal women who attended 5–8 sessions of a group exercise education program. Population 3: Post-menopausal women who attended 9–12 sessions of a group exercise education program.

The comparison distribution will be an F distribution. The hypothesis test will be a one-way between-groups ANOVA. The data were not selected randomly, so we must generalize only with caution. We do not know if the underlying population distributions are normal, but the sample data do not indicate severe skew. To see if we meet the homoscedasticity assumption, we will check to see if the largest variance is no greater than twice the smallest variance. From the calculations below, we see that the largest variance, 387, is not more than twice the smallest, 208.67, so we have met the homoscedasticity assumption. (The following information is taken from the calculation of SS_{within}.)

Sample	<5	5–8	9–12
Squared deviations	400	324	324
	225	441	4
	25	9	289
	9		
Sum of squares	650	774	626
$N - 1$	2	2	3
Variance	**325**	**387**	**208.67**

Summary of Step 2

Null hypothesis: Post-menopausal women in different categories of attendance at a group exercise education program exercise the same average number of minutes per week—H_0: $\mu_1 = \mu_2 = \mu_3$. Research hypothesis: Post-menopausal women in different categories of attendance at a group exercise education program do not exercise the same average number of minutes per week.

Summary of Step 3

$$df_{between} = N_{groups} - 1 = 3 - 1 = 2$$

$$df_1 = 3 - 1 = 2; df_2 = 3 - 1 = 2; df_3 = 4 - 1 = 3$$

$$df_{within} = 2 + 2 + 3 = 7$$

The comparison distribution will be the F distribution with 2 and 7 degrees of freedom.

Summary of Step 4

The critical F statistic based on a p level of 0.05 is 4.74.

Summary of Step 5

$$df_{total} = 2 + 7 = 9 \text{ or } df_{total} = 10 - 1 = 9$$

$$SS_{total} = \Sigma(X - GM)^2 = 12{,}222.40$$

Sample	X	$(X - GM)$	$(X - GM)^2$
<5	155	−24.6	605.16
$M_{<5} = 135$	120	−59.6	3552.16
	130	−49.6	2460.16
5–8	199	19.4	376.36
$M_{5-8} = 181$	160	−19.6	384.16
	184	4.4	19.36
9–12	230	50.4	2540.16
$M_{9-12} = 212$	214	34.4	1183.36
	195	15.4	237.16
	209	29.4	864.36
	$GM = 179.60$		$SS_{total} = \mathbf{12{,}222.40}$

$$SS_{within} = \Sigma(X - M)^2 = 2050.00$$

Sample	X	$(X - M)$	$(X - M)^2$
<5	155	20	400
$M_{<5} = 135$	120	−15	225
	130	−5	25
5–8	199	18	324
$M_{5-8} = 181$	160	−21	441
	184	3	9
9–12	230	18	324
$M_{9-12} = 212$	214	2	4
	195	−17	289
	209	−3	9
	$GM = 179.60$		$SS_{within} = \mathbf{2050.00}$

$$SS_{between} = \Sigma(M - GM)^2 = 10{,}172.40$$

Sample	X	$(M - GM)$	$(M - GM)^2$
<5	155	−44.6	1989.16
$M_{<5} = 135$	120	−44.6	1989.16
	130	−44.6	1989.16
5–8	199	1.4	1.96
$M_{ed} = 181$	160	1.4	1.96
	184	1.4	1.96
9–12	230	32.4	1049.76
$M_{bus} = 212$	214	32.4	1049.76
	195	32.4	1049.76
	209	32.4	1049.76
	$GM = 179.60$		$SS_{between} = \mathbf{10{,}172.40}$

$$SS_{total} = SS_{within} + SS_{between} \; ; 12{,}222.40 = 2050.00 + 10{,}172.40$$

$$MS_{between} = \frac{SS_{between}}{df_{between}} = \frac{10{,}172.40}{2} = 5086.20$$

$$MS_{within} = \frac{SS_{within}}{df_{within}} = \frac{2050.00}{7} = 292.857$$

$$F = \frac{MS_{between}}{MS_{within}} = \frac{5086.20}{292.857} = 17.37$$

Source	SS	df	MS	F
Between	10,172.40	2	5086.200	**17.37**
Within	2050.00	7	292.857	
Total	12,222.40	9		

Summary of Step 6

Our F statistic, 17.37, is beyond the cutoff of 4.74. We can reject the null hypothesis. It appears that post-menopausal women in different categories of attendance at a group exercise education program do exercise a different average number of minutes per week. However, the results from this ANOVA do not tell us where specific differences lie. The ANOVA only tells us that there is at least one difference between means. We must calculate a post-hoc test to determine exactly what pairs of means are different.

Exercises

Clarifying the Concepts

11.1 What is an ANOVA?

11.2 What do the F distributions allow us to do that the t distributions do not?

11.3 The F statistic is a ratio of between-groups variance and within-groups variance. What are these two types of variance?

11.4 What is the difference between a within-groups (repeated-measures) ANOVA and a between-groups ANOVA?

11.5 What are the three assumptions for a between-groups ANOVA?

11.6 The null hypothesis for ANOVA posits no difference among population means, as in other hypothesis tests, but the research hypothesis in this case is a bit different. Why?

11.7 Why is the F statistic always positive?

11.8 In your own words, define the word *source* as you would use it in everyday conversation. Provide at least two different meanings that might be used. Then define the word as a statistician would use it.

11.9 Explain the concept of *sum of squares.*

11.10 The total sum of squares for a between-groups ANOVA is found by adding what two statistics together?

11.11 What is the grand mean?

11.12 How do we calculate the between-groups sum of squares?

11.13 We typically measure effect size with _____ for a z test or a t test and with _____ for an ANOVA.

11.14 What are Cohen's conventions for interpreting effect size using R^2?

11.15 What does *post-hoc* mean, and when are these tests needed with ANOVA?

11.16 Define the symbols in the following formula:
$$N' = \frac{N_{groups}}{\Sigma(1/N)}$$

11.17 Find the error in the statistics language in each of the following statements about z, t, or F distributions or their related tests. Explain why it is incorrect and provide the correct word.

a. The professor reported the mean and standard error for the final exam in the statistics class.

b. Before we can calculate a t statistic, we must know the population mean and the population standard deviation.

c. The researcher calculated the parameters for her three samples so that she could calculate an F statistic and conduct an ANOVA.

d. For her honors project, Evelyn calculated a z statistic so that she could compare a sample of students who had ingested caffeine and a sample of students who had not ingested caffeine on their video game performance mean scores.

11.18 Find the incorrectly used symbol or symbols in each of the following statements or formulas. For each statement or formula, (i) state which symbol(s) is/are used incorrectly, (ii) explain why the symbol(s) in the original statement is/are incorrect, and (iii) state what symbol(s) *should* be used.

a. When calculating an F statistic, the numerator includes the estimate for the between-groups variance, s.

b. $SS_{between} = (X - GM)^2$

c. $SS_{within} = (X - M)$

d. $F = \sqrt{t}$

11.19 What are the four assumptions for a within-groups ANOVA?

11.20 What are order effects?

11.21 Explain the source of variability called "subjects."

Calculating the Statistics

11.22 Calculate each type of degrees of freedom for the following data, assuming a between-groups design:

Group 1: 11, 17, 22, 15

Group 2: 21, 15, 16

Group 3: 7, 8, 3, 10, 6, 4

Group 4: 13, 6, 17, 27, 20

a. $df_{between}$

b. df_{within}

c. df_{total}

11.23 Calculate each type of degrees of freedom for the following data, assuming a between-groups design:

> 1970: 45, 211, 158, 74
> 1980: 92, 128, 382
> 1990: 273, 396, 178, 248, 374

  a. $df_{between}$

  b. df_{within}

  c. df_{total}

11.24 Using the F table and a p level of 0.05, determine the critical value for the degrees of freedom determined in Exercise 11.22.

11.25 Using the F table and a p level of 0.05, determine the critical value for the degrees of freedom determined in Exercise 11.23.

11.26 Calculate the F statistic, writing the ratio accurately, for each of the following cases:

  a. Between-groups variance is 29.4 and within-groups variance is 19.1.

  b. Within-groups variance is 0.27 and between-groups variance is 1.56.

  c. Between-groups variance is 4595 and within-groups variance is 3972.

11.27 Calculate the F statistic, writing the ratio accurately, for each of the following cases:

  a. Between-groups variance is 321.83 and within-groups variance is 177.24.

  b. Between-groups variance is 2.79 and within-groups variance is 2.20.

  c. Within-groups variance is 41.60 and between-groups variance is 34.45.

11.28 An incomplete one-way, between-groups ANOVA source table is shown below. Compute the missing values.

Source	SS	df	MS	F
Between	191.45	—	47.86	—
Within	104.72	32	—	
Total	—	36		

11.29 An incomplete one-way, between-groups ANOVA source table is shown below. Compute the missing values.

Source	SS	df	MS	F
Between	—	2	—	—
Within	89	11	—	
Total	132	—		

11.30 Calculate a mean for each group and a grand mean for these data from Exercise 11.22.

> Group 1: 11, 17, 22, 15
> Group 2: 21, 15, 16
> Group 3: 7, 8, 3, 10, 6, 4
> Group 4: 13, 6, 17, 27, 20

11.31 Calculate a mean for each group and a grand mean for these data from Exercise 11.23.

> 1970: 45, 211, 158, 74
> 1980: 92, 128, 382
> 1990: 273, 396, 178, 248, 374

11.32 Using the data from Exercise 11.22, calculate each of the following for a between-groups design:

  a. Total sum of squares

  b. Within-groups sum of squares

  c. Between-groups sum of squares

11.33 Using the data from Exercise 11.23, calculate each of the following for a between-groups design:

  a. Total sum of squares

  b. Within-groups sum of squares

  c. Between-groups sum of squares

11.34 Using all of your calculations from Exercises 11.22 and 11.32, perform the simple division to complete an entire ANOVA source table for these data.

11.35 Using all of your calculations from Exercises 11.23 and 11.33, perform the simple division to complete an entire ANOVA source table for these data.

11.36 Compute effect size for the data provided below (from Exercise 11.23), assuming a between-groups design. State how large this effect is in terms of Cohen's conventions.

> 1970: 45, 211, 158, 74
> 1980: 92, 128, 382
> 1990: 273, 396, 178, 248, 374

11.37 Calculate Tukey HSD values for the necessary comparisons following the F statistic you calculated in Exercise 11.34. Remember that this F statistic was based on the data originally presented in Exercise 11.22 and that you worked with in Exercise 11.32.

11.38 Each of the following is a calculated F statistic with its degrees of freedom. Using the F table and a p level of .05, estimate the level of significance for each. You can do this by indicating if its likelihood of occurring is greater than or less than a p level shown on the table.

  a. $F = 4.11$, with 3 $df_{between}$ and 30 df_{within}

  b. $F = 1.12$, with 5 $df_{between}$ and 83 df_{within}

  c. $F = 2.28$, with 4 $df_{between}$ and 42 df_{within}

11.39 Calculate each type of degrees of freedom for the following data, assuming a within-groups design:

	Person			
	1	2	3	4
Level 1 of the IV	7	16	3	9
Level 2 of the IV	15	18	18	13
Level 3 of the IV	22	28	26	29

a. $df_{between} = N_{groups} - 1$

b. $df_{subjects} = n - 1$

c. $df_{within} = (df_{between})(df_{subjects})$

d. $df_{total} = df_{between} + df_{subjects} + df_{within}$, or $df_{total} = N_{total} - 1$

11.40 Calculate the four sum of squares values for the data listed in Exercise 11.39 using the source table from Exercise 11.41.

a. $SS_{total} = \Sigma(X - GM)^2$

b. $SS_{between} = \Sigma(M - GM)^2$

c. $SS_{subjects} = \Sigma(M_{participant} - GM)^2$

d. $SS_{within} = SS_{total} - SS_{between} - SS_{subjects}$

11.41 Using all of your calculations in Exercises 11.39 and 11.40, perform the simple division to complete an ANOVA source table for these data.

11.42 Compute effect size for the data provided in Exercise 11.39—using the source table from Exercise 11.41.

	Person			
	1	2	3	4
Level 1 of the IV	7	16	3	9
Level 2 of the IV	15	18	18	13
Level 3 of the IV	22	28	26	29

11.43 Calculate the Tukey *HSD* statistic for the comparisons between level 1 and level 3, as presented in Exercise 11.39, and based on the *F* statistic you calculated in Exercise 11.41.

Applying the Concepts

11.44 Focusing on coverage of the 2004 U.S. presidential election, Julia R. Fox, a telecommunications professor at Indiana University, wondered if *The Daily Show,* despite its comedy format, was a valid source of news. She coded a number of half-hour episodes of *The Daily Show* as well as a number of half-hour episodes of the network news (Indiana University Media Relations, 2006). Fox reported that the average amounts of "video and audio substance" were not statistically significantly different between the two types of shows. Her analyses are de-

scribed as "second-by-second," so for this exercise, assume that all outcome variables are measures of time.

a. As the study is described, what are the independent and dependent variables? For nominal variables, state the levels.

b. As the study is described, what type of hypothesis test would Fox use?

c. Now imagine that Fox added a third category, a cable news channel such as CNN. Based on this new information, state the independent variable or variables and the levels of any nominal independent variables. What hypothesis test would she use?

11.45 For each of the following situations, state whether the distribution of interest is a *z* distribution, a *t* distribution, or an *F* distribution. Explain your answer.

a. A city employee locates a U.S. Census report that includes the mean and standard deviation for income in the state of Wyoming and then takes a random sample of 100 residents of the city of Cheyenne. He wonders whether residents of Cheyenne earn more, on average, than Wyoming residents as a whole.

b. A researcher studies the effect of different contexts on work interruptions. Using discreet video cameras, she observes employees working in enclosed offices in the workplace, in open cubicles in the workplace, and in home offices.

c. An honors student wondered whether an education in statistics reduced the tendency to believe advertising that cited data. He compared social science majors who had taken statistics and social science majors who had not taken statistics with respect to their responses to an interactive advertising assessment.

11.46 For each of the following situations, state whether the distribution of interest is a *z* distribution, a *t* distribution, or an *F* distribution. Explain your answer.

a. A student reads in her *Introduction to Psychology* textbook that the mean IQ is 100. She asks 10 friends what their IQ scores are (they attend a university that assesses everyone's IQ score) to determine whether her friends are smarter than average.

b. Is the presence of books in the home a marker of a stable family? A social worker counted the number of books on view in the living rooms of all the families he visited over the course of one year. He categorized families into four groups: no books visible, only children's books visible, only adult books visible, and both children's and adult books visible. The department for which he worked had stability ratings for each family based on a number of measures.

c. Which television show leads to more learning? A researcher assessed the vocabularies of a sample of children randomly assigned to watch *Sesame Street* as much as they wanted for a year but not to watch *The Wiggles.* She also assessed the vocabularies of a sample of children randomly assigned to watch *The*

Wiggles as much as they wanted for a year but not to watch *Sesame Street*. She compared the average vocabulary scores for the two groups.

11.47 The *z, t,* and *F* distributions are closely linked. In fact, it is possible to use an *F* distribution in all cases in which a *t* or a *z* could be used.

   a. If you calculated an *F* statistic of 4.22 but you could have used a *t* statistic (i.e., the situation met all criteria for using a *t* statistic), what would the *t* statistic have been? Explain your answer.

   b. If you calculated an *F* statistic of 4.22 but you could have used a *z* statistic, what would the *z* statistic have been? Explain your answer.

   c. If you calculated a *t* statistic of 0.67 but you could have used a *z* statistic, what would the *z* statistic have been? Explain your answer.

   d. Cite two reasons that all three types of distributions (i.e., *z, t,* and *F*) are still in use when we really only need an *F* distribution.

11.48 Catherine Ruby (2006), a doctoral student at New York University, conducted an online survey to ascertain the reasons that foreign students chose to attend graduate school in the United States. One of several dependent variables that she considered was reputation; students were asked to rate the importance in their decision of factors such as the reputation of the institution, the institution and program's academic accreditations, and the reputation of the faculty. Students rated factors on a 1–5 scale, and then all reputation ratings were averaged to form a summary score for each respondent. For each of the following scenarios, state the independent variable with its levels (the dependent variable is reputation in all cases). Then state what kind of an ANOVA she would use.

   a. Ruby compared the importance of reputation among graduate students in different types of programs: arts and sciences, education, law, and business.

   b. Imagine that Ruby followed these graduate students for three years and assessed their rating of reputation once a year.

   c. Ruby compared foreign students working toward a master's, a doctorate, or a professional degree (e.g., MBA) on reputation.

   d. Imagine that Ruby followed foreign students from their master's program to their doctoral program to their post-doctoral fellowship, assessing their ratings of reputation once at each level of their training.

11.49 Do people remember names better under different circumstances? In a fictional study, a cognitive psychologist studied memory for names after a group activity that lasted 20 minutes. Participants were not told that this was a study of memory. After the group activity, participants were asked to name the other group members. The researcher randomly assigned 120 participants to one of three conditions: (1) group members introduced themselves once (one introduction only), (2) group members were introduced by the experimenter and by themselves (two introductions), and (3) group members were introduced by the experimenter and themselves and also wore nametags throughout the group activity (two introductions and nametags).

   a. Identify the type of ANOVA that should be used to analyze the data from this study.

   b. State what the researcher could do to redesign this study so it would be analyzed with a one-way within-groups ANOVA. Be specific.

11.50 Does the black grease beneath football players' eyes really reduce glare or just make them look intimidating? In a variation of a study actually conducted at Yale University, 46 participants placed one of three substances below their eyes: black grease, black antiglare stickers, or petroleum jelly. The researchers assessed eye glare using a contrast chart that gives a value for each participant on a scale measure. Every participant was assessed with each of the three substances, one at a time. Black grease led to a reduction in glare compared with the two other conditions, antiglare stickers or petroleum jelly (DeBroff & Pahk, 2003).

   a. List the independent variable, along with its levels.

   b. What is the dependent variable?

   c. What kind of ANOVA is this?

11.51 Refer to the study described in Exercise 11.50.

   a. What is the first assumption for ANOVA? Is it likely that the researchers met this assumption? Explain your answer.

   b. What is the second assumption for ANOVA? How could the researchers check to see if they had met this assumption? Be specific.

   c. What is the third assumption for ANOVA? How could the researchers check to see if they had met this assumption? Be specific.

11.52 Imagine that your cousin, a high school student, has been assigned to an algebra class based on previous performance. Like many high schools, his high school has three levels of algebra classes: (1) one that includes the standard curriculum plus remedial lessons, (2) one that includes the standard curriculum, and (3) one that includes the standard curriculum plus an advanced component. At the end of the semester, students' performance will be assessed on a statewide standardized mathematics exam. These data will be analyzed using a one-way between-groups ANOVA.

   a. Using this example, explain the concept of between-groups variance.

   b. Using this example, explain the concept of within-groups variance.

c. How would you draw a curve for each distribution (1, 2, and 3) that demonstrates the concepts of between-groups variance and within-groups variance, while also showing what you'd expect these three distributions to look like in comparison with one another?

11.53 Researchers asked 180 U.S. students to identify their political viewpoint as most similar to that of the Republicans, most similar to that of the Democrats, or neither. All three groups then completed a religiosity scale. The researchers wondered whether political orientation affected levels of religiosity, a measure that assesses how religious one is, regardless of the specific religion with which a person identifies.

a. What is the independent variable, and what are its levels?

b. What is the dependent variable?

c. What are the populations and what are the samples?

d. Using this example, explain how you would calculate the F statistic.

11.54 Iranian researchers studied factors affecting patients' likelihood of wearing orthodontic appliances, noting that orthodontics is perhaps the area of health care with the highest need for patient cooperation (Behenam & Pooya, 2006). Among their analyses, they compared students in primary school, junior high school, and high school. The data that follow have almost exactly the same means as they found in their study, but with far smaller samples. The score for each student is his or her daily hours of wearing the orthodontic appliance.

> Primary school: 16, 13, 18
>
> Junior high school: 8, 13, 14, 12
>
> High school: 20, 15, 16, 18

a. What is the independent variable? What are its levels?

b. What is the dependent variable?

c. Conduct all six steps of hypothesis testing for a one-way between-groups ANOVA.

d. How would you report the statistics in a journal article?

11.55 In Chapter 10, we introduced a study by Steele and Pinto (2006) that examined whether people's level of trust in their direct supervisor was related to their level of agreement with a policy supported by that leader. Steele and Pinto found that the extent to which subordinates agreed with their supervisor was related to trust and showed no relation to gender, age, time on the job, or length of time working with the supervisor. Let's assume we used a scale that sorted employees into three groups: low trust, moderate trust, and high trust in supervisors. We have presented fictional data regarding level of agreement with a leader's decision for these three groups. The scores presented are the level of agreement with a decision made by a leader, from 1, the least agreement, to 40, the highest level of agreement. (*Note:* These fictional data are different from those presented in Chapter 10.)

> Employees with low trust in their leader: 9, 14, 11, 18
>
> Employees with moderate trust in their leader: 14, 35, 23
>
> Employees with high trust in their leader: 27, 33, 21, 34

a. What is the independent variable? What are its levels?

b. What is the dependent variable?

c. Conduct all six steps of hypothesis testing for a one-way between-groups ANOVA.

11.56 In Exercise 11.54, you conducted an ANOVA on the use of orthodontics appliances by three age groups. Conduct a Tukey *HSD* test. What did you learn by conducting these analyses?

11.57 In Exercise 11.55, you conducted an ANOVA on data regarding employees' trust in supervisors. Conduct a Tukey *HSD* test. What did you learn?

11.58 In How It Works 11.1, we conducted a one-way between-groups ANOVA on an abbreviated data set from research by Irwin and colleagues (2004) on adherence to an exercise regimen. Participants were asked to attend a monthly group education program to help them change their exercise behavior. Attendance was taken and participants were divided into three categories: those who attended fewer than 5 sessions, those who attended between 5 and 8 sessions, and those who attended between 9 and 12 sessions. The dependent variable was number of minutes of exercise per week. Here are the data once again:

> <5 sessions: 155, 120, 130
>
> 5–8 sessions: 199, 160, 184
>
> 9–12 sessions: 230, 214, 195, 209

a. What conclusion did you draw in step 6 of the ANOVA? Why could you not be more specific in your conclusion? That is, why is an additional test necessary when our ANOVA is statistically significant?

b. Conduct a Tukey *HSD* test for this example. State your conclusions based on this test. Show all calculations.

c. If we did not reject the null hypothesis for every possible pair of means, then why can't we conclude that the two means are the same?

11.59 In Exercise 11.54 we used a one-way between-groups ANOVA to explore patients' likelihood of wearing orthodontic appliances. The researchers compared students in primary school, junior high school, and high school. The data presented were hours spent wearing the appliance per day.

> Primary school: 16, 13, 18
> Junior high school: 8, 13, 14, 12
> High school: 20, 15, 16, 18

a. Calculate the appropriate measure of effect size for this sample.

b. Based on Cohen's conventions, is this a small, medium, or large effect size?

c. Why is it useful to have this information in addition to the results of a hypothesis test?

11.60 Two samples of students, one comprised of social science majors and one comprised of students with other majors, completed the CFC. The accompanying tables include the output from software for an independent-samples t test and a one-way between-groups ANOVA on these data.

tual p level to a cutoff p level such as 0.05 to decide whether to reject the null hypothesis. Explain what this "sig." value means.

c. In the ANOVA, the column titled "Mean Square" includes the estimates of variance. Show how the F statistic was calculated from two types of variance. (*Hint:* Look at the far left column to determine which estimate of variance is which.)

d. Looking at the table titled "Group Statistics," how many participants were in each sample?

e. Looking at the table titled "Group Statistics," what is the mean CFC score for the social science majors?

11.61 Based on your knowledge of the relation between the t and F distributions, complete the accompanying software output tables on page 301. The table for the independent-samples t test and the table for the one-way between-groups ANOVA were calculated using the identical fictional data.

Independent Samples Test

	t	Df	Sig. (2-tailed)	Mean Difference	Standard Error Difference	95% Confidence Interval of the Difference	
						Lower	Upper
CFC Scores	-.650	28	.521	-.17500	.26930	-.72664	.37664

ANOVA

CFC Scores

	Sum of Squares	df	Mean Square	F	Sig.
Between Groups	.204	1	.204	.422	.521
Within Groups	13.538	28	.483		
Total	13.742	29			

Group Statistics

Major		N	Mean	Standard Deviation	Standard Error Mean
CFC Scores	Other	10	3.2000	.88819	.28087
	Social Science	20	3.3750	.58208	.13016

a. Demonstrate that the results of the independent-samples t test and the one-way between-groups ANOVA are the same. (*Hint:* Find the t statistic for the t test and the F statistic for the ANOVA.)

b. In statistical software output, "Sig." refers to the actual p level of the statistic. We can compare the ac-

a. What is the F statistic? Show your calculations. (*Hint:* The "Mean Square" column includes the two estimates of variance used to calculate the F statistic.)

b. What is the t statistic? Show your calculations. (*Hint:* Use the F statistic that you calculated in part (a).)

c. In statistical software output, "Sig." refers to the actual p level of the statistic. We can compare the actual p level to a cutoff p level such as 0.05 to decide whether to reject the null hypothesis. For the t test, what is the "Sig."? Explain how you determined this. (*Hint:* Would we expect that the "Sig." for the independent-samples t test be the same as or different from that for the one-way between-groups ANOVA?)

d. In Exercise 11.43, you calculated a Tukey *HSD* test comparing fear in response to the small versus large dog. What can you conclude based on this statistic? (Note that these are the data for Exercises 11.39 through 11.43, on which you've already calculated several statistics. We've now given these data a context.)

11.63 Commercials for chewing gum make claims about how long the flavor will last. In fact, some commercials pres-

Independent Samples Test

			t-test for Equality of Means				
	T	Df	Sig. (2-tailed)	Mean Difference	Standard Error Difference	95% Confidence Interval of the Difference	
						Lower	Upper
GPA		82		-.28251	.12194	-.52508	-.03993

ANOVA

GPA	Sum of Squares	Df	Mean Square	F	Sig.
Between Groups	4.623	1	4.623		.005
Within Groups	42.804	82	.522		
Total	47.427	83			

11.62 Imagine a researcher wanted to assess people's fear of dogs as a function of the size of the dog. He assessed fear among people who indicate they were afraid of dogs, using a 30-point scale from 0 (no fear) to 30 (extreme fear). The researcher exposed each participant to three different dogs, a small dog that weighed 20 pounds, a medium-sized dog weighing 55 pounds, and a large dog weighing 110 pounds, assessing the fear level after each exposure. Here are some hypothetical data; note that these are the data from Exercises 11.39 through 11.43, on which you have already calculated several statistics:

	Person			
	1	2	3	4
Small dog	7	16	3	9
Medium dog	15	18	18	13
Large dog	22	28	26	29

a. State your null and research hypotheses.

b. Consider whether the assumptions of random selection and order effects were met.

c. In Exercise 11.42, you calculated the effect size for these data. Interpret what this statistic tells us.

ent the idea that the flavor lasts too long, affecting sales and profit. Let's put these claims to a test. Imagine a student decides to compare four different gums using five participants. Each randomly selected participant was asked to chew a different piece of gum each day for four days, such that at the end of the four days, each participant had chewed all four types of gum. The order of the gums was randomly determined for each participant. After two hours of chewing, participants recorded the intensity of flavor from 1 (not intense) to 9 (very intense). Here are some hypothetical data:

	Person				
	1	2	3	4	5
Gum 1	4	6	3	4	4
Gum 2	8	6	9	9	8
Gum 3	5	6	7	4	5
Gum 4	2	2	3	2	1

a. Conduct all six steps of the hypothesis test.

b. Are any additional tests warranted? Explain your answer.

Terms

Formulas

$df_{between} = N_{groups} - 1$ (p. 263)

$df_{within} = df_1 + df_2 + \ldots + df_{last}$

(in which df_1, df_2, etc., are the degrees of freedom, $N - 1$, for each sample)

[formula for a one-way between-groups ANOVA] (p. 263)

$df_{total} = df_{between} + df_{within}$

[formula for a one-way between-groups ANOVA] (p. 268)

$df_{total} = N_{total} - 1$ (p. 268)

$GM = \dfrac{\Sigma(X)}{N_{total}}$ (p. 269)

$SS_{total} = \Sigma(X - GM)^2$ (p. 270)

$SS_{within} = \Sigma(X - M)^2$

[formula for a one-way between-groups ANOVA] (p. 271)

$SS_{between} = \Sigma(M - GM)^2$ (p. 272)

$SS_{total} = SS_{within} + SS_{between}$

[alternate formula for a one-way between-groups ANOVA] (p. 272)

$MS_{between} = \dfrac{SS_{between}}{df_{between}}$ (p. 273)

$MS_{within} = \dfrac{SS_{within}}{df_{within}}$ (p. 273)

$F = \dfrac{MS_{between}}{MS_{within}}$ (p. 274)

$R^2 = \dfrac{SS_{between}}{SS_{total}}$ [formula for a one-way between-groups ANOVA] (p. 275)

$HSD = \dfrac{(M_1 - M_2)}{s_M}$, for any two sample means (p. 277)

$s_M = \sqrt{\dfrac{MS_{within}}{N}}$, if equal sample sizes (p. 277)

$N' = \dfrac{N_{groups}}{\Sigma(1/N)}$ (p. 278)

$s_M = \sqrt{\dfrac{MS_{within}}{N'}}$, if unequal sample sizes (p. 278)

$df_{subjects} = n - 1$ (p. 284)

$df_{within} = (df_{between})(df_{subjects})$

[formula for a one-way within-groups ANOVA] (p. 284)

$df_{total} = df_{between} + df_{subjects} + df_{within}$

[formula for a one-way within-groups ANOVA] (p. 284)

$SS_{subjects} = \Sigma(M_{participant} - GM)^2$ (p. 286)

$SS_{within} = SS_{total} - SS_{between} - SS_{subjects}$.

[formula for a one-way within-groups ANOVA] (p. 286)

$MS_{subjects} = \dfrac{SS_{between}}{df_{between}}$ (p. 287)

$MS_{subjects} = \dfrac{SS_{subjects}}{df_{subjects}}$ (p. 287)

$F_{subjects} = \dfrac{MS_{subjects}}{MS_{within}}$ (p. 287)

$R^2 = \dfrac{SS_{between}}{(SS_{total} - SS_{subjects})}$ [formula for a one-way within-groups ANOVA] (p. 288)

Symbols

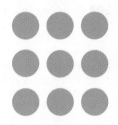

Two-Way ANOVA

BEFORE YOU GO ON

- You should be able to conduct and interpret a one-way ANOVA (Chapter 11).

- You should understand the concept of effect size and the measure of effect size for ANOVA, R^2 (Chapter 11).

A Surprising Interaction
An interaction occurs when two independent variables combine to produce something completely new. In this case, the effect of the normal advertising of Mars candy bars combined with media coverage of the Mars Pathfinder to produce an unexpected increase in candy sales.

In 1997, worldwide media attention was focused on NASA's Mars Pathfinder mission. Because of this event, the Mars candy bar company caught a lucky break and its sales shot up (White, 1997). Here's the funny thing: the Mars candy bar is named after the founder of the company, Forrest Mars, not the planet Mars. But the name association between the candy bar and the planet demonstrates how priming one mental association can unconsciously influence what appears to be an unrelated behavior.

Market researchers wanted to know if priming other types of environmental cues could also influence how people evaluated a consumer product. So researchers conducted several experiments in which students were led to believe they were participating in an advertising campaign for a new digital music player named "ePlay" (Berger & Fitzsimons, 2008).

In one experiment, students were divided into two groups: a dorm with food trays in the dining hall and a dorm without food trays in the dining hall. This was the first independent variable. Students also were randomly assigned to learn one of two different advertising slogans, the second independent variable. One slogan was "Luggage carries your gear, ePlay carries what you want to hear." The other slogan was "Dinner is carried by a tray, music is carried by ePlay." In other words, researchers set up an experiment with two independent variables. The dependent variable was how highly students rated the "ePlay."

With two independent variables and one dependent variable, the experiment contains three comparisons that might influence a consumer's product evaluation: (1) the environmental priming cue (dormitory trays versus no dormitory trays), (2) the advertising slogan the students learned (the luggage–related slogan versus the tray–related slogan), and (3) the combined effects of the environmental cue *and* the advertising slogan. In this study, researchers discovered that the combined effects of the two variables (the environmental cue *and* the advertising slogan) were the most important influence on how highly students rated ePlay. Students who learned the tray–related advertising slogan rated ePlay more highly, on average, if they ate in dining halls that used dormitory trays, an effect that did not occur among students who learned the luggage–related advertising slogan. Priming works!

The two variables combined to influence the dependent variable in a unique way. In this chapter, we examine a hypothesis test that tests for the presence of combined effects, also called *interactions. An* **interaction** *occurs when two or more independent variables have an effect in combination that we do not see when we examine each independent variable*

> ▪ A statistical **interaction** occurs in a factorial design when the two independent variables have an effect in combination that we do not see when we examine each independent variable on its own.
>
> ▪ A **two-way ANOVA** is a hypothesis test that includes two nominal independent variables, regardless of their numbers of levels, and a scale dependent variable.
>
> ▪ A **factorial ANOVA** is a statistical analysis used with one scale dependent variable and at least two nominal independent variables (also called *factors*); also called a *multifactorial ANOVA.*
>
> ▪ **Factor** is a term used to describe an independent variable in a study with more than one independent variable.

on its own. In this chapter, we learn about interactions in relation to a research design that has *two* nominal independent variables, one scale dependent variable, and a between-groups design. We learn the different types of effects that can be explored in a two-way analysis of variance (ANOVA), how the six steps of hypothesis testing apply to this statistical test, and how to calculate an effect size for each of the effects.

Two-Way ANOVA

Media coverage of NASA's mission to the planet Mars primed people to buy more Mars candy bars than usual. Using trays in the dining hall primed students to be more receptive to an advertising slogan that mentioned dining hall trays. Our buying decisions, and many other behaviors, can be influenced by multiple variables, so we need a way to measure the interactive effects of multiple variables.

A two-way ANOVA allows us to compare levels from two independent variables plus the joint effects of those two variables. *A **two-way ANOVA** is a hypothesis test that includes two nominal independent variables, regardless of their numbers of levels, and a scale dependent variable.* We can have ANOVAs with more than two independent variables. As the number of independent variables increases, the number increases in the name of the ANOVA—three-way, four-way, five-way, and so on. Table 12-1 shows a range of possibilities for naming ANOVAs. Regardless of the number of independent variables, we can have different research designs. As with other hypothesis tests, a between-groups design is one in which every participant is in only one condition, and a within-groups design is one in which every participant is in all conditions. A mixed design is one in which at least one of the independent variables is between-groups and at least one is within-groups. In this chapter, we focus on the ANOVA that uses the second adjective from column 1 and the first adjective from column 2: the two-way between-groups ANOVA.

There is a catch-all phrase for two-way, three-way, and higher-order ANOVAs; any ANOVA with at least two independent variables can be called a ***factorial ANOVA***, *a statistical analysis used with one scale dependent variable and at least two nominal independent variables* (also called *factors*). This is also called a *multifactorial ANOVA*. **Factor** *is another word used to describe an independent variable in a study with more than one independent variable.*

In this section, we learn more about the situations in which we use a two-way ANOVA, as well as the language that is used in reference to this type of hypothesis test. Then, we talk about the three effects that we are examining when we conduct a two-way ANOVA.

TABLE 12-1. How to Name an ANOVA

ANOVAs are typically described by two adjectives, one from the first column and one from the second. We always have one descriptor from each column. So, we could have a one-way between-groups ANOVA or a one-way within-groups ANOVA, a two-way between-groups ANOVA or a two-way within-groups ANOVA, and so on. If at least one independent variable is between-groups and at least one is within-groups, it is a mixed-design ANOVA.

Number of Independent Variables: Pick One	Participants in One or All Samples: Pick One	Always Follows Descriptors
One-way	Between-groups	ANOVA
Two-way	Within-groups	
Three-way	Mixed-design	

Why We Use Two-Way ANOVA

To understand the benefits of a two-way ANOVA, let's consider a specific example. Since the mid-1990s, numerous studies (e.g., Bailey & Dresser, 2004; Mitchell, 1999) have documented the potential for grapefruit juice to increase the blood levels of certain medications, sometimes to toxic levels, by boosting the absorption of one or more of the active ingredients. Even scarier, this potentially life-threatening increase cannot be predicted for a given individual; it is found only by trial and error. For that reason, many physicians suggest that patients who take a wide range of medications (from some blood pressure drugs to many antidepressants) avoid grapefruit juice entirely. One commonly used anticholesterol drug whose effect is moderately boosted, sometimes dangerously, by the consumption of grapefruit juice is Lipitor (e.g., Bellosta, Paoletti, & Corsini, 2004). Let's use this particular interaction to understand how a two-way ANOVA gives us much more information with far less effort and expense.

EXAMPLE 12.1

Let's say that an investigator, Dr. Goldstein, wanted to know how to treat cholesterol but only knew how to analyze hypothesis tests that used one independent variable, the one-way ANOVA that we learned about in Chapter 11. She would have to conduct one study to compare the effect of Lipitor on cholesterol levels with the effect of another drug or a placebo. Then she would have to conduct a second study to compare the effect of grapefruit juice on cholesterol levels with that of another beverage or with no beverage, a study that might not even make much sense; after all, no one is predicting grapefruit juice on its own to be a treatment for high cholesterol. So how could she discover whether Lipitor works differently when combined with grapefruit juice?

A single study simultaneously examining medications like Lipitor *and* beverages like grapefruit juice is more efficient than two studies examining each independent variable individually. Two-way ANOVAs allow researchers to examine both hypotheses with the resources, time, and energy of a single study. But a two-way ANOVA yields even more information than two separate experiments.

Specifically, a two-way ANOVA allows researchers to explore exactly what Dr. Goldstein wanted to explore: interactions. Does the effect of some medications, but not others, depend on the particular levels of another independent variable, the beverages that accompany them? A two-way ANOVA can examine (1) the effect of Lipitor versus other medications, (2) the effect of grapefruit juice versus other beverages, *and* (3) the ways in which a drug and a juice might combine to create some entirely new, and often unexpected, effect.

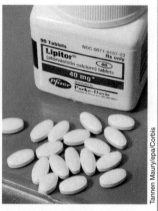

The Perils of Grapefruit Juice Studies have demonstrated that grapefruit juice (a level of one independent variable) can interact with many common medications (levels of a second independent variable) and cause higher levels of active ingredients (the dependent variable) to be absorbed into the bloodstream. The medical journals that physicians read report the results of such two-way ANOVAs because interactions have the potential to be toxic. This is why some physicians recommend that patients who take certain medications avoid grapefruit juice entirely.

The More Specific Vocabulary of Two-Way ANOVAs

Every ANOVA, we learned, has two descriptors, one indicating the number of independent variables and one indicating the research design. Many researchers expand the first descriptor to provide even more information about the independent variables. Let's consider these expanded descriptors in the context of Dr. Gold-

---

TABLE 12-2. Interactions with Grapefruit Juice

A two-way ANOVA allows researchers to examine two independent variables, as well as the ways in which they might interact, simultaneously.

	Lipitor (L)	Zocor (Z)	Placebo (P)
Grapefruit Juice (G)	L & G	Z & G	P & G
Water (W)	L & W	Z & W	P & W

---

stein's research. Were she to conduct just one study that examined both medication and beverage, she'd assign each participant to one level of medication (perhaps Lipitor, another cholesterol medication such as Zocor, or a placebo) *and* to one level of beverage (perhaps grapefruit juice or water). This research design is shown in Table 12-2.

When we draw the design of a study, such as in Table 12-2, we call each box of the design a **cell**, *a box that depicts one unique combination of levels of the independent variables in a factorial design.* When cells contain numbers, they are usually means of the scores of all participants who were assigned to that combination of levels. In Dr. Goldstein's study, participants are assigned to one of the six cells. Each participant is randomly assigned to one of the three levels of the variable medication: Lipitor, Zocor, or placebo. Each level of medication is in one column of the table of cells.

Each participant is *also* assigned to one of the two levels of the variable beverage: grapefruit juice or water. Each level of beverage is in one row of the table of cells. A participant might be assigned to take Lipitor and grapefruit juice (upper-left cell), placebo and water (lower-right cell), or any of the other four combinations. In this case, there are two independent variables, or factors: medication and beverage. Medication, in the columns of the table, has three levels, and beverage, in the rows of the table, has two levels.

This leads us to the new ANOVA vocabulary. Instead of the descriptor *two-way,* many researchers refer to an ANOVA with this arrangement of cells as a *3 × 2 ANOVA* (pronounced "three by two," not "three times two"). As with the *two-way* descriptor, the ANOVA is described with a second adjective—usually *between-groups* or *within-groups.* Because participants would receive only one medication and only one beverage, the hypothesis test for this design could be called either a *two-way between-groups ANOVA* or a *3 × 2 between-groups ANOVA.* (An added benefit to the method of naming ANOVAs by the numbers of levels in each independent variable is the ease of calculating the total number of cells. Simply multiply the levels of the independent variables—the number of rows by the number of columns. In this case, the 3 × 2 ANOVA would have (3 × 2) = 6 cells.)

Two Main Effects and an Interaction

Two-way ANOVAs produce *three* F statistics: one for the first independent variable, one for the second independent variable, and one for the interaction between the two independent variables. The F statistics for each of the two independent variables are referred to as *main effects. A **main effect** occurs in a factorial design when one of the independent variables has an influence on the dependent variable.* We evaluate whether there is a main effect by disregarding the influence of any other independent variables in the study—we temporarily pretend that the other variable doesn't exist.

▦ A **cell** is a box that depicts one unique combination of levels of the independent variables in a factorial design.

▦ A **main effect** occurs in a factorial design when one of the independent variables has an influence on the dependent variable.

So, with two independent variables, Dr. Goldstein would have two possibilities for a main effect. For example, after testing her participants in a two-way ANOVA, she might find a main effect of "type of medication," and she would test for that main effect by temporarily pretending that the variable beverage hasn't even been included in the study. For example, Lipitor and Zocor might both work better than placebo at lowering cholesterol. That's the first F statistic. She also might find a main effect of "beverage," and she would test for that main effect by temporarily pretending that the variable type of medication hasn't even been included in the study. For example, drinking grapefruit juice may reduce cholesterol, at least as compared to water. That's the second F statistic.

> **MASTERING THE CONCEPT**
>
> **12-1:** In a two-way ANOVA, we test three different effects—two main effects, one for each independent variable, and one interaction, the joint effect of the two independent variables.

The third F statistic in a two-way ANOVA has the potential to be the most interesting because it is complicated by multiple, interacting variables. As we discussed earlier, an interaction occurs when the effect of one independent variable on the dependent variable depends on the particular level of the other independent variable. For example, Dr. Goldstein might find that both Lipitor and Zocor (but not placebo) have more extreme effects on cholesterol when taken in combination with grapefruit juice versus water. In other words, the presence of the grapefruit juice changes the effects of Lipitor and Zocor, but not placebo.

Each of the three F statistics has its own between-groups sum of squares (SS), degrees of freedom (df), mean square (MS), and critical value, but they all share a within-groups mean square (MS_{within}). The source table is shown in Table 12-3. The symbols in the body of the table are replaced by the specific values of these statistics in an actual source table.

TABLE 12-3. An Expanded Source Table

This source table is the framework into which we would place the calculations for the two-way between-groups ANOVA with independent variables of medication and beverage. It tells three stories: the two main effects are listed first, then the interaction.

Source	SS	df	MS	F
Medication	$SS_{medication}$	$df_{medication}$	$MS_{medication}$	$F_{medication}$
Beverage	$SS_{beverage}$	$df_{beverage}$	$MS_{beverage}$	$F_{beverage}$
Medication × beverage	$SS_{medication \times beverage}$	$df_{medication \times beverage}$	$MS_{medication \times beverage}$	$F_{medication \times beverage}$
Within	SS_{within}	df_{within}	MS_{within}	
Total	SS_{total}	df_{total}		

CHECK YOUR LEARNING

Reviewing the Concepts

> Factorial ANOVAs are used with multiple independent variables because they allow us to examine several hypotheses in a single study and explore interactions.

> Factorial ANOVAs are often referred to by the levels of their independent variables (e.g., 2 × 2) rather than the number of independent variables (e.g., two-way), and sometimes the independent variables are called *factors*.

> Each unique combination of levels of the independent variables is represented by a cell in the visual depiction of factorial ANOVAs.

> A two-way ANOVA has two main effects (one for each independent variable) and one interaction (the combined influence of both variables). Each effect and interaction has its own set of statistics, including its own F statistic, displayed in an expanded source table.

Clarifying the Concepts

12-1 What is a factorial ANOVA?

12-2 What is an interaction?

Calculating the Statistics

12-3 Determine how many factors are in each of the following designs:

    a. Three diet programs and two exercise programs are combined to assess their impact on weight loss.

    b. Three diet programs, two exercise programs, and three different personal metabolism types are combined to determine their impact on weight loss.

    c. The effect of gift certificate value ($15, $25, $50, and $100) on the amount people spend over that value is investigated.

    d. The effect of gift certificate value ($15, $25, $50, and $100) and store quality (low-end versus high-end) on consumer overspending is investigated.

Applying the Concepts

12-4 Adam Alter, a graduate student at Princeton University, and his advisor, Daniel Oppenheimer, studied whether names of stocks affected selling prices (Alter & Oppenheimer, 2006). They found that stocks with pronounceable ticker-code names, like "BAL," tended to sell at higher prices than did stocks with unpronounceable names, like "BDL." They examined this effect one day, one week, six months, and one year after the stock was offered for sale. The effect was strongest one day after the stock was initially offered.

    a. What are the "participants" in this study?

    b. What are the independent variables and what are their levels?

    c. What is the dependent variable?

    d. Using the new descriptors in Table 12-1, what would you call the hypothesis test that would be used for this study?

    e. Using the new descriptors from page 307, what would you call the hypothesis test (i.e., statistical analysis) that would be used for this study?

Solutions to these Check Your Learning questions can be found in Appendix D.

    f. How many cells are there? Demonstrate how you calculated this answer.

Understanding Interactions in ANOVA

Media attention about NASA's mission to Mars helped sell more Mars candy bars. Media attention primed the word *Mars,* which made Mars candy bars come to mind more easily. Priming, of course, would not increase sales for everybody— there would be exceptions to the rule. For example, diabetics who never eat chocolate, people who hate Mars bars, and people living someplace where they could not purchase Mars bars would all represent interacting exceptions to the rule that priming increases sales of Mars bars. Another kind of exception to the rule occurs when sales increase in the absence of priming. Halloween, for example, temporarily increases sales of Mars bars well above the norm, and sales of Mars candy

■ A **quantitative interaction** is an interaction in which one independent variable exhibits a strengthening or weakening of its effect at one or more levels of the other independent variable, but the direction of the initial effect does not change.

■ A **qualitative interaction** is a particular type of quantitative interaction of two (or more) independent variables in which one independent variable reverses its effect depending on the level of the other independent variable.

bars just before this holiday would increase whether priming is taking place or not. In other words, any subgroup that represents a significant exception in any direction to the general trend in the data might indicate a statistical interaction. An interaction occurs when the effect of one variable depends on the specific level of another variable.

In this section, we explore the concept of an interaction in a two-way ANOVA in more depth. We look at a real-life example of an interaction, then introduce two different types of interaction, quantitative and qualitative, that will help us to better interpret interactions when they occur in our own research.

Interactions and Public Policy

Hurricane Katrina demonstrates the importance of understanding interactions. First, the hurricane itself was an interaction among several weather variables. The devastating effects of the hurricane depended on particular levels of other variables, such as where it made landfall and the speed of its movement across the Gulf of Mexico. We can't understand Hurricane Katrina at a meteorological level without understanding the concept of interactions.

Interactions are relevant for the people affected by Hurricane Katrina as well. For example, we would think that Hurricane Katrina would have been universally bad for the health of all those displaced people—a main effect of a hurricane on health care. However, there were exceptions to that rule, and three researchers from the Tulane University School of Public Health and Tropical Diseases in New Orleans proposed a startling interaction regarding the effects of the hurricane on health care for pregnant women (Buekens, Xiong, & Harville, 2006).

There were women who gave birth in the squalor of the Superdome or in alleys while waiting for rescuers. When it comes to pregnant women, the first priority of disaster relief agencies is to provide obstetrical and neonatal care. Massive relief efforts sometimes mean that access to care for pregnant women is actually improved in the aftermath of a disaster. Of course, the quality of health care certainly didn't improve for everybody, which means that an interaction was involved. So we could create a hypothesis for why the quality of health care might improve for pregnant women in the aftermath of a disaster, while it becomes worse for almost everyone else. In the language of two-way ANOVA, we could hypothesize that the effect of a disaster (one independent variable with two levels: disaster versus no disaster) on the quality of health care (the dependent variable) depends on the type of health care needed (the second independent variable, also with two levels: obstetrics /neonatal versus all other types of health care).

Why might health care improve for pregnant women but not for others? Pregnant women are among the most vulnerable people during a natural catastrophe, so perhaps they were given more attention by the rescue workers. Or perhaps the pregnant women were more assertive in seeking help. Or both. At this point, we don't know how to explain the researchers' findings, so we can only hypothesize. But in our complicated world, the influence of one variable usually depends on a specific level of another variable. Because we need to understand the logic of interactions to understand complicated circumstances, we need to learn how to interpret interactions.

Interpreting Interactions

The two-way between-groups ANOVA allows us to separate the between-groups variance into three finer categories: the two main effects, one for each independent variable, and an interaction effect. The interaction effect is a blended effect resulting from the interaction between the two independent variables; it is not a separate individual variable. The interaction effect is like mixing chocolate syrup into a glass of milk; the two foods blend into something familiar yet new.

Quantitative Interactions Two terms often used to describe interactions are *quantitative* and *qualitative* (e.g., Newton & Rudestam, 1999). *A **quantitative interaction** is an interaction in which one independent variable exhibits a strengthening or weakening of its effect at one or more levels of the other independent variable, but the direction of the initial effect does not change.* More specifically, the effect of one independent variable is modified in the presence of another independent variable.

A **qualitative interaction** *is a particular type of quantitative interaction of two (or more) independent variables in which one independent variable reverses its effect depending on the level of the other independent variable.* In a qualitative interaction, the effect of one variable doesn't just become stronger or weaker; it actually reverses direction in the presence of another variable. Let's first examine the quantitative interaction.

> ◀ **MASTERING THE CONCEPT**
>
> **12-2:** Researchers often describe interactions with one of two terms—*quantitative* or *qualitative*. In a quantitative interaction, the effect of one independent variable is strengthened or weakened at one or more levels of the other independent variable, but the direction of the initial effect does not change. In a qualitative interaction, one independent variable actually reverses its effect depending on the level of the other independent variable.

EXAMPLE 12.2

Our grapefruit juice example is a helpful illustration of a quantitative interaction. Lipitor and Zocor lead to elevations of some liver enzymes in combination with water, but the absorption levels are even higher with grapefruit juice. This effect is not seen with placebo, which has an equal effect regardless of beverage. The effects of Lipitor and Zocor, therefore, depend on what type of beverage they are paired with, and the effect of placebo does not. Let's invent some numbers to demonstrate this. The numbers in the cells in Table 12-4 don't represent actual absorption levels; rather, they are numbers that are easy for us to work with in our understanding of interactions. For this exercise, we will consider every difference between numbers to be statistically significant. (Of course, if we really conducted this study, we would conduct the two-way ANOVA to determine exactly which effects were statistically significant.)

First, we'll consider main effects; then we'll consider the overall pattern that constitutes the interaction. If there is a significant interaction, we then ignore any significant main effects. The significant interaction supersedes any significant main effects.

Table 12-4 includes mean absorption levels for the six cells of the study. It also includes numbers in the margins of the table, to the right of and below the cells. The

TABLE 12-4. A Table of Means

We use a table to display the cell and marginal means so that we can interpret any main effects.

	Lipitor (L)	Zocor (Z)	Placebo (P)	
Grapefruit Juice (G)	60	60	3	41
Water (W)	30	30	3	21
	45	45	3	

■ A **marginal mean** is the mean of a row or a column in a table that shows the cells of a study with a two-way ANOVA design.

numbers in the margins are also means, but for every participant in a given row or in a given column. As you might expect, each of these is called a ***marginal mean***, *the mean of a row or a column in a table that shows the cells of a study with a two-way ANOVA design.* In Table 12-4, for example, the mean across from the row for grapefruit juice, 41, is the mean absorption level of every participant who was assigned to drink grapefruit juice, regardless of the medication level to which he or she was assigned. The mean below the column for placebo, 3, is the mean absorption level of every participant who took the placebo, regardless of the beverage level to which he or she was assigned. (Although we wouldn't expect any absorption with placebo, we gave it a small value, 3, to facilitate our explanation of interactions.)

The easiest way to understand the main effects is to make a smaller table for each, with only the appropriate marginal means. Separate tables let us focus on one main effect at a time without being distracted by the means in the cells. For the main effect of beverage, we construct a table with two cells, as shown in Table 12-5. Notice that we have only the means for beverage, as if medication were never even included in the study. The table makes it easy to see that the absorption level was higher, on average, for grapefruit juice than for water. Still, we would have to conduct a two-way ANOVA and reject the null hypothesis before drawing this conclusion.

Let's now consider the second main effect, that for medication. As before, we construct a table (see Table 12-6) that shows only the means for medication, as if beverage were never even included in the study. We kept the means for beverage in rows and for medication in columns, just as they were in the original table. You may, however, arrange them either way, whichever makes sense to you. Table 12-6 demonstrates that the absorption levels for Lipitor and Zocor were higher, on average, than for placebo, which led to almost no absorption. This result would still need to be verified with a hypothesis test, but we seem to have two main effects: (1) a main effect of beverage (grapefruit juice leads to higher absorption, on average, than water does) and (2) a main effect of medication (Lipitor and Zocor lead to higher absorption, on average, than placebo does).

But that's not the whole story. Grapefruit juice, for example, does not lead to higher absorption, on average, among placebo users. Here's where the interaction comes in. Now we ignore the marginal means and get back to the means in the cells themselves, seen again in Table 12-7. Here we can see the overall pattern by framing it in two different ways. We can start by considering beverage. Does grapefruit juice boost mean absorption levels as compared to water? It depends. It depends on the level of the other independent variable, medication; specifically, it depends on whether the patient is taking one of the two medications or a placebo. We can also frame the question by starting with medication. Do Lipitor and Zocor boost mean absorption levels as compared to placebo? It depends. They do anyway, even when just drinking water, but they do so to a far greater degree when drinking grapefruit juice. This is a quantitative interaction because the *strength* of the effect varies under certain conditions, but not the *direction*.

TABLE 12-5. The Main Effect of Beverage

This table shows only the marginal means that demonstrate the main effect of beverage. Because we have isolated these marginal means, we cannot get distracted or confused by the other means in the table.

Grapefruit Juice	41
Water	21

TABLE 12-6. The Main Effect of Medication

This table shows only the marginal means that demonstrate the main effect of medication. Because we have isolated these marginal means, we cannot get distracted or confused by the other means in the table.

Lipitor (L)	Zocor (Z)	Placebo (P)
45	45	3

TABLE 12-7. Examining the Overall Pattern of Means

A first step in understanding an interaction is examining the overall pattern of means in the cells.

	Lipitor (L)	Zocor (Z)	Placebo (P)
Grapefruit Juice (G)	60	60	3
Water (W)	30	30	3

Yet people sometimes perceive an interaction where there is none. If Lipitor, Zocor, and placebo all had higher mean absorption rates when drinking grapefruit juice (versus water), there would be no interaction. Lipitor and Zocor would *always* lead to a particular increase in average absorption levels versus placebo—this would occur in the presence of any beverage. And grapefruit juice would *always* lead to a particular increase in average absorption levels versus water—this would occur in the presence of any medication. On the other hand, there is an interaction in the example we have been considering because grapefruit juice has a special effect with the two medications that it does not have with placebo. The tendency to see an interaction when there is none can be diminished by constructing a bar graph, as in Figure 12-1.

The bar graph helps us to see the overall pattern, but one more step is necessary. Once we have created our bar graph, we connect each set of bars with a line. We have two choices that match the two ways we framed the interaction in words above. (1) As in Figure 12-2, we could connect the bars for the first independent variable,

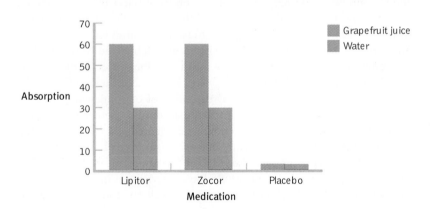

FIGURE 12-1
Bar Graphs and Interactions

Bar graphs help us determine if there really is an interaction. We can look at the pattern of the bars to determine whether there is an interaction. The bars in this graph help us to see that, among those taking placebo, the mean absorption is the same whether the placebo is accompanied by grapefruit juice or water, whereas, among those taking Lipitor or Zocor, the mean absorption is higher when accompanied by grapefruit juice than when accompanied by water.

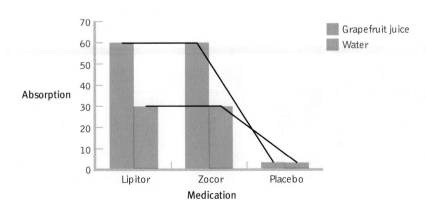

FIGURE 12-2
Are the Lines Parallel? Part I

We add lines to bar graphs to help us to determine whether there really is an interaction. We draw a line connecting the three medications under the grapefruit juice condition. We then draw a line connecting the three medications under the water condition. These two lines intersect, an indication of an interaction that can be confirmed by conducting a hypothesis test.

FIGURE 12-3
Are the Lines Parallel? Part II

There are always two ways to examine the pattern of our bar graphs. Here, we have drawn three lines, one connecting the two beverages under each of the three medication conditions. Were the three lines to continue, the two medication lines would eventually intersect with the horizontal placebo line, an indication of an interaction that can be confirmed by conducting a hypothesis test.

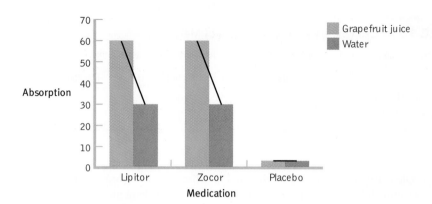

medication. We would connect the three medications for the grapefruit condition, and then we would connect the three medications for the water condition. (2) Alternatively, as in Figure 12-3, we could connect the bars for the two beverages. We would connect the two beverages for Lipitor, then for Zocor, and then for placebo.

In Figure 12-3, notice that the lines do not intersect, but they're not all parallel either. If the lines were long enough, eventually they would intersect. Perfectly parallel lines indicate the likely absence of an interaction, but we almost never see perfectly parallel lines emerging from real-life data sets; real-life data are usually messy. Nonparallel lines may indicate an interaction, but we have to conduct an ANOVA and compare the F statistic with its critical value to be sure. Only if the lines are significantly different from parallel can we reject the null hypothesis that there is no interaction; and we only want to interpret an interaction if we reject the null hypothesis.

Some social scientists refer to an interaction as a significant difference in differences. In the context of the grapefruit juice study, the mean difference between grapefruit juice and water is larger when participants are taking one of the medications than when they are taking placebo. In fact, for those taking placebo, there is no mean difference between grapefruit juice and water. This is an example of a significant difference between differences. Whenever the effect of one independent variable on the dependent variable depends on a particular level of the other independent variable, there is an interaction. This interaction is represented graphically whenever the lines connecting the bars are significantly different from parallel.

However, if grapefruit juice also led to an increase in mean absorption levels among those taking placebo, the graph would look like the one in Figure 12-4. In this case, the mean absorption levels of Lipitor and Zocor do increase with grapefruit juice, but

FIGURE 12-4
Parallel Lines

The three lines are exactly parallel. Were they to continue indefinitely, they would never intersect. Were this true among the population (not just this sample), there would be no interaction.

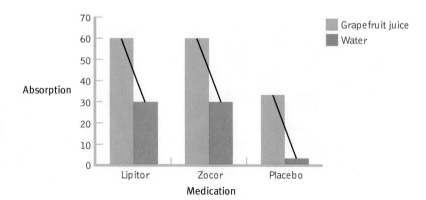

so does the mean absorption level of placebo, and there is likely no interaction. Grapefruit juice has the same effect, regardless of the level of the other independent variable of medication. When in doubt about whether there is an interaction or just two main effects that add up to a greater effect, draw a graph and connect the bars with lines.

Qualitative Interactions Let's recall the definition of a qualitative interaction: a particular type of quantitative interaction of two (or more) independent variables in which the effect of one independent variable reverses its effect depending on the level of the other independent variable.

EXAMPLE 12.3

Here's an example about how people integrate information and make decisions. Do you think that, on average, people make better decisions when they consciously focus on the decision? Or do they make better decisions when the decision-making process is unconscious (i.e., making their decision after being distracted by other tasks)? Which decision-making method do you think is superior, and why?

Researchers conducted a series of studies in which participants were asked to decide between two options following either conscious or unconscious thinking about the choice. The studies were analyzed with two-way ANOVAs (Dijksterhuis, Bos, Nordgren, & van Baaren, 2006).

In one study, participants were asked to choose one of four cars. One car was objectively the best of the four, and one was objectively the worst. Some participants made a less complex decision; they were told 4 characteristics of each car. Some participants made a more complex decision; they were told 12 characteristics of each car. After learning about the characteristics of the cars, half the participants in each group were randomly assigned to think consciously about the cars for four minutes before making a decision. Half were randomly assigned to distract themselves for four minutes by solving anagrams before making a decision. The research design, with two independent variables, is shown in Table 12-8. The

Choosing the Best Car When making decisions, such as which car to buy, do we make better choices after conscious or unconscious deliberation? Research by Dijksterhuis and colleagues (2006) suggests that less complex decisions are typically better when made after conscious deliberation, whereas more complex decisions are typically better when made after unconscious deliberation.

Franco Vogt/Corbis

TABLE 12-8. A Two-Way Between-Groups ANOVA

Dutch researchers designed a study to examine what style of decision making led to the best choices in less complex and more complex situations. Would you predict an interaction? In other words, would the lines connecting bars on a graph be different from parallel? And if they are different from parallel, how are they different? If they are different just in strength, you are predicting a quantitative interaction. If the direction of effect actually reverses, you are predicting a qualitative interaction.

	Conscious Thought	Unconscious Thought (Distraction)
Less Complex (4 Attributes of Each Car)	less complex; conscious	less complex; unconscious
More Complex (12 Attributes of Each Car)	more complex; conscious	more complex; unconscious

TABLE 12-9. Decision-Making Tactics

To understand the main effects and overall pattern of a two-way ANOVA, we start by examining the cell means and marginal means.

	Conscious Thought	Unconscious Thought (Distraction)	
Less Complex	5.5	2.3	3.9
More Complex	0.6	5.0	2.8
	3.05	3.65	

first independent variable is complexity, with two levels: less complex (4 attributes) and more complex (12 attributes). The second independent variable is type of decision making, with two levels: conscious thought and unconscious thought (distraction).

The researchers then evaluated how well people made their decisions; specifically, they calculated a score for each participant that reflected his or her ability to differentiate between the objectively best and objectively worst cars in the group. This score represents the dependent variable, and higher numbers indicate a better ability to differentiate between the best and worst cars. Let's look at Table 12-9, which presents cell means and marginal means for this experiment. Note that the means are approximate and that the marginal means are created by assuming the same number of participants in each cell. As we consider these findings, we will assume that all differences are statistically significant. (In a real research situation, we would conduct an ANOVA to determine whether the main effects and interaction were statistically significant.)

Because there was an overall pattern—an interaction—the researchers did not pay attention to the main effects in this study; an interaction trumps any main effects. However, let's examine the main effects—to get some practice—first for the independent variable of complexity and then for the independent variable of type of decision making, and create tables for each of the two main effects so that we can examine them independently (Tables 12-10 and 12-11). The marginal means indicate that when type of decision making is ignored entirely, people make better decisions, on average, in less complex situations than in more complex situations. Further, the marginal means also suggest that, when complexity of decision is ignored, people make better decisions, on average, when the decision-making process is unconscious than when it is conscious.

However, if there is also a significant interaction, these main effects don't tell the whole story. The overall pattern of cell means renders this knowledge misleading,

TABLE 12-10. Main Effect of Complexity of Decision

These marginal means suggest that, overall, participants are better at making less complex decisions.

Less Complex	3.9
More Complex	2.8

TABLE 12-11. Main Effect of Type of Decision Making

These marginal means suggest that, overall, participants are better at making decisions when the decision making is unconscious—that is, when they are distracted.

Conscious	Unconscious
3.05	3.65

even inaccurate, under certain conditions. The interaction offers far more nuanced information on the best method for making decisions. It demonstrates that the effect of the decision-making method *depends* on the complexity of the decision. Conscious decision making tends to be better than unconscious decision making in less complex situations, but unconscious decision making tends to be better than conscious decision making in more complex situations. This reversal of direction is what makes this a qualitative interaction. It's not just the strength of the effect that changes, but the actual direction!

A bar graph, shown in Figure 12-5, makes the pattern of the data far clearer. We can actually see the qualitative interaction. The direction of the effect of type of decision making in less complex situations is opposite that in more complex situations.

As with a quantitative interaction, we would add lines to determine whether they are parallel (no matter how long the lines were drawn) or intersect (or would do so if extended far enough), as in Figure 12-6. Here we see that the lines intersect without even having to extend them beyond the graph. This is likely an interaction. Further, the fact that the direction reverses indicates that this is a qualitative, not a quantitative, interaction. Type of decision making has an effect on the quality of the decision, on average, but it depends on the complexity of the decision. Those making a less complex decision tend to make better choices if they use conscious thought. Those making a more complex decision tend to make better choices if they use unconscious thought. We would, as usual, verify this finding by conducting a hypothesis test before rejecting the null hypothesis that there is no interaction.

The qualitative interaction of decision-making method and complexity of situation was not likely to have been predicted by common sense. When this occurs, we should be cautious before generalizing the findings. In this case, the research was carefully conducted and the researchers replicated their findings across several situations. For example, the researchers found similar effects in a real-life context when the less complex situation was shopping at a department store that sells clothing and kitchen products, and the more complex situation was purchasing furniture at IKEA. Such an intriguing finding would not have been possible without the inclusion of two independent variables in one study, which required that researchers use a two-way ANOVA capable of testing for two main effects *and* an interaction.

So what do these findings mean for us as we approach the decisions we face every day? Which sunblock should we buy to best protect against UV rays? Should we go to graduate school or get a job following graduation? Should we consciously consider characteristics of sunblocks but "sleep on" graduate school–related factors? Research would suggest yes (Dijksterhuis et al., 2006). Yet, if the history of social science research is any indication, there are other factors that were not included in these studies but likely affect the quality of our decisions. And so the research process continues.

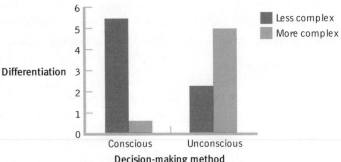

FIGURE 12-5
Graphing Decision-Making Methods

This bar graph displays the traditional form of the interaction far better than does a table or words. We can see that it is a qualitative interaction; there is an actual reversal of direction of the effect of decision-making method in less complex versus more complex situations.

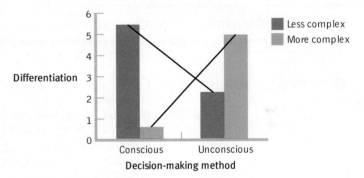

FIGURE 12-6
The Intersecting Lines of a Qualitative Interaction

When we draw two lines, one for the two bars that represent less complex situations and one for the two bars that represent more complex situations, we can easily see that they intersect. Lines that intersect, or would intersect if we extended them, indicate an interaction.

CHECK YOUR LEARNING

Reviewing the Concepts

> A two-way ANOVA is represented by a grid or matrix in which cells represent each unique combination of independent variables. Means are calculated for cells, called *cell means*. Means are also computed for each level of an independent variable, by itself, without regard to the levels of the other independent variable. These means, found in the margins of the grid, are called *marginal means*.

> When there is a statistically significant interaction, the main effects are considered to be modified by an interaction. As a result, we ignore the main effects and focus only on the overall pattern of cell means that reveals the interaction.

> Two categories of interactions describe the overall pattern of cell means—quantitative interactions and qualitative interactions.

> The most common interaction is a quantitative interaction in which the effect of the first independent variable depends on the levels of the second independent variable, but the differences at each level vary only in the strength of the effect.

> Qualitative interactions are those in which the effect of the first independent variable depends on the levels of the second independent variable, but the direction of the effect actually reverses across the levels of the second independent variable.

> There are three ways to identify a statistically significant interaction: (1) visually, whenever the lines connecting the means of each group are significantly different from parallel; (2) conceptually, when we need to use the word or idea of "it depends" to tell the data's story; and (3) statistically, when the p value associated with an interaction in a source table is < 0.05, as with other hypothesis tests. This last option, the statistical analysis, is the only objective way to assess the interaction.

Clarifying the Concepts

12-5 What is the difference between a quantitative interaction and a qualitative interaction?

12-6 Why are main effects ignored when there is an interaction? (We often say they are *trumped* by an interaction.)

Calculating the Statistics

12-7 Data are presented here for two hypothetical independent variables (IV) and their combinations.
IV 1, level A; IV 2, level A: 2, 1, 1, 3
IV 1, level B; IV 2, level A: 5, 4, 3, 4
IV 1, level A; IV 2, level B: 2, 3, 3, 3
IV 1, level B; IV 2, level B: 3, 2, 2, 3

a. Figure out how many cells are in this study's table, and draw a grid to represent them.

b. Calculate cell means and write them in the cells of the grid.

c. Calculate marginal means and write them in the margins of the grid.

d. Draw a bar graph for these data.

Applying the Concepts

12-8 For each of the following situations involving a real-life interaction, (i) state the independent variables, (ii) state the likely dependent variable, (iii) construct a table showing the cells, and (iv) explain whether it describes a qualitative or quantitative interaction.

a. Caroline and Mira are both really smart and do equally well in their psychology class, but something happens to Caroline when she goes to their philosophy class. She just can't keep up, whereas Mira does even better.

b. Our college baseball team has had a great few years. The team plays especially well, scoring more runs, at home versus away if playing teams in its own conference. However, they play especially well at away games (versus home games) if playing teams from another conference.

c. Caffeinated drinks get me wired and make it somewhat difficult to sleep. So does working out in the evenings. When I do both, I'm so wired that I might as well stay up all night.

Solutions to these Check Your Learning questions can be found in Appendix D.

Conducting a Two-Way Between-Groups ANOVA

Advertising agencies understand that interactions can help them to target their advertising campaigns. For example, researchers demonstrated that an increased exposure to *dogs* (linked in our memories to *cats* through familiar phrases such as "it's raining cats and dogs") positively influenced people's evaluations of Puma sneakers (a brand whose name refers to a cat), but only for people who recognized the Puma logo (Berger & Fitzsimons, 2008). The interaction between frequency of exposure to dogs (one independent variable) and whether or not someone could recognize the Puma logo (a second independent variable) *combined* to create a more positive evaluation, on average, of Puma sneakers (the dependent variable). Once again, both variables were needed to produce an interaction.

Behavioral scientists explore interactions by using two-way ANOVAs. Fortunately, hypothesis testing for a two-way between-groups ANOVA uses the same logic as hypothesis testing for a one-way between-groups ANOVA. For example, the null hypothesis is exactly the same: no difference exists between groups. Type I and Type II errors still pose the same threats to our decision making: rejecting the null hypothesis when we shouldn't reject it or not rejecting the null hypothesis when we should reject it. We compare an F statistic to a critical F value to decide whether to reject the null hypothesis. The only way that a two-way ANOVA differs from a one-way ANOVA is that three ideas are being tested and each idea is a separate source of variability.

The three ideas being tested in a two-way ANOVA are the main effect of the first independent variable, the main effect of the second independent variable, and the interaction effect of the two independent variables. A fourth source of variability in a two-way ANOVA is variance we can't explain, more formally referred to as "error," or within-groups variance. Let's learn how to separate and measure these four sources of variance by evaluating a commonly used educational method to improve public health: myth-busting.

The Six Steps of Two-Way ANOVA

Does myth-busting really improve public health? Here are some myths and facts.

EXAMPLE 12.4

From the Web site of the Headquarters Counseling Center (2005) in Lawrence, Kansas:

Myth: "Suicide happens without warning."

Fact: "Most suicidal persons talk about and/or give behavioral clues about their suicidal feelings, thoughts, and intentions."

From the Web site for the World Health Organization (2007):

Myth: "Disasters bring out the worst in human behavior."

Fact: "Although isolated cases of antisocial behavior exist, the majority of people respond spontaneously and generously."

A group of Canadian researchers examined the effectiveness of myth-busting (Skurnik, Yoon, Park, & Schwarz, 2005). They wondered if the effectiveness of debunking false medical claims depends on the age of the person targeted by the message. In one study, they compared two groups of adults: one group of 32 younger adults, ages 18–25, and a second group of 32 older adults, ages 71–86, for a total of 64 participants. Participants were presented with a series of claims and were told that each claim

Do We Remember the Medical Myth or the Fact? Skurnik and colleagues (2005) studied the factors that influenced the misremembering of false medical claims as fact. They asked: When a physician tells a patient a false claim, then debunks it with the facts, does the patient remember the false claim or the facts? A source table will examine each factor in our study and tell us how much of the variability in the dependent variable is explained by that factor.

was either true or false. (In reality, all claims were true, partly because researchers did not want to run the risk that participants would misremember false claims as being true.) In some cases, the claim was presented once, and in other cases, it was repeated three times. (Note that we have altered the study's design somewhat in our description to make the study simpler for our purposes, but the results are the same.)

The two independent variables in this study were age, with two levels (younger and older), and number of repetitions, with two levels (once and three times). The dependent variable, proportion of responses that were wrong after a three-day delay, was calculated for each participant. This was a two-way between-groups ANOVA. Alternatively, we could label it a 2×2 between-groups ANOVA. From this name, we know that the table has four cells: $(2 \times 2) = 4$. There were 64 total participants—16 in each cell. But for our purposes here, we use an example with 12 participants—3 in each cell. Here are the data that we'll use. These data have similar means to those in the actual study, and the F statistics are similar as well.

Experimental Conditions	Proportion of Responses That Were Wrong	Mean
Younger, one repetition	0.25, 0.21, 0.14	0.20
Younger, three repetitions	0.07, 0.13, 0.16	0.12
Older, one repetition	0.27, 0.22, 0.17	0.22
Older, three repetitions	0.33, 0.31, 0.26	0.30

Let's consider the steps of hypothesis testing for a two-way between-groups ANOVA in the context of this example.

STEP 1. Identify the populations, distribution, and assumptions.

The first step of hypothesis testing for a two-way between-groups ANOVA is very similar to that for a one-way between-groups ANOVA. First, we state the populations, but we specify that they are broken down into more than one category. In the current example, there are four populations, so there are four cells (see Table 12-12). With 12 participants, there are 3 in each cell. As we do the calculations, think of the first independent variable, age, as being in the rows of the table, and think of the second independent variable, number of repetitions, as being in the columns of the tables.

There are four populations, each with labels representing the levels of the two independent variables to which they belong.

TABLE 12-12. Studying the Memory of False Claims Using a Two-Way ANOVA

The study of memory for false claims has two independent variables, age (younger, older) and number of repetitions (one, three).

	One Repetition (1)	Three Repetitions (3)
Younger (Y)	Y; 1	Y; 3
Older (O)	O; 1	O; 3

> Population 1 (Y; 1): Younger adults who hear one repetition of a false claim.
>
> Population 2 (Y; 3): Younger adults who hear three repetitions of a false claim.
>
> Population 3 (O; 1): Older adults who hear one repetition of a false claim.
>
> Population 4 (O; 3): Older adults who hear three repetitions of a false claim.

We next consider the characteristics of our data to determine the distributions to which we will compare our sample. We have more than two groups, so we need to consider variances to analyze differences among means. Therefore, we will use the F distributions. Finally, we list the hypothesis test that we would use for that distribution and check the assumptions for that hypothesis test. For F distributions, we will use ANOVA—in this case, a two-way between-groups ANOVA.

The assumptions are the same for all types of ANOVA. First, the sample should be selected randomly. Second, the populations should be distributed normally. Third, the population variances should be equal.

(1) These data were not randomly selected. Younger adults were recruited from a university setting, and older adults were recruited from the local community. Because random sampling was not used, we must be cautious when generalizing from these samples. (2) The researchers did not report whether they investigated the shapes of the distributions of their samples to assess the shapes of the underlying populations. (3) The researchers did not provide standard deviations of the samples as an indication of whether the population spreads might be approximately equal, a condition known as *homoscedasticity*. If we were analyzing our own data, we would explore these assumptions using our sample data.

Summary:

> Population 1 (Y; 1): Younger adults who hear one repetition of a false claim.
>
> Population 2 (Y; 3): Younger adults who hear three repetitions of a false claim.
>
> Population 3 (O; 1): Older adults who hear one repetition of a false claim.
>
> Population 4 (O; 3): Older adults who hear three repetitions of a false claim.

The comparison distributions will be F distributions. The hypothesis test will be a two-way between-groups ANOVA. Assumptions: (1) The data are not from random samples, so we must generalize only with caution. (2) From the published research report, we do not know if the underlying population distributions are normal. (3) We do not know if the population variances are approximately equal (homoscedasticity).

STEP 2. State the null and research hypotheses.

The second step, to state the null and research hypotheses, is similar to that for a one-way between-groups ANOVA, except that we now have three sets of hypotheses, one for each main effect and one for the interaction. Those for the two main effects are the same as those for the one effect of a one-way between-groups ANOVA (see summary section below). If there are only two levels, then we can simply say that means for the two levels are not equal; if there are only two levels and there is a statistically significant difference, then it must be between the means of those two levels. Note that because there are two independent variables, we clarify which variable we are referring to by using initial letters or abbreviations for the levels of each (e.g., Y for younger and O for older). If an independent variable has more than two levels, the research hypothesis would be that the means of any two or more levels of the independent variable are not equal to one another.

The hypotheses for the interaction are typically stated in words, but not in symbols. The null hypothesis is that the effect of one independent variable is not dependent on the levels of the other independent variable. The research hypothesis is that the effect of one independent variable depends on the levels of the other independent variable. It does not matter which independent variable we list first (i.e., "the effect of age is not dependent . . ." or "the effect of number of repetitions is not dependent . . ."). Write the hypotheses in the way that makes the most sense to you.

Summary: The hypotheses for the main effect of the first independent variable, age, are as follows: Null hypothesis: On average, younger adults have the same proportion of responses that are wrong when remembering which claims are myths compared with older adults—H_0: $\mu_Y = \mu_O$. Research hypothesis: On average, younger adults have a different proportion of responses that are wrong when remembering which claims are myths compared with older adults—H_1: $\mu_Y \neq \mu_O$.

The hypotheses for the main effect of the second independent variable, number of repetitions, are as follows: Null hypothesis: On average, those who hear one repetition have the same proportion of responses that are wrong when remembering which claims are myths compared with those who hear three repetitions—H_0: $\mu_1 = \mu_3$. Research hypothesis: On average, those who hear one repetition have a different proportion of responses that are wrong when remembering which claims are myths compared with those who hear three repetitions—H_1: $\mu_1 \neq \mu_3$.

The hypotheses for the interaction of age and number of repetitions are as follows: Null hypothesis: The effect of number of repetitions is not dependent on the levels of age. Research hypothesis: The effect of number of repetitions depends on the levels of age.

> **STEP 3. Determine the characteristics of the comparison distribution.**

The third step is similar to that of a one-way between-groups ANOVA, except that there are three comparison distributions, all of them F distributions. We need to provide the appropriate degrees of freedom for each of these: two main effects and one interaction. As before, the F statistic is a ratio of two types of variance, between-groups variance and within-groups variance. Because there are three effects for a two-way ANOVA, there are three between-groups variance estimates, each with its own degrees of freedom. There is only one within-groups variance estimate for all three, so the within-groups variance (and its degrees of freedom) is the same for all three possible effects.

For each main effect, the between-groups degrees of freedom is calculated as for a one-way ANOVA: the number of groups minus 1. The first independent variable, age, is in the rows of the table of cells, so the between-groups degrees of freedom is:

$$df_{rows(age)} = N_{rows} - 1 = 2 - 1 = 1$$

The second independent variable, number of repetitions, is in the columns of the table of cells, so the between-groups degrees of freedom is:

$$df_{columns(reps)} = N_{columns} - 1 = 2 - 1 = 1$$

We now need a between-groups degrees of freedom for the interaction, which is calculated by multiplying the degrees of freedom for the two main effects:

MASTERING THE FORMULA

12-1: The formula for the between-groups degrees of freedom for the independent variable in the rows of the table of cells is $df_{rows} = N_{rows} - 1$. We subtract 1 from the number of rows, representing levels, for that variable.

MASTERING THE FORMULA

12-2: The formula for the between-groups degrees of freedom for the independent variable in the columns of the table of cells is $df_{columns} = N_{columns} - 1$. We subtract 1 from the number of columns, representing levels, for that variable.

$$df_{interaction} = (df_{rows(age)})(df_{columns(reps)}) = (1)(1) = 1$$

The within-groups degrees of freedom is calculated like that for a one-way between-groups ANOVA, the sum of the degrees of freedom in each of the cells. In the current example, there are 3 participants in each cell, so the within-groups degrees of freedom is calculated as follows, with N representing the number in each cell:

$$df_{Y,1} = N - 1 = 3 - 1 = 2$$

$$df_{Y,3} = N - 1 = 3 - 1 = 2$$

$$df_{O,1} = N - 1 = 3 - 1 = 2$$

$$df_{O,3} = N - 1 = 3 - 1 = 2$$

$$df_{within} = df_{Y,1} + df_{Y,3} + df_{O,1} + df_{O,3} = 2 + 2 + 2 + 2 = 8$$

For a check on our work, we can calculate the total degrees of freedom just as we did for the one-way between-groups ANOVA. We subtract 1 from the total number of participants:

$$df_{total} = N_{total} - 1 = 12 - 1 = 11$$

We can now add up the three between-groups degrees of freedom and the within-groups degrees of freedom to see if they equal 11. If they do not, we can check our calculations to find our error. In this case, they match:

$$11 = 1 + 1 + 1 + 8$$

Finally, for this step, we list the distributions with their degrees of freedom for each of the three effects. Note that, although the between-groups degrees of freedom for each effect are the same in this case, they are often different. For example, if one independent variable had three levels and the other had four, the between-groups degrees of freedom for the main effects would be 2 and 3, respectively, and the between-groups degrees of freedom for the interaction would be 6.

Summary: Main effect of age: F distribution with 1 and 8 degrees of freedom.

Main effect of number of repetitions: F distribution with 1 and 8 degrees of freedom.

Interaction of age and number of repetitions: F distribution with 1 and 8 degrees of freedom. (*Note:* It is helpful to include all degrees of freedom calculations in this step.)

STEP 4. Determine the critical values, or cutoffs.

Again, this step for the two-way between-groups ANOVA is just an expansion of that for the one-way version. We now need three cutoffs, or critical values, but they're determined just as we determined them before. We use the F table in Appendix B. For each main effect and for the interaction, we'll look up the within-groups degrees of freedom, which is always the same for each effect, along the left-hand side and the appropriate between-groups degrees of freedom across the top of the table. The place on the grid where this row and this column intersect contains three numbers. From top to bottom, the table provides cutoffs for p levels of 0.01, 0.05, and 0.10. As usual, we typically use 0.05. In this instance, it

> **MASTERING THE FORMULA**
>
> **12-3:** The formula for the between-groups degrees of freedom for the interaction is $df_{interaction} = (df_{rows})(df_{columns})$. We multiply the degrees of freedom for each of the independent variables.

> **MASTERING THE FORMULA**
>
> **12-4:** To calculate the within-groups degrees of freedom, we first calculate degrees of freedom for each cell. That is, we subtract 1 from the number of participants in each cell. We then sum the degrees of freedom for each cell. For a study in which there are four cells, we'd use this formula: $df_{within} = df_{cell\ 1} + df_{cell\ 2} + df_{cell\ 3} + df_{cell\ 4}$.

> **MASTERING THE FORMULA**
>
> **12-5:** There are two ways to calculate the total degrees of freedom. We can subtract 1 from the total number of participants in the entire study: $df_{total} = N_{total} - 1$. We can also add the three between-groups degrees of freedom and the within-groups of freedom. It's a good idea to calculate it both ways as a check on our work.

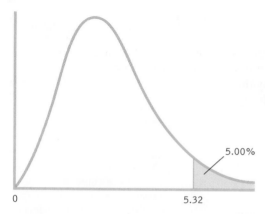

FIGURE 12-7
Determining Cutoffs for an _F_ Distribution

We determine the cutoffs, or critical values, for an _F_ distribution for a two-way between-groups ANOVA just as we did for a one-way between-groups ANOVA, except that we must calculate three cutoffs, one for each main effect and one for the interaction. In this case, the between-groups degrees of freedom are the same for all three, and so the cutoffs are the same.

happens that the critical value is the same for both main effects and for the interaction because the between-groups degrees of freedom is the same for all three. But when the between-groups degrees of freedom are different, as often happens, there are different critical values. Here, we look up the between-groups degrees of freedom of 1, the within-groups degrees of freedom of 8, and a _p_ level of 0.05. The cutoff for all three is 5.32, as seen in Figure 12-7.

Summary: There are three critical values in a two-way ANOVA; in this case, they are all the same, as seen in the curve in Figure 12-7. The critical _F_ value for the main effect of age is 5.32. The critical _F_ value for the main effect of number of repetitions is 5.32. The critical _F_ value for the interaction of age and number of repetitions is 5.32.

STEP 5. Calculate the test statistic.

As with the one-way between-groups ANOVA, the fifth step for the two-way between-groups ANOVA is the most time-consuming. As you might guess, it's similar to what we already learned, but we have to calculate three _F_ statistics instead of one. We learn the logic and the specific calculations for this step in the next section.

STEP 6. Make a decision.

This step is the same as for a one-way between-groups ANOVA, except that we compare each of the three _F_ statistics to its appropriate cutoff _F_ statistic. If the _F_ statistic is beyond the critical value, then we know that it is in the most extreme 5% of possible test statistics _if_ the null hypothesis is true. After making a decision for each _F_ statistic, we present our results in one of three ways.

First, if we are able to reject the null hypothesis for the interaction, then we can draw a specific conclusion with the help of a table and graph. Because we have more than two groups, we use a post-hoc test, such as the one that we learned in Chapter 11. Because there are three effects, post-hoc tests are typically implemented separately for each main effect, if necessary, and for the interaction (Hays, 1994). If the interaction is statistically significant, then it might not matter whether the main effects also are significant; if they are also significant, then those findings are usually qualified by the interaction, and they are not typically described separately. The overall pattern of cell means can tell the whole story.

Second, if we are not able to reject the null hypothesis for the interaction, then we focus on any significant main effects, drawing a specific directional conclusion for each. In this study, each independent variable has only two levels, so there is no need for a post-hoc test. If there were three or more levels, however, then each significant main effect would require a post-hoc test to determine exactly where the differences lie. Third, if we do not reject the null hypothesis for either main effect or the interaction, then we can only conclude that there is insufficient evidence from this study to support our research hypotheses. We will complete step 6 of hypothesis testing for this study in the next section, after we consider the calculations of the source table for a two-way between-groups ANOVA.

Identifying Four Sources of Variability in Two-Way ANOVA

In this section, we complete step 5 for a two-way ANOVA. The calculations for a two-way ANOVA are similar to those for a one-way ANOVA, except that we calculate three _F_ statistics. We use a source table with elements like those shown in Table 12-3.

TABLE 12-13. Calculating the Total Sum of Squares

The total sum of squares is calculated by subtracting the overall mean, called the *grand mean,* from every score to create deviations, then squaring the deviations and summing them: $\Sigma(X - GM)^2 = 0.0672$.

	X	$(X - GM)$	$(X - GM)^2$
Y, 1	0.25	$(0.25 - 0.21) = 0.04$	0.0016
	0.21	$(0.21 - 0.21) = 0.00$	0.0000
	0.14	$(0.14 - 0.21) = -0.07$	0.0049
Y, 3	0.07	$(0.07 - 0.21) = -0.14$	0.0196
	0.13	$(0.13 - 0.21) = -0.08$	0.0064
	0.16	$(0.16 - 0.21) = -0.05$	0.0025
0, 1	0.27	$(0.27 - 0.21) = 0.06$	0.0036
	0.22	$(0.22 - 0.21) = 0.01$	0.0001
	0.17	$(0.17 - 0.21) = -0.04$	0.0016
0, 3	0.33	$(0.33 - 0.21) = 0.12$	0.0144
	0.31	$(0.31 - 0.21) = 0.10$	0.0100
	0.26	$(0.26 - 0.21) = 0.05$	0.0025

First, we calculate the total sum of squares (Table 12-13). We calculate this number in exactly the same way as for a one-way ANOVA. We first calculate the grand mean, the mean of all the individual scores: 0.21. We subtract the grand mean from every score to create deviations, then square the deviations, and finally sum the squared deviations:

$$SS_{total} = \Sigma(X - GM)^2 = 0.0672$$

We now calculate the between-groups sums of squares for the two main effects—the one in the rows and then the one in the columns of the table. Both are calculated similarly to the between-groups sum of squares for a one-way between-groups ANOVA. The table with the cell means and marginal means is shown in Table 12-14. The between-groups sum of squares for the main effect of the independent variable age would be the sum, for every score, of the marginal mean minus the grand mean, squared. We list all 12 scores in Table 12-15, marking the divisions among the cells. For each of the 6 younger participants, those in the top 6 rows of Table 12-15, we subtract the grand mean, 0.21, from the marginal mean, 0.16. For the 6 older participants, those in the bottom 6 rows, we subtract 0.21 from the marginal mean, 0.26.

> ◀ **MASTERING THE FORMULA**
>
> **12-6:** We calculate the total sum of squares using the following formula: $SS_{total} = \Sigma(X - GM)^2$. We subtract the grand mean from every score to create deviations, then square the deviations, and finally sum the squared deviations.

TABLE 12-14. Means for False Medical Claims Study

The study of the misremembering of false medical claims as true had two independent variables, age and number of repetitions. The cell means and marginal means for error rates are shown in the table. The grand mean is 0.21.

	One Repetition (1)	Three Repetitions (3)	
Younger (Y)	0.20	0.12	0.16
Older (O)	0.22	0.30	0.26
	0.21	0.21	0.21

TABLE 12-15. Calculating the Sum of Squares for the First Independent Variable

The sum of squares for the first independent variable is calculated by subtracting the overall mean (the grand mean) from the mean for each level of that variable—in this case, age—to create deviations, then squaring the deviations and summing them: $\Sigma(M_{row(age)} - GM)^2 = 0.03$.

	X	$(M_{row(age)} - GM)$	$(M_{row(age)} - GM)^2$
Y, 1	0.25	$(0.16 - 0.21) = -0.05$	0.0025
	0.21	$(0.16 - 0.21) = -0.05$	0.0025
	0.14	$(0.16 - 0.21) = -0.05$	0.0025
Y, 3	0.07	$(0.16 - 0.21) = -0.05$	0.0025
	0.13	$(0.16 - 0.21) = -0.05$	0.0025
	0.16	$(0.16 - 0.21) = -0.05$	0.0025
0, 1	0.27	$(0.26 - 0.21) = 0.05$	0.0025
	0.22	$(0.26 - 0.21) = 0.05$	0.0025
	0.17	$(0.26 - 0.21) = 0.05$	0.0025
0, 3	0.33	$(0.26 - 0.21) = 0.05$	0.0025
	0.31	$(0.26 - 0.21) = 0.05$	0.0025
	0.26	$(0.26 - 0.21) = 0.05$	0.0025

MASTERING THE FORMULA

12-7: We calculate the between-groups sum of squares for the first independent variable, that in the rows of the table of cells, using the following formula: $SS_{between(rows)} = \Sigma(M_{row} - GM)^2$. For every participant, we subtract the grand mean from the marginal mean for the appropriate row for that participant. We square these deviations, and sum the squared deviations.

We square all of these deviations and then add them to calculate the sum of squares for the rows, the independent variable of age:

$$SS_{between(rows)} = \Sigma(M_{row(age)} - GM)^2 = 0.03$$

We repeat this process for the second possible main effect, that of the independent variable in the columns of the tables (Table 12-16). So the between-groups

TABLE 12-16. Calculating the Sum of Squares for the Second Independent Variable

The sum of squares for the second independent variable is calculated by subtracting the overall mean (the grand mean) from the mean for each level of that variable—in this case, number of repetitions—to create deviations, then squaring the deviations and summing them: $\Sigma(M_{column(reps)} - GM)^2 = 0$.

	X	$(M_{column(reps)} - GM)$	$(M_{column(reps)} - GM)^2$
Y, 1	0.25	$(0.21 - 0.21) = 0$	0
	0.21	$(0.21 - 0.21) = 0$	0
	0.14	$(0.21 - 0.21) = 0$	0
Y, 3	0.07	$(0.21 - 0.21) = 0$	0
	0.13	$(0.21 - 0.21) = 0$	0
	0.16	$(0.21 - 0.21) = 0$	0
0, 1	0.27	$(0.21 - 0.21) = 0$	0
	0.22	$(0.21 - 0.21) = 0$	0
	0.17	$(0.21 - 0.21) = 0$	0
0, 3	0.33	$(0.21 - 0.21) = 0$	0
	0.31	$(0.21 - 0.21) = 0$	0
	0.26	$(0.21 - 0.21) = 0$	0

sum of squares for number of repetitions, then, would be the sum, for every score, of the marginal mean minus the grand mean, squared. We would again list all 12 scores, marking the divisions among the cells. For each of the 6 participants who had one repetition, those in the left-hand column of Table 12-14 and in rows 1–3 and 7–9 of Table 12-16, we'd subtract the grand mean, 0.21, from the marginal mean, 0.21. For each of the 6 participants who had three repetitions, those in the right-hand column of Table 12-14 and in the rows 4–6 and 10–12 of Table 12-16, we'd subtract 0.21 from the marginal mean, 0.21. (*Note:* It is a coincidence that in this case the marginal means are exactly the same.) We'd square all of these deviations and add them to calculate the between-groups sum of squares for the columns, the independent variable of number of repetitions. Again, the calculations for the between-groups sum of squares for each main effect are just like the calculations for the between-groups sum of squares in a one-way between-groups ANOVA:

$$SS_{between(columns)} = \Sigma(M_{column(reps)} - GM)^2 = 0$$

The within-groups sum of squares is calculated in exactly the same way as for the one-way between-groups ANOVA (Table 12-17). For each of the 12 scores, the cell mean is subtracted from the score. The deviations are squared and summed:

$$SS_{within} = \Sigma(X - M_{cell})^2 = 0.018$$

All we need now is the between-groups sum of squares for the interaction. We can calculate this by subtracting the other between-groups sums of squares (those for the two main effects) and the within-groups sum of squares from the total sum of squares. The between-groups sum of squares for the interaction is essentially what is left over when the main effects are accounted for. Mathematically, any variability that is predicted by these variables, but is not directly predicted by either independent

MASTERING THE FORMULA

12-8: We calculate the between-groups sum of squares for the second independent variable, that in the columns of the table of cells, using the following formula: $SS_{between(columns)} = \Sigma(M_{column} - GM)^2$. For every participant, we subtract the grand mean from the marginal mean for the appropriate column for that participant. We square these deviations, and then sum the squared deviations.

MASTERING THE FORMULA

12-9: We calculate the within-groups sum of squares using the following formula: $SS_{within} = \Sigma(X - M_{cell})^2$. For every participant, we subtract the appropriate cell mean from that participant's score. We square these deviations, and sum the squared deviations.

TABLE 12-17. Calculating the Within-Groups Sum of Squares

The within-groups sum of squares is calculated the same way for a two-way ANOVA as for a one-way ANOVA. We take each score and subtract the mean of the cell from which it comes—not the grand mean—to create deviations; then we square the deviations and sum them: $\Sigma(X - M_{cell})^2 = 0.018$.

	X	$\Sigma(X - M_{cell})^2$	$\Sigma(X - M_{cell})^2$
Y, 1	0.25	$(0.25 - 0.20) = 0.05$	0.0025
	0.21	$(0.21 - 0.20) = 0.01$	0.0001
	0.14	$(0.14 - 0.20) = -0.06$	0.0036
Y, 3	0.07	$(0.07 - 0.12) = -0.05$	0.0025
	0.13	$(0.13 - 0.12) = 0.01$	0.0001
	0.16	$(0.16 - 0.12) = 0.04$	0.0016
0, 1	0.27	$(0.27 - 0.22) = 0.05$	0.0025
	0.22	$(0.22 - 0.22) = 0.00$	0.0000
	0.17	$(0.17 - 0.22) = -0.05$	0.0025
0, 3	0.33	$(0.33 - 0.30) = 0.03$	0.0009
	0.31	$(0.31 - 0.30) = 0.01$	0.0001
	0.26	$(0.26 - 0.30) = -0.04$	0.0016

MASTERING THE FORMULA

12-10: To calculate the between-groups sum of squares for the interaction, we subtract the two between-groups sums of squares for the independent variables and the within-groups sum of squares from the total sum of squares. The formula is: $SS_{between(interaction)} = SS_{total} - (SS_{between(rows)} + SS_{between(columns)} + SS_{within})$.

variable on its own, is attributed to the interaction of the two independent variables. The formula is:

$$SS_{between(interaction)} = SS_{total} - (SS_{between(rows)} + SS_{between(columns)} + SS_{within})$$

And the calculations are:

$$SS_{between(interaction)} = 0.0672 - (0.03 + 0 + 0.018) = 0.0192$$

Now we can complete step 6 of hypothesis testing by calculating the F statistics using the formulas in Table 12-18. The results are in the source table (Table 12-19). The main effect of age is statistically significant because the F statistic, 13.04, is larger than the critical value of 5.32. The means tell us that older participants tend to make more mistakes, remembering more medical myths as true, on average, than do younger participants. The main effect of number of repetitions is not statistically significant, however, because the F statistic of 0.00 is not larger than the cutoff of 5.32. It is unusual to have an F statistic of 0.00. Even when there is no statistically significant effect, there is usually some difference among means due to random sampling. The interaction also is statistically significant because the F statistic of 8.26 is larger than the cutoff of 5.32. Therefore, we construct a bar graph of the cell means, as seen in Figure 12-8, to interpret the interaction.

TABLE 12-18. The Expanded Source Table and the Formulas

This source table includes all of the formulas for the calculations necessary to conduct a two-way between-groups ANOVA.

Source	SS	df	MS	F
Age (between/rows)	$\Sigma(M_{between(rows)} - GM)^2$	$N_{rows} - 1$	$\frac{SS_{between(rows)}}{df_{between(rows)}}$	$\frac{MS_{between(rows)}}{MS_{within}}$
Repetitions (between/columns)	$\Sigma(M_{between(columns)} - GM)^2$	$N_{columns} - 1$	$\frac{SS_{between(columns)}}{df_{between(columns)}}$	$\frac{MS_{between(columns)}}{MS_{within}}$
Age × Repetitions (between/interaction)	$SS_{total} - (SS_{between(rows)} + SS_{between(columns)} + SS_{within})$	$(df_{rows})(df_{columns})$	$\frac{SS_{interaction}}{df_{interaction}}$	$\frac{MS_{interaction}}{MS_{within}}$
Within	$\Sigma(X - M_{cell})^2$	$df_{within} = df_{cell1} + df_{cell2} + df_{cell3} + df_{cell4}$ (and so on for any additonal cells)	$\frac{SS_{within}}{df_{within}}$	
Total	$\Sigma(X - GM)^2$	$df_{total} = N_{total} - 1$		

MASTERING THE FORMULA

12-11: The formulas to calculate the four mean squares are in Table 12-18. There are three between-groups mean squares—one for each main effect and one for the interaction—and one within-groups mean square. For each mean square, we divide the appropriate sum of squares by its related degrees of freedom. The formulas for the three F statistics, one for each main effect and one for the interaction, are also in Table 12-18. For each of the three effects, we divide the appropriate between-groups mean square by the within-groups mean square. The denominator is the same in all three cases.

TABLE 12-19. The Expanded Source Table and False Medical Claims

This expanded source table shows the actual sums of squares, degrees of freedom, mean squares, and F statistics for the study on false medical claims.

Source	SS	df	MS	F
Age (A)	0.0300	1	0.0300	13.04
Repetitions (R)	0.0000	1	0.0000	0.00
A × R	0.0192	1	0.0190	8.26
Within	0.0180	8	0.0023	
Total	0.0672	11		

(Note that we could choose to calculate p_{rep} for each of the main effects as well as the interaction. We would use the procedure introduced in earlier chapters in which we use statistical software such as SPSS to determine the specific p values for each effect, and then use Microsoft Excel to determine p_{rep}.)

In Figure 12-8, the lines are not parallel; in fact, they intersect without even having to extend them beyond the graph. We can see that among younger participants, the proportion of responses that were incorrect was *lower,* on average, with three repetitions than with one repetition. Among older participants, the proportion of responses that were incorrect was *higher,* on average, with three repetitions than with one repetition. Does repetition help? It depends. It helps for younger people but is detrimental for older people. Specifically, repetition tends to help younger people distinguish between myth and fact. But the mere repetition of a medical myth tends to lead older people to be more likely to view it as fact. The researchers speculate that older people remember that they are familiar with a statement but forget the context in which they heard it; they forget that it's a false claim. Because the direction of the effect of repetition reverses from one age group to another, this is a qualitative interaction.

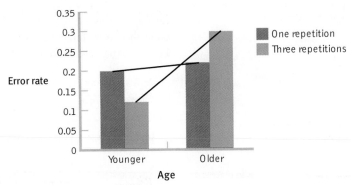

FIGURE 12-8
Interpreting the Interaction

The nonparallel lines demonstrate the interaction. The bars tell us that repetition increases accuracy for younger people but decreases it for older people. Because the direction reverses, this is a qualitative interaction.

Effect Size for Two-Way ANOVA

With two-way ANOVA, as with one-way ANOVA, we calculate R^2 as our measure of effect size. As we learned in Chapter 11, for R^2, we use sums of squares as indicators of variability. For each of the three effects—the two main effects and the interaction—we divide the appropriate between-groups sum of squares by the total sum of squares minus the sums of squares for both of the other effects. We subtract the sums of squares for the other two effects from the total so that we can isolate the effect size for a single effect at a time. For example, if we want to determine effect size for the main effect in the rows, we divide the sum of squares for the rows by the total sum of squares minus the sum of squares for the column and the sum of squares for the interaction.

For the first main effect, the one in the rows of the table of cells, the formula is:

$$R^2_{rows} = \frac{SS_{rows}}{(SS_{total} - SS_{columns} - SS_{interaction})}$$

For the second main effect, the one in the columns of the table of cells, the formula is:

$$R^2_{columns} = \frac{SS_{columns}}{(SS_{total} - SS_{rows} - SS_{interaction})}$$

For the interaction, the formula is:

$$R^2_{interaction} = \frac{SS_{interaction}}{(SS_{total} - SS_{rows} - SS_{columns})}$$

> **MASTERING THE FORMULA**
>
> **12-12:** To calculate effect size for two-way ANOVA, we calculate three R^2 values, one for each main effect and one for the interaction. In each case, we divide the appropriate between-groups sum of squares by the total sum of squares minus the between-groups sums of squares for the other two effects. For example, the effect size for the interaction is calculated using this formula:
>
> $R^2_{interaction} = \frac{SS_{interaction}}{(SS_{total} - SS_{rows} - SS_{columns})}$.

EXAMPLE 12.5

Let's apply this to the ANOVA we just conducted. We can use the statistics in the source table shown in Table 12-19 to calculate R^2 for each main effect and the interaction. Here are the calculations for R^2 for the main effect for age:

$$R^2_{rows(age)} = \frac{SS_{rows(age)}}{(SS_{total} - SS_{columns(repetition)} - SS_{interaction})} = \frac{0.0300}{(0.0672 - 0.000 - 0.0192)} = 0.625$$

Here are the calculations for R^2 for the main effect for repetitions:

$$R^2_{columns(repetions)} = \frac{SS_{columns(repetions)}}{(SS_{total} - SS_{rows(age)} - SS_{interaction})} = \frac{0.000}{(0.0672 - 0.0300 - 0.0192)} = 0.000$$

Here are the calculations for R^2 for the interaction:

$$R^2_{interaction} = \frac{SS_{interaction}}{(SS_{total} - SS_{rows(age)} - SS_{columns(repetions)})} = \frac{0.0192}{(0.0672 - 0.0300 - 0.000)} = 0.516$$

The conventions for R^2 are the same as those presented in Chapter 11 and are shown again here in Table 12-20. From this table, we can see that our R^2 of 0.63 for the main effect of age and 0.52 for the interaction are very large. The R^2 of 0.00 for the main effect of repetitions indicates that there is no observable effect in this study.

TABLE 12-20. Cohen's Conventions for Effect Sizes: R^2

The following guidelines, called *conventions* by statisticians, are meant to help researchers decide how important an effect is. These numbers are not cutoffs, merely rough guidelines to aid researchers in their interpretation of results.

Effect Size	Convention
Small	0.01
Medium	0.06
Large	0.14

CHECK YOUR LEARNING

Reviewing the Concepts

> The six steps of hypothesis testing for a two-way between-groups ANOVA are similar to those for a one-way between-groups ANOVA.

> Because we have the possibility of two main effects and an interaction, each step is broken down into three parts; we have three sets of hypotheses, three comparison distributions, three critical F values, three F statistics, and three conclusions.

> As with other hypothesis tests, we can choose to determine p_{rep} instead of reporting information about our p values for each of our effects.

> An expanded source table helps us to keep track of the calculations.

> Significant F statistics require post-hoc tests to determine where differences lie when there are more than two groups.

> We can calculate a measure of effect size, R^2, for each main effect and for the interaction.

Clarifying the Concepts

12-9 The six steps of hypothesis testing for a two-way between-groups ANOVA are similar to those for a one-way between-groups ANOVA, except for what basic difference?

12-10 What are the four sources of variability in a two-way ANOVA?

Calculating the Statistics

12-11 Compute the three between-groups degrees of freedom (both main effects and the interaction), the within-groups degrees of freedom, and the total degrees of freedom for the following data (IV = independent variable):

IV 1, level A; IV 2, level A: 2, 1, 1, 3
IV 1, level B; IV 2, level A: 5, 4, 3, 4
IV 1, level A; IV 2, level B: 2, 3, 3, 3
IV 1, level B; IV 2, level B: 3, 2, 2, 3

12-12 Using the degrees of freedom you calculated in Check Your Learning 12-11, determine critical values, or cutoffs, using a p level of 0.05, for the F tests of the two main effects and the interaction.

Applying the Concepts

12-13 Researchers studied the effect of e-mail messages on students' final exam grades (Forsyth & Kerr, 1999; Forsyth, Lawrence, Burnette, & Baumeister, 2006). To test for possible interactions, participants included students whose first exam grade was either (1) a C or (2) a D or F. Participants were randomly assigned to receive several e-mails in one of three conditions: e-mails intended to bolster their self-esteem, e-mails intended to enhance their sense of control over their grades, and e-mails with review questions. The accompanying table shows the cell means for the final exam grades (note that some of these are approximate, but all represent actual findings). For simplicity, assume there were 84 participants in the study and that they were evenly divided among cells.

	Self-Esteem (SE)	Sense of Control (C)	Review (R)
C	67.31	69.83	71.12
D/F	47.83	60.98	62.13

a. From step 1 of hypothesis testing, list the populations for this study.

b. Conduct step 2 of hypothesis testing, listing all three sets of hypotheses.

c. Conduct step 3 of hypothesis testing, listing the comparison distributions for this study, including all degrees of freedom.

d. Conduct step 4 of hypothesis testing, listing all three critical F values.

e. The F statistics are 20.84 for the main effect of the independent variable of initial grade, 1.69 for the main effect of the independent variable of type of e-mail, and 3.02 for the interaction. Conduct step 6 of hypothesis testing.

Solutions to these Check Your Learning questions can be found in Appendix D.

REVIEW OF CONCEPTS

Two-Way ANOVA

Factorial ANOVAs (also called *multifactorial ANOVAs*), those with more than one independent variable (or *factor*), permit us to test more than one hypothesis in a single study—a savings of time and resources. They also allow us to examine *interactions* between independent variables. Factorial ANOVAs are often named by referring to the levels of their independent variables (e.g., 2×2) rather than the number of independent variables (e.g., two-way). With a *two-way ANOVA*, we can examine two *main effects,* one for each independent variable, and one interaction, the way in which the two variables might work together to influence the dependent variable. Because we are examining three hypotheses (two main effects and one interaction), we calculate three sets of statistics for a two-way ANOVA.

Understanding Interactions in ANOVA

Researchers typically interpret interactions by examining the overall pattern of cell means. A *cell* is one condition in a study. We typically write the mean of a group in its cell. We write the means for each row to the right of the cells, and the means for each column below the cells; these are called *marginal means.* If the main effect of one independent variable is stronger under certain conditions of the second independent variable, there is a *quantitative interaction.* If the direction of the main effect actually reverses under certain conditions of the second independent variable, there is a *qualitative interaction.*

Conducting a Two-Way Between-Groups ANOVA

A two-way between-groups ANOVA uses the same six steps of hypothesis testing that we have used previously, with only minor changes. Because we have to test for two main effects and one interaction, each step is broken down into three parts, one for each possible effect. Specifically, we have three sets of hypotheses, three comparison distributions, three critical F values, three F statistics, and three conclusions. We use an expanded source table to aid in our calculations of the three F statistics. As with other hypothesis tests, we can calculate p_{rep} instead of reporting information about the p value associated with the statistic. We also can calculate a measure of effect size, R^2, for each of our main effects and for the interaction.

SPSS®

Let's use SPSS to conduct a two-way ANOVA for the data on myth-busting that we used earlier in this chapter.

We can instruct SPSS to analyze our ANOVA by selecting: **Analyze** → General Linear Model → Univariate and selecting the variables. A two-way ANOVA requires two fixed factors (independent variables) and a dependent variable. We select our dependent variable, false memory, by highlighting it and clicking the arrow next to "Dependent Variable." We select our independent variables, age and repetitions, by clicking each of them, then clicking the arrow next to "Fixed Factor(s)." We can include specific descriptive statistics, as well as a measure of effect size, by selecting "Options," then selecting "Descriptive statistics" and "Estimates of effect size."

The screenshot shown here includes the same F statistics that we calculated earlier. The small differences between the ones here and the ones we calculated are due only to rounding decisions. For example, we see that the F statistic for the main effect of age is 13.333. Its p value (which we could use to calculate p_{rep}) is found in the column headed "Sig." and is .006. This is well below the typical p level of 0.05, which tells us that this is a statistically significant effect. The effect size is found in the final column, headed "Partial Eta Squared," which can be interpreted as we learned to interpret R^2. The effect size of .625, which matches the effect size we calculated by hand earlier, indicates that this is a very large effect.

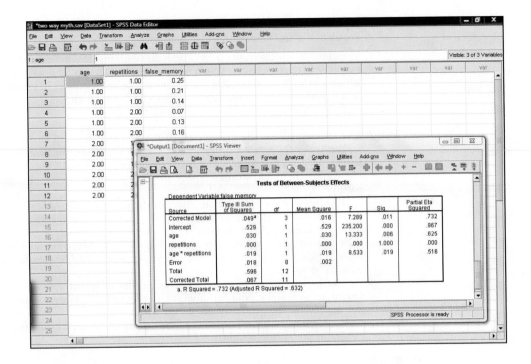

How It Works

12.1 CONDUCTING A TWO-WAY BETWEEN-GROUPS ANOVA

The online dating Web site Match.com allows its users to post personal ads to meet others. Each person is asked to specify a range from the youngest age that would be acceptable in a dating partner to the oldest age that would be acceptable. The following data were randomly selected from the ads of 25-year-old people living in the New York metropolitan area. The scores represent the youngest acceptable ages listed by those in the sample. So, in the first line, the first of the five 25-year-old women who are seeking men states that she will not date a man younger than 26 years old.

> 25-year-old women seeking men: 26, 24, 25, 24, 25
> 25-year-old men seeking women: 18, 21, 22, 22, 18
> 25-year-old women seeking women: 22, 25, 22, 25, 25
> 25-year-old men seeking men: 23, 25, 24, 22, 20

There are two independent variables and one dependent variable. The first independent variable is gender of the seeker, and its levels are male and female. The second independent variable is gender of the person being sought, and its levels are men and women. The dependent variable is the youngest acceptable age of the person being sought. Based on these variables, how can we conduct a two-way between-groups ANOVA on these data? The cell means are:

	Female seekers	Male seekers
Men sought	24.8	22.8
Women sought	23.8	20.2

Here are the six steps of hypothesis testing for this example.

Step 1: Population 1 (women, men): Women seeking men.
Population 2 (men, women): Men seeking women.

Population 3 (women, women): Women seeking women.

Population 4 (men, men): Men seeking men.

The comparison distributions will be F distributions. The hypothesis test will be a two-way between-groups ANOVA. Assumptions: The data are not from random samples, so we must generalize with caution. The homogeneity of variance assumption is violated because the largest variance (3.70) is much larger than the smallest variance (0.70).

Step 2: The hypotheses for the main effect of the first independent variable, gender of seeker, are as follows: Null hypothesis: On average, men and women report the same youngest acceptable ages for their partners, $\mu_1 = \mu_2$. Research hypothesis: On average, men and women report different youngest acceptable ages for their partners, $\mu_1 \neq \mu_2$.

The hypotheses for the main effect of the second independent variable, gender of person sought, are as follows: Null hypothesis: On average, those seeking men and those seeking women report the same youngest acceptable ages for their partners, $\mu_1 = \mu_2$. Research hypothesis: On average, those seeking men and those seeking women report different youngest acceptable ages for their partners, $\mu_1 \neq \mu_2$.

The hypotheses for the interaction of gender of seeker and gender of person sought are as follows: Null hypothesis: The effect of the gender of the seeker does not depend on the gender of the person sought.

Research hypothesis: The effect of the gender of the seeker does depend on the gender of the person sought.

Step 3: $df_{columns(seeker)} = 2 - 1 = 1$

$df_{rows(sought)} = 2 - 1 = 1$

$df_{interaction} = (1)(1) = 1$

$df_{within} = df_{W,M} + df_{M,W} + df_{W,W} + df_{M,M} = 4 + 4 + 4 + 4 = 16$

Main effect of gender of seeker: F distribution with 1 and 16 degrees of freedom
Main effect of gender of sought: F distribution with 1 and 16 degrees of freedom
Interaction of seeker and sought: F distribution with 1 and 16 degrees of freedom

Step 4: Cutoff F for main effect of seeker: 4.49
Cutoff F for main effect of sought: 4.49
Cutoff F for interaction of seeker and sought: 4.49

Step 5: $SS_{total} = \Sigma(X - GM)^2 = 103.800$

$SS_{columns(seeker)} = \Sigma(M_{columns(seeker)} - GM)^2 = 39.200$

$SS_{rows(sought)} = \Sigma(M_{rows(sought)} - GM)^2 = 16.200$

$SS_{within} = \Sigma(X - M_{cell})^2 = 45.200$

$SS_{interaction} = SS_{total} - (SS_{rows} + SS_{columns} + SS_{within}) = 3.200$

Source	SS	df	MS	F
Seeker gender	39.200	1	39.200	13.876
Sought gender	16.200	1	16.200	5.736
Seeker × sought	3.200	1	3.200	1.133
Within	45.200	16	2.825	
Total	103.800	19		

Step 6: There is a significant main effect of gender of the seeker and a significant main effect of gender of the person being sought. We can reject the null hypotheses for both of these main effects. Male seekers are willing to accept younger partners, on average, than are female seekers. Those seeking women are willing to accept younger partners with a younger average age than are those seeking men. We cannot reject the null hypothesis for the interaction; we can only conclude that there is not sufficient evidence that the effect of the gender of the seeker depends on the gender of the person sought.

Exercises

12.1 What is a two-way ANOVA?

12.2 What is a factor?

12.3 In your own words, define the word *cell,* first as you would use it in everyday conversation and then as a statistician would use it.

12.4 What is a four-way within-groups ANOVA?

12.5 What is the difference in information provided when we say *two-way ANOVA* versus *2 × 3 ANOVA*?

12.6 What are the three different F statistics in a two-way ANOVA?

12.7 What is a marginal mean?

12.8 What are the three ways to identify a statistically significant interaction?

12.9 How do bar graphs help us identify and interpret interactions? Explain how the addition of lines to the bar graph can help.

12.10 How do we calculate the between-groups degrees of freedom for an interaction effect?

12.11 In step 6 of our hypothesis testing for a two-way between-groups ANOVA, we make a decision for each F statistic. What are the three possible outcomes with respect to the overall pattern of results?

12.12 When are post-hoc tests needed for a two-way between-groups ANOVA?

12.13 Define the terms in the following formula: $SS_{interaction} = SS_{total} - (SS_{rows} + SS_{columns} + SS_{within})$.

12.14 In your own words, define the word *interaction,* first as you would use it in everyday conversation and then as a statistician would use it.

Calculating the Statistic

12.15 Identify the factors and their levels in the following research designs:

    a. Men's and women's enjoyment of two different sporting events are compared using a 20-point enjoyment scale.

    b. The amount of underage drinking, as documented in formal incident reports, is compared at "dry" college campuses (no alcohol at all regardless of age) and "wet" campuses (those that enforce the legal age for possession of alcohol). Three different types of colleges are considered: state institutions, private schools, and schools with a religious affiliation.

    c. The extent of contact with juvenile authorities is compared for youth across three age groups, considering both gender and family composition (two-parent family, single-parent, or no identified authority figure).

12.16 Calculate the number of cells in each of these studies. Create an empty grid to represent these cells.

    a. Men's and women's enjoyment of two different sporting events are compared using a 20-point enjoyment scale.

    b. The amount of underage drinking, as documented in formal incident reports, is compared at "dry" college campuses (no alcohol at all regardless of age) and "wet" campuses (those that enforce the legal age for possession of alcohol). Three different types of colleges are considered: state institutions, private schools, and schools with a religious affiliation.

    c. The extent of contact with juvenile authorities is compared for youth across three age groups, considering both gender and family composition (two-parent family, single-parent, or no identified authority figure).

12.17 For the following data, calculate cell and marginal means.

	Hockey	Ice Skating
Men	19, 17, 18, 17	6, 4, 8, 3
Women	13, 14, 18, 8	11, 7, 4, 14

12.18 For the following data, calculate cell and marginal means and place them in an appropriate table. Notice the unequal N values.

"Dry" campus, state school: 47, 52, 27, 50
"Dry" campus, private school: 25, 33, 31
"Wet" campus, state school: 77, 61, 55, 48
"Wet" campus, private school: 52, 68, 60

12.19 Draw a bar chart for the data presented in Exercise 12.17.

12.20 Draw a bar chart for the data presented in Exercise 12.18.

12.21 Calculate the five different measures of degrees of freedom for the data presented in Exercise 12.17. Also indicate the critical value for an ANOVA based on each set of degrees of freedom, assuming the p level is 0.01.

12.22 Calculate the five different measures of degrees of freedom for the data presented in Exercise 12.18. Also indicate the critical value for an ANOVA based on each set of degrees of freedom, assuming the p level is 0.05.

12.23 Using the data provided in Exercise 12.17, calculate each sum of squares:

a. Total sum of squares
b. Between-groups sum of squares for the independent variable gender
c. Between-groups sum of squares for the independent variable sporting event
d. Within-groups sum of squares
e. Sum of squares for the interaction

12.24 Using the data provided in Exercise 12.18, calculate each sum of squares:

a. Total sum of squares
b. Between-groups sum of squares for the independent variable campus
c. Between-groups sum of squares for the independent variable school
d. Within-groups sum of squares
e. Sum of squares for the interaction

12.25 Using your work in Exercises 12.21 and 12.23, create a source table.

12.26 Using your work in Exercises 12.22 and 12.24, create a source table.

12.27 Using what you know about the expanded source table, fill in the missing values in the table shown here:

Source	SS	df	MS	F
Gender	248.25	1		
Parenting style	84.34	3		
Gender × style	33.60			
Within	1107.2	36		
Total				

12.28 Using the information in the source table provided here, compute R^2 values for each effect. Using Cohen's conventions, explain what these values mean.

Source	SS	df	MS	F
A (rows)	0.267	1	0.267	0.004
B (columns)	3534.008	2	1767.004	24.432
A × B	5.371	2	2.686	0.037
Within	1157.167	16	72.323	
Total	4696.813	21		

12.29 Using the information in the source table provided here, compute R^2 values for each effect. Using Cohen's conventions, explain what these values mean.

Source	SS	df	MS	F
A (rows)	30.006	1	30.006	0.511
B (columns)	33.482	1	33.482	0.570
A × B	1.720	1	1.720	0.029
Within	587.083	10	58.708	
Total	652.291	13		

Applying the Concepts

12.30 Consider the study we used as an example in this chapter for a two-way between-groups ANOVA. Older and younger people were randomly assigned to hear either one repetition or three repetitions of a health-related myth, accompanied by the accurate information that "busted" the myth.

a. Explain why this study is a between-groups ANOVA.
b. How could this study be redesigned to use a within-groups ANOVA? (*Hint:* Think long term.)

12.31 In a fictional study, a cognitive psychologist studied memory for names after a group activity that lasted 20 minutes. The researcher randomly assigned 120 participants to one of three conditions: (1) group members introduced themselves once (one introduction only), (2) group members were introduced by the experimenter and by themselves (two introductions), and (3) group members were introduced by the experimenter and themselves, and wore nametags throughout the group activity (two introductions and nametags).

a. What could the researcher do to redesign this study so it would be analyzed with a two-way between-groups ANOVA? Be specific. (*Note:* There are several possible ways that the researcher could do this.)

b. What could the researcher do to redesign this study so it would be analyzed with a two-way within-groups ANOVA? Be specific. (*Note:* There are several possible ways the researcher could do this.)

12.32 A researcher wondered about the degree to which age was a factor for those posting personal ads on Match.com. He randomly selected 200 ads and examined data about the posters (the people who posted the ads). Specifically, for each ad, he calculated the difference between the poster's age and the oldest age he or she would be open to in a romantic prospect. So, if someone was 23 years old and would date someone as old as 30, his or her score would be 7; if someone was 25 and would date someone as old as 23, his or her score would be −2. He calculated these scores for all 200 posters and categorized them into male versus female and homosexual versus heterosexual.

a. List any independent variables, along with the levels.

b. What is the dependent variable?

c. What kind of ANOVA is this?

d. Now name the ANOVA using the more specific language that enumerates the numbers of levels.

e. Use your answer to part (d) to calculate the number of cells. Explain how you made this calculation.

f. Draw a table that depicts the cells of this ANOVA.

12.33 A study on motivated skepticism examined whether participants were more likely to be skeptical when it served their self-interest (Ditto & Lopez, 1992). Ninety-three participants completed a fictitious medical test that told them they had high levels of a certain enzyme, TAA. Participants were randomly assigned to be told either that high levels of TAA had potentially unhealthy consequences or that high levels of TAA had potentially healthy consequences. They were also randomly assigned to complete a dependent measure before or after the TAA test. The dependent measure assessed their perception of the accuracy of the TAA test on a scale of 1 (very inaccurate) to 9 (very accurate).

a. State the independent variables and their levels.

b. State the dependent variable.

c. What kind of ANOVA would be used to analyze these data? State the name using the original language as well as the more specific language.

d. Use the more specific language of ANOVA to calculate the number of cells in this research design.

e. Draw a table that depicts the cells of this ANOVA.

12.34 In the study described in Exercise 12.33, Ditto and Lopez (1992) found the following means for those who completed the dependent measure prior to taking the TAA test: unhealthy result, 6.6; healthy result, 6.9. They found the following means for those who completed the dependent measure after taking the TAA test: unhealthy result, 5.6; healthy result, 7.3. From their ANOVA, they reported statistics for two findings. For the main effect of test outcome, they reported the following statistic: $F_{(1,73)} = 7.74, p < 0.01$. For the interaction of test outcome and timing of the dependent measure, they reported the following statistic: $F_{(1,73)} = 4.01, p < 0.05$.

a. Draw a table of cell means that includes the actual means for this study. Include the marginal means and the grand mean. To calculate the marginal means and grand mean, assume that equal numbers of participants were assigned to each cell (even though this was not the case in the actual study).

b. Describe the significant main effect in your own words.

c. Draw a bar graph that depicts the main effect.

d. Why is the main effect misleading on its own?

e. Is the main effect qualified by a statistically significant interaction? Explain. Describe the interaction in your own words.

f. Draw a bar graph that depicts the interaction. Include lines that connect the tops of the bars and show the pattern of the interaction.

g. Is this a quantitative or qualitative interaction? Explain.

12.35 Consider again the study discussed in Exercises 12.33 and 12.34.

a. Change the cell mean for the participants who had a healthy test outcome and who completed the dependent measure prior to the TAA test so that this is now a quantitative interaction.

b. Draw a bar graph depicting the pattern that includes the new cell mean.

c. Change the cell mean for the participants who had a healthy test outcome and who completed the dependent measure prior to the TAA test so that there is now no interaction.

d. Draw a bar graph that depicts the pattern that includes the new cell mean.

12.36 In a study of racism, Nail, Harton, and Decker (2003) had participants read a scenario in which a police officer assaulted a motorist. Half the participants read about an African American officer who assaulted a European American motorist, and half read about a European American officer who assaulted an African American motorist. Participants were categorized into three categories based on political orientation: liberal, moderate, or conservative. Participants were told that the officer was acquitted of assault charges in state court but was found guilty of violating the motorist's rights in federal court. Double jeopardy occurs when an individual is tried twice for the same crime. Participants were asked to rate, on a scale of 1–7, the degree to which the officer had been placed in double jeopardy by the second trial. The researchers reported the interaction as $F(2, 58) = 10.93$, $p < 0.0001$. The means for the *liberal* participants were 3.18 for those who read about the African American officer and 1.91 for those who read about the European American officer. The means for the *moderate* participants were 3.50 for those who read about the African American officer and 3.33 for those who read about the European American officer. The means for the *conservative* participants were 1.25 for those who read about the African American officer and 4.62 for those who read about the European American officer.

a. Draw a table of cell means that includes the actual means for this study.

b. Do the reported statistics indicate that there is a significant interaction? If yes, describe the interaction in your own words.

c. Draw a bar graph that depicts the interaction. Include lines that connect the tops of the bars and show the pattern of the interaction.

d. Is this a quantitative or qualitative interaction? Explain.

12.37 Consider again the study in Exercise 12.36.

a. Change the cell means for the conservative participants who read about an African American officer so that this is now a quantitative interaction.

b. Draw a bar graph that depicts the pattern that includes the new cell means.

c. Change the cell means for the moderate and conservative participants who read about an African American officer so that there is now no interaction.

d. Draw a bar graph that depicts the pattern that includes the new cell means.

12.38 Ratner and Miller (2001) wondered whether people are uncomfortable when they act in a way that's not obviously in their own self-interest. They randomly assigned 33 women and 32 men to read a fictional passage saying that federal funding would soon be cut for research into a gastrointestinal illness that mostly affected either (1) women or (2) men. They were then asked to rate, on a 1–7 scale, how comfortable they would be "attending a meeting of concerned citizens who share your position" on this cause (p. 11). A higher rating indicates a higher level of comfort. The journal article reported the statistics for the interaction as $F(1, 58) = 9.83$, $p < 0.01$. Women who read about women had a mean of 4.88, whereas those who read about men had a mean of 3.56. Men who read about women had a mean of 3.29, whereas those who read about men had a mean of 4.67.

a. What are the independent variables and their levels? What is the dependent variable?

b. What kind of ANOVA did the researchers conduct?

c. Do the reported statistics indicate that there is a significant interaction? Explain your answer.

d. Draw a table that includes the cells of the study and the cell means.

e. Draw a bar graph that depicts these findings.

f. Describe the pattern of the interaction in words. Is this a qualitative or a quantitative interaction? Explain your answer.

12.39 Consider the interaction described in Exercise 12.38.

a. Draw a new table of cells, but change the means for male participants told that the illness affects mostly women so that there is now a quantitative, rather than a qualitative, interaction.

b. Draw a bar graph that represents the means in part (a).

c. Draw a new table of cells, but change the means for male participants told that the illness affects mostly women so that there is no interaction.

d. Draw a bar graph that represents the means in part (c).

12.40 Hugenberg, Miller, and Claypool (2007) conducted a study to better understand the cross-race effect, in which individuals have a difficult time recognizing members of different racial groups—colloquially known as the "they-all-look-the-same-to-me" effect. In a variation on Hugenberg and colleagues' study, white participants viewed either 20 black faces or 20 white faces for three seconds each. Half the participants were told to pay particular attention to distinguishing features of the faces. Later, participants were shown 40 black faces or 40 white faces (the same race as in the prior stage of the experiment), 20 of which were new. Each participant received a score that measured their recognition accuracy. The researchers reported two effects, one for the race of the pictures, $F(1, 136) = 23.06$, $p < 0.001$, and one for the interaction of the race of the pictures and the instructions, $F(1, 136) = 5.27$, $p < 0.05$. When given no instructions, the mean recognition scores were 1.46 for white faces and 1.04 for black faces. When given instructions to pay attention to distinguishing features, the mean recognition scores were 1.38 for white faces and 1.23 for black faces.

a. What are the independent variables and their levels? What is the dependent variable?

b. What kind of ANOVA did the researchers conduct?

c. Do the reported statistics indicate that there is a significant main effect? If yes, describe it.

d. Why is the main effect not sufficient in this situation to understand the findings? Be specific about why the main effect is misleading on its own.

e. Do the reported statistics indicate that there is a significant interaction? Explain your answer.

f. Draw a table that includes the cells of the study and the cell means.

g. Draw a bar graph that depicts these findings.

h. Describe the pattern of the interaction in words. Is this a qualitative or a quantitative interaction? Explain your answer.

12.41 A sample of students from our statistics classes reported their GPAs, indicated their genders, and stated whether they were in the university's Greek system (i.e., in a fraternity or sorority). Following are the GPAs for the different groups of students:

Men in a fraternity: 2.6, 2.4, 2.9, 3.0

Men not in a fraternity: 3.0, 2.9, 3.4, 3.7, 3.0

Women in a sorority: 3.1, 3.0, 3.2, 2.9

Women not in a sorority: 3.4, 3.0, 3.1, 3.1

a. What are the independent variables and their levels? What is the dependent variable?

b. Draw a table that lists the cells of the study design. Include the cell means.

c. Conduct all six steps of hypothesis testing.

d. Draw a bar graph for all significant effects.

e. Is there a significant interaction? If yes, describe it in words, and indicate whether it is a qualitative or a quantitative interaction. Explain.

12.42 The data below are from the same 25-year-old participants described in How It Works 12.1, but now the scores represent the oldest age that would be acceptable in a dating partner.

25-year-old women seeking men: 40, 35, 29, 35, 35

25-year-old men seeking women: 26, 26, 28, 28, 28

25-year-old women seeking women: 35, 35, 30, 35, 45

25-year-old men seeking men: 33, 35, 35, 36, 38

a. What are the independent variables and their levels? What is the dependent variable?

b. Draw a table that lists the cells of the study design. Include the cell means.

c. Conduct all six steps of hypothesis testing.

d. Is there a significant interaction? If yes, describe it in words, indicate whether it is a quantitative or a qualitative interaction, and draw a bar graph.

12.43 Heyman and Ariely (2004) were interested in whether effort and willingness to help were affected by the form and amount of payment offered in return for effort. They predicted that when money was used as payment, in what is called a *money market,* effort would increase as a function of payment level. On the other hand, if effort is performed out of altruism, in what is called a *social market,* the level of effort would be consistently high and unaffected by level of payment. In one of their studies, college students were asked to estimate another student's willingness to help load a sofa into a van in return for a cash payment or no payment (rather than money, these students received candy of equivalent value). Willingness to help was assessed using an 11-

point scale ranging from "not at all likely to help" to "will help for sure." Data are presented here to recreate some of their findings.

Cash payment, low amount of $0.50: 4, 5, 6, 4

Cash payment, moderate amount of $5.00: 7, 8, 8, 7

Candy payment, low amount valued at $0.50: 6, 5, 7, 7

Candy payment, moderate amount valued at $5.00: 8, 6, 5, 5

a. What are the independent variables and their levels?

b. What is the dependent variable?

c. Draw a table that lists the cells of the study design. Include the cell and marginal means.

d. Create a bar graph.

e. Using this graph and the table of cell means, describe what effects you see in the pattern of the data.

12.44 Using the research and data given in Exercise 12.43, complete the following:

a. Write the null and research hypotheses.

b. Complete all of the calculations, and construct a full source table for these data.

c. Determine the critical value for each F test at a p level of 0.05.

d. Draw your conclusions. Is there a significant interaction? If yes, describe it in words and indicate whether it is a qualitative or a quantitative interaction. Explain.

12.45 Expanding on the work of Heyman and Ariely (2004), let's assume a higher level of payment was included and the following data were collected. (Notice that all data are the same as earlier with the addition of new data under a high payment amount.)

Cash payment, low amount of $0.50: 4, 5, 6, 4

Cash payment, moderate amount of $5.00: 7, 8, 8, 7

Cash payment, high amount of $50.00: 9, 8, 7, 8

Candy payment, low amount, valued at $0.50: 6, 5, 7, 7

Candy payment, moderate amount, valued at $5.00: 8, 6, 5, 5

Candy payment, high amount, valued at $50.00: 6, 7, 7, 6

a. What are the independent variables and their levels? What is the dependent variable?

b. Draw a table that lists the cells of the study design. Include the cell and marginal means.

c. Create a new bar graph of these data.

d. Do you think there is a significant interaction? If yes, describe it in words.

e. Now that one independent variable has three levels, what additional analyses are needed? Explain what you would do and why. Where do you think significant differences would exist based on the graph you created?

12.46 Back in How It Works 12.1, we worked through the six steps of hypothesis testing. Using that work, compute the effect size, R^2, for each main effect and the interaction. Also interpret these effect sizes using Cohen's conventions. The source table we constructed is presented here:

Source	SS	df	MS	F
Seeker gender	39.200	1	39.200	13.876
Sought gender	16.200	1	16.200	5.736
Seeker × sought	3.200	1	3.200	1.133
Within	45.200	16	2.825	
Total	103.800	19		

12.47 Using your work from Exercise 12.41, compute the effect size, R^2, for the main effect of gender, membership in a Greek organization, and the interaction of these two variables. Using Cohen's conventions, interpret the effect-size values.

12.48 Using your work from Exercise 12.42, compute the effect size, R^2, for the main effect of gender of the seeker, gender being sought, and the interaction of these two variables. Using Cohen's conventions, interpret the effect-size values.

12.49 Let's follow up on what we learned in Exercise 12.44 about motivating helpful behavior through different forms and levels of payment. Compute the effect size, R^2, for the main effect of form of payment, level of payment, and the interaction of these two variables. Using Cohen's conventions, interpret the effect-size values.

Terms

interaction (p. 305)
two-way ANOVA (p. 305)
factorial ANOVA (p. 305)

factor (p. 305)
cell (p. 307)
main effect (p. 307)

quantitative interaction (p. 311)
qualitative interaction (p. 311)
marginal mean (p. 312)

Formulas

$df_{rows} = N_{rows} - 1$ (p. 322)

$df_{columns} = N_{columns} - 1$ (p. 322)

$df_{within} = df_{cell\ 1} + df_{cell\ 2} + df_{cell\ 3} + df_{cell\ 4}$ (and so on for any additional cells) (p. 323)

$df_{total} = N_{total} - 1$ (p. 323)

$df_{interaction} = (df_{rows})(df_{columns})$ (p. 325)

$SS_{total} = \Sigma(X - GM)^2$ for each score (p. 325)

$SS_{between(rows)} = \Sigma(M_{row} - GM)^2$ for each score (p. 326)

$SS_{between(columns)} = \Sigma(M_{column} - GM)^2$ for each score (p. 327)

$SS_{within} = \Sigma(X - M_{cell})^2$ for each score (p. 327)

$SS_{between(interaction)} = SS_{total} - (SS_{between(rows)} + SS_{between(columns)} + SS_{within})$ (p. 328)

$R^2_{rows} = \dfrac{SS_{rows}}{(SS_{total} - SS_{columns} - SS_{interaction})}$ (p. 329)

$R^2_{columns} = \dfrac{SS_{columns}}{(SS_{total} - SS_{rows} - SS_{interaction})}$ (p. 329)

$R^2_{interaction} = \dfrac{SS_{interaction}}{(SS_{total} - SS_{rows} - SS_{columns})}$ (p. 329)

Correlation

BEFORE YOU GO ON

■ You should know the difference between
   correlational research and experimental
   research (Chapter 1).

■ You should understand how to calculate the
   deviations of scores from a mean (Chapter 4).

■ You should understand the concept of sum of
   squares (Chapter 4).

■ You should understand the concept of effect
   size (Chapter 8).

In Chapter 1, we learned how John Snow's map of the London cholera epidemic displayed a systematic association called a *correlation,* the association (or relation) between two variables. The correlation statistic continues to advance the cause of public health. For example, Paul Krugman (2006) used the idea of correlation in a newspaper column when he asked, "Is being an American bad for your health?" Krugman explained that the United States has higher per capita spending on health care than any country in the world and yet is surpassed by many countries in life expectancy (Krugman cited a study published in the *Journal of the American Medical Association;* Banks, Marmot, Oldfield, & Smith, 2006). Higher per capita health care costs and lower life expectancy is a surprising effect; we would anticipate that spending more on health care would be associated with *increased* life expectancy, not *decreased* life expectancy. So why is the correlation in the opposite direction of what we would expect? Why aren't people in the United States getting as much bang for their health care buck as people in many other countries?

Krugman mentioned the more obvious possible causes: the lack of universal health insurance and the varied quality of health care based on class or race, both of which are problems specific to the United States. But these aren't winning explanations. For example, a comparison of non-Hispanic white people from America and from England (thus taking race out of the equation) yielded a surprising finding: the wealthiest third of Americans have poorer health than do even the *least* wealthy third of the English. This correlation is still in the opposite direction of what we would expect, and it is probable that the wealthiest third of Americans are the most likely to have health insurance. In other words, this particular correlation doesn't seem to be explained by differing levels of health insurance, institutionalized racial bias, or economic class.

So Krugman noted the alarming tendency for Americans to be obese, the difficulty that even insured Americans have in getting preventive health care, and the long workweeks typical in the United States (a mean of 46 hours compared to a mean of 41 in the United Kingdom, France, and Germany). Whatever the cause, Krugman points out, "there's something about [the American] way of life that is seriously bad for our health." *Correlations can't tell us which explanation is right,* but they can force us to think about the possible explanations.

A *correlation* is the association (or relation) between two variables. Correlation gives us new ways to measure behavior and to distinguish among the influences of overlapping variables. In this chapter, we'll discover how to assess the direction and size of the correlation, and we'll identify some of the limitations of correlation. We'll learn how to calculate the most common form of correlation: *r,* the Pearson correlation coefficient. Finally, we'll use the six steps of hypothesis testing to determine if a correlation is statistically significant.

A Correlation between Nationality and Health
Do obstacles in the American healthcare system contribute to poorer health and lower life expectancy?

- A **correlation coefficient** is a statistic that quantifies a relation between two variables.

- A **positive correlation** is an association between two variables such that participants with high scores on one variable tend to have high scores on the other variable as well, and those with low scores on one variable tend to have low scores on the other variable.

Correlation

A correlation is exactly what its name suggests: a co-relation between two variables. Lots of things are co-related: health care costs and longevity, the amount of junk food consumed and the amount of body fat, how many cars travel on a particular road and how often the road needs maintenance. We learned in Chapter 1 that correlational studies examine relations, usually between two scale (interval or ratio) variables. Statisticians calculate a correlation coefficient to help them better understand these relations between variables.

The Characteristics of Correlation

The number that we calculate when we quantify a correlation is called a *coefficient*. Specifically, *a* **correlation coefficient** *is a statistic that quantifies a relation between two variables.* In this chapter, we learn how to quantify a relation—that is, we learn to calculate a correlation coefficient—when the data are linearly related. A linear relation means that the data form an overall pattern through which it would make sense to draw a straight line—that is, the dots on the scatterplot are roughly clustered around a line, rather than, say, a curve.

One of the handy things about the correlation coefficient is that it really can be understood with just a glance. There are only three main characteristics of the correlation coefficient.

1. The correlation coefficient can be either positive or negative.
2. The correlation coefficient always falls between −1.00 and 1.00.
3. It is the strength (also called the *magnitude*) of the coefficient, not its sign, that indicates how large it is.

> ◀ **MASTERING THE CONCEPT**
>
> **13-1:** A correlation coefficient always falls between −1.00 and 1.00. The size of the coefficient, not its sign, indicates how large it is.

The first important characteristic of the correlation coefficient is that it may be either positive or negative. When two variables are related to one another, they are related in one of two directions: positively or negatively. A positive correlation has a positive sign (e.g., 0.32), and a negative correlation has a negative sign (e.g., −0.32). *A* **positive correlation** *is an association between two variables such that participants with high scores on one variable tend to have high scores on the other variable as well, and those with low scores on one variable tend to have low scores on the other variable.* (Contrary to what some people think, when participants with low scores on one variable tend to have low scores on the other, it is *not* a negative correlation.) A positive correlation describes a situation in which participants tend to have similar scores, with respect to the mean and spread, on both variables—whether the scores are low, medium, or high. On a scatterplot, we see data points that are positively correlated as fitting around a line that is sloping upward to the right.

EXAMPLE 13.1

The scatterplot in Figure 13-1 shows a positive correlation between Scholastic Aptitude Test (SAT) score and college grade point average (GPA). For example, the second dot from the left is for a person with a 980 on the SAT and a 2.2 GPA; this person is lower than average on both scores. The upper-right dot is for a person with

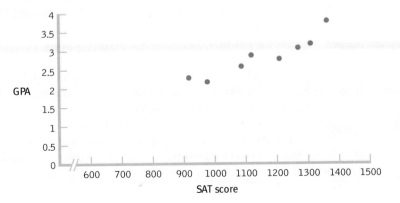

FIGURE 13-1
A Positive Correlation

These data points depict a positive correlation between SAT score and college GPA. Those with higher SAT scores tend to have higher GPAs, and those with lower SAT scores tend to have lower GPAs.

■ A **negative correlation** is an association between two variables in which participants with high scores on one variable tend to have low scores on the other variable.

a 1360 on the SAT and a 3.8 GPA; this person is higher than average on both scores. This makes sense, because we would expect people with higher SAT scores to get better grades, on average.

A **negative correlation** is an association between two variables in which participants with high scores on one variable tend to have low scores on the other variable. On the scatterplot, we see data points that are negatively correlated as fitting around a line that is sloping downward to the right.

EXAMPLE 13.2

The scatterplot in Figure 13-2 shows a negative correlation between nights socializing per week and GPA. For example, the upper-left dot is for a person who goes out one night per week and has a 3.8 GPA; this person is lower than average on nights socializing and higher than average on GPA. The lower-right dot is for a person who goes out six nights per week and has a 2.2 GPA; this person is higher than average on nights socializing and lower than average on GPA. This makes sense, because we would expect people who go out more to get lower grades, on average.

FIGURE 13-2
A Negative Correlation

These data points depict a negative correlation between nights socializing per week and GPA. Those who go out more tend to have lower GPAs, whereas those who go out less tend to have higher GPAs.

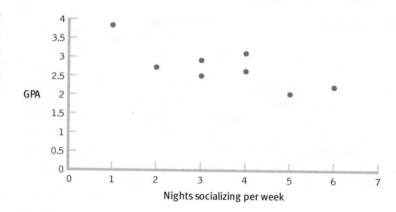

Note that the correlation between health care spending and longevity reported by Krugman (2006) is also a negative correlation. Higher per capita spending on health care was associated with decreased longevity, and lower per capita spending on health care was associated with increased longevity.

A second important characteristic of the correlation coefficient is that it always falls between −1.00 and 1.00. Both −1.00 and 1.00 are perfect correlations. If we calculate a coefficient that is outside this range, we have made a mistake in our calculations. A correlation coefficient of 1.00 indicates a perfect positive correlation because every point on the scatterplot falls in one line, as seen in the imaginary relation between absences and exam grades depicted in Figure 13-3. Higher scores on one variable are associated with higher scores on the other, and lower scores on one variable are associated with lower scores on the other. When a correlation coefficient is either −1.00 or 1.00, knowing somebody's score on one variable is sufficient to know exactly what that person's score is on the other variable. They are perfectly related.

> ▶ **MASTERING THE CONCEPT**
>
> **13-2:** The sign indicates the direction of the correlation, positive or negative. A positive correlation occurs when people who are high on one variable tend to be high on the other as well, and people who are low on one variable tend to be low on the other. A negative correlation occurs when people who are high on one variable tend to be low on the other.

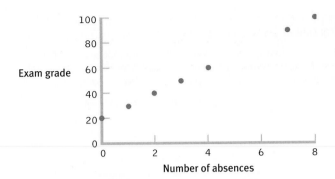

FIGURE 13-3
A Perfect Positive Correlation

When every pair of scores falls on the same line on the scatterplot, with higher scores on one variable associated with higher scores on the other (and lower scores with lower scores), there is a perfect positive correlation of 1.00, a situation that almost never occurs in real life. Also, we would not predict that the number of absences would be positively correlated with exam grade!

A correlation coefficient of −1.00 indicates a perfect negative correlation. Every point on the scatterplot falls in one line, as seen in the imaginary relation between absences and exam grades depicted in Figure 13-4, but now higher scores on one variable go with lower scores on the other variable. As with a perfect positive correlation, knowing one's score on one variable is sufficient to know one's exact score on the other variable. A correlation of 0.00 falls right in the middle of the two extremes and indicates no correlation— no association between the two variables.

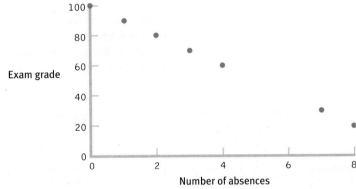

FIGURE 13-4
A Perfect Negative Correlation

When every pair of scores falls on the same line on the scatterplot and higher scores on one variable are associated with lower scores on the other variable, there is a perfect negative correlation of −1.00, a situation that almost never occurs in real life.

The third useful characteristic of the correlation coefficient is that its sign—positive or negative—indicates only the direction of the association, not the strength or size of the association. So a correlation coefficient of −0.35 is the same size as one of 0.35. A correlation coefficient of −0.67 is larger than one of 0.55. Don't be fooled by a negative sign; the sign indicates the direction of the relation, not the strength.

The strength of the correlation is determined by how close to "perfect" the data points are. The closer the data points are to the imaginary line that one could draw through them, the closer to a perfect correlation (either −1.00 or 1.00) and the stronger the relation between the two variables. The farther the points are from this imaginary line, the farther the correlation is from being perfect (so closer to 0.00) and the weaker the relation between the two variables.

The scores in a positive correlation move up and down together, the same way the mercury rises in a thermometer as the temperature goes up. The scores in a negative correlation move up and down in opposition to each other, like a teeter-totter. This is the key to correlation, and it is why knowing the direction of a correlation allows us to use a person's score on one variable to predict his or her score on another variable. Fortunately, we can be far more specific than merely identifying the direction of the correlation between variables. We can also quantify the strength of the correlation between those variables.

So, what magnitude of a correlation coefficient is large enough to be considered important, or worth talking about?

The Teeter-Tottering Negative Correlation When two variables are negatively correlated, a high score on one variable indicates a likely low score on the other variable—just like children on a teeter-totter.

TABLE 13-1. How Strong Is an Association?

Cohen (1988) published guidelines to help researchers determine the strength of a correlation from the correlation coefficient. In social science research, however, it is extremely unusual to have a correlation as high as 0.50, and many have disputed the utility of Cohen's conventions for many social science contexts.

Size of the Correlation	Correlation Coefficient
Small	0.10
Medium	0.30
Large	0.50

We can actually think about correlation coefficients as effect sizes. Cohen (1988) published standards, as seen in Table 13-1, for the size of the correlation coefficient, *r*. Very few findings in the social sciences have correlation coefficients of 0.50 or larger, the number that Cohen has suggested indicates a large correlation. This is usually true because any particular variable is influenced not just by one other variable but by many variables. A student's exam grade, for example, is influenced not only by absences from class but also by attention level in class, hours of studying, interest in the subject matter, IQ, and many more variables. So correlation coefficients are often surprising, usually because we expect a stronger (closer to −1.00 or 1.00) correlation than we actually observe.

When we read that two variables are correlated, we know only that they are associated with each other in some way. The first step in understanding correlation is to ascertain the direction of the association. Is it a positive correlation or a negative correlation? But that's not enough. We also need to know the size of the correlation. Is it small, medium, or large? And how big does the correlation need to be in a given context for it to have practical importance? We learn how to answer these questions later in the chapter, but before we do that, we need to learn a little more about what correlations can and cannot tell us.

Correlation Is Not Causation

As a student of the behavioral sciences, you need to understand what correlations can (and cannot) reveal about the relation between variables. Any two co-occurring events are, by definition, correlated, but they are not necessarily causally related. Correlations provide clues to causality, but they do not demonstrate or test for causality; they only quantify the strength and direction of the relation between variables. This is why your understanding of what correlations can and *cannot* do determines whether your reasoning is scientific. Let's think through the possible causal influences by using an example that we're already familiar with.

Let's say that we calculate a correlation coefficient for the relation between number of absences from statistics class and students' exam grades and that we find a strong negative correlation between these two variables. A professor would likely take this as evidence that students should attend class if they want to earn good grades. The assumption behind this conclusion is that class attendance causes good grades. As teachers who have observed many students study statistics, we do believe that class attendance leads to better grades. But, as researchers, we also have to acknowledge that (1) the pattern isn't true for every student and (2) there might be other explanations for this association.

With any association, we must consider three possible reasons for the pattern. Let's call absences from class variable "A" and exam grade variable "B." We could hypothesize that lower levels of the variable A cause higher levels of the variable B. Yet it is possible, although somewhat less plausible, that the reverse is true. Perhaps those who get good grades get more excited about class and don't want to be absent. In this case, higher levels of the variable B lead to lower levels of the variable A. But even more important is the possibility of a third variable (or more). We'll refer to any third (or fourth or fifth) variable as C. The three possibilities are outlined in Figure 13-5. Because we use the letters A, B, and C to describe the different possibilities, we refer to this as the A-B-C model.

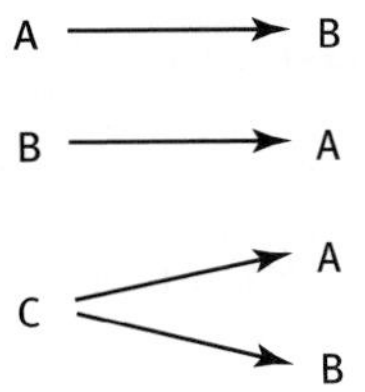

What third variables might lead to a correlation between number of absences and exam grade? A high need for achievement might lead both to better grades and to a realization that skipping class is a bad thing. Having friends in class also might lead students to avoid skipping class and then to get better grades by having study partners. What if it's a morning class? Students who are "morning people" might be more likely to wake up alert, not skip class, and therefore perform better on exam days. The possibilities are limitless. Never confuse correlation with causation.

FIGURE 13-5
Three Possible Causal Explanations for a Correlation

Any correlation could be explained in one of several ways. The first variable (A) might cause the second variable (B). Or the reverse could be true—the second variable (B) could cause the first variable (A). Finally, a third variable, C, could cause both A and B. In fact, there could be many "third" variables.

◀ **MASTERING THE CONCEPT**

13-3: Just because two variables are related doesn't mean one causes the other. It could be that one causes the second, the second causes the first, or a third variable causes both. Correlation does not indicate causation.

CHECK YOUR LEARNING

Reviewing the Concepts
> A correlation coefficient is a statistic that quantifies a relation between two variables.
> The correlation coefficient always falls between -1.00 and 1.00.
> When two variables are related such that people with high scores on one tend to have high scores on the other and people with low scores on one tend to have low scores on the other, we describe them as positively correlated.
> When two variables are related such that people with high scores on one tend to have low scores on the other, we describe them as negatively correlated.
> When two variables are not related, there is no correlation and they have a correlation coefficient close to 0.
> The strength of the correlation, captured by the number value of the coefficient, is independent of its sign. Cohen established standards for evaluating the strength of an association.
> Correlation is not equivalent to causation. In fact, correlation does not help us decide the merits of different causal explanations.
> When two variables are correlated, this association might occur because the first variable (A) causes the second (B) or because the second variable (B) causes the first (A). In addition, a third variable (C) could cause both of the correlated variables (A and B).

Clarifying the Concepts
13-1 There are three main characteristics of the correlation coefficient. What are they?
13-2 Why doesn't correlation indicate causation?

Calculating the Statistics
13-3 Use Cohen's guidelines to describe the strength of the following coefficients:
  a. -0.60
  b. 0.35
  c. 0.04

continued on next page

13-4 Draw a hypothetical scatterplot to depict the following correlation coefficients:

a. −0.60

b. 0.35

c. 0.04

Applying the Concepts

Solutions to these Check Your Learning questions can be found in Appendix D.

13-5 A writer for *Runner's World* magazine debated the merits of running while listening to music (Seymour, 2006). The writer, an avid iPod user, interviewed a clinical psychologist, whose response to the debate about whether to listen to music while running was: "I like to do what the great ones do and try to emulate that. What are the Kenyans doing? Are they running with Walkmans?" Let's say a researcher conducted a study in which he determined the correlation between the percentage of a country's marathon runners who train while using a portable music device and the average marathon finishing time for that country's runners. (Note that in this case the participants are countries, not people.) Let's say the researcher finds a strong positive correlation. That is, the more of a country's runners that train with music, the longer the average marathon finishing time. Remember, in a marathon, a longer time is bad. So this fictional finding is that training with music is associated with *slower* marathon finishing times; the United States, for example, would have a higher percentage of music use and higher (slower) finishing times than Kenya. Using the A-B-C model, provide three possible explanations for this finding.

The Pearson Correlation Coefficient

When we want to understand more about a relation between two variables, such as the relation between spending on health care and longevity, we want to calculate the correlation coefficient so we can know the direction and strength of the relation. There are several kinds of correlation coefficients. The one that we choose to calculate depends on the specific relation between our variables. *The **Pearson correlation coefficient** is a statistic that quantifies a linear relation between two scale variables.* In other words, a single number is used to describe the direction and strength of the relation between two variables when their overall pattern indicates a straight-line relation. The Pearson correlation coefficient is symbolized by the italic letter r when it is a statistic based on sample data. When we're referring to the population parameter for the correlation coefficient, such as when we're writing the hypotheses for significance testing, we use the Greek letter ρ, written as "rho" and pronounced "row," even though it looks a bit like the Latin letter p.

Calculation of the Pearson Correlation Coefficient

The correlation coefficient can be used as a descriptive statistic, simply to describe the direction and strength of an association between two variables. However, it also can be used as an inferential statistic. We can conduct a hypothesis test to determine if the correlation coefficient is significantly different from 0 (no correlation). In this section, we construct a scatterplot from our data and learn how to calculate the correlation coefficient. In the next section, we walk through the steps of hypothesis testing.

EXAMPLE 13.3

Let's consider an example related to your everyday decision making as a student. Every couple of semesters, we have a student who avows that she does not have to attend statistics classes regularly to do well because she can learn it all from the book. What do you think? What relation would you expect between the variables of attendance and exam grades? Table 13-2 displays the data for 10 students in one of our recent sta-

TABLE 13-2. Is Skipping Class Related to Statistics Exam Grades?

Here are the scores for 10 students on two scale variables: number of absences from class in one semester, and the student's exam grade.

Student	Absences	Exam Grade
1	4	82
2	2	98
3	2	76
4	3	68
5	1	84
6	0	99
7	4	67
8	8	58
9	7	50
10	3	78

■ The **Pearson correlation coefficient** is a statistic that quantifies a linear relation between two scale variables.

tistics classes. The second column shows the number of absences over the semester (out of 29 classes total) for each student, and the third column shows each student's final exam grade for the semester.

Before we even start the calculations, we want to construct a scatterplot for these data, seen in Figure 13-6, to be sure that the relation is roughly linear. We can see from this scatterplot that the data, overall, have a pattern through which we could imagine drawing a straight line. So, from this graph, we can confirm that the data have an approximately linear relation, and it is safe to proceed with the calculation of a Pearson correlation coefficient. It's also helpful to use the scatterplot to make a guess about what we'd expect the correlation coefficient to be. If the coefficient that we calculate does not match our expectations, we can go back to find out where we went wrong.

We learned earlier that a positive correlation results when a high score—one above the mean—on one variable tends to indicate a high score—also above the mean—on the other variable. On the other hand, a negative correlation results when a high score

> ◀ **MASTERING THE CONCEPT**
>
> **13-4:** A scatterplot can indicate whether two variables are linearly related. It can also give us a sense of the direction and strength of the relation between the two variables.

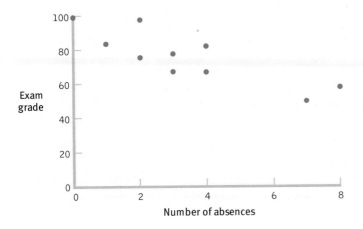

FIGURE 13-6
Always Start with a Scatterplot

Before calculating a correlation coefficient for the relation between number of absences from class and exam grade, we construct a scatterplot. If the relation between the variables appears to be roughly linear, we can calculate a Pearson correlation coefficient. We can also use the scatterplot to make a guess about what we expect from the correlation. Here, the correlation appears to be negative. The pattern of data goes down and to the right, and high scores on one variable are associated with low scores on the other. In addition, we would expect a somewhat large correlation—that is, fairly close to −1.00—because the data are fairly close to forming a straight line.

on one variable—above the mean—tends to indicate a low score—below the mean—on the other variable.

One straightforward way to determine whether an individual falls above or below the mean is to calculate deviations for each score. If participants tend to have two positive deviations (both scores above the mean) or two negative deviations (both scores below the mean), then the two variables are likely to be positively correlated. If participants tend to have one positive deviation (above the mean) and one negative deviation (below the mean), then the two variables are likely to be negatively correlated. We can harness this aspect of deviations to calculate the correlation coefficient. In fact, when we calculate the correlation coefficient, part of the process involves multiplying the deviations for each pair of scores.

Think about why this makes sense. Let's consider a positive correlation. High scores are above the mean and so would have positive deviations. The product of a pair of high scores would be positive. Low scores are below the mean and would have negative deviations. The product of a pair of low scores would also be positive. When we calculate a correlation coefficient, part of the process involves adding up the products of the deviations. If most of these are positive, we get a positive correlation coefficient.

Let's consider a negative correlation. High scores, which are above the mean, would convert to positive deviations. Low scores, which are below the mean, would convert to negative deviations. The product of one positive deviation and one negative deviation would be negative. If most of the products of the deviations are negative, we would get a negative correlation coefficient.

In fact, the process we just described is the calculation of the numerator of the correlation coefficient. Let's try it with our data. Table 13-3 shows us the calculations. The first column has the number of absences for each student. The second column shows the deviations from the mean, 3.40. The third column has the exam grade for each student. The fourth column shows the deviations from the mean for that variable, 76.00. The fifth column shows the products of the deviations. Below the fifth column, we see the sum of the products of the deviations, −304.00.

As you can see in Table 13-3, the pairs of scores tend to fall on either side of the mean—that is, for each student, a negative deviation on one score tends to indicate a

TABLE 13-3. Calculating the Numerator of the Correlation Coefficient

Absences (X)	($X - M_X$)	Exam Grade (Y)	($Y - M_Y$)	($X - M_X$)($Y - M_Y$)
4	0.6	82	6	3.6
2	−1.4	98	22	−30.8
2	−1.4	76	0	0.0
3	−0.4	68	−8	3.2
1	−2.4	84	8	−19.2
0	−3.4	99	23	−78.2
4	0.6	67	−9	−5.4
8	4.6	58	−18	−82.8
7	3.6	50	−26	−93.6
3	−0.4	78	2	−0.8
$M_X = 3.400$		$M_Y = 76.000$		$\Sigma[(X - M_X)(Y - M_Y)] = -304.0$

positive deviation on the other score. For example, student 6 was never absent, so he has a score of 0, which is well below the mean, and he got a 99 on the exam, well above the mean. On the other hand, student 9 was absent 7 times, well above the mean, and she only got a 50 on the exam, well below the mean. So most of the products of the deviations are negative, and when we sum the products, we get a negative total. This indicates a negative correlation.

You might have noticed that this number, -304.0, is not between -1.00 and 1.00. The problem is that this number is influenced by two factors—sample size and variability. First, the more people in the sample, the more deviations there are to contribute to the sum. Second, if the scores in our study are more variable, the deviations would be larger, and so would the sum of the products. So we have to correct for these two factors in our denominator.

It makes sense that we would have to correct for variability. In Chapter 6, we learned that z scores provide an important function in statistics by allowing us to standardize. You may remember that the formula for the z score that we first learned was $z = \dfrac{(X - M)}{SD}$. In the calculations in the numerator of the correlation coefficient, we already subtracted the mean from our scores, but we didn't divide by standard deviation. If we correct for variability in our denominator, that takes care of one of the two factors for which we have to correct.

But we also have to correct for sample size. You may remember that when we calculate standard deviation, the last two steps are (1) dividing the sum of squared deviations by the sample size, N, to remove the influence of the sample size and to calculate variance, and (2) taking the square root of variance to get standard deviation. So to factor in sample size along with standard deviation (which we just mentioned allows us to factor in variability), we can go backward in our calculations. If we multiply variance by sample size, we get the sum of squared deviations, or sum of squares. Because of this, the denominator of the correlation coefficient is based on the sums of squares for both variables. To make the denominator match the numerator, we multiply the two sums of squares together, and then we take their square root, as we would with standard deviation. Table 13-4 shows the calculations for the sum of squares for the two variables, absences and exam grades.

TABLE 13-4. Calculating the Denominator of the Correlation Coefficient

Absences (X)	$(X - M_X)$	$(X - M_X)^2$	Exam Grade (Y)	$(Y - M_Y)$	$(Y - M_Y)^2$
4	0.6	0.36	82	6	36
2	−1.4	1.96	98	22	484
2	−1.4	1.96	76	0	0
3	−0.4	0.16	68	−8	64
1	−2.4	5.76	84	8	64
0	−3.4	11.56	99	23	529
4	0.6	0.36	67	−9	81
8	4.6	21.16	58	−18	324
7	3.6	12.96	50	−26	676
3	−0.4	0.16	78	2	4
		$\Sigma(X - M_X)^2 = 56.4$			$\Sigma(Y - M_Y)^2 = 2262$

We now have all of the ingredients necessary to calculate the correlation coefficient. Here's the formula:

$$r = \frac{\Sigma[(X - M_X)(Y - M_Y)]}{\sqrt{(SS_X)(SS_Y)}}$$

The numerator is the sum of the product of the deviations for each variable.

Step 1: For each score, we calculate the deviation from its mean.

Step 2: For each participant, we multiply the deviations for his or her two scores.

Step 3: We sum the products of the deviations.

The denominator is the square root of the product of the two sums of squares.

Step 1: We calculate a sum of squares for each variable.

Step 2: We multiply the two sums of squares.

Step 3: We take the square root of the product of the sums of squares.

Let's apply the formula for the correlation coefficient to our data:

$$r = \frac{\Sigma[(X - M_X)(Y - M_Y)]}{\sqrt{(SS_X)(SS_Y)}} = \frac{-304.0}{\sqrt{(56.4)(2262.0)}} = \frac{-304.0}{357.179} = -0.851$$

So the Pearson correlation coefficient, r, is -0.85. This is a very strong negative correlation. If we examine the scatterplot in Figure 13-6 carefully, we will notice that there aren't any glaring individual exceptions to this rule. The dots tell a consistent story. So what should our students learn from this result? Go to class! (But remember that correlation is not necessarily causation; other factors are likely at work, too.)

Hypothesis Testing with the Pearson Correlation Coefficient

We said earlier that correlation can be used as a descriptive statistic to simply describe a relation between two variables and that it also can be used as an inferential statistic.

EXAMPLE 13.4

Here we outline the six steps for hypothesis testing with a correlation coefficient. Usually, when we conduct hypothesis testing with correlation, we want to test whether our correlation is statistically significantly different from no correlation—an r of 0.

STEP 1. Identify the population, distribution, and assumptions. Population 1: Students like those whom we studied in Example 13.3. Population 2: Students for whom there is no correlation between number of absences and exam grade.

The comparison distribution is a distribution of correlation coefficients taken from the population, but with the characteristics of our study, such as a sample size of 10. In this case, it is a distribution of all possible correlations between the numbers of absences and exam grades when 10 students are considered.

The first two assumptions are like those for other parametric tests. (1) The data must be randomly selected, or external validity will be limited. In this case, we do not know how the data were selected, so we should generalize with caution. (2) The underlying population distributions for the two variables must be approximately normal. In our study, it's difficult to tell if the distribution is normal because we have so few data points.

MASTERING THE FORMULA

13-1: The formula for the correlation coefficient is: $r = \frac{\Sigma[(X - M_X)(Y - M_Y)]}{\sqrt{(SS_X)(SS_Y)}}$. We divide the sum of the products of the deviations for each variable by the square root of the products of the sums of squares for each variable. This calculation has a built-in standardization procedure: It subtracts a mean from each score and divides by some kind of variability. By using sums of squares in the denominator, it also takes sample size into account.

MASTERING THE CONCEPT

13-5: As with other statistics, we can conduct hypothesis testing with the correlation coefficient. We compare our correlation coefficient to critical values on the r distribution.

The third assumption is specific to correlation: each variable should vary equally, no matter the magnitude of the other variable. That is, number of absences should show the same amount of variability at each level of exam grade; conversely, exam grade should show the same amount of variability at each number of absences. You can get a sense of this by looking at the scatterplot in Figure 13-7. In our study, it's hard to determine whether the amount of variability is the same for each variable across all levels of the other variable because we have so few data points. But it seems as if there's variability of between 10 and 20 points on exam grade at each number of absences. The center of that variability decreases as we increase in number of absences, but the amount of variability stays roughly the same. It also seems that there's variability of between 2 and 3 absences at each exam grade. Again, the center of that variability decreases as exam grade increases, but the amount of variability stays roughly the same.

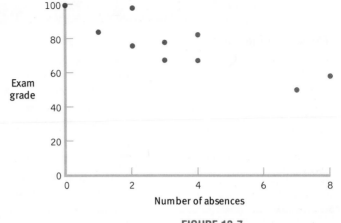

FIGURE 13-7
Using a Scatterplot to Examine the Assumptions

We can use a scatterplot to see whether one variable varies equally at each level of the other variable. With only 10 data points, we can't be certain. But this scatterplot suggests a variability of between 10 and 20 points on exam grade at each number of absences, and a variability of between 2 and 3 absences at each exam grade.

STEP 2. State the null and research hypotheses.

Null hypothesis: There is no correlation between number of absences and exam grade—H_0: $r = 0$. Research hypothesis: There is a correlation between number of absences and exam grade—H_1: $r \neq 0$.

STEP 3. Determine the characteristics of the comparison distribution.

The comparison distribution is an r distribution with degrees of freedom calculated by subtracting 2 from the sample size, which in Pearson correlation is the number of participants rather than the number of scores:

$$df_r = N - 2$$

In our study, degrees of freedom are calculated as follows:

$$df_r = N - 2 = 10 - 2 = 8$$

So the comparison distribution is an r distribution with 8 degrees of freedom.

STEP 4. Determine the critical values, or cutoffs.

Now that we know the degrees of freedom, we can look up the critical values in the r table in Appendix B. Like the z table and the t table, the r table includes only positive values. For a two-tailed test, we'd take the negative and positive version of the critical test statistic indicated in the table. So, the critical values for an r distribution with 8 degrees of freedom for a two-tailed test with a p level of 0.05 are -0.632 and 0.632.

STEP 5. Calculate the test statistic.

We've already calculated our test statistic, r, above. It is -0.85.

STEP 6. Make a decision.

Our test statistic, $r = -0.85$, is larger in magnitude than the critical value of -0.632. We can reject the null hypothesis and conclude that number of absences and exam grade seem to be negatively correlated.

◀ **MASTERING THE FORMULA**

13-2: When conducting hypothesis testing for the Pearson correlation coefficient, r, we calculate degrees of freedom by subtracting 2 from the sample size. In Pearson correlation, the sample size is the number of participants, not the number of scores. The formula is: $df_r = N - 2$.

CHECK YOUR LEARNING

Reviewing the Concepts

> The Pearson correlation coefficient allows us to quantify the relations that we observe.

> Before we calculate a correlation coefficient, we must always construct a scatterplot to be sure the two variables are linearly related.

> Once we have determined that any association is linear, the Pearson correlation coefficient is calculated in three basic steps. (1) We calculate the deviation of each score from its mean, multiply the two deviations for each person, and sum the products of the deviations. (2) We calculate a sum of squares for each variable, multiply the sums of squares, and take the square root. (3) We divide the sum from step 1 by the square root in step 2.

> We can use the six steps of hypothesis testing to determine whether our correlation coefficient is statistically significantly different from 0. We compare our correlation coefficient to critical values on an r distribution.

Clarifying the Concepts

13-6 Define the Pearson correlation coefficient.

13-7 The denominator of the correlation equation corrects for what two issues present in the calculation of the numerator?

Calculating the Statistics

13-8 Create a scatterplot for the following data:

Variable A	Variable B
8.0	14.0
7.0	13.0
6.0	10.0
5.0	9.5
4.0	8.0
5.5	9.0
6.0	12.0
8.0	11.0

13-9 Calculate the correlation coefficient for the data provided in Check Your Learning 13-8 by completing these three steps:

  a. Calculate deviation scores, products of the deviations for each individual, and sum all products. This is the numerator of the correlation coefficient equation.

  b. Calculate the sum of squares for each variable. Then compute the square root of the product of the sums of squares. This is the denominator of the correlation coefficient equation.

  c. Divide the numerator by the denominator to compute the coefficient, r.

Applying the Concepts

13-10 According to social learning theory, children exposed to aggressive behavior, including family violence, are more likely to engage in aggressive behavior than children who do not witness such violence. Let's assume the data you worked with in Check Your Learning 13-8 and 13-9 represent exposure to violence as the first variable (A) and aggressive behavior as the second variable (B). For both variables, higher values indicate higher levels, either of exposure to violence or of incidents of aggressive behavior. You computed the correlation coefficient, step 5 in hypothesis testing, in Check Your Learning 13-9. Now, let's complete the other five steps of hypothesis testing.

  a. Step 1: Identify the population, distribution, and assumptions.

  b. Step 2: State the null and research hypotheses.

Solutions to these Check Your Learning questions can be found in Appendix D.

c. Step 3: Determine the characteristics of the comparison distribution.

d. Step 4: Determine the critical values, or cutoffs, assuming a two-tailed test with a *p* level of 0.05.

e. Step 6: Make a decision, including an evaluation of the size of the correlation using Cohen's guidelines.

REVIEW OF CONCEPTS

Correlation

Correlation is an association between two variables and is quantified by a *correlation coefficient*. A *positive correlation* indicates that a participant who has a high score on one variable is likely to have a high score on the other, and someone with a low score on one variable is likely to have a low score on the other. A *negative correlation* indicates that someone with a high score on one variable is likely to have a low score on the other. All correlation coefficients must fall between −1.00 and 1.00. The strength of the correlation is independent of its sign.

Correlation coefficients can be very useful but also have the ability to mislead. To accurately interpret a correlation coefficient, we must be certain not to confuse correlation with causation. We cannot know the causal direction in which two variables are related from a correlation coefficient, nor can we know if there is a hidden third variable that causes the apparent relation.

The Pearson Correlation Coefficient

The *Pearson correlation coefficient* is used when two scale variables are linearly related, as determined from a scatterplot. Calculating a *correlation coefficient* involves three steps. (1) We calculate the deviation of each score from its mean, multiply the deviations on each variable for each participant, and add the products of the deviations. (2) We multiply the sums of squares for each variable, then take the square root of the product. (3) We divide the sum of the products of the deviations (from step 1) by the square root of the product of the sums of squares (from step 2). We can use the six steps of hypothesis testing to determine whether our correlation coefficient is statistically significantly different from 0. We compare our coefficient to critical values on the *r* distribution.

SPSS®

Instructing SPSS to run a correlation on our variables requires only a few choices, but those choices remind us what a correlation can and *cannot* reveal about the relation between two scale variables. Enter the data for the example used to calculate the correlation coefficient in this chapter: numbers of absences and exam grades. Be sure to put each student's two scores on the same row.

To view a scatterplot of the relations between two variables, select: **Graphs** → Chart Builder → Gallery → Scatter/Dot. Drag the upper-left sample scatterplot to the large box on top. Then select the variables to be included in the scatterplot by dragging the independent variable, absences, to the *x*-axis and the dependent variable, grade, to the *y*-axis. Click "OK."

If the scatterplot indicates that we meet the assumptions for a Pearson correlation coefficient, we can analyze our data. Select: **Analyze** → Correlate → Bivariate. Then select the two variables to be analyzed, absences and grade. "Pearson" will already be checked as the type of correlation coefficient to be calculated. (*Note:* If more than two variables are selected, SPSS will build a correlation matrix of all possible pairs of variables.) After making our choices, we click on "OK" to see the Output screen. The screenshot here shows the output for our Pearson correlation coefficient. Notice that the correlation coefficient is 0.851, the same as the coefficient that we calculated by hand earlier. The two asterisks indicate that it is statistically significant at a *p* level of 0.01.

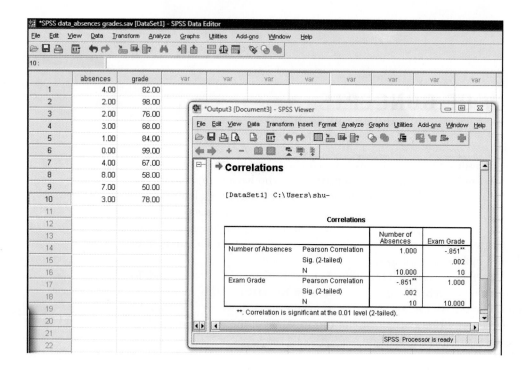

How It Works

13.1: UNDERSTANDING CORRELATION COEFFICIENTS

A researcher gathered data on psychology students' ratings of their likelihood of attending graduate school and the numbers of credits they had completed in their psychology major (Rajecki, Lauer, & Metzner, 1998). Imagine that each of the following numbers represents the Pearson correlation coefficient that quantifies the relation between these two variables. From each coefficient, explain what we know about the relation between the two variables.

  a. 1.00: This correlation coefficient reflects a perfect positive relation between students' ratings of the likelihood of attending graduate school and the number of psychology credits they completed. This correlation is the strongest correlation of the options.

  b. −0.001: This correlation coefficient reflects a lack of relation between students' ratings and the number of psychology credits they completed. This is the weakest correlation of the options.

  c. 0.56: This correlation coefficient reflects a large positive relation between students' ratings and the number of completed psychology credits.

  d. −0.27: This coefficient reflects a medium negative relation between students' ratings and the number of completed psychology credits. (*Note:* This is the actual correlation between these variables found in the study.)

  e. −0.98: This coefficient reflects a large (close to perfect) negative relation between students' ratings and the number of psychology credits they have completed.

    f. 0.09: This coefficient reflects a small positive relation between students' ratings and the number of completed psychology credits.

13.2: CALCULATING THE PEARSON CORRELATION COEFFICIENT

Is age associated with how much people study? Calculate the Pearson correlation coefficient for the accompanying data (taken from students in some of our statistics classes).

Student	Age	Number of Hours Studied Per Week
1	19	5
2	20	20
3	20	8
4	21	12
5	21	18
6	23	25
7	22	15
8	20	10
9	19	14
10	25	15

1. Our first step is to construct a scatterplot:

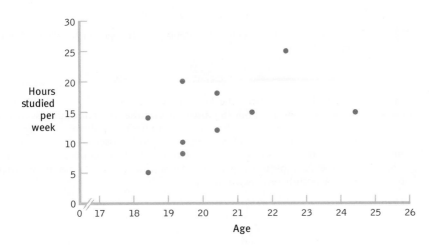

    We can see from this scatterplot that the data, overall, have a pattern through which we could imagine drawing a straight line. So we know the data have an approximately linear relation and it is safe to proceed with the calculation of the Pearson correlation coefficient.

    2. Our next step is to calculate the numerator of the Pearson correlation coefficient. The numerator is the sum of the product of the deviations for each variable. The mean for age is 21, and the mean for hours studied is 14.2. We use these means to calculate each score's deviation from its mean. We then multiply the deviations for each student's two scores, and sum the products of the deviations. Here are the calculations:

Age (X)	($X - M$)	Hours Studied (Y)	($Y - M$)	($X - M$)($Y - M$)
19	−2	5	−9.2	18.4
20	−1	20	5.8	−5.8
20	−1	8	−6.2	6.2
21	0	12	−2.2	0
21	0	18	3.8	0
23	2	25	10.8	21.6
22	1	15	0.8	0.8
20	−1	10	−4.2	4.2
19	−2	14	−0.2	0.4
25	4	15	0.8	3.2
$M_X = 21$		$M_Y = 14.2$		$\Sigma[(X - M_X)(Y - M_Y)] = 49$

The numerator is 49.

3. Our next step is to calculate the denominator of the Pearson correlation coefficient. The denominator is the square root of the product of the two sums of squares. We first calculate a sum of squares for each variable. The calculations are here:

Age (X)	($X - M$)	($X - M$)^2	Hours Studied (Y)	($Y - M$)	($Y - M$)^2
19	−2	4	5	−9.2	84.64
20	−1	1	20	5.8	33.64
20	−1	1	8	−6.2	38.44
21	0	0	12	−2.2	4.84
21	0	0	18	3.8	14.44
23	2	4	25	10.8	116.64
22	1	1	15	0.8	0.64
20	−1	1	10	−4.2	17.64
19	−2	4	14	−0.2	0.04
25	4	16	15	0.8	0.64
$M = 21$	$\Sigma(X - M)^2 = 32$		$M = 14.2$		$\Sigma(Y - M)^2 = 311.6$

We now multiply the two sums of squares, then take the square root of the product of the sums of squares.

$$\sqrt{(SS_X)(SS_Y)} = \sqrt{(32)(311.6)} = 99.856$$

4. Finally, we can put our numerator and denominator together to calculate our Pearson correlation coefficient:

$$r = \frac{\Sigma[(X - M_X)(Y - M_Y)]}{\sqrt{(SS_X)(SS_Y)}} = \frac{49}{99.856} = 0.49$$

5. Now that we have calculated the Pearson correlation coefficient (0.49), we determine what the statistic tells us about the direction and the strength of the association between the two variables (age and number of hours studied). The absence of a sign indicates that this is a positive correlation. Higher ages tend to be associated with longer hours spent studying, and lower ages tend to be associated with fewer hours spent studying. This is what we would expect given that pairs of scores for each student tend to be either both above the mean or both below the mean.

Exercises

Clarifying the Concepts

13.1 What is a correlation coefficient?

13.2 What is a linear relation?

13.3 Describe a perfect correlation, including its possible coefficients.

13.4 What is the difference between a *positive correlation* and a *negative correlation*?

13.5 What *magnitude* of a correlation coefficient is large enough to be considered important, or worth talking about?

13.6 When we have a straight-line relation between two variables, we use a Pearson correlation coefficient. What does this coefficient describe?

13.7 Explain how the correlation coefficient can be used as a descriptive or inferential statistic.

13.8 How are deviation scores used in assessing the relation between variables?

13.9 Explain how the sum of the product of deviations determines the sign of the correlation.

13.10 What are the null and research hypotheses for correlations?

13.11 What are the three basic steps to calculate the Pearson correlation coefficient?

13.12 Describe the third assumption of hypothesis testing with correlation.

Calculating the Statistics

13.13 Determine if the data in each of the graphs provided would result in a negative or positive correlation coefficient.

a.

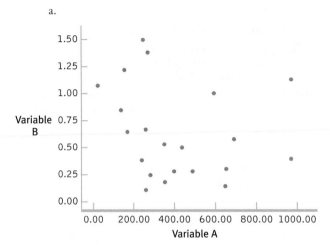

b.

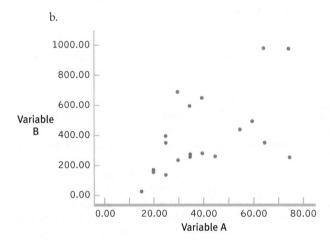

c.

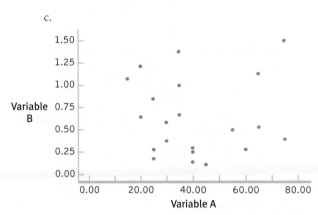

13.14 Decide which of the three correlation coefficient values below goes with each of the scatterplots presented in Exercise 13.13 above.

a. 0.545

b. 0.018

c. −0.20

13.15 Use Cohen's guidelines to describe the strength of the following correlation coefficients:

a. −0.28

b. 0.79

c. 1.0

d. −0.015

13.16 For each of the pairs of correlation coefficients provided, determine which one indicates a stronger relation between variables:

a. −0.28 and −0.31

b. 0.79 and 0.61

c. 1.0 and −1.0

d. −0.15 and 0.13

13.17 Create a scatterplot for the following data:

X	Y
0.13	645
0.27	486
0.49	435
0.57	689
0.84	137
0.64	167

13.18 Create a scatterplot for the following data:

X	Y	X	Y
394	25	276	40
972	75	254	45
349	25	156	20
349	65	248	75
593	35		

13.19 Create a scatterplot for the following data:

X	Y
40	60
45	55
20	30
75	25
15	20
35	40
65	30

13.20 Calculate the correlation coefficient for the data provided in Exercise 13.17 by completing these three steps:

  a. Calculate deviation scores, multiply the deviations for each individual, and sum all products. This is the numerator of the correlation coefficient equation.

  b. Calculate the sum of squares for each variable. Then compute the square root of the product of the sums of squares. This is the denominator of the correlation coefficient equation.

  c. Divide the numerator by the denominator to compute the coefficient, r.

13.21 Calculate the correlation coefficient for the data provided in Exercise 13.18 by completing these three steps:

  a. Calculate deviation scores, multiply the deviations for each individual, and sum all products. This is the numerator of the correlation coefficient equation.

  b. Calculate the sum of squares for each variable. Then compute the square root of the product of the sums of squares. This is the denominator of the correlation coefficient equation.

  c. Divide the numerator by the denominator to compute the coefficient, r.

13.22 Calculate the correlation coefficient for the data provided in Exercise 13.19 by completing these three steps:

  a. Calculate deviation scores, multiply the deviations for each individual, and sum all products. This is the numerator of the correlation coefficient equation.

  b. Calculate the sum of squares for each variable. Then compute the square root of the product of the sums of squares. This is the denominator of the correlation coefficient equation.

  c. Divide the numerator by the denominator to compute the coefficient, r.

13.23 Calculate degrees of freedom for each of the following studies:

  a. Forty students were recruited for a study about the relation between knowledge regarding academic integrity and values held by students, with the idea that students with less knowledge would care less about the issue than students with greater amounts of knowledge.

  b. Twenty-seven couples are surveyed regarding their years together and their relationship satisfaction.

  c. Data are collected to examine the relation between size of dog and rate of bone and joint health issues. Veterinarians from around the country contributed data on 3113 dogs.

  d. Hours spent studying per week was correlated with credit hour load for 72 students.

13.24 Calculate degrees of freedom for the data provided in each of the following:

  a. Exercise 13.17

  b. Exercise 13.18

  c. Exercise 13.19

13.25 Determine the critical values, or cutoffs, assuming a two-tailed test with a p level of 0.05, for each of the designs described in Exercise 13.23.

13.26 Determine the critical values, or cutoffs, assuming a two-tailed test with a p level of 0.05, for the data provided in:

  a. Exercise 13.17

  b. Exercise 13.18

  c. Exercise 13.19

Applying the Concepts

13.27 The *New York Times* reported that an officer of the International Society for Astrological Research, Anne Massey, stated that a certain phase of the planet Mercury, the retrograde phase, leads to breakdowns in areas as wide-ranging as communication and travel (Newman, 2006). The *Times* reporter, Andy Newman, documented the likelihood of breakdown on a number of variables in both phases, retrograde and nonretrograde. Newman discovered that, contrary to Massey's hypothesis, New Jersey Transit commuter trains were less likely to be late, by 0.4%, during the retrograde phase. On the other hand, consistent with Massey's hypothesis, the rate of baggage complaints at LaGuardia airport increased from 5.38 during nonretrograde periods to 5.44 during retrograde periods. Newman's findings were contradictory across all examined variables—rates of theft, computer crashes, traffic disruptions, delayed plane arrivals—with some variables backing Massey and others not. Newman cited a transportation statistics expert, Bruce Schaller, who said, "If all of this is due to randomness, that's the result you'd expect." Astrologer Massey counters that the pattern she predicts would only emerge across thousands of years of data.

  a. Do reporter Newman's data suggest a correlation between Mercury's phase and breakdowns?

  b. How do transportation expert Schaller's statement and Newman's contradictory results relate to what you learned about probability in Chapter 5? Discuss expected relative-frequency probability in your answer.

  c. If there were indeed a small correlation that one could observe only across thousands of years of data, how useful would that knowledge be in terms of predicting events in your own life?

  d. Write a brief response to Massey's contention of a correlation between Mercury's phases and breakdowns in aspects of day-to-day living.

13.28 In the newspaper column discussed at the beginning of this chapter, Paul Krugman (2006) mentioned obesity (as measured by body mass index) as a possible correlate of age at death.

    a. Describe the likely correlation between these variables. Is it likely to be positive or negative? Explain.

    b. Draw a scatterplot that depicts the correlation you described in part (a).

13.29 Does the amount that people exercise correlate with the number of friends they have? The accompanying table contains data collected in some of our statistics classes. The first column shows hours exercised per week and the second column shows the number of close friends reported by each participant.

Exercise	Friends	Exercise	Friends
1.00	4.00	8.00	4.00
.00	3.00	2.00	4.00
1.00	2.00	10.00	4.00
6.00	6.00	5.00	7.00
1.00	3.00	4.00	5.00
6.00	5.00	2.00	6.00
2.00	4.00	7.00	5.00
3.00	5.00	1.00	5.00
5.00	6.00		

    a. Create a scatterplot of these data. Be sure to label both axes.

    b. What does the scatterplot suggest about the relation between these two variables?

    c. Would it be appropriate to calculate a Pearson correlation coefficient? Explain your answer.

13.30 A study on the relation between rejection and depression in adolescents conducted by one of the authors (Nolan, Flynn, & Garber, 2003) also collected data on externalizing behaviors (e.g., acting out in negative ways, such as causing fights) and anxiety. We wondered whether externalizing behaviors were related to feelings of anxiety. Some of the data are presented in the accompanying table.

Externalizing	Anxiety	Externalizing	Anxiety
9.00	37.00	6.00	33.00
7.00	23.00	2.00	26.00
7.00	26.00	6.00	35.00
3.00	21.00	6.00	23.00
11.00	42.00	9.00	28.00

    a. Create a scatterplot of these data. Be sure to label both axes.

    b. What does the scatterplot suggest about the relation between these two variables?

    c. Would it be appropriate to calculate a Pearson correlation coefficient? Explain your answer.

    d. Construct a second scatterplot, but this time add in the data for one more participant who scored 1 on externalizing and 45 on anxiety. Would you expect the correlation coefficient to be positive or negative now? Small in magnitude or large in magnitude?

    e. The Pearson correlation coefficient for the first set of data is 0.61; for the second set of data it is 0.12. Explain why the correlation changed so much with the addition of just one participant.

13.31 Using the data in Exercise 13.30, perform all six steps of hypothesis testing to explore the relation between externalizing and anxiety.

    a. Step 1: Identify the population, distribution, and assumptions.

    b. Step 2: State the null and research hypotheses.

    c. Step 3: Determine the characteristics of the comparison distribution.

    d. Step 4: Determine the critical values, or cutoffs, assuming a two-tailed test with a p level of 0.05.

    e. Step 5: Calculate the test statistic.

    f. Step 6: Make a decision, including an evaluation of the size of the correlation using Cohen's guidelines.

13.32 For each of the following pairs of variables, would you expect a positive correlation or a negative correlation between the two variables? Explain your answer.

    a. How hard the rain is falling and your commuting time

    b. How often you say no to dessert and your body fat

    c. The amount of wine you consume with dinner and your alertness after dinner

13.33 You may be aware of the stereotype about the crazy elderly person who owns a lot of cats. Have you wondered whether the stereotype is true? As a researcher, you decide to interview 100 senior citizens in a retirement complex. You assess all senior citizens on two variables: (1) the number of cats they own and (2) their level of mental health problems (a higher score indicates more problems).

    a. Imagine that you found a positive relation between these two variables. What might you expect for someone who owns a lot of cats? Explain.

    b. Imagine that you found a positive relation between these two variables. What might you expect for someone who owns no cats or just one cat? Explain.

    c. Imagine that you found a negative relation between these two variables. What might you expect for someone who owns a lot of cats? Explain.

d. Imagine that you found a negative relation between these two variables. What might you expect for someone who owns no cats or just one cat? Explain.

13.34 Consider the scenario in Exercise 13.33 again. The two variables under consideration were (1) number of cats owned and (2) level of mental health problems (with a higher score indicating more problems). Each possible relation between these variables would be represented by a different scatterplot. Using data for about 10 participants, draw a scatterplot that depicts a correlation between these variables for each of the following:

a. A weak positive correlation

b. A strong positive correlation

c. A perfect positive correlation

d. A weak negative correlation

e. A strong negative correlation

f. A perfect negative correlation

g. No (or almost no) correlation

13.35 Graduate student Angela Holiday (2007) conducted a study examining perceptions of combat veterans suffering from mental illness. Participants read a description of a person, either a man or a woman, who had recently returned from combat in Iraq and who was suffering from depression. Participants rated the situation (combat in Iraq) with respect to how traumatic they believed it was; they also rated the combat veterans on a range of variables, including scales that assessed how masculine and how feminine they perceived the person to be. Among other analyses, Holiday examined the relation between the perception of the situation as being traumatic and the perception of the veteran as being masculine or feminine. When the person was male, the perception of the situation as traumatic was strongly positively correlated with the perception of the man as feminine but was only weakly positively correlated with the perception of the man as masculine. What would you expect when the person was female? The accompanying table presents some of the data for the perception of the situation as traumatic (on a scale of 1–10, with 10 being the most traumatic) and the perception of the woman as feminine (on a scale of 1–10, with 10 being the most feminine).

Traumatic	Feminine
5	6
6	5
4	6
5	6
7	4
8	5

a. Draw a scatterplot for these data. Does the scatterplot suggest that it is appropriate to calculate a Pearson correlation coefficient? Explain.

b. Calculate the Pearson correlation coefficient.

c. State what the Pearson correlation coefficient tells us about the relation between these two variables.

d. Explain why the pattern of pairs of deviation scores enables us to understand the relation between the two variables. (That is, consider whether pairs of deviations tend to have the same sign or opposite signs.)

13.36 Using the data and your work in Exercise 13.35, perform the remaining five steps of hypothesis testing to explore the relation between trauma and femininity.

a. Step 1: Identify the population, distribution, and assumptions.

b. Step 2: State the null and research hypotheses.

c. Step 3: Determine the characteristics of the comparison distribution.

d. Step 4: Determine the critical values, or cutoffs, assuming a two-tailed test with a p level of 0.05.

e. Step 6: Make a decision, including an evaluation of the size of the correlation using Cohen's guidelines.

13.37 See the description of Holiday's experiment in Exercise 13.35. We calculated the correlation coefficient for the relation between the perception of a situation as traumatic and the perception of a woman's femininity. Now let's look at data to examine the relation between the perception of a situation as traumatic and the perception of a woman's masculinity.

Traumatic	Masculine
5	3
6	3
4	2
5	2
7	4
8	3

a. Draw a scatterplot for these data. Does the scatterplot suggest that it is appropriate to calculate a Pearson correlation coefficient? Explain.

b. Calculate the Pearson correlation coefficient.

c. State what the Pearson correlation coefficient tells us about the relation between these two variables.

d. Explain why the pattern of pairs of deviation scores enables us to understand the relation between the two variables. (That is, consider whether pairs of deviation scores tend to share the same sign or to have opposite signs.)

e. Explain how the relations between the perception of a situation as traumatic and the perception of a woman as either masculine or feminine differ from those same relations with respect to men.

13.38 Using the data and your work in Exercise 13.37, perform the remaining five steps of hypothesis testing to explore the relation between trauma and masculinity.

a. Step 1: Identify the population, distribution, and assumptions.

b. Step 2: State the null and research hypotheses.

c. Step 3: Determine the characteristics of the comparison distribution.

d. Step 4: Determine the critical values, or cutoffs, assuming a two-tailed test with a p level of 0.05.

e. Step 6: Make a decision, including an evaluation of the size of the correlation using Cohen's guidelines.

13.39 A friend tells you that there is a correlation between how late she's running and the amount of traffic. Whenever she's going somewhere and she's behind schedule, there's a lot of traffic. And when she has plenty of time, the traffic is sparser. She tells you that this happens no matter what time of day she's traveling or where she's going. She concludes that she's cursed with respect to traffic.

a. Explain to your friend how other phenomena, such as coincidence, superstition, and the confirmation bias, might explain her conclusion.

b. How could she quantify the relation between these two variables: the degree to which she is late and the amount of traffic? In your answer, be sure to explain how you might operationalize these variables. Of course, these could be operationalized in many different ways.

13.40 The trashy tabloid *Weekly World News* published an article—"Water from Mountain Falls Can Make You a Genius"—stating that drinking water from a special waterfall in a secret location in Switzerland "boosts IQ by 14 points—in the blink of an eye!" (exclamation point in the original). Hans and Inger Thurlemann, two hikers lost in the woods, drank some of the water, noticed an improvement in their thinking, and instantly found their way out of the woods. The more water they drank, the smarter they seemed to get. They credited the "miracle water" with enhancing their IQs. They brought some of the water home to their friends, who also claimed to notice an improvement in their thinking. Use this described correlation to illustrate the importance of random sampling to generalize findings.

13.41 A *New York Times* editorial ("Public vs. Private Schools," 2006) cited a finding by the U.S. Department of Education that standardized test scores were significantly higher among students in private schools than among students in public schools.

a. What are the researchers suggesting with respect to causality?

b. How could this correlation be explained by reversing the direction of hypothesized causality? Be specific.

c. How might a third variable account for this correlation? Be specific. Note that there are many possible third variables.

(*Note:* In the actual study, the difference between types of school disappeared when the researchers statistically controlled for related third variables including race, gender, parents' education, and family income.)

13.42 How safe are convertibles? *USA Today* (Healey, 2006) examined the pros and cons of convertible automobiles. The Insurance Institute for Highway Safety, the newspaper reported, determined that, depending on the model, 52 to 99 drivers of 1 million registered convertibles died in a car crash. The average rate of deaths for all passenger cars was 87. "Counter to conventional wisdom," the reporter wrote, "convertibles generally aren't unsafe."

a. What does the reporter suggest about the safety of convertibles?

b. Can you think of another explanation for the fairly low fatality rates? (*Hint:* The same article reported that convertibles "are often second or third cars.")

c. Given your explanation in part (b), suggest data that might make for a more appropriate comparison.

13.43 As this chapter is being written, March Madness, the final championship series in college basketball in the United States, is in full swing. The national sports media and news media enjoy covering the games and including human interest stories about the young men and women who compete at this elite level. Some of these athletes also compete at the highest level in academics. Although the stereotype of the dumb jock might be strong and ever-present, a fair amount of research shows that athletes maintain decent grades and competitive graduation rates when compared to nonathletes. Let's play with some data to explore the relation between GPA and participation in athletics. Data are presented here for a hypothetical team, including the GPA for each athlete and the average number of minutes played per game.

a. Create a scatterplot of these data and describe your impression of the relation between these variables based on the scatterplot.

b. Compute the Pearson correlation coefficient for these data.

c. Explain why the correlation coefficient you just computed is a descriptive statistic and not an inferential statistic. What would you need to do to make this an inferential statistic?

Minutes	GPA	Minutes	GPA
29.70	3.20	6.88	2.89
32.14	2.88	6.38	2.24
32.72	2.78	15.83	3.35
21.76	3.18	2.50	3.00
18.56	3.46	4.17	2.18
16.23	2.12	16.36	3.50
11.80	2.36		

13.44 Using the data provided in Exercise 13.43, test the hypothesis that grades are related to participation in athletics.

   a. Perform the six steps of hypothesis testing.

   b. What limitations are there to the conclusions you can draw based on this correlation?

   c. How else could you have studied this phenomenon such that you might have been able to draw a more sound, causal conclusion?

13.45 Did you know that sometimes you eat more just because the food is in front of you? Geier, Rozin, and Doros (2006) studied how portion size affected the amount people consumed. They discovered interesting things, such as people eat more M&M's when they are dispensed using a big spoon compared with when a small spoon is used. They investigated this phenomenon with two other food products as well, soft pretzels and Tootsie Roll candies. Not only are their findings informative for individuals who might want to lose weight by reducing their food intake, they are also valuable for restaurants and other reception areas where one might want to save money on the free candies offered by reducing customer consumption rates. Let's explore this last phenomenon. Hypothetical data are presented below for the amount of candy presented in a bowl for customers to take and the amount of candy taken by the end of each day:

Number of Pieces Presented	Number of Pieces Taken
10.00	3.00
25.00	14.00
50.00	26.00
75.00	44.00
100.00	36.00
125.00	57.00
150.00	41.00

   a. Create a scatterplot of these data.

   b. Describe your impression of the relation between these variables based on the scatterplot.

   c. Compute the Pearson correlation coefficient for these data.

   d. Summarize your findings using Cohen's guidelines.

13.46 Let's build on our analysis of the candy data.

   a. Perform the six steps of hypothesis testing.

   b. What limitations are there to the conclusions you can draw based on this correlation?

   c. Use the A–B–C model to explain possible causes for the relation between these variables.

Terms

correlation coefficient (p. 343)

positive correlation (p. 343)

negative correlation (p. 344)

Pearson correlation coefficient (p. 348)

Formulas

$$r = \frac{\Sigma[(X - M_X)(Y - M_Y)]}{\sqrt{(SS_X)(SS_Y)}}$$ (p. 352)

$df_r = N - 2$ (p. 353)

Symbols

r (p. 348)

ρ (p. 348)

Regression

BEFORE YOU GO ON

- You should understand the concept of effect size (Chapter 8).

- You should understand the concept of correlation (Chapter 13).

- You should be able to explain the limitations of correlation (Chapter 13).

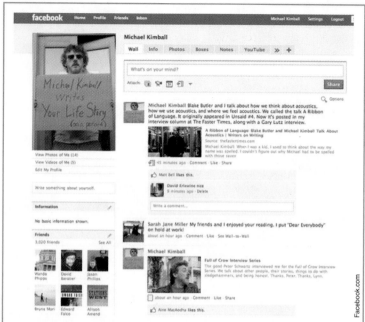

Facebook and Social Capital The prediction tools introduced in this chapter helped researchers determine that increased use of Facebook tends to lead to higher levels of social capital.

In 2004, college student Mark Zuckerman created the social networking site Facebook, which soon exploded in popularity across college campuses. Zuckerman dropped out of college to manage the site, and his company quickly became valued at hundreds of millions of dollars. By 2009, Facebook.com reported having over 250 million active users with over 120 million logging in at least once daily. As Facebook use ballooned, researchers at Michigan State University (Ellison, Steinfeld, & Lampe, 2007) wanted to understand what college students were getting out of their Facebook relationships, an idea known as *social capital*.

To find out, Ellison and colleagues' study focused on the idea of "bridging" social capital, the loose social connections we think of as acquaintances rather than friends. The researchers' hypothesis was that greater use of Facebook would predict more of this type of social capital. Researchers measured this by asking students to rate several items such as "I feel I am part of the MSU community" and "At MSU, I come into contact with new people all the time."

Obviously, many influences determined how much students used Facebook and how much social capital they enjoyed. For example, some students who spend many hours online every day might be more likely to spend lots of that time on Facebook, whereas other students only get online for a few minutes each day to check their e-mail. In addition, answering the research question was complicated by gender, ethnicity, location of residence, and many other factors. In other words, to find out what students were getting out of their Facebook relationships, researchers had to account for the influence of many variables.

The Michigan State University researchers controlled for all of these variables in their study and found that the more students used Facebook, the higher they scored on their measure of social capital. This result suggests that students were indeed using Facebook to bridge social capital.

The analytical methods we learn in this chapter build on correlation to help us to create prediction tools. We learn how to use one scale variable to predict outcome on a second scale variable. Then we discuss the limitations of this method—limitations that are similar to those we encountered with correlation. Finally, we expand this analytical method to allow us to use multiple scale variables to predict outcome on another scale variable.

Simple Linear Regression

Correlation is a marvelous tool that allows us to know the direction and strength of a relation between two variables. We can also use a correlation coefficient to develop a prediction tool. The procedure that we learn in this chapter lets statisticians develop an equation to predict someone's score on a scale dependent variable from his or her score on a scale independent variable. For instance, the research team at Michigan State could predict a high score on a measure of social capital for a student who spends a lot of time on Facebook. Indeed, any time we want to use data on one or

Simple linear regression is a statistical tool that lets us predict an individual's score on the dependent variable from his or her score on one independent variable.

Prediction and Car Insurance
When you call an insurance company for a car insurance estimate, the salesperson asks a number of questions about you (e.g., age, gender, marital status) and about your car (e.g., make, model, year, color). These characteristics are input into a type of statistical equation; the output is your quote. A flashy, expensive car driven by a young, unmarried man leads to a higher quote than a basic sedan driven by a married 50-year-old woman.

more independent variables to predict scores on a dependent variable, we can use this tool.

The real-life examples of statistical prediction tools are numerous. For example, many universities use variables such as high school grade point average (GPA) and Scholastic Aptitude Test (SAT) score to predict the success of prospective students. Similarly, insurance companies input demographic data into an equation to predict the likelihood of a class of people (such as young, male drivers) to submit a claim.

Prediction Versus Relation

The name for the prediction tool that we've been discussing is *regression,* a statistical technique that can provide specific quantitative information that predicts relations between variables. More specifically, **simple linear regression** *is a statistical tool that lets us predict an individual's score on the dependent variable from his or her score on one independent variable.*

Simple linear regression works by calculating the equation for a straight line. Once we have a line, we can look at any point on the *x*-axis and find its corresponding point on the *y*-axis. That corresponding point is what we'd predict for *y*. (*Note:* We must have data that are linearly related in order to use simple linear regression; the data must form an overall pattern through which it would make sense to draw a straight line. Like the Pearson correlation coefficient, simple linear regression would not be used if our data do not form the pattern of a straight line.) Let's consider an example of research that uses regression techniques, and then we'll walk through the steps to develop a regression equation.

> ◀ **MASTERING THE CONCEPT**
>
> **14-1:** Simple linear regression allows us to determine an equation for a straight line that predicts someone's score on a dependent variable from his or her score on the independent variable. We can only use it when our data are approximately linearly related.

Christopher Ruhm, an economist, often uses regression in his research. In one study, Ruhm wanted to explore the reasons for his finding (Ruhm, 2000) that the death rate *decreases* when unemployment goes up—a surprising negative relation between the death rate and an economic indicator. He took this relation a step further, into the realm of prediction: He found that an increase of 1% in unemployment predicted a decrease in the death rate of 0.5%, on average. A *poorer* economy predicted *better* health! It is a surprising finding, so Ruhm (2006) set out to explore the reasons for this negative relation between the economy and health.

Ruhm conducted regression analyses for independent variables related to health (smoking, obesity, and physical activity) and dependent variables related to the economy (income, unemployment, and the length of the workweek). He analyzed data from a sample of nearly 1.5 million participants collected from telephone surveys between 1987 and 2000. Among other things, Ruhm found that a decrease in working hours predicted decreases in smoking, obesity, and physical inactivity. All of these relations could have been identified by correlation alone. So why do we bother with regression? Because regression can take us a step further.

Regression can provide specific quantitative predictions that more precisely explain relations among variables. For example, Ruhm reported that a decrease in the workweek of just one hour predicted a 1% decrease in physical inactivity. So, to explain why the number of working hours predicts one's level of physical inactivity, Ruhm suggested that shorter working hours free up time for physical activity—something he might not have thought of without the more specific quantitative information provided by regression. Let's now calculate a simple linear regression using information that we're already familiar with: z scores.

Regression with z Scores

In Chapter 13 we calculated a Pearson correlation coefficient to quantify the relation between students' numbers of absences from statistics class and their statistics final exam grades; the data for the 10 students in the sample are shown in Table 14-1. Remember, the mean number of absences was 3.400 and the standard deviation was 2.375; the mean exam grade was 76.000 and the standard deviation was 15.040. The Pearson correlation coefficient that we calculated in Chapter 13 was -0.85, an indication of a strong negative relation between the two variables. Now simple linear regression can take us a step further. We can develop an equation to predict students' final exam grades from their numbers of absences. In other words, regression allows us to use one piece of information to make predictions about something else.

Let's say that a student (let's call him Skip) announces on the first day of class that he intends to skip five classes during the semester. We can refer to the size and direction of the correlation (-0.85) as our benchmark to predict his final exam grade. To predict his grade, we unite regression with a statistic we are more familiar with: z scores. If we know Skip's z score on one variable, we can multiply by the correlation coefficient to calculate his z score on the second variable. Remember that z scores indicate

TABLE 14-1. Is Skipping Class Related to Exam Grades?

Here are the scores for 10 students on two scale variables, number of absences from class in one semester and the final exam grade for that semester. The correlation between these variables is -0.85, but regression can take us a step further. We can develop a regression equation to assist with prediction.

Student	Absences	Exam Grade
1	4	82
2	2	98
3	2	76
4	3	68
5	1	84
6	0	99
7	4	67
8	8	58
9	7	50
10	3	78

how far a participant falls from the mean in terms of standard deviations. The formula, called the *standardized regression equation* because it uses z scores, is:

$$z_{\hat{Y}} = (r_{XY})(z_X)$$

The subscripts in the formula indicate that the first z score is for the dependent variable, Y, and that the second z score is for the independent variable, X. The ^ symbol over the subscript Y, called a "hat" by statisticians, refers to the fact that this variable is predicted. This is the z score for "Y hat"—the z score for the *predicted* score on the dependent variable, not the actual score. We cannot, of course, predict the actual score, and the "hat" reminds us of this. When we refer to this score, we can either say "the predicted score for Y" (with no hat, because we have specified with our words that it is predicted) or we can use the hat, $\hat{Y}$, to indicate that it is predicted. (We would not use both expressions because that would be redundant.) The subscripts X and Y for the Pearson correlation coefficient, r, indicate that this is the correlation between variables X and Y.

◄ **MASTERING THE FORMULA**

14-1: The standardized regression equation predicts the z score of a dependent variable, Y, from the z score of an independent variable, X. We simply multiply the independent variable's z score by the Pearson correlation coefficient to get the predicted z score on the dependent variable: $z_{\hat{Y}} = (r_{XY})(z_X)$.

EXAMPLE 14.1

Let's apply the formula to see how it works. If Skip's projected number of absences was identical to the mean number of absences for the entire class, then he'd have a z score of 0. If we multiply that by the correlation coefficient, then he'd have a predicted z score of 0 for final exam grade:

$$z_{\hat{Y}} = (-0.85)(0) = 0$$

So if he's right at the mean on the independent variable, then we'd predict that he'd be right at the mean on the dependent variable.

If Skip missed more classes than average and had a z score of 1.0 on the independent variable (1 standard deviation above the mean), then his predicted score on the dependent variable would be -0.85 (0.85 standard deviations below the mean):

$$z_{\hat{Y}} = (-0.85)(1) = -0.85$$

If his z score was -2 (2 standard deviations below the mean), his predicted z score on the dependent variable would be 1.7 (1.7 standard deviations above the mean):

$$z_{\hat{Y}} = (-0.85)(-2) = 1.7$$

Notice two things. First, because this is a negative correlation, a score above the mean on absences predicts a score below the mean on grade, and vice versa. Second, the predicted z score on the dependent variable is closer to its mean than is the z score on the independent variable. Table 14-2 demonstrates this for several z scores. This regressing of the dependent variable—the fact that it is closer to its mean—is called **regression to the mean,** *the tendency of scores that are particularly high or low to drift toward the mean over time.* In the social sciences, many phenomena demonstrate regression to the mean. For example, parents who are very tall tend to have children who are somewhat shorter than they are, although probably still above average. And parents who are very short tend to have children who are somewhat taller than they are, although probably still below average. We explore this concept in more detail later in this chapter.

When we don't have an someone's z score on the independent variable, we have to perform the additional step of converting his or her raw score to a z score. In

■ **Regression to the mean** is the tendency of scores that are particularly high or low to drift toward the mean over time.

> ## TABLE 14-2. Regression to the Mean
>
> One reason that regression equations are so named is because they predict a z score on the dependent variable that is closer to the mean than is the z score on the independent variable. This phenomenon is often called *regression to the mean*. The following predicted z scores for the dependent variable, Y, were calculated by multiplying the z score for the independent variable, X, by the Pearson correlation coefficient of -0.85.
>
> | z Score for the Independent Variable, X | Predicted z Score for the Dependent Variable, Y |
> |---|---|
> | −2.0 | 1.70 |
> | −1.0 | 0.85 |
> | 0.0 | 0.00 |
> | 1.0 | −0.85 |
> | 2.0 | −1.70 |

addition, when we calculate a predicted z score on the dependent variable, we can use our formula that determines a raw score from a z score. Let's try it with our skipping class and exam grade example using Skip as our subject.

EXAMPLE 14.2

We already know that Skip has announced his plans to skip five classes. What would we predict for his final exam grade?

STEP 1. Calculate the z score.

We first have to calculate Skip's z score on number of absences. Using the mean (3.400) and the standard deviation (2.375) that we calculated in Chapter 13, we calculate:

$$z_X = \frac{(X - M_X)}{SD_X} = \frac{(5 - 3.400)}{2.375} = 0.674$$

STEP 2. Multiply the z score by the correlation coefficient.

We multiply this z score by the correlation coefficient to get his predicted z score on the dependent variable, final exam grade:

$$z_{\hat{Y}} = (-0.85)(0.674) = -0.573$$

STEP 3. Convert the z score to a raw score.

We convert from the z score on Y, -0.573, to a raw score for Y:

$$\hat{Y} = z_{\hat{Y}}(SD_Y) + M_Y = 0.573(15.040) + 76.000 = 67.38$$

- The **intercept** is the predicted value for Y when X is equal to 0, which is the point at which the line crosses, or intercepts, the y-axis.

- The **slope** is the amount that Y is predicted to increase for an increase of 1 in X.

(Note that we use the "hat" symbol, ˆ, to indicate that the raw score, Y, is predicted.) If Skip skipped five classes, this number would be more classes than the typical students skipped, so we would expect that he would earn a lower-than-average grade. And the formula makes this very prediction—that Skip's final exam grade would be 67.38, which is lower than the mean (76.00).

The admissions counselor and the insurance salesperson, however, are unlikely to have the time or interest to do conversions from raw scores to z scores and back. So the z score regression equation is not useful in a practical sense for situations in which we must make ongoing predictions using the same variables. It is very useful, however, as a tool that helps us develop a regression equation we can use with raw scores, a procedure we look at in the next section.

Determining the Regression Equation

You may remember the equation for a line that you learned in geometry class. The version you likely learned was: $y = m(x) + b$. (In this equation, b is the intercept and m is the slope.) In statistics, we use a slightly different version of this formula:

$$\hat{Y} = a + b(X)$$

a is the **intercept**, *the predicted value for Y when X is equal to 0, which is the point at which the line crosses, or intercepts, the y-axis.* In Figure 14-1, the intercept is 5. b is the **slope**, *the amount that Y is predicted to increase for an increase of 1 in X.* In Figure 14-1, the slope is 2. As X increases from 3 to 4, for example, we see an increase in what we predict for Y of 2: from 11 to 13. The equation, therefore, is: $\hat{Y} = 5 + 2(X)$. If the score on X is 6, for example, the predicted score for Y is: $\hat{Y} = 5 + 2(6) = 5 + 12 = 17$. We can verify this on the line in Figure 14-1. Here, we were given the regression equation and regression line, but usually we have to determine these from our data. In this section, we learn the process of calculating a regression equation from data.

Once we have the equation for a line, it's easy to input any value for X to determine our predicted value for Y. Let's imagine that one of Skip's classmates, Allie, anticipates two absences this semester. If we had a regression equation, then we could input Allie's score of 2 on X and find her predicted score on Y. But first we have to develop the regression equation. Using the z score regression equation to find the intercept and slope enables us to "see" where these numbers come from in a way that makes sense (Aron & Aron, 2002). For this, we use the z score regression equation: $z_{\hat{Y}} = (r_{XY})(z_X)$.

MASTERING THE FORMULA

14-2: The simple linear regression equation uses the formula: $\hat{Y} = a + b(X)$. In this formula, X is the raw score on the independent variable and $\hat{Y}$ is the predicted raw score on the dependent variable. a is the intercept of the line, and b is its slope.

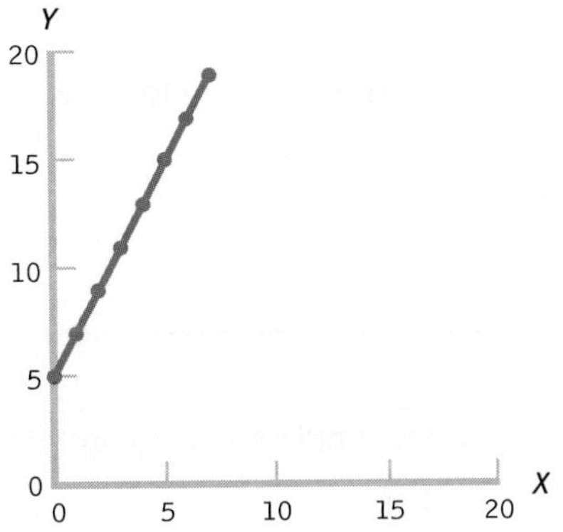

FIGURE 14-1
The Equation for a Line

The equation for a line includes the intercept, the point at which the line crosses the y-axis; here the intercept is 5. It also includes the slope, the amount that $\hat{Y}$ increases for an increase of 1 in X. Here, the slope is 2. The equation, therefore, is: $\hat{Y} = 5 + 2(X)$.

EXAMPLE 14.3

We start by calculating a, the intercept, a process that takes three steps.

STEP 1. Find the z score for X.

We know that the intercept is the point at which the line crosses the y-axis when X is equal to 0. So we start by finding the z score for X using the formula: $z_X = \frac{(X - M_X)}{SD_X}$.

$$z_X = \frac{(X - M_X)}{SD_X} = \frac{(0 - 3.400)}{2.375} = -1.432$$

STEP 2. Use the z score to calculate the predicted score on Y.

We use the z score regression equation, $z_{\hat{Y}} = (r_{XY})(z_X)$, to calculate the predicted score on Y.

$$\hat{Y} = (r_{XY})(z_X) = (-0.85)(-1.432) = 1.217$$

STEP 3. Convert the z score to its raw score.

We convert the z score for $\hat{Y}$ to its raw score using the formula: $\hat{Y} = z_{\hat{Y}}(SD_Y) + M_Y$.

$$\hat{Y} = z_{\hat{Y}}(SD_Y) + M_Y = 1.217(15.040) + 76.000 = 94.304$$

We have our intercept! When X is 0, $\hat{Y}$ is 94.30. That is, we would predict that someone who never misses class would earn a final exam grade of 94.30.

EXAMPLE 14.4

Next, we calculate our slope, a process that is similar to the one for calculating the intercept, but calculating slope takes four steps. We know that the slope is the amount that $\hat{Y}$ increases when X increases by 1. So all we need to do is calculate what we would predict for an X of 1. We can then compare our $\hat{Y}$ for an X of 0 to the $\hat{Y}$ for an X of 1. The difference between the two is the slope.

STEP 1. Find the z score for an X of 1.

We find the z score for an X of 1, using the formula: $z_X = \dfrac{(X - M_X)}{SD_X}$.

$$z_X = \frac{(X - M_X)}{SD_X} = \frac{(1 - 3.400)}{2.375} = -1.011$$

STEP 2. Use the z score to calculate the predicted score on Y.

We use the z score regression equation, $z_{\hat{Y}} = (r_{XY})(z_X)$, to calculate the predicted score on Y.

$$z_{\hat{Y}} = (r_{XY})(z_X) = (-0.85)(-1.011) = 0.859$$

STEP 3. Convert the z score to its raw score.

We convert the z score for $\hat{Y}$ to its raw score, using the formula: $\hat{Y} = z_{\hat{Y}}(SD_Y) + M_Y$.

$$\hat{Y} = z_{\hat{Y}}(SD_Y) + M_Y = 0.859(15.040) + 76.000 = 88.919$$

STEP 4. Find a predicted score.

Our prediction is that a student who misses one class would achieve a final exam grade of 88.919. As X, number of absences, increased from 0 to 1, what happened to $\hat{Y}$? First, ask yourself if it increased or decreased. An increase would mean a positive slope, and a decrease would mean a negative slope. Here, we see a decrease in exam grade as the number of absences increased. Next, determine how much it increased or decreased. In this case, the decrease is 5.385: $94.304 - 88.919 = 5.385$. So the slope here is -5.39.

We now have our intercept and our slope and can put them into the equation: $\hat{Y} = a + b(X)$, which becomes $\hat{Y} = 94.30 - 5.39(X)$. We can use this equation to predict Allie's final exam grade based on her number of absences, two.

$$\hat{Y} = 94.30 - 5.39(X) = 94.30 - 5.39(2) = 83.52$$

Based on the data from our statistics classes, we predict that Allie would earn a final exam grade of 83.52 if she skipped two classes. We could have predicted this same grade for Allie using the z score regression equation. The difference is that now we can input any score into the raw-score regression equation, and it does all the work of converting for us. The admissions counselor or insurance salesperson has an easy formula and doesn't have to know z scores. He or she only has to know how to enter the appropriate number in the computer.

In addition to plugging in a score on X to find a predicted score on Y, we also can draw our regression line to get a visual sense of what it looks like. We do this by calculating two points on the regression line, usually for one low score on X and one high score on X. We would always have $\hat{Y}$ for two scores, 0 and 1 (although in some cases these numbers won't make sense, such as for the variable of human body temperature; you'd never have a temperature that low!). Because these scores are low on the scale for number of absences, we would choose a high score as well; 8 is the highest score in our original data set, so we can use that:

$$\hat{Y} = 94.30 - 5.39(X) = 94.30 - 5.39(8) = 51.18$$

For someone who skipped eight classes, we predict a final exam grade of 51.18. We now have three points, as shown in Table 14-3. It's useful to have three points because the third point serves as a check on the other two. If the three points do not fall in a straight line, we have made an error. (Note that 0 or 1 are not always useful as the low score, particularly if these numbers are far outside the range of values for X.)

We can now plot these three points, as seen in Figure 14-2, just as we would on a scatterplot. We then draw a line through the dots, but it's not just any line. This line is our regression line, which has another name that is wonderfully intuitive: the line of best fit. If you have ever had some clothes tailored to fit your body, perhaps for a wedding or

TABLE 14-3. Drawing a Regression Line

We calculate at least two, and preferably three, pairs of scores for X and $\hat{Y}$. Ideally, at least one is low on the scale for X and at least one is high.

X	$\hat{Y}$
0	94.30
1	88.92
8	51.18

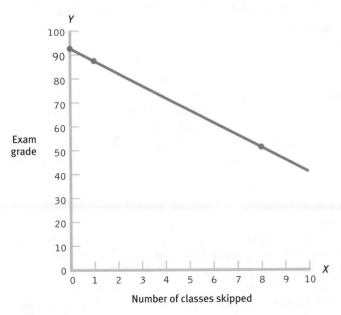

FIGURE 14-2
The Regression Line

To draw a regression line, we plot at least two, and preferably three, pairs of scores for X and $\hat{Y}$. We then draw a line through the dots.

The Line of Best Fit The line of best fit in regression has the same characteristics as tailored clothes; there is nothing we could do to that line that would make it fit our data any better.

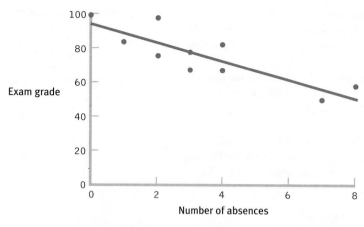

FIGURE 14-3
The Line of Best Fit

The regression line is the line that best fits the points on our scatterplot. Statistically, the regression line is the line that leads to the least amount of error in prediction.

other special occasion, then you know that there really is such a thing as a "best fit." Nothing the tailor could do would make those clothes fit you any better.

The meaning of the line of best fit in regression has the same characteristic as a tailored set of clothes. We couldn't make the line a little steeper, or raise or lower it, in any way that would allow it to represent those dots any better than it already does. When we look at the scatterplot around the line in Figure 14-3, we can observe that the line goes precisely through the middle of our data. This is why statisticians also call the regression line the line of best fit. Statistically, this is the line that leads to the least amount of error in prediction.

Notice that the negative slope means that the line we just drew starts in the upper-left corner of the graph and ends in the lower right. Think of the word *slope,* often used when discussing, say, ski slopes. A negative slope means that the line looks like it's going downhill as we move from left to right. This makes sense because the calculations for the regression equation are based on the correlation coefficient, and the scatterplot associated with a negative correlation coefficient has dots that also go "downhill." If the slope were positive, the line would start in the lower-left corner of the graph and end in the upper right. A positive slope means that the line looks like it's going uphill as we move from left to right. Again, this makes sense, because we base the calculations on a positive correlation coefficient, and the scatterplot associated with a positive correlation coefficient has dots that also go "uphill."

The Standardized Regression Coefficient and Hypothesis Testing with Regression

Our slope tells us the amount that the dependent variable changes as the independent variable increases by 1. So, for the skipping class and exam grades example, our slope of -5.39 tells us that for each additional class skipped, we can predict that the exam grade will be 5.39 points lower. Let's say that another professor uses skipped classes to predict the class grade on a grade point average scale of 0–4. And let's say that we found a slope of -0.23 with these data. For each additional skipped class, we would predict that the grade, in terms of the 0–4 scale, would decrease by 0.23. The problem here is that we can't directly compare one professor's findings with another professor's findings. A decrease of 5.39 is larger than a decrease of 0.23, but they're on different scales so they're not comparable.

This problem might remind you of the problems we faced in comparing scores on different scales. To appropriately compare scores, we standardized them using the z statistic. We can standardize slopes in a similar way by calculating the standardized regression coefficient. *The **standardized regression coefficient**, a standardized version of the slope in a regression equation, is the predicted change in the dependent variable in terms of standard deviations for a 1 standard deviation increase in the independent variable.* It is symbolized by β and is often referred to by its symbol, pronounced "beta," or called a *beta weight*. It is calculated using the formula:

$$\beta = (b)\frac{\sqrt{SS_X}}{\sqrt{SS_Y}}$$

MASTERING THE FORMULA

14-3: The standardized regression coefficient, β, is calculated by multiplying the slope of the regression equation by the quotient of the square root of the sum of squares for the independent variable by the square root of the sum of squares for the dependent variable:

$\beta = (b)\dfrac{\sqrt{SS_X}}{\sqrt{SS_Y}}.$

TABLE 14-4. The Denominator of the Correlation Coefficient: The Calculations for Sums of Squares

Absences (X)	$(X - M_X)$	$(X - M_X)^2$	Exam Grade (Y)	$(Y - M_Y)$	$(Y - M_Y)^2$
4	0.6	0.36	82	6	36
2	−1.4	1.96	98	22	484
2	−1.4	1.96	76	0	0
3	−0.4	0.16	68	−8	64
1	−2.4	5.76	84	8	64
0	−3.4	11.56	99	23	529
4	0.6	0.36	67	−9	81
8	4.6	21.16	58	−18	324
7	3.6	12.96	50	−26	676
3	−0.4	0.16	78	2	4
		$\Sigma(X - M_X)^2 = 56.4$			$\Sigma(Y - M_Y)^2 = 2262$

■ The **standardized regression coefficient**, a standardized version of the slope in a regression equation, is the predicted change in the dependent variable in terms of standard deviations for a 1 standard deviation increase in the independent variable; also called *beta weight*.

We calculated the slope, −5.39, earlier in this chapter. We calculated the sums of squares in Chapter 13. Table 14-4 repeats part of the calculations for the denominator of the correlation coefficient equation. At the bottom of the table, we can see that the sum of squares for the independent variable of classes skipped is 56.4 and the sum of squares for the dependent variable of exam grade is 2262. By inputting these numbers into the formula, we calculate:

$$\beta = (b)\frac{\sqrt{SS_X}}{\sqrt{SS_Y}} = -5.39\frac{\sqrt{56.4}}{\sqrt{2262}} = -5.39\frac{7.510}{47.560} = -5.39(0.159) = -0.857$$

Notice that this result is similar to our Pearson correlation coefficient of 0.85. In fact, for simple linear regression, it is exactly the same. The difference that we see here is due to rounding decisions for both calculations. Both the standardized regression coefficient and the correlation coefficient indicate the change in standard deviation that we expect when the independent variable increases by 1 standard deviation. Note that the correlation coefficient is *not* the same as the standardized regression coefficient when an equation includes more than one independent variable, a situation we'll encounter later in the section on multiple regression.

Because the standardized regression coefficient is the same as the correlation coefficient with simple linear regression, the outcome of hypothesis testing is also identical. The hypothesis-testing process that we used to test whether the correlation coefficient is statistically significantly different from 0 can also be used to test whether the standardized regression coefficient is statistically significantly different from 0. As you'll remember from Chapter 13, the Pearson correlation coefficient, r = −0.85, was larger in magnitude than the critical value of −0.632 (determined based on 8 degrees of freedom and a p level of 0.05). We rejected the null hypothesis and concluded that number of absences and exam grade seemed to be negatively correlated.

◀ **MASTERING THE CONCEPT**

14-2: A standardized regression coefficient is the standardized version of a slope, much like a z statistic is a standardized version of a raw score. For simple linear regression, the standardized regression coefficient is identical to the correlation coefficient. This means that when we conduct hypothesis testing and conclude that a correlation coefficient is statistically significantly different from 0, we can draw the same conclusion about the standardized regression coefficient.

CHECK YOUR LEARNING

Reviewing the Concepts

> Regression builds on correlation, enabling us not only to quantify the relation between two variables, but also to predict a score on a dependent variable from a score on an independent variable.

> With the standardized regression equation, we simply multiply an individual's z score on an independent variable by the Pearson correlation coefficient to predict that individual's z score on a dependent variable.

> The raw-score regression equation is easier to use in that the equation itself does the transformations from raw score to z score and back. We can use it to predict Y for any value of X.

> We use the standardized regression equation to build the regression equation that can predict a raw score on a dependent variable from a raw score on an independent variable.

> We can graph the regression line, $\hat{Y} = a + b(X)$, remembering that it is well named as the line of best fit. The line includes values for the y intercept (a), the value on Y when X is zero, and the slope (b), the change in Y expected for a 1-unit increase in X.

> The slope, which captures the nature of the relation between the variables, can be standardized by calculating the standardized regression coefficient. The standardized regression coefficient tells us the predicted change on the dependent variable in terms of standard deviations for every standard deviation increase in the independent variable.

> With simple linear regression, the standardized regression coefficient is identical to the Pearson correlation coefficient. Because of this fact, hypothesis testing with simple linear regression gives us the same outcome as with correlation.

Clarifying the Concepts

14-1 What is simple linear regression?

14-2 What purpose does the regression line serve?

Calculating the Statistics

14-3 Let's assume we know that women's heights and weights are correlated and the Pearson correlation coefficient is 0.28. Let's also assume that we know the following descriptive statistics: for women's height, the mean is 5 feet, 4 inches (64 inches) with a standard deviation of 2 inches, and for women's weight, the mean is 155 pounds with a standard deviation of 15 pounds. Sarah is 5 feet, 7 inches tall. How much would you predict she weighs? To answer this question, complete the following steps:

a. Transform the raw score for the independent variable into a z score.

b. Calculate the predicted z score for the dependent variable.

c. Transform the z score for the dependent variable back into a raw score.

14-4 Given the following regression line, $\hat{Y} = 12 + 0.67(X)$, make predictions for each of the following:

a. $X = 78$

b. $X = -14$

c. $X = 52$

Applying the Concepts

14-5 In Exercise 13.43, we explored the relation between athletic participation, measured by average minutes played by players on a basketball team, and academic achievement, as measured by GPA. We computed a correlation of 0.344 between these variables. The original, fictional data are presented below. The regression equation for these data is: $\hat{Y} = 2.586 + 0.016(X)$.

Minutes	GPA	Minutes	GPA
29.70	3.20	6.88	2.89
32.14	2.88	6.38	2.24
32.72	2.78	15.83	3.35
21.76	3.18	2.50	3.00
18.56	3.46	4.17	2.18
16.23	2.12	16.36	3.50
11.80	2.36		

a. Interpret both the y-intercept and the slope in this regression equation.

b. Compute the standardized regression coefficient.

c. Explain how the strength of the correlation relates to the utility of the regression line.

Solutions to these Check Your Learning questions can be found in Appendix D.

d. What conclusion would you draw if you performed a hypothesis test for this regression?

Interpretation and Prediction

In this section, we explore how the logic of regression is already a part of our every-day reasoning. Then we address why regression doesn't allows us to designate causation as we interpret our data; for instance, MSU researchers could not say that spending more time on Facebook *caused* students to bridge more social capital. This discussion of causation then leads us to a familiar caution about interpreting the meaning of regression, this time due to the process called *regression to the mean*. Finally, we learn how to calculate effect sizes so we can make interpretations about how well our regression equation predicts behavior.

Regression and Error

For many different reasons, our predictions are full of errors, and that, too, is factored into the regression analysis. For example, we might predict that a student would get a certain grade based on how many classes she skipped, but we could be wrong in our prediction. Other factors, such as her intelligence, the amount of sleep she got the night before, and the number of related classes she's taken all are likely to affect her grade as well. The number of skipped classes is highly unlikely to be a perfect predictor. Statistically speaking, errors in prediction lead directly back to variability, which is often assessed by standard deviation and standard error. But this time, we are concerned with variability around the line of best fit rather than variability around the mean. A graph that includes a line of best fit can give us a sense of how much error there is in a regression equation. That is, as we can see in Figure 14-4, the arrangement of the dots around the line of best fit in a graph tells us something about the error that's likely to occur when we use the regression equation.

We can make a guess about the amount of error by looking at a graph. However, we can go a step further by quantifying the amount of error. The number that describes how far away, on average, the data points are from the line of best fit is called *the standard error of the estimate*, *a statistic indicating the typical distance between a regression line and*

The **standard error of the estimate** is a statistic indicating the typical distance between a regression line and the actual data points.

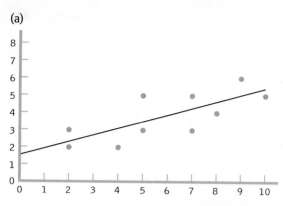

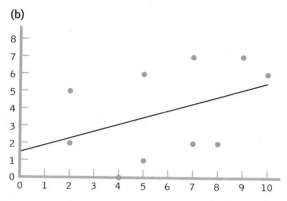

FIGURE 14-4
The Standard Error of the Estimate

Data points clustered closely around the line of best fit as, in graph (a), are described by a small standard error of the estimate. Data points clustered far away from the line of best fit, as in graph (b), are described by a large standard error of the estimate. We enjoy a high level of confidence in the predictive ability of our independent variable when the data points are tightly clustered around the line of best fit, as in (a). That is, there is much less error. And we have a low level of confidence in the predictive ability of our independent variable when the data points vary widely around the line of best fit, as in (b). That is, there is much more error.

the actual data points. The standard error of the estimate is essentially the standard deviation of the actual data points around the regression line. We usually get the standard error of the estimate using software, so its calculation is not covered here.

Applying the Lessons of Correlation to Regression

In addition to understanding the ways in which regression can help us, it is important to understand the limitations associated with using regression. It is extremely rare that the data analyzed in a regression equation are from a true experiment (one that used randomization to assign participants to conditions). Typically, we cannot randomly assign participants to conditions when the independent variable is a scale variable (rather than a nominal variable), as is usually the case with regression. Said another way, if the independent variable is number of absences from class (with a range of 0 to more than 20), then we can't easily randomly assign participants to every possible value. When the data are not from a true experiment, the results are subject to the same limitations in interpretation that we discussed with respect to correlation.

In Chapter 13, we introduced the A-B-C model of understanding correlation. We noted that the correlation between number of absences and exam grade could be explained if skipping class (A) harmed one's grade (B), if a bad grade (B) led one to skip more often (A) because of frustration, or if a third variable (C)—such as intelligence—might lead both to the awareness that going to class is a good thing (A) and to good grades (B). When drawing conclusions from regression, we must consider the same set of possible confounding variables that limited our confidence in our findings following a correlation.

In fact, regression, like correlation, can be wildly inaccurate in its predictions. As with the Pearson correlation coefficient, simple linear regression should be used only if a visual inspection of the scatterplot indicates that it's sensible to proceed. A good statistician examines the data points *before* proceeding (e.g., to check for linearity) and questions causality *after* the statistical analysis (to identify potential confounding variables). A good statistician also considers whether he or she can predict beyond the data. But one more source of error can affect fair-minded interpretations of regression analyses: regression to the mean.

Regression to the Mean

In the study that we considered earlier in this chapter (Ruhm, 2006), economic factors predicted several indicators of health. Ruhm also reported that "the drop in tobacco use disproportionately occurs among heavy smokers, the fall in body weight among the severely obese, and the increase in exercise among those who were completely inactive" (p. 2). What Ruhm describes captures the meaning of the word *regression,* as defined by its early proponents. Those who were most extreme on a given variable regressed (toward the mean). In other words, they became somewhat less extreme on that variable.

Francis Galton (Darwin's cousin) was the first to describe the phenomenon of regression to the mean, and he did so in a number of contexts (Bernstein, 1996). For example, Galton studied sweet peas. Galton asked nine individuals—including Darwin—to plant sweet pea seeds in the widely disparate locations in Britain where they lived. Galton found that the variability among the seeds he sent out to be planted was larger than among the seeds that were produced by these plants. The largest seeds produced seeds smaller than they were. The smallest seeds produced seeds larger than they were. Similarly, among people, Galton documented that, although tall parents tend to have taller-than-average children, their children tend to be a little shorter than their parents. And although short parents tend to have shorter-than-average children, their children tend to be a little taller than their parents. Galton noted that if regression to the mean did *not* occur, with tall people and large sweet peas producing offspring even taller or larger, and short people and small sweet peas producing offspring even shorter or smaller, "the world would consist of nothing but midgets and giants" (quoted in Bernstein, 1996, p. 167).

Regression to the mean is also why so much of the world is described by the bell-shaped curve, another concept often studied by Galton. If regression to the mean did not occur, the size of sweet peas, the heights of individuals, the aggressiveness of personalities, and everything else would look bimodal, like a valley (Figure 14-5a), instead of unimodal, like a hill or what we call the normal, bell-shaped curve (Figure 14-5b).

> **◄ MASTERING THE CONCEPT**
>
> **14-3:** Regression to the mean occurs because extreme scores tend to become less extreme—that is, they tend to regress toward the mean. Very tall parents do tend to have tall children, but usually not as tall as they are, whereas very short parents do tend to have short children, but usually not as short as they are.

Regression to the Mean Tall parents tend to have children who are taller than average but not as tall as they are. Similarly, short parents (like the older parents in this photograph) tend to have children who are shorter than average but not as short as they are. Francis Galton was the first to observe this phenomenon, which came to be called regression to the mean.

(a) 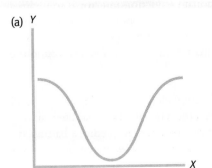   (b)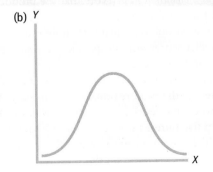

FIGURE 14-5
Regression to the Mean

The distribution on the left (a) demonstrates what most observations of the world would look like if regression to the mean did not occur. Trees would be either enormous or tiny. People would cry constantly or almost never. There would be no "middle ground." Instead, the distribution on the right (b) demonstrates the reality that underlies statistical reasoning: the normal, bell-shaped curve.

TABLE 14-5. Regression to the Mean: Investing

Bernstein (1996) presented these data from *Morningstar*, an investment publication, demonstrating regression to the mean in action. Notice that those categories that showed the highest performances during the first time period (e.g., international stocks) had declined by the second time period, whereas those with the poorest performances in the first time period (e.g., aggressive growth) had improved by the second time period.

5 Years to Objective	5 Years to March 1989	March 1994
International stocks	20.6%	9.4%
Income	14.3%	11.2%
Growth and income	14.2%	11.9%
Growth	13.3%	13.9%
Small company	10.3%	15.9%
Aggressive growth	8.9%	16.1%
Average	13.6%	13.1%

An understanding of regression to the mean can help us make better choices in our daily lives. For example, regression to the mean is a particularly important concept to remember when we begin to save for retirement and have to choose the specific allocations of our savings. Table 14-5 shows data from *Morningstar*, an investment publication. The percentages represent the increase in that investment vehicle over two five-year periods: 1984–1989 and 1989–1994 (Bernstein, 1996). As most descriptions of mutual funds remind potential investors, previous performance is not necessarily indicative of future performance. Perhaps what they really mean is that previous high performances are unlikely to continue increasing indefinitely. Consider regression to the mean in your own investment decisions. It might help you ride out a decrease in a mutual fund rather than panic and sell before the likely drift back toward the mean. And it might help you avoid buying into the fund that's been on top for several years, knowing that it stands a chance of sliding back toward the mean.

Proportionate Reduction in Error

In the previous section, we developed a regression equation to predict a final exam score from number of absences. Now we want to know: How good is this regression equation? Is it worth having students use this equation to predict their own final exam grades from the numbers of classes they plan to skip? To answer this question, we calculate a form of effect size, *the **proportionate reduction in error**—a statistic that quantifies how much more accurate our predictions are when we use the regression line instead of the mean as a prediction tool.* (Note that the proportionate reduction in error is sometimes called the *coefficient of determination*.) More specifically, the proportionate reduction in error is a statistic that quantifies how much more accurate our predictions are when we predict scores using a specific regression equation rather than just predicting the mean for everyone.

If the mean is all we have to go by, then it's a fair predictor. In other words, using the mean is the most reasonable way to predict a baseball player's batting average if all we know is the team average. But if we know that the baseball player has been among the top five hitters for three years in a row, then we are likely to predict a batting average higher than the mean. Why? We have more information. The regression line gives us more information than the mean, and the proportionate reduction in error quan-

■ The **proportionate reduction in error** is a statistic that quantifies how much more accurate our predictions are when we use the regression line instead of the mean as a prediction tool; also called the *coefficient of determination*.

tifies how much better the regression equation predicts a player's batting average than does the mean.

Earlier in this chapter, we noted that if we did not have a regression equation, the best we could do is predict the mean for everyone, regardless of number of absences. The average final exam grade for students in this sample is 76. With no further information, we could only tell our students that our best guess for their statistics grade is a 76. There would obviously be a great deal of error if we predicted the mean for everyone. Some would fall at or near the mean, but many would fall either a good deal lower or a good deal higher than the mean. Using the mean to estimate scores is a reasonable way to proceed if that's all the information we have. But the regression line provides a more precise picture of the relation between variables, so using a regression equation reduces our error. In other words, using the regression equation means that we're not as far off in our predictions as we are when we use the mean.

Less error is the same thing as having a smaller standard error of the estimate. And a smaller standard error of the estimate means that we'd be doing much better in our predictions than if we had a larger one; visually, this means that the actual scores are closer to the regression line. And with a larger standard error of the estimate, we'd be doing much worse in our predictions than if we had a smaller one; visually, the actual scores are farther away from the regression line. As the actual scores are closer to the regression line, we have less error. But we can do more than just quantify the standard deviation around the regression line. We can determine how much better the regression equation is compared to the mean: we calculate the proportion of error that we can eliminate by using the regression equation, rather than the mean, to predict. (In this next section, we learn the long way to calculate this proportion in order to understand exactly what this proportion represents. Then, we learn a shortcut.)

Using our sample, we can calculate the amount of error from using the mean as a predictive tool. We quantify that error by determining how far off an individual's score on the dependent variable (final exam grade) is from the mean, as seen in the column titled "error" in Table 14-6.

TABLE 14-6. Calculating Error When We Predict the Mean for Everyone

If we do not have a regression equation, the best we can do is predict the mean for Y for every participant. When we do that, we will, of course, have some error, because not everyone will have exactly the mean value on Y. This table presents the squared errors for each participant when we predict the mean for each of them.

Student	Grade (Y)	Mean For Y	Error	Squared Error
1	82	76	6	36
2	98	76	22	484
3	76	76	0	0
4	68	76	−8	64
5	84	76	8	64
6	99	76	23	529
7	67	76	−9	81
8	58	76	−18	324
9	50	76	−26	676
10	78	76	2	4

EXAMPLE 14.5

For example, for student 1, the error is $82 - 76 = 6$. We then square these errors for all 10 students and sum them. This is another type of sum of squares: the sum of squared errors. Here, the sum of squared errors is 2262 (the sum of the values in column 5). This is a measure of the error that would result if we predicted the mean for every person in our sample. We'll call this particular type of sum of squared errors the *sum of squares total*, SS_{total}, because it represents the worst-case scenario, the total error we would have if there was no regression equation. We can visualize this error on a graph that depicts a horizontal line for the mean, as seen in Figure 14-6. We can add the actual points, as we would in a scatterplot, and draw vertical lines from each point to the mean. These vertical lines give us a visual sense of the error that results from predicting the mean for everyone.

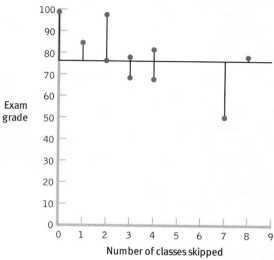

FIGURE 14-6
Visualizing Error

A graph with a horizontal line for the mean, 76, can allow us to visualize the error that would result if we predicted the mean for everyone. We draw lines for each person's point on a scatterplot to the mean. Those lines are a visual representation of error.

The regression equation can't make our predictions any worse than just predicting the mean for everyone. But it's not worth the time and effort to use a regression equation if it doesn't lead to a substantial improvement over just predicting the mean. There will still be error with a regression equation, but there will be less error. As with the mean, we can calculate the amount of error from using the regression equation with our sample. We can then see how much better we do with the regression equation than with the mean. So let's quantify that error by determining how far each prediction is from the actual score on the dependent variable for each participant in our sample.

First, we have to calculate what we would predict for each student if we used the regression equation. We do this by plugging each X into the regression equation. Here are our calculations using the equation $\hat{Y} = 94.30 - 5.39(X)$:

$$\hat{Y} = 94.30 - 5.39(4); \hat{Y} = 72.74$$

$$\hat{Y} = 94.30 - 5.39(2); \hat{Y} = 83.52$$

$$\hat{Y} = 94.30 - 5.39(2); \hat{Y} = 83.52$$

$$\hat{Y} = 94.30 - 5.39(3); \hat{Y} = 78.13$$

$$\hat{Y} = 94.30 - 5.39(1); \hat{Y} = 88.91$$

$$\hat{Y} = 94.30 - 5.39(0); \hat{Y} = 94.30$$

$$\hat{Y} = 94.30 - 5.39(4); \hat{Y} = 72.74$$

$$\hat{Y} = 94.30 - 5.39(8); \hat{Y} = 51.18$$

$$\hat{Y} = 94.30 - 5.39(7); \hat{Y} = 56.57$$

$$\hat{Y} = 94.30 - 5.39(3); \hat{Y} = 78.13$$

The $\hat{Y}$'s, or predicted scores for Y, that we just calculated are presented in Table 14-7, where the errors are calculated based on the predicted scores, rather than the mean. For example, for student 1, the error is $82 - 72.74 = 9.26$. As before, we square the errors and sum them. The sum of squared errors based on the regression equation

TABLE 14-7. Calculating Error When We Use the Regression Equation to Predict

When we use a regression equation for prediction, as opposed to the mean, we will have less error. We will, however, still have some error because not every participant will fall exactly on the regression line. This table presents the squared errors for each participant when we predict each one's score on Y using the regression equation.

Student	Absences (X)	Grade (Y)	Predicted for Y	Error	Squared Error
1	4	82	72.74	9.26	85.748
2	2	98	83.52	14.48	209.670
3	2	76	83.52	−7.52	56.550
4	3	68	78.13	−10.13	102.617
5	1	84	88.91	−4.91	24.108
6	0	99	94.30	4.70	22.090
7	4	67	72.74	−5.74	32.948
8	8	58	51.18	6.82	46.512
9	7	50	56.57	−6.57	43.165
10	3	78	78.13	0.13	0.017

is 623.425. We call this the *sum of squared error, SS_error*, because it represents the error that we'd have if we predicted Y using our regression equation.

As before, we can visualize this error on a graph that includes the regression line, as seen in Figure 14-7. We again add the actual points, as in a scatterplot, and we draw vertical lines from each point to the regression line. These vertical lines give us a visual sense of the error that results from predicting Y for everyone using the regression equation. Notice that these vertical lines in Figure 14-7 tend to be shorter than those connecting each person's point with the mean in Figure 14-6.

So how much better did we do? Our error if we predict using the mean for everyone in this sample is 2262. The error if we predict using the regression equation for everyone in this sample is 623.425. Remember that this measure of how well the regression equation predicts is called the proportionate *reduction* in error. What we want to know is how much error we have gotten rid of—reduced—by using the regression equation instead of the mean. The amount of error we've reduced is 2262 − 623.425 = 1638.575. But the word *proportionate* indicates that we want a proportion of the total error that we have reduced, so we set up a ratio to determine this. We have reduced 1638.575 of the original 2262, or

$$\frac{1638.575}{2262} = 0.724$$

We have reduced 0.724, or 72.4%, of the original error by using the regression equation versus using the mean to predict

FIGURE 14-7
Visualizing Error

A graph that depicts the regression line allows us to visualize the error that would result if we predicted Y for everyone using the regression equation. We draw lines for each person's point on a scatterplot to the regression line. Those lines are a visual representation of error.

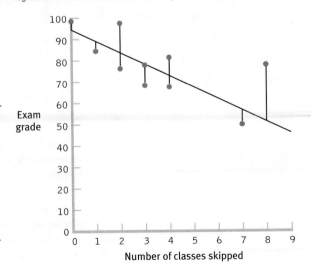

Y. This ratio can be calculated using an equation that represents what we just calculated: the proportionate reduction in error, symbolized as

$$r^2 = \frac{(SS_{total} - SS_{error})}{SS_{total}} = \frac{(2262 - 623.425)}{2262} = 0.724$$

MASTERING THE FORMULA

14-4: The proportionate reduction in error is calculated by subtracting the error generated using the regression equation as a prediction tool from the total error that would occur if we used the mean as everyone's predicted score. We then divide this difference by the total error: $r^2 = \frac{(SS_{total} - SS_{error})}{SS_{total}}$. We can interpret the proportionate reduction in error as we did the effect size estimate for ANOVA. It represents the same statistic.

To recap, the worst-case scenario is predicting the mean for everyone, but if it's all the information we have, then it's much better than having no information at all. The error using the mean, the total of the sum of squares, or sum of squares total, is 2262. The regression equation that used the independent variable of number of absences to predict the dependent variable of final exam grade still led to error, but less error. The error using the regression equation, the sum of squares error, is 623.425. Knowing these two numbers enables us to determine the proportion of error that we reduced by using the regression equation to predict, rather than merely predicting the mean for everyone. We calculate the reduction in error by determining the amount of error we got rid of. We do this by taking a ratio, the amount of error we reduced over the total amount of error. In short, we simply have to do the following:

1. Determine the error associated with using the mean as our predictor.
2. Determine the error associated with using the regression equation as our predictor.
3. Subtract the error associated with the regression equation from the error associated with the mean.
4. Divide the difference (calculated in step 3) by the error associated with using the mean.

MASTERING THE CONCEPT

14-4: Proportionate reduction in error is the effect size used with regression. It is the same number we calculated as the effect-size estimate for ANOVA. It tells us the proportion of error that is eliminated when we predict scores on the dependent variable using the regression equation versus simply predicting that everyone is at the mean on the dependent variable.

The proportionate reduction in error tells us how good our regression equation is. Here is another way to state it: the proportionate reduction in error is a measure of the amount of variance in the dependent variable that is explained by the independent variable. Did you notice the symbol for the proportionate reduction in error? The symbol is r^2. Perhaps you see the connection with another number we have calculated. Yes, we could simply square the correlation coefficient! The longer calculations are necessary, however, to see the difference between the error in prediction from using the regression equation and the error in prediction from simply predicting the mean for everyone. Once you have calculated the proportionate reduction in error the long way a few times, you'll have a good sense of exactly what you're calculating. In addition to the relation of the proportionate reduction in error to the correlation coefficient, it also is the same as another number we've calculated, the effect size for ANOVA, R^2. In both cases, this number represents the proportion of variance in the dependent variable that is explained by the independent variable.

Because the proportionate reduction in error can be calculated by squaring the correlation coefficient, we can have a sense of the amount of error that would be reduced simply by looking at the correlation coefficient. A correlation coefficient that is high in magnitude, whether negative or positive, indicates a strong relation between two variables. If two variables are highly related, it makes sense that one of them is going to be a good predictor of the other. And it makes sense that when we use one variable to predict the other, we're going to reduce error. A high correlation coefficient (whether positive or negative) indicates a high proportionate reduction in error, and both indicate a useful regression equation. So, once the long calculations have given us a sense of what r^2 means, we can simply square our correlation coefficient to assess our regression equation. Better yet, we can let the computer do it for us. But now we have some sense of where that number comes from.

CHECK YOUR LEARNING

Reviewing the Concepts

> Findings from regression analyses are subject to the same types of limitations as correlation. Regression, like correlation, does not tell us about causation.

> Individuals with extreme scores at one point in time tend to have less extreme scores (scores closer to the mean) at a later point in time, a phenomenon called regression to the mean.

> Error based on the mean is referred to as the sum of squares total (SS_{total}), whereas error based on the regression equation is referred to as the sum of squared error (SS_{error}).

> Proportionate reduction in error, r^2, determines the amount of error we have eliminated by using a particular regression equation to predict an individual's score on the dependent variable versus simply predicting the mean on the dependent variable for that person.

Clarifying the Concepts

14-6 Distinguish error of prediction when the mean is used from the standard error of the estimate.

14-7 Explain how the strength of the correlation is related to the proportionate reduction in error for regression.

Calculating the Statistics

14-8 Data are provided here with descriptive statistics, a correlation coefficient and a regression equation: $r = -0.77$, $\hat{Y} = 7.846 - 0.431(X)$

X	Y
5	6
6	5
4	6
5	6
7	4
8	5
$M_X = 5.833$	$M_Y = 5.333$
$SD_X = 1.344$	$SD_Y = 0.745$

a. Using this information, calculate the sum of squared error for the mean, SS_{total}.

b. Now, using the regression equation provided, calculate the sum of squared error for the regression equation, SS_{error}.

c. Using your work, calculate the proportionate reduction in error for these data.

d. Check that this calculation of r^2 equals the square of the correlation coefficient.

Applying the Concepts

14-9 Many athletes and sports fans believe that an appearance on the cover of *Sports Illustrated* (SI) is a curse. The tendency for SI cover subjects to face imminent bad sporting luck is documented in the pages of (what else?) *Sports Illustrated* and even

continued on next page

has a name, the "SI jinx" (Wolff, 2002). Players or teams, shortly after appearing on the cover, often have a particularly poor performance, a tendency especially pronounced among individual athletes rather than teams, and among those who were described on the cover with superlatives, such as *best*. In fact, of 2456 covers, SI counted 913 "victims." And their potential victims have noticed: after the New England Patriots football team won their league championship in 1996, their coach at the time, Bill Parcells, called his daughter, an SI staffer, and ordered: "No cover." Using your knowledge about the limitations of regression, what would you tell Coach Parcells?

Solutions to these Check Your Learning questions can be found in Appendix D.

Multiple Regression

In regression analysis, we explain more of the variability in our dependent variable if we can discover genuine predictors that are separate and distinct. This involves *orthogonal variables, independent variables that make separate and distinct contributions in the prediction of a dependent variable, as compared with other variables.* Orthogonal variables do not overlap each other. For example, the study we discussed earlier explored whether Facebook use predicted social capital. It is likely that a person's personality also predicts social capital; for example, we would expect extroverted, or outgoing, people to be more likely to have this kind of social capital than introverted, or shy, people. It would be useful to separate the effects of Facebook use and extroversion on social capital.

Multiple pieces of evidence are usually better than one. The behavioral sciences frequently use multiple pieces of evidence to reach conclusions. So the statistical technique we consider next is a way of quantifying (1) whether multiple pieces of evidence really are better than one and (2) precisely how much better each additional piece of evidence actually is.

Understanding the Equation

Just as a regression equation using one independent variable is a better predictor than the mean, a regression equation using more than one independent variable is likely to be an even better predictor. And this makes sense in the same way that knowing a baseball player's historical batting average *plus* knowing that the player continues to suffer from a serious injury is likely to change our prediction yet again. So it is not surprising that multiple regression is far more common than simple linear regression. *Multiple regression is a statistical technique that includes two or more predictor variables in a prediction equation.* More specifically, multiple regression is a statistical technique that develops an equation that predicts scores on a single dependent variable by using more than one independent variable.

Let's examine an equation that might be used to predict final exam grade from two variables, number of absences *and* score on the mathematics portion of the SAT. Table 14–8 repeats the data from Table 14–1, with the added variable of SAT score. (Note that although the scores on number of absences and final exam grade are real-life data from our statistics classes, the SAT scores are fictional.)

The computer gives us the printout seen in Figure 14–8. The column in which we're interested is the one labeled "B" under "unstandardized coefficients." The first number, across from "(constant)," is the intercept, so called because the intercept does

> **MASTERING THE CONCEPT**
>
> **14-5:** Multiple regression predicts scores on a single dependent variable from scores on more than one independent variable. Because behavior tends to be influenced by many factors, multiple regression allows us to better predict a given outcome.

TABLE 14-8. Predicting Exam Grade from Two Variables

Multiple regression allows us to develop a regression equation that predicts a dependent variable from two or more independent variables. Here, we will use these data to develop a regression equation that predicts exam grade from number of absences *and* SAT score.

Student	Absences	SAT	Exam Grade
1	4	620	82
2	2	750	98
3	2	500	76
4	3	520	68
5	1	540	84
6	0	690	99
7	4	590	67
8	8	490	58
9	7	450	50
10	3	560	78

- An **orthogonal variable** is an independent variable that makes a separate and distinct contribution in the prediction of a dependent variable, as compared with another variable.

- **Multiple regression** is a statistical technique that includes two or more predictor variables in a prediction equation.

not change; it is not multiplied by any value of an independent variable. The intercept here is 33.422. The second number is the slope for the independent variable, number of absences. Number of absences is negatively correlated with final exam grade, so the slope, -3.340, is negative. The third number in this column is the slope for the independent variable of SAT score. As we might guess, SAT score and final exam grade are positively correlated; a student with a high SAT score tends to have a higher final exam grade. So, the slope, 0.094, is positive. We can put these numbers into a regression equation:

$$\hat{Y} = 33.422 - 3.34(X_1) + 0.094(X_2)$$

Once we have developed our multiple regression equation, we can input raw scores on number of absences and mathematics SAT score to determine an individual's predicted score on Y. Imagine that our student, Allie, scored 600 on the mathematics portion of the SAT. We already know she planned to miss two classes this semester. What would we predict for her final exam grade?

$$\hat{Y} = 33.422 - 3.34(X_1) + 0.094(X_2) = 33.422 - 3.34(2) + 0.094(600)$$
$$= 33.422 - 6.68 + 56.4 = 83.142$$

FIGURE 14-8
Software Output for Regression

Computer software provides the information necessary for the multiple regression equation. All necessary coefficients are in column B under "unstandardized coefficients." The constant, 33.422, is the intercept; the number next to "number of absences," -3.340, is the slope for that independent variable; and the number next to "SAT," .094, is the slope for that independent variable.

Coefficients(a)

Model		Unstandardized Coefficients		Standardized Coefficients	t	Sig.
		B	Std. Error	Beta		
1	(Constant)	33.422	13.584		2.460	.043
	number of absences	-3.340	.773	-.527	-4.320	.003
	SAT	.094	.021	.558	4.569	.003

a Dependent Variable: mean exam grade

Based on these two variables, we predict a final exam grade of 83.142 for Allie. And how good is this multiple regression equation? From software, we calculated that the proportionate reduction in error for this equation is a whopping 0.93. We have reduced 93% of the error that would result from predicting the mean of 76 for everyone by using a multiple regression equation with the independent variables of number of absences and SAT score. Compared to using averages, the multiple regression equation represents a significant advance in our ability to predict human behavior.

When we calculate proportionate reduction in error for a multiple regression, the symbol changes slightly. The symbol is now R^2 instead of r^2. The capitalization of this statistic is an indication that the proportionate reduction in error is based on more than one independent variable.

Multiple Regression in Everyday Life

With the development of increasingly more powerful computers and the availability of ever-larger amounts of computerized data, tools based on multiple regression have proliferated. Now the general public can access many of them online (Darlin, 2006). Bing Travel (formerly Farecast.com) predicts the price of an airline ticket for specific routes, travel dates, and, most important, purchase dates. Using the same data available to travel agents, along with additional independent variables such as the weather and even which sports teams' fans might be traveling to a championship game, Bing Travel mimics the regression equations used by the airlines. Airlines predict how much money potential travelers are willing to pay on a given date for a given flight and use these predictions to adjust their fares so they can earn the most money.

Bing Travel is an attempt at an end run, using mathematical prediction tools, to help savvy airline consumers either to beat or to wait out the airlines' price hikes. In 2007, Bing Travel's precursor, Farecast.com, claimed a 74.5% accuracy rate for its predictions. Zillow.com does for real estate what Bing Travel does for airline tickets. Using archival land record data, Zillow.com predicts U.S. housing prices and claims to be accurate within 10% of the actual selling price of a given home. Another company, Inrix, predicts the dependent variable, traffic, using the independent variables of the traveling speeds of vehicles that have been outfitted with global positioning satellite (GPS) systems, the weather, and information about events such as rock concerts. It even suggests, via cell phone or in-car navigation systems, alternative routes for gridlocked drivers. As of March 2009, Inrix was available in all major metropolitan areas in the United States, the United Kingdom, and the Netherlands, as well as in parts of 16 other European countries. In addition, it sells its predictions to other companies, such as the news media or navigation device companies. Like the future of visual displays of data, the future of the regression equation is limited only by the creativity of the rising generation of behavioral scientists and statisticians.

CHECK YOUR LEARNING

Reviewing the Concepts

> Multiple regression is used when we want to predict a dependent variable from more than one independent variable. Ideally, these variables are distinct from each other such that they contribute uniquely to our predictions.

> We can develop a multiple regression equation and input specific scores for each independent variable to determine the predicted score on the dependent variable.

> Multiple regression is the backbone of many online tools that we can use for predicting everyday variables such as traffic or home prices.

Clarifying the Concepts 14-10 What is multiple regression, and what are its benefits over simple linear regression?

Calculating the Statistics 14-11 Write the equation for the line of prediction using the following output from a multiple regression analysis:

Coefficients[a]

Model		Unstandardized Coefficients		Standardized Coefficients	t	Sig.
		B	Std. Error	Beta		
1	(Constant)	5.251	4.084		1.286	.225
	Variable A	.060	.107	.168	.562	.585
	Variable B	1.105	.437	.758	2.531	.028

a. Dependent Variable: Outcome variable

14-12 Use the equation for the line you created in Check Your Learning 14-11 to make predictions for each of the following:

a. $X_1 = 40, X_2 = 14$

b. $X_1 = 101, X_2 = 39$

c. $X_1 = 76, X_2 = 20$

Applying the Concepts 14-13 The accompanying computer printout shows a regression equation that predicts GPA from three independent variables: hours slept per night, hours studied per week, and admiration for Pamela Anderson, the B-level actress whom many view as tacky. The data are from some of our statistics classes. (*Note:* Hypothesis testing shows that all three independent variables are statistically significant predictors of GPA!)

Coefficients(a)

Model		Unstandardized Coefficients		Standardized Coefficients	t	Sig.
		B	Std. Error	Beta		
1	(Constant)	2.695	.228		11.829	.000
	Hours Slept Per Night	.069	.032	.173	2.186	.030
	Hours Studied Per Week	.015	.006	.209	2.637	.009
	Level of Admiration for Pamela Anderson	-.072	.025	-.229	-2.882	.005

a Dependent Variable: GPA

a. What is the regression equation based on these data?

b. If someone reports that they typically sleep six hours a night, study twenty hours per week, and have a Pamela Anderson admiration level of 4 (on a scale of 1–7, with 7 indicating the highest level of admiration), what would you predict for his GPA?

c. What does the negative sign in the slope for the independent variable, level of admiration for Pamela Anderson, tell you about this variable's predictive association with grade point average?

Solutions to these Check Your Learning questions can be found in Appendix D.

REVIEW OF CONCEPTS

Simple Linear Regression

Regression is an expansion of correlation in that it allows us not only to quantify a relation between two variables but also to quantify one variable's ability to predict another variable. We can predict a dependent variable's z score from an independent variable's z score, or we can do a bit more initial work and predict a dependent variable's raw score from an independent variable's raw score. The latter method uses the equation for a line with an *intercept* and a *slope*.

We are using *simple linear regression* when we predict one dependent variable from one independent variable when the two variables are linearly related. We can graph this line using the regression equation, plugging in low and high values of X and plotting those values with their associated predicted values on Y, then connecting the dots to form the regression line.

Just as we can standardize a raw score by converting it to a z score, we can standardize a slope by converting it to a *standardized regression coefficient*. This number indicates the predicted change on the dependent variable in terms of standard deviation for every standard deviation increase in the independent variable. For simple linear regression, the standardized regression coefficient is the same as the Pearson correlation coefficient. Hypothesis testing that determines whether the correlation coefficient is statistically significantly different from 0 also indicates whether the standardized regression coefficient is statistically significantly different from 0.

Interpretation and Prediction

A regression equation is rarely a perfect predictor of scores on the dependent variable. There is always some prediction error, which can be quantified by the *standard error of the estimate*, the number that describes the typical amount that an observation falls from the regression line. In addition, regression suffers from the same drawbacks as correlation. For example, we cannot know if the predictive relation is causal; the posited direction could be the reverse (with Y causally predicting X), or there could be a third variable at work.

When we use regression, we must also be aware of the phenomenon called *regression to the mean*, in which extreme values tend to become less extreme over time. Finally, we also must consider the degree to which an independent variable predicts a dependent variable. To do this, we can calculate the *proportionate reduction in error*, symbolized as r^2. The proportionate reduction in error tells us how much better our prediction is with the regression equation than with the mean as the only predictive tool.

Multiple Regression

We use *multiple regression* when we have more than one independent variable, as is usual in most research in the behavioral sciences. Multiple regression is particularly useful when we have *orthogonal variables*, independent variables that make separate contributions to the prediction of a dependent variable. Multiple regression has led to the development of many Web-based prediction tools that allow us to make educated guesses about such outcomes as airplane ticket prices.

SPSS®

The most common form of regression analysis on SPSS uses at least two scale variables: an independent variable (predictor) and a dependent variable (the variable being predicted). Let's use our absences and exam grade data as an example. Once again, begin by visualizing the data.

Request the scatterplot of the data by selecting: **Graphs** → Chart Builder → Gallery → Scatter/Dot. Drag the upper-left sample graph to the large box on top. Then select the variables to be included in the scatterplot by dragging the independent variable, absences, to the *x*-axis and the dependent variable, exam grade, to the *y*-axis. Click "OK." Then click on the graph to make changes. To add the regression line, click "Elements," then "Fit Line at Total." Choose "Linear," then click "Apply."

To analyze the linear regression, select: **Analyze** → Regression → Linear. Select "absences" as the independent (predictor) variable and "grade" as the dependent variable being predicted.

As usual, click on "OK" to see the Output screen. Part of the output is shown in the screenshot here. In the box titled "Model Summary," we can see the correlation coefficient of .851 under "R" and the proportionate reduction of error, .724, under "R Square." In the box titled "Coefficients," we can look in the first column under "B" to determine the regression equation. The intercept, 94.326, is across from "(Constant)," and the slope, −5.390, is across from "Number of Absences." (Any slight differences from the numbers we calculated earlier are due to rounding decisions.)

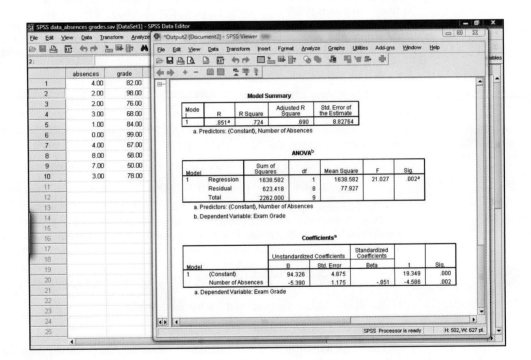

How It Works

14.1: REGRESSION WITH *z* SCORES

Shannon Callahan, a student in the Experimental Psychology master's program at Seton Hall University, conducted a study that examined evaluations of faculty members on Ratemyprofessor.com. She wondered if professors who were rated high on "clarity" were more likely to be viewed as "easy." Callahan found a significant correlation of 0.267 between the average easiness rating a professor garnered and the average rating he or she received with respect to clarity of teaching.

If we know that a professor's z score on clarity is 2.2 (an indication that he is very clear), we could predict his z score on easiness:

$$z_{\hat{Y}} = (r_{XY})(z_X) = (0.267)(2.2) = 0.59$$

When there's a positive correlation, we predict a z score above the mean when his original z score is above the mean.

And if a professor's z score on clarity is -1.8 (an indication that she's not very clear), we could predict her z score on easiness:

$$z_{\hat{Y}} = (r_{XY})(z_X) = (0.267)(-1.8) = -0.48$$

When there's a positive correlation, we predict a z score below the mean when her original z score is below the mean.

14.2: REGRESSION WITH RAW SCORES

Using Shannon Callahan's data, let's develop the regression equation so that we can work directly with raw scores. To do this, we need a little more information. For this data set, the mean clarity score is 3.673 with a standard deviation of 0.890, and the mean easiness score is 2.843 with a standard deviation of 0.701. As noted before, the correlation between these variables is 0.267.

To calculate the regression equation, we need to find the intercept and the slope. We determine the *intercept* by calculating what we predict for Y (easiness) when X (clarity) equals 0. Given the means, the standard deviations, and the correlation calculated above, we first find z_X:

$$z_X = \frac{(X - M_X)}{SD_X} = \frac{(0 - 3.673)}{0.890} = -4.124$$

We then calculate the predicted z score for easiness:

$$z_{\hat{Y}} = (r_{XY})(z_X) = (0.267)(-4.124) = -1.101$$

Finally, we transform the predicted easiness z score into the predicted easiness raw score:

$$\hat{Y} = z_{\hat{Y}}(SD_Y) + M_Y = -1.101(0.701) + 2.843 = 2.071$$

The intercept, therefore, is 2.071.

To determine the *slope,* we calculate what we would predict for Y (easiness) when X (clarity) equals 1 and determine how much that differs from what we would predict when X equals 0. The z score for X corresponding to our raw score of 1 is:

$$z_X = \frac{(X - M_X)}{SD_X} = \frac{(1 - 3.673)}{0.890} = -3.003$$

We then calculate the predicted z score for easiness:

$$z_{\hat{Y}} = (r_{XY})(z_X) = (0.267)(-3.003) = -0.801$$

Finally, we transform the predicted easiness z score into the predicted easiness raw score:

$$\hat{Y} = z_{\hat{Y}}(SD_Y) + M_Y = -0.801(0.701) + 2.843 = 2.281$$

The difference between our predicted Y when X equals 1 (2.281) and that when X equals 0 (2.071) yields our slope, which is $2.281 - 2.071 = 0.210$. So, the regression equation is:

$$\hat{Y} = 2.07 + 0.21(X)$$

We can then use this regression equation to calculate a professor's predicted easiness score from her clarity score. Let's say a professor has a clarity score of 3.2. We would use the regression equation to predict her easiness score as follows:

$$\hat{Y} = 2.07 + 0.21(X) = 2.07 + 0.21(3.2) = 0.141$$

This result makes sense because she is below the mean on clarity, so, given that there is a positive correlation, we predict her score to fall below the mean on easiness.

Exercises

Clarifying the Concepts

14.1 What does regression add above and beyond what we learn from correlation?

14.2 How does the regression line relate to the correlation of the two variables?

14.3 Is there any difference between $\hat{Y}$ and a predicted score for Y?

14.4 What do each of the symbols stand for in the formula for the regression equation: $z_{\hat{Y}} = (r_{XY})(z_X)$?

14.5 The equation for a line is $\hat{Y} = a + b(X)$. Define the symbols a and b.

14.6 What are the three steps to calculate the intercept?

14.7 When is the intercept not meaningful or useful?

14.8 What does the slope tell us?

14.9 Why do we also call the regression line the line of best fit?

14.10 How are the sign of the correlation coefficient and the sign of the slope related?

14.11 What is the difference between a small standard error of the estimate and a large one?

14.12 Explain why explanations of the causes behind relations explored with regression are limited in the same way they were with correlation.

14.13 What is the connection between regression to the mean and the bell-shaped curve?

14.14 Explain why the regression equation is a better source of predictions than the mean.

14.15 What is the SS_{total}?

14.16 When drawing error lines between data points and the regression line, why is it important that these lines be perfectly vertical?

14.17 What are the basic steps to calculate the proportionate reduction in error?

14.18 What information does the proportionate reduction in error give us?

14.19 What is an orthogonal variable?

Calculating the Statistics

14.20 Using the following information, make a prediction for Y given an X score of 8:

> Variable X: $M = 12$, $SD = 3$
> Variable Y: $M = 74$, $SD = 18$
> Pearson correlation of variables X and $Y = 0.46$

  a. Transpose the raw score for the independent variable to a z score.

  b. Calculate the predicted z score for the dependent variable.

  c. Transpose the z score for the dependent variable back into a raw score.

14.21 Let's assume we know that age is related to bone density, with a Pearson correlation coefficient of -0.19. (Notice the correlation is negative, indicating bone density is lower at older ages than at younger ages.) Assume we also know the following descriptive statistics:

> Age of people studied: 55 years on average, with a standard deviation of 12 years
> Bone density of people studied: 1000 mg/cm² on average, with a standard deviation of 95 mg/cm²

Virginia is 76 years old. What would you predict her bone density to be? To answer this question, complete the following steps:

  a. Transpose the raw score for the independent variable to a z score.

  b. Calculate the predicted z score for the dependent variable.

  c. Transpose the z score for the dependent variable back into a raw score.

14.22 Given the regression line $\hat{Y} = -6 + 0.41(X)$, make predictions for each of the following:

  a. $X = 25$

  b. $X = 50$

  c. $X = 75$

14.23 Given the regression line $\hat{Y} = 49 - 0.18(X)$, make predictions for each of the following:

  a. $X = -31$

  b. $X = 65$

  c. $X = 14$

14.24 Using the following information from Exercise 14.20, complete the following:

> Variable X: $M = 12$, $SD = 3$
> Variable Y: $M = 74$, $SD = 18$
> Pearson correlation of variables X and $Y = 0.46$

  a. Calculate the y-intercept, a.

  b. Calculate the slope, b.

  c. Write the equation for the regression line.

  d. Draw the regression line, basing your line on predicted Y values for X values of 0, 1, and 18.

14.25 Using the following information from Exercise 14.21, complete the following:

Age is related to bone density, with a Pearson coefficient of −0.19.

Age of people studied: 55 years on average, with a standard deviation of 12 years

Bone density of people studied: 1000 mg/cm² on average, with a standard deviation of 95 mg/cm²

a. Calculate the y-intercept, a.

b. Calculate the slope, b.

c. Write the equation for the regression line.

d. Draw the regression line, basing your line on predicted Y values for X values of 0, 1, and 48 years of age.

14.26 Data are provided here with descriptive statistics, a correlation coefficient, and a regression equation: $r = 0.426$, $\hat{Y} = 219.974 + 186.595(X)$.

X	Y
0.13	200.00
0.27	98.00
0.49	543.00
0.57	385.00
0.84	420.00
1.12	312.00
$M_X = 0.57$	$M_Y = 326.333$
$SD_X = 0.333$	$SD_Y = 145.752$

Using this information, compute the following estimates of prediction error:

a. Calculate the sum of squared error for the mean, SS_{total}.

b. Now, using the regression equation provided, calculate the sum of squared error for the regression equation, SS_{error}.

c. Using your work, calculate the proportionate reduction in error for these data.

d. Check that this calculation of r^2 equals the square of the correlation coefficient.

14.27 Data are provided here with descriptive statistics, a correlation coefficient, and a regression equation: $r = 0.52$, $\hat{Y} = 2.643 + 0.469(X)$.

X	Y
4.00	6.00
6.00	3.00
7.00	7.00
8.00	5.00
9.00	4.00
10.00	12.00
12.00	9.00
14.00	8.00
$M_X = 8.75$	$M_Y = 6.75$
$SD_X = 3.031$	$SD_Y = 2.727$

Using this information, compute the following estimates of prediction error:

a. Calculate the sum of squared error for the mean, SS_{total}.

b. Now, using the regression equation provided, calculate the sum of squared error for the regression equation, SS_{error}.

c. Using your work, calculate the proportionate reduction in error for these data.

d. Check that this calculation of r^2 equals the square of the correlation coefficient.

14.28 Write the equation for the line of prediction using the following output from a multiple regression analysis:

Coefficients[a]

Model		Unstandardized Coefficients		Standardized Coefficients	t	Sig.
		B	Std. Error	Beta		
1	(Constant)	3.977	1.193		3.333	.001
	Variable 1	.414	.096	.458	4.313	.000
	Variable 2	-.019	.011	-.181	-1.704	.093

a. Dependent Variable: Outcome (Y)

14.29 Write the equation for the line of prediction using the following output from a multiple regression analysis:

Coefficients[a]

Model		Unstandardized Coefficients		Standardized Coefficients	t	Sig.
		B	Std. Error	Beta		
1	(Constant)	1.675	.563		2.972	.004
	SAT	.001	.000	.321	2.953	.004
	Rank	-.008	.003	-.279	-2.566	.012

a. Dependent Variable: GPA

14.30 Use the equation for the line you created in Exercise 14.28 to make predictions for each of the following:

a. Variable 1 = 6, variable 2 = 60

b. Variable 1 = 9, variable 2 = 54.3

c. Variable 1 = 13, variable 2 = 44.8

14.31 Use the equation for the line you created in Exercise 14.29 to make predictions for each of the following:

a. SAT = 1030, rank = 41

b. SAT = 860, rank = 22

c. SAT = 1060, rank = 8

14.32 Compute the standardized regression coefficient for the data presented in Exercise 14.26. Remember, $r = 0.426$, and the regression equation is $\hat{Y} = 219.974 + 186.595(X)$.

X	Y
0.13	200.00
0.27	98.00
0.49	543.00
0.57	385.00
0.84	420.00
1.12	312.00
$M_X = 0.57$	$M_Y = 326.333$
$SD_X = 0.333$	$SD_Y = 145.752$

14.33 Compute the standardized regression coefficient for the data presented in Exercise 14.27. Remember, $r = 0.52$, and the regression equation is: $\hat{Y} = 2.643 + 0.469(X)$.

X	Y
4.00	6.00
6.00	3.00
7.00	7.00
8.00	5.00
9.00	4.00
10.00	12.00
12.00	9.00
14.00	8.00
$M_X = 8.75$	$M_Y = 6.75$
$SD_X = 3.031$	$SD_Y = 2.727$

Applying the Concepts

14.34 Several studies have found a correlation between weight and blood pressure.

a. Explain what is meant by a correlation between these two variables.

b. If you were to examine these two variables with simple linear regression instead of correlation, how would you frame the question? (*Hint:* The research question for correlation would be: Is weight related to blood pressure?)

c. What is the difference between simple linear regression and multiple regression?

d. If you were to conduct a multiple regression instead of a simple linear regression, what other independent variables might you include?

14.35 Running a football stadium for an NFL team involves innumerable predictions. For example, when stocking up on food and beverages for sale at the game, it helps to have an idea of how much will be sold. In the football stadiums in colder climates, stadium managers use expected outdoor temperature to predict sales of hot chocolate.

a. What is the independent variable in this example?

b. What is the dependent variable?

c. As the value of the independent variable increases, what can we predict would happen to the value of the dependent variable?

d. What other variables might predict this dependent variable? Name at least three.

14.36 In How It Works 13.2, we calculated the correlation coefficient between students' age and number of hours they study per week. The correlation between these two variables is 0.49.

a. Elif's z score for age is -0.82. What would we predict for the z score for the number of hours she studies per week?

b. John's z score for age is 1.2. What would we predict for the z score for the number of hours he studies per week?

c. Eugene's z score for age is 0. What would we predict for the z score for the number of hours he studies per week?

d. For part (c). explain why the concept of *regression* to the mean is not relevant (and why you didn't really need the formula).

14.37 A study of Consideration of Future Consequences (CFC) found a mean score of 3.51, with a standard deviation of 0.61, for the 664 students in the sample (Petrocelli, 2003).

a. Imagine that your z score on the CFC score was -1.2. What would your raw score be? Use symbolic notation and the formula. Explain why this answer makes sense.

b. Imagine that your z score on the CFC score was 0.66. What would your raw score be? Use symbolic notation and the formula. Explain why this answer makes sense.

14.38 The verbal subtest of the GRE has a population mean of 500 and a population standard deviation of 100 by design (the quantitative subtest has the same mean and standard deviation).

a. Convert the following z scores to raw scores *without* using a formula: (i) 1.5, (ii) −0.5, (iii) −2.0.

b. Now convert the same z scores to raw scores using symbolic notation and the formula: (i) 1.5, (ii) −0.5, (iii) −2.0.

14.39 In How It Works 13.2, we calculated the correlation coefficient between students' age and number of hours they study per week. The mean for age is 21, and the standard deviation is 1.789. The mean for hours studied is 14.2, and the standard deviation is 5.582. The correlation between these two variables is 0.49. Use the z-score formula.

a. Joâo is 24 years old. What would we predict for the number of hours he studies per week?

b. Kimberly is 19 years old. What would we predict for the number of hours she studies per week?

c. Seung is 45 years old. Why might it not be a good idea to predict how many hours per week he studies?

d. From a mathematical perspective, why is the word *regression* used? [*Hint:* Look at parts (a) and (b), and discuss the scores on the first variable with respect to their mean versus the predicted scores on the second variable with respect to their mean.]

14.40 A regression analysis of data from some of our statistics classes yielded the following regression equation for the independent variable, hours studied, and the dependent variable, grade point average (GPA): $\hat{Y} = 2.96 + 0.02(X)$.

a. If you plan to study 8 hours per week, what would you predict for your grade?

b. If you plan to study 10 hours per week, what would you predict for your grade?

c. Create a graph and draw the regression line based on these two pairs of scores, plus the X value 11 and its predicted score on Y.

d. Do some algebra, and determine the number of hours you'd have to study to have a predicted GPA of the maximum possible, 4.0. Why is it misleading

to make predictions for anyone who plans to study this many hours (or more)?

14.41 Exercise 14.39 used the example from How It Works 13.2 on whether age can predict how much people study. Recall that the mean for age is 21, and the standard deviation is 1.789. The mean for hours studied is 14.2, and the standard deviation is 5.582. The correlation coefficient is 0.49.

a. Calculate the regression equation.

b. Use the regression equation to predict the number of hours studied for a 17-year-old student and for a 22-year-old student.

c. Using the four pairs of scores that you have [age and predicted hours studied from part (b), and the predicted scores for a score of 0 and 1 from calculating the regression equation], create a graph that includes the regression line.

d. Why is it misleading to include the ages 0 and 1 on the graph?

14.42 Researchers studied whether corporate political contributions predicted profits (Cooper, Gulen, & Ovtchinnikov, 2007). From archival data, they determined how many political candidates each company supported with financial contributions, as well as each company's profit in terms of a percentage. The accompanying table shows data for five companies. (*Note:* The data points are hypothetical but are based on averages for companies falling in the 2nd, 4th, 6th, and 8th deciles in terms of candidates supported. A decile is a range of 10%, so the 2nd decile includes those with percentiles between 10 and 19.9.)

Number of Candidates Supported	Profit (%)
6	12.37
17	12.91
39	12.59
62	13.43
98	13.42

a. Create a scatterplot for these scores.

b. Calculate the mean and standard deviation for the variable number of candidates supported.

c. Calculate the mean and standard deviation for the variable profit.

d. Calculate the correlation between number of candidates supported and profit.

e. Calculate the regression equation for the prediction of profit from number of candidates supported.

f. Create a graph and draw the regression line.

g. What do these data suggest about the political process?

h. What third variables might be at play here?

14.43 Exercises 14.39 and 14.41 used the example from How It Works 13.2 on whether age can predict how much people study.

a. Construct a graph that includes both the scatterplot for these data and the regression line as determined in Exercise 14.41. Draw vertical lines to connect each dot on the scatterplot with the regression line.

b. Construct a second graph that includes both the scatterplot and a line for the mean for hours studied, 14.2. The line will be a horizontal line beginning at 14.2 on the y-axis. Draw vertical lines to connect each dot on the scatterplot with the regression line.

c. Part (a) is a depiction of the error if we use the regression equation to predict hours studied. Part (b) is a depiction of the error if we use the mean to predict hours studied (i.e., if we predict that everyone has the mean of 14.2 on hours studied per week). Which one appears to have less error? Briefly explain why the error is less in one situation.

14.44 Exercises 14.39, 14.41, and 14.43 used the example from How It Works 13.2 on whether age can predict how much people study. Here are the data once again.

Student	Age	Number of Hours Studied (per week)
1	19	5
2	20	20
3	20	8
4	21	12
5	21	18
6	23	25
7	22	15
8	20	10
9	19	14
10	25	15

a. Calculate the proportionate reduction in error the long way.

b. Explain what the proportionate reduction in error that you calculated in part (a) tells us. Be specific about what it tells us about predicting using the regression equation versus predicting using the mean.

c. Demonstrate how the proportionate reduction in error could be calculated using the short way. Why does this make sense? That is, why does the correlation coefficient give us a sense of how useful the regression equation will be?

14.45 Does one's cola consumption predict one's bone mineral density? Using regression analyses, nutrition researchers found that older women who drank more cola (but not more of other carbonated drinks) tended to have lower bone mineral density, a risk factor for osteoporosis (Tucker et al., 2006). Cola intake, therefore, does seem to predict bone mineral density.

a. Explain why we cannot conclude that cola intake causes a decrease in bone mineral density.

b. The researchers included a number of possible third variables in their regression analyses. Among the included variables were physical activity score, smoking, alcohol use, and calcium intake. They included the possible third variables first, and then added the bone density measure. Why would they have used multiple regression in this case? Explain.

c. How might physical activity play a role as a third variable? Discuss its possible relation to both bone density and cola consumption.

d. How might calcium intake play a role as a third variable? Discuss its possible relation to both bone density and cola consumption.

14.46 Does the level of precipitation predict violence? Dubner and Levitt (2006b) reported on various studies that found links between rain and violence. They mentioned one study by Miguel, Satyanath, and Sergenti that found that decreased rain was linked with an increased likelihood of civil war across a number of African countries they examined. Referring to the study's authors, Dubner and Levitt state, "The causal effect of a drought, they argue, was frighteningly strong."

a. What is the independent variable in this study?

b. What is the dependent variable?

c. What possible third variables might play a role in this connection? That is, is it just the lack of rain that's causing violence, or is it something else? (*Hint:* Consider the likely economic base of many African countries.)

14.47 Are podcasts a drain on students' time, or does the information they contain help students do better in school? You collect data on the number of podcasts each student downloads per month and each student's GPA. When we calculate regression equations (just as when we calculate correlation coefficients), it's important to construct a scatterplot first. Let's say that it turns out that really poor students don't download podcasts very often, maybe because they don't use their computers much at all, and really good students don't download podcasts very often, maybe because they're too busy studying to have time to listen. Explain how this might present a problem if we calculate a simple linear regression equation to predict GPA from number of podcasts downloaded, and explain how a scatterplot might help us to identify the problem.

14.48 A researcher conducted a study in which students with problems learning mathematics were offered the opportunity to purchase time with special tutors; the number of weeks that students met with their tutors varied from 1 to 20. He found that the number of weeks of tutoring predicted mathematics performance in these children and recommended that parents of such children send them for tutoring for as many weeks as possible—for two years if they could afford it. List three problems with that interpretation. Be sure to explain why each of these poses a problem.

14.49 Consider again the example used in Exercise 14.48. As before, the researcher is interested in predicting mathematics ability with the ultimate goal of identifying ways to improve mathematics performance. If you were to develop a multiple regression equation instead of a simple linear regression equation, what additional variables might be good independent variables? List at least one variable that can be manipulated (e.g., weeks of tutoring) and at least one variable that cannot be manipulated (e.g., parents' years of education).

14.50 We analyzed data from a larger data set that one of the authors used for previous research (Nolan, Flynn, & Garber, 2003). In the current analyses, we used regression to look at factors that predict anxiety over a three-year period. Here is the output for the regression analysis examining whether depression at year 1 predicted anxiety at year 3.

Coefficients(a)

	Unstandardized Coefficients		Standardized Coefficients	t	Sig.
	B	Std. Error	Beta		
(Constant)	24.698	.566		43.665	.000
Depression Year 1	.161	.048	.235	3.333	.001

a Dependent Variable: Anxiety Year 3

a. From this software output, write the regression equation.

b. As depression at year 1 increases by 1 point, what happens to the predicted anxiety level for year 3? Be specific.

c. If someone has a depression score of 10 at year 1, what would we predict for her anxiety score at year 3?

d. If someone has a depression score of 2 at year 1, what would we predict for his anxiety score at year 3?

14.51 We conducted a second regression analysis on the data from Exercise 14.50. In addition to depression at year 1, we included a second independent variable to predict anxiety at year 3. We also included anxiety at year 1. (We might expect that the best predictor of anxiety at a later point in time is one's anxiety at an earlier point in time.) Here is the output for that analysis.

Coefficients(a)

	Unstandardized Coefficients		Standardized Coefficients	t	Sig.
	B	Std. Error	Beta		
(Constant)	17.038	1.484		11.482	.000
Depression Year 1	-.013	.055	-.019	-.237	.813
Anxiety Year 1	.307	.056	.442	5.521	.000

a Dependent Variable: Anxiety Year 3

a. From this software output, write the regression equation.

b. As the first independent variable, depression at year 1, increases by 1 point, what happens to the predicted score on anxiety at year 3?

c. As the second independent variable, anxiety at year 1, increases by 1 point, what happens to the predicted score on anxiety at year 3?

d. Compare the predictive utility of depression at year 1 using the regression equation in Exercise 14.50 and using this regression equation. In which regression equation is depression at year 1 a better predictor? Given that we're using the same sample, is depression at year 1 actually better at predicting anxiety at year 3 in one situation versus the other? Why do you think there's a difference?

e. The table below is the correlation matrix for the three variables. As you can see, all three are highly correlated with each other. If we look at the intersection of each pair of variables, the number next to the words "Pearson correlation" is the correlation coefficient. For example, the correlation between "Anxiety year 1" and "Depression year 1" is .549. Which two variables show the strongest correlation? How might this explain the fact that depression at year 1 seems to be a better predictor when it's the only independent variable than when anxiety at year 1 also is included? What does this tell us about the importance of including third variables in our regression analyses when possible?

f. Let's say you want to add a fourth independent variable. You have to choose among three possible independent variables: (1) a variable highly correlated with both independent variables and the dependent variable, (2) a variable highly correlated with the dependent variable but not correlated with either independent variable, and (3) a variable not correlated with either of the independent variables or with the dependent variable. Which of the three variables is likely to make the multiple regression equation better? That is, which is likely to increase the proportionate reduction in error? Explain.

14.52 Using the data about age and number of hours studied, and your work from Exercise 14.41, answer the following questions:

a. Compute the standardized regression coefficient.

b. How does this coefficient relate to other information you know?

c. Draw a conclusion about your analysis based on what you know about hypothesis testing with regression.

14.53 Using the data about political contributions and corporate profits, and your work from Exercise 14.42, answer the following questions:

a. Compute the standardized regression coefficient.

b. How does this coefficient relate to other information you know?

c. Draw a conclusion about your analysis based on what you know about hypothesis testing with regression.

Correlations

		Depression Year 1	Anxiety Year 1	Anxiety Year 3
Depression Year 1	Pearson Correlation	1	.549(**)	.235(**)
	Sig. (2-tailed)		.000	.001
	N	240	240	192
Anxiety Year 1	Pearson Correlation	.549(**)	1	.432(**)
	Sig. (2-tailed)	.000		.000
	N	240	240	192
Anxiety Year 3	Pearson Correlation	.235(**)	.432(**)	1
	Sig. (2-tailed)	.001	.000	
	N	192	192	192

** Correlation is significant at the 0.01 level (2-tailed).

Terms

simple linear regression (p. 367)
regression to the mean (p. 369)
intercept (p. 371)
slope (p. 371)
standardized regression coefficient (p. 374)
standard error of the estimate (p. 377)
proportionate reduction in error (p. 380)
orthogonal variable (p. 386)
multiple regression (p. 386)

Formulas

$$z_{\hat{Y}} = (r_{XY})(z_X) \qquad \text{(p. 369)}$$
$$\hat{Y} = a + b(X) \qquad \text{(p. 371)}$$

$$\beta = (b)\frac{\sqrt{SS_X}}{\sqrt{SS_Y}} \qquad \text{(p. 374)}$$

$$r^2 = \frac{(SS_{total} - SS_{error})}{SS_{total}} \qquad \text{(p. 384)}$$

Symbols

$\hat{Y}$	(p. 369)	β	(p. 374)	SS_{error}	(p. 383)
a	(p. 371)	SS_{total}	(p. 382)	r^2	(p. 384)
b	(p. 371)				

Chi Square and Other Nonparametric Tests

BEFORE YOU GO ON

- You should be able to differentiate between a parametric and a nonparametric hypothesis test (Chapter 7).

- You should know the six steps of hypothesis testing (Chapter 7).

- You should understand the concept of effect size (Chapter 8).

- You should understand the concept of correlation (Chapter 13).

- You should know when to use an independent-samples *t* test (Chapter 10).

Does LeBron James have a "hot hand"?
Studies of baseball, basketball, and many other sports tell the same story: you may feel as if you have a "hot hand," but the pattern is only a strongly felt illusion. In basketball, success or failure on a previous shot does not influence the outcome of the next shot.

You can't believe everything you think (Gilovich, 1991; Kida, 2006). The "hot hand" in basketball, the "hot seat" at the poker table, and "Big Mo" in football all represent the same false perception—the idea that somebody can't miss or lose. People often perceive a predictable pattern where only chance exists. No matter how strongly we may be "feeling it," the evidence from most sports (bowling being a notable exception) comes to the same conclusion: we falsely believe that the hot streak will continue (Alter & Oppenheimer, 2006a).

In the study that started hot hand research, both basketball players and basketball fans were found to believe that a player's chance of hitting a shot is greater after a make than a miss (Gilovich, Vallone, & Tversky, 1985). But the shooting records of the Philadelphia 76ers do not support the hot hand theory. Neither did a study of free throw records of the Boston Celtics. And a controlled study of 14 men and 12 women from Cornell University's basketball teams demonstrated that the players believed the outcome of the previous shot somehow influenced the next shot but did *not* perform that way (Gilovich et al., 1985).

We seem to have an attachment to falsely perceiving patterns amidst random events, but it is the fundamental job of statistical inference to bypass such human perceptual biases. Separating pattern from chance helps us to decide whether what we have observed is actually different from what we could have expected by chance. Nonparametric hypothesis tests, such as the ones we learn about in this chapter, allow us to explore hypotheses about data that do not have a scale dependent variable.

In this chapter, we learn specific guidelines for when we should use a nonparametric test, and then we look at several nonparametric tests. We explore two types of tests based on the chi-square distribution that are used with nominal data. Finally, we examine two tests that can be used with ordinal data: a nonparametric version of the correlation coefficient and a nonparametric version of the independent-samples *t* test. For example, Vergin (2000) used a chi-square test, based on the chi-square distribution, to compare winning streaks in major league baseball and in the National Basketball Association. Vergin was able to do this because the chi-square distribution lets us test the hot hand theory by comparing what we observe with what we can expect by chance.

The chi-square statistic allows us to test relations between variables when they are nominal. As long as we can count the frequency of any event and assign each frequency to one category, the chi-square statistic lets us test for the independence of those categories and estimate effect sizes.

Nonparametric Statistics

Most statistical studies of sporting events confirm that the hot hand is a myth. For example, researchers analyzed how well players shot a basketball after a commentator identified them as being "on fire" and found that such comments represented historical commentary but did not predict future success (Koehler & Conley, 2003). However, such uncontrolled field studies often violate assumptions for hypothesis testing (most importantly the assumption that the data are drawn from a normally distributed population). Fortunately, nonparametric statistics provide a way to analyze data that violate this important assumption for parametric hypothesis testing.

As we learned in Chapter 7, a nonparametric test is a statistical analysis that is *not* based on a set of assumptions about the population. Nonparametric tests are hypothesis tests, just as parametric tests are. Both use precisely the same logic, but nonparametric tests are statistical tools that should be reserved for particular statistical circumstances.

An Example of a Nonparametric Test

Let's look at an example in which the data require us to use a nonparametric test.

EXAMPLE 15.1

A team of Israeli physician-researchers, led by Dr. Shevach Friedler, a trained mime as well as a physician (Ryan, 2006), found that live entertainment by clowns—yes, clowns!—was associated with higher rates of conception (Rockwell, 2006). Out of 93 women receiving in vitro fertilization (IVF) treatment, 35% who were entertained by a clown conceived, compared with 19% in a group that did not enjoy the entertaining clown. Friedler had a professional clown entertain the women during the 15 minutes after embryo transfer (Brinn, 2006).

Let's consider the variables of interest in the clown study. The independent variable is type of post-IVF treatment, with two levels (clown therapy versus no clown therapy). The dependent variable is outcome, with two levels (becomes pregnant versus does not become pregnant). The hypothesis is that whether a woman becomes pregnant depends on whether she receives clown therapy. We record what level (pregnancy, no pregnancy) of a category each participant falls in. This means that we have encountered a new situation: both the independent variable and the dependent variable are nominal (Table 15-1).

This new situation calls for a new statistic and a new hypothesis test. Specifically, a situation with all nominal variables requires the chi-square distribution. The chi-square statistic is symbolized as χ^2 (pronounced "kai square"—rhymes with *sky*).

TABLE 15-1. A Summary of Research Designs

We have encountered several research designs so far, most of which fall in one of two categories. Some designs—those listed in category I—include a scale independent variable and a scale dependent variable. Other designs—those listed in category II—include a nominal independent variable and a scale dependent variable. Until now, we have not encountered a research design with a nominal independent variable and a nominal dependent variable, or a research design with ordinal variables.

I. Scale Independent Variable and Scale Dependent Variable	II. Nominal Independent Variable and Scale Dependent Variable
Correlation	z test
Regression	All kinds of t tests
	All kinds of ANOVAs

When to Use Nonparametric Tests

The three circumstances in which we commonly use a nonparametric test are (1) when the dependent variable is nominal (for example, in the clown study, our dependent variable—whether a woman becomes pregnant—is nominal), (2) when either the independent variable or the dependent variable is ordinal, or (3) when the sample size is small and we suspect that the underlying population of interest is skewed.

The first circumstance, when a dependent variable is nominal, is fairly common. Because you can't be just a little bit pregnant, the dependent variable in the clown study is nominal—whether a woman becomes pregnant. Each woman in the study is placed in a category on the dependent variable, rather than receiving a score.

The second circumstance in which we use a nonparametric test occurs when either our independent variable or dependent variable is ordinal. Recall that an ordinal variable is one in which the participants are ranked, such as class rank in high school or the finishing rankings in a marathon.

◀ **MASTERING THE CONCEPT**

15-1: We use nonparametric tests when (1) the dependent variable is nominal, (2) either the independent variable or the dependent variable is ordinal, or (3) the sample size is small and we suspect that the underlying population distribution is not normal.

■ **Chi-square test for goodness-of-fit** is a nonparametric hypothesis test used with one nominal variable.

■ **Chi-square test for independence** is a nonparametric hypothesis test used with two nominal variables.

The third circumstance that calls for a nonparametric statistic is when we have a small sample size and we suspect that the population of interest is from a skewed distribution. For example, if we wanted to study brain patterns on functional magnetic resonance imaging (fMRI) tests among people who have won the Nobel Prize in literature, we would be very unlikely to recruit a sample of at least 30 people (the number needed to transform a skewed distribution into a normal distribution), no matter how hard we tried or how much we paid people to participate.

In this chapter, we learn techniques for dealing with these three situations. It's important, however, to note that we use a nonparametric test when we cannot use a parametric test—when we have no choice. Nonparametric tests greatly expand the range of variables available for statistical analysis, but they have two main limitations. One limitation is that confidence intervals and effect-size measures are not typically available for nominal or ordinal data. A second limitation is that nonparametric tests tend to have less statistical power than parametric tests. This increases the risk of a Type II error: we are less likely to reject the null hypothesis when we should reject it—that is, when there is a real difference between groups. So, when we can use a parametric test, we should. But when we cannot, nonparametric tests are there for us.

CHECK YOUR LEARNING

Reviewing the Concepts

> We use a nonparametric test when we cannot meet the assumptions of a parametric test, primarily the assumptions of having a scale dependent variable and a normally distributed population.

> The most common situations in which we use a nonparametric test are when we have a nominal dependent variable, any ordinal variable, or a small sample in which the data for the dependent variable suggest that the underlying population distribution might be skewed.

> We use the chi-square statistic when all variables are nominal.

Clarifying the Concepts

15-1 Distinguish parametric tests from nonparametric tests.

15-2 When do we use nonparametric tests?

Calculating the Statistics

15-3 For each of the following situations, identify the independent and dependent variables and how they are measured (nominal, ordinal, or scale).

a. Bernstein (1996) reported that Francis Galton created a "beauty map" by recording the numbers of women he encountered in different cities in England who were either pretty or not so pretty. London women, he found, were the most likely to be pretty and Aberdeen women the least likely.

b. Imagine that Galton instead gave every woman a beauty score on a scale of 1–10 and then compared means for the women in each of five cities. Let's say he found, again, that London women were the prettiest, on average, and Aberdeen the least pretty, on average.

c. Galton was infamous for discounting the intelligence of most women (Bernstein, 1996). Imagine that he assessed the intelligence of 50 women and then applied the beauty scale mentioned in part (b). Let's say he found that women with higher intelligence were more likely to be pretty, whereas women with lower intelligence were less likely to be pretty.

d. Imagine that Galton ranked 50 women on a scale of 1–50 on their beauty and on their intelligence. Let's say he again found that women with higher intelligence tended to be more beautiful, whereas women with lower intelligence tended to be less beautiful.

Applying the Concepts	15-4	For each of the situations listed in Check Your Learning 15-3, state the category (I or II) from Table 15-1 from which you would choose the appropriate hypothesis test. If you would not choose a test from either category I or II, simply list category III— other. Explain why you chose I, II, or III.
Solutions to these Check Your Learning questions can be found in Appendix D.		

Chi-Square Tests

Hot hand research has moved beyond individual performance and tested the popular idea of whether momentum (Big Mo) actually influences team performance. Big Mo is sometimes believed in so strongly that Super Bowl coach Mike Holmgren wrestled with the decision over whether to rest key players in the last game of the season when the game's outcome would not affect the team's seeding in the playoffs. Holmgren declared, "I don't want to lose momentum." The reality, however, is that Big Mo doesn't exist. Researchers have found that many people strongly believed in Big Mo but that the data are not a good fit with their belief in momentum (Vergin, 2000).

The notion of a "good fit" is a way of expressing the relation between variables in one of the most commonly used forms of chi-square analysis: *the **chi-square test for goodness-of-fit**, a nonparametric hypothesis test used with one nominal variable.* A second, related chi-square hypothesis test is *the **chi-square test for independence**, a nonparametric hypothesis test used with two nominal variables.* These two tests are the most commonly used of all the nonparametric tests, and both involve the same six steps of hypothesis testing that we use for parametric tests.

Both chi-square tests are calculated with the chi-square statistic: χ^2. Both chi-square statistics are based on the chi-square distribution. As with t and F distributions, there are also several chi-square distributions, depending on the degrees of freedom.

> ◀ **MASTERING THE CONCEPT**
>
> **15-2:** When we only have nominal variables, we use the chi-square statistic. Specifically, we use a chi-square test for goodness-of-fit when we have one nominal variable, and we use a chi-square test for independence when we have two nominal variables.

Chi-Square Test for Goodness-of-Fit

The chi-square test for goodness-of-fit calculates a statistic based on just one variable. There is no independent variable or dependent variable, just one categorical variable with two or more categories into which participants are placed. In fact, the chi-square test for goodness-of-fit received its name because it measures how good the fit is between the observed data in the various categories of a single nominal variable and the data we would expect according to the null hypothesis. If there's a really good fit with the null hypothesis, then we cannot reject the null hypothesis. If we're hoping to receive empirical support for our research hypothesis, then we're actually hoping for a *bad fit* between our observed data and what we expect according to the null hypothesis. Let's look at an example.

EXAMPLE 15.2

Researchers reported that the best soccer players in the world were more likely to have been born early in the year than later (Dubner & Levitt, 2006a). As one example, they reported that 52 elite youth players in Germany (those on the national youth teams and from whom the World Cup players are frequently drawn) were born in January,

Are Elite Soccer Players Born in the Early Months of the Year?
Researchers reported that elite soccer players are far more likely to be born in the first three months of the year than in the last three months of the year (Dubner & Levitt, 2006). Based on data on elite German youth soccer players, a chi-square test for goodness-of-fit showed a significant effect: players were significantly more likely to have been born in the first three months than in the last three months of the year.

February, or March, whereas only 4 players were born in October, November, or December. (Those born in other months were not included in this study.)

Based on the null hypothesis, we would expect that the time of year in which one was born would *not* affect one's likelihood of becoming an elite soccer player. Based on the research hypothesis, we would expect that the time of year in which one was born *would* affect one's likelihood of becoming an elite soccer player. Given an assumption that births are evenly distributed across the months of the year, the null hypothesis would posit equal numbers, or frequencies, of elite soccer players born in the first three months and the last three months of the year. With 56 participants in the study (52 born in the first three months and 4 in the last three months), equal frequencies would lead us to expect 28 players born in the first three months and 28 in the last three months just by chance.

We conduct our chi-square test for goodness-of-fit using the six steps of hypothesis testing. You'll notice many similarities with other hypothesis tests.

STEP 1. Identify the populations, distribution, and assumptions.

There are always two populations when conducting a chi-square test: one population that matches the frequencies of participants like those we observed, and another population that matches the frequencies of participants like those we would expect according to the null hypothesis. In the current case, we'd have a population of elite German youth soccer players with birth dates like those we observed, and a population of elite German youth soccer players with birth dates like those in the general population.

The comparison distribution is a chi-square distribution. There's just one nominal variable, birth months, so we'll conduct a chi-square test for goodness-of-fit.

The first assumption is that the variable of interest is nominal. The second assumption is that each observation must be independent of all the other observations. This means that no single participant can be in more than one category. The third assumption is that participants should be randomly selected. If not, we will be limited in our ability to generalize beyond our sample. Finally, the fourth assumption is that there should be a minimum number of expected participants in every cell in a table of cells. A common guideline is that the minimum expected frequency in each cell should be no lower than 5 (or, preferably, 10). However, an alternative guideline (Delucchi, 1983) suggests that there should be at least five times as many participants as cells. The chi-square tests seem robust to violations of this last assumption.

Summary: Population 1: Elite German youth soccer players with birth dates like those we observed. Population 2: Elite German youth soccer players with birth dates like those in the general population.

The comparison distribution is a chi-square distribution. The hypothesis test will be a chi-square test for goodness-of-fit because we have one nominal variable only, birth months. This study meets three of the four assumptions. (1) The one variable is nominal. (2) Every participant is in only one cell (a soccer player can have a birth date in only one category). (3) This is not a randomly selected sample of all elite soccer players, however. The sample includes only German youth soccer players in the elite leagues. We must be cautious in generalizing beyond young German elite players. (4) There are more than five times as many participants as cells (the table has two cells, and $2 \times 5 = 10$). We have 56 participants, far more than the 10 necessary to meet this guideline.

STEP 2. State the null and research hypotheses.

For chi-square tests, it's easiest to state the hypotheses in words only, rather than in both words and symbols.

Summary: Null hypothesis: Elite German youth soccer players have the same pattern of birth months as do those in the general population. Research hypothesis: Elite German youth soccer players have a different pattern of birth months from those in the general population.

STEP 3. Determine the characteristics of the comparison distribution.

Our only task at this step is to determine the degrees of freedom. In most previous hypothesis tests, the degrees of freedom have been based on sample size. For the chi-square hypothesis tests, however, the degrees of freedom are based on the numbers of categories, or cells, in which participants can be counted. The degrees of freedom for a chi-square test for goodness-of-fit is the number of categories minus 1:

$$df_{\chi^2} = k - 1$$

◀ **MASTERING THE FORMULA**

15-1: We calculate the degrees of freedom for the chi-square test for goodness-of-fit by subtracting 1 from the number of categories, represented in the formula by k. The formula is: $df_{\chi^2} = k - 1$.

Here, k is the symbol for the number of categories. Our current example has only two categories: each soccer player in this study was born either in the first three months of the year or in the last three months of the year:

$$df_{\chi^2} = 2 - 1 = 1$$

Summary: The comparison distribution is a chi-square distribution, which has 1 degree of freedom: $df_{\chi^2} = 2 - 1 = 1$.

STEP 4. Determine the critical value, or cutoff.

To determine the cutoff, or critical value, for the chi-square statistic, we use the chi-square table in Appendix B. χ^2 is based on squares and can never be negative, so there is just one critical value. An excerpt from Appendix B that applies to our soccer study is given in Table 15-2. We look under the p level

TABLE 15-2. Excerpt from the χ^2 Table

We use the χ^2 table to determine critical values for a given p level, based on the degrees of freedom.

	Proportion in Critical Region		
df	0.10	0.05	0.01
1	2.706	3.841	6.635
2	4.605	5.992	9.211
3	6.252	7.815	11.345
.			
.			
.			

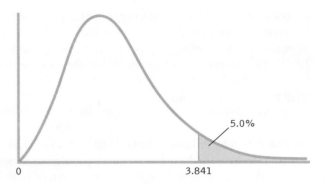

FIGURE 15-1
Determining the Cutoff for a Chi-Square Statistic

We look up the critical value for a chi-square statistic, based on a certain p level and degrees of freedom, in the chi-square table. Because the chi-square statistic is squared, it is never negative, so there is only one critical value.

that we're using, usually 0.05, and across from our degrees of freedom, in this case, 1. For this situation, our critical chi-square statistic is 3.841.

Summary: Our critical χ^2, based on a p level of 0.05 and 1 degree of freedom, is 3.841, as seen in the curve in Figure 15-1.

STEP 5. Calculate the test statistic. To calculate a chi-square statistic, we first determine our observed frequencies and our expected frequencies, as seen in Table 15-3. The expected frequencies are determined from the information we have about the general population. In this case, we estimate that, in the general population, about half of all births (only, of course, among those born in the first or last three months of the year) occur in the first three months of the year, a proportion of 0.50.

$$(0.50)(56) = 28$$

Of the 56 elite German youth soccer players in the study, we would expect to find that 28 of them were born in the first three months of the year (versus the last three months of the year) if these youth soccer players are no different from the general population with respect to birth date. Similarly, we would expect a proportion of $1 - 0.50 = 0.50$ of these soccer players to have been born in the last three months of the year:

$$(0.50)(56) = 28$$

These numbers are identical only because the proportions are 0.50 and 0.50. If the proportion expected for the first three months of the year, based on the general pop-

TABLE 15-3. Observed Frequencies and Expected Frequencies

The first step in calculating the chi-square statistic is creating two tables, one with cells that display the observed frequencies of birth dates among elite German youth soccer players and one with cells that display the expected frequencies.

Observed (when elite players were born)	
First Three Months of the Year	Last Three Months of the Year
52	4
Expected (from the general population)	
First Three Months of the Year	Last Three Months of the Year
28	28

TABLE 15-4. The Chi-Square Calculations

As with many other statistics, we calculate the chi-square statistic using columns to keep track of our work. We calculate the difference between the observed frequency and the expected frequency, square the difference, then divide each square by its appropriate expected frequency. Finally, we add up the numbers in the sixth column to find our chi-square statistic.

Column 1	2	3	4	5	6
Category	Observed (O)	Expected (E)	$O - E$	$(O - E)^2$	$\dfrac{(O-E)^2}{E}$
First three months	52	28	24	576	20.571
Last three months	4	28	−24	576	20.571

ulation, were 0.60, then we would expect a proportion of $1 - 0.60 = 0.40$ for the last three months of the year.

The next step in calculating the chi-square statistic is to calculate a sort of sum of squared differences. We start by determining the difference between each observed frequency and its matching expected frequency. This is usually done in columns, so we'll use this format even though we have only two categories. The first three columns of Table 15-4 show us the categories, observed frequencies, and expected frequencies, respectively. The fourth column, using O for observed and E for expected, displays the differences. As in the past, if we sum the differences, we get 0; they cancel out because some are positive and some are negative. We solve this problem as we have in the past—by squaring the differences, as shown in the fifth column. Next, however, we have a step that we haven't seen before with squared differences. We divide each squared difference by the expected value for its cell, as seen in the sixth column. The numbers in the sixth column are the ones we'll sum.

As an example, here are the calculations for the category "first three months":

$$O - E = (52 - 28) = 24$$

$$(O - E)^2 = (24)^2 = 576$$

$$\frac{(O - E)^2}{E} = \frac{576}{28} = 20.571$$

Once we have the table completed, the last step is easy. We just add up the numbers in the sixth column. In this case, the chi-square statistic is $20.571 + 20.571 = 41.14$. We can finish our formula by adding a summation sign to the formula in the sixth column. Note that we don't have to divide this sum by anything, as we've done with other statistics. We already did our dividing before we summed. This sum is the chi-square statistic. Here is the formula:

$$\chi^2 = \Sigma \left[\frac{(O - E)^2}{E} \right]$$

Summary: $\chi^2 = \Sigma \left[\dfrac{(O - E)^2}{E} \right] = (20.571 + 20.571) = 41.1$

STEP 6. Make a decision.

This last step is identical to the one used in every other hypothesis test we've encountered. We reject the null hypothesis if our test statistic is beyond the critical value, and

> **MASTERING THE FORMULA**
>
> **15-2:** The formula for the chi-square statistic is $\chi^2 = \Sigma \left[\dfrac{(O - E)^2}{E} \right]$. For each cell, we subtract the expected count, E, from the observed count, O. Then we square each difference and divide the square by the expected count. Finally, we sum the calculations for each of the cells.

FIGURE 15-2
Making a Decision

As with other hypothesis tests, we make a decision with a chi-square test by comparing our test statistic to the cutoff, or critical value. 41.14 would be *far* to the right of 3.841.

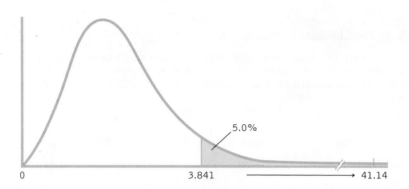

we fail to reject the null hypothesis if our test statistic is not beyond the critical value. In this case, our test statistic, 41.14, is far beyond the cutoff, 3.841, as seen in Figure 15-2. So we reject the null hypothesis. Because there are only two categories, it's clear where the difference lies. It appears that elite German youth soccer players are more likely to have been born in the first three months of the year, and less likely to have been born in the last three months of the year, than members of the general population. (If we had failed to reject the null hypothesis, we could only have concluded that these data did not provide sufficient evidence to show that German youth soccer players have a different likelihood of being born in the first, versus last, three months of the year from those in the general population.)

Summary: Reject the null hypothesis; it appears that elite German youth soccer players are more likely to have been born in the first three months of the year, and less likely to have been born in the last three months of the year, than those in the general population.

We would report these statistics in a journal article in almost the same format that we've seen previously. We report the degrees of freedom, the value of the test statistic, and whether the p value associated with the test statistic was less than or greater than the cutoff based on the p level of 0.05. (As usual, we would report the actual p level if we conducted this hypothesis test using software. Also, we could report p_{rep} instead by determining the exact p value of our test statistic using statistical software, then inputting it into the p_{rep} formula in Excel.) In addition, we report the sample size in parentheses with the degrees of freedom. In the current example, the statistics would read:

$$\chi^2(1, N = 56) = 41.14, p < 0.05$$

The researchers who conducted this study asked why this association might occur and offered four ideas: "a) certain astrological signs confer superior soccer skills; b) winter-born babies tend to have higher oxygen capacity, which increases soccer stamina; c) soccer-mad parents are more likely to conceive children in springtime, at the annual peak of soccer mania; d) none of the above" (Dubner & Levitt, 2006a). What's your guess?

The researchers picked (d) and offered one possible answer (Dubner & Levitt, 2006a): soccer leagues have age limits, and the cutoff date for each of these leagues is December 31. Those born in January, almost a year before the cutoff, are likely to be physically larger and psychologically more mature than their counterparts born 11 months later in December, just before the cutoff. The January players are more likely to be chosen for the best soccer leagues and therefore are more likely to receive the kind of practice and feedback that leads to superiority. All this from a simple chi-square test for goodness-of-fit!

Chi-Square Test for Independence

The chi-square test for goodness-of-fit analyzes just one nominal variable. The chi-square test for independence analyzes *two* nominal variables.

With the chi-square test for independence, however, we do not have to identify a specific independent variable and dependent variable. Like the correlation coefficient, the chi-square statistic is identical even if we switch the independent variable and dependent variable. The main reason we identify a specific independent variable and dependent variable is to help us articulate our hypotheses. The chi-square test for independence is so named because we are trying to determine

Clown Therapy Israeli researchers tested whether entertainment by a clown led to higher pregnancy rates after in vitro fertilization treatment. Their study had two nominal variables—entertainment (clown, no clown) and pregnancy (pregnant, not pregnant)—and could have been analyzed with a chi-square test for independence.

whether the two variables—no matter which one we consider to be the independent variable—are independent of each other. In this next example, we ask whether pregnancy rates are independent of (that is, depend on) whether one is entertained by a clown after in vitro fertilization IVF treatment.

EXAMPLE 15.3

In the clown study reported by the mass media (Ryan, 2006), 186 women were randomly assigned to receive IVF treatment only or to receive IVF treatment followed by 15 minutes of clown entertainment. Eighteen out of 93 who received only the IVF treatment became pregnant, whereas 33 of the 93 who received both IVF treatment and clown entertainment became pregnant. So, 18 out of 93, or 19%, got pregnant with just IVF, 33 out of 93, or 35%, got pregnant with IVF and clown therapy. Both differ from the overall rate—51 out of 186, or 27.4%. The cells for these observed frequencies are in Table 15-5. The table of cells for a chi-square test for independence is called a *contingency table* because we are trying to see if the outcome of one variable (becoming pregnant versus not becoming pregnant) is contingent upon the other variable (clown versus no clown). Let's implement the six steps of hypothesis testing for a chi-square test for independence.

STEP 1. Identify the populations, distribution, and assumptions.

Population 1: Women receiving IVF treatment like the women we observed. Population 2: Women receiving IVF treatment for whom the presence of a clown is not associated with eventual pregnancy.

The comparison distribution is a chi-square distribution. The hypothesis test will be a chi-square test for independence because we have two nominal variables. This study meets three of the four assumptions. (1) The two variables are nominal. (2) Every partic-

---

TABLE 15-5. Observed Pregnancy Rates

This table depicts the cells and their frequencies for the study on whether entertainment by a clown is associated with pregnancy rates among women undergoing in vitro fertilization.

	Observed	
	Pregnant	Not Pregnant
Clown	33	60
No Clown	18	75

ipant is in only one cell. (3) The participants were not, however, randomly selected from the population of all women undergoing IVF treatment. We must be cautious in generalizing beyond the sample of Israeli women at this particular hospital. (4) There are more than five times as many participants as cells (186 participants and 4 cells—4 × 5 = 20). We have far more participants, 186, than the 20 necessary to meet this guideline.

STEP 2. State the null and research hypotheses.

Null hypothesis: Pregnancy rates are independent of whether one is entertained by a clown after IVF treatment. Research hypothesis: Pregnancy rates depend on whether one is entertained by a clown after IVF treatment.

STEP 3. Determine the characteristics of the comparison distribution.

For a chi-square test for independence, we calculate degrees of freedom for each variable and then multiply the two to get the overall degrees of freedom. The degrees of freedom for the variable in the rows of the contingency table is:

$$df_{row} = k_{row} - 1$$

The degrees of freedom for the variable in the columns of the contingency table is:

$$df_{column} = k_{column} - 1$$

The overall degrees of freedom is:

$$df_{\chi^2} = (df_{row})(df_{column})$$

To expand this last formula, we write:

$$df_{\chi^2} = (k_{row} - 1)(k_{column} - 1)$$

The comparison distribution is a chi-square distribution, which has 1 degree of freedom:

$$df_{\chi^2} = (k_{row} - 1)(k_{column} - 1) = (2 - 1)(2 - 1) = 1$$

MASTERING THE FORMULA

15-3: To calculate the degrees of freedom for the chi-square test for independence, we first have to calculate the degrees of freedom for each variable. For the variable in the rows, we subtract 1 from the number of categories in the rows: $df_{row} = k_{row} - 1$. For the variable in the columns, we subtract 1 from the number of categories in the columns: $df_{column} = k_{column} - 1$. We multiply these two numbers to get the overall degrees of freedom: $df_{\chi^2} = (df_{row})(df_{column})$. To combine all the calculations, we can use the following formula instead: $df_{\chi^2} = (k_{row} - 1)(k_{column} - 1)$.

STEP 4. Determine the critical values, or cutoffs.

Our critical value, or cutoff, for the chi-square statistic based on a p level of 0.05 and 1 degree of freedom is 3.841 (Figure 15-3).

STEP 5. Calculate the test statistic.

The next step, the determination of the appropriate expected frequencies, is the most important in the calculation of the chi-square test for independence. We have already calculated that 27.4% of all women in the study became pregnant. If pregnancy rates are independent of whether a woman is entertained by a clown, then we would expect 27.4% of the women who were entertained by a clown to become pregnant and 27.4% of women who were not entertained by a clown to become pregnant. Based on this percentage, 100 − 27.4 = 72.6% of women in the study did not become pregnant. We would expect, therefore, 72.6% of women who were entertained by a clown to fail to become pregnant and 72.6% of women who were not entertained by a clown to fail to become pregnant. Again, we're expecting the same pregnancy and nonpregnancy rates in both groups—those who were and were not entertained by clowns.

Table 15-6 shows our observed data once again, now with totals for each row, each column, and the whole table.

From Table 15-6, we see that 93 women were entertained by a clown after IVF treatment. As we calculated above, we would expect 27.4% of them to become pregnant:

$$(0.274)(93) = 25.482$$

Of the 93 women who were not entertained by a clown, we would expect 27.4% of them to become pregnant if clown entertainment is independent of pregnancy rates:

$$(0.274)(93) = 25.482$$

We now repeat the same procedure for not becoming pregnant. We would expect 72.6% of women in both groups to fail to become pregnant. For the women who were entertained by a clown, we would expect 72.6% of them to fail to become pregnant:

$$(0.726)(93) = 67.518$$

For the women who were not entertained by a clown, we would expect 72.6% of them to fail to become pregnant:

$$(0.726)(93) = 67.518$$

(Note that the two expected frequencies for the first row are the same as the two expected frequencies for the second row, but only because the same number of people were in each clown condition, 93. If these two numbers were different, we would not see the same frequencies in the two rows.)

The method of calculating the expected frequencies that we described above is ideal because it is directly based on our own thinking about the frequencies in the rows and in the columns. Sometimes, however, our thinking can get muddled, particularly when the two (or more) row totals do not match and the two (or more) column totals do not match. For these situations, a simple set of rules leads to accurate expected frequencies. For each cell, we divide its column total ($Total_{column}$) by the grand total (N) and multiply that by the row total ($Total_{row}$):

$$\frac{Total_{column}}{N}(Total_{row})$$

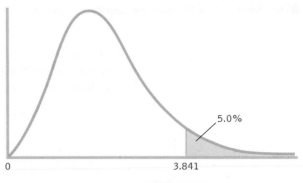

FIGURE 15-3
The Cutoff for a Chi-Square Test for Independence

The shaded region is beyond the critical value for a chi-square test for independence with a p level of 0.05 and 1 degree of freedom. If the test statistic falls within this shaded area, we will reject the null hypothesis.

MASTERING THE FORMULA

15-4: When conducting a chi-square test for independence, we can calculate the expected frequency in each cell by taking the total for the column that the cell is in, dividing it by the total in the study, and then multiplying by the total for the row that the cell is in: $\frac{Total_{column}}{N}(Total_{row})$.

TABLE 15-6. Observed Frequencies with Totals

This table includes the observed frequencies for each of the four cells, along with row totals (93, 93), column totals (51, 135), and the grand total for the whole table (186).

	Observed		
	Pregnant	Not Pregnant	
Clown	33	60	93
No clown	18	75	93
	51	135	186

As an example, the observed frequency of those who became pregnant and were entertained by a clown is 33. The row total for this cell is 93. The column total is 51. The grand total, N, is 186. The expected frequency, therefore, is:

$$\frac{Total_{column}}{N}(Total_{row}) = \frac{51}{186}(93) = (0.274)(93) = 25.482$$

Notice that this result is identical to what we calculated without a formula. The middle step above shows that, even with the formula, we actually did calculate the pregnancy rate overall, by dividing the column total (51) by the grand total (186). We then calculated how many in that row of 93 participants we would expect to get pregnant using this overall rate:

$$(0.274)(93) = 25.482$$

The formula follows our logic, but it also keeps us on track when there are multiple calculations.

As a final check on our calculations, shown in Table 15-7, we can add up the frequencies to be sure that they still match the row, column, and grand totals. For example, if we add the two numbers in the first column, 25.482 and 25.482, we get 50.964 (different from 51 only because of rounding decisions). If we had made the mistake of dividing the 186 participants into cells by dividing by 4, we would have had 46.5 in each cell; then the total for the first column would have been 46.5 + 46.5 = 93, not a match with 51. This final check ensures that we have the appropriate expected frequencies in the cells.

The remainder of the fifth step is identical to that for a chi-square test for goodness-of-fit, as seen in Table 15-8. As before, we calculate the difference between each ob-

TABLE 15-7. Expected Frequencies with Totals

This table includes the expected frequencies for each of the four cells. The expected frequencies should still add up to the row totals (93, 93), column totals (51, 135), and the grand total for the whole table (186).

	Expected		
	Pregnant	Not Pregnant	
Clown	25.482	67.518	93
No clown	25.482	67.518	93
	51	135	186

TABLE 15-8. The Chi-Square Calculations

For the calculations for the chi-square test for independence, we use the same format as we did for the chi-square test for goodness-of-fit. We calculate the difference between the observed frequency and the expected frequency, square the difference, then divide each square by its appropriate expected frequency. Finally, we add up the numbers in the last column, and that's our chi-square statistic.

Category	Observed (O)	Expected (E)	$O - E$	$(O - E)^2$	$\frac{(O-E)^2}{E}$
Clown; pregnant	33	25.482	7.518	56.520	2.218
Clown; not pregnant	60	67.518	−7.518	56.520	0.837
No clown; pregnant	18	25.482	−7.482	55.980	2.197
No clown; not pregnant	75	67.518	7.482	55.980	0.829

▪ **Cramer's *V*** is the standard effect size used with the chi-square test for independence; also called *Cramer's phi*, symbolized as φ.

served frequency and its matching expected frequency, square these differences, and divide each squared difference by the appropriate expected frequency. We add up the numbers in the final column of our table to calculate our chi-square statistic:

$$\chi^2 = \Sigma\left[\frac{(O - E)^2}{E}\right] = (2.218 + 0.837 + 2.197 + 0.829) = 6.081$$

STEP 6. Make a decision.

Reject the null hypothesis; it appears that pregnancy rates depend on whether a woman receives clown entertainment following IVF treatment (Figure 15-4).

The statistics, as reported in a journal article, would follow the format we learned for a chi-square test for goodness-of-fit, as well as for other hypothesis tests in earlier chapters. We report the degrees of freedom and sample size, the value of the test statistic, and whether the p value associated with the test statistic was less than or greater than the critical value based on the p level of 0.05. (We would report the actual p level if we conducted this hypothesis test using software. Or we could choose to calculate and report p_{rep}.) In the current example, the statistics would read:

$$\chi^2(1, N = 186) = 6.08, p < 0.05$$

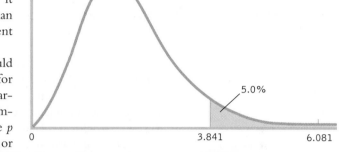

FIGURE 15-4
The Decision

Because the chi-square statistic, 6.081, is beyond the critical value, 3.841, we can reject the null hypothesis. It is unlikely that the pregnancy rates for those who received clown therapy versus those who did not were this different from each other just by chance.

Cramer's *V*, the Effect Size for Chi Square

A hypothesis test tells us only that there is a likely effect—that the observed effect was unlikely to have occurred merely by chance if the null hypothesis were true. But a hypothesis test, including any based on the chi-square statistic, does not tell us how large the effect is. We have to calculate an additional statistic, an effect size, before we can make claims about the importance of a study's finding.

Cramer's V, also called *Cramer's phi* and symbolized as φ (pronounced "fie"—rhymes with fly), is the standard effect size used with the chi-square test for independence. Once we have calculated our test statistic, it is easy to calculate Cramer's V by hand. The formula is:

$$\text{Cramer's } V = \sqrt{\frac{\chi^2}{(N)(df_{row/column})}}$$

χ^2 is the test statistic we just calculated, N is the total number of participants in the study (the lower-right number in the contingency table), and $df_{row/column}$ is the degrees of freedom for either the category in the rows or the category in the columns, whichever is smaller.

> **MASTERING THE FORMULA**
>
> **15-5:** The formula for Cramer's V, the effect size typically used with the chi-square statistic, is Cramer's $V =$ $\sqrt{\frac{\chi^2}{(N)(df_{row/column})}}$. The numerator is the chi-square statistic, χ^2. The denominator is the product of the sample size, N, and either the degrees of freedom for the rows or the degrees of freedom for the columns, whichever is smaller. We take the square root of this quotient to get Cramer's V.

EXAMPLE 15.4

For the clown example, we calculated a chi-square statistic of 6.081, there were 186 participants, and the degrees of freedom for both categories were 1. When neither degrees of freedom is smaller than the other, of course, it doesn't matter which one we choose. Our effect size for the clown study, therefore, is:

$$\text{Cramer's } V = \sqrt{\frac{\chi^2}{(N)(df_{row/column})}} = \sqrt{\frac{6.081}{(186)(1)}} = \sqrt{0.033} = 0.181$$

TABLE 15-9. Conventions for Determining Effect Size Based on Cramer's *V*

Jacob Cohen (1992) developed guidelines to determine whether particular effect sizes should be considered small, medium, or large. The effect-size guidelines vary depending on the size of the contingency table. There are different guidelines based on whether the smaller of the two degrees of freedom (row or column) is 1, 2, or 3.

Effect Size	When $df_{row/column} = 1$	When $df_{row/column} = 2$	When $df_{row/column} = 3$
Small	0.10	0.07	0.06
Medium	0.30	0.21	0.17
Large	0.50	0.35	0.29

Now that we have our effect size, what does it mean? As with other effect sizes, Jacob Cohen (1992) has developed guidelines, shown in Table 15-9, for determining whether a particular effect is small, medium, or large. The guidelines vary based on the size of the contingency table. When the smaller of the two degrees of freedom for the row and column is 1, we use the guidelines in the second column. When the smaller of the two degrees of freedom is 2, we use the guidelines in the third column. And when it is 3, we use the guidelines in the fourth column. As with the other guidelines for judging effect sizes, such as those for Cohen's *d*, the guidelines are not cutoffs. Rather, they are rough indicators to help researchers gauge a finding's importance.

Our effect size for the clowning and pregnancy study was 0.18. The smaller of the two degrees of freedom, that for the row and that for the column, was 1 (in fact, both were 1). So we use the second column in Table 15-9. Our Cramer's *V* falls about halfway between the effect-size guidelines for a small effect (0.10) and a medium effect (0.30). We would call this a small-to-medium effect. We can build on our report of the statistics by adding the Cramer's *V* to the end:

$$\chi^2(1, N = 186) = 6.08, p < 0.05, \text{Cramer's } V = 0.18$$

CHECK YOUR LEARNING

Reviewing the Concepts

> The chi-square tests are used when all variables are nominal.

> The chi-square test for goodness-of-fit is used with one nominal variable.

> The chi-square test for independence is used with two nominal variables; usually one can be thought of as the independent variable and one as the dependent variable.

> Both chi-square hypothesis tests use the same six steps of hypothesis testing with which we are familiar.

> After completing the hypothesis test, it is wise to calculate an effect size as well. The appropriate effect-size measure for the chi-square test for independence is Cramer's *V*.

Clarifying the Concepts

15-5 When do we use chi-square tests?

15-6 What are observed frequencies and expected frequencies?

Calculating the Statistics

15-7 Imagine a town that boasts clear blue skies 80% of the time. You get to work in that town one summer for 78 days and record the following data. (*Note:* For each day, you picked just one label.)

Clear blue skies: 59 days

Cloudy/hazy/gray skies: 19 days

a. Calculate degrees of freedom for this chi-square test for goodness-of-fit.

b. Determine the observed and expected frequencies.

c. Calculate the differences and squared differences between frequencies, and calculate the chi-square statistic. Use the six-column format provided here.

Category	Observed (O)	Expected (E)	$O - E$	$(O - E)^2$	$\dfrac{(O - E)^2}{E}$
Clear blue skies					
Unclear skies					

Applying the Concepts

15-8 The Chicago Police Department conducted a study comparing two types of lineups for suspect identification: simultaneous lineups and sequential lineups (Mecklenburg, Malpass, & Ebbesen, 2006). In simultaneous lineups, witnesses saw the suspects all at once, either live or in photographs, and then made their selection. In sequential lineups, witnesses saw the people in the lineup one at a time, either live or in photographs, and said yes or no to suspects one at a time. After numerous high-profile cases in which DNA evidence exonerated people who had been convicted, including many on death row, many police departments shifted to sequential lineups in the hope of reducing incorrect identifications. Several previous studies had indicated the superiority of sequential lineups with respect to accuracy. Over one year, three jurisdictions in Illinois compared the two types of lineups. Of 319 simultaneous lineups, 191 led to identification of the suspect, 8 led to identification of another person in the lineup, and 120 led to no identification. Of 229 sequential lineups, 102 led to identification of the suspect, 20 led to identification of another person in the lineup, and 107 led to no identification.

a. Who or what would the participants in this study be? Identify the independent variable and its levels as well as the dependent variable and its levels.

b. Conduct all six steps of hypothesis testing.

c. Calculate the appropriate measure of effect size for this study.

d. Report the statistics as you would in a journal article.

Solutions to these Check Your Learning questions can be found in Appendix D.

e. Why is this study an example of the importance of using two-tailed rather than one-tailed hypothesis tests?

Other Nonparametric Tests

The logic of the nonparametric statistics used with ordinal data should be familiar to you. In this section, we consider two nonparametric tests, listed along with their parametric equivalents in Table 15-10. First, we learn the nonparametric equivalent for the Pearson correlation coefficient, the Spearman rank-order correlation coefficient—

TABLE 15-10. Parametric and Nonparametric Partners

Most parametric hypothesis tests have at least one equivalent nonparametric alternative. Here, the parametric tests call for scale dependent variables, and their nonparametric counterparts call for ordinal dependent variables.

Design	Parametric Test	Nonparametric Test
Association between two variables	Pearson correlation coefficient	Spearman rank-order correlation coefficient
Two groups; between-groups design	Independent-samples t test	Mann–Whitney U test

a nonparametric statistic that quantifies the association between two ordinal variables. Second, we learn a nonparametric equivalent for the independent-samples *t* test, the Mann–Whitney *U* test—a nonparametric hypothesis test used when there are two groups, a between-groups design, and an ordinal dependent variable.

Spearman Rank-Order Correlation Coefficient

Many daily observations represent rank-ordered data. For example, a person may prefer Chunky Monkey ice cream to Chubby Hubby ice cream but would not be able to specify that he liked it precisely twice as much. When we collect ranked data, we analyze it using nonparametric statistics. The ***Spearman rank–order correlation coefficient*** *is a nonparametric statistic that quantifies the association between two ordinal variables.*

To see how the Spearman rank-order correlation coefficient works, let's look at a study that uses two ordinal variables. In March 2006, the University of Chicago News Office published a press release headlined "Americans and Venezuelans Lead the World in National Pride." Researchers surveyed individuals in 33 countries (Smith & Kim, 2006) and developed two different kinds of national pride scores: pride in specific accomplishments of their nations (which they called *domain-specific national pride*) and a more general national pride. The accomplishment-related national pride scale asked respondents to rate their level of pride in their countries' accomplishments in specific areas such as international political influence, social security, equality across societal groups, science and technology, and sports. The general national pride scale included questions related to a country's general superiority over other countries.

▶ **MASTERING THE CONCEPT**

15-3: We calculate a Spearman rank-order correlation coefficient to quantify the association between two ordinal variables. It is the nonparametric equivalent of the Pearson correlation coefficient.

The researchers first developed two sets of national pride scores—accomplishment-related and general—for each country. They then converted the scores to ranks and reported the rankings of the 33 countries in the study. When results on the two scales were merged, Venezuela and the United States were tied for first place. These findings suggest many hypotheses about what creates and inflates national pride. Because the researchers provided ordinal data, we have to use nonparametric statistics designed for use with ordinal data.

We wondered about other possible precursors of high levels of national pride. What traits, such as competitiveness, might be associated with national pride? What categories of nations, such as those with communist histories versus those without communist histories, might have higher levels of national pride than other categories of nations?

As so often happens with descriptive data such as national rankings, we started wondering how the descriptive data might be related to other variables. Specifically, we wondered whether accomplishment-related national pride is related to the underlying trait of competitiveness. So we randomly selected 10 countries from this list and compiled their scores for accomplishment-related national pride. We also located rankings of competitiveness compiled by an international business school (IMD International, 2001).

National Pride University of Chicago researchers ranked 33 countries in terms of national pride. Venezuela, along with the United States, came out on top. Ordinal data such as these are analyzed using nonparametric statistics.

A correlation between these variables, if found, would be evidence that countries' levels of accomplishment-related national pride are tied to levels of competitiveness. This research question involves two variables. The competitiveness variable we borrowed from the business school rankings was already ordinal. However, the accomplishment-related national pride variable was initially a scale variable. When even one of the

■ The **Spearman rank-order correlation coefficient** is a nonparametric statistic that quantifies the association between two ordinal variables.

TABLE 15-11. Converting Pride Scores to Ranks

When we convert scale data to ordinal data, we simply arrange the data from highest to lowest (or lowest to highest if that makes more sense) and then rank them. These are the data for accomplishment-related national pride. In cases of ties, we average the two ranks that these participants—countries, in this case—would hold.

Country	Pride Score	Pride Rank
United States	4.00	1
South Africa	2.70	2
Austria	2.40	3.5
Canada	2.40	3.5
Chile	2.30	5
Japan	1.80	6
Hungary	1.60	7
France	1.50	8
Norway	1.30	9
Slovenia	1.10	10

---

variables is ordinal, we use the Spearman rank-order correlation coefficient (often called just the Spearman correlation coefficient, or Spearman's rho). Its symbol is almost like that for the Pearson correlation coefficient, but it has a subscript S to indicate that it is Spearman's correlation coefficient: r_S.

To convert scale data, we simply organize our data from highest to lowest (or lowest to highest if that makes more sense) and then rank them. Table 15-11 shows the conversion from scale data to ordinal data for accomplishment-related national pride. Sometimes, as seen for Austria and Canada, we have a tie. Both of these countries had an accomplishment-related national pride score of 2.4. When we rank the data, these countries take the third and fourth positions, but they must have the same rank because their scores are the same. So we take the average of the two ranks they would hold if the scores were different: $(3 + 4)/2 = 3.5$. Both of these countries receive the rank of 3.5. We handle tied ranks in this way no matter what nonparametric test for ordinal data we're using—not just for the Spearman correlation.

Now that we have our ranks, we can compute our Spearman correlation coefficient.

EXAMPLE 15.5

We first need to include both sets of ranks in the same table, as in the second and third columns in Table 15-12. We then calculate the difference (D) between each pair of ranks, as in the fourth column. The differences always add up to 0, so we must square the differences, as in the last column. As we have frequently done with squared differences in the past, we sum them—another variation on the concept of a sum of squares. The sum of these squared differences is:

$$\Sigma D^2 = (0 + 64 + 2.25 + 0.25 + 0 + 1 + 1 + 4 + 25 + 1) = 98.5$$

The formula for calculating the Spearman correlation coefficient includes the sum of the squared differences that we just calculated, 98.5. The formula is:

$$r_S = 1 - \frac{6(\Sigma D^2)}{N(N^2 - 1)}$$

MASTERING THE FORMULA

15-6: The formula for the Spearman correlation coefficient is $r_S = 1 - \frac{6(\Sigma D^2)}{N(N^2 - 1)}$. The numerator includes a constant, 6, as well as the sum of the squared differences between ranks for each participant. The denominator is calculated by multiplying the sample size, N, by the square of the sample size minus 1.

TABLE 15-12. Calculating a Spearman Correlation Coefficient

The first step in calculating a Spearman correlation coefficient is creating a table that includes the ranks for all participants—countries, in this case—on both variables of interest (accomplishment-related national pride and competitiveness). We then calculate differences for each participant (i.e., country) and square each difference.

Country	Pride Rank	Competitiveness Rank	Difference (D)	Squared Difference (D^2)
United States	1	1	0	0
South Africa	2	10	−8	64
Austria	3.5	2	1.5	2.25
Canada	3.5	3	0.5	0.25
Chile	5	5	0	0
Japan	6	7	−1	1
Hungary	7	8	−1	1
France	8	6	2	4
Norway	9	4	5	25
Slovenia	10	9	1	1

In addition to the sum of squared differences, the only other information we need is the sample size, N, which is 10 in this example. (The number 6 is a constant; it is always included in the calculation of the Spearman correlation coefficient.) Our Spearman correlation coefficient, therefore, is:

$$r_S = 1 - \frac{6(\Sigma D^2)}{N(N^2 - 1)} = 1 - \frac{6(98.5)}{10(100 - 1)} = 0.40$$

The Spearman correlation coefficient is 0.40.

The interpretation of the Spearman correlation coefficient is identical to that for the Pearson correlation coefficient. The coefficient can range from −1, a perfect negative correlation, to 1, a perfect positive correlation. A correlation coefficient of 0 indicates no relation between the two variables. As with the Pearson correlation coefficient, it is not the sign of the Spearman correlation coefficient that indicates the strength of a relation. So, for example, a coefficient of −0.66 indicates a stronger association than does a coefficient of 0.23. Finally, as with the Pearson correlation coefficient, we can implement the six steps of hypothesis testing to determine whether the Spearman correlation coefficient is statistically significantly different from 0. If we do, we can find the critical values in the chi-square table in Appendix B.

The easiest way to get a sense of how the Spearman correlation coefficient works may surprise you: just eyeball the data. Let's take a closer look at the individual data points in Table 15-12.

The country ranked number one in competitiveness (the United States) is also ranked number one in accomplishment-related national pride. This sounds like the start of a positive correlation because the nation highest on one variable is also highest on the other variable. Now look at the lowest-ranked (10th) nation in national pride, Slovenia. This country is ranked next to lowest (9th) in competitiveness. This looks like more evidence for a positive correlation because the nation low on one variable is also low on the other variable. After these two initial observations, the two

▪ The **Mann–Whitney *U* test** is a nonparametric hypothesis test used when there are two groups, a between-groups design, and an ordinal dependent variable.

variables of competitiveness and accomplishment-related national pride seem to be moving up and down together: a positive correlation.

But wait! The country ranked 10th in competitiveness (South Africa) is ranked 2nd in accomplishment-related national pride. This sounds like evidence for a negative correlation because the nation low on one variable ranks high on the other variable. As we continue to eyeball the data, we notice that the pattern is not quite as clear as we might hope, which is precisely why we need a mathematical formula—to clarify the relation between the two variables. In this case (as we already know), the Spearman rank-order correlation is positive (0.40), in spite of the individual exceptions to the rule (South Africa and Norway).

As with the Pearson correlation coefficient, the Spearman correlation coefficient does not tell us about causation. It is possible that there is a causal relation in one of two directions. The relation between competitiveness (variable A) and accomplishment-related national pride (variable B) is 0.40, a fairly strong positive correlation. It is possible that competitiveness (variable A) causes a country to feel prouder (variable B) of its accomplishments. On the other hand, it is possible that accomplishment-related national pride (variable B) causes competitiveness (variable A). Finally, it is also possible that a third variable, C, causes both of the other two variables (A and B). For example, a high gross domestic product (variable C) might cause both a sense of competitiveness with other economic powerhouses (variable A) and a feeling of national pride at this economic accomplishment (variable B). A strong correlation indicates only a strong association; we can draw no conclusions about causation.

Mann–Whitney *U* Test

Most parametric hypothesis tests have nonparametric equivalents. In this section, we learn how to conduct one of the most common of these tests—the Mann–Whitney *U* test, the nonparametric equivalent of the independent-samples *t* test. The **Mann–Whitney U test** is a nonparametric hypothesis test used when there are two groups, a between-groups design, and an ordinal dependent variable. It is symbolized as *U*. Let's use this new statistic to test more hypotheses about the ranked data on national pride.

> ◀ **MASTERING THE CONCEPT**
>
> **15-4:** We conduct a Mann–Whitney *U* test to compare two independent groups with respect to an ordinal dependent variable. It is the nonparametric equivalent of the independent-samples *t* test.

EXAMPLE 15.6

The researchers observed that countries with recent communist pasts tended to have lower ranks on national pride (Smith & Kim, 2006). Let's choose 10 European countries, 5 of which were communist during part of the previous century. Our independent variable is type of country, with two levels: formerly communist and not formerly communist. The dependent variable is rank on accomplishment-related national pride. As in previous situations, we may have started with ordinal data, or we may have converted scale data to ordinal data because we were far from meeting the assumptions of a parametric test. Table 15-13 shows the accomplishment-related national pride scores for the 10 countries.

As noted earlier, nonparametric tests use the same six steps of hypothesis testing as parametric tests but are usually easier to calculate.

STEP 1. Identify the assumptions.

There are three assumptions. (1) The dependent variable must be ordinal. (2) We should use random selection; otherwise, our ability to generalize will be limited. (3) Ideally, no ranks are tied. The Mann–Whitney *U* test is robust with respect to violations of the third assumption; if there are only a few ties, then it is usually safe to proceed.

> **TABLE 15-13.** Comparing Two Groups
>
> Here are the data for two samples: European countries that were recently communist and European countries that were not recently communist. The data in this table are scale; because we do not meet the assumptions for a parametric test, we have to convert our data from scale to ordinal as one step of our calculations.
>
> | Country | Pride Score |
> |---|---|
> | *Noncommunist* | |
> | Ireland | 2.90 |
> | Austria | 2.40 |
> | Spain | 1.60 |
> | Portugal | 1.60 |
> | Sweden | 1.20 |
> | *Communist* | |
> | Hungary | 1.60 |
> | Czech Republic | 1.30 |
> | Slovenia | 1.10 |
> | Slovakia | 1.10 |
> | Poland | 0.90 |

Summary: (1) We need to convert our data from scale to ordinal. (2) The researchers did not indicate whether they used random selection to choose the European countries in the sample, so we must be cautious when generalizing from these results. (3) There are some ties, but we will assume that there are not so many as to render the results of the test invalid.

STEP 2. State the null and research hypotheses.	We state the null and research hypotheses only in words, not in symbols.

Summary: Null hypothesis: European countries with recent communist histories and those without recent communist histories do not tend to differ in accomplishment-related national pride. Research hypothesis: European countries with recent communist histories and those without recent communist histories tend to differ in accomplishment-related national pride.

STEP 3. Determine the characteristics of the comparison distribution.	The Mann–Whitney U test compares the two distributions—those represented by our two samples. There is no comparison distri-

bution in the sense of a parametric test. To complete step 4 and find a cutoff, or critical value, we need two pieces of information—the sample size for the first group and the sample size for the second group.

Summary: There are five countries in the communist group and five countries in the noncommunist group.

STEP 4. Determine the critical values, or cutoffs.	There are two Mann–Whitney U tables. We use Table B.8A (for a one-tailed test) or Table B.8B (for a two-tailed test) from Ap-

pendix B to determine the cutoff, or critical value, for the Mann–Whitney U test. In the tables, we find the sample size for our first group across the top row and the sample size for our second group down the left-hand column. The table includes only critical values for a hypothesis test with a p level of 0.05. There are two differences between this critical value and those we considered with parametric tests. First, we calculate two test statistics, but we only compare the *smaller* one with the critical value. Second, we want our test statistic to be equal to or *smaller than* the critical value.

Summary: The cutoff, or critical value, for a Mann–Whitney U test with two groups of five participants (countries), a p level of 0.05, and a two-tailed test is 2. (*Note:* Remember that we want the *smaller* of our test statistics to be equal to or *smaller than* this critical value.)

| STEP 5. Calculate the test statistic. | As noted above, we calculate two test statistics for a Mann–Whitney U test, one for |

each group. We start our calculations by organizing our data by raw score from highest to lowest in one single column and then by rank in the next column, as shown in Table 15-14. For the two sets of tied scores, we took the average of the ranks they would have held and applied that rank to the tied scores. For example, Spain, Portugal, and Hungary all received scores of 1.60; they would have been ranked 3, 4, and 5, but because they're tied, they all received the average of these three scores, 4. (We have chosen to give the highest score a rank of 1, as did the researchers.) We include the group membership of each participant (country) next to its score and rank: C indicates a formerly communist country and NC represents a noncommunist country. The final two columns separate the ranks by group; from these columns we can easily see that the noncommunist countries tend to hold the higher ranks, and the communist countries, the lower ranks.

TABLE 15-14. Organizing Data for a Mann–Whitney U Test

To conduct a Mann–Whitney U test, we first organize our data. We organize the raw scores from lowest to highest in a single column, then rank them in an adjacent column. Notice that when scores are tied, we average the ranks of the two or three tied scores. The next column includes the group to which each country belongs—a recently communist country (C) or a noncommunist (NC) country. The last two columns separate the ranks by group.

Country	Pride Score	Pride Rank	Type Of Country	NC Ranks	C Ranks
Ireland	2.90	1	NC	1	
Austria	2.40	2	NC	2	
Spain	1.60	4	NC	4	
Portugal	1.60	4	NC	4	
Hungary	1.60	4	C		4
Czech Republic	1.30	6	C		6
Sweden	1.20	7	NC	7	
Slovenia	1.10	8.5	C		8.5
Slovakia	1.10	8.5	C		8.5
Poland	0.90	10	C		10

Before we continue, we sum the ranks (R) for each group and add subscripts to indicate which group is which:

$$\Sigma R_{NC} = 1 + 2 + 4 + 4 + 7 = 18$$

$$\Sigma R_C = 4 + 6 + 8.5 + 8.5 + 10 = 37$$

The formula for the first group, with the n's referring to sample size in a particular group, is:

$$U_{NC} = (n_{NC})(n_C) + \frac{n_{NC}(n_{NC} + 1)}{2} - \Sigma R_{NC} = (5)(5) + \frac{5(5 + 1)}{2} - 18 = 25 + 15 - 18 = 22$$

The formula for the second group is:

MASTERING THE FORMULA ▶

15-7: The formula for the first group in a Mann–Whitney U test is $U_1 = (n_1)(n_2) + \frac{n_1(n_1 + 1)}{2} - \Sigma R_1$. The formula for the second group is $U_2 = (n_1)(n_2) + \frac{n_2(n_2 + 1)}{2} - \Sigma R_2$. The symbol n refers to the sample size for a particular group. In these formulas, the first group is labeled 1 and the second group is labeled 2. ΣR refers to the sum of the ranks for a particular group.

$$U_C = (n_{NC})(n_C) + \frac{n_C(n_C + 1)}{2} - \Sigma R_C = (5)(5) + \frac{5(5 + 1)}{2} - 37 = 25 + 15 - 37 = 3$$

Summary: $U_{NC} = 22$; $U_C = 3$.

STEP 6. Make a decision.

For a Mann–Whitney U test, we compare only our smaller test statistic, 3, with the critical value, 2. This test statistic is not smaller than the critical value, so we fail to reject the null hypothesis. We cannot conclude that the two groups are different with respect to accomplishment-related national pride rankings. The researchers were able to conclude that the two groups tended to be different, but remember, they used more countries in their analyses (Smith & Kim, 2006). We selected just 10 of the European countries on their list. As with parametric tests, increased sample sizes lead to increased statistical power.

Summary: The test statistic, 3, is not smaller than the critical value, 2. We cannot reject the null hypothesis. We can conclude only that insufficient evidence exists to show the two groups are different with respect to accomplishment-related national pride rankings.

After completing our hypothesis test, we want to present the primary statistical information in a report. In our write-up, we list our two groups and their sample sizes, but there are no degrees of freedom. In addition, we report only the smaller test statistic; because this is the standard, we do not need to include a subscript. (Note that we could choose to calculate and report p_{rep} instead.) Thus, the statistics read:

$$U = 3, p > 0.05$$

CHECK YOUR LEARNING

Reviewing the Concepts

> When we want to determine a correlation between two ordinal variables, we calculate a Spearman correlation coefficient, which is interpreted in the same way as the Pearson correlation coefficient.

> We use the Mann–Whitney U test in place of the independent-samples t test when there is an ordinal dependent variable.

> Nonparametric hypothesis tests use the same six steps of hypothesis testing that are used for parametric tests, but the steps and the calculations tend to be simpler.

| Clarifying the Concepts | 15-9 | Describe a common situation in which we use nonparametric tests other than chi-square tests. |
| | 15-10 | What is the difference between the Spearman rank-order correlation coefficient and the Mann–Whitney *U* test? |

| Calculating the Statistics | 15-11 | Convert the following scale data to ordinal or ranked data, starting with a rank of 1 for the smallest data point. |

Observation	Variable 1	Variable 2
1	1.3	54.39
2	1.8	50.11
3	1.2	53.39
4	1.06	44.89
5	1.8	48.5

15-12 Compute the Spearman correlation coefficient for the data listed in Check Your Learning 15-11.

| Applying the Concepts | 15-13 | Researchers provided accomplishment-related national pride scores for a number of countries (Kim & Smith, 2006). We selected seven countries for which English is the primary language and seven countries for which it is not. We wondered whether English-speaking countries would be different on the variable of accomplishment-related national pride than would non-English-speaking countries. The data are in the accompanying table. Conduct a Mann–Whitney *U* test on these data. Remember to organize the data in one column before starting. |

English-Speaking Countries	Pride Score	Non-English-Speaking Countries	Pride Score
United States	4.00	Chile	2.30
Australia	2.90	Japan	1.80
Ireland	2.90	France	1.50
South Africa	2.70	Czech Republic	1.30
New Zealand	2.60	Norway	1.30
Canada	2.40	Slovenia	1.10
Great Britain	2.20	South Korea	1.00

Solutions to these Check Your Learning questions can be found in Appendix D.

REVIEW OF CONCEPTS

Nonparametric Statistics

Nonparametric hypothesis tests are used when we do not meet the assumptions of a parametric test. This often occurs when we have a nominal dependent variable, an ordinal independent or dependent variable, or a small sample in which the data suggest a skewed population distribution. Given the choice, we should use a parametric test because these tests tend to have more statistical power and because we can more frequently calculate confidence intervals and effect sizes for parametric hypothesis tests.

Chi-Square Tests

When we have a nominal dependent variable, we analyze our data using a chi-square test. We use the *chi-square test for goodness-of-fit* when we have only one variable and it is nominal. We use the *chi-square test for independence* when we have two nominal variables; typically, for the purposes of articulating a hypothesis, one variable is thought of as the independent variable and the other is thought of as the dependent variable. With both chi-square tests, we analyze whether the data that we observe match what we would expect according to the null hypothesis. Both tests use the same basic six steps of hypothesis testing that we learned previously. We usually calculate an effect size as well; the most commonly calculated effect size with chi square is *Cramer's V*, also called *Cramer's phi*.

Other Nonparametric Tests

Nonparametric hypothesis tests have been developed as replacements for most parametric tests when there are severe violations of assumptions. The nonparametric parallel to the Pearson correlation coefficient is the *Spearman rank-order correlation coefficient*, a statistic that is interpreted just like its parametric cousin with respect to magnitude and direction. The *Mann–Whitney U test* is used in situations in which we would have used the independent-samples *t* test. The same six steps of hypothesis testing are used for both parametric and nonparametric tests, but the steps and the calculations for the nonparametric tests tend to be simpler.

SPSS®

In SPSS, we would conduct a chi-square test for independence by first entering our data. Each participant would get a score on each variable. For the pregnancy and clown entertainment data, we would have two columns: one for a woman's status with respect to entertainment by a clown (yes or no) and another for her pregnancy status (yes or no). We can use the numbers 1 and 2 to represent the levels of these variables. We would then select: **Analyze** → Descriptive Statistics → Crosstabs (select a nominal variable for the row and a nominal variable for the column; we selected entertainment-by-clown status for the rows and pregnancy status for the columns, but it doesn't matter which we choose) → Statistics → Chi-Square and Phi & Cramer's V (for effect sizes) → Continue. We can also select "Cells" and then click "Row" under percentages to give us the percentage of women who got pregnant in each clown condition. Click "Continue," and then click "OK" to run the analysis.

Most of the output, along with a view of some of the data, can be seen in the accompanying screenshot. In the top box of the output, we can see the percentages of women who did or did not become pregnant in each condition. For example, 35.5% of women who were entertained by a clown

became pregnant. We can also see that the chi-square statistic (in the box labeled "Chi-Square Tests" and in the row titled "Pearson Chi-Square") is 6.078, the same as the one we calculated by hand earlier. In the box titled "Symmetric Measures," we can see the Cramer's *V* statistic of .181, also the same as we calculated earlier. (Any slight differences we see in this table versus what we calculated earlier are due to rounding decisions.)

Let's conduct a Mann–Whitney *U* test on the country data we used when comparing communist and noncommunist countries on accomplishment-related pride. In SPSS, we would conduct a Mann–Whitney *U* test by selecting: **Analyze** → Nonparametric Tests → 2 Independent-Samples Tests. Select "Mann-Whitney U" as the test type. Select "Descriptive" under "Options" if you want the descriptive data as well. The dependent variable, rankings on accomplishment-related national pride, goes under "Test Variable List," and the independent variable, political system (noncommunist versus communist), goes under "Grouping Variable." Be sure to define your groups by clicking "Define Groups" and telling SPSS what you have called each of your conditions (e.g., 1 and 2 for noncommunist and communist, respectively). The output will give us the same value for the Mann–Whitney U statistic, 3, that we calculated earlier. (*Note:* You may enter either scale or ordinal data as the dependent variable. SPSS automatically ranks the data. If the data are already ranked, no change is made to the values. If the data are scale, they are converted to ranks.)

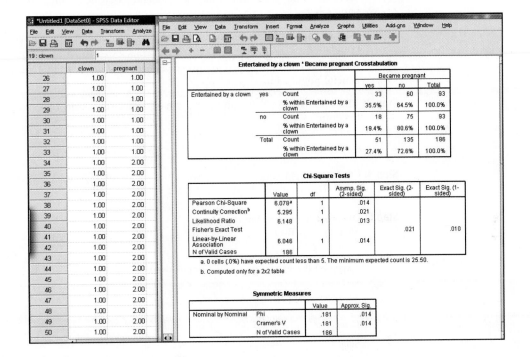

How It Works

15.1: CONDUCTING THE CHI-SQUARE TEST FOR GOODNESS-OF-FIT

Gary Steinman (2006), an obstetrician and gynecologist, studied whether a woman's diet could affect the likelihood that she would have twins. Insulin-like growth factor (IGF), often found in diets that include animal products, is hypothesized to lead to higher rates of twin births. Rates of twin births have increased, along with rates of IGF in animal products, a direct result of growth hormones aimed at increasing the production of products like milk and beef. Steinman wondered whether women who were vegans (those who eat neither meat nor dairy products) would have lower rates of twin births than would women who were vegetarians and consumed dairy products or who ate meat. Steinman reported that, in the general population, 1.9% of births result in twins (without the aid of reproductive technologies). In Steinman's study of 1042 vegans who gave birth (without reproductive technologies), four sets of twins were born. How can we use Steinman's data to conduct the six steps of hypothesis testing for a chi-square test for goodness-of-fit?

Step 1: Population 1: Vegans who recently gave birth like those whom we observed.

Population 2: Vegans who recently gave birth who are like the general population of mostly nonvegans.

The comparison distribution is a chi-square distribution. The hypothesis test will be a chi-square test for goodness-of-fit because we have one nominal variable only. This study meets three of the four assumptions. (1) The one variable is nominal. (2) Every participant is in only one cell (a vegan woman is not counted as having twins *and* as having one child, or singleton). (3) There are far more than five times as many participants as cells (there are 1042 participants and only two cells). (4) The participants were not, however, randomly selected. We learn from the published research paper that participants were recruited with the assistance of "various vegan societies." This limits our ability to generalize beyond women like those in our sample.

Step 2: Null hypothesis: Vegan women give birth to twins at the same rate as the general population.

Research hypothesis: Vegan women give birth to twins at a different rate from the general population.

Step 3: The comparison distribution is a chi-square distribution that has 1 degree of freedom:

$$df_{\chi^2} = 2 - 1 = 1$$

Step 4: Our critical chi-square statistic, based on a *p* level of 0.05 and 1 degree of freedom, is 3.841, as seen in the curve in Figure 15-1.

Step 5: Observed (among vegan mothers)

Singleton	Twins
1038	4

Expected (based on the general population)

Singleton	Twins
1022.202	19.798

Category	Observed (O)	Expected (E)	O − E	(O − E)²	$\frac{(O-E)^2}{E}$
Singleton	1038	1022.202	15.798	249.577	0.244
Twins	4	19.798	−15.798	249.577	12.606

$$\chi^2 = \sum\left(\frac{(O-E)^2}{E}\right) = 0.244 + 12.606 = 12.85$$

Step 6: Reject the null hypothesis; it appears that vegan mothers are less likely to have twins than are mothers in the general population.

The statistics, as reported in a journal article, would read:

$$\chi^2(1, N = 1042) = 12.85, p < 0.05$$

15.2: CONDUCTING THE CHI-SQUARE TEST FOR INDEPENDENCE

Do people who move far from their hometown have a more exciting life? Since 1972, the General Social Survey (GSS) has asked approximately 40,000 adults in the United States numerous questions about their lives. During several years of the GSS, participants were asked, "In general, do you find life exciting, pretty routine, or dull?", a variable called LIFE, and also were asked, "When you were 16 years old, were you living in the same (city/town/country)?", a variable called MOBILE16. How can we use these data to conduct the six steps of hypothesis testing for a chi-square test for independence?

In this case, there are two nominal variables. The independent variable is where a person lives relative to when she or he was 16 years old (same city, same state but different city, different state). The dependent variable is how the person finds life (exciting, routine, dull). Here are the data:

	Exciting	Routine	Dull
Same City	4890	6010	637
Same State/Different City	3368	3488	337
Different State	4604	4139	434

Step 1: Population 1: People like those in this sample.

Population 2: People from a population in which a person's characterization of life as exciting, routine, or dull does not depend on where that person is living relative to when she was 16 years old.

The comparison distribution is a chi-square distribution. The hypothesis test will be a chi-square test for independence because we have two nominal variables. This study meets all four assumptions: (1) the two variables are nominal; (2) every participant is in only one cell; (3) there are more than five times as many participants as there are cells (there are 27,907 participants and 9 cells); and (4) the GSS sample uses a form of random selection.

Step 2: Null hypothesis: The proportion of people who find life to be exciting, routine, or dull does not depend on where they live relative to when they were 16 years old.

Research hypothesis: The proportion of people finding life exciting, routine, or dull differs depending on where they live relative to when they were 16 years old.

Step 3: The comparison distribution is a chi-square distribution that has four degrees of freedom:

$$df_{\chi^2} = (k_{row} - 1)(k_{column} - 1) = (3 - 1)(3 - 1) = 4$$

Step 4: Our critical chi-square statistic, based on a p level of 0.05 and 2 degrees of freedom, is 9.49.

Step 5:

	OBSERVED (EXPECTED IN PARENTHESES)			
	Exciting	Routine	Dull	
Same City	4890	6010	637	11,537
	(5317.264)	(5637.656)	(582.08)	
Same State/Different City	3368	3488	337	7193
	(3315.167)	(3514.923)	(362.911)	
Different State	4604	4139	434	9178
	(4230.030)	(4484.910)	(463.060)	
	12,862	13,637	1408	27,907

$$\frac{Total_{column}}{N}(Total_{row}) = \frac{12,862}{27,907}(11,537) = 5317.264$$

$$\frac{Total_{column}}{N}(Total_{row}) = \frac{12,862}{27,907}(7193) = 3315.167$$

$$\frac{Total_{column}}{N}(Total_{row}) = \frac{12,862}{27,907}(9178) = 4230.030$$

$$\frac{Total_{column}}{N}(Total_{row}) = \frac{13,637}{27,907}(11,537) = 5637.656$$

$$\frac{Total_{column}}{N}(Total_{row}) = \frac{13,637}{27,907}(7193) = 3514.923$$

$$\frac{Total_{column}}{N}(Total_{row}) = \frac{13,637}{27,907}(9178) = 4484.910$$

$$\frac{Total_{column}}{N}(Total_{row}) = \frac{1408}{27,907}(11,537) = 582.080$$

$$\frac{Total_{column}}{N}(Total_{row}) = \frac{1408}{27,907}(7193) = 362.911$$

$$\frac{Total_{column}}{N}(Total_{row}) = \frac{1408}{27,907}(9178) = 463.060$$

Category	$(O - E)^2$	$\dfrac{(O - E)^2}{E}$
Same city; exciting	182,554.530	34.332
Same city; routine	138,640.050	24.592
Same city; dull	3,016.206	5.182
Same state/different city; exciting	2,791.326	0.842
Same state/different city; routine	724.848	0.206
Same state/different city; dull	671.380	1.850
Different state; exciting	139,853.560	33.062
Different state; routine	119,653.730	26.679
Different state; dull	844.484	1.824

$$\chi^2 = \Sigma\left(\frac{(O-E)^2}{E}\right) = 128.559$$

Step 6: Reject the null hypothesis. Our calculated chi-square value exceeds our critical value. How exciting a person finds life does appear to depend on where she or he lives relative to when she or he was 16 years old.

We'd present these statistics in a journal article as: $\chi^2(4) = 128.56, p < 0.05$.

15.3: CALCULATING CRAMER'S *V*

What is the effect size, Cramer's *V*, for the chi-square test for independence we conducted in How It Works 15.2?

$$V = \sqrt{\frac{\chi^2}{(N)(df_{row/column})}} = \sqrt{\frac{128.559}{(27,907)(2)}} = \sqrt{\frac{128.559}{55,814}} = 0.048$$

According to Cohen's conventions, this is a small effect size. With this piece of information, we'd present the statistics in a journal article as:

$$\chi^2(4, N = 27,907) = 128.56, p < 0.05, \text{Cramer's } V = 0.05$$

15.4: CALCULATING THE SPEARMAN RANK-ORDER CORRELATION COEFFICIENT

The accompanying table includes ranks for accomplishment-related national pride, along with numbers of medals won at the 2000 Sydney Olympics by the same countries in our random sample. (Of course, this might not be the best way to operationalize the variable of Olympic performance; perhaps we should be ranking Olympic medals per capita.) How can we calculate the Spearman correlation coefficient for these two variables?

Country	Pride Rank	Olympic Medals
United States	1	97
South Africa	2	5
Austria	3	3
Canada	4	14
Chile	5	1
Japan	6	18
Hungary	7	17
France	8	38
Norway	9	10
Slovenia	10	2

First, we have to convert the numbers of Olympic medals to ranks. Then we can calculate our correlation coefficient.

Country	Pride Rank	Olympic Medals	Medals Rank	Difference (D)	Squared Difference (D^2)
United States	1	97	1	0	0
South Africa	2	5	7	−5	25
Austria	3	3	8	−5	25
Canada	4	14	5	−1	1
Chile	5	1	10	−5	25
Japan	6	18	3	3	9
Hungary	7	17	4	3	9
France	8	38	2	6	36
Norway	9	10	6	3	9
Slovenia	10	2	9	1	1

$$\Sigma D^2 = (0 + 25 + 25 + 1 + 25 + 9 + 9 + 36 + 9 + 1) = 140$$

$$r_S = 1 - \frac{6(\Sigma D^2)}{N(N^2 - 1)} = 1 - \frac{6(140)}{10(10^2 - 1)} = 1 - \frac{840}{10(100 - 1)}$$
$$= 1 - \frac{840}{990} = 1 - 0.848 = 0.152$$

The Spearman correlation coefficient of 0.152 indicates a small, positive association. Even if we had scale data on both variables, we would not have wanted to use the scale data for Olympic medals because the United States, with a score of 98, appears to be an outlier. Its score is likely to inflate the strength of the correlation.

15.5: CONDUCTING THE MANN-WHITNEY *U* TEST

In what region do political science graduate programs tend to have the best rankings—on the East Coast (E) or in the Midwest (M)? Here are data from *U.S. News & World Report's* 2005 online rankings of graduate schools. These are the top 13 doctoral programs in political science that are either on the East Coast or in the Midwest. Schools listed at the same rank are tied.

1	Harvard University (E)
2	University of Michigan–Ann Arbor (M)
3	Princeton (E)
4	Yale University (E)
5.5	Duke University (E)
5.5	University of Chicago (M)
7.5	Columbia University (E)
7.5	Massachusetts Institute of Technology (E)
10	Ohio State University (M)
10	University of North Carolina–Chapel Hill (E)
10	University of Rochester (E)
12.5	University of Wisconsin–Madison (M)
12.5	Washington University in St. Louis (M)

How can we conduct a Mann-Whitney *U* test for this example? The independent variable is the region of the country, and its levels are East Coast and Midwest. The dependent variable is the *U.S. News & World Report* ranking.

Step 1: This study meets three of the four assumptions. (1) We need to convert our data from scale to ordinal. (2) The researchers did not use random selection, so our ability to generalize beyond this sample is limited. (3) There are some ties, but we will assume that there are not so many as to render the results of the test invalid.

Step 2: Null hypothesis: Political science programs on the East Coast and those in the Midwest do not tend to differ in national ranking.

Research hypothesis: Political science programs on the East Coast and those in the Midwest tend to differ in national ranking.

Step 3: There are eight political science programs on the East Coast and five in the Midwest.

Step 4: The cutoff, or critical value, for a Mann–Whitney U test with one group of 8 programs and one group of 5 programs, a p level of 0.05, and a two-tailed test is 8.

Step 5:

School	Rank	East Coast Rank	Midwest Rank
Harvard	1	1	
Michigan, Ann Arbor	2		2
Princeton	3	3	
Yale	4	4	
Duke	5.5	5.5	
Chicago	5.5		5.5
Columbia	7.5	7.5	
MIT	7.5	7.5	
Ohio State	10		10
North Carolina, Chapel Hill	10	10	
Rochester	10	10	
Wisconsin	12.5		12.5
Washington University in St. Louis	12.5		12.5

Before we continue, we sum the ranks for each group and add subscripts to indicate which group is which:

$$\Sigma R_E = 1 + 3 + 4 + 5.5 + 7.5 + 7.5 + 10 + 10 = 48.5$$

$$\Sigma R_M = 2 + 5.5 + 10 + 12.5 + 12.5 = 42.5$$

The formula for the first group is:

$$U_E = (n_E)(n_M) + \frac{n_E(n_E + 1)}{2} - \Sigma R_E$$

$$= (8)(5) + \frac{8(8 + 1)}{2} - 48.5 = 40 + 36 - 48.5 = 27.5$$

The formula for the second group is:

$$U_M = (n_E)(n_M) + \frac{n_M(n_M + 1)}{2} - \Sigma R_M$$

$$= (8)(5) + \frac{5(5 + 1)}{2} - 42.5 = 40 + 15 - 42.5 = 12.5$$

Step 6: For a Mann–Whitney U test, we compare only our smaller test statistic, 12.5, with the critical value, 8. This test statistic is not smaller than the critical value, so we fail to reject the null hypothesis. We cannot conclude that the two groups tend to differ with respect to national rankings.

In a journal article, the statistics would read:

$$U = 12.5, p > 0.05$$

Exercises

Clarifying the Concepts

15.1 Distinguish nominal, ordinal, and scale data.

15.2 What are the three main situations in which we use a nonparametric test?

15.3 What is the difference between the chi-square test for goodness-of-fit and the chi-square test for independence?

15.4 What are the four assumptions for the chi-square tests?

15.5 List two ways in which statisticians use the word *independence* or *independent* with respect to concepts introduced earlier in this book. Then describe how *independence* is used by statisticians with respect to chi square.

15.6 What are the hypotheses when conducting the chi-square test for goodness-of-fit?

15.7 How are the degrees of freedom for the chi-square hypothesis tests different from those of most other hypothesis tests?

15.8 Why is there just one critical value for a chi-square test, even when the hypothesis is a two-tailed test?

15.9 What information is presented in a contingency table in the chi-square test for independence?

15.10 What measure of effect size is used with chi square?

15.11 Define the symbols in the following formula: $\chi^2 = \Sigma\left[\dfrac{(O-E)^2}{E}\right]$.

15.12 What is the formula $\dfrac{Total_{column}}{N}(Total_{row})$ used for?

15.13 Why do we sometimes convert scale data to ordinal data?

15.14 When the data on at least one variable are ordinal, the data on any scale variable must be converted from scale to ordinal. How do we convert a scale variable into an ordinal one?

15.15 When do we use the Mann–Whitney U test?

15.16 What are the assumptions of the Mann–Whitney U test?

15.17 Explain how the relation between ranks is the core of the Spearman rank-order correlation.

15.18 Define the symbols in the following term: $r_S = 1 - \dfrac{6(\Sigma D^2)}{N(N^2-1)}$.

Calculating the Statistics

15.19 In order to compute statistics, we need to have working formulas. For each of the following, (i) identify the incorrect symbol, (ii) state what the correct symbol should be, and (iii) explain why the initial symbol was incorrect.

a. For the chi-square test for goodness-of-fit: $df_{\chi^2} = N - 1$

b. For the chi-square test for independence: $df_{\chi^2} = (k_{row} - 1) + (k_{column} - 1)$

c. $\chi^2 = \Sigma\left[\dfrac{(M-E)^2}{E}\right]$

d. Cramer's $V = \sqrt{\dfrac{\chi^2}{(N)(k_{row/column})}}$

e. Expected frequency for each cell $= \dfrac{k_{column}}{N(k_{row})}$

f. $r = 1 - \dfrac{6(\Sigma D^2)}{N(N^2-1)}$

g. $U_1 = (n_1)(n_2) + \dfrac{n_1(n_1+1)}{2} - \Sigma R_1^2$

15.20 For each of the following, identify the independent variable(s), dependent variable(s), and the level of measurement (nominal, ordinal, scale).

a. The number of loads of laundry washed per month was tracked for women and men living in college dorms.

b. A researcher interested in people's need to maintain social image collected data on the number of miles on someone's car and his/her rank for "need for approval" out of the 183 people studied.

c. A professor of social science was interested in whether involvement in campus life is significantly impacted by whether a student lives on or off campus. Thirty-seven students living on campus and 37 students living off campus were asked whether they were an active member of a club.

15.21 Use this calculation table for the chi-square test for goodness-of-fit to complete this exercise.

Category	Observed (O)	Expected (E)	O − E	(O − E)²	$\dfrac{(O-E)^2}{E}$
1	48	60			
2	46	30			
3	6	10			

a. Calculate degrees of freedom for this chi-square test for goodness-of-fit.

b. Perform all of the calculations to complete this table.

c. Compute the chi-square statistic.

15.22 Use this calculation table for the chi-square test for goodness-of-fit to complete this exercise.

Category	Observed (O)	Expected (E)	O − E	(O − E)²	$\frac{(O - E)^2}{E}$
1	750	625			
2	650	625			
3	600	625			
4	500	625			

a. Calculate degrees of freedom for this chi-square test for goodness-of-fit.

b. Perform all of the calculations to complete this table.

c. Compute the chi-square statistic.

15.23 Below are some data to use in a chi-square test for independence. Calculate the degrees of freedom for this test.

	Observed Accidents	No Accidents	
Rain	19	26	45
No Rain	20	71	91
	39	97	136

15.24 Using the data presented in Exercise 15.23, complete this table of expected frequencies.

	Expected Accidents	No Accidents
Rain		
No Rain		

15.25 Using the data presented in Exercise 15.23 and the work you did in Exercise 15.24, calculate the test statistic.

15.26 Calculate the appropriate measure of effect size for the data presented in Exercise 15.23 and the statistic calculated in Exercise 15.25.

15.27 Convert the following scale data to ordinal or ranked data, starting with a rank of 1 for the smallest data point.

Count	Variable X	Variable Y
1	134.5	64.00
2	186	60.00
3	157	61.50
4	129	66.25
5	147	65.50
6	133	62.00
7	141	62.50
8	147	62.00
9	136	63.00
10	147	65.50

15.28 Convert the following scale data to ordinal or ranked data, starting with a rank of 1 for the smallest data point.

Count	Variable X	Variable Y
1	$1250	25
2	$1400	21
3	$1100	32
4	$1450	54
5	$1600	38
6	$2100	62
7	$3750	43
8	$1300	32

15.29 Compute the Spearman correlation for the data listed in Exercise 15.27.

15.30 Compute the Spearman correlation for the data listed in Exercise 15.28.

15.31 Compute the Mann–Whitney U test on the following data:

Group 1	Ordinal Dependent Variable	Group 2	Ordinal Dependent Variable
1	1	1	11
2	2.5	2	9
3	8	3	2.5
4	4	4	5
5	6	5	7
6	10	6	12

15.32 Compute the Mann–Whitney U test on the following data:

Group 1	Scale Dependent Variable	Group 2	Scale Dependent Variable
1	8	9	3
2	5	10	4
3	5	11	2
4	7	12	1
5	10	13	1
6	14	14	5
7	9	15	6
8	11		

Applying the Concepts

15.33 For each of the following research questions, state whether a parametric or nonparametric hypothesis test is more appropriate. Explain your answers.

a. Are women more or less likely than men to be economics majors?

b. At a small company with 15 staff and 1 top boss, do those with a college education tend to make a different amount of money from those without one?

c. At your high school, did athletes or nonathletes tend to have higher grade point averages?

d. At your high school, did athletes or nonathletes tend to have higher class ranks?

e. Compare car accidents in which the occupants were wearing seat belts with accidents in which the occupants were not wearing seat belts. Do seat belts seem to make a difference in the numbers of accidents that lead to no injuries, nonfatal injuries, and fatal injuries?

f. Compare car accidents in which the occupants were wearing seat belts with accidents in which the occupants were not wearing seat belts. Were those wearing seat belts driving at slower speeds, on average, than those not wearing seat belts?

15.34 Weinberg, Fleisher, and Hashimoto (2007) studied almost 50,000 students' evaluations of their professors in almost 400 economics courses at The Ohio State University over a 10-year period. For each of their findings, outlined below, state (i) the independent variable or variables, and their levels where appropriate; (ii) the de-

pendent variable(s); and (iii) what category of research design is being used:

I—scale independent variable(s) and scale dependent variable

II—nominal independent variable(s) and scale dependent variable

III—only nominal variables

Explain your answer to part (iii).

a. The researchers found that students' ratings of their professors were predictive of grades in the class for which the professor was evaluated.

b. The researchers also found that students' ratings of their professors were not predictive of grades for other, related future classes. (The researchers stated that these first two findings suggest that student ratings of professors are tied to their current grades but not to learning—which would affect future grades.)

c. The researchers found that male professors received statistically significantly higher student ratings, on average, than did female professors.

d. The researchers reported, however, that average levels of students learning (as assessed by grades in related future classes) were not statistically significantly different for those who had male and those who had female professors.

e. The researchers might have been interested in whether there were proportionally more female professors teaching upper-level than lower-level courses and proportionally more male professors teaching lower-level than upper-level courses (perhaps a reason for the lower average ratings of female professors).

f. The researchers found no statistically significant differences in average student evaluations among non–tenure-track lecturers, graduate student teaching associates, and tenure-track faculty members.

15.35 A *New York Times* article on grade inflation reported several findings related to a tendency for average grades to rise over the years and a tendency for the top-ranked institutions to give the highest average grades (Archibold, 1998). For each of the findings outlined below, state (i) the independent variable or variables, and their levels where appropriate; (ii) the dependent variable(s); and (iii) what category of research design is being used:

I—scale independent variable(s) and scale dependent variable

II—nominal independent variable(s) and scale dependent variable

III—only nominal variables

Explain your answer to part (iii).

   a. In 1969, 7% of all grades were A's; in 1994, 25% of all grades were A's.

   b. The average GPA for the graduating students of elite schools is 3.2; the average GPA for graduating students at selective schools (the level below elite schools) is 3.04; and the average GPA for graduating students at state colleges is 2.95.

   c. At Dartmouth College, an elite university, SAT scores of incoming students have increased along with their subsequent college GPAs (perhaps an explanation for grade inflation).

15.36 Here are three ways to assess one's performance in high school: (1) GPA at graduation, (2) whether one graduated with honors (as indicated by graduating with a GPA of at least 3.5), and (3) class rank at graduation. For example, Abdul had a 3.98 GPA, graduated with honors, and was ranked 10th in his class.

   a. Which of these variables could be considered to be a nominal variable? Explain.

   b. Which of these variables is most clearly an ordinal variable? Explain.

   c. Which of these variables is a scale variable? Explain.

   d. Which of these variables gives us the most information about Abdul's performance?

   e. If we were to use one of these variables in an analysis, which variable (as the dependent variable) would lead to the lowest chance of a Type II error? Explain why.

15.37 CNN.com reported on a 2005 study that ranked the world's cities in terms of how livable they are using a range of criteria related to stability, health care, culture and environment, education, and infrastructure. Vancouver came out on top. For each of the following research questions, state which nonparametric hypothesis test is most appropriate: Spearman rank-order correlation coefficient or Mann–Whitney U test. Explain your answers.

   a. Which cities tend to receive higher rankings—those north or south of the equator?

   b. Are the livability rankings related to a city's economic status (assessed by rank)?

15.38 "Do Immigrants Make Us Safer?" asked the title of a *New York Times Magazine* article (Press, 2006). The article reported findings from several studies, including several conducted by Harvard sociologist Robert Sampson in Chicago. For each of the following findings, draw the table of cells that would comprise the research design. Include the labels for each row and column.

   a. Mexicans were more likely to be married (versus single) than U.S.-born blacks or whites.

   b. People living in immigrant neighborhoods were 15% less likely than were people living in nonimmigrant neighborhoods to commit crimes. This finding was true among both those living in households headed by a married couple and those living in households not headed by a married couple.

   c. The crime rate was higher among second-generation than among first-generation immigrants; moreover, the crime rate was higher among third-generation than among second-generation immigrants.

15.39 Across all of India, there are only 933 girls for every 1000 boys (Lloyd, 2006), evidence of a bias that leads many parents to illegally select for boys or to kill their infant girls. (Note that this translates into a proportion of girls of 0.483.) In Punjab, a region of India in which residents tend to be more educated than in other regions, there are only 798 girls for every 1000 boys. Assume that you are a researcher interested in whether sex selection is more or less prevalent in educated regions of India and that 1798 children from Punjab constitute the entire sample. (*Hint:* You will use the proportions from the national database for comparison.)

   a. How many variables are there in this study? What are the levels of any variable you identified?

   b. What hypothesis test would be used to analyze these data? Justify your answer.

   c. Conduct the six steps of hypothesis testing for this example. (*Note:* Be sure to use the correct proportions for the expected values, not the actual numbers for the population.)

   d. Report the statistics as you would in a journal article.

15.40 Richards (2006) reported data from a study by the *American Prospect* on the genders of op-ed writers who covered the topic of abortion in the *New York Times*. Over a two-year period, the *American Prospect* counted 124 articles that discussed abortion (from a wide range of political and ideological perspectives). Of these, just 21 were written by women.

   a. How many variables are there in this study? What are the levels of any variable you identified?

   b. What hypothesis test would be used to analyze these data? Justify your answer.

   c. Conduct the six steps of hypothesis testing for this example.

   d. Report the statistics as you would in a journal article.

15.41 In a classic prisoner's dilemma game with money for prizes, players who cooperate with each other both earn good prizes. If, however, your opposing player cooperates but you do not (the term used is *defect*), you receive an even bigger payout and your opponent receives nothing. If you cooperate but your opposing player defects, he or she receives that bigger payout and you receive nothing. If you both defect, you each get a small prize. Because of this, most players of such games choose to defect, knowing that if they cooperate but their partners don't, they won't win anything. The strategies of U.S. and Chinese students were compared. The researchers hypothesized that those from the market economy (United States) would cooperate less (i.e., would defect more often) than would those from the nonmarket economy (China).

	Defect	Cooperate
China	31	36
United States	41	14

a. How many variables are there in this study? What are the levels of any variables you identified?

b. What hypothesis test would be used to analyze these data? Justify your answer.

c. Conduct the six steps of hypothesis testing for this example, using the above data.

d. Calculate the appropriate measure of effect size. According to Cohen's conventions, what size effect is this?

e. Report the statistics as you would in a journal article.

15.42 Grimberg, Kutikov, and Cucchiara (2005) wondered whether gender bias was evident in referrals of children for poor growth. They believed that boys were more likely to be referred even when there was no problem—bad for boys because families of short boys might falsely view their height as a medical problem. They also believed that girls were less likely to be referred even when there was a problem—bad for girls because real problems might not be diagnosed and treated. They studied all new patients at The Children's Hospital of Philadelphia Diagnostic and Research Growth Center who were referred for potential problems related to short stature. Of the 182 boys who were referred, 27 had an underlying medical problem, 86 did not but were below norms for their age, and 69 were of normal height according to growth charts. Of the 96 girls who were referred, 39 had an underlying medical problem, 38 did not but were below norms for their age, and 19 were of normal height according to growth charts.

a. How many variables are there in this study? What are the levels of any variable you identified?

b. What hypothesis test would be used to analyze these data? Justify your answer.

c. Conduct the six steps of hypothesis testing for this example.

d. Calculate the appropriate measure of effect size. According to Cohen's conventions, what size effect is this?

e. Report the statistics as you would in a journal article.

15.43 Refer to the prisoner's dilemma example in Exercise 15.41.

a. Draw a table that includes the conditional proportions for participants from China and from the United States. (The conditional proportions are the proportions of Chinese who defect or cooperate and the proportions of Americans who defect or cooperate.)

b. Create a graph with bars showing the proportions for all four conditions.

c. Create a graph with two bars showing just the proportions for the defections for each country.

15.44 Refer to the study of poor growth in children in Exercise 15.42.

a. Draw a table that includes the conditional proportions for boys and for girls—that is the proportion of boys in each condition and the proportion of girls in each condition.

b. Create a graph with bars showing the proportions for all six conditions.

15.45 Here are some monthly cell phone bills, in dollars, for college students:

```
100 60   35   50   50   50 60 65
  0 75 100   55   50   40 80
200 30   50 108 500 100 45
 40 45   50   40   40 100 80
```

a. Convert these data from scale to ordinal. (Don't forget to put them in order first.) What happens to an outlier when you convert these data to ordinal?

b. Roughly, what shape would the distribution of these data take? Would they likely be normally distributed? Explain why the distribution of ordinal data is never normal.

c. Why does it not matter if the ordinal variable is normally distributed? (*Hint:* Think about what kind of hypothesis test you would conduct.)

15.46 In fantasy baseball, groups of 12 league participants conduct a draft in which they can "buy" any baseball players from any teams across one of the leagues (i.e., the

American League or National League). These makeshift teams are compared on the basis of the combined statistics of the individual baseball players. Statistics such as home runs are awarded points, and each fantasy team receives a total score of all combined points for its baseball players, regardless of their real-life team. Many in the fantasy and real-life baseball worlds have wondered how success in fantasy leagues maps onto the real-life success of winning baseball games. Walker (2006) compared the fantasy league performances of the players for each American League team with their actual American League finishes for the 2004 season, the year the Red Sox broke the legendary "curse" against them and won the World Series. The data, sorted from highest to lowest fantasy league score, are shown in the accompanying table.

Team	Fantasy League Points	Actual American League Finish
Boston	117.5	2
New York	109.5	1
Anaheim	108	3.5
Minnesota	97	3.5
Texas	85	6
Chicago	80	7
Cleveland	79	8
Oakland	77	5
Baltimore	74.5	9
Detroit	68.5	10
Seattle	51	13
Tampa Bay	47.5	11
Toronto	35.5	12
Kansas City	20	14

a. What are the two variables of interest? For each variable, state whether it's scale or ordinal.

b. Calculate the Spearman correlation coefficient for these two variables. Remember to convert any scale variables to ranks.

c. What does the coefficient tell us about the relation between these two variables?

d. Why couldn't we calculate a Pearson correlation coefficient for these data?

15.47 Does speed in completing a test correlate with one's grade? Here are test scores for eight students in one of our statistics classes. They are arranged in order from the

student who turned in the test first to the student who turned in the test last.

98 74 87 92 88 93 62 67

a. What are the two variables of interest? For each variable, state whether it's scale or ordinal.

b. Calculate the Spearman correlation coefficient for these two variables. Remember to convert any scale variables to ranks.

c. What does the coefficient tell us about the relation between these two variables?

d. Why couldn't we calculate a Pearson correlation coefficient for these data?

15.48 Consider again the two variables described in Exercise 15.47, test grade and speed in taking the test. Imagine that each of the following numbers represents the Spearman correlation coefficient that quantifies the relation between these two variables—test grade converted to ranks such that the top grade of 98 is ranked 1, and speed in taking the test with the fastest person ranked 1. What does each coefficient suggest about the relation between the variables? Using the guidelines for the Pearson correlation coefficient, indicate whether each coefficient is roughly small (0.10), medium (0.30), or large (0.50). Specify which of these coefficients suggests the strongest relation between the two variables as well as which coefficient suggests the weakest relation between the two variables. [You calculated the actual correlation between these variables in Exercise 15.47(b).]

a. 1.00

b. −0.001

c. 0.52

d. −0.27

e. −0.98

f. 0.09

15.49 Exercise 15.47 presented data to enable you to calculate the Spearman correlation coefficient that quantifies the relation between the speed of taking the test and the test grade.

a. Does this correlation coefficient suggest that students should take their tests as quickly as possible? That is, does it indicate that taking the test quickly *causes* a good grade? Explain your answer.

b. What third variables might be responsible for this correlation? That is, what third variables might cause both speedy test-taking and a good test grade?

15.50 Do public or private universities tend to have better sociology graduate programs? *U.S. News & World Report* publishes online rankings of graduate schools across a range of disciplines. Here is their 2005 list of the top 21 doctoral programs in sociology, along with an indication of whether they're public or private institutions. Schools listed at the same rank are tied.

1	University of Wisconsin, Madison (public)
2	University of California, Berkeley (public)
3	University of Michigan, Ann Arbor (public)
4.5	University of Chicago (private)
4.5	University of North Carolina (public)
6.5	Princeton University (private)
6.5	Stanford University (private)
8.5	Harvard University (private)
8.5	University of California, Los Angeles (public)
10	University of Pennsylvania (private)
12	Columbia University (private)
12	Indiana University, Bloomington (public)
12	Northwestern University (private)
15	Cornell University (private)
15	Duke University (private)
15	University of Texas, Austin (public)
18	Pennsylvania State University, University Park (public)
18	University of Arizona (public)
18	University of Washington (public)
20.5	The Ohio State University (public)
20.5	Yale University (private)

a. What is the independent variable, and what are its levels? What is the dependent variable?

b. Is this a between-groups or within-groups design? Explain.

c. Why do we have to use a nonparametric hypothesis test for these data?

d. Conduct all six steps of hypothesis testing for a Mann–Whitney U test.

e. How would you present these statistics in a journal article?

15.51 Do red states (U.S. states whose residents tend to vote Republican) have different voter turnouts from blue states (U.S. states whose residents tend to vote Democratic)? The accompanying table shows voter turnouts (in percentages) for the 2004 presidential election for eight randomly selected red states and eight randomly selected blue states.

Red States	Voted in 2004 Election (%)	Blue States	Voted in 2004 Election (%)
Georgia	57.38	California	60.01
Idaho	64.89	Illinois	60.73
Indiana	55.69	Maine	73.40
Louisiana	60.78	New Jersey	64.54
Missouri	66.89	Oregon	70.50
Montana	64.36	Vermont	66.19
Texas	53.35	Washington	67.42
Virginia	61.50	Wisconsin	76.73

a. What is the independent variable, and what are its levels? What is the dependent variable?

b. Is this a between-groups or within-groups design? Explain.

c. Conduct all six steps of hypothesis testing for a Mann–Whitney U test.

d. How would you present these statistics in a journal article?

15.52 Spanish researchers reported the following: "Using the Mann-Whitney nonparametrical statistical test on the gender differences, we found a significant difference between boys and girls in Group 1 for overall [aggression] ($U = 44.00$, $p = 0.004$) and received aggression ($U = 48.00$, $p = 0.005$). So, in their dreams, younger boys not only had a higher level of general aggression but also received more *severe* aggressive acts than girls of the same age" (emphasis in original) (Oberst, Charles, & Chamarro, 2005 p. 175).

a. What is the independent variable, and what are its levels? What is the dependent variable?

b. Is this a between-groups or within-groups design?

c. What hypothesis test did the researchers conduct? Why might they have chosen a nonparametric test?

d. Describe what they found in your own words.

e. Can we conclude that gender caused a difference in levels of aggression in dreams? Explain. Provide at least two reasons why gender might not cause certain levels of aggression in dreams even though these variables are associated.

Terms

chi-square test for goodness-of-fit (p. 405)

chi-square test for independence (p. 405)

Cramer's V (Cramer's phi) (p. 415)

Spearman rank-order correlation coefficient (p. 418)

Mann–Whitney U test (p. 421)

Formulas

$df_{\chi^2} = k - 1$ (degrees of freedom for chi-square test for goodness-of-fit) (p. 407)

$\chi^2 = \Sigma\left[\dfrac{(O - E)^2}{E}\right]$ (p. 409)

$df_{\chi^2} = (k_{row} - 1)(k_{column} - 1)$ (degrees of freedom for chi-square test for independence) (p. 412)

Expected frequency for each cell

$= \dfrac{Total_{column}}{N}(Total_{row})$, where we use the overall number of participants, N, along with the totals for the rows and columns for each particular cell (p. 413)

Crame's $V = \sqrt{\dfrac{\chi^2}{(N)(df_{row/column})}}$ (p. 415)

$r_S = 1 - \dfrac{6(\Sigma D^2)}{N(N^2 - 1)}$ (p. 419)

$U_1 = (n_1)(n_2) + \dfrac{n_1(n_1 + 1)}{2} = \Sigma R_1$ (p. 424)

$U_2 = (n_1)(n_2) + \dfrac{n_2(n_2 + 1)}{2} = \Sigma R_2$ (p. 424)

Symbols

χ^2 (p. 405)

k (p. 407)

Cramer's V (p. 415)

Cramer's φ (p. 415)

r_S (p. 419)

U (p. 421)

Reference for Basic Mathematics

This appendix serves as a reference for the basic mathematical operations that are used in the book. We provide quick reference tables to help you with symbols and notation; instruction on the order of operations for equations with multiple operations; guidelines for converting fractions, decimals, and percentages; and examples of how to solve basic algebraic equations. Some of you will need a more extensive review than is presented in these pages. That review, which involves greater detail and instruction, can be found on the book's companion Web site. Most of you will be familiar with much of this material. However, the inclusion of this reference can help you to solve problems throughout this book, particularly when you come across material that appears unfamiliar.

We include a diagnostic quiz for you to assess your current comfort level with this material. Following the diagnostic test, we provide instruction and reference tables for each section so that you can review the concepts, apply the concepts through worked problems, and review your skills with a brief self-quiz.

A.1 Diagnostic Test: Skills Evaluation

This diagnostic test is divided into four parts that correspond to the sections of the basic mathematics review that follows. The purpose of the diagnostic test is to help you understand which areas you need to review prior to completing work in this book. (Answers to each of the questions can be found at the end of the review on page A-6.)

SECTION 1 (Symbols and Notation: Arithmetic Operations)

1. $8 + 2 + 14 + 4 = $ _____
2. $4 \times (-6) = $ _____
3. $22 - (-4) + 3 = $ _____
4. $8 \times 6 = $ _____
5. $36 \div (-9) = $ _____
6. $13 + (-2) + 8 = $ _____
7. $44 \div 11 = $ _____
8. $-6 \, (-3) = $ _____
9. $-6 - 8 = $ _____
10. $-14 \, / \, -2 = $ _____

SECTION 2 (Order of Operations)

1. $3 \times (6 + 4) - 30 = $ _____
2. $4 + 6(2 + 1) + 6 = $ _____
3. $(3 - 6) \times 2 + 5 = $ _____
4. $4 + 6 \times 2 = $ _____
5. $16/2 + 6(3 - 1) = $ _____
6. $2^2 \, (12 - 8) = $ _____
7. $5 - 3(4 - 1) = $ _____
8. $7 \times 2 - (9 - 3) \times 2 = $ _____
9. $15 \div 5 + (6 + 2)/2 = $ _____
10. $15 - 3^2 + 5(2) = $ _____

SECTION 3 (Proportions: Fractions, Decimals, and Percentages)

1. Convert 0.42 into a fraction _____
2. Convert $^6/_{10}$ into a decimal _____
3. Convert $^4/_5$ into a percentage _____
4. $^6/_{13} + {}^4/_{13} = $ _____
5. $0.8 \times 0.42 = $ _____
6. 40% of 120 = _____
7. $^2/_7 + {}^2/_5 = $ _____
8. $^2/_5 \times 80 = $ _____
9. $^1/_4 \div {}^1/_3 = $ _____
10. $^4/_7 \times {}^5/_9 = $ _____

SECTION 4 (Solving Equations with a Single Unknown Variable)

1. $5X - 13 = 7$ _____
2. $3(X - 2) = 9$ _____
3. $X/3 + 2 = 10$ _____
4. $X(-3) + 2 = -16$ _____
5. $X(6 - 4) + 3 = 15$ _____
6. $X/4 + 3 = 6$ _____
7. $3X + (-9)/(-3) = 24$ _____
8. $9 + X/4 = 12$ _____
9. $4X - 5 = 19$ _____
10. $5 + (-2) + 3X = 9$ _____

A.2 Symbols And Notation: Arithmetic Operations

SYMBOLS AND NOTATION

The basic mathematical symbols used throughout this textbook are located in Table A.1. These include the most common arithmetic operations, and most of you will find that you are familiar with them. However, it is worth your time to review the reference table and material that outline the operations using positive and negative numbers. For those of you who have spent little time solving math equations recently, familiarizing yourselves with this material can be quite helpful in avoiding common mistakes.

ARITHMETIC OPERATIONS: Worked Examples

Adding, Subtracting, Multiplying, and Dividing with Positive and Negative Numbers

1. Adding with positive numbers: Add the two (or series of) numbers to produce a sum.
   a. $4 + 7 = 11$
   b. $7 + 4 + 9 = 20$
   c. $4 + 6 + 7 + 2 = 19$

2. Adding with negative numbers: Sum the absolute values of each number and place a negative sign in front of the sum. (*Hint:* When a positive sign directly precedes a negative sign, change both signs to a single negative sign.)
   a. $-6 + (-4) = -10$
      $-6 - 4 = -10$

   b. $-3 + (-2) = -5$
      $-3 - 2 = -5$

3. Adding two numbers with opposite signs: Find the difference between the two numbers and assign the sign (positive or negative) of the larger number.
   a. $17 + (-9) = 8$
   b. $-16 + 10 = -6$

4. Subtracting one number from another number. (*Hint:* When subtracting a negative number from another number, two negative signs come in sequence, as in part (a). To solve the equations, change the two sequential negative signs into a single positive sign.)
   a. $5 - (-4) = 9$
      $5 + 4 = 9$
   b. $5 - 8 = -3$
   c. $-6 - 3 = -9$

5. Multiplying two positive numbers produces a positive result.
   a. $6 \times 9 = 54$
   b. $6(9) = 54$
   c. $4 \times 3 = 12$
   d. $4(3) = 12$

6. Multiplying two negative numbers produces a positive result.
   a. $-3 \times -9 = 27$
   b. $-3(-9) = 27$
   c. $-4 \times (-3) = 12$
   d. $-4(-3) = 12$

7. Multiplying one positive and one negative number produces a negative result.
   a. $-3 \times 9 = -27$
   b. $-3(9) = -27$
   c. $4 \times (-3) = -12$
   d. $4(-3) = -12$

8. Dividing two positive numbers produces a positive result.
   a. $12 \div 4 = 3$
   b. $12 / 4 = 3$
   c. $16 \div 8 = 2$
   d. $16 / 8 = 2$

9. Dividing two negative numbers produces a positive result.
   a. $-12 \div -4 = 3$
   b. $-12 / -4 = 3$
   c. $-16 \div (-8) = 2$
   d. $^-16 / (-8) = 2$

10. Dividing a positive number by a negative number (or dividing a negative number by a positive number) produces a negative result.
    a. $-12 \div 4 = -3$
    b. $-12 / 4 = -3$
    c. $16 \div (-8) = -2$
    d. $16 / (-8) = -2$

TABLE A.1 Symbols and Notations

$+$	Addition	$8 + 3 = 11$
$-$	Subtraction	$14 - 6 = 8$
$\times, ()$	Multiplication	$4 \times 3 = 12, 4(3) = 12$
$4, /$	Division	$12 \div 6 = 2, {}^{12}/_6 = 2$
$>$	Greater than	$7 > 5$
$<$	Less than	$4 < 9$
$\geq$	Greater than or equal to	$7 \geq 5, 4 \geq 4$
$\leq$	Less than or equal to	$5 \leq 9, 6 \leq 6$
$\neq$	Not equal to	$5 \neq 3$

SELF-QUIZ #1: Symbols and Notation: Arithmetic Operations

(Answers to this quiz can be found on page A-7.)

1. $4 \times 7 =$

2. $6 + 3 + 9 =$

3. $-6 - 3 =$

4. $-27 / 3 =$

5. $4(9) =$

6. $12 + (-5) =$

7. $16(-3) =$

8. $-24 / -3 =$

9. $75 \div 5 =$

10. $-7(-4) =$

A.3 Order Of Operations

Equations and formulas often include a number of mathematical operations combining addition, subtraction, multiplication, and division. Some will also include exponents and square roots. In complex equations with more than one operation, it is important to perform the operations in a specific sequence. Deviating from this sequence can produce a wrong answer. Table A.2 lists the order of operations for quick reference.

ORDER OF OPERATIONS: Worked Examples

1. $-3 + 6(4) - 7 =$ — Multiplication
   $-3 + 24 - 7 =$ — Addition
   $21 - 7 =$ — Subtraction
   $14 = 14$ — Answer

2. $2(8) + 6 / 3 \times 8 =$ — Multiplication. Remember to move left to right.
   $16 + 6 / 3 \times 8 =$ — Division
   $16 + 2 \times 8 =$ — Multiplication
   $16 + 16 =$ — Addition
   $32 = 32$ — Answer

3. $3^2 + 6 / 3 - 12(2) =$ — Square (raise exponent)
   $9 + 6 / 3 - 12(2) =$ — Division
   $9 + 2 - 12(2) =$ — Multiplication
   $9 + 2 - 24 =$ — Addition
   $11 - 24 =$ — Subtraction
   $-13 = -13$ — Answer

4. $(10 + 6) - 6^2 / 4 + 3(10) =$ — Within parentheses
   $16 - 6^2 / 4 + 3(10) =$ — Square (raise exponent)
   $16 - 36 / 4 + 3(10) =$ — Division
   $16 - 9 + 3(10) =$ — Multiplication
   $16 - 9 + 30 =$ — Subtraction
   $7 + 30 =$ — Addition
   $37 = 37$ — Answer

5. $8 + (-4) + 3(12 - 8) =$ — Within parentheses
   $8 + (-4) + 3(4) =$ — Multiplication
   $8 + (-4) + 12 =$ — Addition
   $4 + 12 =$ — Addition
   $16 = 16$ — Answer

SELF-QUIZ #2: Order of Operations

(Answers to this quiz can be found on page A-7.)

1. $3(7) - 12/3 + 2 =$

2. $4/2 + 6 - 2(3) =$

3. $-5(4) + 16 =$

4. $8 + (-16)/4 =$

5. $6 - 3 + 5 - 3(5) + 10 =$

6. $4^2/8 - 4(3) + (8 - 3) =$

7. $(14 - 6) + 72/9 + 4 =$

8. $(54 - 18)/4 + 7 \times 3 =$

9. $32 - 4(3 + 4) + 8 =$

10. $100 \times 3 - 87 =$

TABLE A.2 Order of Operations

Rule of Operation	Example
1. Calculations within parentheses are completed first.	1a. $(6 + 2) - 4 \times 3 / 2^2 + 6 =$ 1b. $8 - 4 \times 3 / 2^2 + 6 =$
2. Squaring (or raising to another exponent) is completed second.	2a. $8 - 4 \times 3 / 2^2 + 6 =$ 2b. $8 - 4 \times 3 / 4 + 6 =$
3. From **left** to **right**, complete all multiplication and division operations. This may require multiple steps.	3a. $8 - 4 \times 3 / 4 + 6 =$ 3b. $8 - 12 / 4 + 6 =$ 3c. $8 - 12 / 4 + 6 =$ 3d. $8 - 3 + 6 =$
4. Last, complete all the addition and subtraction operations.	4a. $8 - 3 + 6 =$ 4b. $5 + 6 =$ 4c. $11 = 11$

A.4 Proportions: Fractions, Decimals, And Percentages

A proportion is a part in relation to a whole. When we look at fractions, we understand the denominator (the bottom number) to be the number of equal parts in the whole. The numerator represents the proportion of parts of that whole that are present. Fractions can be converted into decimals by dividing the numerator by the denominator. Decimals can then be converted into percentages by multiplying by 100 (Table A.3). It is important to use the percentage symbol (%) when differentiating decimals from percentages. Additionally, decimals are often rounded to the nearest hundredth before they are converted into a percentage.

FRACTIONS

Equivalent Fractions

The same proportion can be expressed in a number of equivalent fractions. Equivalent fractions are found by multiplying both the numerator and the denominator by the same number.

$$^1/_2 = {}^2/_4 = {}^6/_{12} = {}^{30}/_{60}$$

In this case, we multiply each side of $^1/_2$ by 2 to reach the equivalent $^2/_4$, then by 3 to reach the equivalent $^6/_{12}$, then by 5 to reach the equivalent $^{30}/_{60}$. Or we could have multiplied the numerator and denominator of the original $^1/_2$ by 30 to reach our concluding $^{30}/_{60}$.

Now fractions can also be reduced to a simpler form by dividing the numerator and denominator by the same number. Be sure to divide each by a number that will result in a whole number for both the numerator and the denominator.

$$^{25}/_{75} = {}^5/_{15} = {}^1/_3$$

By dividing each side by 5, the fraction was reduced from $^{25}/_{75}$ to $^5/_{15}$. By further dividing by 5, we reduce the fraction to its simplest form, $^1/_3$. Or we could have divided the numerator and denominator of the original $^{25}/_{75}$ by 25, resulting in the simplest expression of this fraction, $^1/_3$.

Adding and Subtracting Fractions (with the same denominator)

Finding equivalent fractions is essential to adding and subtracting two or more fractions. In order to add or subtract, each fraction must have the same denominator. If the two fractions already have the same denominator, add or subtract the numbers in the numerators only.

$$^2/_7 + {}^1/_7 = {}^3/_7 \qquad ^4/_5 - {}^3/_5 = {}^1/_5$$

In each of these instances, we are adding or subtracting from the same whole (or same pie, as in lines one and two of Table A.3). In the first equation, we are increasing our proportion of 2 by 1 to equal 3 pieces of the whole. In the second equation, we are reducing the number of proportions from 4 by 3 to equal just 1 piece of the whole.

Adding and Subtracting Fractions (with different denominators)

When adding or subtracting two proportions with different denominators, it is necessary to find a common denominator before performing the operation. It is often easiest to multiply each side (numerator and denominator) by the number equal to the denominator of the other fraction. This provides an easy route to finding a common denominator.

$$^2/_5 + {}^1/_6 =$$

Multiply the numerator and denominator of $^2/_5$ by 6, equaling $^{12}/_{30}$

Multiply the numerator and denominator of $^1/_6$ by 5, equaling $^5/_{30}$

$$^{12}/_{30} + {}^5/_{30} = {}^{17}/_{30}$$

Multiplying Fractions

When multiplying fractions, it is not necessary to find common denominators. Just multiply the two numerators in each fraction and the two denominators in each fraction.

$$^4/_7 \times {}^5/_8 = (4 \times 5)/(7 \times 8) = {}^{20}/_{56}$$

(*Note:* This fraction can be reduced to a simpler equivalent by dividing both the numerator and denominator by 4. The result is $^5/_{14}$.)

Dividing Fractions

When dividing a fraction by another fraction, invert the second fraction and multiply as above.

$$^1/_3 \div {}^2/_3 = {}^1/_3 \times {}^3/_2 = (1 \times 3) / (3 \times 2) = {}^3/_6$$

(*Note:* This can be reduced to a simpler equivalent by dividing both the numerator and denominator by 3. The result is one-half, $^1/_2$.)

SELF-QUIZ #3: Fractions

(Answers to this quiz can be found on page A-7.)

1. $^2/_5 + {}^1/_5 =$
2. $^2/_7 \times {}^4/_5 =$
3. $^{11}/_{15} - {}^2/_5 =$
4. $^3/_5 \div {}^6/_8 =$
5. $^3/_8 + {}^1/_4 =$
6. $^1/_8 \div {}^4/_5 =$
7. $^8/_9 - {}^5/_9 + {}^2/_9 =$
8. $^2/_7 + {}^1/_3 =$
9. $^4/_{15} \times {}^3/_5 =$
10. $^6/_7 - {}^3/_4 =$

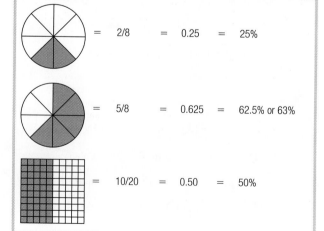

TABLE A.3 Proportions: Converting Fractions to Decimals to Percentages

=	2/8	= 0.25	= 25%
=	5/8	= 0.625	= 62.5% or 63%
=	10/20	= 0.50	= 50%

DECIMALS

Converting Decimals to Fractions

Decimals represent proportions of a whole similar to fractions. Each decimal place represents a factor of 10. So the first decimal place represents a number over 10, the second decimal place represents a number over 100, the third decimal place represents a number over 1000, the fourth decimal place represents a number over 10,000, and so on.

To convert a decimal to a fraction, take the number as the numerator and place it over 10, 100, 1000, and so on based on how many numbers are to the right of the decimal point. For example,

$$0.6 = {}^{6}/_{10} \qquad 0.58 = {}^{58}/_{100}$$
$$0.926 = {}^{926}/_{1000} \qquad 0.7841 = {}^{7841}/_{10,000}$$

Adding and Subtracting Decimals

When adding or subtracting decimal points, it is necessary to keep the decimal points in a vertical line. Then add or subtract each vertical row as you normally would.

$$\begin{array}{r} 3.83 \\ +1.358 \\ \hline 5.188 \end{array} \qquad \begin{array}{r} 4.4992 \\ -1.738 \\ \hline 2.7612 \end{array}$$

Multiplying Decimals

Multiplying decimals requires two basic steps. First, multiply the two decimals just as you would any numbers, paying no concern to where the decimal point is located. Once you have completed that operation, add the number of places to the right of the decimal in each number and count off that many decimal points in the solution line. That is your answer, which you may round up to three decimal places (two for the final answer).

$$\begin{array}{r} 4.26 \text{ (two decimal places)} \\ \times 0.398 \text{ (three decimal places)} \\ \hline 3408 \\ 3834 \\ 1278 \\ \hline 1.69548 \text{ (five decimal places)} \end{array}$$

$$\begin{array}{r} 0.532 \text{ (three decimal places)} \\ \times 0.8 \text{ (one decimal place)} \\ \hline 0.4256 \text{ (four decimal places)} \end{array}$$

Dividing Decimals

When dividing decimals, it is easiest to multiply each decimal by the factor of 10 associated with the number of places to the right of the decimal point. So, if one of the numbers has two numbers to the right of the decimal point and the other number has three, each number should be multiplied by 1000. For example,

$$0.7 \div 1.32 = {}^{0.7}/_{1.32}$$

Then multiply each side by the factor of 10 associated with the most spaces to the right of the decimal point in either number. In this case, that is 2, so we multiply each side by 100.

$$0.7 \times 100 = 70$$
$$1.32 \times 100 = 132$$

So, our new fraction is ${}^{70}/_{132}$.

SELF-QUIZ #4: Decimals

(Answers to this quiz can be found on page A-7.)

1. $1.83 \times 0.68 =$
2. $2.637 + 4.2 =$
3. $1.894 - 0.62 =$
4. $0.35 \div 0.7 =$
5. $3.419 \times 0.12 =$
6. ${}^{0.82}/_{1.74} =$
7. $0.125 \div 0.625 =$
8. $0.44 \times 0.163 =$
9. $0.8 + 1.239 =$
10. $13.288 - 4.46 =$

PERCENTAGES

Converting Percentages to Fractions or Decimals

Convert a percentage into a fraction by removing the percentage symbol and placing the number over a denominator of 100.

$$82\% = {}^{82}/_{100} \quad \text{or} \quad {}^{41}/_{50} \quad \text{or} \quad 0.82$$
$$20\% = {}^{20}/_{100} \quad \text{or} \quad {}^{1}/_{5} \quad \text{or} \quad 0.2$$

Multiplying with Percentages

In statistics, it is often necessary to determine the percentage of a whole number when analyzing data. To multiply with a percentage, convert the percentage to a decimal (Table A.3) and solve the equation. To convert a percentage to a decimal, remove the percentage symbol and move the decimal point two places to the left.

$$80\% \text{ of } 45 = 80\% \times 45 = 0.80 \times 45 = 36$$
$$25\% \text{ of } 94 = 25\% \times 94 = 0.25 \times 94 = 23.5$$

SELF-QUIZ #5: Percentages

(Answers to this quiz can be found on page A-7.)

1. $45\% \times 100 =$
2. $22\% \text{ of } 80 =$
3. $35\% \text{ of } 90 =$
4. $80\% \times 23 =$
5. $58\% \times 60 =$
6. $32 \times 16\% =$
7. $125 \times 73\% =$
8. $24 \times 75\% =$
9. $69\% \text{ of } 224 =$
10. $51\% \times 37 =$

A.5 Solving Equations With A Single Unknown Variable

When solving equations with an unknown variable, isolate the unknown variable on one side of the equation. By isolating the variable, you free up the other side of the equation so you can solve it to a single number, thus providing you with the value of the variable.

To isolate the variable, add, subtract, multiply, or divide each side of the equation to solve operations on the side of the equation that contains the variable (Table A.4).

SOLVING EQUATIONS WITH A SINGLE UNKNOWN VARIABLE: Worked Examples

1.
$$X + 12 = 42$$
$$X + 12 - 12 = 42 - 12$$
$$X = 30$$

2.
$$X - 13 = -5$$
$$X - 13 + 13 = -5 + 13$$
$$X = 8$$

3.
$$(X - 3)/6 = 2$$
$$(X - 3)/6 \times 6 = 2 \times 6$$
$$X - 3 = 12$$
$$X - 3 + 3 = 12 + 3$$
$$X = 15$$

4.
$$(3X + 4)/2 = 8$$
$$(3X + 4)/2 \times 2 = 8 \times 2$$
$$3X + 4 = 16$$
$$3X + 4 - 4 = 16 - 4$$
$$3X = 12$$
$$3X/3 = 12/3$$
$$X = 4$$

5.
$$(X - 2)/3 = 7$$
$$(X - 2)/3 \times 3 = 7 \times 3$$
$$X - 2 = 21$$
$$X - 2 + 2 = 21 + 2$$
$$X = 23$$

SELF-QUIZ #6: Solving Equations with a Single Unknown Variable

(Answers to this quiz can be found on page A.7.)

1. $7X = 42$
   $X =$

2. $87 - X + 16 = 57$
   $X =$

3. $X - 17 = -6$
   $X =$

4. $5X - 4 = 21$
   $X =$

5. $X - 10 = -4$
   $X =$

6. $X / 8 = 20$
   $X =$

7. $(X + 17)/3 = 10$
   $X =$

TABLE A.4 Solving Equations With A Single Variable

Addition
$$X + 7 = 18$$
$$X + 7 - 7 = 18 - 7$$
$$X = 11$$

Subtracting 7 from each side zeros the addition operation.

Subtraction
$$X - 13 = 27$$
$$X - 13 + 13 = 27 + 13$$
$$X = 40$$

Adding 13 to each side zeros the subtraction operation.

Multiplication
$$X \times 5 = 20$$
$$X \times 5/5 = 20/5$$
$$X = 4$$

Dividing each side by 5 zeros the multiplication operation.

Division
$$X/5 = 40$$
$$X/5 \times 5 = 40 \times 5$$
$$X = 200$$

Multiplying each side by 5 zeros the division operation.

Multiple Operations
$$4X + 6 = 18$$
$$4X + 6 - 6 = 18 - 6$$
$$4X = 12$$
$$4X/4 = 12/4$$
$$X = 3$$

When isolating a variable, work *backward* through the order of operations (see Table A.2). Isolate addition and subtraction operations first. Then isolate operations for multiplication and division.

---

8. $2(X + 4) = 24$
   $X =$

9. $X(3 + 12) - 20 = 40$
   $X =$

10. $34 - X/6 = 27$
    $X =$

A.6 Answers To Diagnostic Test And Self-Quizzes

Answers to Diagnostic Test

Section 1

1. 28; 2. −24; 3. 29; 4. 48; 5. −4; 6. 19; 7. 4; 8. 18; 9. −14; 10. 7

Section 2

1. 0; 2. 28; 3. −1; 4. 16; 5. 20; 6. 16; 7. −4; 8. 2; 9. 7; 10. 16

Section 3

1. $^{42}/_{100}$ or $^{21}/_{50}$; 2. 0.6; 3. 80%; 4. $^{10}/_{13}$; 5. 0.336; 6. 48; 7. $^{24}/_{35}$; 8. 32; 9. $^{3}/_{4}$; 10. $^{20}/_{63}$

Section 4

1. 4; 2. 5; 3. 24; 4. 6; 5. 6; 6. 12; 7. 7; 8. 12; 9. 6; 10. 2

Answers for Self-Quiz #1: Symbols and Notation

1. 28; 2. 18; 3. −9; 4. −9; 5. 36; 6. 7; 7. −48; 8. 8; 9. 15; 10. 28

Answers for Self-Quiz #2: Order of Operations

1. 19; 2. 2; 3. −4; 4. 4; 5. 3; 6. −5; 7. 20; 8. 30; 9. 12; 10. 213

Answers for Self-Quiz #3: Fractions

1. $^3/_5$; 2. $^8/_{35}$; 3. $^1/_3$ or $^5/_{15}$ or $^{25}/_{75}$; 4. $^{24}/_{30}$ or $^4/_5$; 5. $^5/_8$; 6. $^5/_{32}$; 7. $^5/_9$; 8. $^{13}/_{21}$; 9. $^{12}/_{75}$ or $^4/_{25}$; 10. $^3/_{28}$

Answers for Self-Quiz #4: Decimals

1. 1.244; 2. 6.837; 3. 1.274; 4. $^{35}/_{70}$ or $^1/_2$ or 0.5; 5. 0.41028; 6. $^{82}/_{174}$ or $^{41}/_{87}$ or 0.47; 7. $^{125}/_{625}$ or $^1/_5$ or 0.2; 8. 0.07172; 9. 2.039; 10. 8.828

Answers for Self-Quiz #5: Percentages

1. 45; 2. 17.6; 3. 31.5; 4. 18.4; 5. 34.8; 6. 5.12; 7. 91.25; 8. 18; 9. 154.56; 10. 18.87

Answers for Self-Quiz #6: Solving Equations with a Single Unknown Variable

1. 6; 2. 46; 3. 11; 4. 5; 5. 6; 6. 160; 7. 13; 8. 8; 9. 4; 10. 42

Statistical Tables

TABLE B.1 THE z DISTRIBUTION

Normal curve columns represent percentage between the mean and the
z score and percentage beyond the z score in the tail.

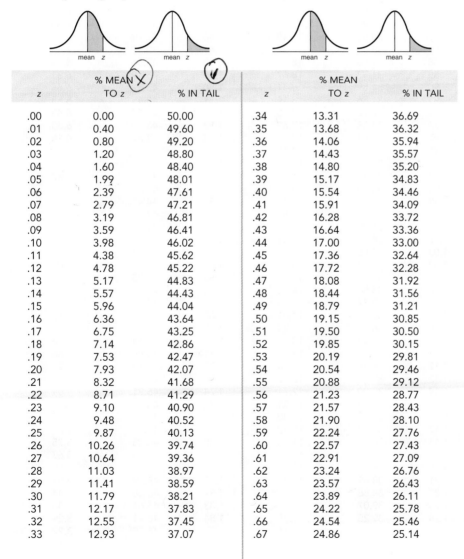

z	% MEAN TO z	% IN TAIL	z	% MEAN TO z	% IN TAIL
.00	0.00	50.00	.34	13.31	36.69
.01	0.40	49.60	.35	13.68	36.32
.02	0.80	49.20	.36	14.06	35.94
.03	1.20	48.80	.37	14.43	35.57
.04	1.60	48.40	.38	14.80	35.20
.05	1.99	48.01	.39	15.17	34.83
.06	2.39	47.61	.40	15.54	34.46
.07	2.79	47.21	.41	15.91	34.09
.08	3.19	46.81	.42	16.28	33.72
.09	3.59	46.41	.43	16.64	33.36
.10	3.98	46.02	.44	17.00	33.00
.11	4.38	45.62	.45	17.36	32.64
.12	4.78	45.22	.46	17.72	32.28
.13	5.17	44.83	.47	18.08	31.92
.14	5.57	44.43	.48	18.44	31.56
.15	5.96	44.04	.49	18.79	31.21
.16	6.36	43.64	.50	19.15	30.85
.17	6.75	43.25	.51	19.50	30.50
.18	7.14	42.86	.52	19.85	30.15
.19	7.53	42.47	.53	20.19	29.81
.20	7.93	42.07	.54	20.54	29.46
.21	8.32	41.68	.55	20.88	29.12
.22	8.71	41.29	.56	21.23	28.77
.23	9.10	40.90	.57	21.57	28.43
.24	9.48	40.52	.58	21.90	28.10
.25	9.87	40.13	.59	22.24	27.76
.26	10.26	39.74	.60	22.57	27.43
.27	10.64	39.36	.61	22.91	27.09
.28	11.03	38.97	.62	23.24	26.76
.29	11.41	38.59	.63	23.57	26.43
.30	11.79	38.21	.64	23.89	26.11
.31	12.17	37.83	.65	24.22	25.78
.32	12.55	37.45	.66	24.54	25.46
.33	12.93	37.07	.67	24.86	25.14

z	% MEAN TO z	% IN TAIL	z	% MEAN TO z	% IN TAIL
.68	25.17	24.83	1.28	39.97	10.03
.69	25.49	24.51	1.29	40.15	9.85
.70	25.80	24.20	1.30	40.32	9.68
.71	26.11	23.89	1.31	40.49	9.51
.72	26.42	23.58	1.32	40.66	9.34
.73	26.73	23.27	1.33	40.82	9.18
.74	27.04	22.96	1.34	40.99	9.01
.75	27.34	22.66	1.35	41.15	8.85
.76	27.64	22.36	1.36	41.31	8.69
.77	27.94	22.06	1.37	41.47	8.53
.78	28.23	21.77	1.38	41.62	8.38
.79	28.52	21.48	1.39	41.77	8.23
.80	28.81	21.19	1.40	41.92	8.08
.81	29.10	20.90	1.41	42.07	7.93
.82	29.39	20.61	1.42	42.22	7.78
.83	29.67	20.33	1.43	42.36	7.64
.84	29.95	20.05	1.44	42.51	7.49
.85	30.23	19.77	1.45	42.65	7.35
.86	30.51	19.49	1.46	42.79	7.21
.87	30.78	19.22	1.47	42.92	7.08
.88	31.06	18.94	1.48	43.06	6.94
.89	31.33	18.67	1.49	43.19	6.81
.90	31.59	18.41	1.50	43.32	6.68
.91	31.86	18.14	1.51	43.45	6.55
.92	32.12	17.88	1.52	43.57	6.43
.93	32.38	17.62	1.53	43.70	6.30
.94	32.64	17.36	1.54	43.82	6.18
.95	32.89	17.11	1.55	43.94	6.06
.96	33.15	16.85	1.56	44.06	5.94
.97	33.40	16.60	1.57	44.18	5.82
.98	33.65	16.35	1.58	44.29	5.71
.99	33.89	16.11	1.59	44.41	5.59
1.00	34.13	15.87	1.60	44.52	5.48
1.01	34.38	15.62	1.61	44.63	5.37
1.02	34.61	15.39	1.62	44.74	5.26
1.03	34.85	15.15	1.63	44.84	5.16
1.04	35.08	14.92	1.64	44.95	5.05
1.05	35.31	14.69	1.65	45.05	4.95
1.06	35.54	14.46	1.66	45.15	4.85
1.07	35.77	14.23	1.67	45.25	4.75
1.08	35.99	14.01	1.68	45.35	4.65
1.09	36.21	13.79	1.69	45.45	4.55
1.10	36.43	13.57	1.70	45.54	4.46
1.11	36.65	13.35	1.71	45.64	4.36
1.12	36.86	13.14	1.72	45.73	4.27
1.13	37.08	12.92	1.73	45.82	4.18
1.14	37.29	12.71	1.74	45.91	4.09
1.15	37.49	12.51	1.75	45.99	4.01
1.16	37.70	12.30	1.76	46.08	3.92
1.17	37.90	12.10	1.77	46.16	3.84
1.18	38.10	11.90	1.78	46.25	3.75
1.19	38.30	11.70	1.79	46.33	3.67
1.20	38.49	11.51	1.80	46.41	3.59
1.21	38.69	11.31	1.81	46.49	3.51
1.22	38.88	11.12	1.82	46.56	3.44
1.23	39.07	10.93	1.83	46.64	3.36
1.24	39.25	10.75	1.84	46.71	3.29
1.25	39.44	10.56	1.85	46.78	3.22
1.26	39.62	10.38	1.86	46.86	3.14
1.27	39.80	10.20	1.87	46.93	3.07

TABLE B.1 continued

z	% MEAN TO z	% IN TAIL	z	% MEAN TO z	% IN TAIL
1.88	46.99	3.01	2.46	49.31	.69
1.89	47.06	2.94	2.47	49.32	.68
1.90	47.13	2.87	2.48	49.34	.66
1.91	47.19	2.81	2.49	49.36	.64
1.92	47.26	2.74	2.50	49.38	.62
1.93	47.32	2.68	2.51	49.40	.60
1.94	47.38	2.62	2.52	49.41	.59
1.95	47.44	2.56	2.53	49.43	.57
1.96	47.50	2.50	2.54	49.45	.55
1.97	47.56	2.44	2.55	49.46	.54
1.98	47.61	2.39	2.56	49.48	.52
1.99	47.67	2.33	2.57	49.49	.51
2.00	47.72	2.28	2.58	49.51	.49
2.01	47.78	2.22	2.59	49.52	.48
2.02	47.83	2.17	2.60	49.53	.47
2.03	47.88	2.12	2.61	49.55	.45
2.04	47.93	2.07	2.62	49.56	.44
2.05	47.98	2.02	2.63	49.57	.43
2.06	48.03	1.97	2.64	49.59	.41
2.07	48.08	1.92	2.65	49.60	.40
2.08	48.12	1.88	2.66	49.61	.39
2.09	48.17	1.83	2.67	49.62	.38
2.10	48.21	1.79	2.68	49.63	.37
2.11	48.26	1.74	2.69	49.64	.36
2.12	48.30	1.70	2.70	49.65	.35
2.13	48.34	1.66	2.71	49.66	.34
2.14	48.38	1.62	2.72	49.67	.33
2.15	48.42	1.58	2.73	49.68	.32
2.16	48.46	1.54	2.74	49.69	.31
2.17	48.50	1.50	2.75	49.70	.30
2.18	48.54	1.46	2.76	49.71	.29
2.19	48.57	1.43	2.77	49.72	.28
2.20	48.61	1.39	2.78	49.73	.27
2.21	48.64	1.36	2.79	49.74	.26
2.22	48.68	1.32	2.80	49.74	.26
2.23	48.71	1.29	2.81	49.75	.25
2.24	48.75	1.25	2.82	49.76	.24
2.25	48.78	1.22	2.83	49.77	.23
2.26	48.81	1.19	2.84	49.77	.23
2.27	48.84	1.16	2.85	49.78	.22
2.28	48.87	1.13	2.86	49.79	.21
2.29	48.90	1.10	2.87	49.79	.21
2.30	48.93	1.07	2.88	49.80	.20
2.31	48.96	1.04	2.89	49.81	.19
2.32	48.98	1.02	2.90	49.81	.19
2.33	49.01	.99	2.91	49.82	.18
2.34	49.04	.96	2.92	49.82	.18
2.35	49.06	.94	2.93	49.83	.17
2.36	49.09	.91	2.94	49.84	.16
2.37	49.11	.89	2.95	49.84	.16
2.38	49.13	.87	2.96	49.85	.15
2.39	49.16	.84	2.97	49.85	.15
2.40	49.18	.82	2.98	49.86	.14
2.41	49.20	.80	2.99	49.86	.14
2.42	49.22	.78	3.00	49.87	.13
2.43	49.25	.75	3.50	49.98	.02
2.44	49.27	.73	4.00	50.00	.00
2.45	49.29	.71	4.50	50.00	.00

TABLE B.2 THE *t* DISTRIBUTIONS

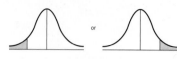

One-Tailed Tests   **Two-Tailed Tests**

df	.10	.05	.01	.10	.05	.01
1	3.078	6.314	31.821	6.314	12.706	63.657
2	1.886	2.920	6.965	2.920	4.303	9.925
3	1.638	2.353	4.541	2.353	3.182	5.841
4	1.533	2.132	3.747	2.132	2.776	4.604
5	1.476	2.015	3.365	2.015	2.571	4.032
6	1.440	1.943	3.143	1.943	2.447	3.708
7	1.415	1.895	2.998	1.895	2.365	3.500
8	1.397	1.860	2.897	1.860	2.306	3.356
9	1.383	1.833	2.822	1.833	2.262	3.250
10	1.372	1.813	2.764	1.813	2.228	3.170
11	1.364	1.796	2.718	1.796	2.201	3.106
12	1.356	1.783	2.681	1.783	2.179	3.055
13	1.350	1.771	2.651	1.771	2.161	3.013
14	1.345	1.762	2.625	1.762	2.145	2.977
15	1.341	1.753	2.603	1.753	2.132	2.947
16	1.337	1.746	2.584	1.746	2.120	2.921
17	1.334	1.740	2.567	1.740	2.110	2.898
18	1.331	1.734	2.553	1.734	2.101	2.879
19	1.328	1.729	2.540	1.729	2.093	2.861
20	1.326	1.725	2.528	1.725	2.086	2.846
21	1.323	1.721	2.518	1.721	2.080	2.832
22	1.321	1.717	2.509	1.717	2.074	2.819
23	1.320	1.714	2.500	1.714	2.069	2.808
24	1.318	1.711	2.492	1.711	2.064	2.797
25	1.317	1.708	2.485	1.708	2.060	2.788
26	1.315	1.706	2.479	1.706	2.056	2.779
27	1.314	1.704	2.473	1.704	2.052	2.771
28	1.313	1.701	2.467	1.701	2.049	2.764
29	1.312	1.699	2.462	1.699	2.045	2.757
30	1.311	1.698	2.458	1.698	2.043	2.750
35	1.306	1.690	2.438	1.690	2.030	2.724
40	1.303	1.684	2.424	1.684	2.021	2.705
60	1.296	1.671	2.390	1.671	2.001	2.661
80	1.292	1.664	2.374	1.664	1.990	2.639
100	1.290	1.660	2.364	1.660	1.984	2.626
120	1.289	1.658	2.358	1.658	1.980	2.617
∞	1.282	1.645	2.327	1.645	1.960	2.576

TABLE B.3 THE *F* DISTRIBUTIONS

WITHIN-GROUPS df	SIGNIFICANCE (p) LEVEL	BETWEEN-GROUPS DEGREES OF FREEDOM					
		1	2	3	4	5	6
1	.01	4,052	5,000	5,404	5,625	5,764	5,859
	.05	162	200	216	225	230	234
	.10	39.9	49.5	53.6	55.8	57.2	58.2
2	.01	98.50	99.00	99.17	99.25	99.30	99.33
	.05	18.51	19.00	19.17	19.25	19.30	19.33
	.10	8.53	9.00	9.16	9.24	9.29	9.33

WITHIN-GROUPS *df*	SIGNIF-ICANCE (*p*) LEVEL	BETWEEN-GROUPS DEGREES OF FREEDOM					
		1	2	3	4	5	6
3	.01	34.12	30.82	29.46	28.71	28.24	27.91
	.05	10.13	9.55	9.28	9.12	9.01	8.94
	.10	5.54	5.46	5.39	5.34	5.31	5.28
4	.01	21.20	18.00	16.70	15.98	15.52	15.21
	.05	7.71	6.95	6.59	6.39	6.26	6.16
	.10	4.55	4.33	4.19	4.11	4.05	4.01
5	.01	16.26	13.27	12.06	11.39	10.97	10.67
	.05	6.61	5.79	5.41	5.19	5.05	4.95
	.10	4.06	3.78	3.62	3.52	3.45	3.41
6	.01	13.75	10.93	9.78	9.15	8.75	8.47
	.05	5.99	5.14	4.76	4.53	4.39	4.28
	.10	3.78	3.46	3.29	3.18	3.11	3.06
7	.01	12.25	9.55	8.45	7.85	7.46	7.19
	.05	5.59	4.74	4.35	4.12	3.97	3.87
	.10	3.59	3.26	3.08	2.96	2.88	2.83
8	.01	11.26	8.65	7.59	7.01	6.63	6.37
	.05	5.32	4.46	4.07	3.84	3.69	3.58
	.10	3.46	3.11	2.92	2.81	2.73	2.67
9	.01	10.56	8.02	6.99	6.42	6.06	5.80
	.05	5.12	4.26	3.86	3.63	3.48	3.37
	.10	3.36	3.01	2.81	2.69	2.61	2.55
10	.01	10.05	7.56	6.55	6.00	5.64	5.39
	.05	4.97	4.10	3.71	3.48	3.33	3.22
	.10	3.29	2.93	2.73	2.61	2.52	2.46
11	.01	9.65	7.21	6.22	5.67	5.32	5.07
	.05	4.85	3.98	3.59	3.36	3.20	3.10
	.10	3.23	2.86	2.66	2.54	2.45	2.39
12	.01	9.33	6.93	5.95	5.41	5.07	4.82
	.05	4.75	3.89	3.49	3.26	3.11	3.00
	.10	3.18	2.81	2.61	2.48	2.40	2.33
13	.01	9.07	6.70	5.74	5.21	4.86	4.62
	.05	4.67	3.81	3.41	3.18	3.03	2.92
	.10	3.14	2.76	2.56	2.43	2.35	2.28
14	.01	8.86	6.52	5.56	5.04	4.70	4.46
	.05	4.60	3.74	3.34	3.11	2.96	2.85
	.10	3.10	2.73	2.52	2.40	2.31	2.24
15	.01	8.68	6.36	5.42	4.89	4.56	4.32
	.05	4.54	3.68	3.29	3.06	2.90	2.79
	.10	3.07	2.70	2.49	2.36	2.27	2.21
16	.01	8.53	6.23	5.29	4.77	4.44	4.20
	.05	4.49	3.63	3.24	3.01	2.85	2.74
	.10	3.05	2.67	2.46	2.33	2.24	2.18
17	.01	8.40	6.11	5.19	4.67	4.34	4.10
	.05	4.45	3.59	3.20	2.97	2.81	2.70
	.10	3.03	2.65	2.44	2.31	2.22	2.15
18	.01	8.29	6.01	5.09	4.58	4.25	4.02
	.05	4.41	3.56	3.16	2.93	2.77	2.66
	.10	3.01	2.62	2.42	2.29	2.20	2.13
19	.01	8.19	5.93	5.01	4.50	4.17	3.94
	.05	4.38	3.52	3.13	2.90	2.74	2.63
	.10	2.99	2.61	2.40	2.27	2.18	2.11

WITHIN-GROUPS df	SIGNIF-ICANCE (p) LEVEL	BETWEEN-GROUPS DEGREES OF FREEDOM					
		1	2	3	4	5	6
20	.01	8.10	5.85	4.94	4.43	4.10	3.87
	.05	4.35	3.49	3.10	2.87	2.71	2.60
	.10	2.98	2.59	2.38	2.25	2.16	2.09
21	.01	8.02	5.78	4.88	4.37	4.04	3.81
	.05	4.33	3.47	3.07	2.84	2.69	2.57
	.10	2.96	2.58	2.37	2.23	2.14	2.08
22	.01	7.95	5.72	4.82	4.31	3.99	3.76
	.05	4.30	3.44	3.05	2.82	2.66	2.55
	.10	2.95	2.56	2.35	2.22	2.13	2.06
23	.01	7.88	5.66	4.77	4.26	3.94	3.71
	.05	4.28	3.42	3.03	2.80	2.64	2.53
	.10	2.94	2.55	2.34	2.21	2.12	2.05
24	.01	7.82	5.61	4.72	4.22	3.90	3.67
	.05	4.26	3.40	3.01	2.78	2.62	2.51
	.10	2.93	2.54	2.33	2.20	2.10	2.04
25	.01	7.77	5.57	4.68	4.18	3.86	3.63
	.05	4.24	3.39	2.99	2.76	2.60	2.49
	.10	2.92	2.53	2.32	2.19	2.09	2.03
26	.01	7.72	5.53	4.64	4.14	3.82	3.59
	.05	4.23	3.37	2.98	2.74	2.59	2.48
	.10	2.91	2.52	2.31	2.18	2.08	2.01
27	.01	7.68	5.49	4.60	4.11	3.79	3.56
	.05	4.21	3.36	2.96	2.73	2.57	2.46
	.10	2.90	2.51	2.30	2.17	2.07	2.01
28	.01	7.64	5.45	4.57	4.08	3.75	3.53
	.05	4.20	3.34	2.95	2.72	2.56	2.45
	.10	2.89	2.50	2.29	2.16	2.07	2.00
29	.01	7.60	5.42	4.54	4.05	3.73	3.50
	.05	4.18	3.33	2.94	2.70	2.55	2.43
	.10	2.89	2.50	2.28	2.15	2.06	1.99
30	.01	7.56	5.39	4.51	4.02	3.70	3.47
	.05	4.17	3.32	2.92	2.69	2.53	2.42
	.10	2.88	2.49	2.28	2.14	2.05	1.98
35	.01	7.42	5.27	4.40	3.91	3.59	3.37
	.05	4.12	3.27	2.88	2.64	2.49	2.37
	.10	2.86	2.46	2.25	2.11	2.02	1.95
40	.01	7.32	5.18	4.31	3.83	3.51	3.29
	.05	4.09	3.23	2.84	2.61	2.45	2.34
	.10	2.84	2.44	2.23	2.09	2.00	1.93
45	.01	7.23	5.11	4.25	3.77	3.46	3.23
	.05	4.06	3.21	2.81	2.58	2.42	2.31
	.10	2.82	2.43	2.21	2.08	1.98	1.91
50	.01	7.17	5.06	4.20	3.72	3.41	3.19
	.05	4.04	3.18	2.79	2.56	2.40	2.29
	.10	2.81	2.41	2.20	2.06	1.97	1.90
55	.01	7.12	5.01	4.16	3.68	3.37	3.15
	.05	4.02	3.17	2.77	2.54	2.38	2.27
	.10	2.80	2.40	2.19	2.05	1.96	1.89
60	.01	7.08	4.98	4.13	3.65	3.34	3.12
	.05	4.00	3.15	2.76	2.53	2.37	2.26
	.10	2.79	2.39	2.18	2.04	1.95	1.88

TABLE B.3 continued

WITHIN-GROUPS df	SIGNIF-ICANCE (p) LEVEL	BETWEEN-GROUPS DEGREES OF FREEDOM					
		1	2	3	4	5	6
65	.01	**7.04**	**4.95**	**4.10**	**3.62**	**3.31**	**3.09**
	.05	3.99	3.14	2.75	2.51	2.36	2.24
	.10	2.79	2.39	2.17	2.03	1.94	1.87
70	.01	**7.01**	**4.92**	**4.08**	**3.60**	**3.29**	**3.07**
	.05	3.98	3.13	2.74	2.50	2.35	2.23
	.10	2.78	2.38	2.16	2.03	1.93	1.86
75	.01	**6.99**	**4.90**	**4.06**	**3.58**	**3.27**	**3.05**
	.05	3.97	3.12	2.73	2.49	2.34	2.22
	.10	2.77	2.38	2.16	2.02	1.93	1.86
80	.01	**6.96**	**4.88**	**4.04**	**3.56**	**3.26**	**3.04**
	.05	3.96	3.11	2.72	2.49	2.33	2.22
	.10	2.77	2.37	2.15	2.02	1.92	1.85
85	.01	**6.94**	**4.86**	**4.02**	**3.55**	**3.24**	**3.02**
	.05	3.95	3.10	2.71	2.48	2.32	2.21
	.10	2.77	2.37	2.15	2.01	1.92	1.85
90	.01	**6.93**	**4.85**	**4.01**	**3.54**	**3.23**	**3.01**
	.05	3.95	3.10	2.71	2.47	2.32	2.20
	.10	2.76	2.36	2.15	2.01	1.91	1.84
95	.01	**6.91**	**4.84**	**4.00**	**3.52**	**3.22**	**3.00**
	.05	3.94	3.09	2.70	2.47	2.31	2.20
	.10	2.76	2.36	2.14	2.01	1.91	1.84
100	.01	**6.90**	**4.82**	**3.98**	**3.51**	**3.21**	**2.99**
	.05	3.94	3.09	2.70	2.46	2.31	2.19
	.10	2.76	2.36	2.14	2.00	1.91	1.83
200	.01	**6.76**	**4.71**	**3.88**	**3.41**	**3.11**	**2.89**
	.05	3.89	3.04	2.65	2.42	2.26	2.14
	.10	273	2.33	2.11	1.97	1.88	1.80
1000	.01	**6.66**	**4.63**	**3.80**	**3.34**	**3.04**	**2.82**
	.05	3.85	3.00	2.61	2.38	2.22	2.11
	.10	2.71	2.31	2.09	1.95	1.85	1.78
∞	.01	**6.64**	**4.61**	**3.78**	**3.32**	**3.02**	**2.80**
	.05	3.84	3.00	2.61	2.37	2.22	2.10
	.10	2.71	2.30	2.08	1.95	1.85	1.78

TABLE B.4 THE CHI-SQUARE DISTRIBUTIONS

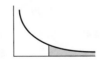

df	SIGNIFICANCE (p) LEVEL		
	.10	.05	.01
1	2.706	3.841	6.635
2	4.605	5.992	9.211
3	6.252	7.815	11.345
4	7.780	9.488	13.277
5	9.237	11.071	15.087
6	10.645	12.592	16.812
7	12.017	14.067	18.475
8	13.362	15.507	20.090
9	14.684	16.919	21.666
10	15.987	18.307	23.209

TABLE B.5 THE q STATISTIC (TUKEY *HSD* TEST)

WITHIN-GROUPS df	SIGNIF-ICANCE (p) LEVEL	2	3	4	5	6	7	8	9	10	11	12
						k = NUMBER OF TREATMENTS (LEVELS)						
5	.05	3.64	4.60	5.22	5.67	6.03	6.33	6.58	6.80	6.99	7.17	7.32
	.01	5.70	6.98	7.80	8.42	8.91	9.32	9.67	9.97	10.24	10.48	10.70
6	.05	3.46	4.34	4.90	5.30	5.63	5.90	6.12	6.32	6.49	6.65	6.79
	.01	5.24	6.33	7.03	7.56	7.97	8.32	8.61	8.87	9.10	9.30	9.48
7	.05	3.34	4.16	4.68	5.06	5.36	5.61	5.82	6.00	6.16	6.30	6.43
	.01	4.95	5.92	6.54	7.01	7.37	7.68	7.94	8.17	8.37	8.55	8.71
8	.05	3.26	4.04	4.53	4.89	5.17	5.40	5.60	5.77	5.92	6.05	6.18
	.01	4.75	5.64	6.20	6.62	6.96	7.24	7.47	7.68	7.86	8.03	8.18
9	.05	3.20	3.95	4.41	4.76	5.02	5.24	5.43	5.59	5.74	5.87	5.98
	.01	4.60	5.43	5.96	6.35	6.66	6.91	7.13	7.33	7.49	7.65	7.78
10	.05	3.15	3.88	4.33	4.65	4.91	5.12	5.30	5.46	5.60	5.72	5.83
	.01	4.48	5.27	5.77	6.14	6.43	6.67	6.87	7.05	7.21	7.36	7.49
11	.05	3.11	3.82	4.26	4.57	4.82	5.03	5.20	5.35	5.49	5.61	5.71
	.01	4.39	5.15	5.62	5.97	6.25	6.48	6.67	6.84	6.99	7.13	7.25
12	.05	3.08	3.77	4.20	4.51	4.75	4.95	5.12	5.27	5.39	5.51	5.61
	.01	4.32	5.05	5.50	5.84	6.10	6.32	6.51	6.67	6.81	6.94	7.06
13	.05	3.06	3.73	4.15	4.45	4.69	4.88	5.05	5.19	5.32	5.43	5.53
	.01	4.26	4.96	5.40	5.73	5.98	6.19	6.37	6.53	6.67	6.79	6.90
14	.05	3.03	3.70	4.11	4.41	4.64	4.83	4.99	5.13	5.25	5.36	5.46
	.01	4.21	4.89	5.32	5.63	5.88	6.08	6.26	6.41	6.54	6.66	6.77
15	.05	3.01	3.67	4.08	4.37	4.59	4.78	4.94	5.08	5.20	5.31	5.40
	.01	4.17	4.84	5.25	5.56	5.80	5.99	6.16	6.31	6.44	6.55	6.66
16	.05	3.00	3.65	4.05	4.33	4.56	4.74	4.90	5.03	5.15	5.26	5.35
	.01	4.13	4.79	5.19	5.49	5.72	5.92	6.08	6.22	6.35	6.46	6.56
17	.05	2.98	3.63	4.02	4.30	4.52	4.70	4.86	4.99	5.11	5.21	5.31
	.01	4.10	4.74	5.14	5.43	5.66	5.85	6.01	6.15	6.27	6.38	6.48
18	.05	2.97	3.61	4.00	4.28	4.49	4.67	4.82	4.96	5.07	5.17	5.27
	.01	4.07	4.70	5.09	5.38	5.60	5.79	5.94	6.08	6.20	6.31	6.41
19	.05	2.96	3.59	3.98	4.25	4.47	4.65	4.79	4.92	5.04	5.14	5.23
	.01	4.05	4.67	5.05	5.33	5.55	5.73	5.89	6.02	6.14	6.25	634
20	.05	2.95	3.58	3.96	4.23	4.45	4.62	4.77	4.90	5.01	5.11	5.20
	.01	4.02	4.64	5.02	5.29	5.51	5.69	5.84	5.97	6.09	6.19	6.28
24	.05	2.92	3.53	3.90	4.17	4.37	4.54	4.68	4.81	4.92	5.01	5.10
	.01	3.96	4.55	4.91	5.17	5.37	5.54	5.69	5.81	5.92	6.02	6.11
30	.05	2.89	3.49	3.85	4.10	4.30	4.46	4.60	4.72	4.82	4.92	5.00
	.01	3.89	4.45	4.80	5.05	5.24	5.40	5.54	5.65	5.76	5.85	5.93

WITHIN-GROUPS df	SIGNIF-ICANCE (p) LEVEL	\(k\) = NUMBER OF TREATMENTS (LEVELS)										
		2	3	4	5	6	7	8	9	10	11	12
40	.05	2.86	3.44	3.79	4.04	4.23	4.39	4.52	4.63	4.73	4.82	4.90
	.01	3.82	4.37	4.70	4.93	5.11	5.26	5.39	5.50	5.60	5.69	5.76
60	.05	2.83	3.40	3.74	3.98	4.16	4.31	4.44	4.55	4.65	4.73	4.81
	.01	3.76	4.28	4.59	4.82	4.99	5.13	5.25	5.36	5.45	5.53	5.60
120	.05	2.80	3.36	3.68	3.92	4.10	4.24	4.36	4.47	4.56	4.64	4.71
	.01	3.70	4.20	4.50	4.71	4.87	5.01	5.12	5.21	5.30	5.37	5.44
∞	.05	2.77	3.31	3.63	3.86	4.03	4.17	4.28	4.39	4.47	4.55	4.62
	.01	3.64	4.12	4.40	4.60	4.76	4.88	4.99	5.08	5.16	5.23	5.29

TABLE B.6 THE PEARSON CORRELATION COEFFICIENT

To be significant, the sample correlation coefficient, *r*, must be greater than or equal to the critical value in the table.

LEVEL OF SIGNIFICANCE FOR ONE-TAILED TEST			LEVEL OF SIGNIFICANCE FOR TWO-TAILED TEST		
df = N − 2	.005	.01	df = N − 2	.05	.01
1	.988	.9995	1	.997	.9999
2	.900	.980	2	.950	.990
3	.805	.934	3	.878	.959
4	.729	.882	4	.811	.917
5	.669	.833	5	.754	.874
6	.622	.789	6	.707	.834
7	.582	.750	7	.666	.798
8	.549	.716	8	.632	.765
9	.521	.685	9	.602	.735
10	.497	.658	10	.576	.708
11	.476	.634	11	.553	.684
12	.458	.612	12	.532	.661
13	.441	.592	13	.514	.641
14	.426	.574	14	.497	.623
15	.412	.558	15	.482	.606
16	.400	.542	16	.468	.590
17	.389	.528	17	.456	.575
18	.378	.516	18	.444	.561
19	.369	.503	19	.433	.549
20	.360	.492	20	.423	.537
21	.352	.482	21	.413	.526
22	.344	.472	22	.404	.515
23	.337	.462	23	.396	.505
24	.330	.453	24	.388	.496
25	.323	.445	25	.381	.487
26	.317	.437	26	.374	.479
27	.311	.430	27	.367	.471
28	.306	.423	28	.361	.463
29	.301	.416	29	.355	.456
30	.296	.409	30	.349	.449
35	.275	.381	35	.325	.418
40	.257	.358	40	.304	.393
45	.243	.338	45	.288	.372
50	.231	.322	50	.273	.354
60	.211	.295	60	.250	.325

	LEVEL OF SIGNIFICANCE FOR ONE-TAILED TEST			LEVEL OF SIGNIFICANCE FOR TWO-TAILED TEST	
$df = N - 2$	.05	.01	$df = N - 2$	.05	.01
70	.195	.274	70	.232	.302
80	.183	.256	80	.217	.283
90	.173	.242	90	.205	.267
100	.164	.230	100	.195	.254

TABLE B.7 THE SPEARMAN CORRELATION COEFFICIENT

To be significant, the sample correlation coefficient, r_s, must be greater than or equal to the critical value in the table.

	LEVEL OF SIGNIFICANCE FOR ONE-TAILED TEST			LEVEL OF SIGNIFICANCE FOR TWO-TAILED TEST	
N	.05	.01	N	.05	.01
4	1.000	—	4	—	—
5	0.900	1.000	5	1.000	—
6	0.829	0.943	6	0.886	1.000
7	0.714	0.893	7	0.786	0.929
8	0.643	0.833	8	0.738	0.881
9	0.600	0.783	9	0.700	0.833
10	0.564	0.745	10	0.648	0.794
11	0.536	0.709	11	0.618	0.755
12	0.503	0.671	12	0.587	0.727
13	0.484	0.648	13	0.560	0.703
14	0.464	0.622	14	0.538	0.675
15	0.443	0.604	15	0.521	0.654
16	0.429	0.582	16	0.503	0.635
17	0.414	0.566	17	0.485	0.615
18	0.401	0.550	18	0.472	0.600
19	0.391	0.535	19	0.460	0.584
20	0.380	0.520	20	0.447	0.570
21	0.370	0.508	21	0.435	0.556
22	0.361	0.496	22	0.425	0.544
23	0.353	0.486	23	0.415	0.532
24	0.344	0.476	24	0.406	0.521
25	0.337	0.466	25	0.398	0.511
26	0.331	0.457	26	0.390	0.501
27	0.324	0.448	27	0.382	0.491
28	0.317	0.440	28	0.375	0.483
29	0.312	0.433	29	0.368	0.475
30	0.306	0.425	30	0.362	0.467
35	0.283	0.394	35	0.335	0.433
40	0.264	0.368	40	0.313	0.405
45	0.248	0.347	45	0.294	0.382
50	0.235	0.329	50	0.279	0.363
60	0.214	0.300	60	0.255	0.331
70	0.190	0.278	70	0.235	0.307
80	0.185	0.260	80	0.220	0.287
90	0.174	0.245	90	0.207	0.271
100	0.165	0.233	100	0.197	0.257

TABLE B.8A MANN-WHITNEY U FOR A p LEVEL OF .05 FOR A ONE-TAILED TEST

To be statistically significant, the smaller U must be equal to or less than the value in the table.

N_A/N_B	1	2	3	4	5	6	7	8	9	10	11	12	13	14	15	16	17	18	19	20
1	—	—	—	—	—	—	—	—	—	—	—	—	—	—	—	—	—	—	0	0
2	—	—	—	—	0	0	0	1	1	1	1	2	2	2	3	3	3	4	4	4
3	—	—	0	0	1	2	2	3	3	4	5	5	6	7	7	8	9	9	10	11
4	—	—	0	1	2	3	4	5	6	7	8	9	10	11	12	14	15	16	17	18
5	—	0	1	2	4	5	6	8	9	11	12	13	15	16	18	19	20	22	23	25
6	—	0	2	3	5	7	8	10	12	14	16	17	19	21	23	25	26	28	30	32
7	—	0	2	4	6	8	11	13	15	17	19	21	24	26	28	30	33	35	37	39
8	—	1	3	5	8	10	13	15	18	20	23	26	28	31	33	36	39	41	44	47
9	—	1	3	6	9	12	15	18	21	24	27	30	33	36	39	42	45	48	51	54
10	—	1	4	7	11	14	17	20	24	27	31	34	37	41	44	48	51	55	58	62
11	—	1	5	8	12	16	19	23	27	31	34	38	42	46	50	54	57	61	65	69
12	—	2	5	9	13	17	21	26	30	34	38	42	47	51	55	60	64	68	72	77
13	—	2	6	10	15	19	24	28	33	37	42	47	51	56	61	65	70	75	80	84
14	—	2	7	11	16	21	26	31	36	41	46	51	56	61	66	71	77	82	87	92
15	—	3	7	12	18	23	28	33	39	44	50	55	61	66	72	77	83	88	94	100
16	—	3	8	14	19	25	30	36	42	48	54	60	65	71	77	83	89	95	101	107
17	—	3	9	15	20	26	33	39	45	51	57	64	70	77	83	89	96	102	109	115
18	—	4	9	16	22	28	35	41	48	55	61	68	75	82	88	95	102	109	116	123
19	0	4	10	17	23	30	37	44	51	58	65	72	80	87	94	101	109	116	123	130
20	0	4	11	18	25	32	39	47	54	62	69	77	84	92	100	107	115	123	130	138

TABLE B.8B MANN-WHITNEY U FOR A p LEVEL OF .05 FOR A TWO-TAILED TEST

To be statistically significant, the smaller U must be equal to or less than the value in the table.

N_A/N_B	1	2	3	4	5	6	7	8	9	10	11	12	13	14	15	16	17	18	19	20
1	—	—	—	—	—	—	—	—	—	—	—	—	—	—	—	—	—	—	—	—
2	—	—	—	—	—	—	—	0	0	0	0	1	1	1	1	1	2	2	2	2
3	—	—	—	—	0	1	1	2	2	3	3	4	4	5	5	6	6	7	7	8
4	—	—	—	0	1	2	3	4	4	5	6	7	8	9	10	11	11	12	13	13
5	—	—	0	1	2	3	5	6	7	8	9	11	12	13	14	15	17	18	19	20
6	—	—	1	2	3	5	6	8	10	11	13	14	16	17	19	21	22	24	25	27
7	—	—	1	3	5	6	8	10	12	14	16	18	20	22	24	26	28	30	32	34
8	—	0	2	4	6	8	10	13	15	17	19	22	24	26	29	31	34	36	38	41
9	—	0	2	4	7	10	12	15	17	20	23	26	28	31	34	37	39	42	45	48
10	—	0	3	5	8	11	14	17	20	23	26	29	33	36	39	42	45	48	52	55
11	—	0	3	6	9	13	16	19	23	26	30	33	37	40	44	47	51	55	58	62
12	—	1	4	7	11	14	18	22	26	29	33	37	41	45	49	53	57	61	65	69
13	—	1	4	8	12	16	20	24	28	33	37	41	45	50	54	59	63	67	72	76
14	—	1	5	9	13	17	22	26	31	36	40	45	50	55	59	64	67	74	78	83
15	—	1	5	10	14	19	24	29	34	39	44	49	54	59	64	70	75	80	85	90
16	—	1	6	11	15	21	26	31	37	42	47	53	59	64	70	75	81	86	92	98
17	—	2	6	11	17	22	28	34	39	45	51	57	63	67	75	81	87	93	99	105
18	—	2	7	12	18	24	30	36	42	48	55	61	67	74	80	86	93	99	106	112
19	—	2	7	13	19	25	32	38	45	52	58	65	72	78	85	92	99	106	113	119
20	—	2	8	13	20	27	34	41	48	55	62	69	76	83	90	98	105	112	119	127

TABLE B.9 WILCOXON SIGNED-RANKS TEST FOR MATCHED PAIRS (T)

	LEVEL OF SIGNIFICANCE (p LEVEL) FOR ONE-TAILED TEST			LEVEL OF SIGNIFICANCE (p LEVEL) FOR TWO-TAILED TEST	
N	.05	.01	N	.05	.01
5	0	—	5	—	—
6	2	—	6	0	—
7	3	0	7	2	—
8	5	1	8	3	0
9	8	3	9	5	1
10	10	5	10	8	3
11	13	7	11	10	5
12	17	9	12	13	7
13	21	12	13	17	9
14	25	15	14	21	12
15	30	19	15	25	15
16	35	23	16	29	19
17	41	27	17	34	23
18	47	32	18	40	27
19	53	37	19	46	32
20	60	43	20	52	37
21	67	49	21	58	42
22	75	55	22	65	48
23	83	62	23	73	54
24	91	69	24	81	61
25	100	76	25	89	68
26	110	84	26	98	75
27	119	92	27	107	83
28	130	101	28	116	91
29	140	110	29	126	100
30	151	120	30	137	109
31	163	130	31	147	118
32	175	140	32	159	128
33	187	151	33	170	138
34	200	162	34	182	148
35	213	173	35	195	159
36	227	185	36	208	171
37	241	198	37	221	182
38	256	211	38	235	194
39	271	224	39	249	207
40	286	238	40	264	220
41	302	252	41	279	233
42	319	266	42	294	247
43	336	281	43	310	261
44	353	296	44	327	276
45	371	312	45	343	291
46	389	328	46	361	307
47	407	345	47	378	322
48	426	362	48	396	339
49	446	379	49	415	355
50	466	397	50	434	373

TABLE B.10 RANDOM DIGITS

19223	95034	05756	28713	96409	12531	42544	82853
73676	47150	99400	01927	27754	42648	82425	36290
45467	71709	77558	00095	32863	29485	82226	90056
52711	38889	93074	60227	40011	85848	48767	52573
95592	94007	69971	91481	60779	53791	17297	59335
68417	35013	15529	72765	85089	57067	50211	47487
82739	57890	20807	47511	81676	55300	94383	14893
60940	72024	17868	24943	61790	90656	87964	18883
36009	19365	15412	39638	85453	46816	83485	41979
38448	48789	18338	24697	39364	42006	76688	08708
81486	69487	60513	09297	00412	71238	27649	39950
59636	88804	04634	71197	19352	73089	84898	45785
62568	70206	40325	03699	71080	22553	11486	11776
45149	32992	75730	66280	03819	56202	02938	70915
61041	77684	94322	24709	73698	14526	31893	32592
14459	26056	31424	80371	65103	62253	50490	61181
38167	98532	62183	70632	23417	26185	41448	75532
73190	32533	04470	29669	84407	90785	65956	86382
95857	07118	87664	92099	58806	66979	98624	84826
35476	55972	39421	65850	04266	35435	43742	11937
71487	09984	29077	14863	61683	47052	62224	51025
13873	81598	95052	90908	73592	75186	87136	95761
54580	81507	27102	56027	55892	33063	41842	81868
71035	09001	43367	49497	72719	96758	27611	91596
96746	12149	37823	71868	18442	35119	62103	39244
96927	19931	36809	74192	77567	88741	48409	41903
43909	99477	25330	64359	40085	16925	85117	36071
15689	14227	06565	14374	13352	49367	81982	87209
36759	58984	68288	22913	18638	54303	00795	08727
69051	64817	87174	09517	84534	06489	87201	97245
05007	16632	81194	14873	04197	85576	45195	96565
68732	55259	84292	08796	43165	93739	31685	97150
45740	41807	65561	33302	07051	93623	18132	09547
27816	78416	18329	21337	35213	37741	04312	68508
66925	55658	39100	78458	11206	19876	87151	31260
08421	44753	77377	28744	75592	08563	79140	92454
53645	66812	61421	47836	12609	15373	98481	14592
66831	68908	40772	21558	47781	33586	79177	06928
55588	99404	70708	41098	43563	56934	48394	51719
12975	13258	13048	45144	72321	81940	00360	02428
96767	35964	23822	96012	94591	65194	50842	53372
72829	50232	97892	63408	77919	44575	24870	04178
88565	42628	17797	49376	61762	16953	88604	12724
62964	88145	83083	69453	46109	59505	69680	00900
19687	12633	57857	95806	09931	02150	43163	58636
37609	59057	66967	83401	60705	02384	90597	93600
54973	86278	88737	74351	47500	84552	19909	67181
00694	05977	19664	65441	20903	62371	22725	53340
71546	05233	53946	68743	72460	27601	45403	88692
07511	88915	41267	16853	84569	79367	32337	03316

Solutions to Odd-Numbered End-of-Chapter Problems

CHAPTER 1

1.1 Descriptive statistics organize, summarize, and communicate a group of numerical observations. Inferential statistics use sample data to make general estimates about the larger population.

1.3 The four types of variables are nominal, ordinal, interval, and ratio. A nominal variable is used for observations that have categories, or names, as their values. An ordinal variable is used for observations that have rankings (i.e., 1st, 2nd, 3rd, . . .) as their values. An interval variable has numbers as its values; the distance (or interval) between pairs of consecutive numbers is assumed to be equal. Finally, a ratio variable meets the criteria for interval variables but also has a meaningful zero point. Interval and ratio variables are both often referred to as scale variables.

1.5 Discrete variables can only be represented by specific numbers, usually whole numbers; continuous variables can take on any values, including those with great decimal precision (e.g., 1.597).

1.7 A confounding variable (also called a confound) is any variable that systematically varies with the independent variable so that we cannot logically determine which variable affects the dependent variable. Researchers attempt to control confounding variables in experiments by randomly assigning participants to conditions. The hope with random assignment is that the confounding variable will be spread equally across the different conditions of the study, thus neutralizing its effects.

1.9 An operational definition specifies the operations or procedures used to measure or manipulate an independent or dependent variable.

1.11 When conducting experiments, the researcher randomly assigns participants to conditions or levels of the independent variable. When random assignment is not possible, such as when studying something like gender or marital status, correlational research is used. Correlational research allows us to examine how variables are related to each other; experimental research allows us to make assertions about how an independent variable causes an effect in a dependent variable.

1.13 **a.** "This was an experiment."

b. ". . . the independent variable of caffeine on hours of sleep . . ."

c. "A university assessed the validity of a commonly used scale . . ."

d. "In a between-groups experiment on calcium and osteoporosis . . ."

e. "A researcher studied a sample of 20 rats to determine . . ."

1.15 **a.** 73 people

b. All people who shop in grocery stores similar to the one where data were collected

1.17 Inferential statistic

1.19 **a.** Answers may vary, but people could be labeled as having a "healthy diet" or an "unhealthy diet."

b. Answers may vary, but there could be groupings such as "no items," "minimal items," "some items," and "many items."

c. Answers may vary, but the number of items could be counted or weighed.

1.21 The independent variables are physical distance and emotional distance. The dependent variable is accuracy of memory.

1.23 Answers may vary, but accuracy of memory could be operationalized as the number of facts correctly recalled.

1.25 **a.** The average weight for a 10-year-old girl was 77.4 pounds in 1963 and nearly 88 pounds in 2002.

b. No; the CDC would not be able to weigh every single girl in the United States because it would be too expensive and time-consuming.

c. It is a descriptive statistic because it is a numerical summary of a sample. It is an inferential statistic because the researchers drew conclusions about the population's average weight based on this information from a sample.

1.27 **a.** Ordinal

b. Scale

c. Nominal

1.29 **a.** Discrete

b. Continuous

c. Discrete

d. Discrete

e. Continuous

1.31 **a.** The independent variables are temperature and rainfall. Both are continuous, interval variables.

b. The dependent variable is experts' ratings. These are discrete, interval variables.

c. The researchers wanted to know if the wine experts are consistent in their ratings—that is, if they're reliable.

d. This observation would suggest that Robert Parker's judgments are valid. His ratings seem to be measuring what they intend to measure—wine quality.

1.33 **a.** There are several possible answers to this question. The developers of this Web site might, for example, hypothesize that the region of the world in which one grew up predicts different personality profiles based on region.

b. The independent variable would be region and the dependent variable would be personality profile.

1.35 **a.** Age: teenagers and adults in their 30s

b. Spanking: spanking and not spanking

c. Meetings: go to meetings and participate online

d. Studying: with others and alone

e. Beverage: caffeinated and decaffeinated

1.37 **a.** The independent variable is CFC level; the dependent variables are credit card debt and the tendency to buy on impulse.

b. There are many possible answers to this question. As one example, the scale might have asked, "When you go grocery shopping, how often do you buy an item that is not on your list?"

1.39 **a.** Researchers could have randomly assigned some people who are HIV-positive to take the oral vaccine and other people who are HIV-positive not to take the oral vaccine. The second group would likely take a placebo.

b. This would have been a between-groups experiment because the people who are HIV-positive would have been in only one group: either vaccine or no vaccine (i.e., placebo).

c. This limits the researchers' ability to draw causal conclusions because the participants who received the vaccine may have been different in some way from those who did not receive the vaccine. There may have been a confounding variable that led to these findings. For example, those who received the vaccine might have had better access to health care and better sanitary conditions to begin with, making them less likely to contract cholera regardless of the vaccine's effectiveness.

1.41 We could recruit a sample of people who are HIV-positive. Half would be randomly assigned to take the oral vaccine; half would be randomly assigned to take a placebo. They would be followed to determine whether they developed cholera.

1.43 **a.** An experiment requires random assignment to conditions. It would not be ethical to randomly assign some people to smoke and some people not to smoke, so this research had to be correlational.

b. Other unhealthy behaviors have been associated with smoking, such as poor diet and infrequent exercise. These other unhealthy behaviors might be confounded with smoking.

c. The tobacco industry could claim it was not the smoking that was harming people, but rather the other activities in which smokers tend to engage or fail to engage that were harming them.

d. One could randomly assign people to either a smoking group or a nonsmoking group. Confounding variables could be controlled through random assignment and by attempting to control the diet and lifestyles of those participating in the research.

1.45 **a.** This is experimental because students are randomly assigned to one of the recycling incentive conditions.

b. Answers may vary, but one hypothesis could be "Students fined for not recycling will report lower concerns for the environment than those rewarded for recycling."

CHAPTER 2

2.1 Raw scores are the original data, to which nothing has been done.

2.3 A frequency table is a visual depiction of data that shows how often each value occurred; that is, it shows how many scores are at each value. Values are listed in one column, and the numbers of individuals with scores at that value are listed in the second column. A grouped frequency table is a visual depiction of data that reports the frequency within each given interval rather than the frequency for each specific value.

2.5 A histogram looks like a bar graph but is typically used to depict scale data with the values (or midpoints of intervals) of the variable on the x-axis and the frequencies on the y-axis. A frequency polygon is a line graph with the x-axis representing values (or midpoints of intervals) and the y-axis representing frequencies; a point is placed at the frequency for each value (or midpoint), and the points are connected.

2.7 In everyday conversation, we use the word *distribution* in a number of different contexts, from the distribution of food to marketing distribution. In statistics, we use the word *distribution* in a very particular way. We are interested in the way that a set of scores, such as a set of grades, is distributed. That is, we are interested in the overall pattern of our data—what the shape is, where the data tend to cluster, and how they trail off.

2.9 With positively skewed data, the distribution's tail extends to the right, in a positive direction, and with negatively skewed data, the distribution's tail extends to the left, in a negative direction.

2.11 17.95% and 40.67%

2.13 0.04, 198.22, and 17.89

2.15 Five

2.17 The full range of data is 68 minus 2, plus 1, or 67. The range (67) divided by the desired 7 intervals gives us an interval size of 9.57, or 10 with rounding. The 7 intervals are: 0–9, 10–19, 20–29, 30–39, 40–49, 50–59, and 60–69.

2.19 25 shows

2.21 Serial killers would create positive skew, adding high numbers of murders to the data that are clustered around 1.

2.23 **a.** For the college population, the range of age extends farther to the right (with greater years) than to the left, creating positive skew.

b. The limited access to college of minors who are youthful prodigies creates a sort of floor effect where low scores are less possible.

2.25 **a.**

YEARS TO COMPLETE	FREQUENCY
15	2
14	1
13	1
12	1
11	1
10	2
9	4
8	9
7	11
6	10

b. 30

c. A grouped frequency table is not necessary here. These data are relatively easy to interpret in the frequency table. Grouped frequency tables are useful when the list of data is long and difficult to interpret.

d. These data are clustered around 6 to 8 years with a long trail of data out to greater years to complete. These data show positive skew.

2.27 **a.**

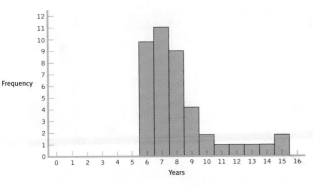

b. Eight

c. The data are clustered around 6 to 8 years with a tail of data extending to greater years, creating positive skew.

2.29 **a.**

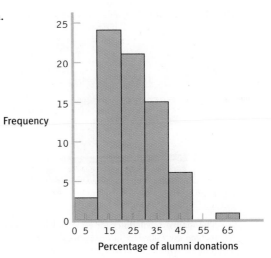

b.

c. There is one unusual score—61. The distribution appears to be positively skewed. The center of the distribution seems to be in the 10–29 range.

2.31 **a.**

INTERVALS	FREQUENCIES
60–69	1
50–59	7
40–49	10
30–39	7
20–29	2
10–19	3

b.

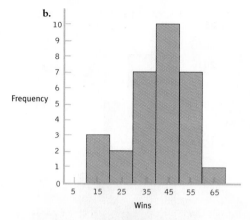

c. The summary will differ for each student but should include the following information: the data appear to be roughly symmetric, maybe a bit negatively skewed.

d. There are many possible answers to this question. For example, one might ask whether teams with older players do better or worse than those with younger players. Another study might examine whether team budget relates to wins; there's a salary cap, but some teams might choose to pay the "luxury tax" in order to spend more. Does spending make a difference?

2.33 a.

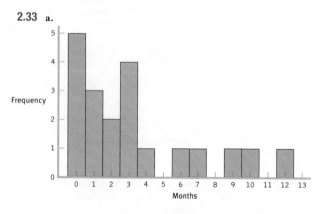

b.

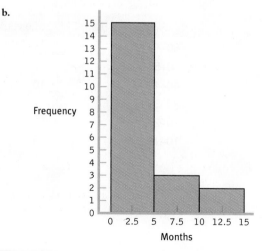

2.35 a. These data are centered around the 3-month period with positive skew extending the data out to the 12-month period.

b. The bulk of the data would need to be shifted from the 3-month period to approximately 12 months, so that group of women might be the focus of attention. Perhaps early contact at the hospital and at follow-up visits after birth would help encourage mothers to nurse, and to nurse longer. One could also consider studying the women who create the positive skew to learn what unique characteristics or knowledge they have that influenced their behavior.

2.37 a. Frequency table

b. Grouped frequency table, histogram, or frequency polygon

c. Grouped frequency table, histogram, or frequency polygon

d. Frequency table, histogram, or frequency polygon

2.39 a. A histogram of grouped frequencies

b. Approximately 32

c. Approximately 27

2.41 a.

INTERVAL	FREQUENCY
18–20	2
15–17	6
12–14	2
9–11	3
6–8	7
3–5	8
0–2	2

b.

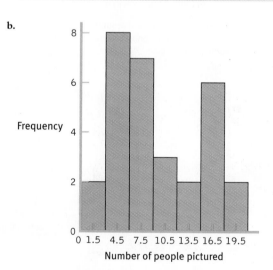

2.43 The column for faculty shows a high point from 0–7 friends. The column for students shows two high points around 4–11 and 16–19 with some high outliers creating positive skew.

CHAPTER 3

3.1 The false face validity lie, the biased scale lie, the sneaky sample lie, the extrapolation lie, the inaccurate values lie, and the outright lie.

3.3 With scale data, a scatterplot allows for a helpful visual analysis of the relation between two variables. If the data points appear to fall approximately along a straight line, this indicates a linear relation. If the data form a line that changes direction along its path, a nonlinear relation may be present. If the data points show no particular relation, it is possible that the two variables are not related.

3.5 Bar graphs are visual depictions of data when the independent variable is nominal and the dependent variable is scale. Each bar typically represents the mean value of the dependent variable for each category. A Pareto chart is a specific type of bar graph in which the categories along the x-axis are ordered from highest bar on the left to lowest bar on the right.

3.7 A pictorial graph is a visual depiction of data typically used for a nominal independent variable with very few levels (categories) and a scale dependent variable. Each category uses a picture or symbol to represent its value on the scale dependent variable. A pie chart is a graph in the shape of a circle with a slice for every category. The size of each slice represents the proportion (or percentage) of each category. In most cases, a bar graph is preferable to a pictorial graph or a pie chart.

3.9 The independent variable typically goes on the horizontal x-axis and the dependent variable goes on the vertical y-axis.

3.11 Moiré vibrations are any patterns that computers provide as options to fill in bars or other elements of a graph. Grids refer to a background pattern, almost like graph paper, on which the data representations, such as bars, are superimposed. Ducks are features of the data that have been dressed up to be something other than merely data.

3.13 Sorting people into the categories of "alumni who donated money" and "alumni who did not donate money" creates nominal data. We would show the mean ages for two categories in a bar graph.

3.15 Nonlinear, because the data change direction around 4.00 on the x-axis.

3.17 These graphs are missing titles and axis labels. The axes are also missing 0 values.

3.19 The y-axis should go down to 0.

3.21 **a.** 3.20%

  b. 3.22%

  c. 2.80%

3.23 These data have a minimum value of 273 and a maximum value of 342. Because the minimum value is far from 0, it is not practical to have the axis start at 0, so cut marks would be used. We might then include every 10th value starting at 270: 270, 280, 290, 300, 310, 320, 330, 340, 350.

3.25 **a.** The independent variable is height, and the dependent variable is attractiveness. Both are scale variables.

  b. The best graph for these data would be a scatterplot (which also might include a line of best fit if the relation is linear) because there are two scale variables.

  c. It would not be practical to start the axis at 0. With the data clustered from 58 to 71 inches, a 0 start to the axis would mean that a large portion of the graph would be empty. We would use cut marks to indicate that the axis did not include all values from 0 to 71.

3.27 **a.** The independent variable is country, and the dependent variable is male suicide rate.

  b. Country is a nominal variable and suicide rate is a scale variable.

  c. The best graph for these data would be a Pareto chart. Because there are 20 categories along the x-axis, it is best to arrange them in order from highest to lowest.

  d. A time series plot could show year on the x-axis and suicide rate on the y-axis. Each country would be represented by a different color line.

3.29 **a.**

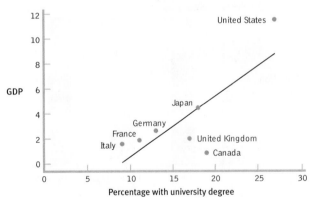

Relation Between Percentage with University Degree and GDP (in trillions of $US)

  b. The percentage of residents with a university degree appears to be related to GDP. As the percentage with a university degree increases, so does GDP.

  c. It is possible that an educated populace has the skills to make that country productive and profitable. Conversely, it is possible that a productive and profitable country has the money needed for the populace to be educated.

3.31 **a.** The independent variable is type of academic institution. It is nominal, with levels private national, public national, and liberal arts.

  b. The dependent variable is alumni donation rate. It is a scale variable, the units are percentages, and the range of values is from 9 to 66.

c. The defaults will differ depending on the software used. Here is one example.

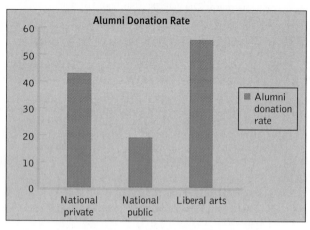

d. The redesigns will differ depending on the software used. In this example, we have added a clear title, labeled the *x*-axis, omitted the key, and labeled the *y*-axis (being sure that it reads from left to right). We also toned down the unnecessary color in the background, and cut some of the extra numbers from the *y*-axis. Finally, we removed the black box from around the graph.

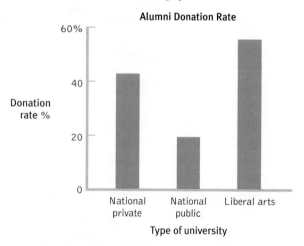

e. These data suggest that more alumni of liberal arts colleges than of national private or natonal public universities donate to their institutions. Moreover, more alumni of national private universities than of national public universities donate.

f. There are many possible answers to this question. One might want to identify characteristics of alumni who donate, methods of soliciting donations that result in the best outcomes, or characteristics of universities within a given category (e.g., liberal arts) that have the highest rates.

3.33 a. One independent variable is time frame; it has two levels: 1945–1950 and 1996–1998. The other independent variable is type of graduate program; it also has two levels: clinical psychology and experimental psychology.

b. The dependent variable is percentage of graduates who had a mentor while in graduate school.

c.

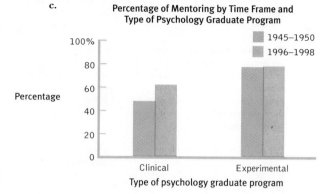

d. These data suggest that clinical psychology graduate students were more likely to have been mentored if they were in school in the 1996–1998 time frame than if they were in school during the 1945–1950 time frame. There does not appear to be such a difference among experimental psychology students.

e. This was not a true experiment. Students were not randomly assigned to time period or type of graduate program.

3.35 a. Pictures could be used instead of bars. For example, dollar signs might be used to represent the three quantities.

b. If the dollar signs become wider as they get taller, as often happens with pictorial graphs, the overall size would be proportionally larger than the increase in donation rate it is meant to represent. A bar graph is not subject to this problem, because graphmakers are not likely to make bars wider as they get taller.

3.37 a.

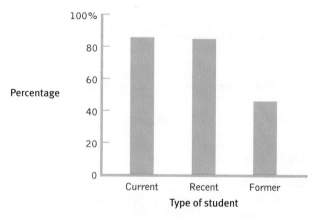

b. The default options that students choose to override will differ. For the bar graph here, we (1) added a title, (2) labeled the *x*-axis, (3) labeled the *y*-axis, (4) rotated the *y*-axis label so that it read from left to right, (5) eliminated the box around the whole graph, (6) eliminated the right and top borders around the part of the graph that contains the bars, (7) eliminated the grid lines, (8) muted the color of the axes, (9) eliminated background color, and (10) eliminated the black lines around the bars themselves.

3.39 Each student's advice will differ. The following are examples of advice.

    a. The shrinking doctor: Replace the pictures with bars. Space the three years out in relation to their actual values (right now 1964 and 1975 are a good deal farther apart than are 1975 and 1990). Include a more descriptive title as the main title.

    b. Workforce participation: Eliminate all the pictures. A falling line now indicates an *increase* in percentage; notice that 40% is at the top and 80% is at the bottom. Make the *y*-axis go from highest to lowest, starting from 0. Eliminate the three-dimensional effect to make the lines easier to compare. Make it clear where the data point for each year falls by including a tick mark for each number on the *x*-axis.

3.41 **a.** The graph proposes that Type I regrets of action are initially intense but decline over the years, while Type II regrets of inaction are initially mild but become more intense over the years.

    b. There are two independent variables: type of regret (a nominal variable) and age (a continuous scale variable). There is one dependent variable: intensity of regrets (also a continuous scale variable).

    c. This is a graph of a theory. No data have been collected, so there are no statistics of any kind.

    d. The story that this theoretical relation suggests is that regrets over things you have done are intense shortly after the actual behavior but decline over the years. In contrast, regrets over things you have not done but wish you had done are initially low in intensity but become more intense as the years go by.

CHAPTER 4

4.1 The mean is the arithmetic average of a group of scores; it is calculated by summing all the scores and dividing by the total number of scores. The median is the middle score of all the scores in a sample where the scores are arranged in ascending order. If there is no single middle score, the median is the mean of the two middle scores. The mode is the most common score of all the scores in a sample.

4.3 The mean takes into account the actual numeric value of each score. The mean is the mathematic center of the data. It is the center balance point in the data such that the sum of the deviations (rather than the number of deviations) below the mean equals the sum of deviations above the mean.

4.5 The mode is typically used in three situations: (1) when one score dominates the distribution, (2) to describe bimodal or multimodal distributions, and (3) when nominal data are summarized.

4.7 The mean is affected by outliers because the numeric value of the outlier is used in the computation of the mean. The

median typically is not affected by outliers because its computation is based on the data in the middle of the distribution, and outliers lie at the extremes of the distribution.

4.9 The standard deviation is a measure of variability in terms of the values of the measure used to assess the variable, whereas the variance is squared values. Squared values simply don't make sense to us, so we take the square root of the variance and report this value, the standard deviation.

4.11 The mean is calculated as

$$M = \frac{\Sigma X}{N} = (15 + 34 + 32 + 46 + 22 + 36 + 34 + 28 + 52 + 28)/10 = 327/10 = 32.7$$

    The median is found by arranging the scores in numeric order—15, 22, 28, 28, 32, 34, 34, 36, 46, 52—then dividing the number of scores, 10, by 2 and adding ½ to get 5.5. The mean of the 5th and 6th score in our ordered list of scores is our median—(32 + 34)/2 = 33—so 33 is the median.

    The mode is the most common score. In these data, two scores appear twice, so we have two modes, 28 and 34.

4.13 Adding the value of 112 to the data from Exercise 4.11 changes the calculation of the mean in the following way:

$$(15 + 34 + 32 + 46 + 22 + 36 + 34 + 28 + 52 + 28 + 112)/11 = 439/11 = 39.91$$

The mean gets larger with this outlier.

    There are now 11 data points, so the median is the 6th value in the ordered list, which is 34.

    The modes are unchanged at 28 and 34.

    This outlier increases the mean by approximately 7 values; it increases the median by 1; and it does not affect the mode at all.

4.15 The range is: $X_{highest} - X_{lowest} = 52 - 15 = 37$

    The variance is: $SD^2 = \dfrac{\Sigma(X - M)^2}{N}$

    We start by calculating the mean, which is 32.7. We then calculate the deviation of each score from the mean and the square of that deviation.

X	X − M	(X − M)²
15	−17.7	313.29
34	1.3	1.69
32	−0.7	0.49
46	13.3	176.89
22	−10.7	114.49
36	3.3	10.89
34	1.3	1.69
28	−4.7	22.09
52	19.3	372.49
28	−4.7	22.09

$$SD^2 = \frac{\Sigma(X - M)^2}{N} = \frac{1036.1}{10} = 103.61$$

The standard deviation is: $SD = \sqrt{SD^2}$ or $SD = \sqrt{\dfrac{\Sigma(X - M)^2}{N}}$

$$= \sqrt{103.61} = 10.18$$

4.17 The range would change from $X_{highest} - X_{lowest} = \$61,774 - \$38,862 = \$22,912$ to $X_{highest} - X_{lowest} = \$97,582 - \$38,862 = \$58,720$

4.19 The range is: $X_{highest} - X_{lowest} = 61 - 9 = 52$

4.21 The mean is calculated as

$$M = \frac{\Sigma X}{N} = (-47 + -46 + -38 + -20 \ldots + -46)/12$$
$$= -163/12 = -13.58°F$$

The median is found by arranging the temperatures in numeric order:

$$-47, -46, -46, -38, -20, -20, -5, -2, 8, 9, 20, 24$$

There are 12 data points, so the mean of the 6th and 7th data points gives us the median: $(-20 + -5)/2 = -25/2 = -12.5°F$.

There are two modes: both -46 and -20 were recorded twice.

4.23 For the wind gust data, we could create 10-mph intervals and calculate the mode as the interval that occurs most often. There are four recorded gusts in the 160–169 mph interval, three in the 170–179 interval, and only one in the other intervals. So, the 160-mph interval could be presented as our mode.

4.25 For the record low temperature data, the range is: $X_{highest} - X_{lowest} = 24 - (-47) = 71°F$

The variance is: $SD^2 = \frac{\Sigma(X - M)^2}{N}$

We start by calculating the mean, which is $-13.58°F$. We then calculate the deviation of each score from the mean and the square of that deviation.

X	X − M	(X − M)²
−47	−60.58	3669.94
−46	−59.58	3549.78
−46	−59.58	3549.78
−38	−51.58	2660.50
−20	−33.58	1127.62
−20	−33.58	1127.62
−5	−18.58	345.22
−2	−15.58	242.74
8	−5.58	31.14
9	−4.58	20.98
20	6.42	41.22
24	10.42	108.58

$$SD^2 = \frac{\Sigma(X - M)^2}{N} = \frac{16,475.08}{12} = 1372.92 \text{ is our variance.}$$

The standard deviation is: $SD = \sqrt{SD^2}$ or $SD = \sqrt{\frac{\Sigma(X - M)^2}{N}}$

$= \sqrt{1372.92} = 37.05°F$

4.27 The word "normal" implies that extreme temperatures, or rare weather events, were excluded from the calculation. In

this case, it is probably a median that is presented. We know that the median is less affected by extreme scores than the mean.

4.29 It may not make sense to average weather across the different months in a state like New Hampshire that has wide seasonal variations in weather. We might want to create seasonal data by grouping the summer months or winter months together. We also might want to consider the tourism industry in this area and present data for peak times (e.g., leaf-viewing season in the fall).

4.31 a. $M = \frac{\Sigma X}{N} = (0.755 + 0.721 + 0.708 + 0.773 \ldots + 0.650 + 0.651)/11 = 7.698/11 = 0.70$

b. First, we arrange the scores in order: 0.477, 0.617, 0.650, 0.651, 0.708, 0.721, 0.747, 0.755, 0.773, 0.782, 0.817. There are 11 scores: $(11/2) + 0.5 = 6$. Thus, the median is the 6th score, which is 0.721.

c. The mean is lower than the median; this suggests that the data are somewhat skewed. The score of 0.477 is likely pulling the mean down but would not affect the median.

4.33 a. The answers will be different for each student, but most ads promote a product that offers purportedly fast, easy, substantial weight loss.

b. The answers will be different for each student, but such ads typically offer little or no data. Testimonials abound.

c. It would be most useful to see a median; the mean could be skewed higher by the occasional person who loses a great deal of weight (and maybe not even from this diet product specifically). The mean would not be representative of the typical person's weight loss.

d. We would tell a friend to look at the data for the *typical* person—the median, or middle score. The company clearly chooses the biggest "losers" for its ad testimonials.

4.35 a. Range $= X_{highest} - X_{lowest} = 83 - 32 = 51$

b. There are several possible answers to this question. For example, we might wonder whether classroom size relates to participation or whether the gender balance affects participation.

4.37 a. This is a parameter because it is the mean of *all* members of the population of interest, French-speaking Canadians living in Ontario.

b. This is a parameter because it is the mean of *all* members of the population of interest, National Basketball Association teams.

c. This is a statistic because it is the mean for only the sample who participated in the GSS, not for all Americans.

d. This is a statistic because it is the mean percentage for the sample of schools that participated in the NSSE, not all schools in the United States.

4.39 a. Bimodal. There would be newborn infants and mothers of childbearing age.

b. Unimodal. Most people would fall in the middle, with some exhibiting no depression and others reporting to be very depressed.

c. Unimodal. Most people would score around 500, with some scoring down toward 200 and others up toward 800.

d. Bimodal. The developed countries would charge much more for the drug than the developing countries.

4.41 For these data, it would probably be fair to present the mean. Because we are analyzing all states, the healthy size of our data set helps to minimize the effects of any outlier states. If we are unsure of what measure of central tendency to present, we should go ahead and present all three: the mean, median, and mode.

4.43 **a.** These averages are probably means. As we learned in this chapter, the mean is the most commonly presented measure of central tendency.

b. TV viewing habits might vary significantly by age group studied. If the researchers were not consistent in assessing the habits of similar people across the different countries, then the influence of age as a confounding variable could be important here.

c. If we were interested in age (or gender or level of education or any other variable) as it relates to viewing habits, we might select participants based on that characteristic.

4.45 The Guinness World Record organization relies on extreme observations. These are the data points used in computing the range of a distribution. If we want to know the range of human height, we could go to the record book and compute the range by taking the height of the tallest person ever recorded and subtracting the height of the shortest person ever recorded. The Guinness World Record database tells us very little about what is typical; in this case, average is not extraordinary!

CHAPTER 5

5.1 It is rare to have access to an entire population. That is why we study samples and use inferential statistics to estimate what is happening in the population.

5.3 Generalizability refers to the ability of researchers to apply findings from one sample or in one context to other samples or contexts.

5.5 Random sampling means that every member of a population has an equal chance of being selected to participate in a study. Random assignment means that each selected participant has an equal chance of being in any of the experimental conditions.

5.7 Random assignment is a process in which every participant (regardless of how he or she was selected) has an equal chance of being in any of the experimental conditions. This avoids bias across experimental conditions.

5.9 A proportion is the mathematical calculation of how often something occurred out of the number of trials performed; probability is a statement of the likelihood of an outcome over the long run.

5.11 In general, a control group is a level of the independent variable that is designed to match the experimental group—the group receiving the treatment or intervention of interest—in all ways but the experimental manipulation itself.

5.13 We can reject the null hypothesis and support our research hypothesis, or we can fail to reject the null hypothesis and acknowledge that we did not find any support for our research hypothesis. Conclusions are made in relation to the null hypothesis. The language of hypothesis testing avoids statements about accepting either hypothesis.

5.15 The numbers as two-digit sequences read: 23, 79, 85, 54, 25, 32, 45, and 43. Our four trucks would be numbers 23, 25, 32, and 43.

5.17 Ignoring all numbers other than those from 1 to 3, we observe the following sequence: 3, 1, 2, 2, 3, 1, 2, 1, 1. So the first person is assigned to the 3rd condition, the second person to the 1st condition, and so on.

5.19 The probability of an event occurring is equal to the number of successes divided by the number of total trials over the long run. The formula here would be: $71/489 = 0.145$.

5.21 **a.** 1.73%

b. 80%

c. 37.19%

5.23 The number 6 appears four times in the top two rows, which contain 60 numbers, so we would estimate the probability to be 4/60, or 0.067.

5.25 Six out of 16 gives a Type II error rate of 0.38.

5.27 One out of 29 gives a Type I error rate of 0.03.

5.29 **a.** The targeted population is the 5000 school psychologists with doctoral degrees.

b. The researcher would like to recruit 100 of these doctoral-level school psychologists.

c. The researcher would number the members of the population from 0001 to 5000, then select the first 100 four-digit numbers from a random numbers table that are between 0001 and 5000, ignoring doubles (e.g., two 2549's).

d. The first 10 participants would be: 449, 3524, 2463, 3824, 4586, 2510, 2500, 1881, 1196, 1599 and 3896.

5.31 **a.** There are two levels of the independent variable; these levels would be given numbers, such as 0 and 1 for "improving" and "declining," respectively. A random numbers table or computerized random numbers generator would be used to generate a list of 0's and 1's. Each participant would be assigned to the condition that matched the next number on the random numbers list. If a random numbers table was used, any numbers except 0 and 1 would be ignored. Thus, if the first three relevant numbers were 0, 0, and 1, then the first participant would read the article about the improving job market, as would the second. The third would read the article about the declining job market. As soon as 50 participants were assigned to one of the levels of the independent variable, the remaining individuals would be assigned to the other condition.

b. With 0 representing "improving" and 1 representing "declining," the first 10 participants would be assigned to a condition as follows: 0010001001.

c. These numbers don't appear to be random because there are so many more 0's than 1's. In the short run, lists of randomly generated numbers may not appear to be random. It is only in the long run that proportions tend to reflect the actual underlying probabilities.

5.33 **a.** (i) We could identify the population of U.S. physicians in the AMA and so could use random selection to generate our sample. In such a study, the researcher could generalize to the population of all AMA physicians. (ii) We could not, however, randomly assign participants to be men or women. We would have to take participants according to their gender.

b. (i) We could not identify the entire population—that is, all preterm infants. We could not, therefore, recruit a random sample. The researcher likely wanted to generalize to all children who were born preterm but must use caution because the sample was not randomly selected. (ii) Moreover, we could not randomly assign participants to be born preterm or full term. We would have to study participants in the conditions in which they were born.

c. (i) Because the entire population—students who came to the counseling center because of depression or anxiety—could be identified, the researcher could use random sampling. The researcher can generalize, therefore, to all students who come to the counseling center for depression or anxiety. (ii) The researcher, however, could not use random assignment. Participants could not be assigned to depression versus anxiety conditions.

d. (i) The population of interest is likely all people who use laptops, clearly not a population that can be identified in its entirety. Thus, random sampling is not possible. Although the researcher likely wanted to generalize to all people who use laptops, he is limited by his inability to use random selection. (ii) The researcher could, however, use random assignment, assigning participants to use a Mac, PC, or new laptop.

5.35 a. The typical respondent is likely more concerned with her looks and her outfits than is the average *Cosmo* reader who does not respond. (In turn, the average *Cosmo* reader who does not respond is likely more concerned with her looks and her outfits than is the average non-*Cosmo* reader.)

b. Volunteer samples tend to be composed of people who care more deeply about the issue at hand than do those in the general population to which researchers likely want to generalize.

c. There are many possible answers to this question. As one example, the quiz provides very few options. It is certainly possible that a hip woman might adopt a look other than that of Lauryn Hill, the Indigo Girls, or glam Madonna.

5.37 a. This scenario describes selection. Random sampling was used. The participants were the counseling centers themselves, and every counseling center at a Canadian university had an equal chance of being selected to participate in this study.

b. This scenario describes assignment. Each monkey was assigned randomly to one of the two conditions. Each monkey had an equal chance of being assigned to each condition.

c. This scenario describes selection. This is a volunteer sample. All participants signed up voluntarily to take part in the study.

d. This scenario describes selection. This is a convenience sample. The researcher used a readily available pool of potential participants: Introduction to Psychology students.

5.39 a. *Probability* refers to the proportion of aces that we expect to see in the long run. In the long run, given 4 aces out of 52 cards, we would expect the proportion of aces to be 4/52 = 0.077.

b. *Proportion* refers to the observed fraction of cards that are aces—the number of successes divided by the number of trials. In this case, the proportion of aces is 5/15 = 0.333.

c. *Percentage* refers to the proportion multiplied by 100: 0.333(100) = 33.3. Thus, 33.3% of the cards drawn were aces.

d. Although 0.333 is far from 0.077, we would expect a great deal of fluctuation in the short run. These data are not sufficient to determine whether the deck is stacked.

5.41 a. The null hypothesis is that the average tendency to develop false memories is either unchanged or is lowered by the repetition of false information. The research hypothesis is that false memories are higher, on average, when false information is repeated than when it is not.

b. The null hypothesis is that outcome is the same or worse whether or not structured assessments are used. The research hypothesis is that average outcome is better when structured assessments are used than when they are not used.

c. The null hypothesis is that mean employee morale is the same whether employees work in enclosed offices or cubicles. The research hypothesis is that mean employee morale is different when employees work in enclosed offices versus cubicles.

d. The null hypothesis is that ability to speak one's native language is the same, on average, whether or not a second language is taught to children from birth. The research hypothesis is that the ability to speak one's native language is different, on average, when a second language is taught from birth than when no second language is taught.

5.43 a. If this conclusion is incorrect, we have made a Type I error. We have rejected the null hypothesis when the null hypothesis is really true. (Of course, we never know whether we have made an error! We just have to acknowledge the possibility.)

b. If this conclusion is incorrect, we have made a Type I error. We have rejected the null hypothesis when the null hypothesis is really true.

c. If this conclusion is incorrect, we have made a Type II error. We have failed to reject the null hypothesis when the null hypothesis is not true.

d. If this conclusion is incorrect, we have made a Type II error. We have failed to reject the null hypothesis when the null hypothesis is not true.

5.45 a. The population of interest is male students with alcohol problems. The sample is the 64 students who were ordered to meet with a school counselor.

b. Random selection was not used. The sample was comprised of 64 male students who had been ordered to meet with a school counselor; they were not chosen out of all male students with alcohol problems.

c. Random assignment was used. Each participant had an equal chance of being assigned to each of the two conditions.

d. The independent variable is type of counseling. It has two levels: BMI and AE. The dependent variable is number of alcohol-related problems at follow-up.

e. The null hypothesis is that the mean number of alcohol-related problems is the same regardless of type of counseling (BMI or AE). The research hypothesis is that students who undergo BMI have different mean numbers of alcohol-related problems at follow-up than do students who participate in AE.

f. The researchers rejected the null hypothesis.

g. If the researchers were incorrect in their decision, they made a Type I error. If this is the case, they rejected the null hypothesis when the null hypothesis was true. The consequences of this type of error are that a new treatment that is no better, on average, than the standard treatment would be implemented. This might lead to unnecessary costs to train counselors to implement the new treatment.

CHAPTER 6

6.1 In everyday conversation, the word *normal* is used to refer to events or objects that are common or that typically occur. Statisticians use the word to refer to distributions that conform to the bell-shaped curve, with a peak in the middle, where most of the observations lie, and symmetric areas underneath the curve on either size of the midpoint. This normal curve represents the pattern of occurrence of many different kinds of events.

6.3 The distribution of sample scores approaches normal as the sample size increases, assuming the population is normally distributed.

6.5 A z score is a way to standardize data; it expresses how far a data point is from the mean of its distribution in terms of standard deviations.

6.7 The mean is 0 and the standard deviation is 1.0.

6.9 The μ indicates that it is the mean of a *population,* and the subscript M indicates that the population is composed of *sample means*—the means of all possible samples of a given size from a particular population of individual scores.

6.11 The z statistic tells us how many standard errors a sample mean is from the population mean.

6.13 a.

Solutions

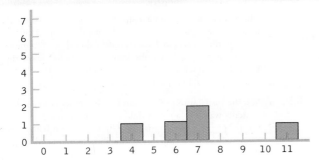

b.

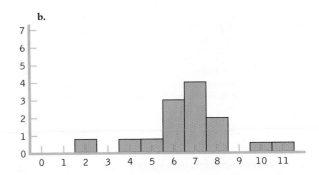

c.

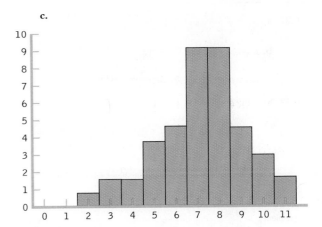

d. As the sample size is increasing, the distribution is approaching the shape of the normal curve.

6.15 a. $z = \dfrac{1000 - 1179}{164} = -1.09$

b. $z = \dfrac{721 - 1179}{164} = -2.79$

c. $z = \dfrac{1531 - 1179}{164} = 2.15$

d. $z = \dfrac{1184 - 1179}{164} = 0.03$

6.17 $z = \dfrac{203 - 250}{47} = -1.0$

$z = \dfrac{297 - 250}{47} = +1.0$

Each of these scores is 47 points away from the mean, which is the value of our standard deviation. The z scores of -1.0 and 1.0 express that the first score, 203, is 1 standard deviation below the mean, whereas the other score, 297, is 1 standard deviation above the mean.

6.19 a. $X = z(\sigma) + \mu = -0.23(164) + 1179 = 1141.28$

b. $X = 1.41(164) + 1179 = 1410.24$

c. $X = 2.06(164) + 1179 = 1516.84$

d. $X = 0.03(164) + 1179 = 1183.92$

6.21 a. $X = z(\sigma) + \mu = 1.5(100) + 500 = 650$

b. $X = z(\sigma) + \mu = -0.5(100) + 500 = 450$

c. $X = z(\sigma) + \mu = -2.0(100) + 500 = 300$

6.23 **a.** $z = \dfrac{45 - 51}{4} = -1.5$

$z = \dfrac{732 - 765}{23} = -1.43$

b. Both of these scores fall below the mean of their distribution, resulting in negative z scores. One score (45) is a little farther below its mean than the other (732).

6.25 **a.** 50%

b. 82% (34 + 34 + 14)

c. 4% (2 + 2)

d. 48% (34 + 14)

e. 100%

6.27 **a.** $\mu_M = \mu = 55$, and $\sigma_M = \dfrac{8}{\sqrt{30}} = 1.46$

b. $\mu_M = \mu = 55$, and $\sigma_M = \dfrac{8}{\sqrt{300}} = 0.46$

c. $\mu_M = \mu = 55$, and $\sigma_M = \dfrac{8}{\sqrt{3000}} = 0.15$

6.29 **a.** Histogram for the 10 scores:

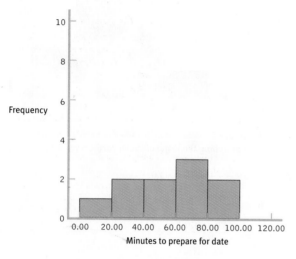

b. Histogram for all 40 scores:

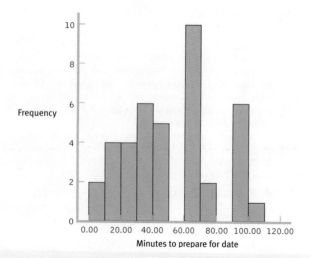

c. The shape of the distribution became more normal as the number of scores increased. If we added more scores, the distribution would become more and more normal. This occurs because many physical, psychological, and behavioral variables are normally distributed. With smaller samples, this might not be clear. But as the sample size approaches the size of the population, the shape of the sample distribution approaches that of the population.

d. This is a distribution of scores because each individual score is represented in the histogram on its own, not as part of a mean.

e. There are several possible answers to this question. For example, instead of using retrospective self-reports, we could have had students call a number or send an e-mail as they began to get ready; they would then have called the same number or sent another e-mail when they were ready. This would have led to scores that would be closer to the actual time it took students to get ready.

f. There are several possible answers to this question. For example, we could examine whether there was a mean gender difference in time spent getting ready for a date.

6.31 **a.** The mean of the z distribution is always 0.

b. $z = \dfrac{(X - \mu)}{\sigma} = \dfrac{(6.65 - 6.65)}{1.24} = 0$

c. The standard deviation of the z distribution is always 1.

d. A student 1 standard deviation above the mean would have a score of $6.65 + 1.24 = 7.89$. This person's z score would be: $z = \dfrac{(X - \mu)}{\sigma} = \dfrac{(7.89 - 6.65)}{1.24} = 1$

e. The answer will differ for each student but will involve substituting one's own score for X in this equation:

$z = \dfrac{(X - 6.65)}{1.24}$

6.33 **a.** It would not make sense because we would be comparing a mean to a distribution of scores. Because the distribution of scores would include some extreme scores, it would have a larger spread. The distribution of means includes sample means; within a given sample, the occasional extreme score is balanced by less extreme scores, and so the overall distribution has a smaller spread. Means are less likely to be extreme than are scores. A sample mean, therefore, is unlikely to appear extreme when compared to the wider range of scores.

b. $\mu_M = \mu = 3.51$

$\sigma_M = \dfrac{\sigma}{\sqrt{N}} = \dfrac{0.61}{\sqrt{40}} = 0.096$

c. $z = \dfrac{(M - \mu_M)}{\sigma_M} = \dfrac{(3.62 - 3.51)}{0.096} = 1.15$

d. This sample mean is about 1 standard deviation above the mean, and we know that about 34% of a distribution falls between the mean and 1 standard deviation above the mean (i.e., a z statistic of 1). We also know that 50% fall below the mean, because the z distribution is symmetric. The percentile would be about $50 + 34 = 84\%$.

6.35 **a.** Yes, the distribution of the number of movies college students watch in a year would likely approximate a normal curve. You can imagine that a small number of students watch an enormous number of movies and that a small number watch very few but that most watch a moderate number of movies between these two extremes.

b. Yes, the number of full-page advertisements in magazines is likely to approximate a normal curve. We could find magazines that have no or just one or two full-page advertisements and some that are chock full of them, but most magazines have some intermediate number of full-page advertisements.

c. Yes, human birth weights in Canada could be expected to approximate a normal curve. Few infants would weigh in at the extremes of very light or very heavy, and the weight of most infants would cluster around some intermediate value.

6.37 a. $z = \frac{(X - \mu)}{\sigma} = \frac{(95 - 81.71)}{13.07} = 1.02$

b. $z = \frac{(X - \mu)}{\sigma} = \frac{(10 - 8.13)}{3.70} = 0.51$

c. According to these data, the Red Sox had a better regular season (they had a higher z score) than did the Patriots.

d. The Patriots would have had to win 12 regular season games to have a slightly higher z score than the Red Sox:

$$z = \frac{(X - \mu)}{\sigma} = \frac{(12 - 8.13)}{3.70} = 1.05$$

e. There are several possible answers to this question. For example, we could have summed the teams' scores for every game (as compared to other teams' scores within their leagues).

6.39 a. $X = z(\sigma) + \mu = -0.18(10.83) + 81.00 = 79$ games (rounded to a whole number)

b. $X = z(\sigma) + \mu = -1.475(3.39) + 8.0 = 3$ games (rounded to a whole number)

c. Fifty percent of scores fall below the mean, so 34% (84 − 50 = 34) fall between the mean and the Steelers' score. We know that 34% of scores fall between the mean and a z score of 1.0, so the Steelers have a z score of 1.0. $X = z(\sigma) + \mu = 1(3.39) + 8.0 = 11$ games (rounded to a whole number).

d. We can examine our answers to be sure that negative z scores match up with answers that are below the mean and positive z scores match up with answers that are above the mean.

6.41 a. $\mu = 50; \sigma = 10$

b. $\mu_M = \mu = 50; \sigma_M = \frac{\sigma}{\sqrt{N}} = \frac{10}{\sqrt{95}} = 1.03$

c. When we calculate the mean of the scores for 95 individuals, the most extreme MMPI-2 depression scores will likely be balanced by scores toward the middle, as well as scores that are extreme in the other direction. It would be rare to have an extreme mean of the scores for 95 individuals. Thus, the spread is smaller than is the spread for all of the individual MMPI-2 depression scores.

6.43 a. These are the data for a distribution of scores rather than means because they have been obtained by entering each individual score into the analysis.

b. Comparing the size of the mean and the standard deviation suggests that there is positive skew. A person can't have fewer than zero friends, so the distribution would have to extend in a positive direction to have a standard deviation larger than the mean.

c. Because the mean is larger than either the median or the mode, it suggests that the distribution is positively skewed. There are extreme scores in the positive end of the distribution that are causing the mean to be more extreme.

d. You would compare this person to the distribution of scores. When making a comparison of an individual score, we must use the distribution of scores.

e. You would compare this sample to the distribution of means. When making a comparison involving a sample mean, we must use the distribution of means because it has a different pattern of variability from the distribution of scores (it has less variability).

f. $\mu_M = \mu = 7.44$. The number of individuals in the sample as reported in part (e) is 80. Substituting 80 in our standard error equation yields $\sigma_M = \frac{\sigma}{\sqrt{N}} = \frac{10.98}{\sqrt{80}} = 1.23$.

g. The distribution of means is likely to be a normal curve. Because the sample of 80 is well above the 30 recommended to see the central limit theorem at work, we expect that the distribution of the sample means will approximate a normal distribution.

6.45 a. You would compare this sample mean to a distribution of means. When we are making a comparison involving a sample mean, we need to use the distribution of means because it is this distribution that indicates the variability we are likely to see in sample means.

b. $z = \frac{(M - \mu_M)}{\sigma_M} = \frac{(8.7 - 7.44)}{1.23} = 1.02$.

This z score of 1.02 is approximately 1 standard deviation above the mean. Because 50% of the sample are below the mean and 34% are between the mean and 1 standard deviation above it, this sample would be at approximately the 84th percentile.

c. It does make sense to calculate a percentile for this sample. Given the central limit theorem and the size of the sample used to calculate the mean (80), we would expect the distribution of the sample means to be approximately normal.

CHAPTER 7

7.1 A percentile tells you the percentage of scores that fall below a certain point on a distribution.

7.3 We add the percentage between the mean and the positive z score to 50%, which is the percentage of scores below the mean (50% of scores are on each side of the mean).

7-5 In statistics, assumptions are the characteristics we ideally require the population from which we are sampling to have so that we can make accurate inferences.

7.7 *Parametric tests* are statistical analyses based on a set of assumptions about the population. By contrast, *nonparametric tests* are statistical analyses that are not based on a set of assumptions about the population.

7.9 *Critical values,* often called simply *cutoffs,* are the test statistic values beyond which we reject the null hypothesis. The *critical region* refers to the area in the tails of the distribution in which we reject the null hypothesis if our test statistic falls there.

7.11 A *statistically significant* finding is one in which we have rejected the null hypothesis because the pattern in the data differed from what we would expect by chance. The word *significant* is another one of those statistical terms with a very particular meaning. The phrase does not necessarily mean that the finding is important or meaningful; it means that we are justified in believing that the pattern in the data is genuine.

7.13 *Critical region* may have been chosen because values of a test statistic that are significant appear in a particular area, or region, on the normal distribution.

7.15 For a one-tailed test, the critical region (usually 5%, or a *p* level of 0.05) is placed in only one tail of the distribution; for a two-tailed test, the critical region must be split in half and shared between both tails (usually 2.5%, or 0.025, in each tail).

7.17 **a.** The percentage above is calculated as the area between this negative *z* score and the mean plus the 50% of the distribution above the mean. So, 3.19% + 50% = 53.19%.

b. The percentage below is calculated as the area below the mean, 50%, minus the area between this negative *z* score and the mean, 3.19%, or 46.81%.

c. The percentage at least as extreme is computed by taking the area beyond our *z* score, which is 46.81%, and doubling that to account for both sides of the curve. We get 93.62%.

7.19 **a.** 0.05

b. 0.83

c. 0.51

7.21 To get 2.5% in each tail, we use *z* values of ±1.96.

7.23 **a.** 5% in the one tail

b. 10% in the one tail

c. 1% in the one tail

7.25 $\mu_M = \mu = 500$

$$\sigma_M = \frac{\sigma}{\sqrt{N}} = \frac{100}{\sqrt{132}} = 8.70$$

7.27 **a.** Fail to reject the null hypothesis because -0.94 does not exceed the cutoff of -2.58.

b. Fail to reject the null hypothesis because 2.12 does not exceed the cutoff of 2.58.

c. The *z* statistic for which 49.6% of data fall between it and the mean occurs at ±2.65, which is more extreme than our cutoffs, so we would reject the null hypothesis.

7.29 **a.** $z = \frac{(X - \mu)}{\sigma} = \frac{58 - 63.80}{2.66} = -2.18$

b. 48.54% of the data fall between this *z* score and the mean. Because this is a negative *z* score, we add that amount to the 50% above the mean to get the percentage of girls taller than Elena, which is 98.54%.

c. 1.46% are shorter. This can be calculated two ways: (1) as 50% − 48.54%, or (2) as 100% of the distribution minus the percentage taller than she is, 98.54%.

d. At 58 inches, she is 5.8 inches shorter than the national average of 63.80 inches. She would have to grow 5.8 inches.

e. The 75th percentile is found by finding the *z* score that has 25% of scores between it and the mean, and therefore 25% in the tail. A *z* score of +0.67 gets us the closest, with

24.86% between it and the mean. Using this *z* score we can compute a raw score as:

$$X = 0.67(2.66) + 63.80 = 65.58 \text{ inches}$$

f. Elena would have to grow 7.58 inches to get to 65.58 inches.

7.31 **a.** $z = \frac{(M - \mu_M)}{\sigma_M} = \frac{62.6 - 63.8}{\frac{2.66}{\sqrt{33}}} = -2.59$

b. The *z* statistic indicates that this sample mean is 2.59 standard deviations below the expected mean for samples of size 33. In other words, this sample of girls has a mean height well below average.

c. The percentile rank is 0.48%, meaning that less than half of 1% of means is expected to have this value or less.

7.33 **a.** The percentage of scores between this *z* score and the mean is 36.43%; add this to the 50% below the mean to get the percentile score of 86.43%.

b. This score is a little more than 1 standard deviation above the mean, so you outperformed most other students in the class.

c. The original score is $X = z(\sigma) + \mu = 1.10(3) + 41 = 44.3$.

7.35 **a.** $\mu_M = \mu = 67$ inches

$$\sigma_M = \frac{\sigma}{\sqrt{N}} = \frac{3.19}{\sqrt{57}} = 0.423$$

b. $z = \frac{(M - \mu_M)}{\sigma_M} = \frac{68.1 - 67}{0.423} = 2.60$

c. 0.47% of sample means based on samples of size 57 would be taller.

d. Means as extreme or more extreme than this mean happen 0.94% of the time.

e. This result is well within the 5% cutoff region, as it happens less than 1% of the time.

7.37 **a.** This is a nondirectional hypothesis because no expected result is expressed.

b. This is a directional hypothesis because better grades are expected.

c. This hypothesis is nondirectional because any change is of interest.

7.39 **a.** We calculate the *z* scores for raw scores of 20 and 35 (and draw a curve with those *z* scores on it):

$$z = \frac{(X - \mu)}{\sigma} = \frac{(20 - 100)}{15} = -5.333$$

$$z = \frac{(X - \mu)}{\sigma} = \frac{(35 - 100)}{15} = -4.333$$

The table tells us that 50% of scores fall between the mean and these *z* scores. In other words, based on a normal distribution, almost no one has an IQ score between these numbers.

b. We calculate the *z* scores for raw scores of 50 and 70 (and draw a curve with those *z* scores on it):

$$z = \frac{(X - \mu)}{\sigma} = \frac{(50 - 100)}{15} = -3.333$$

$$z = \frac{(X - \mu)}{\sigma} = \frac{(70 - 100)}{15} = -2.000$$

So 49.95% fall between the mean and a z score of -3.333, and 47.72% fall between the mean and a z score of -2.000. Therefore, $49.95 - 47.72 = 2.23\%$ fall between these two z scores if IQ scores indeed are normally distributed.

c. $z = \dfrac{(X - \mu)}{\sigma} = \dfrac{(66 - 100)}{15} = -2.267$. (We then draw a curve with this z score on it.) So 48.84% of scores fall between the mean and a z score of -2.267. Therefore, $50 - 48.84 = 1.16\%$ of scores fall below an IQ of 66. This individual is at the 1.16th percentile.

d. We start by drawing a curve and shading the lowest 3%. We look up $50 - 3 = 47\%$ on the z table. The z score associated with 47% is 1.88, and we add a negative sign because the score is below the mean: -1.88. We calculate the raw score for this z score: $X = z(\sigma) + \mu = -1.88(15) + 100 = 71.8$. This individual would not be classified as having a mental disability because he has an IQ score above 70.

7.41 a. Null hypothesis: Adult psychiatric inpatients have the same intrasubtest scatter, on average, as normal adults. $H_0: \mu_1 = \mu_2$
Research hypothesis: Adult psychiatric inpatients have different intrasubtest scatter, on average, from normal adults. $H_1: \mu_1 \neq \mu_2$

b. Null hypothesis: Adult psychiatric inpatients do not have less intrasubtest scatter, on average, than normal adults. $H_0: \mu_1 \geq \mu_2$
Research hypothesis: Adult psychiatric inpatients have less intrasubtest scatter, on average, than normal adults. $H_1: \mu_1 < \mu_2$

7.43 a. Null hypothesis: Division I-AA games have the same average point spread as do Division I-A games. $H_0: \mu_1 = \mu_2$
Research hypothesis: Division I-AA games have a different average point spread than do Division I-A games. $H_1: \mu_1 \neq \mu_2$

b. Null hypothesis: Division I-AA games do not have a greater average point spread than do Division I-A games. $H_0: \mu_1 \leq \mu_2$
Research hypothesis: Division I-AA games have a greater point spread on average than do Division I-A games. $H_1: \mu_1 > \mu_2$

7.45 a. *Step 1:* Population 1 is Canadian adults. Population 2 is English adults. The comparison distribution will be a distribution of means. The hypothesis test will be a z test because we have only one sample and we know the population mean and the standard deviation. This study meets two of the three assumptions and may meet the third. The dependent variable appears to be scale. In addition, there are 30 participants in the sample, indicating that the comparison distribution will be normal. The data were not likely randomly selected, however, so we must be cautious when generalizing.
Step 2: Null hypothesis: Canadian adults have the same average GNT scores as do English adults. $H_0: \mu_1 = \mu_2$
Research hypothesis: Canadian adults have different average GNT scores from English adults. $H_0: \mu_1 \neq \mu_2$
Step 3: $\mu_M = \mu = 20.4$; $\sigma_M = \dfrac{\sigma}{\sqrt{N}} = \dfrac{3.2}{\sqrt{30}} = 0.584$
Step 4: Our cutoff z statistics, based on a p level of 0.05 and a two-tailed test, are -1.96 and 1.96. (*Note:* It is helpful to draw a picture of the normal curve and include these z statistics on it.)

Step 5: $z = \dfrac{(M - \mu_M)}{\sigma_M} = \dfrac{(17.5 - 20.4)}{0.584} = -4.97$. (*Note:* It is helpful to add this z statistic to your drawing of the normal curve that includes the cutoff z statistics.)
Step 6: Reject the null hypothesis. It appears that Canadian adults have lower average GNT scores than English adults.

b. Sometimes the people on whom the test was normed have characteristics in common that other people might not have. Often, when a test that was normed with one cultural group is used with another cultural group, the average scores are lower, not because the groups are actually different on the variable of interest but because some items are biased toward one group.

7.47 a. *Step 4:* Our cutoff z statistics, based on a p level of 0.01 and a two-tailed test, are -2.58 and 2.58. (*Note:* It is helpful to draw a picture of the normal curve and include these z statistics on it.)

b. *Step 6:* Reject the null hypothesis; it appears that Canadian adults have lower average GNT scores than English adults.

c. A p level of 0.01 leads to more extreme cutoff statistics than a p level of 0.05, making it more difficult to reject the null hypothesis. When the tails are limited to 1% versus 5%, the tails beyond the cutoffs are smaller and the cutoffs are more extreme.

d. The difference between the mean of the population and the mean of the sample is identical in both cases, as is the test statistic. The only aspect that is affected is the critical value.

CHAPTER 8

8.1 There may be a statistically significant difference between group means, but the difference might not be meaningful or have real-life application.

8.3 Confidence intervals add details to our hypothesis test. Specifically, they tell us a range of sample statistics we could expect if we conducted repeated hypothesis tests using samples from the same population.

8.5 In everyday language, we use the word *effect* to refer to the outcome of some event. Statisticians use the word in a similar way when they look at effect sizes. They want to assess a given outcome. For statisticians, the outcome is any change in a dependent variable, and the event creating the outcome is an independent variable. When statisticians calculate an effect size, they are calculating the size of an outcome.

8.7 In many hypothesis tests, we are comparing whether two distributions are truly different. If the two distributions overlap a lot, then we would probably find a small effect size and not be willing to conclude that the distributions are necessarily different. If the distributions do not overlap much, this would be evidence for a larger effect or a real difference between them.

8.9 According to Cohen's guidelines for interpreting the d statistic, a small effect is around 0.2, a medium effect is around 0.5, and a large effect is around 0.8.

8.11 In everyday language, we use the word *power* to mean either an ability to get something done or an ability to make others do things. Statisticians use the word *power* to refer to the ability to detect an effect, given that one exists.

8.13 80%

8.15 Power is our ability to reject the null hypothesis when we should do just that. Effect size is a measure of the difference between observed statistics, without consideration of sample size. Larger effects are easy to detect and make rejecting the null hypothesis easier than with smaller effects. High power allows researchers to detect small effects.

8.17 31% to 39% of respondents were suspicious of steroid use among world-record-breaking athletes in track-and-field.

8.19 44% to 50% of Americans reported feeling safer with a gun in the home.

8.21 **a.** z values of ± 1.28 put 10.03% in each tail.
b. z values of ± 1.44 put 7.49% in each tail.
c. z values of ± 2.58 put 0.49% in each tail, without going over.

8.23 z values of ± 1.28 put 10.03% in each tail, so we will use those as our critical values for the 80% confidence interval. Our standard error is calculated as:

$$\sigma_M = \frac{\sigma}{\sqrt{N}} = \frac{1.3}{\sqrt{78}} = 0.147$$

Now we can calculate the lower and upper bounds of the confidence interval.

$$M_{lower} = -z(\sigma_M) + M_{sample} = -1.28(0.147) + 4.1$$
$$= 3.912 \text{ hours}$$

$$M_{upper} = z(\sigma_M) + M_{sample} = 1.28(0.147) + 4.1 = 4.288 \text{ hours}$$

The 80% confidence interval can be expressed as [3.91, 4.29].

8.25 **a.** $\sigma_M = \frac{\sigma}{\sqrt{N}} = \frac{136}{\sqrt{12}} = 39.26$

b. $\sigma_M = \frac{\sigma}{\sqrt{N}} = \frac{136}{\sqrt{39}} = 21.78$

c. $\sigma_M = \frac{\sigma}{\sqrt{N}} = \frac{136}{\sqrt{188}} = 9.92$

8.27 Cohen's $d = \frac{(M - \mu)}{\sigma} = \frac{(1057 - 1014)}{136} = 0.32$

8.29 **a.** Small
b. Small
c. Large

8.31 **a.** The percentage beyond the z statistic of 2.23 is 1.29%. Converted to a proportion by dividing by 100, we get 0.0129.

b. For -1.82, the percentage in the tail is 3.51%. As a proportion, it is 0.0351.

c. For 0.33, the percentage in the tail is 37.07%. As a proportion, it is 0.3707.

8.33 **a.** Using the formula =NORMSDIST(NORMSINV (1-.0129)/(SQRT(2))), we get a p_{rep} of 0.9425.

b. Using the formula =NORMSDIST(NORMSINV (1-.0351)/(SQRT(2))), we get a p_{rep} of 0.8998.

c. Using the formula =NORMSDIST(NORMSINV (1-.3707)/(SQRT(2))), we get a p_{rep} of 0.5922.

8.35 *Step 1:* We know the following about population 1: $\mu = 16$ hours and $\sigma = 1.7$ hours. We assume the following about population 2 based on the sample: $N = 37$ infants and $M = 14.9$ hours. Standard error was given:

$$\sigma_M = \frac{\sigma}{\sqrt{N}} = \frac{1.7}{\sqrt{37}} = 0.279$$

Step 2: Because we are testing whether those in the sample sleep *fewer* hours, on average, than those in the population, we will conduct a one-tailed test focused on the low end of the distribution.

We need to find the critical value that marks where 5% of the data fall in the tail of population 1. We know that the z critical value for a one-tailed test is -1.64. Using that z we can calculate a raw score.

$$M = z(\sigma_M) + \mu_M = -1.64(0.279) + 16 = 15.542$$

This mean of 15.54 hours marks the point beyond which 5% of all means based on samples of 37 observations will fall, assuming that population 1 is true.

Step 3: For the second distribution, centered around 14.9 hours, we need to calculate how often means of 15.54 (our cutoff) and less occur. We do this by calculating the z statistic for the raw mean of 15.54 with respect to the sample mean of 14.9.

$$z = \frac{15.542 - 14.9}{0.279} = 2.30$$

We now look up this z on the table and find that 48.93% falls between the mean and this positive z value. We add this amount to 50%, the percent of the distribution below the mean, to compute power at 98.93%.

8.37 (Numbered steps indicate steps in the z test.)
a. *Step 3:*

$$\mu_M = \mu = 3.51; \sigma_M = \frac{\sigma}{\sqrt{N}} = \frac{0.61}{\sqrt{5}} = 0.273$$

Step 5:

$$z = \frac{(M - \mu_M)}{\sigma_M} = \frac{(3.7 - 3.51)}{0.273} = 0.696$$

b. *Step 3:*

$$\mu_M = \mu = 3.51; \sigma_M = \frac{\sigma}{\sqrt{N}} = \frac{0.61}{\sqrt{1000}} = 0.019$$

Step 5:

$$z = \frac{(M - \mu_M)}{\sigma_M} = \frac{(3.7 - 3.51)}{0.019} = 10.0$$

c. *Step 3:*

$$\mu_M = \mu = 3.51; \sigma_M = \frac{\sigma}{\sqrt{N}} = \frac{0.61}{\sqrt{1,000,000}} = 0.0006$$

Step 5:

$$z = \frac{(M - \mu_M)}{\sigma_M} = \frac{(3.7 - 3.51)}{0.0006} = 316.667$$

d. As sample size increases, the standard error decreases. This makes sense because means derived from larger samples would be less extreme—that is, would have less spread. As standard error decreases, the test statistic becomes larger. A larger test statistic is more likely to fall in the tails of the distribution, beyond the critical values.

e. An identical difference between means might lead to different conclusions based on sample size. If the sample size is large enough, even a small difference can lead to a large test statistic. The larger the sample size, the larger the test statistic, and the easier it is to reject the null hypothesis. So a significant finding might be small and not practically important.

8.39 **a.** (1) You could use a one-tailed, rather than a two-tailed, test. (2) You could use a less stringent p level (0.05 versus 0.01). (3) You could use a much larger sample size.

b. None of these tactics would change the actual difference between samples. This is a potential problem with hypothesis testing because an identical difference between means could be statistically significant under some circumstances but not others. Statistical significance, therefore, does not necessarily translate into importance of a finding.

8.41 **a.** A statistically significant difference just indicates that the difference between the means is unlikely to be due to chance. It does not tell us that there is no overlap in the distributions of the two populations we are considering. It is likely that there is overlap between the distributions and that some players with three children actually perform better than some players with two or fewer children. The drawings of distributions will vary; the two curves will overlap, but the mean of the distribution representing two or fewer children should be farther to the right than the mean of the distribution representing three or more children.

b. A difference can be statistically significant even if it is very small. In fact, if you have enough observations in your sample, even a tiny difference will approach statistical significance. Statistical significance does not indicate the importance or size of an effect—we need measures of effect size, which are not influenced by sample size, to understand the importance of an effect. These measures of effect size allow us to compare different predictors of performance. For example, in this case, it is likely that other aspects of a player's stats are more strongly associated with his performance and therefore would have a larger effect size. We could make our decision about whom to include in the fantasy team on the basis of the largest predictors of performance.

c. Even if the association is true, we cannot conclude that having a third child causes a decline in baseball performance. There are a number of possible causal explanations for this relation. It could be the reverse; perhaps those players who are not performing as well in their career end up devoting more time to family and therefore not playing well causes more children. Alternatively, a third variable could explain both having three children and poorer baseball performance. For example, perhaps less competitive or more laid-back players have more children and also perform more poorly.

d. The sample size for this analysis is likely small, so the statistical power to detect an effect is likely small as well.

8.43 **a.** z values of ± 1.28 put 10.03% in each tail, so we will use those as our critical values for the 80% confidence interval. Our standard error is calculated as:

$$\sigma_M = \frac{\sigma}{\sqrt{N}} = \frac{12.128}{\sqrt{4}} = 6.064$$

Now we can calculate the lower and upper bounds of the confidence interval.

$$M_{lower} = -z(\sigma_M) + M_{sample} = -1.28(6.064) + 8.75$$
$$= 0.99 \text{ points}$$

$$M_{upper} = z(\sigma_M) + M_{sample} = 1.28(6.064) + 8.75$$
$$= 16.51 \text{ points}$$

The 80% confidence interval around the mean of 8.75 is [0.99, 16.51].

b. The null-hypothesized mean of 16.189 still falls within this confidence interval, although just barely. We can see that the confidence interval became narrow, or smaller, as we dropped in confidence.

c. Because the z distribution and other normal distributions have tails that extend to infinity, there are no true bounds to the curve. We could say with 100% confidence that someone's height will be between 0 and 10 feet, but that range of heights is so wide that we are not adding any information to what people already know. In statistics, we push ourselves to have both high precision and high confidence in our estimates.

8.45 **a.** To determine p_{rep}, first we convert our test statistic to a p value. The z table in Appendix B gives us a percentage beyond the z statistic of 10.93%. Doubled, this is 21.86%. Converted to a proportion by dividing by 100, we get a p value of 0.2186. We then use Microsoft Excel to determine p_{rep}. Using the formula =NORMSDIST(NORMSINV (1-.2186)/(SQRT(2))), we get 0.7086.

b. If we were to replicate this study with a sample of the same size drawn from the same population, we would expect to get the same effect 70.86% of the time.

8.47 **a.** We know that the cutoffs for the 95% confidence interval are $z = \pm 1.96$. Our standard error is calculated as:

$$\sigma_M = \frac{\sigma}{\sqrt{N}} = \frac{6.5}{\sqrt{9}} = 2.167$$

Now we can calculate the lower and upper bounds of the confidence interval.

$$M_{lower} = -z(\sigma_M) + M_{sample} = -1.96(2.167) + 138$$
$$= 133.75 \text{ mph}$$

$$M_{upper} = z(\sigma_M) + M_{sample} = 1.96(2.167) + 138$$
$$= 142.25 \text{ mph}$$

The 95% confidence interval can be expressed as [133.75, 142.25].

Because the population mean of 135 mph falls within our confidence interval around the new mean, we cannot conclude anything exciting about our program. We do not have evidence to support that it changed the speed of a tennis serve.

b. Cohen's $d = \frac{(M - \mu)}{\sigma} = \frac{(138 - 135)}{6.5} = 0.46$, a medium effect size.

8.49 **a.** For the z statistic of -4.97, we get a percentage of 0.0000. Using 0.000001 in Excel, we get p_{rep} of 0.9996.

b. The z statistic was -1.57, giving 5.82% in one tail and 11.64% in two tails. This gives a proportion of 0.1164. Using Excel, we get p_{rep} of 0.8006.

c. As sample size increases, the likelihood of replicating an effect—given a sample of the same size from the same population—also increases. All else being equal, it increases from 80.06% with a sample of 3 to almost 100% with a sample of 30.

8.51 **a.** *Step 1:* We know the following about population 1: $\mu = 16$ hours and $\sigma = 1.7$ hours. We know the following about population 2: $N = 37$ infants and $M = 14.9$ hours. Standard error is calculated as:

$$\sigma_M = \frac{\sigma}{\sqrt{N}} = \frac{1.7}{\sqrt{37}} = 0.279$$

Step 2: Because we are testing whether the sample sleeps fewer hours, we will conduct a one-tailed test focused on the low end of the distribution.

We need to find the cutoff that marks where 1% of the data fall in the tail of population 1. The z critical value at which 1% of the distribution falls in the tail is -2.33. Using that z value we can calculate a raw score.

$$M = z(\sigma_M) + \mu_M = -2.33(0.279) + 16 = 15.349 \text{ hours}$$

This mean of 15.349 hours marks the point beyond which 1% of all means based on samples of 37 observations will fall, assuming that population 1 is true.

Step 3: For the second distribution, centered around 14.9 hours, we need to calculate how often means of 15.349 (our cutoff) and less occur. We do this by calculating the z statistic for the raw mean of 15.359 with respect to the sample mean of 14.9.

$$z = \frac{15.349 - 14.9}{0.279} = 1.609$$

We now look up this z statistic on the table and find that 44.63% falls between the mean and this positive z value. We add this amount to 50%, the percent of the distribution below the mean, to compute power at 94.63%. Power is calculated, in this case, as the proportion of means that would fall between the z value and the tail of interest.

b. Making alpha smaller (from 5% to 1%) reduced our power by around 5%. Alpha is the cutoff for rejecting the null hypothesis. If we reduce the chance of rejecting the null hypothesis, then we reduce the probability of rejecting it when it should be rejected, which is power.

c. We hesitate to use an alpha much larger than the standard 5% because we do not want to increase our chances of making a Type I error, falsely rejecting the null hypothesis when it is accurate.

8.53 a. $\sigma_M = \frac{1.7}{\sqrt{37}} = 0.279$ $z = \frac{14.9 - 16}{0.279} = -3.94$

This exceeds either a one-tailed (-1.64) or two-tailed (-1.96) cutoff, so we reject the null hypothesis and conclude that these infants sleep less, on average, than those in the population.

b. $\sigma_M = \frac{1.7}{\sqrt{4}} = 0.85$ $z = \frac{14.9 - 16}{0.85} = -1.29$

This falls short of both critical values, so with either hypothesis test, we would fail to reject the null hypothesis. We cannot conclude anything based on these data.

8.55 a. *Step 1:* To calculate statistical power, we need to know the mean of population 1, which is $\mu_1 = 16.189$, and the population standard deviation, which is $\sigma = 12.128$. We need to calculate standard error based on our expected sample size of $N = 4$. In this case, our standard error is $\sigma_M = \frac{\sigma}{\sqrt{N}} = \frac{12.12}{\sqrt{4}} = 6.064$. Finally, the mean of population 2 (which, for the sake of calculating statistical power, we're assuming is represented by the mean of our sample) is 6.25.

Step 2: Looking only at population 1, we find the raw mean (of this distribution of means) that marks off the

bottom 5% of the distribution; we choose the bottom 5% because the sample mean is lower than the mean of population 1. To find the raw mean, we find the critical z value for that point, -1.645, and convert it to a raw mean: $M = z(\sigma_M) + \mu_M = -1.64(6.064) + 16.189 = 6.244$. See the accompanying figure, which shows where this mean falls on the distribution with respect to the mean of population 1.

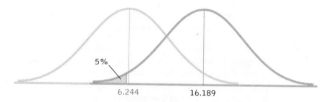

Step 3: At this step, we're focusing just on the second distribution, the one centered around 6.25. The accompanying figure shows where the raw mean of 6.244 falls relative to the mean of population 2 (the sample mean), 6.25. (You'll notice that they are almost exactly the same.) We will now compare the raw mean we just calculated, 6.244, with the mean of population 2, 6.25, by calculating the z statistic for 6.244 with respect to 6.25:

$$z = \frac{6.244 - 6.25}{6.064} = 0.0009$$

We now look up the z value of 0.0009 in the z table, and we find that approximately 50% of the distribution falls on either side of the z value. So 50% falls beyond that z value in the second distribution. (The critical z value from the first distribution is essentially at the mean of the second distribution, the one centered around the sample mean.) In this case, our statistical power to detect an effect is about 50%. If the population represented by the second distribution really does exist, we have a 50% chance of randomly selecting a sample with a mean different enough from that in population 1 that we will reject the null hypothesis.

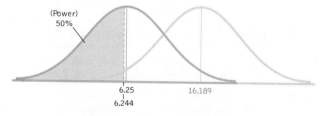

b. Statistical power of 80% is typically considered acceptable. Because our statistical power for this study was low relative to that, 50%, we should be cautious about saying that there is no difference between the point spreads of the two divisions. We may just not have had enough statistical power to detect a real difference.

c. Your results with G★Power should agree with what you calculated in part (a), with some possible slight difference due to decimal precision.

CHAPTER 9

9.1 The t distributions are used when we do not know the population standard deviation or are comparing only two groups.

9.3 For both tests, standard error is calculated as the standard deviation divided by the square root of N. For the z test, the population standard deviation is calculated with N in the denominator. For the t test, the standard deviation for the population is estimated by dividing the sum of squared deviations by $N - 1$.

9.5 t stands for the t statistic, M is the sample mean, μ_M is the mean of the distribution of means, and s_M is the standard error as estimated from a sample.

9.7 A distribution of mean differences is constructed by measuring the difference scores for a sample of individuals and then averaging those differences. This process is performed repeatedly, using the same population and samples of the same size. Once a collection of mean differences is gathered, they can be distributed on a graph (in most cases, they form a bell-shaped curve).

9.9 *Free to vary* refers to the number of scores that can take on different values if we know a given parameter.

9.11 As the sample size increases, we can feel more confident in our estimate of variability in the population. Remember, this estimate of variability (s) is calculated with $N - 1$ in the denominator in order to inflate the estimate somewhat. As our sample increases from 10 to 100, and then up to 1000, subtracting 1 from N has less of an impact on the overall calculation. As this happens, our t distribution approaches the z distribution, where we in fact knew the population standard deviation and did not need to estimate it.

9.13 We could report p_{rep} instead of the p value.

9.15 The term *paired-samples* is used to describe a test that compares an individual's scores in both conditions; it is also called a *paired-samples t test. Independent-samples* refer to groups that do not overlap in any way, including membership; the observations made in one group in no way relate or depend on the observations made in another group.

9.17 a. First we need to calculate the mean:

$$M = \frac{\Sigma X}{N} = \frac{93 + 97 + 91 + 88 + 103 + 94 + 97}{7}$$
$$= \frac{663}{7} = 94.714$$

We then calculate the deviation of each score from the mean and the square of that deviation.

X	$X - M$	$(X - M)^2$
93	−1.714	2.938
97	2.286	5.226
91	−3.714	13.794
88	−6.714	45.078
103	8.286	68.658
94	−0.714	0.510
97	2.286	5.226

The standard deviation is:

$$SD = \sqrt{\frac{\Sigma(X - M)^2}{N}} = \sqrt{\frac{141.430}{7}} = \sqrt{20.204} = 4.49$$

b. When estimating the population variability, we calculate s:

$$s = \sqrt{\frac{\Sigma(X - M)^2}{N - 1}} = \sqrt{\frac{141.430}{7 - 1}} = \sqrt{23.572} = 4.86$$

9.19 $s_M = \frac{s}{\sqrt{N}} = \frac{4.86}{\sqrt{7}} = 1.84$

9.21 $t = \frac{(M - \mu_M)}{s_M} = \frac{(94.714 - 96)}{1.84} = -0.70$

9.23 a. Because 73 df is not on our table, we go to 60 df (we do not go to the closest value, which would be 80, because we want to be conservative and go to the next lowest value for df) to find our critical value of 1.296 in the upper tail. If we are looking in the lower tail, our critical value is −1.296.

b. ± 1.984

c. Either −2.438 or +2.438

9.25 a. This is a two-tailed test with $df = 25$, so the critical t value is ±2.060.

b. $df = 17$, so the t critical value is either −2.567 or +2.567, depending on which tail is of interest.

c. ±2.043

9.27 a. $t = \frac{(M - \mu_M)}{s_M} = \frac{(8.5 - 7)}{\frac{2.1}{\sqrt{41}}} = 4.57$

b. $M_{lower} = -t(s_M) + M_{sample} = -2.705(0.328) + 8.5 = 7.61$
$M_{upper} = t(s_M) + M_{sample} = 2.705(0.328) + 8.5 = 9.39$

c. $d = \frac{(M - \bar{\mu})}{s} = \frac{(8.5 - 7)}{2.1} = 0.71$

9.29 a. $s_M = \frac{s}{\sqrt{N}} = \frac{1.42}{\sqrt{13}} = 0.394$

$t = \frac{(-0.77 - 0)}{0.394} = -1.95$

b. $M_{lower} = -t(s_M) + M_{sample} = -2.179(0.394) + (-0.77) = -1.63$
$M_{upper} = t(s_M) + M_{sample} = 2.179(0.394) + (-0.77) = 0.09$

c. $d = \frac{(M - \mu)}{s} = \frac{(-0.77 - 0)}{1.42} = -0.54$

9.31 a. ±1.96

b. Either −2.33 or +2.33, depending on the tail of interest

c. ±1.96

d. The critical z values are lower than the critical t values, making it easier to reject the null hypothesis when conducting a z test. Decisions using the t distributions are more conservative because of the chance we may have poorly estimated the population standard deviation.

9.33 a. The appropriate mean: $\mu_M = \mu = 11.72$

The calculations for the appropriate standard deviation (in this case, standard error, s_M): $M =$
$\frac{\Sigma X}{N} = \frac{(25.62 + 13.09 + 8.74 + 17.63 + 2.80 + 4.42)}{6} = 12.05$

X	X − M	(X − M)²
25.62	13.57.8	184.145
13.09	1.04	1.082
8.74	−3.31	10.956
17.63	5.58	31.136
2.80	−9.25	85.563
4.42	−7.63	58.217

Numerator: $\Sigma(X - M)^2 = \Sigma(184.145 + 1.082 + 10.956 + 31.136 + 85.563 + 58.217) = 371.099$

$$s = \sqrt{\frac{\Sigma(X-M)^2}{(N-1)}} = \sqrt{\frac{371.099}{(6-1)}} = \sqrt{74.220}$$
$$= 8.615$$
$$s_M = \frac{s}{\sqrt{N}} = \frac{8.615}{\sqrt{6}} = 3.517$$

b. $t = \dfrac{(M - \mu_M)}{s_M} = \dfrac{(12.05 - 11.72)}{3.517} = 0.09$

c. p_{rep} is 0.1496. This tells us that, if we were to replicate this study by drawing a sample of the same size from the same population, we would obtain an effect in the same direction 14.96% of the time.

d. There are several possible answers to this question. Among the hypotheses that could be examined are whether the length of stay on death row depends on gender, race, or age. Specifically, given prior evidence of a racial bias in the implementation of the death penalty, we might hypothesize that black and Hispanic prisoners have shorter times to execution than do prisoners overall.

e. We would need to know the population standard deviation. If we were really interested in this, we could calculate the standard deviation from the online execution list.

9.35 a. $M_{lower} = -t(s_M) + M_{sample} = -2.571(3.517) + 12.05 = 3.01$ years
$M_{upper} = t(s_M) + M_{sample} = 2.571(3.517) + 12.05 = 21.09$ years

b. Because the population mean of 11.72 years is within the very large range of the confidence interval, we fail to reject the null hypothesis. This confidence interval is so large, it is not useful. The size of the confidence interval is caused by the large variability in the sample (s_M) and the small sample size (resulting in a large critical t value).

9.37 a. Population 1 is local stores before the big box store opens. Population 2 is local stores after the big box store opens.

b. The comparison distribution would be a distribution of mean differences. The participants, local stores, are the same in both samples. Thus, we can calculate a difference score for each participant and a mean difference score for the study. The mean difference score will be compared to a distribution of all possible mean difference scores for a sample of this size and based on the null hypothesis.

c. Because we have two samples and all participants are in both samples, we would use a paired-samples t test.

d. (1) The dependent variable, earnings, is scale. (2) The sample includes 20 local stores in one area before a specific big box store opens; they were not randomly selected, so we must be cautious about generalizing from this sample. (3) We do not know if the population distributions are normal, and we have fewer than 30 participants (i.e., 20); we should examine our sample data as an indication of whether the underlying populations are likely to be normally distributed.

e. There may have been changes other than the opening of a big box store. A local factory, employing a large percentage of town residents, might have closed. The economy might have entered a recession or boomed. It may have been rainy every day one October and sunny every day the other. These other differences, not related to the big box store opening, could have led to any changes.

9.39 a. *Step 1:* Population 1 is male U.S. Marines following a month-long training exercise. Population 2 is college men. The comparison distribution will be a distribution of means.

The hypothesis test will be a single-sample t test because we have only one sample and we know the population mean but not the standard deviation. This study meets one of the three assumptions and may meet another. The dependent variable, anger, appears to be scale. The data were not likely randomly selected, so we must be cautious with respect to generalizing to all Marines who complete this training. We do not know whether the population is normally distributed, and there are not at least 30 participants. However, the data from our sample do not suggest a skewed distribution.

Step 2: Null hypothesis: Male U.S. Marines after a month-long training exercise have the same average anger levels as college men—$H_0: \mu_1 = \mu_2$.

Research hypothesis: Male U.S. Marines after a month-long training exercise have different average anger levels from college men—$H_1: \mu_1 \neq \mu_2$.

Step 3: $\mu_M = \mu = 8.90$; $s_M = 0.495$

X	X − M	(X − M)²
14	0.667	0.445
12	−1.333	1.777
13	−0.333	0.111
12	−1.333	1.777
14	0.667	0.445
15	1.667	2.779

$M = 13.333$

$SS = \Sigma(X - M)^2 = \Sigma(0.445 + 1.777 + 0.111 + 1.777 + 0.445 + 2.779) = 7.334$

$$s = \sqrt{\frac{\Sigma(X-M)^2}{N-1}} = \sqrt{\frac{SS}{(N-1)}} = \sqrt{\frac{7.334}{6-1}}$$
$$= \sqrt{1.468} = 1.212$$
$$s_M = \frac{s}{\sqrt{N}} = \frac{1.212}{\sqrt{6}} = 0.495$$

Step 4: $df = N - 1 = 6 - 1 = 5$; our critical values, based on 5 degrees of freedom, a p level of 0.05, and a two-tailed test, are −2.571 and 2.571. (*Note:* It is helpful to draw a curve that includes these cutoffs.)

Step 5: $t = \dfrac{(M - \mu_M)}{s_M} = \dfrac{(13.333 - 8.90)}{0.495} = 8.96$

(*Note:* It is helpful to add this t statistic to the curve that you drew in step 4.)

Step 6: Reject the null hypothesis. It appears that male U.S. Marines just after a month-long training exercise have higher average anger levels than college men; $t(5) = 8.96$, $p < 0.05$.

b. $t = \dfrac{(M - \mu_M)}{s_M} = \dfrac{(13.333 - 9.20)}{0.495} = 8.35$; reject the null

hypothesis; it appears that male U.S. Marines just after a month-long training exercise have higher average anger levels than adult men; $t(5) = 8.35$, $p < 0.05$.

c. $t = \dfrac{(M - \mu_M)}{s_M} = \dfrac{(13.333 - 13.5)}{0.495} = 0.34$; fail to reject the null

hypothesis; we conclude that there is no evidence from this study to support the research hypothesis; $t(5) = -0.34$, $p > 0.05$.

d. We can conclude that Marines' anger scores just after high-altitude, cold-weather training are, on average, higher than those of college men and adult men. We cannot conclude, however, that they are higher, on average, than those of male psychiatric outpatients. With respect to the latter difference, we can only conclude that there is no evidence to support that there is a difference between Marines' mean anger scores and those of male psychiatric outpatients.

9.41 a. We know from the problem that $\mu_M = \mu = 15$ days. Now we need to calculate the mean of our sample:

$$M = \frac{\Sigma X}{N} = (10 + 11 + 8 + 14 + 13 + 12 + 12 + 27) / 8$$
$$= 107/8 = 13.375$$

X	X − M	(X − M)²
10	−3.375	11.391
11	−2.375	5.641
8	−5.375	28.891
14	0.625	0.391
13	−0.375	0.141
12	−1.375	1.891
12	−1.375	1.891
27	13.625	185.641

The estimate of the population variability is calculated as:

$$s = \sqrt{\frac{\Sigma(X - M)^2}{N - 1}} = \sqrt{\frac{235.878}{8 - 1}} = \sqrt{33.697} = 5.805$$

The standard error is calculated as:

$$s_M = \frac{s}{\sqrt{N}} = \frac{5.805}{\sqrt{8}} = 2.052$$

$$t = \frac{(13.375 - 15)}{2.052} = -0.79$$

b. $df = N - 1 = 8 - 1 = 7$

For a two-tailed test with a p level of 0.05 and 7 degrees of freedom, the cutoffs are ± 2.365. Because our t test statistic fails to exceed our cutoffs, we fail to reject the null hypothesis. We cannot conclude that this small business is any different from the national average when it comes to amount of paid days off.

c. For a p level of 0.454, p_{rep} is 0.5326.

d. The confidence interval is calculated as:

$M_{lower} = -t(s_M) + M_{sample} = -2.365(2.052) + 13.375$
$= 8.52$ paid days off
$M_{upper} = t(s_M) + M_{sample} = 2.365(2.052) + 13.375$
$= 18.23$ paid days off

e. $d = \dfrac{(M - \mu)}{s} = \dfrac{(13.375 - 15)}{5.805} = -0.28$

This is a small effect.

9.43 a. We know from the problem that $\mu_M = \mu = 15$ days. Now we need to calculate the mean of our sample:

$$M = \frac{\Sigma X}{N} = (10 + 11 + 8 + 14 + 13 + 12 + 12) / 7$$
$$= 80/7 = 11.429 \text{ days}$$

X	X − M	(X − M)²
10	−1.429	2.042
11	−0.429	0.184
8	−3.429	11.758
14	2.571	6.610
13	1.571	2.468
12	0.571	0.326
12	0.571	0.326

The estimate of the population variability is calculated as:

$$s = \sqrt{\frac{\Sigma(X - M)^2}{N - 1}} = \sqrt{\frac{23.714}{7 - 1}} = \sqrt{3.952} = 1.988$$

The standard error is calculated as:

$$s_M = \frac{s}{\sqrt{N}} = \frac{1.988}{\sqrt{7}} = 0.751$$

$$t = \frac{(11.429 - 15)}{0.751} = -4.75$$

b. $df = N - 1 = 7 - 1 = 6$

For a two-tailed test with a p level of 0.05 and 6 degrees of freedom, the cutoffs are ± 2.447. Our test statistic far exceeds these cutoffs, so we can reject the null hypothesis and conclude that this group of employees gets fewer paid days off, on average, compared to the population.

c. For a p level of 0.003, p_{rep} is 0.9740.

d. $d = \dfrac{(M - \mu)}{s} = \dfrac{(11.43 - 15)}{1.99} = -1.79$

This is a large effect.

e. Because the owner's large data point, 27 days, was taken out of the analyses, the mean number of paid days off went down a little; this created a larger difference in the numerator of the t test and Cohen's d. More significantly, perhaps, the estimate of variability in the population also went down (from 5.80 to 1.99). This had a great impact on the calculation of t and d, resulting in a statistically significant difference being observed, and also affected p_{rep} such that there is now a high probability of finding an effect in the same direction with the same size sample from this population.

9.45 $d = \dfrac{(M - \mu)}{s} = \dfrac{(0.1 - 0)}{0.138} = 0.72$

This is a medium-to-large effect size. This might indicate that, if we continue to investigate our hypothesis, we might attain statistical significance. The easiest way to do this is to increase our sample size. We could use a power calculator to estimate how large our sample would need to be to find an effect of this size.

9.47 **a.** *Step 2:* Null hypothesis: The average Stroop reaction time of highly hypnotizable individuals who receive a posthypnotic suggestion is greater than or equal to that of highly hypnotizable individuals who receive no posthypnotic suggestion—$H_0: \mu_1 \geq \mu_2$.

Research hypothesis: Highly hypnotizable individuals who receive a posthypnotic suggestion will have faster (i.e., lower number) average Stroop reaction times than highly hypnotizable individuals who receive no posthypnotic suggestion—$H_1: \mu_1 < \mu_2$.

b. *Step 4:* $df = N - 1 = 6 - 1 = 5$; our critical value, based on 5 degrees of freedom, a p level of 0.05, and a one-tailed test, is -2.015. (*Note:* It is helpful to draw a curve that includes this cutoff.)

c. *Step 6:* Reject the null hypothesis; it appears that highly hypnotizable people have faster Stroop reaction times when they receive a posthypnotic suggestion than when they do not.

d. It is easier to reject the null hypothesis with a one-tailed test. Although we rejected the null hypothesis under both conditions, the critical t value is less extreme with a one-tailed test because the entire 0.05 (5%) critical region is in one tail instead of divided between two.

e. The difference between the means of the samples is identical, as is the test statistic. The only aspect that is affected is the critical value.

9.49 **a.** *Step 3:* $\mu_M = \mu = 0$; $s_M = 0.850$

(*Note:* Remember to cross out the original scores once you have created the difference scores so you won't be tempted to use them in your calculations.)

X	Y	DIFFERENCE	X − M	(X − M)²
~~12.6~~	~~8.5~~	−4.1	−0.8	0.64
~~13.8~~	~~9.6~~	−4.2	−0.9	0.81
~~11.6~~	~~10.0~~	−1.6	1.7	2.89

$M_{difference} = -3.3$

$SS = \Sigma(X - M)^2 = \Sigma(0.64 + 0.81 + 2.89) = 4.34$

$s = \sqrt{\dfrac{\Sigma(X-M)^2}{(N-1)}} = \sqrt{\dfrac{SS}{(N-1)}} = \sqrt{\dfrac{4.34}{(3-1)}}$
$= \sqrt{2.17} = 1.473$

$s_M = \dfrac{s}{\sqrt{N}} = \dfrac{1.473}{\sqrt{3}} = 0.850$

Step 4: $df = N - 1 = 3 - 1 = 2$; our critical values, based on 2 degrees of freedom, a p level of 0.05, and a two-tailed test, are -4.303 and 4.303. (*Note:* It is helpful to draw a curve that includes these cutoffs.)

Step 5: $t = \dfrac{(M_{difference} - \mu_{difference})}{s_M} = \dfrac{(-3.3 - 0)}{0.850} = -3.38$

(*Note:* It is helpful to add this t statistic to the curve that you drew in step 4.)

b. This test statistic is no longer beyond the critical value. Reducing the sample size makes it more difficult to reject the null hypothesis because it results in a larger standard error and therefore a smaller test statistic. It also results in more extreme critical values.

CHAPTER 10

10.1 An independent-samples t test is used when we do not know the population parameters and are comparing two groups that are composed of nonoverlapping, unrelated participants or observations.

10.3 Independent events are things that do not affect each other. For example, the lunch you buy today does not impact the mean hours of sleep per night the authors of this book get.

10.5 The comparison distribution for the paired-samples t test is made up of *mean differences*—the average of many difference scores. The comparison distribution for the independent-samples t test is made up of *differences between means*, or the differences we can expect to see between group means if the null hypothesis is true.

10.7 Both of these represent corrected variance within a group (s^2), but one is for the X variable and the other is for the Y variable. Because these are corrected measures of variance, $N - 1$ is in the denominator.

10.9 We assume that larger samples do a better job of estimating the population than smaller samples, so we would want the variability measure based on the larger sample to count more.

10.11 We can take the confidence interval's upper bound and lower bound, compare those to the point estimate in our numerator, and get our margin of error. So, if we predict a score of 7 with a confidence interval of [4.3, 9.7], we can also express this as a margin of error of 2.7 points (7 ± 2.7). Confidence interval and margin of error are simply two ways to say the same thing.

10.13 The size of the confidence interval size relates to the range of scores being predicted. So, a 95% confidence interval that spans a range from 2 to 12 is larger than a 95% confidence interval from 5 to 6. Although the percentage range has stayed the same, the width of the distribution has changed. Larger ranges mean less precision in making predictions; smaller ranges indicate we are doing a better job of predicting the phenomenon within the population.

10.15 Guidelines for interpreting the size of an effect based on Cohen's d were presented in Chapter 8. Those guidelines state that 0.2 is a small effect, 0.5 is a medium effect, and 0.8 is a large effect.

10.17 Group 1 is treated as our X variable; $M_X = 95.8$.

X	X − M	(X − M)²
97	1.2	1.44
83	−12.8	163.84
105	9.2	84.64
102	6.2	38.44
92	−3.8	14.44

$s_X^2 = \dfrac{\Sigma(X-M)^2}{N-1} = \dfrac{(1.44 + 163.84 + 84.64 + 38.44 + 14.44)}{5-1} = 75.7$

Group 2 is treated as our Y variable; $M_Y = 104$.

Y	Y − M	(Y − M)²
111	7	49
103	−1	1
96	−8	64
106	2	4

$$s_Y^2 = \frac{\Sigma(Y - M)^2}{N - 1} = \frac{(49 + 1 + 64 + 4)}{4 - 1} = 39.333$$

10.19 Treating group 1 as X and group 2 as Y, $df_X = N - 1 = 5 - 1 = 4$, $df_Y = 4 - 1 = 3$, and $df_{total} = df_X + df_Y = 4 + 3 = 7$.

10.21 ±2.365

10.23 $s_{pooled}^2 = \left(\frac{df_X}{df_{total}}\right)s_X^2 + \left(\frac{df_Y}{df_{total}}\right)s_Y^2 = \left(\frac{4}{7}\right)75.7 + \left(\frac{3}{7}\right)39.333$
$= 43.257 + 16.857 = 60.114$

10.25 For group 1: $s_{M_X}^2 = \frac{s_{pooled}^2}{N_X} = \frac{60.114}{5} = 12.023$

For group 2: $s_{M_Y}^2 = \frac{s_{pooled}^2}{N_Y} = \frac{60.114}{4} = 15.029$

10.27 The variance of the distribution of differences between means is:

$$s_{difference}^2 = s_{M_X}^2 = s_{M_Y}^2 + 12.023 + 15.029 = 27.052$$

The standard deviation of the distribution of differences between means is:

$$s_{difference} = \sqrt{s_{difference}^2} = \sqrt{27.052} = 5.201$$

10.29 $t = \frac{(M_X - M_Y) - (\mu_X - \mu_Y)}{s_{difference}} = \frac{(95.8 - 104) - (0)}{5.201} = -1.58$

10.31 The critical t values for the 95% confidence interval for a df of 7 are −2.365 and 2.365.

$(M_X - M_Y)_{lower} = -t(s_{difference}) + (M_X - M_Y)_{sample}$
$(M_X - M_Y)_{lower} = -2.365(5.201) + (-8.2) = -20.50$

$(M_X - M_Y)_{upper} = t(s_{difference}) + (M_X - M_Y)_{sample}$
$(M_X - M_Y)_{upper} = 2.365(5.201) + (-8.2) = 4.10$

The confidence interval is [−20.50, 4.10].

10.33 To calculate Cohen's d, we need to calculate the pooled standard deviation for our data:

$$s_{pooled} = \sqrt{s_{pooled}^2} = \sqrt{60.114} = 7.753$$

Cohen's $d = \frac{(M_X - M_Y) - (\mu_X - \mu_Y)}{s_{pooled}} = \frac{(95.8 - 104) - (0)}{7.753}$
$= -1.058$

10.35 a. df_{total} is 35, and the cutoffs are −2.030 and 2.030.
b. df_{total} is 26, and the cutoffs are −2.779 and 2.779.
c. −1.740 and 1.740

10.37 a. *Step 1:* Population 1 is highly hypnotizable people who receive a posthypnotic suggestion. Population 2 is highly hypnotizable people who do not receive a posthypnotic

suggestion. The comparison distribution will be a distribution of differences between means. The hypothesis test will be an independent-samples t test because we have two samples and every participant is in only one sample. This study meets one of the three assumptions and may meet another. The dependent variable, reaction time in seconds, is scale. The data were not likely randomly selected, so we should be cautious when generalizing beyond our sample. We do not know whether the population is normally distributed, and there are fewer than 30 participants, but our sample data do not suggest skew.

Step 2: Null hypothesis: Highly hypnotizable individuals who receive a posthypnotic suggestion have the same average Stroop reaction times as highly hypnotizable individuals who receive no posthypnotic suggestion— $H_0: \mu_1 = \mu_2$.

Research hypothesis: Highly hypnotizable individuals who receive a posthypnotic suggestion have different average Stroop reaction times from highly hypnotizable individuals who receive no posthypnotic suggestion— $H_1: \mu_1 \neq \mu_2$.

Step 3: $(\mu_1 - \mu_2) = 0$; $s_{difference} = 0.463$
Calculations:

$M_X = 12.55$

X	X − M	(X − M)²
12.6	0.05	0.003
13.8	1.25	1.563
11.6	−0.95	0.903
12.2	−0.35	0.123
12.1	−0.45	0.203
13.0	0.45	0.203

$$s_Y^2 = \frac{\Sigma(X - M)^2}{N - 1}$$
$$= \frac{(0.003 + 1.563 + 0.903 + 0.123 + 0.203 + 0.203)}{6 - 1}$$
$$= 0.600$$

$M_Y = 9.5$

Y	Y − M	(Y − M)²
8.5	−1.0	1.000
9.6	0.1	0.010
10.0	0.5	0.250
9.2	−0.3	0.090
8.9	−0.6	0.360
10.8	1.3	1.690

$$s_X^2 = \frac{\Sigma(Y - M)^2}{N - 1}$$
$$= \frac{(1.0 + 0.01 + 0.25 + 0.09 + 0.36 + 1.69)}{6 - 1}$$
$$= 0.680$$

$df_X = N - 1 = 6 - 1 = 5$
$df_Y = N - 1 = 6 - 1 = 5$
$df_{total} = df_X + df_Y = 5 + 5 = 10$

$$s_{pooled}^2 = \left(\frac{df_X}{df_{total}}\right)s_X^2 + \left(\frac{df_Y}{df_{total}}\right)s_Y^2$$
$$= \left(\frac{5}{10}\right)0.600 + \left(\frac{5}{10}\right)0.680$$
$$= 0.300 + 0.340 = 0.640$$

$$s_{M_X}^2 = \frac{s_{pooled}^2}{N} = \frac{0.640}{6} = 0.107$$
$$s_{M_Y}^2 = \frac{s_{pooled}^2}{N} = \frac{0.640}{6} = 0.107$$
$$s_{difference}^2 = s_{M_X}^2 + s_{M_X}^2 = 0.107 + 0.107 = 0.214$$
$$s_{difference} = \sqrt{s_{difference}^2} = \sqrt{0.214} = 0.463$$

Step 4: Our critical values, based on a two-tailed test, a *p* level of 0.05, and df_{total} of 10, are -2.228 and 2.228. (*Note:* It is helpful to draw a curve that includes these cutoffs.)

Step 5: $t = \frac{(12.55 - 9.50) - (0)}{0.463} = \frac{3.05}{0.463} = 6.59$. (*Note:* It is helpful to add this *t* statistic to the curve that you drew in step 4.)

Step 6: Reject the null hypothesis; it appears that highly hypnotizable people have faster Stroop reaction times when they receive a posthypnotic suggestion than when they do not.

b. $t(10) = 6.59, p < 0.05$

10.39 a. *Step 1:* Population 1 consists of garbage cans with the odor-shield bags. Population 2 consists of garbage cans with the standard bags. The comparison distribution is a distribution of differences between means. We will use an independent-samples *t* test because no bag can be in both conditions, and we have two groups. Of the three assumptions, we meet one because the dependent variable, number of larvae, is a scale variable. We do not know whether the data were randomly selected and whether the population is normally distributed, and we have a small *N*, so we should be cautious in drawing conclusions.

Step 2: Null hypothesis: There is no mean difference in the number of larvae between the two types of bags—$H_0: \mu_1 = \mu_2$.

Research hypothesis: Bags with the odor shield attract a different mean number of flies, as reflected in larvae, from the standard bags—$H_1: \mu_1 \neq \mu_2$.

Step 3: $(\mu_1 = \mu_2) = 0$; $s_{difference} \approx 3.474$
Calculations:

$$M_X = 18.667$$

X	X − M	(X − M)²
23	4.333	18.775
19	0.333	0.111
14	−4.667	21.781

$$s_X^2 = \frac{\Sigma(X - M)^2}{N - 1} = \frac{(18.775 + 0.111 + 21.781)}{3 - 1} = 20.334$$

$$M_Y = 9.25$$

Y	Y − M	(Y − M)²
10	0.75	0.563
15	5.75	33.063
8	−1.25	1.563
4	−5.25	27.563

$$s_Y^2 = \frac{\Sigma(Y - M)^2}{N - 1} = \frac{(0.563 + 33.063 + 1.563 + 27.563)}{4 - 1} = 20.917$$

$$df_X = N - 1 = 3 - 1 = 2$$
$$df_Y = N - 1 = 4 - 1 = 3$$
$$df_{total} = df_X + df_Y = 2 + 3 = 5$$
$$s_{pooled}^2 = \left(\frac{df_X}{df_{total}}\right)s_X^2 + \left(\frac{df_Y}{df_{total}}\right)s_Y^2 = \left(\frac{2}{5}\right)20.334 + \left(\frac{3}{5}\right)20.917$$
$$= 8.134 + 12.550 = 20.684$$

$$s_{M_X}^2 = \frac{s_{pooled}^2}{N_X} = \frac{20.684}{3} = 6.895$$

$$s_{M_Y}^2 = \frac{s_{pooled}^2}{N_Y} = \frac{20.684}{4} = 5.171$$

$$s_{difference}^2 = s_{M_X}^2 + s_{M_Y}^2 = 6.895 + 5.171 = 12.066$$

$$s_{difference} = \sqrt{s_{difference}^2} = \sqrt{12.066} = 3.474$$

Step 4: The critical values, based on a two-tailed test, a *p* level of 0.05, and a df_{total} of 5, are -2.571 and 2.571.

Step 5: $t = \frac{(M_X - M_Y) - (\mu_X - \mu_Y)}{s_{difference}} = \frac{(18.667 - 9.25) - (0)}{3.474}$
$= 2.71$

Step 6: Reject the null hypothesis and conclude that the number of larvae is greater on average when odor-shield bags are used than when standard bags are used.

b. $t(5) = 2.71, p < 0.05$

c. There are many variables we might want to control, including the material contained in each garbage bag, the location of the garbage can (inside a garage versus outside), and the time of year the study was conducted.

d. Using Excel and the formula =NORMSDIST(NORMSINV (1-.042)/(SQRT(2))), we determine p_{rep} is 0.89.

10.41 a. *Step 1:* Population 1 consists of mothers, and population 2 is nonmothers. The comparison distribution will be a distribution of differences between means. We will use an independent-samples *t* test because someone is either identified as being a mother or not being a mother; both conditions, in this case, cannot be true. Of the three assumptions, we meet one because the dependent variable, decibel level, is a scale variable. We do not know whether the data were randomly selected and whether the population is normally distributed, and we have a small *N*, so we will be cautious in drawing conclusions.

Step 2: Null hypothesis: There is no difference in sound sensitivity, as reflected in the minimum level of detection, between mothers and nonmothers—$H_0: \mu_1 = \mu_2$.

Research hypothesis: There is a difference in sensitivity between the two groups—$H_1: \mu_1 \neq \mu_2$.

Step 3: $(\mu_1 = \mu_2) = 0$; $s_{difference} = 9.581$

Calculations:

$$M_X = 47$$

X	X − M	(X − M)²
33	−14	196
55	8	64
39	−8	64
41	−6	36
67	20	400

$$s_X^2 = \frac{\Sigma(X - M)^2}{N - 1} = \frac{(196 + 64 + 64 + 36 + 400)}{5 - 1} = 190$$

$$M_Y = 58.333$$

Y	Y − M	(Y − M)²
56	−2.333	5.443
48	−10.333	106.771
71	12.667	160.453

$$s_Y^2 = \frac{\Sigma(Y - M)^2}{N - 1} = \frac{(5.443 + 106.771 + 160.453)}{3 - 1} = 136.334$$

$$df_X = N - 1 = 5 - 1 = 4$$
$$df_Y = N - 1 = 3 - 1 = 2$$
$$df_{total} = df_X + df_Y = 4 + 2 = 6$$

$$s_{pooled}^2 = \left(\frac{df_X}{df_{total}}\right)s_X^2 + \left(\frac{df_Y}{df_{total}}\right)s_Y^2 = \left(\frac{4}{6}\right)190 + \left(\frac{2}{6}\right)136.334$$
$$= 126.667 + 45.445 = 172.112$$

$$s_{M_X}^2 = \frac{s_{pooled}^2}{N_X} = \frac{172.112}{5} = 34.422$$

$$s_{M_Y}^2 = \frac{s_{pooled}^2}{N_Y} = \frac{172.112}{3} = 57.371$$

$$s_{difference}^2 = s_{M_X}^2 + s_{M_Y}^2 = 34.422 + 57.371 = 91.793$$
$$s_{difference} = \sqrt{s_{difference}^2} = \sqrt{91.793} = 9.581$$

Step 4: The critical values, based on a two-tailed test, a p level of 0.05, and a df_{total} of 6, are −2.447 and 2.447.

Step 5: $t = \dfrac{(M_X - M_Y) - (\mu_X - \mu_Y)}{s_{difference}} = \dfrac{(47 - 58.333) - (0)}{9.581}$

$$= -1.183$$

Step 6: Fail to reject the null hypothesis. We do not have enough evidence, based on these data, to conclude that mothers have more sensitive hearing, on average, when compared to nonmothers.

b. $t(6) = -1.183, p > 0.05$

c. Using Excel and the formula =NORMSDIST (NORMSINV(1-.282)/(SQRT(2))), we determine p_{rep} is 0.66.

10.43 a. To calculate the 95% confidence interval, we find the t statistics that correspond to a p level of 0.05—that is, the values that mark off the most extreme 0.025 in each tail—which are −2.447 and 2.447. We then calculate:

$$(M_X - M_Y)_{lower} = -t(s_{difference}) + (M_X - M_Y)_{sample}$$
$$= -2.447(13.335) + (32.25 - 56.50)$$
$$= -32.631 + (-24.25) = -56.881$$

$$(M_X - M_Y)_{upper} = t(s_{difference}) + (M_X - M_Y)_{sample}$$
$$= 2.447(13.335) + (32.25 - 56.50)$$
$$= 32.631 + (-24.25) = 8.381$$

The 95% confidence interval around the difference between means of 24.25 is [−56.88, 8.38].

b. To calculate the 90% confidence interval, we find the t statistics that correspond to a p level of 0.10—that is, the values that mark off the most extreme 0.05 in each tail—which are −1.943 and 1.943. We then calculate:

$$(M_X - M_Y)_{lower} = -t(s_{difference}) + (M_X - M_Y)_{sample}$$
$$= -1.943(13.335) + (32.25 - 56.50)$$
$$= -25.910 + (-24.25) = -50.160$$

$$(M_X - M_Y)_{Upper} = t(s_{difference}) + (M_X - M_Y)_{Sample}$$
$$= 1.943(12.95) + (32.25 - 56.50)$$
$$= 25.910 + (-24.25) = 1.660$$

The 90% confidence interval around the difference between means of 24.25 is [−50.16, 1.66].

c. The 90% confidence interval has a narrower range than the 95% confidence interval. When calculating the 95% confidence interval, we are describing the range in which we think a larger portion of our sample means would fall if we were to repeatedly sample from this population (95% as opposed to 90%), so we have a larger range within which those means are likely to fall.

10.45 a. $(M_X - M_Y)_{lower} = -t(s_{difference}) + (M_X - M_Y)_{sample}$
$$(M_X - M_Y)_{lower} = -2.776(3.815) + (10.333 - 8.333)$$
$$= -8.590$$

$$(M_X - M_Y)_{upper} = t(s_{difference}) + (M_X - M_Y)_{sample}$$
$$(M_X - M_Y)_{upper} = 2.776(3.815) + (10.333 - 8.333)$$
$$= 12.590$$

b. The 95% confidence interval around the difference between means of 2 drinks is [−8.590, 12.590]. What we learn from this confidence interval is that there is great variability in the plausible difference between means for these data, reflected in the wide range. We also notice that 0 is within the confidence interval, so we cannot assume a difference between these groups.

c. On average, the difference in the amount of drinking between people who stayed at all-inclusive resorts versus noninclusive resorts was 2 drinks, with a margin of error of 10.59 drinks.

10.47 a. The appropriate measure of effect size for a t statistic is Cohen's d, which is calculated as

$$d = \frac{(M_X - M_Y) - (\mu_X - \mu_Y)}{s_{pooled}}$$
$$= \frac{(12.55 - 9.5) - (0)}{\sqrt{0.640}} = 3.81$$

b. Based on Cohen's conventions, this is a large effect size.

c. It is useful to have effect-size information because the hypothesis test tells us only whether we were likely to have obtained our sample mean by chance. The effect size tells us the magnitude of the effect, giving us a sense of how important or practical this finding is, and allows us to standardize the results of the study so that we can compare across studies. Here, we know that there's a large effect.

10.49 **a.** $s_{pooled} = \sqrt{s^2_{pooled}} = \sqrt{20.684} = 4.548$

Cohen's $d = \dfrac{(M_X - M_Y) - (\mu_X - \mu_Y)}{s_{pooled}} = \dfrac{(18.667 - 9.25) - (0)}{4.548}$

$= 2.071$

b. This is a large effect.

c. Effect size tells us how big the difference we observed between means was, without the influence of sample size. Often, this measure helps us decide whether we want to continue along our current research lines; that is, if a strong effect is indicated but we fail to reject the null hypothesis, we might want to continue collecting data to increase our statistical power.

10.51 **a.** $s_{pooled} = \sqrt{s^2_{pooled}} = \sqrt{172.112} = 13.119$

Cohen's $d = \dfrac{(M_X - M_Y) - (\mu_X - \mu_Y)}{s_{pooled}} = \dfrac{(47 - 58.333) - (0)}{13.119}$

$= -0.864$

b. This is a large effect.

c. Effect size tells us how big the difference we observed between means was, without the influence of sample size. Often, this measure helps us decide whether we want to continue along our current research lines. In this case, the large effect would encourage us to collect more data to increase statistical power.

10.53 **a.** We would use a single-sample t test because we have one sample of figure skaters and are comparing that sample to a population (women with eating disorders) for which we know the mean.

b. We would use an independent-samples t test because we have two samples, and no participant can be in both samples. One cannot have both a high level and a low level of knowledge about a topic.

c. We would use a paired-samples t test because we have two samples, but every student is assigned to both samples—one night of sleep loss and one night of no sleep loss.

10.55 **a.** Waters is predicting lower levels of obesity among children who are in the Edible Schoolyard program than among children who are not in this program. Waters and others who believe in her program are likely to notice successes and overlook failures. Solid research is necessary before instituting such a program nationally, even though it sounds extremely promising.

b. Students could be randomly assigned to participate in the Edible Schoolyard program or to continue with their usual lunch plan. The independent variable is the program, with two levels (Edible Schoolyard, control), and the dependent variable could be weight. Weight is easily operationalized by weighing children, perhaps after one year in the program.

c. We would use an independent-samples t test because there are two samples and no student is in both samples.

d. *Step 1*: Population 1 is all students who participated in the Edible Schoolyard program. Population 2 is all students who did not participate in the Edible Schoolyard program. The comparison distribution will be a distribution of differences between means. The hypothesis test will be an independent-samples t test. This study meets all three assumptions. The dependent variable, weight, is scale. The data would be collected using a form of random selection. In addition, there would be more than 30 participants in the sample,

indicating that the comparison distribution would likely be normal.

e. *Step 2*: Null hypothesis: Students who participate in the Edible Schoolyard program weigh the same, on average, as students who do not participate—$H_0: \mu_1 = \mu_2$.

Research hypothesis: Students who participate in the Edible Schoolyard program have different weights, on average, from students who do not participate—$H_1: \mu_1 \neq \mu_2$.

f. The dependent variable could be nutrition knowledge, as assessed by a test, or body mass index (BMI).

g. There are many possible confounds when we do not conduct a controlled experiment. For example, the Berkeley school might be different to begin with. After all, the school allowed Waters to begin the program, and perhaps it had already emphasized nutrition. Random selection allows us to have faith in our ability to generalize beyond our sample. Random assignment allows us to eliminate confounds, other variables that may explain any differences between groups.

CHAPTER 11

11.1 An ANOVA is a hypothesis test with at least one nominal independent variable (with at least three total groups) and a scale dependent variable.

11.3 Between-groups variance is an estimate of the population variance based on the differences among the means; within-groups variance is an estimate of the population variance based on the differences within each of the three (or more) sample distributions.

11.5 The three assumptions are that the participants were randomly selected, the underlying populations are normally distributed, and the underlying variances of the different conditions are similar, or *homoscedastic*.

11.7 The F statistic is calculated as the ratio of two variances. Variability, and the variance measure of it, is always positive—it always exists. Variance is calculated as the sum of squared deviations, and squaring both positive and negative values makes them positive.

11.9 With sums of squares, we add up all the squared values. Deviations from the mean always sum to 0. By squaring these deviations, we can sum them and they will not sum to 0. Sums of squares are measures of variability of scores from the mean.

11.11 The grand mean is the mean of every score in a study, regardless of which sample the score came from.

11.13 Cohen's d; R^2

11.15 *Post-hoc* means "after this." These tests are needed when our ANOVA is significant and we want to discover where the significant differences exist between our groups.

11.17 **a.** *Standard error* is wrong. The professor is reporting the spread for a distribution of scores, the *standard deviation*.

b. *t statistic* is wrong. We do not use the population standard deviation to calculate a t statistic. The sentence should say z *statistic* instead.

c. *Parameters* is wrong. Parameters are numbers that describe populations, not samples. The researcher calculated the *statistics*.

d. *z statistic* is wrong. Evelyn is comparing two means; thus, she would have calculated a *t statistic*.

11.19 The four assumptions are that (1) the data are randomly selected, (2) the underlying population distributions are normal, (3) the variability is similar across groups, or homoscedasticity, and (4) there are no order effects.

11.21 The "subjects" variability is noise in the data caused by each individual's personal variability. It is calculated by comparing each person's mean response across all levels of the independent variable with the grand mean, the overall mean response across all levels of the independent variable.

11.23 **a.** $df_{between} = N_{groups} - 1 = 3 - 1 = 2$

b. $df_{within} = df_1 + df_2 + \ldots + df_{last} = (4 - 1) + (3 - 1) + (5 - 1) = 3 + 2 + 4 = 9$

c. $df_{total} = df_{between} + df_{within} = 2 + 9 = 11$

11.25 The critical value for a between-groups degrees of freedom of 2 and a within-groups degrees of freedom of 9 at a *p* level of 0.05 is 4.26.

11.27 **a.** $F = \dfrac{\text{between-groups variance}}{\text{within-groups variance}} = \dfrac{321.83}{177.24} = 1.82$

b. $F = \dfrac{2.79}{2.20} = 1.27$

c. $F = \dfrac{34.45}{41.60} = 0.83$

11.29

SOURCE	SS	df	MS	F
Between	43	2	21.5	**2.66**
Within	89	11	8.09	
Total	132	13		

11.31 $M_{1970} = \dfrac{\Sigma(X)}{N} = \dfrac{45 + 211 + 158 + 74}{4} = 122$

$M_{1980} = \dfrac{\Sigma(X)}{N} = \dfrac{92 + 128 + 382}{3} = 200.67$

$M_{1990} = \dfrac{\Sigma(X)}{N} = \dfrac{273 + 396 + 178 + 248 + 374}{5} = 293.80$

$GM = \dfrac{\Sigma(X)}{N_{total}} = \dfrac{\left(\begin{array}{c}45 + 211 + 158 + 74 + 92 + 128 + \\ 382 + 273 + 396 + 178 + 248 + 374\end{array}\right)}{12} = 213.25$

11.33 (*Note:* The total sum of squares will not exactly equal the sum of the between-groups and within-groups sums of squares because of rounding error.)

a. Total sum of squares is calculated here as $SS_{total} = \Sigma(X - GM)^2$:

SAMPLE	X	(X − GM)	(X − GM)²
1970	45	−168.25	28,308.06
$M_{1970} = 122$	211	−2.25	5.06
	158	−55.25	3,052.56
	74	−139.25	19,390.56
1980	92	−121.25	14,701.56
$M_{1980} = 200.67$	128	−85.25	7,267.56
	382	168.75	28,476.56
1990	273	59.75	3,570.06
$M_{1990} = 293.8$	396	182.75	33,397.56
	178	−35.25	1,242.56
	248	34.75	1,207.56
	374	160.75	25,840.56
	GM = 213.25		SS_{total} = **166,460.25**

b. Within-groups sum of squares is calculated here as $SS_{within} = \Sigma(X - M)^2$:

SAMPLE	X	(X − M)	(X − M)²
1970	45	−77	5,929.00
$M_{1970} = 122$	211	89	7,921.00
	158	36	1,296.00
	74	−48	2,304.00
1980	92	−108.67	11,809.17
$M_{1980} = 200.67$	128	−72.67	5,280.93
	382	181.33	32,880.57
1990	273	−20.8	432.64
$M_{1990} = 293.8$	396	102.2	10,444.84
	178	−115.8	13,409.64
	248	−45.8	2,097.64
	374	80.2	6,432.04
	GM = 213.25		SS_{within} = **100,237.47**

c. Between-groups sum of squares is calculated here as $SS_{between} = \Sigma(M - GM)^2$:

SAMPLE	X	(M − GM)	(M − GM)²
1970	45	−91.25	8326.563
$M_{1970} = 122$	211	−91.25	8326.563
	158	−91.25	8326.563
	74	−91.25	8326.563
1980	92	−12.58	158.2564
$M_{1980} = 200.67$	128	−12.58	158.2564
	382	−12.58	158.2564
1990	273	80.55	6488.303
$M_{1990} = 293.8$	396	80.55	6488.303
	178	80.55	6488.303
	248	80.55	6488.303
	374	80.55	6488.303

GM = 213.25 $SS_{between}$ = **66,222.53**

11.35 $MS_{between} = \dfrac{SS_{between}}{df_{between}} = \dfrac{66,222.53}{2} = 33,111,27$

$MS_{within} = \dfrac{SS_{within}}{df_{within}} = \dfrac{100,237.47}{9} = 11,137.50$

$F = \dfrac{MS_{between}}{MS_{within}} = \dfrac{33,111.27}{11,137.50} = 2.97$

SOURCE	SS	df	MS	F
Between	66,222.53	2	33,111.27	**2.97**
Within	100,237.47	9	11,137.50	
Total	166,460.25	11		

11.37 Because we have unequal sample sizes, we must calculate a weighted sample size.

$N' = \dfrac{N_{groups}}{\Sigma\left(\frac{1}{N}\right)} = \dfrac{4}{\left(\frac{1}{4} + \frac{1}{3} + \frac{1}{6} + \frac{1}{5}\right)} = \dfrac{4}{0.25 + 0.33 + 0.17 + 0.20}$

$= \dfrac{4}{0.95} = 4.21$

$s_M = \sqrt{\dfrac{MS_{within}}{N'}} = \sqrt{\dfrac{25.85}{4.21}} = 2.48$

Now we can compare our three groups.

Group 1 ($M = 16.25$) versus group 2 ($M = 17.33$):

$HSD = \dfrac{16.25 - 17.33}{2.48} = -0.44$

Group 1 ($M = 16.25$) versus group 3 ($M = 6.33$):

$HSD = \dfrac{16.25 - 6.33}{2.48} = 4.0$

Group 1 ($M = 16.25$) versus group 4 ($M = 16.6$):

$HSD = \dfrac{16.25 - 16.6}{2.48} = -0.14$

Group 2 ($M = 17.33$) versus group 3 ($M = 6.33$):

$HSD = \dfrac{17.33 - 6.33}{2.48} = 4.44$

Group 2 ($M = 17.33$) versus group 4 ($M = 16.6$):

$HSD = \dfrac{17.33 - 16.6}{2.48} = 0.29$

Group 3 ($M = 6.33$) versus group 4 ($M = 16.6$):

$HSD = \dfrac{6.33 - 16.6}{2.48} = -4.14$

11.39 a. $df_{between} = N_{groups} - 1 = 3 - 1 = 2$

b. $df_{subjects} = n - 1 = 4 - 1 = 3$

c. $df_{within} = (df_{between})(df_{subjects}) = (2)(3) = 6$

d. $df_{total} = df_{between} + df_{subjects} + df_{within} = 2 + 3 + 6 = 11$, or we can calculate it as $df_{total} = N_{total} - 1 = 12 - 1 = 11$

11.41 $MS_{between} = \dfrac{SS_{between}}{df_{between}} = \dfrac{618.504}{2} = 309.252$

$MS_{subjects} = \dfrac{SS_{subjects}}{df_{subjects}} = \dfrac{62.001}{3} = 20.667$

$MS_{within} = \dfrac{SS_{within}}{df_{within}} = \dfrac{73.495}{6} = 12.249$

$F_{between} = \dfrac{MS_{between}}{MS_{within}} = \dfrac{309.252}{12.249} = 25.247$

$F_{subjects} = \dfrac{MS_{subjects}}{MS_{within}} = \dfrac{20.667}{12.249} = 1.687$

SOURCE	SS	df	MS	F
Between-groups	618.504	2	309.252	25.25
Subjects	62.001	3	20.667	1.69
Within-groups	73.495	6	12.249	
Total	754	11		

11.43 $s_M = \sqrt{\dfrac{MS_{within}}{N}} = \sqrt{\dfrac{12.249}{4}} = 1.75$

The Tukey HSD statistic comparing level 1 and level 3 would be:

$HSD = \dfrac{M_{level\,1} - M_{level\,3}}{S_M} = \dfrac{8.75 - 26.25}{1.75} = -10$

11.45 a. z distribution; we know both the mean and standard deviation for the income of the population, everyone in Wyoming.

b. F distribution; we are comparing the means of three samples—employees in enclosed workplace offices, in open workplace cubicles, and in home offices.

c. t distribution; we are comparing the means of two samples—social science majors who had taken statistics and social science majors who had not taken statistics.

11.47 a. The F statistic is the square of the t statistic. We can take the square root of the F statistic to get the t statistic: $\sqrt{4.22} = 2.05$.

b. With infinitely large samples, the t distribution reduces to the z distribution. This means that the F statistic is also the square of the z statistic (just as with the t statistic). We can take the square root of the F statistic to get the z statistic: $\sqrt{4.22} = 2.05$.

c. The t statistic is the same as the z statistic—in this case, 0.67.

d. First, it is easier to gain a deep understanding of hypothesis testing when we first learn the simple z test and then build to the more complicated tests. Second, historically, statisticians calculated test statistics by hand rather than using a computer. Thus, it made sense to use the far less time-consuming z test or t test when possible, rather than the more complicated ANOVA (based on the F statistic). Statisticians continue to use the simplest test possible as a matter of convention.

11.49 a. A one-way between-groups ANOVA should be used.

b. The researcher could have some members of the same group introduced only once, others introduced twice, and others introduced twice and also wearing nametags. The researcher could then ask the participants to remember all the names of those working in their group. This way, all participants would be in all three experimental conditions.

11.51 a. The first assumption of ANOVA is that the samples are randomly selected from their populations. It is unlikely that the researchers met this assumption. The study description indicates that the researchers were from Yale University and does not mention any techniques the researchers might have used to obtain participants from across the nation. So it is likely that the Yale researchers used a sample of participants from their local area.

b. The second assumption is that the population distribution is normal. Although we do not know the exact distribution of the population of scores, there are more than 30 participants in the study. When there are at least 30 participants in a sample, the distribution of sample means will be approximately normal even if the underlying distribution of scores is not. So it is likely that the distribution of sample means is normal and that this assumption was met.

c. The third assumption is homoscedasticity—that our samples come from populations with equal variances. It is not possible to tell whether this assumption was met on the basis of the study description. The researchers could assess whether this assumption was met by comparing the variance of each of the three treatment groups to ensure that the largest variance is no larger than two times the smallest variance.

11.53 a. The independent variable is political viewpoint, with the levels Republican, Democrat, and neither.

b. The dependent variable is religiosity.

c. The populations are all Republicans, all Democrats, and all who categorize themselves as neither. The samples are the Republicans, Democrats, and people who say they are neither among the 180 students.

d. First, we would calculate the between-groups variance. This involves calculating a measure of variability among the three sample means—the religiosity scores of the Republicans, Democrats, and others. Then we would calculate the within-groups variance; this is essentially an average of the variability within each of the three samples. Finally,

we would divide the between-groups variance by the within-groups variance. If the variability among the means is much larger than the variability within each sample, this provides evidence that the means are different from each other.

11.55 a. Level of trust in the leader is the independent variable. It has three levels: low, moderate, and high.

b. The dependent variable is level of agreement with a policy supported by the leader or supervisor.

c. *Step 1:* Population 1 is employees with low trust in their leader. Population 2 is employees with moderate trust in their leader. Population 3 is employees with high trust in their leader.

The comparison distribution will be an F distribution. The hypothesis test will be a one-way, between-groups ANOVA. We do not know if employees were randomly selected. We also do not know if the underlying distributions are normal, and our sample sizes are small so we must proceed with caution. To check the final assumption, that we have homoscedastic variances, we will calculate variance for each group.

SAMPLE	LOW TRUST	MODERATE TRUST	HIGH TRUST
Squared deviations	16	100	3.06
	1	121	18.06
	4	1	60.06
	25		27.56
Sum of squares	46	222	108.75
$N - 1$	3	2	3
Variance	**15.33**	**111**	**36.25**

Because the largest variance, 111, is much more than twice as large as the smallest variance, we can conclude we have heteroscedastic variances. Violation of this third assumption of homoscedastic samples means we should proceed with caution. Because these data are intended to give you practice calculating statistics, proceed with your analyses. When conducting real research, we would want to have much larger sample sizes and to more carefully consider meeting the assumptions.

Step 2: Null hypothesis: There are no mean differences between these three groups: the mean level of agreement with a policy does not vary across the three trust levels.

Research hypothesis: There are mean differences between some or all of these groups: the mean level of agreement depends on trust.

Step 3: $df_{between} = N_{groups} - 1 = 3 - 1 = 2$

$df_{within} = df_1 + df_2 + \ldots + df_{last}$
$= (4 - 1) + (3 - 1) + (4 - 1) = 3 + 2 + 3 = 8$

The comparison distribution will be the F distribution with 2 and 8 degrees of freedom.

Step 4: The critical value for the F statistic based on a p level of 0.05 is 4.46.

Step 5: $df_{total} = df_{between} + df_{within} = 2 + 8 = 10$

$$GM = 21.727$$

Total sum of squares is calculated here as $SS_{total} = \Sigma(X - GM)^2$:

SAMPLE	X	(X − GM)	(X − GM)²
Low trust	9	−12.727	161.98
$M_{low} = 13$	14	−7.727	59.71
	11	−10.727	115.07
	18	−3.727	13.89
Moderate trust	14	−7.727	59.71
$M_{mod} = 24$	35	13.273	176.17
	23	1.273	1.62
High trust	27	5.273	27.80
$M_{high} = 28.75$	33	11.273	127.08
	21	−0.727	0.53
	34	12.273	150.63
	GM = 21.727		SS_{total} = **894.18**

Within-groups sum of squares is calculated here as $SS_{within} = \Sigma(X - M)^2$:

SAMPLE	X	(X − M)	(X − M)²
Low trust	9	−4	16.00
$M_{low} = 13$	14	1	1.00
	11	−2	4.00
	18	5	25.00
Moderate trust	14	−10	100.00
$M_{mod} = 24$	35	11	121.00
	23	−1	1.00
High trust	27	−1.75	3.06
$M_{high} = 28.75$	33	4.25	18.06
	21	−7.75	60.06
	34	5.25	27.56
	GM = 21.727		SS_{within} = **376.75**

Between-groups sum of squares is calculated here as $SS_{between} = \Sigma(M - GM)^2$:

SAMPLE	X	(M − GM)	(M − GM)²
Low trust	9	−8.73	76.16
$M_{low} = 13$	14	−8.73	76.16
	11	−8.73	76.16
	18	−8.73	76.16
Moderate trust	14	2.27	5.17
$M_{mod} = 24$	35	2.27	5.17
	23	2.27	5.17
High trust	27	7.02	49.32
$M_{high} = 28.75$	33	7.02	49.32
	21	7.02	49.32
	34	7.02	49.32
	GM = 21.727		$SS_{between}$ = **517.43**

$$MS_{between} = \frac{SS_{between}}{df_{between}} = \frac{517.43}{2} = 258.715$$

$$MS_{within} = \frac{SS_{within}}{df_{within}} = \frac{376.75}{8} = 47.093$$

$$F = \frac{MS_{between}}{MS_{within}} = \frac{258.715}{47.093} = 5.49$$

SOURCE	SS	df	MS	F
Between	517.43	2	258.72	5.49
Within	376.75	8	47.09	
Total	894.18	10		

Step 6: Our F statistic, 5.49, is beyond our cutoff of 4.46, so we can reject the null hypothesis. The mean level of agreement with a policy supported by a supervisor varies across level of trust in that supervisor. Remember, our research design and data did not meet the three assumptions of this statistical test, so we should be careful in interpreting this finding.

11.57 Because we have unequal sample sizes, we must calculate a weighted sample size.

$$N' = \frac{N_{groups}}{\Sigma\left(\frac{1}{N}\right)} = \frac{3}{\left(\frac{1}{4} + \frac{1}{3} + \frac{1}{4}\right)} = \frac{3}{0.25 + 0.33 + 0.25} = \frac{3}{0.83} = 3.61$$

$$s_M = \sqrt{\frac{MS_{within}}{N'}}, \text{ then equals } \sqrt{\frac{47.093}{3.61}} = 3.61$$

Now we can compare our three groups.

Low trust ($M = 13$) versus moderate trust ($M = 24$):

$$HSD = \frac{13 - 24}{3.61} = -3.047$$

Low trust ($M = 13$) versus high trust ($M = 28.75$):

$$HSD = \frac{13 - 28.75}{3.61} = -4.363$$

Moderate trust ($M = 24$) versus high trust ($M = 28.75$):

$$HSD = \frac{24 - 28.75}{3.61} = -1.316$$

According to the q table, the critical value is 4.04 for a p level of 0.05 when you are comparing three groups and have a within-groups degrees of freedom of 8. We obtained one q value (-4.363) that exceeds this cutoff. Based on our calculations, there is a statistically significant difference between the mean level of agreement by employees with low trust in their supervisors compared to those with high trust.

Because the sample sizes here were so small and we did not meet the three assumptions of ANOVA, we should be careful in making strong statements about this finding. In fact, these preliminary findings would encourage additional research.

11.59 a. The appropriate measure of effect size is $R^2 = \frac{SS_{between}}{SS_{total}} = \frac{63.475}{111.642} = 0.57$.

b. According to Cohen's conventions, this is a large effect size.

c. It is useful to have this information because hypothesis testing tells us only whether year in school is a significant factor affecting how long patients wear their appliances. R^2 gives us an indication of how large this effect is—or how much of the variability in appliance wearing can be accounted for by year in school. Here, there's a large effect.

11.61 a. $F = \dfrac{MS_{between}}{MS_{within}} = \dfrac{4.623}{0.522} = 8.856$

b. $t = \sqrt{F} = \sqrt{8.856} = 2.98$

c. The "Sig." for t is the same as that for the ANOVA, 0.005, because the F distribution reduces to the t distribution when we are dealing with two groups.

11.63 a. *Step 1:* Four different populations are being compared here: one for the people who chew gum 1, and one for each of the other three types of gum. The comparison distribution will be the F distribution, and we will calculate a one-way, within-groups ANOVA. Regarding our assumptions, we know that the participants were randomly selected and that the order of presentation of the gum was also randomly determined. We do not know anything about the underlying population distributions, and we must be careful when assessing homoscedasticity with such a small sample. We will proceed with caution.

Step 2: Null hypothesis: People report the same flavor intensity, on average, across the different gum types.

Research hypothesis: People do not report the same flavor intensity, on average, across the different gum types.

Step 3: We determine the characteristics of the comparison distribution by computing our degrees of freedom.

$$df_{between} = N_{groups} - 1 = 4 - 1 = 3$$

$$df_{subjects} = n - 1 = 5 - 1 = 4$$

$$df_{within} = (df_{between})(df_{subjects}) = (3)(4) = 12$$

$df_{total} = df_{between} + df_{subjects} + df_{within} = 3 + 4 + 12 = 19;$ we can also calculate it as: $df_{total} = N_{total} - 1 = 20 - 1 = 19$

We will use the F distribution with 3 and 12 degrees of freedom.

Step 4: The critical value for F with 3 and 12 degrees of freedom at a p level of 0.05 is 3.49.

Step 5: Calculate the test statistic.

$$SS_{total} = \Sigma(X - GM)^2 = 111.8$$

GUM	RATING (X)	(X − GM)	(X − GM)²
1	4	−0.9	0.81
1	6	1.1	1.21
1	3	−1.9	3.61
1	4	−0.9	0.81
1	4	−0.9	0.81
2	8	3.1	9.61
2	6	1.1	1.21
2	9	4.1	16.81
2	9	4.1	16.81
2	8	3.1	9.61
3	5	0.1	0.01
3	6	1.1	1.21
3	7	2.1	4.41
3	4	−0.9	0.81
3	5	0.1	0.01
4	2	−2.9	8.41
4	2	−2.9	8.41
4	3	−1.9	3.61
4	2	−2.9	8.41
4	1	−3.9	15.21
	GM = 4.9		$\Sigma(X - GM)^2 = 111.8$

$$SS_{between} = \Sigma(M - GM)^2 = 93.80$$

GUM	RATING (X)	GROUP MEAN	(M − GM)	(M − GM)²
1	4	4.2	−0.7	0.49
1	6	4.2	−0.7	0.49
1	3	4.2	−0.7	0.49
1	4	4.2	−0.7	0.49
1	4	4.2	−0.7	0.49
2	8	8	3.1	9.61
2	6	8	3.1	9.61
2	9	8	3.1	9.61
2	9	8	3.1	9.61
2	8	8	3.1	9.61
3	5	5.4	0.5	0.25
3	6	5.4	0.5	0.25
3	7	5.4	0.5	0.25
3	4	5.4	0.5	0.25
3	5	5.4	0.5	0.25
4	2	2	−2.9	8.41
4	2	2	−2.9	8.41
4	3	2	−2.9	8.41
4	2	2	−2.9	8.41
4	1	2	−2.9	8.41
	GM = 4.9			$\Sigma(M - GM)^2 = 93.8$

$$SS_{subjects} = \Sigma(M_{participant} - GM)^2 = 2.3$$

PARTICIPANT	GUM	RATING (X)	PARTICIPANT MEAN	$(M_{PARTICIPANT} - GM)$	$(M_{PARTICIPANT} - GM)^2$
1	1	4	4.75	−0.15	0.023
2	1	6	5	0.1	0.010
3	1	3	5.5	0.6	0.360
4	1	4	4.75	−0.15	0.023
5	1	4	4.5	−0.4	0.160
1	2	8	4.75	−0.15	0.023
2	2	6	5	0.1	0.010
3	2	9	5.5	0.6	0.360
4	2	9	4.75	−0.15	0.023
5	2	8	4.5	−0.4	0.160
1	3	5	4.75	−0.15	0.023
2	3	6	5	0.1	0.010
3	3	7	5.5	0.6	0.360
4	3	4	4.75	−0.15	0.023
5	3	5	4.5	−0.4	0.160
1	4	2	4.75	−0.15	0.023
2	4	2	5	0.1	0.010
3	4	3	5.5	0.6	0.360
4	4	2	4.75	−0.15	0.023
5	4	1	4.5	−0.4	0.160

$$GM = 4.9 \qquad \Sigma(M_{participant} - GM)^2 = 2.3$$

$$SS_{within} = SS_{total} - SS_{between} - SS_{subjects}$$
$$= 111.8 - 93.8 - 2.3 = 15.7$$

$$MS_{between} = \frac{SS_{between}}{df_{between}} = \frac{93.8}{3} = 31.267$$

$$MS_{within} = \frac{SS_{within}}{df_{within}} = \frac{15.7}{12} = 1.308$$

$$MS_{subjects} = \frac{SS_{subjects}}{df_{subjects}} = \frac{2.3}{4} = 0.575$$

$$F_{between} = \frac{MS_{between}}{MS_{within}} = \frac{31.267}{1.308} = 23.90$$

$$F_{subjects} = \frac{MS_{subjects}}{MS_{within}} = \frac{0.575}{1.308} = 0.439$$

SOURCE	SS	df	MS	F
Between	93.80	3	31.267	23.90
Subjects	2.3	4	0.575	0.44
Within	15.7	12	1.308	
Total	111.8	19		

Step 6: Our F statistic, 23.90, is well beyond our critical value of 3.49, so we would reject the null hypothesis and conclude that there are mean differences in the intensity of flavor. We cannot conclude which gums are different, however, without a post-hoc test.

b. Yes; because we computed a significant *F* statistic, we would want to compute Tukey *HSD* statistics, or conduct some other post-hoc test, to determine where the significant mean differences are within our data. Also, computing the effect size can give us an indication of just how large or important our finding is.

CHAPTER 12

12.1 A two-way ANOVA is a hypothesis test that includes two nominal independent variables and a scale dependent variable.

12.3 In everyday conversation the word *cell* conjures up images of a prison or a small room in which someone is forced to stay, or of one of the building blocks of a plant or animal. In statistics, the word *cell* refers to a single condition in a factorial ANOVA that is characterized by its values on each of the independent variables.

12.5 A two-way ANOVA has two independent variables. When we express that as a 2 × 3 ANOVA, we get added detail; the first number tells us that the first independent variable has two levels, and the second number tells us that the other independent variable has three levels.

12.7 A marginal mean is the mean of a row or a column in a table that shows the cells of a study with a two-way ANOVA design.

12.9 Bar graphs allow us to visually depict the relative changes across the different levels of each independent variable. By adding lines that connect the bars within each series, we can assess whether the lines appear parallel, significantly different from parallel, or intersecting. Intersecting and significantly unparallel lines are indications of interactions.

12.11 First, we may be able to reject the null hypothesis for the interaction. (If the interaction is statistically significant, then it might not matter whether the main effects are significant; if they also are significant, then those findings are usually qualified by the interaction and they are not described separately. The overall pattern of cell means can tell the whole story.) Second, if we are not able to reject the null hypothesis for the interaction, then we focus on any significant main effects, drawing a specific directional conclusion for each. Third, if we do not reject the null hypothesis for either main effect or the interaction, then we can only conclude that there is insufficient evidence from this study to support our research hypotheses.

12.13 This is the formula for the between-groups sum of squares for the interaction; we can calculate this by subtracting the other between-groups sums of squares (those for the two main effects) and the within-groups sum of squares from the total sum of squares. (The between-groups sum of squares for the interaction is essentially what is left over when the main effects are accounted for.)

12.15 a. There are two independent variables or factors: gender and sporting event. Gender has two levels, male and female, and sporting event has two levels.

b. Type of campus is one factor that has two levels, dry or wet. The second factor is type of college, which has three levels, including state, private, and religious.

c. Age group is the first factor, with three levels; gender is a second factor, with two levels; and family composition is the last factor, with three levels.

12.17

	HOCKEY	ICE SKATING	
Men	$M = (19 + 17 + 18 + 17)/4 = 17.75$	$M = (6 + 4 + 8 + 3)/4 = 5.25$	$(17.75 + 5.25)/2 = 11.50$
Women	$M = (13 + 14 + 18 + 8)/4 = 13.25$	$M = (11 + 7 + 4 + 14)/4 = 9$	$(13.25 + 9)/2 = 11.125$
	$(17.75 + 13.25)/2 = 15.5$	$(5.25 + 9)/2 = 7.125$	

12.19

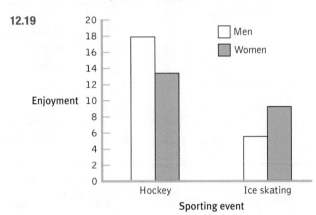

12.21 $df_{rows(gender)} = N_{rows} - 1 = 2 - 1 = 1$

$df_{columns(sport)} = N_{columns} - 1 = 2 - 1 = 1$

$df_{interaction} = (df_{rows})(df_{columns}) = (1)(1) = 1$

$df_{within} = df_{M,H} + df_{M,S} + df_{W,H} + df_{W,S} = 3 + 3 + 3 + 3 = 12$

$df_{total} = N_{total} - 1 = 16 - 1 = 15$

We can also check that this answer is correct by adding all of the other degrees of freedom together:

$$1 + 1 + 1 + 12 = 15$$

The critical value for an F distribution with 1 and 12 degrees of freedom, at a p level of 0.01, is 9.33.

12.23 a. $GM = 11.313$.

$SS_{total} = \Sigma(X - GM)^2$ for each score $= 475.438$

	X	$(X - GM)$	$(X - GM)^2$
Men, hockey	19	7.687	59.090
	17	5.687	32.342
	18	6.687	44.716
	17	5.687	32.342
Men, skating	6	−5.313	28.228
	4	−7.313	53.480
	8	−3.313	10.976
	3	−8.313	69.106
Women, hockey	13	1.687	2.846
	14	2.687	7.220
	18	6.687	44.716
	8	−3.313	10.976
Women, skating	11	−0.313	0.098
	7	−4.313	18.602
	4	−7.313	53.480
	14	2.687	7.220
			$\Sigma = 475.438$

b. Sum of squares for gender: $SS_{between(rows)} = \Sigma(M_{row} - GM)^2$ for each score $= 0.560$

	X	$(M_{ROW} - GM)$	$(M_{ROW} - GM)^2$
Men, hockey	19	0.188	0.035
	17	0.188	0.035
	18	0.188	0.035
	17	0.188	0.035
Men, skating	6	0.188	0.035
	4	0.188	0.035
	8	0.188	0.035
	3	0.188	0.035
Women, hockey	13	−0.188	0.035
	14	−0.188	0.035
	18	−0.188	0.035
	8	−0.188	0.035
Women, skating	11	−0.188	0.035
	7	−0.188	0.035
	4	−0.188	0.035
	14	−0.188	0.035
			$\Sigma = 0.560$

c. Sum of squares for sporting event: $SS_{between(columns)} = \Sigma(M_{column} - GM)^2$ for each score $= 280.560$

	X	$(M_{COLUMN} - GM)$	$(M_{COLUMN} - GM)^2$
Men, hockey	19	4.187	17.531
	17	4.187	17.531
	18	4.187	17.531
	17	4.187	17.531
Men, skating	6	−4.188	17.539
	4	−4.188	17.539
	8	−4.188	17.539
	3	−4.188	17.539
Women, hockey	13	4.187	17.531
	14	4.187	17.531
	18	4.187	17.531
	8	4.187	17.531
Women, skating	11	−4.188	17.539
	7	−4.188	17.539
	4	−4.188	17.539
	14	−4.188	17.539
			$\Sigma = 280.560$

d. $SS_{within} = \Sigma(X - M_{cell})^2$ for each score $= 126.256$

	X	$(X - M_{CELL})$	$(X - M_{CELL})^2$
Men, hockey	19	1.25	1.563
	17	−0.75	0.563
	18	0.25	0.063
	17	−0.75	0.563
Men, skating	6	0.75	0.563
	4	−1.25	1.563
	8	2.75	7.563
	3	−2.25	5.063
Women, hockey	13	−0.25	0.063
	14	0.75	0.563
	18	4.75	22.563
	8	−5.25	27.563
Women, skating	11	2	4.000
	7	−2	4.000
	4	−5	25.000
	14	5	25.000
			$\Sigma = 126.256$

e. The sum of squares for the interaction is found through subtraction. We subtract all other sources from the total sum of squares, and the remaining amount is the sum of squares for the interaction.

$$SS_{gender \times sport} = SS_{total} - (SS_{gender} + SS_{sport} + SS_{within})$$

$$SS_{gender \times sport} = 475.438 - (0.560 + 280.560 + 126.256)$$
$$= 68.062$$

12.25

SOURCE	SS	df	MS	F
Gender	0.560	1	0.560	0.053
Sporting event	280.560	1	280.560	26.667
Gender × sport	68.062	1	68.062	6.469
Within	126.256	12	10.521	
Total	475.438	15		

12.27

SOURCE	SS	df	MS	F
Gender	248.25	1	248.25	8.072
Parenting style	84.34	3	28.113	0.914
Gender × style	33.60	3	11.20	0.364
Within	1107.2	36	30.756	
Total	1473.39	43		

12.29 For the main effect A:

$$R^2_{rows} = \frac{SS_{rows}}{(SS_{total} - SS_{columns} - SS_{interaction})} = \frac{30.006}{(652.291 - 33.482 - 1.720)}$$
$$= 0.049$$

According to Cohen's conventions, this is approaching a medium effect size.

For the main effect B:

$$R^2_{columns} = \frac{SS_{columns}}{(SS_{total} - SS_{rows} - SS_{interaction})} = \frac{33.482}{(652.291 - 30.006 - 1.720)}$$
$$= 0.054$$

According to Cohen's conventions, this is approaching a medium effect size.

For the interaction:

$$R^2_{interaction} = \frac{SS_{interaction}}{(SS_{total} - SS_{rows} - SS_{columns})} = \frac{1.720}{(652.291 - 30.006 - 33.482)}$$
$$= 0.003$$

According to Cohen's conventions, this is smaller than a small effect size.

12.31 **a.** There are many possible answers to this question. In addition to using how they were introduced as the independent variable, the researcher could also assess whether having a priori knowledge that they will be tested on their group members' names affects memory. The levels for this second independent variable would be that participants are told of the upcoming memory test or that participants are not told of the upcoming memory test. If the researcher randomly assigned participants to the different treatment conditions, this study would require a two-way between-groups ANOVA.

b. There are many possible answers to this question. In addition to using how they were introduced as the independent variable, the researcher could also assess whether participants remembered names differently depending on whether the group members were of the same gender as or a different gender from the participant. This would be a within-groups manipulation because every participant would be exposed to members who were of the same gender as the participant and those who were of a different gender from the participant.

12.33 **a.** There are two independent variables. One independent variable is what participants were told regarding the consequences of high TAA. Its levels are unhealthy consequences and healthy consequences. The second independent variable is the timing of the recording of participants' perceptions of the accuracy of the TAA test. Its levels are before taking the TAA test and after taking the TAA test.

b. The dependent variable is the participants' perceptions of the accuracy of the TAA test on the 1–9-point scale.

c. A two-way between-groups ANOVA would be used to analyze these data. More precisely, a 2 × 2 ANOVA would be used.

d. There would be 4 cells in this research design. This number is obtained by multiplying the number of levels of each independent variable (2 × 2).

e.

	PERCEPTION BEFORE	PERCEPTION AFTER
TOLD HEALTHY	healthy; before	healthy; after
TOLD UNHEALTHY	unhealthy; before	unhealthy; after

12.35 **a.**

	PERCEPTION BEFORE	PERCEPTION AFTER
TOLD HEALTHY	**4.2**	5.6
TOLD UNHEALTHY	6.9	7.3

Note: There are several cell means that would work.

b. Bar graph of the quantitative interaction with the new cell mean, 4.2:

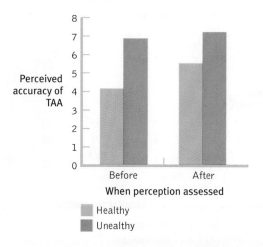

c.

	PERCEPTION BEFORE	PERCEPTION AFTER
TOLD HEALTHY	**5.2**	5.6
TOLD UNHEALTHY	6.9	7.3

d. Bar graph including the new cell mean, 5.2:

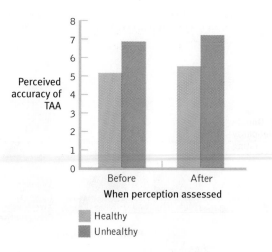

12.37 a.

	LIBERAL	MODERATE	CONSERVATIVE
AFRICAN AMERICAN	3.18	3.50	**4.90**
EUROPEAN AMERICAN	1.91	3.33	4.62

Note: There are several cell means that would work.

b. Bar graph depicting the quantitative interaction that results from including the new cell mean, 4.90:

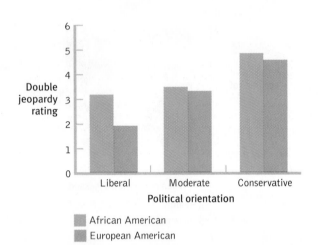

c.

	LIBERAL	MODERATE	CONSERVATIVE
AFRICAN AMERICAN	3.18	**4.60**	**5.89**
EUROPEAN AMERICAN	1.91	3.33	4.62

d. Bar graph depicting the absence of an interaction that results from the two new cell means, 4.60 and 5.89:

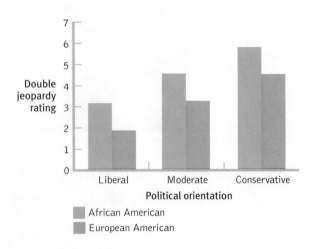

12.39 a.

	FEMALE PARTICIPANTS	MALE PARTICIPANTS
ILLNESS AFFECTS WOMEN	4.88	**4.80**
ILLNESS AFFECTS MEN	3.56	4.67

Note: There are several cell means that would work.

b. Bar graph for the means:

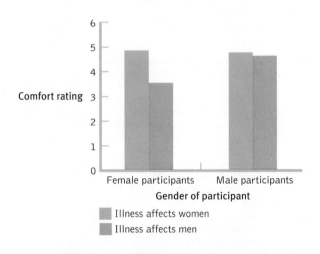

c.

	FEMALE PARTICIPANTS	MALE PARTICIPANTS
ILLNESS AFFECTS WOMEN	4.88	**5.99**
ILLNESS AFFECTS MEN	3.56	4.67

d. Bar graph for the new means:

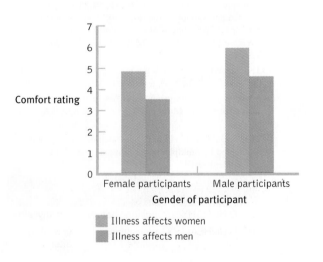

12.41 **a.** The first independent variable is the gender of the student, and its levels are men and women. The second independent variable is membership in the Greek system, and its levels are member and nonmember. The dependent variable is GPA.

b.

	MEN	WOMEN
MEMBER	2.725	3.05
NONMEMBER	3.200	3.15

c. *Step 1:* Population 1 (men, member) is men who are members of a fraternity. Population 2 (men, nonmember) is men who are not members of a fraternity. Population 3 (women, member) is women who are members of a sorority. Population 4 (women, nonmembers) is women who are not members of a sorority. The comparison distributions will be F distributions. The hypothesis test will be a two-way between-groups ANOVA. Assumptions: The data are not from random samples, so we must generalize with caution. The homogeneity of variance assumption is violated because the largest variance (0.115) is much larger than the smallest variance (0.017).

Step 2: Main effect of first independent variable—Greek membership:

Null hypothesis: On average, students who are members in Greek organizations will have the same GPAs as students who are not in Greek organizations—$\mu_G = \mu_{NG}$.

Research hypothesis: On average, students who are members in Greek organizations will have different GPAs from those who are not members—$\mu_G \neq \mu_{NG}$.

Main effect of second independent variable—gender:

Null hypothesis: On average, men and women have the same GPAs—$\mu_M = \mu_W$.

Research hypothesis: On average, men and women have different GPAs—$\mu_M \neq \mu_W$.

Interaction: Greek membership $\times$ gender:

Null hypothesis: The effect of Greek membership does not depend on gender.

Research hypothesis: The effect of Greek membership does depend on gender.

Step 3: $df_{columns(gender)} = 2 - 1 = 1$

$df_{rows(Greek)} = 2 - 1 = 1$

$df_{interaction} = (1)(1) = 1$

$df_{within} = df_{G,M} + df_{NG,M} + df_{G,W} + df_{NG,W}$
$= 3 + 4 + 3 + 3 = 13$

Main effect of gender: F distribution with 1 and 13 degrees of freedom

Main effect of Greek membership: F distribution with 1 and 13 degrees of freedom

Interaction of membership and gender: F distribution with 1 and 13 degrees of freedom

Step 4: Cutoff F for main effect of gender: 4.67

Cutoff F for main effect of Greek membership: 4.67

Cutoff F for interaction of gender and membership: 4.67

Step 5: $SS_{total} = \Sigma(X - GM)^2 = 1.401$

$SS_{column(gender)} = \Sigma(M_{column(gender)} - GM)^2 = 0.348$

$SS_{row(Greek)} = \Sigma(M_{row(Greek)} - GM)^2 = 0.08$

$SS_{within} = \Sigma(X - M_{cell})^2 = 0.828$

$SS_{interaction} = SS_{total} - (SS_{row(Greek)} + SS_{column(gender)}) + SS_{within} = 0.145$

SOURCE	SS	df	MS	F
GENDER	0.348	1	0.348	5.467
GREEK	0.080	1	0.080	1.251
GENDER $\times$ GREEK	0.145	1	0.145	2.266
WITHIN	0.828	13	0.064	
TOTAL	1.401	16		

Step 6: There is a statistically significant effect of Greek membership. It appears that those who are not members of the Greek system have higher GPAs, on average, than those who are members. There is no statistically significant main effect of gender; we can only conclude that there is insufficient evidence that men and women have different GPAs, on average. There is no statistically significant interaction; we can only conclude that there is insufficient evidence that the effect of Greek membership depends on gender.

d. There is a statistically significant main effect of Greek membership. On average, members of Greek organizations have lower GPAs than nonmembers.

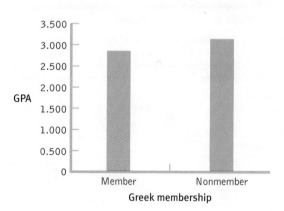

e. There is not a statistically significant interaction.

12.43 **a.** The first independent variable, type of payment, has two levels, cash and candy. The second independent variable, level of payment, has two levels, $0.50 and $5.00.

b. The dependent variable is willingness to help, as assessed via an 11-point scale.

c.

	LOW AMOUNT	MODERATE AMOUNT	
CASH PAYMENT	4.75	7.5	6.125
CANDY PAYMENT	6.25	6	6.125
	5.5	6.75	

d.

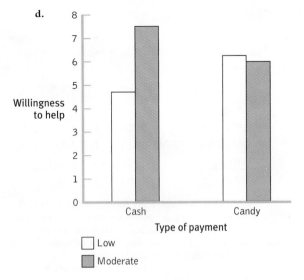

Willingness to help (y-axis: 0 to 8)
Type of payment (x-axis: Cash, Candy)

☐ Low
▨ Moderate

e. At first, based on the marginal means in the table, it looks as if there is a main effect for amount of payment but not for type of payment; however, the bar graph helps us to see that there is really an interaction. The effect for amount of payment only seems to occurs for the cash payment system. So, the amount of payment does seem to affect mean willingness to help, but only when cash is used to compensate efforts. When candy is used, the amount given does not seem to affect mean willingness to help.

12.45 **a.** The independent variables are type of payment, with two levels still, and level of payment, with three levels now (low, moderate, and high). The dependent variable is still willingness to help, as assessed with the 11-point scale.

b.

	LOW AMOUNT	MODERATE AMOUNT	HIGH AMOUNT	
Cash payment	4.75	7.5	8	6.75
Candy payment	6.25	6	6.5	6.25
	5.5	6.75	7.25	

c.

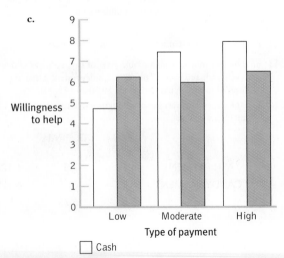

Willingness to help (y-axis: 0 to 9)
Type of payment (x-axis: Low, Moderate, High)

☐ Cash
▨ Candy

d. There does seem to be the same qualitative interaction still, such that the effect of the level of payment depends on the type of payment. When candy payments are used, the level seems to have no mean impact. However, when cash payments are used, a low level leads to a lower willingness to help, on average, than when candy is used, and a moderate or high level leads to a higher willingness to help, on average, than when candy is used.

e. Post-hoc tests would be needed. Specifically, we would need to compare the three levels of payment to see where specific significant differences exist. Based on the graph we created, it appears as if willingness to help in the low cash payment condition is significantly lower, on average, than in the moderate and high conditions for cash payments.

12.47 For the main effect of Greek membership:

$$R^2_{Greek} = \frac{SS_{Greek}}{(SS_{total} - SS_{gender} - SS_{interaction})} = \frac{0.348}{(1.401 - 0.08 - 0.148)}$$
$$= 0.297$$

According to Cohen's conventions, this is a large effect size.
For the main effect of gender:

$$R^2_{gender} = \frac{SS_{gender}}{(SS_{total} - SS_{Greek} - SS_{interaction})} = \frac{0.08}{(1.401 - 0.348 - 0.148)}$$
$$= 0.088$$

According to Cohen's conventions, this is a medium effect size.
For the interaction:

$$R^2_{interaction} = \frac{SS_{interaction}}{(SS_{total} - SS_{Greek} - SS_{gender})} = \frac{0.148}{(1.401 - 0.348 - 0.08)}$$
$$= 0.152$$

According to Cohen's conventions, this is a large effect size.

12.49 For the main effect of type of payment:

$$R^2_{type} = \frac{SS_{type}}{(SS_{total} - SS_{level} - SS_{interaction})} = \frac{0}{(27.846 - 6.256 - 9.086)} = 0$$

We do not need to refer to Cohen's guidelines to know that there is no effect here, and therefore no effect size.
For the main effect of level of payment:

$$R^2_{level} = \frac{SS_{level}}{(SS_{total} - SS_{type} - SS_{interaction})} = \frac{6.25}{(27.846 - 0 - 9.086)} = 0.333$$

According to Cohen's conventions, this is a large effect size.
For the interaction:

$$R^2_{interaction} = \frac{SS_{interaction}}{(SS_{total} - SS_{type} - SS_{level})} = \frac{9}{(27.846 - 0 - 6.256)} = 0.419$$

According to Cohen's conventions, this is a large effect size.

CHAPTER 13

13.1 A correlation coefficient is a statistic that quantifies the relation between two variables.

13.3 A perfect relation occurs when our data points fall exactly on the line we fit through our data. A perfect relation results in a correlation coefficient of −1.0 or 1.0.

13.5 According to Cohen (1988), a correlation coefficient of 0.50 is a large correlation, and 0.30 is a medium one. However, it is unusual in social science research to have a correlation as high as 0.50. The decision of whether a correlation is worth talking about is sometimes based on whether it is statistically significant, as well as what practical effect a correlation of a certain size indicates.

13.7 When used to capture the relation between two variables, the correlation coefficient is a descriptive statistic. When used to draw conclusions about the greater population, such as with hypothesis testing, the coefficient serves as an inferential statistic.

13.9 Positive products of deviations, indicating a positive correlation, occur when each member of a pair of scores tends to result in a positive deviation or when each member tends to result in a negative deviation. Negative products of deviations, indicating a negative correlation, occur when members of a pair of scores tend to result in opposite-valued deviations (one negative and the other positive).

13.11 (1) We calculate the deviation of each score from its mean, multiply the two deviations for each participant, and sum the products of the deviations. (2) We calculate a sum of squares for each variable, multiply the two sums of squares, and take the square root of the product of the sums of squares. (3) We divide the sum from step 1 by the square root in step 2.

13.13 **a.** These data appear to be negatively correlated.
b. These data appear to be positively correlated.
c. Neither; these data appear have a very small correlation, if any.

13.15 **a.** −0.28 is a medium correlation.
b. 0.79 is a large correlation.
c. 1.0 is a perfect correlation.
d. −0.015 is almost no correlation.

13.17

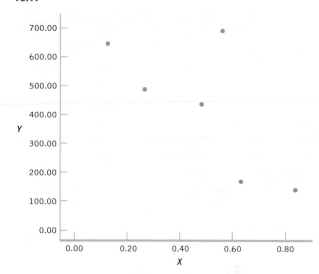

13.19

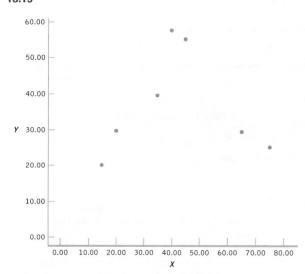

13.21 **a.**

X	(X − M_X)	Y	(Y − M_Y)	(X − M_X)(Y − M_Y)
394	−5	25	−20	100
972	573	75	30	17,190
349	−50	25	−20	1,000
349	−50	65	20	−1,000
593	194	35	−10	−1,940
276	−123	40	−5	615
254	−145	45	0	0
156	−243	20	−25	6,075
248	−151	75	30	−4,530
$M_X = 399$		$M_Y = 45$		$\Sigma[(X − M_X)(Y − M_Y)] = 17,510$

b.

X	$(X - M_X)$	$(X - M_X)^2$	Y	$(Y - M_Y)$	$(Y - M_Y)^2$
394	−5	25	25	−20	400
972	573	328,329	75	30	900
349	−50	2,500	25	−20	400
349	−50	2,500	65	20	400
593	194	37,636	35	−10	100
276	−123	15,129	40	−5	25
254	−145	21,025	45	0	0
156	−243	59,049	20	−25	625
248	−151	22,801	75	30	900
		$\Sigma(X - M_X)^2 =$ 488,994			$\Sigma(Y - M_Y)^2 =$ 3750

$$\sqrt{(SS_X)(SS_Y)} = \sqrt{(488,994)(3750)} = \sqrt{1,833,727,500} = 42,822.0$$

c. $r = \dfrac{\Sigma[(X - M_X)(Y - M_Y)]}{\sqrt{(SS_X)(SS_Y)}} = \dfrac{17,510}{42,822.045} = 0.409$

13.23 a. $df_r = N - 2 = 40 - 2 = 38$
 b. $df_r = N - 2 = 27 - 2 = 25$
 c. $df_r = N - 2 = 3113 - 2 = 3111$
 d. $df_r = N - 2 = 72 - 2 = 70$

13.25 a. Because $df = 38$ is not on the table, we look under $df = 35$, which has cutoffs of −0.325 and 0.325. When we cannot look up our exact degrees of freedom, we choose the degrees of freedom that give us the more conservative critical values. These are the critical values that are more extreme.
 b. −0.381 and 0.381
 c. The highest degrees of freedom listed on the table is 100, with cutoffs of −0.195 and 0.195.
 d. −0.232 and 0.232

13.27 a. Newman's data do not suggest a correlation between Mercury's phases and breakdowns. There was no consistency in the report of breakdowns during one of the phases.
 b. Given that there are two phases of Mercury (and assuming they're equal in length), half of the breakdowns that occur would be expected to occur during the retrograde phase and the other half during the nonretrograde phase, just by chance. Expected relative-frequency probability refers to the expected frequency of events. So in this example we would expect 50% of breakdowns to occur during the retrograde phase and 50% during the nonretrograde phase. If we base our conclusions on only a small number of observations of breakdowns, the observed relative-frequency probability is more likely to differ from the expected relative-frequency probability because we are less likely to have a representative sample of breakdowns.
 c. This correlation would not be useful in predicting events in your own life because no relation would be observed in this limited time span.
 d. Available data do not support the idea that a correlation exists between Mercury's phases and breakdowns.

13.29 a. The accompanying scatterplot depicts the relation between hours of exercise and number of friends. Note that you could also have chosen to put exercise along the y-axis and friends along the x-axis.

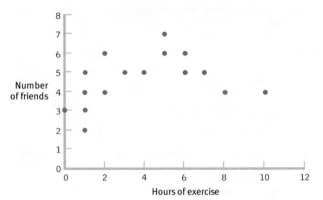

b. The scatterplot suggests that as the number of hours of exercise each week increases from 0 to 5, there is an increase in the number of friends, but as the hours of exercise continues to increase past 5, there is a decrease in the number of friends.
 c. It would not be appropriate to calculate a Pearson correlation coefficient with this set of data. The scatterplot suggests a nonlinear relation between exercise and number of friends, and the Pearson correlation coefficient measures only the extent of linear relation between two variables.

13.31 a. Population 1: Adolescents like those we studied. Population 2: Adolescents for whom there is no relation between externalizing behavior and anxiety. The comparison distribution is made up of correlation coefficients based on many, many samples of our size, 10 people, randomly selected from the population.
  We do not know if our data were randomly selected (first assumption), so we must be cautious when generalizing our findings. We also do not know if the underlying population distribution for externalizing behaviors and anxiety in adolescents is normally distributed (second assumption). Our sample size is too small to make any conclusions about this assumption, so we should proceed with caution. The third assumption, unique to correlation, is that the variability of one variable is equal across the levels of the other variable. Because we have such a small data set, it is difficult to evaluate this. However, we can see from the scatterplot that our data are somewhat consistently variable.
 b. Null hypothesis: There is no correlation between externalizing behavior and anxiety among adolescents— H_0: $r = 0$.
  Research hypothesis: There is a correlation between externalizing behavior and anxiety among adolescents— H_1: $r \neq 0$.
 c. The comparison distribution is a distribution of Pearson correlations, r, with the following degrees of freedom: $df_r = N - 2 = 10 - 2 = 8$.

d. The critical values for an r distribution with 8 degrees of freedom for a two-tailed test with a p level of 0.05 are −0.632 and 0.632.

e. The Pearson correlation coefficient is calculated in three steps. First, we calculate the numerator:

X	$(X - M_X)$	Y	$(Y - M_Y)$	$(X - M_X)(Y - M_Y)$
9	2.40	37	7.60	18.24
7	0.40	23	−6.40	−2.56
7	0.40	26	−3.40	−1.36
3	−3.60	21	−8.40	30.24
11	4.40	42	12.60	55.44
6	−0.60	33	3.60	−2.16
2	−4.60	26	−3.40	15.64
6	−0.60	35	5.60	−3.36
6	−0.60	23	−6.40	3.84
9	2.40	28	−1.40	−3.36
$M_X = 6.60$		$M_Y = 29.40$		$\Sigma[(X - M_X)(Y - M_Y)] = 110.60$

Second, we calculate the denominator:

X	$(X - M_X)$	$(X - M_X)^2$	Y	$(Y - M_Y)$	$(Y - M_Y)^2$
9	2.40	5.76	37	7.60	57.76
7	0.40	0.16	23	−6.40	40.96
7	0.40	0.16	26	−3.40	11.56
3	−3.60	12.96	21	−8.40	70.56
11	4.40	19.36	42	12.60	158.76
6	−0.60	0.36	33	3.60	12.96
2	−4.60	21.16	26	−3.40	11.56
6	−0.60	0.36	35	5.60	31.36
6	−0.60	0.36	23	−6.40	40.96
9	2.40	5.76	28	−1.40	1.96
		$\Sigma(X - M_X)^2 =$ 66.40			$\Sigma(Y - M_Y)^2 =$ 438.40

$$\sqrt{(SS_X)(SS_Y)} = \sqrt{(66.40)(438.40)} = \sqrt{29{,}109.76} = 170.616$$

Finally, we compute r:

$$r = \frac{\Sigma[(X - M_X)(Y - M_Y)]}{\sqrt{(SS_X)(SS_Y)}} = \frac{110.60}{170.6158} = 0.648$$

f. Our test statistic, $r = 0.648$, is larger in magnitude than the critical value of 0.632. We can reject the null hypothesis and conclude that there is a strong positive correlation between the number of externalizing behaviors performed by adolescents and their level of anxiety.

13.33 a. You would expect a person who owns a lot of cats to tend to have many mental health problems. Because the two variables are positively correlated, as cat ownership increases, the number of mental health problems tends to increase.

b. You would expect a person who owns no cats or just one cat to tend to have few mental health problems. Because the variables are positively correlated, people who have a low score on one variable are also likely to have a low score on the other variable.

c. You would expect a person who owns a lot of cats to tend to have few mental health problems. Because the two variables are negatively related, as one variable increases, the other variable tends to decrease. This means a person owning lots of cats would likely have a low score on the mental health variable.

d. You would expect a person who owns no cats or just one cat to tend to have many mental health problems. Because the two variables are negatively related, as one variable decreases, the other variable tends to increase, which means that a person with fewer cats would likely have more mental health problems.

13.35 a. The accompanying scatterplot depicts a negative linear relation between perceived femininity and perceived trauma. Because the relation appears linear, it is appropriate to calculate the Pearson correlation coefficient for these data.

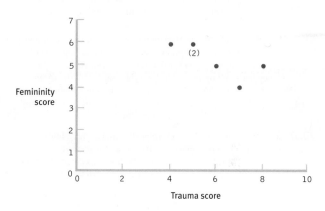

b. The Pearson correlation coefficient is calculated in three steps. Step 1 is calculating the numerator:

X	$(X - M_X)$	Y	$(Y - M_Y)$	$(X - M_X)(Y - M_Y)$
5	−0.833	6	0.667	−0.556
6	0.167	5	−0.333	−0.056
4	−1.833	6	0.667	−1.223
5	−0.833	6	0.667	−0.556
7	1.167	4	−1.333	−1.556
8	2.167	5	−0.333	−0.722
$M_X =$ 5.833		$M_Y =$ 5.333		$\Sigma[(X - M_X)(Y - M_Y)] =$ −4.669

Step 2 is calculating the denominator:

X	$(X - M_X)$	$(X - M_X)^2$	Y	$(Y - M_Y)$	$(Y - M_Y)^2$
5	−0.833	0.692	6	0.667	0.445
6	0.167	0.028	5	−0.333	0.111
4	−1.833	3.360	6	0.667	0.445
5	−0.833	0.694	6	0.667	0.445
7	1.167	1.362	4	−1.333	1.777
8	2.167	4.696	5	−0.333	0.111
		$\Sigma(X - M_X)^2 =$ 10.834			$\Sigma(Y - M_Y)^2 =$ 3.334

$$\sqrt{(SS_X)(SS_Y)} = \sqrt{(10.834)(3.334)} = \sqrt{36.121} = 6.010$$

Step 3 is computing r:

$$r = \frac{\Sigma[(X - M_X)(Y - M_Y)]}{\sqrt{(SS_X)(SS_Y)}} = \frac{-4.6667}{6.0092} = -0.777$$

c. The correlation coefficient reveals a strong negative relation between perceived femininity and perceived trauma; as trauma increases, perceived femininity tends to decrease.

d. Those participants who had positive deviation scores on trauma had negative deviation scores on femininity (and vice versa), meaning that when a person's score on one variable was above the mean for that variable (positive deviation), his or her score on the second variable was below the mean for that variable (negative deviation). So, having a high score on one variable was associated with having a low score on the other, which is a negative correlation.

13.37 a. The accompanying scatterplot depicts a positive linear relation between perceived trauma and perceived masculinity. The data appear to be linearly related; therefore, it is appropriate to calculate a Pearson correlation coefficient.

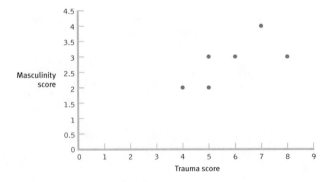

b. The Pearson correlation coefficient is calculated in three steps. Step 1 is calculating the numerator:

X	$(X - M_X)$	Y	$(Y - M_Y)$	$(X - M_X)(Y - M_Y)$
5	−0.833	3	0.167	−0.139
6	0.167	3	0.167	0.028
4	−1.833	2	−0.833	1.527
5	−0.833	2	−0.833	0.694
7	1.167	4	1.167	1.362
8	2.167	3	0.167	0.362
$M_X = 5.833$		$M_Y = 2.833$		$\Sigma[(X - M_X)(Y - M_Y)] = 3.834$

Step 2 is calculating the denominator:

X	$(X - M_X)$	$(X - M_X)^2$	Y	$(Y - M_Y)$	$(Y - M_Y)^2$
5	−0.833	0.694	3	0.167	0.028
6	0.167	0.028	3	0.167	0.028
4	−1.833	3.360	2	−0.833	0.694
5	−0.833	0.694	2	−0.833	0.694
7	1.167	1.362	4	1.167	1.362
8	2.167	4.696	3	0.167	0.028
		$\Sigma(X - M_X)^2 =$ 10.834			$\Sigma(Y - M_Y)^2 =$ 2.834

$$\sqrt{(SS_X)(SS_Y)} = \sqrt{(10.834)(2.834)} = \sqrt{30.704} = 5.541$$

Step 3 is computing r:

$$r = \frac{\Sigma[(X - M_X)(Y - M_Y)]}{\sqrt{(SS_X)(SS_Y)}} = \frac{3.8333}{5.5402} = 0.692$$

c. The correlation indicates that a large positive relation exists between perceived trauma and perceived masculinity.

d. For most of the participants, the sign of the deviation for the traumatic variable is the same as that for the masculinity variable, which indicates that those participants scoring above the mean on one variable also tended to score above the mean on the second variable (and likewise with the lowest scores). Because the scores for each participant tend to fall on the same side of the mean, this is a positive relation.

e. When the person was a woman, the perception of the situation as traumatic was strongly negatively correlated with the perception of the woman as feminine. This relation is opposite that observed when the person was a man. When the person was a man, the perception of the situation as traumatic was strongly positively correlated with the perception of the man as feminine. Regardless of whether the person was a man or a woman, there was a positive correlation between the perception of the situation as traumatic and perception of masculinity, but the observed correlation was stronger for the perceptions of women than for the perceptions of men.

13.39 a. Because your friend is running late, she is likely more concerned about traffic than she otherwise would be. Thus, she may take note of traffic only when she is running late, leading her to believe that the amount of traffic correlates with how late she is. Furthermore, having this belief, in the future she may think only of cases that confirm her belief that a relation exists between how late she is and traffic conditions, reflecting a confirmation bias. Alternatively, traffic conditions might be worse when your friend is running late, but that could be a coincidence. A more systematic study of the relation between your friend's behavior and traffic conditions would be required before she could conclude that a relation exists.

b. There are a number of possible answers to this question. For example, we could operationalize the degree to which she is late as the number of minutes past her intended departure time that she gets in the car. We could operationalize the amount of traffic as the number of minutes the car is being driven at less than the speed limit (given that your friend would normally drive right at the speed limit).

13.41 a. The researchers are suggesting that attending a private school causes a student to have better test scores.

b. It could be that those students who perform better on standardized tests tend to choose to go to private schools over public schools.

c. There are many possible answers. For example, the socioeconomic status of the student's family may account for both better test scores and private school attendance, with higher socioeconomic status causing both improved test scores and private school attendance.

13.43 a. It appears that the data are somewhat positively correlated.

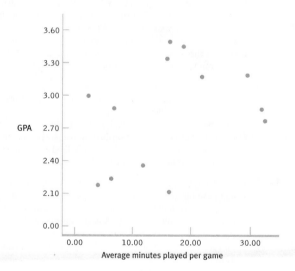

b. The Pearson correlation coefficient is calculated in three steps. Step 1 is calculating the numerator:

X	$(X - M_X)$	Y	$(Y - M_Y)$	$(X - M_X)(Y - M_Y)$
29.70	13.16	3.20	0.34	4.474
32.14	15.60	2.88	0.02	0.312
32.72	16.18	2.78	−0.08	−1.294
21.76	5.22	3.18	0.32	1.670
18.56	2.02	3.46	0.60	1.212
16.23	−0.31	2.12	−0.74	0.229
11.80	−4.74	2.36	−0.50	2.370
6.88	−9.66	2.89	0.03	−0.290
6.38	−10.16	2.24	−0.62	6.299
15.83	−0.71	3.35	0.49	−0.348
2.50	−14.04	3.00	0.14	−1.966
4.17	−12.37	2.18	−0.68	8.412
16.36	−0.18	3.50	0.64	−0.115
$M_X = 16.54$		$M_Y = 2.86$		$\Sigma[(X - M_X)(Y - M_Y)] = 20.966$

Step 2 is calculating the denominator:

X	$(X - M_X)$	$(X - M_X)^2$	Y	$(Y - M_Y)$	$(Y - M_Y)^2$
29.70	13.16	173.186	3.20	0.34	0.116
32.14	15.60	243.360	2.88	0.02	0.000
32.72	16.18	261.792	2.78	−0.08	0.006
21.76	5.22	27.248	3.18	0.32	0.102
18.56	2.02	4.080	3.46	0.60	0.360
16.23	−0.31	0.096	2.12	−0.74	0.548
11.80	−4.74	22.468	2.36	−0.50	0.250
6.88	−9.66	93.316	2.89	0.03	0.001
6.38	−10.16	103.226	2.24	−0.62	0.384
15.83	−0.71	0.504	3.35	0.49	0.240
2.50	−14.04	197.122	3.00	0.14	0.020
4.17	−12.37	153.017	2.18	−0.68	0.462
16.36	−0.18	0.032	3.50	0.64	0.410
		$\Sigma(X - M_X)^2 = 1279.447$			$\Sigma(Y - M_Y)^2 = 2.899$

$$\sqrt{(SS_X)(SS_Y)} = \sqrt{(1279.447)(2.899)} = \sqrt{3709.117} = 60.903$$

Step 3 is computing r:

$$r = \frac{\Sigma[(X - M_X)(Y - M_Y)]}{\sqrt{(SS_X)(SS_Y)}} = \frac{20.966}{60.9025} = 0.344$$

c. We computed the correlation for these data to explore whether there was a relation between GPA and playing time for the members of this team. If we were interested in making a statement about athletes in general, an inferential analysis, we would want to collect more data from a random or representative sample and conduct a hypothesis test.

13.45 **a.**

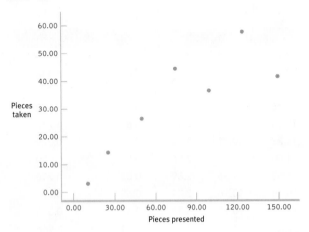

b. These variables seem to be strongly positively correlated, such that small presentation sizes are paired with fewer pieces taken and large presentations are paired with more pieces of candy taken.

c. The Pearson correlation coefficient is calculated in three steps. Step 1 is calculating the numerator:

X	$(X - M_X)$	Y	$(Y - M_Y)$	$(X - M_X)(Y - M_Y)$
10	−66	3	−29	1914
25	−51	14	−18	918
50	−26	26	−6	156
75	−1	44	12	−12
100	24	36	4	96
125	49	57	25	1225
150	74	41	9	666
$M_X = 76$		$M_Y = 32$		$\Sigma[(X - M_X)(Y - M_Y)] = 4963$

Step 2 is calculating the denominator:

X	$(X - M_X)$	$(X - M_X)^2$	Y	$(Y - M_Y)$	$(Y - M_Y)^2$
10	−66	4356	3	−29	841
25	−51	2601	14	−18	324
50	−26	676	26	−6	36
75	−1	1	44	12	144
100	24	576	36	4	16
125	49	2401	57	25	625
150	74	5476	41	9	81
		$\Sigma(X - M_X)^2 =$ 16,087			$\Sigma(Y - M_Y)^2 =$ 2067

$$\sqrt{(SS_X)(SS_Y)} = \sqrt{(16,087)(2067)} = \sqrt{33,251,829} = 5766.440$$

Step 3 is computing r:

$$r = \frac{\Sigma[(X - M_X)(Y - M_Y)]}{\sqrt{(SS_X)(SS_Y)}} = \frac{4963}{5766.440} = 0.861$$

d. According to Cohen, an r of 0.861 is a strong correlation. In fact, we learned in the text that correlations of this magnitude are very rare in the social sciences. Such a strong relation means that we could fit these data very well with a straight line. We can conclude that, in our data, when a small amount of candy was presented, a smaller amount tended to be taken by people, but when a larger amount of candy was presented, a much greater amount tended to be taken. One might be able to save money on candy by always leaving just a small amount out for people to take.

CHAPTER 14

14.1 Regression allows us to make predictions based on the relation established in the correlation. Regression also allows us to consider the contributions of several variables.

14.3 There is no difference between these two terms. They are two options for expressing the same thing.

14.5 a is the *intercept,* the predicted value for Y when X is equal to 0, which is the point at which the line crosses, or intercepts, the y-axis. b is the *slope,* the amount that Y is predicted to increase for an increase of 1 in X.

14.7 The intercept is not meaningful or useful when it is impossible to observe a value of 0 for X. If height is being used to predict weight, it would not make sense to talk about the weight of someone with no height.

14.9 The line of best fit in regression means that we couldn't make the line a little steeper, or raise or lower it, in any way that would allow it to represent those dots any better than it already does. This is why we can look at the scatterplot around this line and observe that the line goes precisely through the middle of the dots. Statistically, this is the line that leads to the least amount of error in prediction.

14.11 Data points clustered closely around the line of best fit are described by a small standard error of the estimate, and we enjoy a high level of confidence in the predictive ability of our independent variable as a result. Data points clustered far away from the line of best fit are described by a large standard error of the estimate, and as a result we have a low level of confidence in the predictive ability of our independent variable.

14.13 If regression to the mean did not occur, every distribution would look bimodal, like a valley. Instead, the end result of the phenomenon of regression to the mean is that things look unimodal, like a hill or what we call the normal, bell-shaped curve. Remember that the center of the bell-shaped curve is the mean, and this is where the bulk of data clusters thanks to regression to the mean.

14.15 The sum of squares total, SS_{total}, represents the worst-case scenario, the total error we would have in our predictions if there was no regression equation and we had to predict the mean for everybody.

14.17 (1) Determine the error associated with using the mean as our predictor. (2) Determine the error associated with using the regression equation as our predictor. (3) Subtract the error associated with the regression equation from the error associated with the mean. (4) Divide the difference (calculated in step 3) by the error associated with using the mean.

14.19 An orthogonal variable is an independent variable that makes a separate and distinct contribution in the prediction of a dependent variable, as compared with another independent variable.

14.21 **a.** $z_X = \dfrac{X - M_X}{SD_X} = \dfrac{76 - 55}{12} = 1.75$

b. $z_{\hat{Y}} = (r_{XY})(z_X) = (-0.19)(1.75) = -0.333$

c. $\hat{Y} = z_{\hat{Y}}(SD_Y) + M_Y = (-0.333)(95) + 1000 = 968.37$

14.23 **a.** $\hat{Y} = 49 + (-0.18)(X) = 49 + (-0.18)(-31) = 54.58$

b. $\hat{Y} = 49 + (-0.18)(65) = 37.3$

c. $\hat{Y} = 49 + (-0.18)(14) = 46.48$

14.25 **a.** The y-intercept occurs when X is equal to 0. We start by finding a z score:

$$z_X = \frac{X - M_X}{SD_X} = \frac{0 - 55}{12} = -4.583$$

This is the z score for an X of 0. Now we need to figure out the predicted z score on Y for this X value:

$$z_{\hat{Y}} = (r_{XY})(z_X) = (-0.19)(-4.583) = 0.871$$

The final step is to convert the z score on this predicted Y to a raw score:

$$\hat{Y} = z_{\hat{Y}}(SD_Y) + M_Y = (0.871)(95) + 1000 = 1082.745$$

This is our y-intercept.

b. The slope can be found by comparing the predicted Y value for an X value of 0 (the intercept) and an X value of 1. Using the same steps as in part (a), we can compute the predicted Y score for an X value of 1.

$$z_X = \frac{X - M_X}{SD_X} = \frac{1 - 55}{12} = -4.5$$

This is the z score for an X of 1. Now we need to figure out the predicted z score on Y for this X value:

$$z_{\hat{Y}} = (r_{XY})(z_X) = (-0.19)(-4.5) = 0.855$$

The final step is to convert the z score on this predicted Y to a raw score:

$$\hat{Y} = z_{\hat{Y}}(SD_Y) + M_Y = (0.855)(95) + 1000 = 1081.225$$

We compute the slope by measuring the change in Y with this 1-unit increase in X:

$$1081.225 - 1082.745 = -1.52$$

This is our slope.

c. $\hat{Y} = 1082.745 - 1.52(X)$

d. In order to draw the line, we have one more $\hat{Y}$ value to compute. This time we can use our regression equation to make the prediction:

$$\hat{Y} = 1082.745 - 1.52(48) = 1009.785$$

Now we can draw the regression line.

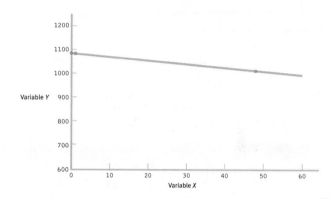

14.27 **a.** The sum of squared error for the mean, SS_{total}:

X	Y	MEAN FOR Y	ERROR	SQUARED ERROR
4	6	6.75	−0.75	0.563
6	3	6.75	−3.75	14.063
7	7	6.75	0.25	0.063
8	5	6.75	−1.75	3.063
9	4	6.75	−2.75	7.563
10	12	6.75	5.25	27.563
12	9	6.75	2.25	5.063
14	8	6.75	1.25	1.563

$$SS_{total} = S(Y - M_Y)^2 = 59.504$$

b. The sum of squared error for the regression equation, SS_{error}:

X	Y	REGRESSION EQUATION	$\hat{Y}$	ERROR $(Y - \hat{Y})$	SQUARED ERROR
4	6	$\hat{Y} = 2.643 + 0.469(4)$	= 4.519	1.481	2.193
6	3	$\hat{Y} = 2.643 + 0.469(6)$	= 5.457	−2.457	6.037
7	7	$\hat{Y} = 2.643 + 0.469(7)$	= 5.926	1.074	1.153
8	5	$\hat{Y} = 2.643 + 0.469(8)$	= 6.395	−1.395	1.946
9	4	$\hat{Y} = 2.643 + 0.469(9)$	= 6.864	−2.864	8.202
10	12	$\hat{Y} = 2.643 + 0.469(10)$	= 7.333	4.667	21.781
12	9	$\hat{Y} = 2.643 + 0.469(12)$	= 8.271	0.729	0.531
14	8	$\hat{Y} = 2.643 + 0.469(14)$	= 9.209	−1.209	1.462

$$SS_{error} = \Sigma(Y - \hat{Y})^2 = 43.306$$

c. The proportionate reduction in error for these data:

$$r^2 = \frac{(SS_{total} - SS_{error})}{SS_{total}} = \frac{(59.504 - 43.306)}{59.504} = 0.272$$

d. This calculation of r^2, 0.272, equals the square of the correlation coefficient, $r^2 = (0.52)(0.52) = 0.270$. These numbers are slightly different due to rounding error.

14.29 $\hat{Y} = 1.675 + (0.001)(X_{SAT}) + (-0.008)(X_{rank})$; or $\hat{Y} = 1.675 + 0.001 (X_{SAT}) - 0.008(X_{rank})$

14.31 **a.** $\hat{Y} = 1.675 + (0.001)(1030) + (-0.008)(41) = 1.675 + 1.03 - 0.328 = 2.377$

b. $\hat{Y} = 1.675 + (0.001)(860) + (-0.008)(22) = 1.675 + 0.86 - 0.176 = 2.359$

c. $\hat{Y} = 1.675 + (0.001)(1060) + (-0.008)(8) = 1.675 + 1.06 - 0.064 = 2.671$

14.33 The standardized regression coefficient is equal to our correlation coefficient for simple linear regression, 0.52. We can also check that this is correct by computing β:

X	$(X - M_X)$	$(X - M_X)^2$	Y	$(Y - M_Y)$	$(Y - M_Y)^2$
4	−4.75	22.563	6	−0.75	0.563
6	−2.75	7.563	3	−3.75	14.063
7	−1.75	3.063	7	0.25	0.063
8	−0.75	0.563	5	−1.75	3.063
9	0.25	0.063	4	−2.75	7.563
10	1.25	1.563	12	5.25	27.563
12	3.25	10.563	9	2.25	5.063
14	5.25	27.563	8	1.25	1.563
		$\Sigma(X - M_X)^2 =$ 73.504			$\Sigma(Y - M_Y)^2 =$ 59.504

$$\beta = (b)\frac{\sqrt{SS_X}}{\sqrt{SS_Y}} = 0.469\frac{\sqrt{73.504}}{\sqrt{59.504}} = 0.469(8.573/7.714) = 0.521$$

14.35 **a.** Outdoor temperature is the independent variable.

b. Number of hot chocolates sold is the dependent variable.

c. As the outdoor temperature increases, we would expect the sale of hot chocolate to decrease.

d. There are several possible answers to this question. For example, the number of fans in attendance may positively predict the number of hot chocolates sold. The number of children in attendance may also positively predict the number of hot chocolates sold. The number of alternative hot beverage choices may negatively predict the number of hot chocolates sold.

14.37 **a.** $X = z(\sigma) + \mu = -1.2(0.61) + 3.51 = 2.778$. This answer makes sense because the raw score of 2.778 is a bit more than 1 standard deviation below the mean of 3.51.

b. $X = z(\sigma) + \mu = 0.66(0.61) + 3.51 = 3.913$. This answer makes sense because the raw score of 3.913 is slightly more than 0.5 standard deviation above the mean of 3.51.

14.39 **a.** To predict the number of hours he studies per week, we use the formula: $z_{\hat{y}} = (r_{XY})(z_X)$ to find the z score for the number of hours he studies; then we can transform the z score into his raw score. First, translate his raw score for age into a z score for age: $z_X = \frac{(X - M_X)}{SD_X} = \frac{(24 - 21)}{1.789} = 1.677$. Then calculate his predicted z score for number of hours studied: $z_{\hat{y}} = (r_{XY})(z_X) = (0.49)(1.677) = 0.82$. Finally, translate the z score for hours studied into the raw score for hours studied: $\hat{Y} = 0.82(5.582) + 14.2 = 18.777$.

b. First, translate age raw score into an age z score:

$$z_X = \frac{(X - M_X)}{SD_X} = \frac{(19 - 21)}{1.789} = -1.118.$$ Then calculate the predicted z score for hours studied: $z_{\hat{y}} = (r_{XY})(z_X) = (0.49)(-1.118) = -0.548$. Finally, translate the z score for hours studied into the raw score for hours studied: $\hat{Y} = -0.548(5.582) + 14.2 = 11.141$.

c. Seung's age is well above the mean age of the students sampled. The relation that exists for traditional-aged students may not exist for students who are much older. Extrapolating beyond the range of the observed data may lead to erroneous conclusions.

d. From a mathematical perspective, the word *regression* refers to a tendency for extreme scores to drift toward the mean. In the calculation of regression, the predicted score is closer to its mean (i.e., less extreme) than the score used for prediction. For example, in part (a) the z score used for predicting was 1.677 and the predicted z score was 0.82, a less extreme score. Similarly, in part (b) the z score used for predicting was −1.118 and the predicted z score was −0.548—again, a less extreme score.

14.41 **a.** First, we'll calculate what we would predict for Y when X equals 0; that number, −17.908, is our intercept.

$$z_X = \frac{(X - M_X)}{SD_X} = \frac{(0 - 21)}{1.789} = -11.738$$

$$z_{\hat{Y}} = (r_{XY})(z_X) = (0.49)(-11.738) = -5.752$$

$$\hat{Y} = z_{\hat{Y}}(SD_Y) + M_Y = -5.752(5.582) + 14.2 = -17.908$$

Note that the reason this prediction is negative (it doesn't make sense to have a negative number of hours) is that the number for age, 0, is not a number that would actually be used in this situation—it's another example of the dangers of extrapolation, but it still is necessary to determine our regression equation.

Then we'll calculate what we would predict for Y when X equals 1: the amount that that number, −16.378, differs from the prediction when X equals 0 is the slope.

$$z_X = \frac{(X - M_X)}{SD_X} = \frac{(1 - 21)}{1.789} = -11.179$$

$$z_{\hat{Y}} = (r_{XY})(z_X) = (0.49)(-11.179) = -5.478$$

$$\hat{Y} = z_{\hat{Y}}(SD_Y) + M_Y = -5.478(5.582) + 14.2 = -16.378$$

When X equals 0, −17.908 is the prediction for Y. When X equals 1, −16.378 is the prediction for Y. The latter number is 1.530 higher [−16.378 − (−17.908) = 1.530]—that is, more positive—than the former. Remember when you're calculating the difference to consider whether the prediction for Y was more positive or more negative when X increased from 0 to 1.

Thus, the regression equation is: $\hat{Y} = -17.91 + 1.53(X)$

b. Substituting 17 for X in the regression equation for part (a) yields 8.1. Substituting 22 for X in the regression equation yields 15.75. We would predict that a 17-year-old would study 8.1 hours and a 22-year-old would study 15.75 hours.

c. The accompanying graph depicts the regression line for predicting hours studied per week from a person's age.

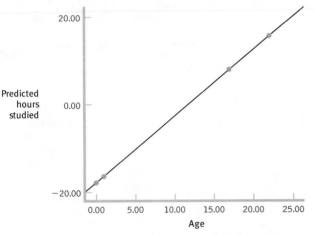

d. It is misleading to include the ages 0 and 1 on the graph because people of that age would never be college students.

14.43 **a.** The accompanying graph shows the scatterplot and regression line relating age and number of hours studied. Vertical lines from each observed data point are drawn to the regression line to represent the error in prediction from the regression equation.

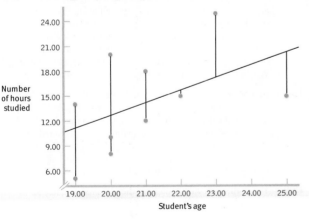

b. The accompanying scatterplot relating age and number of hours studied includes a horizontal line at the mean number of hours studied. Vertical lines between the observed data points and the mean represent the amount of error in predicting from the mean.

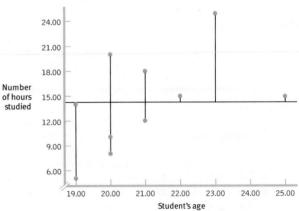

c. There appears to be less error in part (a), where the regression line is used to predict hours studied. This occurs because the regression line is the line that minimizes the distance between the observed scores and the line drawn through them. That is, the regression line is the *one* line that can be drawn through the data that produces the minimum error.

14.45 **a.** We cannot conclude that cola consumption causes a decrease in bone mineral density because there are a number of different kinds of causal relations that could lead to the predictive relation observed by Tucker and colleagues (2006). There may be some characteristic about these older women that both causes them to drink cola and leads to a decrease in bone mineral density. For example, perhaps overall poorer health habits lead to an increased consumption of cola and a decrease in bone mineral density.

b. Multiple regression allows us to assess the contributions of more than one independent variable to the outcome, dependent variable. Performing this multiple regression allowed the researchers to explore the unique contributions of a third variable, such as physical activity, in addition to bone density.

c. Physical activity might produce an increase in bone mineral density, as exercise is known to increase bone density. Conversely, it is possible that physical activity might produce a decrease in cola consumption because people who exercise more might drink beverages that are more likely to keep them hydrated (such as water or sports drinks).

d. Calcium intake should produce an increase in bone mineral density, thereby producing a positive relation between calcium intake and bone density. It is possible that consumption of cola inhibits the body's ability to absorb calcium. As such, it could interact with calcium intake and ultimately counteract any positive effects of calcium on bone mineral density, producing a negative relation between cola consumption and bone density.

14.47 If really poor students and really good students do not download podcasts very often, then the relation between number of podcasts downloaded and GPA is nonlinear. In such a case, it would be inappropriate to calculate a linear regression to predict GPA from podcasts. Constructing a scatterplot of our data would enable us to tell if there was a linear relation in our data and allow us to assess whether it would be appropriate to use regression analysis.

14.49 There are many additional variables the researcher might include in the regression. One independent variable that could be manipulated is the cost of the tutoring sessions. A second independent variable (which could not be manipulated) is the wealth of the students' families. The researcher might also consider using the gender of the student as an independent variable.

14.51 **a.** $\hat{Y} = 17.038 + 0.307(X_1) - 0.01(X_2)$, or predicted year-3 anxiety = $17.038 + 0.307$(year-1 anxiety) $- 0.013$(year-1 depression)

b. As depression increases by 1 point, predicted anxiety at year 3 decreases, on average, by 0.013.

c. As year-1 anxiety increases by 1 point, the predicted anxiety at year 3 increases, on average, by 0.307.

d. Depression at year 1 is a better predictor in the simple linear regression than in the multiple regression. The two regression equations differ because the multiple regression has included another predictor: anxiety at year 1.

e. The two variables with the strongest correlation are anxiety at year 1 and depression at year 1. This correlation accounts for why the slopes for depression at year 1 differ in the simple and multiple regressions. Depression at year 1 and anxiety at year 1 are highly correlated and commonly predict anxiety at year 3. Once anxiety is accounted for, depression no longer uniquely predicts anxiety at year 3. If we had not included the additional predictor of anxiety at year 1 in this analysis, we would have concluded that depression was related to year-3 anxiety. By including anxiety at year 1, however, we learn that depression at year 1 is not a predictor of year-3 anxiety over and above anxiety at year 1.

f. Choosing option (2), a variable that is highly correlated with the dependent variable but not correlated with either independent variable, would increase the predictive power of the multiple regression equation. Because the variable you are choosing is highly correlated with the dependent variable, we know it will be a good predictor of the dependent variable. Also, because the variable is not correlated with other independent variables in the regression equation (i.e., it is orthogonal to the other variables), it will make a unique contribution in accounting for variance in anxiety at year 3, resulting in an increase in the proportionate reduction in error.

14.53 **a.** Here are the computations needed to compute β:

X	$(X - M_X)$	$(X - M_X)^2$	Y	$(Y - M_Y)$	$(Y - M_Y)^2$
6	−38.4	1475.56	12.37	−0.574	0.329
17	−27.4	750.76	12.91	−0.034	0.001
39	−5.4	29.16	12.59	−0.354	0.125
62	17.6	309.76	13.43	0.486	0.236
98	53.6	2872.96	13.42	0.476	0.227
		$\Sigma(X - M_X)^2 =$ 5437.20			$\Sigma(Y - M_Y)^2 =$ 0.918

$$\beta = (b)\frac{\sqrt{SS_X}}{\sqrt{SS_Y}} = 0.011\frac{\sqrt{5437.20}}{\sqrt{0.918}} = 0.011(73.737/0.958) = 0.847$$

b. The standardized regression coefficient is equal to our correlation coefficient, 0.834, for simple linear regression. The numbers are slightly different due to rounding decisions.

c. The hypothesis test for regression is the same as that for correlation. The critical values for r with 3 degrees of freedom at a p level of 0.05 are -0.878 and 0.878. With a correlation of 0.834, we fail to exceed the cutoff and therefore fail to reject the null hypothesis. The same is true then for our regression. We do not have a statistically significant regression and should be careful not to claim that our slope is different from 0.

CHAPTER 15

15.1 Nominal data are those that are categorical in nature; they cannot be ordered in any meaningful way, and they are often thought of as simply named. Ordinal data can be ordered, but we cannot assume even distances between points of equal separation. For example, the difference between the second and third scores may not be the same as the difference between the seventh and the eighth. Scale data are measured on either the interval or ratio level; we can assume equal intervals between points along these measures.

15.3 The chi-square test for goodness-of-fit is a nonparametric hypothesis test used with one nominal variable. The chi-square test for independence is a nonparametric test used with two nominal variables.

15.5 Throughout the book, we have referred to independent variables, those variables that we hypothesize to have an effect on the dependent variable. We also described how statisticians refer to observations that are independent of one another, such as a between-groups research design requiring that observations be taken from independent samples. Here, with regard to chi square, *independence* takes on a similar meaning. We are testing whether the effect of one variable is independent of the other—that the proportion of cases across the levels of one variable does not depend on the levels of the other variable.

15.7 In most previous hypothesis tests, the degrees of freedom have been based on sample size. For the chi-square hypothesis tests, however, the degrees of freedom are based on the numbers of categories, or cells, in which participants can be counted. For example, the degrees of freedom for the chi-square test for goodness-of-fit is the number of categories minus 1: $df_{\chi^2} = k - 1$. Here, k is the symbol for the number of categories.

15.9 The contingency table presents the observed frequencies for each cell in the study.

15.11 This is the formula to calculate the chi-square statistic, which is the sum, for each cell, of the squared difference between each observed frequency and its matching expected frequency, divided by the expected value for its cell.

15.13 When we are concerned about meeting the assumptions of a parametric test, we can convert scale data to ordinal data and use a nonparametric test.

15.15 We use the Mann–Whitney U test when there are two groups, a between-groups design, and an ordinal dependent variable.

15.17 In all correlations, we assess the relative position of a score on one variable with its position on the other variable. In the case of the Spearman rank-order correlation, we examine how ranks on one variable relate to ranks on the other variable. For example, with a positive correlation, scores that rank low on one variable tend to rank low on the other, and scores that rank high on one variable tend to rank high on the other. For a negative correlation, low ranks on one variable tend to be associated with high ranks on the other.

15.19 **a.** (i) N is incorrect. (ii) k is the correct symbol. (iii) Degrees of freedom for the chi-square test of goodness-of-fit is based on the number of groups, symbolized by k.

   b. (i) $+$ is incorrect. (ii) The multiplication symbol is the correct symbol. (iii) When obtaining the degrees of freedom for the chi-square test for independence, we multiply the degrees of freedom associated with each variable.

   c. (i) M is incorrect. (ii) O is the correct symbol. (iii) Calculation of chi square involves calculating the difference between observed (O) and expected frequencies.

   d. (i) k is incorrect. (ii) df is the correct symbol. (iii) Calculation of Cramer's V involves dividing by the degrees of freedom, not the number of groups.

   e. (i) Both ks are incorrect. (ii) *Total* is the correct symbol. (iii) Calculation of the expected values is based on the total counts for the rows and the columns, not the numbers of categories.

   f. (i) The r is incorrect. (ii) r_S is the correct symbol. (iii) This is the formula for the Spearman rank-order correlation, which requires the subscript S.

   g. (i) ΣR_1^2 is incorrect. (ii) ΣR_1 is the correct symbol. (iii) In the Mann–Whitney U test, we do not square the ranks before we sum them; we just sum the ranks.

15.21 **a.** $df_{\chi^2} = k - 1 = 3 - 1 = 2$

   b.

CATEGORY	OBSERVED (O)	EXPECTED (E)	O − E	$(O - E)^2$	$\dfrac{(O - E)^2}{E}$
1	48	60	48 − 60 = −12	144	2.4
2	46	30	46 − 30 = 16	256	8.533
3	6	10	6 − 10 = −4	16	1.6

   c. $\chi^2 = \Sigma\left[\dfrac{(O - E)^2}{E}\right] = 2.4 + 8.533 + 1.6 = 12.$

15.23 $df_{\chi^2} = (k_{row} - 1)(k_{column} - 1)\ 5\ (2 - 1)(2 - 1) = 1$

15.25

CATEGORY	OBSERVED (O)	EXPECTED (E)	O − E	$(O - E)^2$	$\dfrac{(O - E)^2}{E}$
Rain, accidents	19	12.904	6.096	37.161	2.880
Rain, no accidents	26	32.096	−6.096	37.161	1.158
No rain, accidents	20	26.096	−6.096	37.161	1.424
No rain, no accidents	71	64.904	6.096	37.161	0.573

$\chi^2 = \Sigma\left[\dfrac{(O - E)^2}{E}\right] = 2.880 + 1.158 + 1.424 + 0.573 = 6.035$

15.27

COUNT	VARIABLE X	RANK X	VARIABLE Y	RANK Y
1	134.5	3	64.00	7
2	186	10	60.00	1
3	157	9	61.50	2
4	129	1	66.25	10
5	147	7	65.50	8.5
6	133	2	62.00	3.5
7	141	5	62.50	5
8	147	7	62.00	3.5
9	136	4	63.00	6
10	147	7	65.50	8.5

15.29

COUNT	RANK X	RANK Y	DIFFERENCE	SQUARED DIFFERENCE
1	3	7	−4	16
2	10	1	9	81
3	9	2	7	49
4	1	10	−9	81
5	7	8.5	−1.5	2.25
6	2	3.5	−1.5	2.25
7	5	5	0	0
8	7	3.5	3.5	12.25
9	4	6	−2	4
10	7	8.5	−1.5	2.25

$$r_S = 1 - \frac{6(\Sigma D^2)}{N(N^2 - 1)} = 1 - \frac{6(250)}{10(100 - 1)} = 1 - \frac{1500}{990}$$
$$= 1 - 1.515 = -0.515$$

15.31 $\Sigma R_{group1} = 1 + 2.5 + 8 + 4 + 6 + 10 = 31.5$

$\Sigma R_{group2} = 11 + 9 + 2.5 + 5 + 7 + 12 = 46.5$

The formula for the first group is:

$$U_{group1} = (n_{group1})(n_{group2}) + \frac{n_{group1}(n_{group1} + 1)}{2} - \Sigma R_{group1}$$

$$= (6)(6) + \frac{6(6 + 1)}{2} - 31.5 = 36 + 21 - 31.5 = 25.5$$

The formula for the second group is:

$$U_{group2} = (n_{group1})(n_{group2}) + \frac{n_{group2}(n_{group2} + 1)}{2} - \Sigma R_{group2}$$

$$= (6)(6) + \frac{6(6 + 1)}{2} - 46.5 = 36 + 21 - 46.5 = 10.5$$

Our test statistic would be 10.5, because it is the smaller of the two.

15.33 **a.** A nonparametric test would be appropriate because both of the variables are nominal: gender and major.

b. A nonparametric test is more appropriate for this question because the sample size is small and the data are unlikely to be normal; the "top boss" is likely to have a much higher income than the other employees. This outlier would lead to a nonnormal distribution.

c. A parametric test would be appropriate because the independent variable (type of student: athlete versus nonathlete) is nominal and the dependent variable (grade point average) is scale.

d. A nonparametric test would be appropriate because the independent variable (athlete versus nonathlete) is nominal and the dependent variable (class rank) is ordinal.

e. A nonparametric test would be appropriate because the research question is about the relation between two nominal variables: seat-belt wearing and degree of injuries.

f. A parametric test would be appropriate because the independent variable (seat-belt use: no seat belt versus seat belt) is nominal and the dependent variable (speed) is scale.

15.35 **a.** (i) Year. (ii) Grades received. (iii) This is a category III research design because the independent variable, year, is nominal and the dependent variable, grade (A or not), could also be considered nominal.

b. (i) Type of school. (ii) Average GPA of graduating students. (iii) This is a category II research design because the independent variable, type of school, is nominal and the dependent variable, GPA, is scale.

c. (i) SAT scores of incoming students. (ii) College GPA. (iii) This is a category I research design because both the independent variable and the dependent variable are scale.

15.37 **a.** The Mann–Whitney U test would be most appropriate because it is a nonparametric equivalent to the independent-samples t test. It is used when we have a nominal independent variable with two levels (here, they are north and south of the equator), a between-groups research design, and an ordinal dependent variable (here, it is the ranking of the city).

b. The Spearman rank-order correlation would be most appropriate because we are asking a question about the relation between two ordinal variables.

15.39 **a.** There is one variable, gender of the children. Its levels are girls and boys.

b. A chi-square test for goodness-of-fit would be used because we have one sample, the children from Punjab, and we are comparing proportions of children that fall within each level of gender (a nominal variable) to expectations based on national proportions.

c. *Step 1:* Population 1 is children with gender proportions like those that we observed in Punjab. Population 2 is children with gender proportions similar to those in India as a whole. The comparison distribution is a chi-square distribution. The hypothesis test will be a chi-square test for goodness-of-fit because we have only one nominal variable. This study meets three of the four assumptions. (1) The variable under study is nominal. (2) Each observation is independent of the others. (3) There are more than five times as many participants as there are cells (there are 1798 children in the sample and only 2 cells). (4) We do not know, however, whether this is a randomly selected sample of the more educated people, so we must generalize with caution.

Step 2: Null hypothesis: The proportions of boys and girls in Punjab are the same as those in India as a whole.

Research hypothesis: The proportions of boys and girls in Punjab are different from those in India as a whole.

Step 3: The comparison distribution is a chi-square distribution that has 1 degree of freedom: $df_{\chi2} = 2 - 1 = 1$.

Step 4: Our critical χ^2, based on a p level of 0.05 and 1 degree of freedom, is 3.841.

Step 5:

OBSERVED (PROPORTIONS OF BOYS AND GIRLS)	
BOYS	GIRLS
1000	798

EXPECTED (FROM THE GENERAL POPULATION)	
BOYS	GIRLS
929.566	868.434

CATEGORY	OBSERVED (O)	EXPECTED (E)	O − E	(O − E)²	$\frac{(O - E)^2}{E}$
Boys	1000	929.566	70.434	4960.948	5.337
Girls	798	868.434	−70.434	4960.948	5.713

$$\chi^2 = \Sigma\left[\frac{(O - E)^2}{E}\right] = 5.337 + 5.713 = 11.05$$

Step 6: Reject the null hypothesis. Our calculated chi-square value exceeds our critical value. It appears that the proportion of girls in Punjab is less than that in the general population of India.

d. $\chi^2(1, N = 1798) = 11.05, p < 0.05$

15.41 **a.** There are two variables in this study. The independent variable is the country the student is from (United States, China). The dependent variable is the choice the student made (defect, cooperate).

b. A chi-square test for independence would be used because we have data on two nominal variables.

c. *Step 1:* Population 1 contains students like those in this sample. Population 2 contains students from a population in which country of origin and choice to defect or cooperate are independent. The comparison distribution is a chi-square distribution. The hypothesis test will be a chi-square test for independence because we have two nominal variables. This study meets three of the four assumptions. (1) The two variables are nominal; (2) every participant is in only one cell; and (3) there are more than five times as many participants as there are cells (there are 122 participants and 4 cells). (4) The students were not randomly selected, however, so we should use caution when generalizing beyond this sample.

Step 2: Null hypothesis: The proportion of Chinese students who choose to defect as opposed to cooperate is similar to the proportion for U.S. students.

Research hypothesis: The proportion of Chinese students who choose to defect as opposed to cooperate is different from the proportion for U.S. students.

Step 3: The comparison distribution is a chi-square distribution that has 1 degree of freedom: $df_{\chi 2} = (k_{row} - 1)(k_{column} - 1) = (2 - 1)(2 - 1) = 1$.

Step 4: Our cutoff χ^2, based on a p level of 0.05 and 1 degree of freedom, is 3.841.

Step 5:

	OBSERVED		
	DEFECT	COOPERATE	
China	31	36	67
United States	41	14	55
	72	50	122

$$\frac{Total_{column}}{N}(Total_{row}) = \frac{72}{122}(67) = 39.541$$

$$\frac{Total_{column}}{N}(Total_{row}) = \frac{72}{122}(55) = 32.459$$

$$\frac{Total_{column}}{N}(Total_{row}) = \frac{50}{122}(67) = 27.459$$

$$\frac{Total_{column}}{N}(Total_{row}) = \frac{50}{122}(55) = 22.541$$

	EXPECTED		
	DEFECT	COOPERATE	
China	39.541	27.459	67
United States	32.459	22.541	55
	72	50	122

CATEGORY	OBSERVED (O)	EXPECTED (E)	O − E	(O − E)²	$\frac{(O-E)^2}{E}$
China; defect	31	39.451	−8.541	72.949	1.849
China; cooperate	36	27.459	8.541	72.949	2.657
U.S.; defect	41	32.459	8.541	72.949	2.247
U.S.; cooperate	14	22.541	−8.541	72.949	3.236

$$\chi^2 = \Sigma\left[\frac{(O-E)^2}{E}\right] = 1.849 + 2.657 + 2.247 + 3.236 = 9.989$$

Step 6: Reject the null hypothesis. Our calculated chi-square value exceeds our critical value. It appears that the proportion of participants who choose to defect is higher among U.S. students than among Chinese students.

d. Cramer's $V = \sqrt{\dfrac{\chi^2}{(N)(df_{row/column})}} = \sqrt{\dfrac{9.989}{(122)(1)}} = 0.286$. According to Cohen's conventions, this is a medium effect.

e. $\chi^2(1, N = 122) = 9.99, p < 0.05$, Cramer's $V = 0.29$

15.43 a. The accompanying table shows the conditional proportions.

	DEFECT	COOPERATE	
China	0.463	0.537	1.00
United States	0.745	0.255	1.00

b. The accompanying graph shows the conditional proportions for all four conditions.

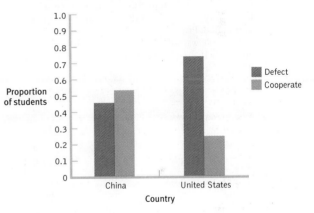

c. The accompanying graph shows only the bar for defects.

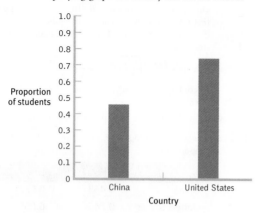

15.45 a. The accompanying table shows the ordered data and corresponding ranks. When converted to ordinal data, the outlier is still at the top of the distribution but is no longer very different from the rest of the scores in the distribution. Prior to converting to ordinal data, the outlier, 500, was well above the next-highest observation, 200. Now the scores of 500 and 200 are ranked 29 and 28, respectively.

PHONE BILL	PHONE RANK	PHONE BILL (CONT.)	PHONE RANK (CONT.)
0	1	55	16
30	2	60	17.5
35	3	60	17.5
40	5.5	65	19
40	5.5	75	20
40	5.5	80	21.5
40	5.5	80	21.5
45	8.5	100	24.5
45	8.5	100	24.5
50	12.5	100	24.5
50	12.5	100	24.5
50	12.5	108	27
50	12.5	200	28
50	12.5	500	29
50	12.5		

b. The distribution is likely to be somewhat rectangular and not normal. However, the distribution of ordinal data is never normal because each score is assigned a rank, which means that each individual raw score usually has a different rank from the others. In most cases (unless there are ties), all frequencies would be 1.

c. It does not matter that the ordinal transformation is not normally distributed because we would be using nonparametric statistics to analyze the data. Nonparametric statistics do not require the assumption that the underlying distribution is normal.

15.47 a. The first variable of interest is test grade, which is a scale variable. The second variable of interest is the order in which students completed the test, which is an ordinal variable.

b. The accompanying table shows test grade converted to ranks, difference scores, and squared differences.

GRADE PERCENTAGE	GRADE SPEED	RANK	D	D^2
98	1	1	0	0
93	6	2	4	16
92	4	3	1	1
88	5	4	1	1
87	3	5	−2	4
74	2	6	−4	16
67	8	7	1	1
62	7	8	−1	1

We calculate the Spearman correlation coefficient as:

$$r_S = 1 - \frac{6(\Sigma D)^2}{N(N^2 - 1)} = 1 - \frac{6(40)}{8(64 - 1)} = 1 - \frac{240}{504} = 0.524$$

c. The coefficient tells us that there is a rather large positive relation between the two variables. Students who completed the test more quickly also tended to score higher.

d. We could not have calculated a Pearson correlation coefficient because one of our variables, order in which students turned in the test, is ordinal.

15.49 a. This correlation does not indicate that students should attempt to take their tests as quickly as possible. Correlation does not provide evidence for a particular causal relation. A number of underlying causal relations could produce this observed correlation.

b. A third variable that might cause both speedy test-taking and a good test grade is knowledge of the material. Students with better knowledge of and more practice with the material would be able to get through the test more quickly and get a better grade.

15.51 a. The independent variable is type of state, and its levels are red and blue. The dependent variable is the percentage of registered voters who voted.

b. This is a between-groups design because each state is either a red state or a blue state but cannot be both.

c. *Step 1:* We need to convert our data to an ordinal measure. The states were randomly selected, so we can assume that they are representative of their populations. Finally, there are no tied ranks.

Step 2: Null hypothesis: There is no difference between the voter turnout in red and blue states.

Research hypothesis: There is a difference between the voter turnout in red and blue states.

Step 3: There are eight red and eight blue states.

Step 4: The critical value for a Mann–Whitney U test with two groups of eight, a p level of 0.05, and a two-tailed test is 15. The smaller calculated statistic needs to be less than or equal to this critical value to be considered statistically significant.

Step 5:

STATE	TURNOUT	TURNOUT RANK	STATE TYPE	RED RANK	BLUE RANK
Wisconsin	76.73	1	Blue		1
Maine	73.4	2	Blue		2
Oregon	70.5	3	Blue		3
Washington	67.42	4	Blue		4
Missouri	66.89	5	Red	5	
Vermont	66.19	6	Blue		6
Idaho	64.89	7	Red	7	
New Jersey	64.54	8	Blue		8
Montana	64.36	9	Red	9	
Virginia	61.5	10	Red	10	
Louisiana	60.78	11	Red	11	
Illinois	60.73	12	Blue		12
California	60.01	13	Blue		13
Georgia	57.38	14	Red	14	
Indiana	55.69	15	Red	15	
Texas	53.35	16	Red	16	

$$\Sigma R_{red} = 5 + 7 + 9 + 10 + 11 + 14 + 15 + 16 = 87$$
$$\Sigma R_{blue} = 1 + 2 + 3 + 4 + 6 + 8 + 12 + 13 = 49$$

$$U_{red} = (8)(8) + \frac{8(8+1)}{2} - 87 = 13$$

$$U_{blue} = (8)(8) + \frac{8(8+1)}{2} - 49 = 51$$

Step 6: The smaller calculated U, 13, is less than the critical value of 15, so we reject the null hypothesis. There is a statistically significant difference between voter turnout in red and blue states. Voter turnout tends to be higher in blue states than in red states.

d. $U = 13, p < 0.05$

Solutions to Check Your Learning Problems

CHAPTER 1

1-1 Data from samples are used in inferential statistics (to make an inference about the larger population).

1-2   **a.** The average grade for your statistics class would be a descriptive statistic because it's being used only to describe the tendency of people in your class with respect to a statistics grade.

  b. In this case, the average grade would be an inferential statistic because it is being used to estimate the results of a population of students taking statistics.

1-3   **a.** 100 selected students

  b. 12,500 students at the university

  c. The 100 students in the sample have an average score of 18, a moderately high stress level.

  d. The entire population of students at this university has a moderately high stress level, on average. The sample mean, 18, is an estimate of the unknown population mean.

1-4 Discrete observations can take on only specific values, usually whole numbers; continuous observations can take on a full range of values.

1-5   **a.** These data are continuous because they can take on a full range of values.

  b. The variable is measured on a ratio scale because there is a true zero point.

  c. On an ordinal scale, Lorna's score would be 2 (or 2nd).

1-6   **a.** The levels of gender, male and female, have no numerical meaning even if they are arbitrarily labeled 1 and 2.

  b. The three levels of hair length (short, mid-length, and very long) are arranged in order, but we do not know the magnitude of the differences in length.

  c. The distances between probability scores are assumed to be equal.

1-7 independent, dependent

1-8   **a.** There are two independent variables: beverage and subject to be remembered. The dependent variable is memory.

  b. Beverage has two levels: caffeine and no caffeine. The subject to be remembered has three levels: numbers, word lists, and aspects of a story.

1-9   **a.** Whether or not a student declared a major

  b. Declared a major; did not declare a major

  c. Anxiety score

  d. The scores would be consistent over time unless a student's anxiety level changed.

  e. The anxiety scale was actually measuring anxiety.

1-10 Experimental research involves random assignment to conditions; correlational research examines associations where random assignment is not possible and variables are not manipulated.

1-11 Random assignment helps to distribute confounding variables evenly across all conditions so that the levels of the independent variable are what truly vary across groups or conditions.

1-12 Rank in high school class and high school grade point average (GPA) are good examples.

1-13   **a.** Researchers could randomly assign a certain number of women to be told about a gender difference on the test and randomly assign a certain number of other women to be told that no gender difference existed on this test.

  b. If researchers did not use random assignment, any gender differences might be due to confounding variables. The women in the two groups might be different in some way (e.g., in math ability or belief in stereotypes) to begin with.

  c. There are many possible confounds. Women who already believed the stereotype might do so because they had always performed poorly in mathematics, whereas those who did not believe the stereotype might be those who always did particularly well in math. Women who believed the stereotype might be those who were discouraged from studying math because "girls can't do math," whereas those who did not believe the stereotype might be those who were encouraged to study math because "girls are just as good as boys in math."

  d. Math performance is operationalized as scores on a math test.

  e. Researchers could have two math tests that are similar in difficulty. All women would take the first test after being told that women tend not to do as well as men on this test. After taking that test, they would be given the second test after being told that women tend to do as well as men on this test.

CHAPTER 2

2-1 Frequency tables, grouped frequency tables, histograms, and frequency polygons

2-2 A frequency is a count of how many times a score appears. A grouped frequency is a count for a defined interval, or group, of scores.

2-3 **a.** Grouped frequency table:

INTERVALS	FREQUENCIES
50–59	2
40–49	1
30–39	1
20–29	2
10–19	4
0–9	7

b. Histogram:

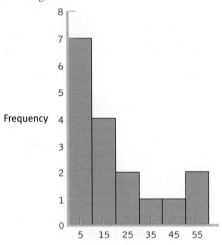

Number of students belonging to an ethnic minority group

c. Frequency polygon:

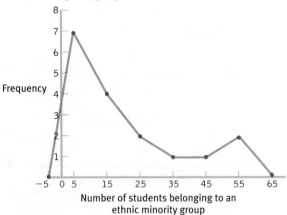

Number of students belonging to an ethnic minority group

2-4 **a.** We can now get a sense of the overall pattern of the data.

b. Percentages might be more useful because they allow us to compare programs. Two programs might have the same number of minority students, but if one program has far more students overall, it is less diverse than one with fewer students overall.

c. It is possible that schools did not provide data if they had no or few minority students. Thus, this data set might be composed of the schools with more diverse student bodies.

This is a volunteer sample; schools are not obligated to report these data.

2-5 A normal distribution is a specific distribution that is symmetric around a center high point: It looks like a bell. A skewed distribution is asymmetric or lopsided to the left or to the right, with a long tail of data to one side.

2-6 negative; positive

2-7 Positive skew

2-8 **a.** Early-onset Alzheimer's disease would create negative skew in the distribution for age of onset.

b. Because all humans eventually die, there is a sort of ceiling effect.

2-9 Being aware of these exceptional early-onset cases allows medical practitioners to be open to such surprising diagnoses. In addition, exceptional cases like these often give us great insight into the underlying mechanisms of disease.

CHAPTER 3

3-1 The purpose of a graph is to reveal and clarify relations between variables.

3-2 Five miles per gallon change (from 22 to 27) and $\frac{5}{22}(100) = 22.7\%$ change

3-3 The graph on the left is misleading. It shows a sharp decline in annual traffic deaths in Connecticut from 1955 to 1956, but we cannot draw valid conclusions from just two data points. The graph on the right is a more accurate and complete depiction of the data. It includes nine, rather than two, data points and suggests that the sharp one-year decline is the beginning of a clear downward trend in traffic fatalities that extends through 1959. It also shows that there had been previous one-year declines of similar magnitude—from 1951 to 1952 and from 1953 to 1954.

3-4 Scatterplots and line graphs both depict the relation between two scale variables.

3-5 The data can almost always be presented more clearly in a table or in a bar graph.

3-6 The line graph known as a time plot or time series plot allow us to do so.

3-7 **a.** A scatterplot is the best graph choice to depict the relation between two scale variables such as depression and stress.

b. A time plot, or time series plot, is the best graph choice to depict the change in a scale variable, such as number of facilities, over time.

c. For one scale variable, such as number of siblings, the best graph choice would be either a frequency histogram or frequency polygon.

d. In this case, there is a nominal variable (region of the United States) and a scale variable (years of education). The best choice would be a bar graph, with one bar depicting the mean years of education for each region. A Pareto chart would arrange the bars from highest to lowest, allowing for easier comparisons.

e. Calories and hours are both scale variables, and the question is about prediction rather than relation. In this case, we'd calculate and graph a line of best fit.

3-8 Chartjunk is any unnecessary information or feature in a graph that detracts from the viewer's understanding.

3-9 **a.** Scatterplot or line graph

b. Bar graph

c. Scatterplot or line graph

3-10

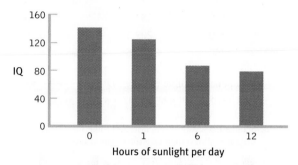

The Effect of Sunlight on IQ Scores

The accompanying graph improves on the chartjunk graph in several ways. First, it has a clear, specific caption. Second, all axes are labeled left to right. Third, there are no abbreviations. The units of measurement, IQ and hours of sunlight per day, are included. The y-axis has 0 as its minimum, the colors are simple and muted, and all chartjunk has been eliminated. This graph wasn't as much fun to create, but it offers a far clearer presentation of the data! (*Note:* We are treating hours as a nominal variable.)

CHAPTER 4

4-1 Statistics are calculated for samples; they are usually symbolized by Latin letters (e.g., M and s). Parameters are calculated for populations; they are usually symbolized by Greek letters (e.g., μ and σ).

4-2 Mean, because the calculation of the mean takes into account the numeric value of each data point, including that outlier.

4-3 **a.** $M = \dfrac{\Sigma X}{N} = (10 + 8 + 22 + 5 + 6 + 1 + 19 + 8 + 13$

$+ 12 + 8)/11 = 112/11 = 10.18$

The median is found by arranging the scores in numeric order—1, 5, 6, 8, 8, 8, 10, 12, 13, 19, 22—then dividing the total number of scores, 11, by 2 and adding ½ to get 6. The 6th score in our ordered list of scores is the median, and in this case the 6th score is the number 8.

The mode is the most common score. In these data, the score 8 occurs most often (three times), so 8 is our mode.

b. $M = \dfrac{\Sigma X}{N} = (122.5 + 123.8 + 121.2 + 125.8 + 120.2$

$+ 123.8 + 120.5 + 119.8 + 126.3 + 123.6)/10$

$= 1227.5/10 = 122.75$

The data ordered are: 119.8, 120.2, 120.5, 121.2, 122.5, 123.6, 123.8, 123.8, 125.8, 126.3. Again, we find the median by ordering the data, and then dividing the number of scores (here there are 10 scores) by 2 and adding ½. In this case, we get 5.5, so the mean of the 5th and 6th data points is the median. The median is $(122.5 + 123.6)/2 = 123.05$.

The mode is 123.8, which occurs twice in these data.

c. $M = \dfrac{\Sigma X}{N} = (0.100 + 0.866 + 0.781 + 0.555 + 0.222$

$+ 0.245 + 0.234)/7 = 3.003/7 = 0.429$.

Note that three decimal places are included here (rather than the standard two places used throughout this book) because the data are carried out to three decimal places.

The median is found by first ordering the data: 0.100, 0.222, 0.234, 0.245, 0.555, 0.781, 0.866. Then the total number of scores, 7, is divided by 2 to get 3.5, to which ½ is added to get 4. So, the 4th score, 0.245, is our median.

There is no mode in these data. All scores occur once.

4-4 **a.** $M = \dfrac{\Sigma X}{N} = (1 + 0 + 1 + 2 + 5 + \ldots 4 + 6)/20$

$= 50/20 = 2.50$

b. In this case, the scores would comprise a sample taken from the whole population, and this mean would be a statistic. The symbol, therefore, would be either M or $\bar{X}$.

c. In this case, the scores would constitute the entire population of interest, and the mean would be a parameter. Thus, the symbol would be μ.

d. To find the median, we would arrange the scores in order: 0, 0, 1,1, 1, 1, 2, 2, 2, 2, 2, 2, 3, 3, 3, 3, 4, 5, 6, 7. We would then divide the total number of scores, 20, by 2 and add ½, which is 10.5. The median, therefore, is the mean of the 10th and 11th scores. Both of these scores are 2; therefore, the median is 2.

e. The mode is the most common score—in this case, there are six 2's, so the mode is 2.

f. The mean is a little higher than the median. This indicates that there are potential outliers pulling the mean higher; outliers would not affect the median.

4-5 Variability is the concept of variety in data, often measured as deviation around some center.

4-6 The range tells us the span of our data, from highest to lowest. It is based on just two scores. The standard deviation tells us how far the typical score falls from the mean. The standard deviation takes every score into account.

4-7 **a.** The range is: $X_{highest} - X_{lowest} = 22 - 1 = 21$

The variance is: $SD^2 = \dfrac{\Sigma(X - M)^2}{N}$

We start by calculating the mean, which is 10.18. We then calculate the deviation of each score from the mean and the square of that deviation.

X	X − M	(X − M)²
10	−0.18	0.03
8	−2.18	4.75
22	11.82	139.71
5	−5.18	26.83
6	−4.18	17.47
1	−9.18	84.27
19	8.82	77.79
8	−2.18	4.75
13	2.82	7.95
12	1.82	3.31
8	−2.18	4.75

$$SD^2 = \frac{\Sigma(X - M)^2}{N} = \frac{371.61}{11} = 33.78$$

The standard deviation is: $SD = \sqrt{SD^2}$ or

$$SD = \sqrt{\frac{\Sigma(X - M)^2}{N}} = \sqrt{33.78} = 5.81$$

b. The range is: $X_{highest} - X_{lowest} = 126.3 - 119.8 = 6.5$

The variance is: $SD^2 = \dfrac{\Sigma(X - M)^2}{N}$

We start by calculating the mean, which is 122.75. We then calculate the deviation of each score from the mean and the square of that deviation.

X	X − M	(X − M)²
122.5	−0.25	0.06
123.8	1.05	1.10
121.2	−1.55	2.40
125.8	3.05	9.30
120.2	−2.55	6.50
123.8	1.05	1.10
120.5	−2.25	5.06
119.8	−2.95	8.70
126.3	3.55	12.60
123.6	0.85	0.72

$$SD^2 = \dfrac{\Sigma(X - M)^2}{N} = \dfrac{47.56}{10} = 4.76$$

The standard deviation is: $SD = \sqrt{SD^2}$ or

$$SD = \sqrt{\dfrac{\Sigma(X - M)^2}{N}} = \sqrt{4.76} = 2.18$$

c. The range is: $X_{highest} - X_{lowest} = 0.866 - 0.100 = 0.766$

The variance is: $SD^2 = \dfrac{\Sigma(X - M)^2}{N}$

We start by calculating the mean, which is 0.429. We then calculate the deviation of each score from the mean and the square of that deviation.

X	X − M	(X − M)²
0.100	−0.33	0.11
0.866	0.44	0.19
0.781	0.35	0.12
0.555	0.13	0.02
0.222	−0.21	0.04
0.245	−0.18	0.03
0.234	−0.20	0.04

$$SD^2 = \dfrac{\Sigma(X - M)^2}{N} = \dfrac{0.55}{7} = 0.08$$

The standard deviation is: $SD = \sqrt{SD^2}$ or

$$SD = \sqrt{\dfrac{\Sigma(X - M)^2}{N}} = \sqrt{0.08} = 0.28$$

4-8 **a.** range $= X_{highest} - X_{lowest} = 1460 - 450 = 1010$

b. We do not know whether scores cluster at some point in the distribution—for example, near one end of the distribution—or whether the scores are more evenly spread out.

c. The formula for variance is $SD^2 = \dfrac{\Sigma(X - M)^2}{N}$.

The first step is to calculate the mean, which is 927.50. We then create three columns: one for the scores, one for the

deviations of the scores from the mean, and one for the squares of the deviations.

X	X − M	(X − M)²
450	−477.5	228,006.25
670	−257.5	66,306.25
1130	202.5	41,006.25
1460	532.5	283,556.25

We can now calculate variance: $SD^2 = \dfrac{\Sigma(X - M)^2}{N} =$ (228,006.25 + 66,306.25 + 41,006.25 + 283,556.25)/4 = 618,875/4 = 154,718.75.

d. Standard deviation is calculated just like we calculated variance, but we then take the square root.

$$SD = \sqrt{\dfrac{\Sigma(X - M)^2}{N}} = \sqrt{154,718.75} = 393.34.$$

e. If the researcher were interested only in these four students, these scores would represent the entire population of interest, and the variance and standard deviation would be parameters. Therefore, the symbols would be σ^2 and σ, respectively.

f. If the researcher hoped to generalize from these four students to all students at the university, these scores would represent a sample, and the variance and standard deviation would be statistics. Therefore, the symbols would be SD^2, s^2, or MS for variance and SD or s for standard deviation.

CHAPTER 5

5-1 The risks of sampling are that we might not have a representative sample, and sometimes this is difficult to know. In this case, we might make conclusions about the population that are inaccurate.

5-2 The numbers in the fourth row, reading across, are 59808 08391 45427 26842 83609. Each person is assigned a number from 01 to 80. We then read the numbers from the table as two-digit numbers: 59, 80, 80, 83, 91, 45, 42, 72, 68, and so on. We ignore repeat numbers (e.g., 80) and numbers that exceed our sample of 80. So, the six people chosen would have the assigned numbers: 59, 80, 45, 42, 72, and 68.

5-3 Reading down from the first column, then the second, and so on, noting only the appearance of 0s and 1s, we see the numbers 0, 0, 0, 0, 1, and 0 (ending in the 6th column). Using these numbers, we could assign the first through the 4th and the 6th people to the group designated as 0, and the 5th person to the group designated as 1. If we want an equal number of people in each of the two groups, we would assign the first three people to the 0 group and the last three to the 1 group, because we pulled three 0's first.

5-4 **a.** The likely population is all patients who will undergo surgery; the researcher would not be able to access this population, and therefore random selection could not be used. Random assignment, however, could be used. The psychologist could randomly assign half of the patients to counseling and half to a control group.

b. The population is all children in this school system; the psychologist could identify all of these children and thus could use random selection. The psychologist also could use random assignment. She could randomly assign half the children to the interactive CD-ROM textbook and half to the printed textbook.

   c. The population is patients in therapy; because the whole population could not be identified, random selection could not be used. Moreover, random assignment could not be used. It is not possible to assign people to either have or not have a diagnosed personality disorder.

5-5 We regularly make personal assessments about how probable we think an event is, but we base these evaluations on our opinions about things rather than on systematic data collection. Statisticians are interested in objective probabilities, based on unbiased research.

5-6   **a.** $probability = \frac{successes}{trials} = 5/100 = 0.50$

   b. $8/50 = 0.16$

   c. $130/1044 = 0.12$

5-7   **a.** In the short run, we might see a wide range of numbers of successes. It would not be surprising to have several in a row or none in a row. In the short run, our observations seem almost like chaos.

   b. Given the assumptions listed for this problem, in the long run, we'd expect 0.50, or 50%, to be women, although there would likely be strings of men and of women along the way.

5-8 When we reject the null hypothesis, we are saying we reject the idea that there is no mean difference in the dependent variable across the levels of our independent variable. Rejecting the null hypothesis means we can support our research hypothesis that there is a mean difference.

5-9 The null hypothesis assumes no mean difference would be observed, so the mean difference in grades would be zero.

5-10 **a.** The null hypothesis is that a decrease in temperature does not affect mean academic performance (or does not decrease mean academic performance).

   b. The research hypothesis is that a decrease in temperature does affect mean academic performance (or decreases mean academic performance).

   c. The researchers would reject the null hypothesis.

   d. The researchers would fail to reject the null hypothesis.

5-11 A Type I error occurs when we reject the null hypothesis, but the null hypothesis is correct. A Type II error occurs when we fail to reject the null hypothesis, but the null hypothesis is false.

5-12 In this scenario, a Type I error would be imprisoning a person who is really innocent, and 7 convictions out of 280 innocent people calculates to be 0.025, or 2.5%.

5-13 In this scenario, a Type II error would be failing to convict a guilty person, and 11 acquittals for every 35 guilty people calculates to be 0.314, or 31.4%.

5-14 **a.** If the virtual-reality glasses really don't have any effect, this is a Type I error, which occurs when the null hypothesis is rejected but is really true.

   b. If the virtual-reality glasses really do have an effect, this is a Type II error, which occurs when the researchers fail to reject the null hypothesis, but the null hypothesis is not true.

CHAPTER 6

6-1 Unimodal means there is one mode or high point to the curve. Symmetric means the left and right sides of the curve have the same shape and are mirror images of each other.

6-2 **a.**

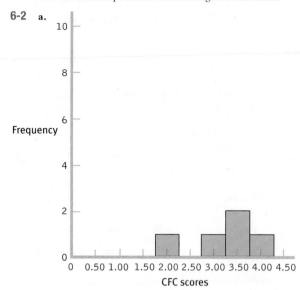

   b.

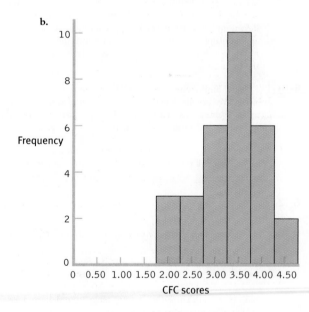

6-3 The shape of the distribution becomes more normal as the size of the sample increases (although the larger sample appears to be somewhat negatively skewed).

6-4 In standardization, we convert individual scores to standardized scores for which we know the percentiles.

6-5 The numeric value tells us how many standard deviations a score is from the mean of the distribution. The sign tells us whether the score is above or below the mean.

6-6 **a.** $z = \frac{(X - \mu)}{\sigma} = \frac{11.5 - 14}{2.5} = -1.0$

b. $z = \dfrac{(X - \mu)}{\sigma} = \dfrac{18 - 14}{2.5} = 1.6$

6-7 **a.** $X = z(\sigma) + \mu = 2(2.5) + 14 = 19$

b. $X = z(\sigma) + \mu = -1.4(2.5) + 14 = 10.5$

6-8 **a.** $z = \dfrac{(X - \mu)}{\sigma} = \dfrac{2.3 - 3.51}{0.61} = -1.98$; approximately 2% of students have a CFC score of 2.3 or less.

b. $z = \dfrac{(X - \mu)}{\sigma} = \dfrac{4.7 - 3.5}{0.61} = 1.95$; this score is at approximately the 98th percentile.

c. This student has a z score of 1.

d. $X = z(\sigma) + \mu = 1(0.61) + 3.51 = 4.12$; this answer makes sense because 4.12 is above the mean of 3.51 as a z score of 1 would indicate.

6-9 **a.** Nicole, because her score is above the mean for her measure, whereas Samantha's personal score is below the mean.

b. Samantha's z score is $z = \dfrac{(X - \mu)}{\sigma} = \dfrac{84 - 93}{4.5} = -2.0$

Nicole's z score is $z = \dfrac{(X - \mu)}{\sigma} = \dfrac{332 - 312}{20} = 1.0$

Nicole is in better health, being 1 standard deviation above the mean, whereas Samantha is 2 standard deviations below the mean.

c. We can conclude that approximately 98% of the population is in better health than Samantha, who is 2 standard deviations below the mean. We can conclude that approximately 16% of the population is in better health than Nicole, who is 1 standard deviation above the mean.

6-10 The central limit theorem asserts that a distribution of sample means approaches the shape of the normal curve as sample size increases. It also asserts that the spread of the distribution of sample means gets smaller as the sample size gets larger.

6-11 A distribution of means is composed of many means that are calculated from all possible samples of a particular size from the same population.

6-12 $\sigma_M = \dfrac{\sigma}{\sqrt{N}} = \dfrac{11}{\sqrt{35}} = 1.86$

6-13 **a.** The scores range from 2.0 to 4.5; which gives us a range of 2.5.

b. The means are 3.4 for the first row, 3.4 for the second row, and 3.15 for the third row [e.g., for the first row, $M = (3.5 + 3.5 + 3.0 + 4.0 + 2.0 + 4.0 + 2.0 + 4.0 + 3.5 + 4.5)/10 = 3.4$]. These three means range from 3.15 to 3.40; which gives us a range of 0.25.

c. The range is smaller for the means of samples of 10 scores than for the individual scores because the more extreme scores will be balanced by lower scores when samples of 10 are taken. Individual scores are not attenuated in that way.

d. The mean of the distribution of means will be the same as the mean of the individual scores: $\mu_M = \mu = 3.32$. The standard error will be smaller than the standard deviation; we must divide by the square root of the sample size of 10: $\sigma_M = \dfrac{\sigma}{\sqrt{N}} = \dfrac{0.69}{\sqrt{10}} = 0.22$

CHAPTER 7

7-1 The mean, μ, and standard deviation, σ, of the population must be known.

7-2 Raw scores are used to compute z scores, and z scores are used to determine what percentage of scores fall below and above that particular position on the distribution. A z score can also be used to compute a raw score.

7-3 Because the curve is symmetric, the same percentage of scores (41.47%) lies between the mean and a z score of -1.37 as between the mean and a z score of 1.37.

7-4 Fifty percent of scores fall below the mean, and 12.93% fall between the mean and a z score of 0.33.

$$50\% + 12.93\% = 62.93\%$$

7-5 **a.** $\mu_M = \mu = 156.8$

$\sigma_M = \dfrac{\sigma}{\sqrt{N}} = \dfrac{14.6}{\sqrt{36}} = 2.433$

$z = \dfrac{(M - \mu_M)}{\sigma_M} = \dfrac{(164.6 - 156.8)}{2.433} = 3.21$

50% below the mean; 49.9% above the mean; $50 + 49.9 = 99.9$th percentile

b. $100 - 99.9 = 0.1\%$ of samples of this size scored higher than the students at Baylor.

c. At the 99.9th percentile, these 36 students from Baylor are truly outstanding. If these students are representative of their majors, clearly, these results reflect positively on Baylor's Psychology and Neuroscience Department.

7-6 For most parametric hypothesis tests, we assume that (1) the dependent variable is assessed on a scale measure—that is, equal changes are reflected by equal distances on the measure; (2) the participants are randomly selected, meaning everyone has the same chance of being selected; and (3) the distribution of the population of interest is approximately normal.

7-7 If a test statistic is more extreme than the critical value, then the null hypothesis is rejected. If a test statistic is less extreme than the critical value, then we fail to reject the null hypothesis.

7-8 If the null hypothesis is true, he will reject it 8% of the time.

7-9 **a.** 0.15

b. 0.03

c. 0.055

7-10 **a.** (1) The dependent variable—diagnosis (correct vs. incorrect)—is nominal, not scale, so this assumption is not met. Based only on this, we should not proceed with a hypothesis test based on a z distribution. (2) The samples include only outpatients seen over two specific months and only those at one community mental health center. The sample is not randomly selected, so we must be cautious about generalizing from it. (3) The populations are not normally distributed because the dependent variable is nominal.

b. (1) The dependent variable, health score, is likely scale. (2) The paticipants were randomly selected; all wild cats in zoos in North America had an equal chance of being selected for this study. (3) The data are not normally distributed; we are told that a few animals had very high scores, so the data are likely positively skewed. Moreover, there are fewer than 30 participants in this study. It probably is not a good idea to proceed with a hypothesis test based on a z distribution.

7-11 A directional test indicates that either a mean increase or a mean decrease in the dependent variable is hypothesized, but not both. A nondirectional test does not indicate a direction of mean difference for the research hypothesis, just that there is a mean difference.

7-12 $\mu_M = \mu = 1090$

$$\sigma_M = \frac{\sigma}{\sqrt{N}} = \frac{87}{\sqrt{53}} = 11.95$$

7-13 $z = \frac{(M - \mu_M)}{\sigma_M} = \frac{(1094 - 1090)}{11.95} = 0.33$

7-14 *Step 1:* Population 1 is coffee drinkers who spend the day in coffee shops/cybercafés. Population 2 is all coffee drinkers in the United States. The comparison distribution will be a distribution of means. The hypothesis test will be a z test because we have only one sample and we know the population mean and the standard deviation. This study meets two of the three assumptions and may meet the third. The dependent variable, the number of cups coffee drinkers drank, is scale. In addition, there are more than 30 participants in the sample, indicating that the comparison distribution is normal. The data were not randomly selected, however, so we must be cautious when generalizing.

Step 2: The null hypothesis is that people who spend the day working in the coffee shop/cybercafé drink the same amount of coffee, on average, as those in the general U.S. population ($H_0: \mu_1 = \mu_2$).

The research hypothesis is that people who spend the day in coffee shops/cybercafés drink a different amount of coffee, on average, than those in the general U.S. population ($H_1: \mu_1 \neq \mu_2$).

Step 3:

$$\mu_M = \mu = 3.10$$

$$\sigma_M = \frac{\sigma}{\sqrt{N}} = \frac{0.9}{\sqrt{34}} = 0.15$$

Step 4: Our cutoff z statistics are -1.96 and 1.96.

Step 5:

$$z = \frac{(M - \mu_M)}{\sigma_M} = \frac{(3.17 - 3.10)}{0.15} = 0.47$$

Step 6: Because our z statistic does not exceed our cutoffs, we fail to reject the null hypothesis. We did not find any evidence that our sample was different from what was normally expected according to the null hypothesis.

CHAPTER 8

8-1 Interval estimates provide a range of scores in which we have some confidence the population statistic will fall, whereas point estimates use just a single value to describe the population.

8-2 The interval estimate is 17% to 25% (21% $-$ 4% = 17% and 21% + 4% = 25%), whereas the point estimate is 21%.

8-3 a. First, we draw a normal curve with the sample mean, 3.7, in the center. Then we put the bounds of the 95% confidence interval on either end, writing the appropriate percentages

under the segments of the curve: 2.5% beyond the cutoffs on either end and 47.5% between the mean and each cutoff. Now we look up the z statistics for these cutoffs; the z statistic associated with 47.5%, the percentage between the mean and the z statistic, is 1.96. Thus, the cutoffs are -1.96 and 1.96. Next, we calculate standard error so that we can convert these z statistics to raw means:

$$\sigma_M = \frac{\sigma}{\sqrt{N}} = \frac{0.61}{\sqrt{45}} = 0.091$$

$M_{lower} = -z(\sigma_M) + M_{sample} = -1.96(0.091) + 3.7 = 3.52$

$M_{upper} = z(\sigma_M) + M_{sample} = 1.96(0.091) + 3.7 = 3.88$

Finally, we check to be sure our answer makes sense by demonstrating that each end of the confidence interval is the same distance from the mean: $3.52 - 3.7 = -0.18$ and $3.88 - 3.7 = 0.18$. The confidence interval is [3.52, 3.88].

b. If we were to conduct this study over and over, determining the limits of a 95% confidence interval for each new sample, we would expect the population mean to fall in that interval 95% of the time. Thus, it provides a range of plausible values for the population mean. Because the null-hypothesized population mean of 3.51 is not a plausible value, we can conclude that those who attended the discussion group have higher CFC scores than those who did not. This conclusion matches that of the hypothesis test, in which we rejected the null hypothesis.

c. The confidence interval is superior to the hypothesis test because not only does it lead to the same conclusion but it also gives us an interval estimate, rather than a point estimate, of the population mean.

8-4 Statistical significance means that the observation met our standard for special events, typically something that occurs less than 5% of the time. Practical importance means that the outcome really matters.

8-5 Effect size is a standardized value that indicates the size of a difference with respect to a measure of spread but is not affected by sample size.

8-6 p_{rep} is the probability of replicating a specific effect given a particular population and sample size.

8-7 Cohen's $d = \frac{(M - \mu)}{\sigma} = \frac{(105 - 100)}{15} = 0.33$

8-8 Using the formula =NORMSDIST(NORMSINV (1-.22)/(SQRT(2))) in Microsoft Excel, p_{rep} is 0.71.

8-9 a. We would calculate Cohen's d, the effect size appropriate for data analyzed with a z test. We use standard deviation in the denominator, rather than standard error, because effect sizes are for distributions of scores rather than distributions of means.

Cohen's $d = \frac{(M - \mu)}{\sigma} = \frac{(3.7 - 3.51)}{0.61} = -0.31$

b. Cohen's conventions indicate that 0.2 is a small effect and 0.5 is a medium effect. This effect size, therefore, would be considered a small-to-medium effect.

c. If the career discussion group is easily implemented in terms of time and money, the small-to-medium effect might be worth the effort. For university students, a higher level of Consideration of Future Consequences might translate into a higher level of readiness for life after graduation, a premise that we could study.

8-10 Three ways to increase power are to increase alpha, to conduct a one-tailed test rather than a two-tailed test, and to increase *N*. All three of these techniques serve to increase the chance of rejecting the null hypothesis.

8-11 *Step 1:* We know the following about population 1: $\mu = 3.51$, $\sigma = 0.61$. We assume the following about population 2 based on the information from our sample: $N = 45$, $M = 3.7$. We need to calculate standard error based on the standard deviation for population 1 and the size of our sample:

$$\sigma_M = \frac{\sigma}{\sqrt{N}} = \frac{0.61}{\sqrt{45}} = 0.09$$

Step 2: Because the sample mean is higher than the population mean, we will conduct this one-tailed test by examining only the high end of the distribution. We need to find the cutoff that marks where 5% of the data fall in the tail. We know that the *z* cutoff for a one-tailed test is 1.64. Using that *z* statistic, we can calculate a raw score.

$$M = z(\sigma_M) + \mu_M = 1.64(0.09) + 3.51 = 3.658$$

This mean of 3.658 marks the point beyond which 5% of all means based on samples of 45 observations will fall.

Step 3: For the second distribution, centered around 3.7, we need to calculate how often means of 3.658 (our cutoff) and greater occur. We do this by calculating the *z* statistic for the raw mean of 3.658 with respect to the sample mean of 3.7.

$$z = \frac{3.658 - 3.7}{0.09} = -0.47$$

We now look up this *z* statistic on the table and find that 31.92% falls toward the tail and 18.08% falls between this *z* statistic and the mean. We calculate power as the proportion of observations between this *z* statistic and the tail of interest, which is at the high end. So, we would add 18.08% and 50% to get our statistical power of 68.08%.

8-12 **a.** Our statistical power calculation means that, if the second population really does exist, we have a 68.08% chance of observing a sample mean, based on 45 observations, that will allow us to reject the null hypothesis. We fall somewhat short of the desired 80% statistical power.

b. We can increase statistical power by increasing the sample size, extending or enhancing our career discussion group such that we create a bigger effect, or by changing alpha.

CHAPTER 9

9-1 The *t* statistic indicates the distance of a sample mean from a population mean in terms of the estimated standard error.

9-2 A single-sample *t* test is a hypothesis test in which we compare data from one sample to a population for which we know the mean but not the standard deviation.

A paired-samples *t* test is a hypothesis test used to compare two means for a within-groups design in which every participant is in both samples.

The independent-samples *t* test is a hypothesis test used to compare two means for a between-groups design in which each participant is assigned to only one condition.

9-3 First we need to calculate the mean:

$$M = \frac{\Sigma X}{N} = (6 + 3 + 7 + 6 + 4 + 5) / 6 = 31/6 = 5.167$$

We then calculate the deviation of each score from the mean and the square of that deviation.

X	X − M	(X − M)²
6	0.833	0.694
3	−2.167	4.696
7	1.833	3.360
6	0.833	0.694
4	−1.167	1.362
5	−0.167	0.028

The standard deviation is:

$$SD = \sqrt{\frac{\Sigma(X-M)^2}{N}} = \sqrt{\frac{10.834}{6}} = \sqrt{1.806} = 1.344$$

When estimating the population variability, we calculate *s*:

$$s = \sqrt{\frac{\Sigma(X-M)^2}{N-1}} = \sqrt{\frac{10.834}{6-1}} = \sqrt{2.167} = 1.472$$

9-4 $s_M = \dfrac{s}{\sqrt{N}} = \dfrac{1.472}{\sqrt{6}} = 0.601$

9-5 **a.** We will use a distribution of means, specifically a *t* distribution. It is a distribution of means because we have a sample consisting of more than one individual. It is a *t* distribution because we are comparing one sample to a population, but we know only the population mean, not its standard deviation.

b. The appropriate mean: $\mu_M = \mu = 25$

The calculations for the appropriate standard deviation (in this case, standard error, s_M):

$$M = \frac{\Sigma X}{N} = \frac{(20 + 19 + 27 + 24 + 18)}{5} = 21.6$$

X	X − M	(X − M)²
20	−1.6	2.56
19	−2.6	6.76
27	5.4	29.16
24	2.4	5.76
18	−3.6	12.96

Numerator: $\Sigma(X - M)^2 = (2.56 + 6.76 + 29.16 + 5.76 + 12.96) = 57.2$

$$s = \sqrt{\frac{\Sigma(X-M)^2}{(N-1)}} = \sqrt{\frac{57.2}{5-1}}$$
$$= \sqrt{14.3} = 3.782$$
$$s_M = \frac{s}{\sqrt{N}} = \frac{3.782}{\sqrt{5}} = 1.691$$

c. $t = \dfrac{(M - \mu_M)}{s_M} = \dfrac{(21.6 - 25)}{1.691} = -2.01$

9-6 *Degrees of freedom* is the number of scores that are free to vary, or take on any value, when estimating a population parameter from a sample.

9-7 A single-sample *t* test has more uses than a *z* test because we only need to know the population mean (and not the population standard deviation).

9-8 **a.** $df = N - 1 = 35 - 1 = 34$

b. $df = N - 1 = 14 - 1 = 13$

9-9 **a.** ± 2.201

b. either -2.584 or $+2.584$, depending on the tail of interest

9-10 *Step 1:* Population 1 is our sample of six students. Population 2 is all university students.

The distribution will be a distribution of means, and we will use a single-sample t test. We meet the assumption that the dependent variable is scale. We do not know if our sample was randomly selected, and we do not know if the population variable is normally distributed. Some caution should be exercised when drawing conclusions from these data.

Step 2: The null hypothesis is $H_0: \mu_1 = \mu_2$; that is, students we're working with miss the same number of classes, on average, as the population.

The research hypothesis is $H_1: \mu_1 \neq \mu_2$; that is, students we're working with miss a different number of classes, on average, from the population.

Step 3: $\mu_M = \mu = 3.7$

$M = \dfrac{\Sigma X}{N} = (6 + 3 + 7 + 6 + 4 + 5) / 6 = 31/6 = 5.167$

$s = \sqrt{\dfrac{\Sigma(X - M)^2}{N - 1}} = \sqrt{\dfrac{10.834}{6 - 1}} = \sqrt{2.167} = 1.472$

$s_M = \dfrac{s}{\sqrt{N}} = \dfrac{1.472}{\sqrt{6}} = 0.601$

Step 4: $df = N - 1 = 6 - 1 = 5$

For a two-tailed test with a p level of 0.05 and 5 degrees of freedom, the cutoffs are ± 2.571.

Step 5: $t = \dfrac{(M - \mu_M)}{s_M} = \dfrac{(5.167 - 3.7)}{0.601} = 2.441$

Step 6: Because our calculated t value falls short of the critical values, we fail to reject the null hypothesis.

9-11 For a paired-samples t test, we calculate a difference score for every individual. We then compare the average difference observed to the average difference we would expect based on the null hypothesis. If no change is expected, then all difference scores should average to 0.

9-12 An individual difference score is a calculation of change for each participant. For example, we might subtract weight before the holiday break from weight after the break to evaluate how many pounds an individual lost or gained.

9-13 We want to subtract the before-lunch energy level from the after-lunch energy level to get values that reflect loss of energy as a negative value and an increase of energy with food as a positive value. The mean of these differences is -1.4.

BEFORE LUNCH	AFTER LUNCH	AFTER − BEFORE
6	3	$3 - 6 = -3$
5	2	$2 - 5 = -3$
4	6	$6 - 4 = +2$
5	4	$4 - 5 = -1$
7	5	$5 - 7 = -2$

9-14 **a.** *Step 1:* Population 1 is students for whom we're measuring energy levels before lunch. Population 2 is students for whom we're measuring energy levels after lunch.

The comparison distribution is a distribution of mean difference scores. We use the paired-samples t test because each participant contributes a score to each of the two samples we are comparing.

We meet the assumption that the dependent variable is a scale measurement. However, we do not know if our participants were randomly selected or if the population is normally distributed, and our sample is less than 30.

Step 2: The null hypothesis is that there is no difference in mean energy levels before and after lunch—$H_0: \mu_1 = \mu_2$.

Our research hypothesis is that there is a mean difference in energy levels— $H_1: \mu_1 \neq \mu_2$.

Step 3:

DIFFERENCE SCORES	DIFFERENCE − MEAN DIFFERENCE	SQUARED DEVIATION
-3	-1.6	2.56
-3	-1.6	2.56
$+2$	3.4	11.56
-1	0.4	0.16
-2	-0.6	0.36

$M_{difference} = -1.4$

$s = \sqrt{\dfrac{\Sigma(X - M)^2}{N - 1}} = \sqrt{\dfrac{17.2}{5 - 1}} = \sqrt{4.3} = 2.074$

$s_M = \dfrac{s}{\sqrt{N}} = \dfrac{2.074}{\sqrt{5}} = 0.928$

$\mu_M = 0, s_M = 0.928$

Step 4: Our degrees of freedom are $5 - 1 = 4$, and the cutoffs, based on a two-tailed test and a p level of 0.05, are ± 2.776.

Step 5: $t = \dfrac{(-1.4 - 0)}{0.928} = -1.51$

Step 6: Because our test statistic, -1.51, failed to exceed our critical value of -2.776, we fail to reject the null hypothesis.

b. $M_{lower} = -t(s_M) + M_{sample} = -2.776(0.928) + (-1.4) = -3.98$

$M_{upper} = t(s_M) + M_{sample} = 2.776(0.928) + (-1.4) = 1.18$

Notice that the confidence interval spans 0, our null-hypothesized difference between energy levels before and after lunch. Because the null value is within the confidence interval, we would fail to reject the null hypothesis.

c. $d = \dfrac{(M - \mu)}{s} = \dfrac{(-1.4 - 0)}{2.074} = -0.68$

This is a medium-to-large effect size according to Cohen's guidelines.

CHAPTER 10

10-1 When the data we are comparing were collected using the same participants in both conditions, a paired-samples t test is used; each participant contributes two values to the analysis. When we are comparing two independent groups, and no participant is in more than one condition, we use an independent-samples t test.

10-2 Pooled variance is a weighted combination of the variability in both groups in an independent-samples t test.

10-3 **a.** Group 1 is treated as our X variable; its mean is 3.0.

X	X − M	(X − M)²
3	0	0
2	−1	1
4	1	1
6	3	9
1	−2	4
2	−1	1

$$s_X^2 = \frac{\Sigma(X - M)^2}{N - 1} = \frac{(0 + 1 + 1 + 9 + 4 + 1)}{6 - 1} = 3.2$$

Group 2 is treated as our Y variable; its mean is 4.6.

Y	Y − M	(Y − M)²
5	0.4	0.16
4	−0.6	0.36
6	1.4	1.96
2	−2.6	6.76
6	1.4	1.96

$$s_Y^2 = \frac{\Sigma(Y - M)^2}{N - 1} = \frac{(0.16 + 0.36 + 1.96 + 6.76 + 1.96)}{5 - 1} = 2.8$$

b. $df_X = N - 1 = 6 - 1 = 5$

$df_Y = N - 1 = 5 - 1 = 4$

$df_{total} = df_X + df_Y = 5 + 4 = 9$

$s_{pooled}^2 = \left(\frac{df_X}{df_{total}}\right)s_X^2 + \left(\frac{df_Y}{df_{total}}\right)s_Y^2 = \left(\frac{5}{9}\right)3.2 + \left(\frac{4}{9}\right)2.8$

$= 1.778 + 1.244 = 3.022$

c. The variance version of standard error is calculated for each sample as:

$$s_{M_X}^2 = \frac{s_{pooled}^2}{N_X} = \frac{3.022}{6} = 0.504$$

$$s_{M_Y}^2 = \frac{s_{pooled}^2}{N_Y} = \frac{3.022}{5} = 0.604$$

d. The variance of the distribution of differences between means is:

$$s_{difference}^2 = s_{M_X}^2 + s_{M_Y}^2 = 0.504 + 0.604 = 1.108$$

This can be converted to standard deviation units by taking the square root:

$$s_{difference} = \sqrt{s_{difference}^2} = \sqrt{1.108} = 1.053$$

e. $t = \dfrac{(M_X - M_Y) - (\mu_X - \mu_Y)}{s_{difference}} = \dfrac{(3 - 4.6) - (0)}{1.053} = -1.519$

10-4 **a.** The null hypothesis asserts that there are no average between-group differences; employees with low trust in their leader show the same mean level of agreement with decisions as those with high trust in their leader. Symbolically, this would be written $H_0: \mu_1 = \mu_2$.

The research hypothesis asserts that mean level of agreement is different between the two groups—H_1: $\mu_1 \neq \mu_2$.

b. Our critical values, based on a two-tailed test, a p level of 0.05, and df_{total} of 9, are −2.262 and 2.262.

The t value we calculated, −1.519, does not exceed the cutoff of −2.262, so we fail to reject the null hypothesis.

c. Based on these results, we did not find evidence that mean level of agreement with a decision is different across the two levels of trust, $t(9) = -1.519, p > 0.05$.

d. Despite having similar means for the two groups, we failed to reject the null hypothesis, whereas the original researchers rejected the null hypothesis. Our failure to reject the null hypothesis is likely due to the low statistical power from the small samples we used.

10-5 We calculate confidence intervals to determine a range of plausible values for the population parameter based on our data.

10-6 Effect size tells us how large or small the difference we observed is, regardless of sample size. Even when a result is statistically significant, it might not be important. Effect size helps us evaluate practical significance.

10-7 **a.** The upper and lower bounds of the confidence interval are calculated as:

$$(M_X - M_Y)_{lower} = -t(s_{difference}) + (M_X - M_Y)_{sample}$$
$$(M_X - M_Y)_{lower} = -2.262(1.053) + (-1.6) = -3.98$$
$$(M_X - M_Y)_{upper} = t(s_{difference}) + (M_X - M_Y)_{sample}$$
$$(M_X - M_Y)_{upper} = 2.262(1.053) + (-1.6) = 0.78$$

The confidence interval is [−3.98, 0.78].

b. To calculate Cohen's d, we need to calculate the pooled standard deviation for our data:

$$s_{pooled} = \sqrt{s_{pooled}^2} = \sqrt{3.022} = 1.738$$

$$\text{Cohen's } d = \frac{(M_X - M_Y) - (\mu_X - \mu_Y)}{s_{pooled}} = \frac{(3 - 4.6) - (0)}{1.738}$$

$$= -0.92$$

10-8 The confidence interval tells us a range of differences between means in which we could expect the population mean difference to fall 95% of the time, based on samples of this size. Whereas the hypothesis test evaluates the point estimate of the difference between means—(3 − 4.6), or −1.6, in this case—the confidence interval gives us a range, or interval estimate, of [−3.98, 0.78].

10-9 The effect size we calculated, Cohen's d of −0.92, is a large effect according to Cohen's guidelines. Beyond the hypothesis test and confidence interval, which both lead us to fail to reject the null hypothesis, the size of the effect indicates that we might be on to a real effect here. We might want to increase statistical power by collecting more data in an effort to better test this relation.

CHAPTER 11

11-1 The F statistic is a ratio of between-groups variance and within-groups variance.

11-2 The two types of research design are within-groups design and between-groups design.

11-3 **a.** $F = \dfrac{\text{between-groups variance}}{\text{within-groups variance}} = \dfrac{8.6}{3.7} = 2.324$

b. $F = \dfrac{102.4}{123.77} = 0.827$

c. $F = \dfrac{45.2}{32.1} = 1.408$

11-4 **a.** We would use an F distribution because there are more than two groups.

b. We would determine the variance among the three sample means—the means for those in the control group, for those in the two-hour communication ban, and for those in the four-hour communication ban.

c. We would determine the variance within each of the three samples, and we would take a weighted average of the three variances.

11-5 If the F statistic is beyond the cutoff, then we can reject the null hypothesis—meaning that there is a significant mean difference (or differences) somewhere in our data, but we do not know where the difference lies.

11-6 If we are able to reject the null hypothesis when conducting an ANOVA, then we must also conduct a post-hoc test, such as a Tukey HSD test, to determine which pairs of means are significantly different from one another.

11-7 **a.** $df_{between} = N_{groups} - 1 = 3 - 1 = 2$

b. $df_{within} = df_1 + df_2 + \ldots + df_{last} = (4 - 1) + (4 - 1) + (3 - 1) = 3 + 3 + 2 = 8$

c. $df_{total} = df_{between} + df_{within} = 2 + 8 = 10$

11-8 $GM = \dfrac{\Sigma(X)}{N_{total}}$

$= \dfrac{(37 + 30 + 22 + 29 + 49 + 52 + 41 + 39 + 36 + 49 + 42)}{11}$

$= 38.73$

11-9 **a.** Total sum of squares is calculated here as $SS_{total} = \Sigma(X - GM)^2$:

SAMPLE	X	(X − GM)	(X − GM)²
Group 1	37	−1.73	2.99
M₁ = 29.5	30	−8.73	76.21
	22	−16.73	279.89
	29	−9.73	94.67
Group 2	49	10.27	105.47
M₂ = 45.25	52	13.27	176.09
	41	2.27	5.15
	39	0.27	0.07
Group 3	36	−2.73	7.45
M₃ = 42.33	49	10.27	105.47
	42	3.27	10.69
GM = 38.73			SS_total = **864.18**

b. Within-groups sum of squares is calculated here as $SS_{within} = \Sigma(X - M)^2$:

SAMPLE	X	(X − M)	(X − M)²
Group 1	37	7.5	56.25
M₁ = 29.5	30	0.5	0.25
	22	−7.5	56.25
	29	−0.5	0.25
Group 2	49	3.75	14.06
M₂ = 45.25	52	6.75	45.56
	41	−4.25	18.06
	39	−6.25	39.06
Group 3	36	−6.33	40.07
M₃ = 42.33	49	6.67	44.49
	42	−0.33	0.11
GM = 38.73			SS_within = **314.42**

c. Between-groups sum of squares is calculated here as $SS_{between} = \Sigma(M - GM)^2$:

SAMPLE	X	(M − GM)	(M − GM)²
Group 1	37	−9.23	85.19
M₁ = 29.5	30	−9.23	85.19
	22	−9.23	85.19
	29	−9.23	85.19
Group 2	49	6.52	42.51
M₂ = 45.25	52	6.52	42.51
	41	6.52	42.51
	39	6.52	42.51
Group 3	36	3.6	12.96
M₃ = 42.33	49	3.6	12.96
	42	3.6	12.96
GM = 38.73		SS_between = **549.68**	

11-10 $MS_{between} = \dfrac{SS_{between}}{df_{between}} = \dfrac{549.68}{2} = 274.84$

$MS_{within} = \dfrac{SS_{within}}{df_{within}} = \dfrac{314.42}{8} = 39.30$

$F = \dfrac{MS_{between}}{MS_{within}} = \dfrac{274.84}{39.30} = 6.99$

SOURCE	SS	df	MS	F
Between	549.68	2	**274.84**	**6.99**
Within	314.42	8	**39.30**	
Total	864.1	10		

11-11 **a.** According to the null hypothesis, there would be no mean differences in efficacy between these three treatment conditions; they would all come from one underlying distribution. The research hypothesis states that there are mean differences in efficacy across some or all of these treatment conditions.

b. There are three assumptions: that the participants were selected randomly, that the underlying populations are normally distributed, and that the underlying populations have similar variances. Although we can't say much about the first two assumptions, we can assess the last one using our sample data.

SAMPLE	GROUP 1	GROUP 2	GROUP 3
Squared deviations	56.25	14.06	40.07
of scores from	0.25	45.56	44.49
sample means:	56.25	18.06	0.11
	0.25	39.06	
Sum of squares:	113	116.75	84.67
$N - 1$:	3	3	2
Variance:	**37.67**	**38.92**	**42.34**

Because these variances are all close together, with the biggest being no more than twice as large as the smallest, we can conclude that we met the third assumption of homoscedastic samples.

c. The critical value for F with a p value of .05, 2 between-groups degrees of freedom, and 8 within-groups degrees of freedom is 4.46. Our F statistic exceeds this cutoff, so we can reject the null hypothesis. There are mean differences between these three groups, but we do not know where.

d. Because we rejected the null hypothesis, we need to perform post-hoc tests to assess which groups have significant differences between them. We'll conduct a Tukey HSD test.

Because we have unequal sample sizes, we must calculate a weighted sample size.

$$N' = \frac{N_{groups}}{\Sigma\left(\frac{1}{N}\right)} = \frac{3}{\left(\frac{1}{4}+\frac{1}{4}+\frac{1}{3}\right)} = \frac{3}{0.25 + 0.25 + 0.33} = \frac{3}{0.83} = 3.61$$

$$s_M = \sqrt{\frac{MS_{within}}{N'}}, \text{ then equals } \sqrt{\frac{39.30}{3.61}} = 3.30$$

Now we can compare our three treatment groups. Psychodynamic therapy ($M = 29.50$) versus interpersonal therapy ($M = 45.25$):

$$HSD = \frac{29.50 - 45.25}{3.30} = -4.77$$

Psychodynamic therapy ($M = 29.5$) versus cognitive-behavioral therapy ($M = 42.33$):

$$HSD = \frac{29.50 - 42.33}{3.30} = -3.89$$

Interpersonal therapy ($M = 45.25$) versus cognitive-behavioral therapy ($M = 42.33$):

$$HSD = \frac{45.25 - 42.33}{3.30} = 0.88$$

We look up the critical value for this post-hoc test on the q table. We look in the row for 8 within-groups degrees of freedom, and then in the column for 3 treatment groups.

At a p level of 0.05, the value in the q table is 4.04, so the cutoffs are -4.04 and 4.04.

We have just one significant difference between psychodynamic therapy and interpersonal therapy: Tukey $HSD = -4.77$. Specifically, clients responded at statistically significantly higher rates to interpersonal therapy than to psychodynamic therapy, with an average improvement of 15.75 points on this scale.

e. Effect size is calculated as $R^2 = \frac{SS_{between}}{SS_{total}} = \frac{549.68}{864.18} = 0.64$.

According to Cohen's conventions for R^2, this is a very large effect.

11-12 For the one-way within-groups ANOVA, we calculate two types of variability that occur within groups: subjects variability and within-groups variability. Subjects variability assesses how much each person's mean differs from the others', assessed by comparing each person's mean score to the grand mean. We then compute within-groups variability as the remainder once between-groups and subjects variability are subtracted from the total sum of squares.

11-13 a. $df_{between} = N_{groups} - 1 = 3 - 1 = 2$

b. $df_{subjects} = n - 1 = 3 - 1 = 2$

c. $df_{within} = (df_{between})(df_{subjects}) = (2)(2) = 4$

d. $df_{total} = df_{between} + df_{subjects} + df_{within} = 2 + 2 + 4 = 8$; or we can calculate it as $df_{total} = N_{total} - 1 = 9 - 1 = 8$

11-14 a. $SS_{total} = \Sigma(X - GM)^2 = 24.886$

GROUP	RATING (X)	(X − GM)	(X − GM)²
1	7	0.111	0.012
1	9	2.111	4.456
1	8	1.111	1.234
2	5	−1.889	3.568
2	8	1.111	1.234
2	9	2.111	4.456
3	6	−0.889	0.790
3	4	−2.889	8.346
3	6	−0.889	0.790
	GM = 6.889		Σ(X − GM)² = 24.886

b. $SS_{between} = \Sigma(M - GM)^2 = 11.556$

GROUP	RATING (X)	GROUP MEAN	(M − GM)	(M − GM)²
1	7	8	1.111	1.234
1	9	8	1.111	1.234
1	8	8	1.111	1.234
2	5	7.333	0.444	0.197
2	8	7.333	0.444	0.197
2	9	7.333	0.444	0.197
3	6	5.333	−1.556	2.421
3	4	5.333	−1.556	2.421
3	6	5.333	−1.556	2.421
	GM = 6.889			Σ(M − GM)² = 11.556

c. $SS_{subject} = \Sigma(M_{participant} - GM)^2 = 4.221$

PARTICIPANT	GROUP	RATING (X)	PARTICIPANT MEAN	$(M_{PARTICIPANT} - GM)$	$(M_{PARTICIPANT} - GM)^2$
1	1	7	6	−0.889	0.790
2	1	9	7	0.111	0.012
3	1	8	7.667	0.778	0.605
1	2	5	6	−0.889	0.790
2	2	8	7	0.111	0.012
3	2	9	7.667	0.778	0.605
1	3	6	6	−0.889	0.790
2	3	4	7	0.111	0.012
3	3	6	7.667	0.778	0.605

$GM = 6.889$ $\Sigma(M_{participant} - GM)^2 = 4.221$

d. $SS_{within} = SS_{total} - SS_{between} - SS_{subjects} = 24.886 - 11.556 - 4.221 = 9.109$

11-15 $MS_{between} = \dfrac{SS_{between}}{df_{between}} = \dfrac{11.556}{2} = 5.778$

$MS_{subjects} = \dfrac{SS_{subjects}}{df_{subjects}} = \dfrac{4.221}{2} = 2.111$

$MS_{within} = \dfrac{SS_{within}}{df_{within}} = \dfrac{9.109}{4} = 2.277$

$F_{between} = \dfrac{MS_{between}}{MS_{within}} = \dfrac{5.778}{2.277} = 2.538$

$F_{subjects} = \dfrac{MS_{subjects}}{MS_{within}} = \dfrac{2.111}{2.277} = 0.927$

SOURCE	SS	df	MS	F
Between-groups	11.556	2	5.778	2.54
Subjects	4.221	2	2.111	0.93
Within-groups	9.109	4	2.277	
Total	24.886	8		

11-16 a. Null hypothesis: People rate the driving experience of these three cars the same, on average. Research hypothesis: People do not rate the driving experience of these three cars the same, on average.

b. Order effects are addressed by counterbalancing. We could create a list of random orders of the three cars to be driven. Then, as a new customer arrives, we would assign him or her the next random order on the list. With a large enough sample size (much larger than the three participants we used in this example), we could feel confident that this assumption would be met with this approach.

c. Our critical value for the *F* statistic for a *p* level of 0.05 and 2 and 4 degrees of freedom is 6.95. Our between-groups *F* statistic of 2.538 does not exceed this critical value. We cannot reject the null hypothesis, so we cannot conclude that there are differences among mean ratings of cars.

d. Because our *F* statistic does not exceed the critical value, we fail to reject our null hypothesis. As a result, Tukey *HSD* tests are not needed. However, we might want to calculate a measure of overall effect size in order to get a sense of whether to pursue additional research.

CHAPTER 12

12-1 A factorial ANOVA is a statistical analysis used with one scale dependent variable and at least two nominal independent variables (also called *factors*).

12-2 A statistical interaction occurs in a factorial design when the two independent variables have an effect in combination that we do not see when we examine each independent variable on its own.

12-3 a. There are two factors: diet programs and exercise programs.

b. There are three factors: diet programs, exercise programs, and metabolism type.

c. There is one factor: gift certificate value.

d. There are two factors: gift certificate value and store quality.

12-4 a. The participants are the stocks themselves.

b. One independent variable is the type of ticker-code name, with two levels: pronounceable and unpronounceable. The second independent variable is time lapsed since the stock was initially offered, with four levels: one day, one week, six months, and one year.

c. The dependent variable is the stocks' selling price.

d. This would be a two-way mixed-design ANOVA.

e. This would be a mixed-design 2 × 4 ANOVA.

f. This study would have eight cells: 2 × 4 = 8

12-5 A *quantitative interaction* is an interaction in which one independent variable exhibits a strengthening or weakening of its effect at one or more levels of the other independent variable, but the direction of the initial effect does not change. More specifically, the effect of one independent variable is modified in the presence of another independent variable. A *qualitative interaction* is a particular type of quantitative interaction of two (or more) independent variables in which one independent variable reverses its effect depending on the level of the other independent variable. In a qualitative interaction, the effect of one variable doesn't just become stronger or weaker; it actually reverses direction in the presence of another variable.

12-6 An interaction indicates that the effect of one independent variable depends on the level of the other independent variable(s). The main effect alone cannot be interpreted because the effect of that one variable depends on another.

12-7 a. There are four cells.

		IV 2	
		LEVEL A	LEVEL B
IV 1	Level A		
	Level B		

b.

		IV 2	
		LEVEL A	LEVEL B
IV 1	Level A	$M = (2 + 1 + 1 + 3)/4$ $= 1.75$	$M = (2 + 3 + 3 + 3)/4$ $= 2.75$
	Level B	$M = (5 + 4 + 3 + 4)/4$ $= 4$	$M = (3 + 2 + 2 + 3)/4$ $= 2.5$

c. Because the sample size is the same for each cell, we can compute marginal means as simply the average between cell means.

		IV 2		MARGINAL MEAN
		LEVEL A	LEVEL B	
IV 1	Level A	1.75	2.75	2.25
	Level B	4	2.5	3.25
	Marginal Mean	2.875	2.625	

d.

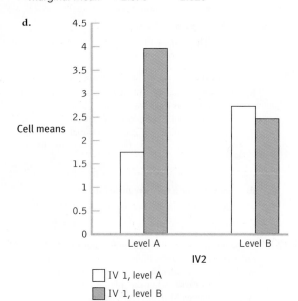

12-8 **a. i.** Independent variables: student (Caroline, Mira); class (philosophy, psychology)

ii. Dependent variable: performance in class

iii.

	CAROLINE	MIRA
Philosophy Class		
Psychology Class		

iv. This describes a qualitative interaction because the direction of the effect reverses. Caroline does worse in philosophy class than in psychology class, whereas Mira does better.

b. i. Independent variables: game location (home, away); team (own conference, other conference)

ii. Dependent variable: number of runs

iii.

	HOME	AWAY
Own Conference		
Other Conference		

iv. This describes a qualitative interaction because the direction of the effect reverses. The team does worse at home against teams in the other conference but does well against those teams while away; the team does better at home against teams in their own conference, but performs poorly against teams in their own conference when away.

c. i. Independent variables: amount of caffeine (caffeine, none); exercise (worked out, did not work out)

ii. Dependent variable: amount of sleep

iii.

	CAFFEINE	NO CAFFEINE
Working Out		
Not Working Out		

iv. This describes a quantitative interaction because the effect of working out is particularly strong in the presence of caffeine versus no caffeine (and the presence of caffeine is particularly strong in the presence of working out versus not). The direction of the effect of either independent variable, however, does not change depending on the level of the other independent variable.

12-9 Because we have the possibility of two main effects and an interaction, each step is broken down into three parts; we have three sets of hypotheses, three comparison distributions, three F critical values, three F statistics, and three conclusions.

12-10 Variability is associated with the two main effects, the interaction, and the within-groups component.

12-11 $df_{IV\ 1} = df_{rows} = N_{rows} - 1 = 2 - 1 = 1$

$df_{IV\ 2} = df_{columns} = N_{columns} - 1 = 2 - 1 = 1$

$df_{interaction} = (df_{rows})(df_{columns}) = (1)(1) = 1$

$df_{within} = df_{1A,2A} + df_{1A,2B} + df_{1B,2A} + df_{1B,2B}$
$= 3 + 3 + 3 + 3 = 12$

$df_{total} = N_{total} - 1 = 16 - 1 = 15$

We can also check that this calculation is correct by adding all of the other degrees of freedom together: $1 + 1 + 1 + 12 = 15$.

12-12 The critical value for the main effect of the first independent variable, based on a between-groups degrees of freedom of 1 and a within-groups degrees of freedom of 12, is 4.75. The critical value for the main effect of the second independent variable, based on 1 and 12 degrees of freedom, is 4.75. The critical value for the interaction, based on 1 and 12 degrees of freedom, is 4.75.

12-13 **a.** Population 1 is students who received an initial grade of C who received e-mail messages aimed at bolstering self-esteem. Population 2 is students who received an initial grade of C who received e-mail messages aimed at bolstering their sense of control over their grades. Population 3 is students who received an initial grade of C who received e-mail messages with just review questions. Population 4 is students who received an initial grade of D or F who received e-mail messages aimed at bolstering self-esteem. Population 5 is students who received an initial grade of D or F who received e-mail messages aimed at bolstering their sense of control over their grades. Population 6 is students who received an initial grade of D or F who received e-mail messages with just review questions.

b. Main effect of first independent variable—initial grade:

Null hypothesis: The mean final exam grade of students with an initial grade of C is the same as that of students with an initial grade of D or F. $H_0: \mu_C = \mu_{D/F}$.

Research hypothesis: The mean final exam grade of students with an initial grade of C is not the same as that of students with an initial grade of D or F. $H_0: \mu_C \neq \mu_{D/F}$.

Main effect of second independent variable—type of e-mail:

Null hypothesis: On average, the mean exam grades among those receiving different types of e-mails are the same—$H_0: \mu_{SE} = \mu_C = \mu_R$. Research hypothesis: On average, the mean exam grades among those receiving different types of e-mails are not the same.

Interaction: Initial grade $\times$ type of e-mail:

Null hypothesis: The effect of type of e-mail is not dependent on the levels of initial grade. Research hypothesis: The effect of type of e-mail depends on the levels of initial grade.

c. $df_{between/grade} = N_{groups} - 1 = 2 - 1 = 1$

$df_{between/e-mail} = N_{groups} - 1 = 3 - 1 = 2$

$df_{interaction} = (df_{between/grade})(df_{between/e-mail}) = (1)(2) = 2$

$df_{C,SE} = N - 1 = 14 - 1 = 13$

$df_{C,C} = N - 1 = 14 - 1 = 13$

$df_{C,R} = N - 1 = 14 - 1 = 13$

$df_{D/F,SE} = N - 1 = 14 - 1 = 13$

$df_{D/F,C} = N - 1 = 14 - 1 = 13$

$df_{D/F,R} = N - 1 = 14 - 1 = 13$

$df_{within} = df_{C,SE} + df_{C,C} + df_{C,R} + df_{D/F,SE} + df_{D/F,C} + df_{D/F,R}$
$= 13 + 13 + 13 + 13 + 13 + 13 = 78$

Main effect of initial grade: F distribution with 1 and 78 degrees of freedom

Main effect of type of e-mail: F distribution with 2 and 78 degrees of freedom

Main effect of interaction of initial grade and type of e-mail: F distribution with 2 and 78 degrees of freedom

d. Note that when the specific degrees of freedom is not in the F table, you should choose the more conservative—that is, larger—cutoff. In this case, go with the cutoffs for a within-groups degrees of freedom of 75 rather than 80. The three cutoffs are:

Main effect of initial grade: 3.97

Main effect of type of e-mail: 3.12

Interaction of initial grade and type of e-mail: 3.12

e. There is a significant main effect of initial grade because the F statistic, 20.84, is larger than the critical value of 3.97. The marginal means, seen in the accompanying table, tell us that students who earned a C on the initial exam have higher scores on the final exam, on average, than do students who earned a D or an F on the initial exam. There is no statistically significant main effect of type of e-mail, however. The F statistic of 1.69 is not larger than the critical value of 3.12. Had this main effect been significant, we would have conducted a post-hoc test to determine where the differences were. There also is not a significant interaction. The F statistic of 3.02 is not larger than the critical value of 3.12. (Had we used a cutoff based on a p level of 0.10, we

would have rejected the null hypothesis for the interaction. The cutoff for a p level of 0.10 is 2.77.) If we had rejected the null hypothesis for the interaction, we would have examined the cell means in tabular and graph form.

	SELF-ESTEEM	SENSE OF CONTROL	REVIEW	
C	67.31	69.83	71.12	69.42
D/F	47.83	60.98	62.13	56.98
	57.57	65.41	66.63	

CHAPTER 13

13-1 (1) The correlation coefficient can be either positive or negative. (2) The correlation coefficient always falls between −1.00 and 1.00. (3) It is the strength, also called the *magnitude,* of the coefficient, not its sign, that indicates how large it is.

13-2 When two variables are correlated, there can be multiple explanations for that association. The first variable can cause the second variable; the second variable can cause the first variable; or a third variable can cause both the first and second variables. In fact, there may be more than one "third" variable causing both the first and second variables.

13-3 **a.** According to Cohen, this is a large (strong) correlation. Note that the sign (negative in this case) is not related to the assessment of strength.

b. This is just above a medium correlation.

c. This is lower than the guideline for a small correlation, 0.10.

13-4 Students will draw a variety of different scatterplots. The important thing to note is the closeness of data points to an imaginary line drawn through the data.

a. A scatterplot for a correlation coefficient of −0.60 might look like this:

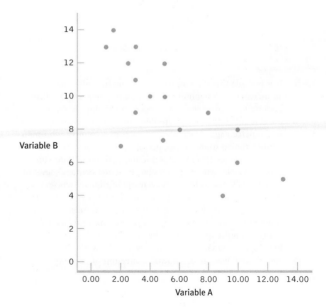

b. A scatterplot for a correlation coefficient of 0.35 might look like this:

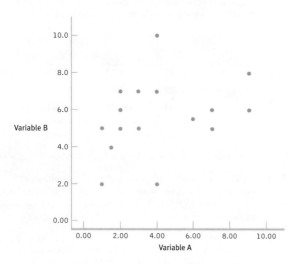

c. A scatterplot for a correlation coefficient of 0.04 might look like this:

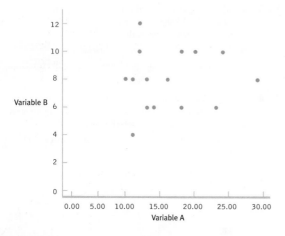

13-5 It is possible that training while listening to music (A) causes an increase in a country's average finishing time (B), perhaps because music decreases one's focus on running. It also is possible that high average finishing times (B) cause an increase in the percentage of marathon runners in a country who train while listening to music (A), perhaps because slow runners tend to get bored and need music to get through their runs. It also is possible that a third variable, such as a country's level of wealth (C), causes a higher percentage of runners who train while listening to music (because of the higher presence of technology in wealthy countries) (A) and also causes higher (slower) finishing times (perhaps because long-distance running is a less popular sport in wealthy countries with access to so many sport and entertainment options) (B). Without a true experiment, we cannot know the direction of causality.

13-6 The Pearson correlation coefficient is a statistic that quantifies a linear relation between two scale variables. Specifically, it describes the direction and strength of the relation between the variables.

13-7 The two issues are variability and sample size.

13-8

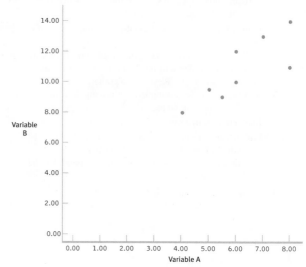

13-9 a.

VARIABLE A (X)	$(X - M_X)$	VARIABLE B (Y)	$(Y - M_Y)$	$(X - M_X)(Y - M_Y)$
8	1.813	14	3.188	5.777
7	0.813	13	2.188	1.777
6	−0.188	10	−0.813	0.152
5	−1.188	9.5	−1.313	1.559
4	−2.188	8	−2.813	6.152
5.5	−0.688	9	−1.813	1.246
6	−0.188	12	1.188	−0.223
8	1.813	11	0.188	0.340
$M_X =$ 6.1875		$M_Y =$ 10.8125		$\Sigma[(X - M_X)(Y - M_Y)] = 16.781$

b.

VARIABLE A (X)	$(X - M_X)$	$(X - M_X)^2$	VARIABLE B (Y)	$(Y - M_Y)$	$(Y - M_Y)^2$
8	1.813	3.285	14	3.188	10.160
7	0.813	0.660	13	2.188	4.785
6	−0.188	0.035	10	−0.813	0.660
5	−1.188	1.410	9.5	−1.313	1.723
4	−2.188	4.785	8	−2.813	7.910
5.5	−0.688	0.473	9	−1.813	3.285
6	−0.188	0.035	12	1.188	1.410
8	1.813	3.285	11	0.188	0.035
		$\Sigma(X - M_X)^2 = 13.969$			$\Sigma(Y - M_Y)^2 = 29.969$

$$\sqrt{(SS_X)(SS_Y)} = \sqrt{(13.969)(29.969)} = \sqrt{418.637} = 20.461$$

c. $r = \dfrac{\Sigma[(X - M_X)(Y - M_Y)]}{\sqrt{(SS_X)(SS_Y)}} = \dfrac{16.781}{20.461} = 0.82$

13-10 a. Population 1: Children like those we studied. Population 2: Children for whom there is no relation between observed and performed acts of aggression. The comparison distribution is made up of correlations based on samples of our size, 8 people, selected from the population.

We do not know if our data were randomly selected, the first assumption, so we must be cautious when generalizing our findings. We also do not know if the underlying population distributions for witnessed aggression and performed acts of aggression by children are normally distributed. Our sample size is too small to make any conclusions about this assumption, so we should proceed with caution. The third assumption, unique to correlations, is that the variability of one variable is equal across the levels of the other variable. Because we have such a small data set, it is difficult to evaluate this. However, we can see from the scatterplot that our data are somewhat consistently variable.

b. Null hypothesis: There is no correlation between the levels of witnessed and performed acts of aggression among children—H_0: $r = 0$. Research hypothesis: There is a correlation between the levels of witnessed and performed acts of aggression among children—H_1: $r \neq 0$.

c. The comparison distribution is a distribution of Pearson correlations, r, with the following degrees of freedom: $df_r = N - 2 = 8 - 2 = 6$.

d. The critical values for an r distribution with 6 degrees of freedom for a two-tailed test with a p level of 0.05 are −0.707 and 0.707.

e. Our test statistic, $r = 0.82$, is larger in magnitude than the critical value of 0.707. We can reject the null hypothesis and conclude that a strong positive correlation exists between the number of witnessed acts of aggression and the number of acts of aggression performed by children.

CHAPTER 14

14-1 Simple linear regression is a statistical tool that lets statisticians predict the score of a dependent variable from the score on an independent variable.

14-2 The regression line allows us to make predictions about one variable based on what we know about another variable. It gives us a visual representation of what we believe is the underlying relation between our variables, based on the data we have available to us.

14-3 a. $z_X = \dfrac{X - M_X}{SD_X} = \dfrac{67 - 64}{2} = 1.5$

b. $z_{\hat{Y}} = (r_{XY})(z_X) = (0.28)(1.5) = 0.42$

c. $\hat{Y} = z_{\hat{Y}}(SD_Y) + M_Y = (0.42)(15) + 155 = 161.3$ pounds

14-4 a. $\hat{Y} = 12 + 0.67(X) = 12 + 0.67(78) = 64.26$

b. $\hat{Y} = 12 + 0.67(-14) = 2.62$

c. $\hat{Y} = 12 + 0.67(52) = 46.84$

14-5 a. The y-intercept, 2.586, is the GPA we might expect if someone played no minutes. The slope of 0.016 is the increase in GPA that we would expect for each one-minute increase in playing time. Because our correlation is positive, it makes sense that our slope is also positive.

b. The standardized regression coefficient is equal to our correlation coefficient for simple linear regression, 0.344. We can also check that this is correct by computing β:

X	$(X - M_X)$	$(X - M_X)^2$	Y	$(Y - M_Y)$	$(Y - M_Y)^2$
29.70	13.159	173.159	3.20	0.343	0.118
32.14	15.599	243.329	2.88	0.023	0.001
32.72	16.179	261.760	2.78	−0.077	0.001
21.76	5.219	27.238	3.18	0.323	0.104
18.56	2.019	4.076	3.46	0.603	0.364
16.23	−0.311	0.097	2.12	−0.737	0.543
11.80	−4.741	22.477	2.36	−0.497	0.247
6.88	−9.661	93.335	2.89	0.033	0.001
6.38	−10.161	103.246	2.24	−0.617	0.381
15.83	−0.711	0.506	3.35	0.493	0.243
2.50	−14.041	197.150	3.00	0.143	0.020
4.17	−12.371	153.042	2.18	−0.677	0.458
16.36	−0.181	0.033	3.50	0.643	0.413

$\Sigma(X - M_X)^2 = 1279.448$ $\Sigma(Y - M_Y)^2 = 2.894$

$$\beta = (b)\dfrac{\sqrt{SS_X}}{\sqrt{SS_Y}} = (0.016)\dfrac{\sqrt{1279.448}}{\sqrt{2.894}} = 0.336$$

There is some difference due to rounding error, but in both cases, these numbers would be expressed as 0.34.

c. Strong correlations indicate strong linear relations between variables. Because of this, when we have a strong correlation, we have a more useful regression line, resulting in more accurate predictions.

d. According to the hypothesis test for the correlation, this r value, 0.34, fails to reach statistical significance. The critical values for r with 11 degrees of freedom at a p level of 0.05 are −0.553 and 0.553. In this chapter, we learned that the outcome of hypothesis testing is the same for simple linear regression as it is for correlation, so we know we also do not have a statistically significant regression.

14-6 The standard error of the estimate is a statistic that indicates the typical distance between a regression line and the actual data points. When we do not have enough information to compute a regression equation, we often use the mean as our "best guess." The error of prediction when the mean is used is typically greater than the standard error of the estimate.

14-7 Strong correlations mean highly accurate predictions with regression. This translates into a large proportionate reduction in error.

14-8 a.

X	Y	MEAN FOR Y	ERROR	SQUARED ERROR
5	6	5.333	0.667	0.445
6	5	5.333	−0.333	0.111
4	6	5.333	0.667	0.445
5	6	5.333	0.667	0.445
7	4	5.333	−1.333	1.777
8	5	5.333	−0.333	0.111

$SS_{total} = \Sigma(Y - M_Y)^2 = 3.334$

b.

X	Y	REGRESSION EQUATION	$\hat{Y}$	ERROR $(Y - \hat{Y})$	SQUARED ERROR
5	6	$\hat{Y} = 7.846 - 0.431\ (5) =$	5.691	0.309	0.095
6	5	$\hat{Y} = 7.846 - 0.431\ (6) =$	5.26	−0.26	0.068
4	6	$\hat{Y} = 7.846 - 0.431\ (4) =$	6.122	−0.122	0.015
5	6	$\hat{Y} = 7.846 - 0.431\ (5) =$	5.691	0.309	0.095
7	4	$\hat{Y} = 7.846 - 0.431\ (7) =$	4.829	−0.829	0.687
8	5	$\hat{Y} = 7.846 - 0.431\ (8) =$	4.398	0.602	0.362

$$SS_{error} = \Sigma(Y - \hat{Y})^2$$
$$= 1.322$$

c. We have reduced error from 3.334 to 1.322, which is a reduction of 2.012. Now we calculate this reduction as a proportion of the total error:

$$\frac{2.012}{3.334} = 0.603$$

This can also be written as:

$$r^2 = \frac{(SS_{total} - SS_{error})}{SS_{total}} = \frac{(3.334 - 1.322)}{3.334} = 0.603$$

We have reduced 0.603, or 60.3%, of error using the regression equation as an improvement over the use of the mean as our predictor.

d. $r^2 = (-0.77)(-0.77) = 0.593$, which closely matches our calculation of r^2 above, 0.603. These numbers are slightly different due to rounding error.

14-9 Tell Coach Parcells that prediction suffers from the same limitations as correlation. First, just because two variables are associated doesn't mean one causes the other. This is not a true experiment, and if we didn't randomly assign athletes to appear on a *Sports Illustrated* cover or not, then we cannot determine if a cover appearance causes sporting failure. Moreover, we have a limited range; by definition, those lauded on the cover are the best in sports. Would the association be different among those with a wider range of athletic ability? Finally, and most important, there is the very strong possibility of regression to the mean. Those chosen for a cover appearance are at the very top of their game. There is nowhere to go but down, so it is not surprising that those who merit a cover appearance would soon thereafter experience a decline. There's likely no need to avoid that cover, Coach.

14-10 Multiple regression is a statistical tool that predicts a dependent variable by using two or more independent variables as predictors. It is an improvement over simple linear regression, which only allows one independent variable to inform predictions.

14-11 $\hat{Y} = 5.251 + 0.06(X_1) + 1.105(X_2)$

14-12 a. $\hat{Y} = 5.251 + 0.06(40) + 1.105(14) = 23.121$
   b. $\hat{Y} = 5.251 + 0.06(101) + 1.105(39) = 54.406$
   c. $\hat{Y} = 5.251 + 0.06(76) + 1.105(20) = 31.911$

14-13 a. $\hat{Y} = 2.695 + 0.069(X_1) + 0.015(X_2) - 0.072(X_3)$
   b. $\hat{Y} = 2.695 + 0.069(6) + 0.015(20) - 0.072(4) = 3.121$
   c. The negative sign in the slope (−0.072) tells us that those with higher levels of admiration for Pamela Anderson tend to have lower GPAs, and those with lower levels of admiration for Pamela Anderson tend to have higher GPAs.

CHAPTER 15

15-1 A nonparametric test is a statistical analysis that is not based on a set of assumptions about the population, whereas parametric tests are based on assumptions about the population. Nonparametric tests are sometimes referred to as *distribution-free tests* because the data do not need to conform to any particular distribution, normal or otherwise.

15-2 We use nonparametric tests when we do not have a scale dependent variable. We also use them when our data violate the assumptions about the population that parametric tests make. The three most common situations that call for nonparametric tests are (1) having a nominal dependent variable, (2) having one or more ordinal variables, and (3) having a small sample size with possible skew.

15-3 a. The independent variable is city, a nominal variable. The dependent variable is whether a woman is pretty or not so pretty, a nominal variable.
   b. The independent variable is city, a nominal variable. The dependent variable is beauty, assessed on a scale of 1–10. This is a scale variable.
   c. The independent variable is intelligence, likely a scale variable. The dependent variable is beauty, assessed on a scale of 1–10. This is a scale variable.
   d. The independent variable is ranking on intelligence, an ordinal variable. The dependent variable is ranking on beauty, also an ordinal variable.

15-4 a. We'd choose a hypothesis test from category III. We'd use a nonparametric test because the dependent variable is nominal and would not meet the primary assumption of a normally distributed dependent variable, even with a large sample.
   b. We'd choose a test from category II because the independent variable is nominal and the dependent variable is scale. (In fact, we'd use a one-way between-groups ANOVA because there is only one independent variable and it has more than two levels.)
   c. We'd choose a hypothesis test from category I because we have a scale independent variable and a scale dependent variable. (If we were assessing the relation between these variables, we'd use the Pearson correlation coefficient. If we wondered whether intelligence predicted beauty, we'd use simple linear regression.)
   d. We'd choose a hypothesis from category III because both the independent and dependent variables are ordinal. We would not meet the assumption of having a normal distribution of the dependent variable, even if we had a large sample.

15-5 We use chi-square tests when all variables are nominal.

15-6 Observed frequencies indicate how often something happened in a given category with the data we collected. Expected frequencies indicate how often something happens in a given category based on what we know about the population or based on our null hypothesis.

15-7 a. $df_{\chi^2} = k - 1 = 2 - 1 = 1$

b. Observed:

CLEAR BLUE SKIES	UNCLEAR SKIES
59 days	19 days

Expected:

CLEAR BLUE SKIES	UNCLEAR SKIES
$(78)(0.80) = 62.4$	$(78)(0.20) = 15.6$ days

c.

CATEGORY	OBSERVED (O)	EXPECTED (E)	$O - E$	$(O - E)^2$	$\dfrac{(O - E)^2}{E}$
Clear blue skies	59	62.4	−3.4	11.56	0.185
Unclear skies	19	15.6	3.4	11.56	0.741

$$\chi^2 = \Sigma\left[\frac{(O - E)^2}{E}\right] = 0.185 + 0.741 = 0.926$$

15-8 **a.** The participants are the lineups. The independent variable is type of lineup (simultaneous, sequential), and the dependent variable is outcome of the lineup (suspect identification, other identification, no identification).

b. *Step 1:* Population 1 is police lineups like those we observed.

Population 2 is police lineups for which type of lineup and outcome are independent. The comparison distribution is a chi-square distribution. The hypothesis test is a chi-square test for independence because we have two nominal variables. This study meets three of the four assumptions. The two variables are nominal; every participant (lineup) is in only one cell; and there are more than five times as many participants as cells (8 participants and 6 cells).

Step 2: Null hypothesis: Lineup outcome is independent of type of lineup.

Research hypothesis: Lineup outcome depends on type of lineup.

Step 3: The comparison distribution is a chi-square distribution with 2 degrees of freedom:

$$df_{\chi^2} = (k_{row} - 1)(k_{column} - 1) = (2 - 1)(3 - 1) = (1)(2) = 2.$$

Step 4: Our cutoff chi-square statistic, based on a p level of 0.05 and 2 degrees of freedom, is 5.992. (*Note:* Include drawing of the chi-square distribution with the cutoff.)

Step 5:

	OBSERVED			
	SUSPECT ID	OTHER ID	NO ID	
Simultaneous	191	8	120	319
Sequential	102	20	107	229
	293	28	227	548

We can calculate the expected frequencies in one of two ways. First, we can think about it. Out of the total of 548 lineups, 293 led to identification of the suspect, an identification rate of $293/548 = 0.535$, or 53.5%. If identification were independent of type of lineup, we would expect the same rate for each type of lineup. For the 319 simultaneous lineups, we would expect: $(0.535)(319) = 170.665$. For the 299 sequential lineups, we would expect: $(0.535)(229) = 122.515$. Or we can use our formula. For these same two cells (the column labeled "suspect ID"), we calculate:

$$\frac{Total_{column}}{N}(Total_{row}) = \frac{293}{548}(319) = (0.535)(319) = 170.665$$

$$\frac{Total_{column}}{N}(Total_{row}) = \frac{293}{548}(229) = (0.535)(229) = 122.515$$

For the column labeled "other ID":

$$\frac{Total_{column}}{N}(Total_{row}) = \frac{28}{548}(319) = (0.051)(319) = 16.269$$

$$\frac{Total_{column}}{N}(Total_{row}) = \frac{28}{548}(229) = (0.051)(229) = 11.679$$

For the column labeled "no ID":

$$\frac{Total_{column}}{N}(Total_{row}) = \frac{227}{548}(319) = (0.414)(319) = 132.066$$

$$\frac{Total_{column}}{N}(Total_{row}) = \frac{227}{548}(229) = (0.414)(229) = 94.806$$

	EXPECTED			
	SUSPECT ID	OTHER ID	NO ID	
Simultaneous	170.665	16.269	132.066	319
Sequential	122.515	11.679	94.806	229
	293	28	227	548

CATEGORY	OBSERVED (O)	EXPECTED (E)	O − E	(O − E)²	$\frac{(O − E)^2}{E}$
Sim; suspect	191	170.665	20.335	413.512	2.423
Sim; other	8	16.269	−8.269	68.376	4.203
Sim; no	120	132.066	−12.066	145.588	1.102
Seq; suspect	102	122.515	−20.515	420.865	3.435
Seq; other	20	11.679	8.321	69.239	5.929
Seq; no	107	94.806	12.194	148.694	1.568

$$\chi^2 = \Sigma\left(\frac{(O − E)^2}{E}\right) = (2.423 + 4.203 + 1.102 + 3.435 + 5.929 + 1.568) = 18.660$$

Step 6: Reject the null hypothesis. It appears that the outcome of a lineup depends on the type of lineup. In general, simultaneous lineups tend to lead to a higher rate than expected of suspect identification, lower rates than expected of identification of other members of the lineup, and lower rates than expected of no identification at all. (*Note:* Add the test statistic to the drawing that included the cutoff).

c. Cramer's $V = \sqrt{\frac{\chi^2}{(N)(df_{row/column})}} = \sqrt{\frac{18.660}{(548)(1)}} = \sqrt{0.034} = 0.18.$ This is a small-to-medium effect.

d. $\chi^2(1, N = 548) = 18.66, p < 0.05$, Cramer's $V = 0.18.$

e. The findings of this study were opposite to what had been expected by the investigators; the report of results noted that, prior to this study, police departments believed that the sequential lineup led to more accurate identification of suspects. This situation occurs frequently in behavioral research, a reminder of the importance of conducting two-tailed hypothesis tests. (Of course, the fact that this study produced different results doesn't end the debate. Future researchers should explore why there are different findings in different contexts in an effort to target the best lineup procedures based on specific situations.)

15-9 When we have ordinal data.

15-10 The Spearman rank-order correlation coefficient is a nonparametric statistic that quantifies the association between two ordinal variables. The Mann–Whitney U test is a nonparametric hypothesis test used when there are two groups, a between-groups design, and an ordinal dependent variable.

15-11

OBSERVATION	VARIABLE 1 SCORE	RANK	VARIABLE 2 SCORE	RANK
1	1.3	3	54.39	5
2	1.8	4.5	50.11	3
3	1.2	2	53.39	4
4	1.06	1	44.89	1
5	1.8	4.5	48.5	2

15-12

OBSERVATION	VARIABLE 1 RANK	VARIABLE 2 RANK	DIFFERENCE	SQUARED DIFFERENCE
1	3	5	−2	4
2	4.5	3	1.5	2.25
3	2	4	−2	4
4	1	1	0	0
5	4.5	2	2.5	6.25

$$r_S = 1 - \frac{6(\Sigma D)^2}{N(N^2 − 1)} = 1 - \frac{6(16.5)}{5(25 − 1)} = 1 - \frac{99}{120} = 1 - 0.825 = 0.175$$

15-13 a. *Step 1:* We convert our data from scale to ordinal. The researchers did not indicate whether they used random selection to choose the countries in the sample, so we must be cautious when generalizing from these results. There are some ties, but we will assume that there are not so many as to render the results of the test invalid.

Step 2: Null hypothesis: Countries in which English is a primary language and countries in which English is not a primary language do not tend to differ in accomplishment-related national pride.

Research hypothesis: Countries in which English is a primary language and countries in which English is not a primary language tend to differ in accomplishment-related national pride.

Step 3: There are seven countries in the English-speaking group and seven countries in the non-English-speaking group.

Step 4: The cutoff, or critical value, for a Mann–Whitney U test with two groups of seven participants (countries), a p level of 0.05, and a two-tailed test is 8.

Step 5: (*Note:* E stands for English-speaking, and NE stands for non-English-speaking.)

COUNTRY	PRIDE SCORE	PRIDE RANK	ENGLISH LANGUAGE	OTHER RANKS	RANKS
United States	4.0	1	E	1	
Australia	2.9	2.5	E	2.5	
Ireland	2.9	2.5	E	2.5	
South Africa	2.7	4	E	4	
New Zealand	2.6	5	E	5	
Canada	2.4	6	E	6	
Chile	2.3	7	NE		7
Great Britain	2.2	8	E	8	
Japan	1.8	9	NE		9
France	1.5	10	NE		10
Czech Republic	1.3	11.5	NE		11.5
Norway	1.3	11.5	NE		11.5
Slovenia	1.1	13	NE		13
South Korea	1.0	14	NE		14

$$\sum R_E = 1 + 2.5 + 2.5 + 4 + 5 + 6 + 8 = 29$$
$$\sum R_{NE} = 7 + 9 + 10 + 11.5 + 11.5 + 13 + 14 = 76$$

$$U_E = (n_E)(n_{NE}) + \frac{n_E(n_E + 1)}{2} - \Sigma R_E$$
$$= (7)(7) + \frac{7(7 + 1)}{2} - 29 = 49 + 28 - 29 = 48$$

$$U_{NE} = (n_E)(n_{NE}) + \frac{n_{NE}(n_{NE} + 1)}{2} - \Sigma R_{NE}$$
$$= (7)(7) + \frac{7(7 + 1)}{2} - 76 = 49 + 28 - 76 = 1$$

$$U_E = 48; U_{NE} = 1$$

Step 6: The smaller test statistic, 1, is smaller than the critical value, 8. We can reject the null hypothesis; it appears that English-speaking countries tend to have higher accomplishment-related national pride than non-English-speaking countries.

Choosing the Appropriate Statistical Test

We have learned four categories of statistical tests:

1. Statistical tests in which all variables are scale

2. Statistical tests in which the independent variable (or variables) is nominal, but the dependent variable is scale

3. Statistical tests in which all variables are nominal

4. Statistical tests in which any variable is ordinal

Category 1: Two Scale Variables

If we have a research design with only scale variables, we have two choices about how to analyze the data. The only question we have to ask ourselves is whether the research question pertains to an association (or relation) between two variables or to the degree to which one variable predicts the other. If the research question is about association, then we choose the Pearson correlation coefficient. If it is about prediction, then we choose regression. The decisions for category 1 are represented in Table E-1.

Category 2: Nominal Independent Variable(s) And Scale Dependent Variable

If our research design includes one or more nominal independent variables and a scale dependent variable, then we have several choices. The next question pertains to the number of independent variables.

1. If there is *just one independent variable,* then we ask ourselves how many levels it has.

TABLE E-1 Category 1 Statistics

When both the independent variable and the dependent variable are interval, we calculate either a Pearson correlation coefficient or a regression equation.

Research Question: Association (Relation)	Research Question: Prediction
Pearson correlation coefficient	Regression equation

---

a. If there are *two levels, but just one sample*—that is, one level is represented by the sample and one level by the population—then we use either a z test or a single-sample t test. It is unusual to know enough about a population that we only need to collect data from a single sample. If this is the case, however, and we know *both* the population mean and standard deviation, then we can use a z test. If this is the case and we know *only* the population mean (but not the standard deviation), then we use the single-sample t test.

b. If there are *two levels, each represented by a sample* (either a single sample in which everyone participates in both levels or two different samples, one for each level), then we use either a paired-samples t test (if all participants are in both levels of the independent variable) or an independent-samples t test (if participants are in only one level of the independent variable).

c. If there are three or more levels, then we use a form of a one-way ANOVA. We examine the research design to determine if it is a between-groups ANOVA (participants in just one level of the independent variable) or a within-groups ANOVA (participants in all levels of the independent variable).

2. If there are *at least two independent variables,* we must use a form of ANOVA. Remember, we name ANOVAs according to the number of independent variables (one-way, two-way, three-way) and the research design (between-groups, within-groups).

The decisions about data that fall into category 2 and have one independent variable are summarized in Table E-2. For those with two or more independent variables, see Table 12-1.

Category 3: One Or Two Nominal Variables

If we have a design with only nominal variables—that is, counts, not means, in the cells—then we have two choices; both nonparametric tests. The only question we have to ask ourselves is whether there are one or two nominal variables. If there is one nominal variable, then we choose the chi-square test for goodness-of-fit. If there are two nominal variables, then we choose the chi-square test for independence. The decision for category 3 is represented in Table E-3.

TABLE E-2 Category 2 Statistics

When there are one or more nominal independent variables and a scale dependent variable, we have several choices. Start by selecting the appropriate number of independent variables. For *one independent variable*, use the accompanying chart. To use this chart, look at the first two columns, those that identify the number of levels of the independent variable and the number of samples. For two levels but one sample, it's a choice between the *z* test and single-sample *t* test; for two levels and two samples, it's a choice between the paired-samples *t* test and the independent-samples *t* test. For three or more levels (and the matching number of samples), we use either a one-way within-groups ANOVA or a one-way between-groups ANOVA. For *two independent variables* or *three independent variables*, we'll use a form of ANOVA and refer to Table 12-1 on naming ANOVAs. One independent variable:

NUMBER OF LEVELS OF INDEPENDENT VARIABLE	NUMBER OF SAMPLES	INFORMATION ABOUT POPULATION	HYPOTHESIS TEST
Two	One (compared to the population)	Mean and standard deviation	*z* test
Two	One (compared to the population)	Mean only	Single-sample *t* test

NUMBER OF LEVELS OF INDEPENDENT VARIABLE	NUMBER OF SAMPLES	RESEARCH DESIGN	HYPOTHESIS TEST
Two	Two	Within-groups	Paired-samples *t* test
Two	Two	Between-groups	Independent-samples *t* test
Three (or more)	Three (or more)	Between-groups	One-way between-groups ANOVA
Three (or more)	Three (or more)	Within-groups	One-way within-groups ANOVA

TABLE E-3 Category 3 Statistics

When we have only nominal variables, then we choose one of the two chi-square tests.

ONE NOMINAL VARIABLE	TWO NOMINAL VARIABLES
Chi-square test for goodness-of-fit	Chi-square test for independence

TABLE E-4 Category 4 Statistics

When at least one variable is ordinal, we use a nonparametric test. If both variables are ordinal, or can be converted to ordinal, and we are interested in quantifying the relation between them, we use the Spearman rank-order correlation coefficient. If the independent variable is nominal, with two levels, the dependent variable is ordinal, and there is a between-groups design, we use a Mann-Whitney *U* test.

TYPE OF INDEPENDENT VARIABLE (AND NUMBER OF LEVELS IF APPLICABLE)	RESEARCH DESIGN	QUESTION TO BE ANSWERED	HYPOTHESIS TEST
Ordinal	Not applicable	Are two variables related?	Spearman rank-order correlation coefficient
Nominal (two levels)	Between-groups	Are two groups different?	Mann–Whitney *U* test

TABLE E-5 Nonparametric Statistics and Their Parametric Counterparts

Every parametric hypothesis test has at least one nonparametric counterpart. If our data are far from meeting the assumptions for a parametric test or at least one variable is ordinal, we should use the appropriate nonparametric test instead of a parametric test.

DESIGN	PARAMETRIC TEST	NONPARAMETRIC TEST
Association between two variables	Pearson correlation coefficient	Spearman rank-order correlation coefficient
Two groups; between-groups design	Independent-samples *t* test	Mann–Whitney *U* test

Category 4: At Least One Ordinal Variable

If we have a design with even one ordinal variable or a design in which our data indicate that it makes sense to convert our data from scale to ordinal, then we have two choices, as seen in Table E-4. Both of these choices parallel a parametric hypothesis test, as seen in Table E-5. (Other parametric tests have nonparametric equivalents, but we did not learn them in this book.) For situations in which we want to investigate the relation between two ordinal variables, we use the Spearman rank-order correlation coefficient. When we have a between-groups design with two groups, we use a Mann–Whitney U test.

The decisions we've outlined above are summarized in Figure E-1.

FIGURE E-1.
Choosing the Appropriate Hypothesis Test.

By asking the right questions about our variables and research design, we can choose the appropriate hypothesis test for our research.

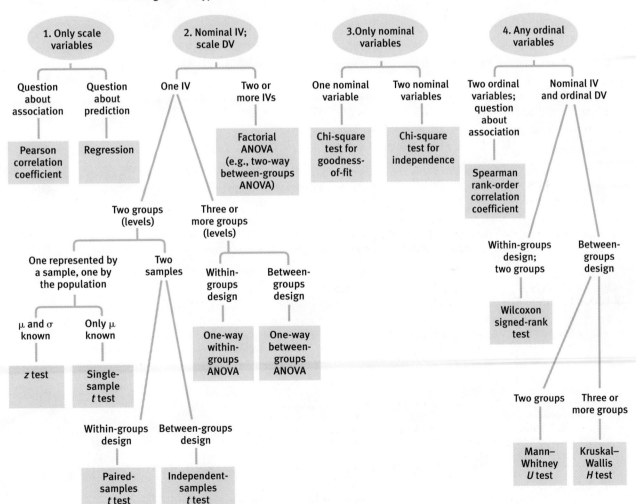

Four Categories of Hypothesis Tests (IV = independent variable; DV = dependent variable)

Reporting Statistics

Overview Of Reporting Statistics

In Chapter 10, we described a study about gender differences in humor (Azim, Mobbs, Jo, Menon, & Reiss, 2005). Let's recap the results of the analyses and then use this information to report statistics in the Methods and Results sections of a paper written in the style of the American Psychological Association (APA). In the analyses of the humor data, we used fictional data that had the same means as the actual study by Azim and colleagues. We used the following raw data:

> Percentage of cartoons labeled as "funny."
>
> Women: 84, 97, 58, 90
>
> Men: 88, 90, 52, 97, 86

We conducted an independent-samples t test on these data and found a test statistic, t, of -0.03. This test statistic was not beyond the cutoff, so we failed to reject the null hypothesis. We can *not* conclude that men and women, on average, find different percentages of the cartoons to be funny; we can only conclude that this study did not provide evidence that women and men are different on this variable. We noted that the statistics, as reported in a journal article, would include the symbol for the statistic, the degrees of freedom, the value of the test statistic, and, for statistics calculated by hand, whether the p value associated with the test statistic was less than or greater than the cutoff p level of 0.05. In the humor example, the statistics would read:

$$t(7) = -0.03, p > 0.05$$

(Note that we explained how to conduct this test using software in the SPSS section of Chapter 10. When we conducted this hypothesis test using SPSS, we got an exact p value of 0.977, so we would say $p = 0.98$ instead of $p > 0.05$ if we had used software.) In Chapter 10, we also noted that we would report the means and standard deviations for the two samples:

> Women: $M = 82.25$, $SD = 17.02$; Men: $M = 82.60$, $SD = 18.13$

We also calculated a confidence interval for these data. The 95% confidence interval, centered around the difference between means of $82.25 - 82.60 = -0.35$, is $[-28.37, 27.67]$.

We also calculated the effect size for this study, a Cohen's d of -0.02. We now have sufficient information to write up these findings.

There are three topics to consider when reporting statistics, all covered in various sections of the *Publication Manual of the American Psychological Association* (APA, 2010):

1. In the Methods section, we justify our study by including information about the statistical power, reliability, and validity of any measures we used.

2. In the Results section, we report the traditional statistics, which include any relevant descriptive statistics and often the results of hypothesis testing.

3. In the Results section, we report the newer statistics that are now required by the APA, including effect sizes and confidence intervals (APA, 2010).

Justify The Study

Researchers should first report the results of the statistical power analyses that were conducted prior to data collection. Then researchers should report any information related to the reliability and validity of the measured variables. This information usually goes in the Methods section of the paper.

To summarize this aspect of the findings, we include:

- statistical power analyses
- psychometric data for each scale used (reliability and validity information)

Report Traditional Statistics

The Results section should include any relevant summary statistics. For analyses with a scale dependent variable, include means, standard deviations, and sample sizes for each cell in the research design. For analyses with a nominal dependent variable (chi-square analyses), include the frequencies (counts) for each cell; there won't be means or standard deviations because there are no scores on a scale measure. Summary statistics are sometimes presented first in a Results section but are more typically presented after a description of each hypothesis test. If there are only two or three cells, then the summary statistics are typically presented in the text; if there are more cells, then a table or figure should display these numbers.

Reports of hypothesis tests typically begin by reiterating the hypothesis to be tested and then describing the test that was conducted, including the independent and dependent variables. The results of the hypothesis test are then presented, usually including the symbol for the statistic, the degrees of freedom, the actual value of the statistic, and, if using software, the p value associated with that statistic. Alternately, researchers might choose to report p_{rep} instead of p. The format for reporting this information has been presented after each hypothesis test in this text and is presented again in Table F-1. After the statistics are presented, a brief statement summarizes the results, indicating the direction of any effects. This brief statement does not draw conclusions beyond the actual finding. In the Results section, researchers do not discuss the finding in terms of the

TABLE F-1. The Format for the Results of a Hypothesis Test

There is a general format for reporting the results of hypothesis tests. The symbol for the statistic is followed by the degrees of freedom in parentheses, then the value of the test statistic, and finally the exact p value associated with that test statistic. This table presents the way that format would be implemented for several of the test statistics discussed in this text. (Note that you will only have the exact p value if you use software. If you conduct a test by hand, you may report whether the p value is greater than or less than 0.05.)

Symbol	Degrees of Freedom	Value of Test Statistic	Information about the Cutoff	Effect Size	Example
z	(df)	$= XX,$	$p = 0.XX$	$d = XX$	$z(54) = 0.60, p = 0.45, d = 0.08$
t	(df)	$= XX,$	$p = 0.XX$	$d = XX$	$t(146) = 2.29, p = 0.024, d = 0.50$
F	$(df_{Between}, df_{Within})$	$= XX,$	$p = 0.XX$	$R^2 = XX$	$F(2, 142) = 6.63, p = 0.002, R^2 = 0.09$
χ^2	$(df, N = XX)$	$= XX,$	$p = 0.XX$	$V = XX$	$\chi^2(1, N = 147) = 0.58, p = 0.447, V = 0.06$
U	None	$= XX,$	$p = 0.XX$	None	$U = 19, p = 0.14$

general theories in the field or in terms of its potential implications or applications (which go, appropriately enough, in the Discussion section). Researchers should present the results of all hypothesis tests that they conducted, even those in which they failed to reject the null hypothesis.

To summarize this aspect of Results sections:

- Include summary statistics: means, standard deviations, and sample sizes for each cell when the dependent variable is scale, and frequencies (counts) for each cell when the dependent variable is nominal. These are often included after each hypothesis test.
- For each hypothesis test conducted:
  - Include a brief summary of the hypotheses and hypothesis test.
  - Report the results of hypothesis testing: the symbol for the statistic used, degrees of freedom, the actual value of the statistic, and the p value associated with this statistic (if using software) or p_{rep}.
  - Provide a statement that summarizes the results of hypothesis testing.
  - Use tables and figures to clarify patterns in the findings.
- Include all results, even for findings that are not statistically significant.

The statistics for our study from Chapter 10 that compared the mean percentages of cartoons that women and men found funny might be reported as follows:

> To examine the hypothesis that women and men, on average, find different percentages of cartoons funny, we conducted an independent-samples t test. The independent variable was gender, with two levels: female and male. The dependent variable was the percentage of cartoons deemed funny. There was not a statistically significant effect of gender, $t(7) = -0.03, p = 0.98$; this study does not provide evidence that women ($M = 82.25, SD = 17.02$) and men ($M = 82.60, SD = 18.13$) deem, on average, different percentages of cartoons to be funny. The difference between the mean percentages for women and men is just 0.35%.

Reporting Newer Statistics

It is no longer enough to simply present the descriptive statistics and the results of the hypothesis test. As of the 2010 edition of its *Publication Manual*, APA requires the inclusion of effect sizes and confidence inter-

vals when relevant. The effect-size estimate is often included as part of the report of the statistics, just after the p value. There is often a statement that indicates the size of the effect in words, not just in numbers. The confidence interval can be presented after the effect size abbreviated as "95% CI" with the actual interval in brackets.

Note that nonparametric tests often do not have associated measures of effect size or confidence intervals. In these cases, researchers should provide enough descriptive information for readers to interpret the findings.

To summarize this aspect of the Results sections, we include:

- Effect sizes, along with a statement about the size of the effect
- Confidence intervals when possible, along with a statement interpreting the confidence interval in the context of the study.

For the study on humor, we might report the effect size as part of the traditional statistics that we described above:

> There was not a statistically significant effect of gender, $t(7) = -0.03, p = 0.98, d = -0.02$, 95% CI [−28.37, 27.67]; this was a small, almost nonexistent, effect. In fact, there is only a 0.35% difference between the mean percentages for women and men. This study does not provide evidence that men and women, on average, rate different percentages of cartoons as funny.

For the humor study, we can now pull the parts together. Here is how the results would be reported:

> To examine the hypothesis that women and men, on average, find different percentages of cartoons funny, we conducted an independent-samples t test. The independent variable was gender, with two levels: female and male. The dependent variable was the percentage of cartoons deemed funny. There was not a statistically significant effect of gender, $t(7) = -0.03, p = 0.98, d = -0.02$, 95% CI [−28.37, 27.67]; this was a small, almost nonexistent, effect. Based on the hypothesis test and the confidence interval, this study does not provide evidence that women ($M = 82.25, SD = 17.02$) and men ($M = 82.60, SD = 18.13$) deem, on average, different percentages of cartoons to be funny. In fact, there is only a very small difference between the mean percentages for women and men, just 0.35%.

GLOSSARY

A

analysis of variance (ANOVA) A hypothesis test typically used with one or more nominal independent variables (with at least three groups overall) and a scale dependent variable.

assumption A characteristic that we ideally require the population from which we are sampling to have so that we can make accurate inferences.

B

bar graph A visual depiction of data when the independent variable is nominal and the dependent variable is scale. Each bar typically represents the average value of the dependent variable for each category.

between-groups ANOVA A hypothesis test in which there are more than two samples and each sample is composed of different participants.

between-groups variance An estimate of the population variance based on the differences among the means.

between-groups research design An experimental design in which participants experience one, and only one, level of the independent variable.

bimodal Describes a distribution that has two modes, or most common scores.

C

ceiling effect A situation in which a constraint prevents a variable from taking on values above a given number.

cell A box that depicts one unique combination of levels of the independent variables in a factorial design.

central limit theorem The idea that a distribution of sample means is a more normal distribution than a distribution of scores, even when the population distribution is not normal.

central tendency A descriptive statistic that best represents the center of a data set, the particular value that all the other data seem to be gathering around.

chartjunk Any unnecessary information or feature in a graph that distracts from a viewer's ability to understand the data.

chi-square test for goodness-of-fit A nonparametric hypothesis test used with one nominal variable.

chi-square test for independence A nonparametric hypothesis test used with two nominal variables.

Cohen's *d* A measure of effect size that assesses the difference between two means in terms of standard deviation, not standard error.

confidence interval An interval estimate, based on the sample statistic, that includes the population mean a certain percentage of the time, were we to sample from the same population repeatedly.

confounding variable A variable that systematically covaries with the independent variable so that we cannot logically determine which variable is at work; also called a *confound*.

control group A level of the independent variable that is designed to match the experimental group in all ways but the experimental manipulation itself.

continuous observation Observed data point that can take on a full range of values (e.g., numbers out to several decimal points); there is an infinite number of potential values.

convenience sample A subset of a population whose members are chosen strictly because they are readily available, as opposed to randomly selecting participants from the entire population of interest.

correlation An association between two or more variables.

correlation coefficient A statistic that quantifies a relation between two variables.

Cramer's *V* The standard effect size used with the chi-square test for independence; also called Cramer's phi, symbolized as φ.

critical region The area in the tails of the distribution within which we will reject the null hypothesis if our test statistic falls there.

critical value A test statistic value beyond which we will reject the null hypothesis; often called a *cutoff*.

D

degrees of freedom The number of scores that are free to vary when estimating a population parameter from a sample.

dependent variable The outcome variable that we hypothesize to be related to, or caused by, changes in the independent variable.

descriptive statistic A statistic that organizes, summarizes, and communicates a group of numerical observations.

deviation from the mean The amount that a score in a sample differs from the mean of the sample; also called the *deviation*.

discrete observation Observed data point that can take on only specific values (e.g., whole numbers); no other values can exist between these numbers.

distribution of means A distribution composed of many means that are calculated from all possible samples of a given size, all taken from the same population.

duck A type of chartjunk in which features of the data have been dressed up to be something other than merely data.

E

effect size A standardized value that indicates the size of a difference with respect to a measure of spread but is not affected by sample size.

expected relative-frequency probability The likelihood of an event occurring based on the actual outcome of many, many trials.

experiment A study in which participants are randomly assigned to a condition or level of one or more independent variables.

experimental group A level of the independent variable that receives the treatment or intervention of interest in an experiment.

F

F statistic A ratio of two measures of variance: (1) between-groups variance, which indicates differences among sample means, and (2) within-groups variance, which is essentially an average of the sample variances.

factor Describes an independent variable in a study with more than one independent variable.

factorial ANOVA A statistical analysis used with one scale dependent variable and at least two nominal independent variables (sometimes called *factors*); also called a *multifactorial ANOVA*.

floor effect A situation in which a constraint prevents a variable from taking values below a certain point.

frequency distribution A distribution that describes the pattern of a set of numbers by displaying a count or proportion for each possible value of a variable.

frequency polygon A line graph with the x-axis representing values (or midpoints of intervals) and the y-axis representing frequencies. A dot is placed at the frequency for each value (or midpoint), and the dots are connected.

frequency table A visual depiction of data that shows how often each value occurred; that is, how many scores were at each value. Values are listed in one column and the numbers of individuals with scores at that value are listed in the second column.

G

generalizability The ability to apply findings from one sample or in one context to other samples or contexts; also called *external validity*.

grand mean The mean of every score in a study, regardless of which sample the score came from.

grid A type of chartjunk that takes the form of a background pattern, almost like graph paper, on which the data representations, such as bars, are superimposed.

grouped frequency table A visual depiction of data that reports the frequencies within a given interval rather than the frequencies for a specific value.

H

heteroscedastic Describes populations that have different variances.

histogram A graph similar to a bar graph typically used to depict scale data with the values of the variable on the x-axis and the frequencies on the y-axis.

homoscedastic Describes populations that have the same variance; also called *homogeneity of variance*.

hypothesis testing The process of drawing conclusions about whether a particular relation between variables is supported by the evidence.

I

independent-samples *t* test A hypothesis test used to compare two means for a between-groups design, a situation in which each participant is assigned to only one condition.

independent variable A variable that we either manipulate or observe to determine its effects on the dependent variable.

inferential statistic Statistical technique that uses sample data to make general estimates about the larger population.

interaction The statistical result achieved in a factorial design when the two independent variables have an effect in combination that we do not see when we examine each independent variable on its own.

intercept The predicted value for Y when X is equal to 0, or the point at which the line crosses, or intercepts, the y-axis.

interval estimate A range of plausible values for the population parameter, based on a sample statistic.

interval variable A variable that has numbers as its values; the distance (or interval) between pairs of consecutive numbers is assumed to be equal.

L

level A discrete value or condition that a variable can take on.

line graph A graph used to illustrate the relation between different scale variables; sometimes the line represents the predicted y scores for each x value and sometimes the line represents change in a variable over time.

linear relation A relation between two variables best described by a straight line.

M

main effect A result occuring in a factorial design when one of the independent variables has an influence on the dependent variable.

Mann–Whitney *U* test A nonparametric hypothesis test used when there are two groups, a between-groups design and an ordinal dependent variable.

marginal mean The mean of a row or a column in a table that shows the cells of a study with a two-way ANOVA design.

mean The arithmetic average of a group of scores. It is calculated by summing all the scores and dividing by the total number of scores.

median The middle score of all the scores in a sample when the scores are arranged in ascending order. If there is no single middle score, the median is the mean of the two middle scores.

mode The most common score of all the scores in a sample.

moiré vibration A type of chartjunk that takes the form of any of the patterns that computers provide as options to fill in bars on a graph.

multimodal Describes a distribution that has more than two modes, or most common scores.

multiple regression A statistical technique that includes two or more predictor variables in a prediction equation.

N

negative correlation An association between two variables in which participants with high scores on one variable tend to have low scores on the other variable.

negatively skewed Describes an asymmetric distribution whose tail extends to the left, in a negative direction.

nominal variable A variable used for observations that have categories, or names, as their values.

nonlinear relation A relation between variables best described by a line that breaks or curves in some way.

nonparametric test An inferential statistical analysis that is not based on a set of assumptions about the population.

normal curve A specific bell-shaped curve that is unimodal, symmetric, and defined mathematically.

normal distribution A specific frequency distribution in the shape of a bell-shaped, symmetric, unimodal curve.

null hypothesis A statement that postulates that there is no difference between populations or that the difference is in a direction opposite from that anticipated by the researcher.

O

one-tailed test A hypothesis test in which the research hypothesis is directional, positing either a mean decrease or a mean increase in the dependent variable, but not both, as a result of the independent variable.

one-way ANOVA A hypothesis test that includes one nominal independent variable with more than two levels and a scale dependent variable.

operational definition The operations or procedures used to measure or manipulate a variable.

ordinal variable A variable used for observations that have rankings (i.e., 1st, 2nd, 3rd. . .) as their values.

orthogonal variable An independent variable that makes a separate and distinct contribution to the prediction of a dependent variable, as compared with another variable.

outcome In reference to probability, the result of a trial.

outlier An extreme score that is either very high or very low in comparison with the rest of the scores in a sample.

P

p_{rep} The probability of replicating an effect given a particular population and sample size.

p level The probability used to determine the critical values, or cutoffs, in hypothesis testing; also called *alpha*.

paired-samples t test A test used to compare two means for a within-groups design, a situation in which every participant is in both samples; also called a *dependent-samples t test*.

parameter A number based on the whole population; it is usually symbolized by a Greek letter.

parametric test An inferential statistical analysis that is based on a set of assumptions about the population.

Pareto chart A type of bar graph in which the categories along the x-axis are ordered from highest bar on the left to lowest bar on the right.

Pearson correlation coefficient A statistic that quantifies a linear relation between two scale variables.

personal probability The likelihood of an event occurring based on an individual's opinion or judgment; also called *subjective probability*.

pictorial graph A visual depiction of data typically used for an independent variable with very few levels (categories) and a scale dependent variable. Each category uses a picture or symbol to represent its value on the scale dependent variable.

pie chart A graph in the shape of a circle with a slice for every category. The size of each slice represents the proportion (or percentage) of each category.

point estimate A summary statistic from a sample that is just one number as an estimate of the population parameter.

pooled variance A weighted average of the two estimates of variance—one from each sample—that are calculated when conducting an independent-samples t test.

population All of the possible observations about which we'd like to know something.

positive correlation An association between two variables such that participants with high scores on one variable tend to have high scores on the other variable as well, and those with low scores on one variable tend to have low scores on the other variable as well.

positively skewed Describes an asymmetric distribution whose tail extends to the right, in a positive direction.

post-hoc test A statistical procedure frequently carried out after we reject the null hypothesis in an analysis of variance; it allows us to make multiple comparisons among several means.

probability The likelihood that a certain outcome will occur out of all possible outcomes.

proportionate reduction in error A statistic that quantifies how much more accurate our predictions are when we use the regression line instead of the mean as a prediction tool; also called the *coefficient of determination*.

Q

qualitative interaction A particular type of quantitative interaction of two (or more) independent variables in which one independent variable reverses its effect depending on the level of the other independent variable.

quantitative interaction An interaction in which one independent variable exhibits a strengthening or weakening of its effect at one or more levels of the other independent variable but the direction of the initial effect does not change.

R

random assignment The protocol established for an experiment whereby every participant in a study has an equal chance of being assigned to any of the groups, or experimental conditions, in the study.

random sample A subset of a population selected using a method that ensures that every member of the population has an equal chance of being selected into the study.

range A measure of variability calculated by subtracting the lowest score (the minimum) from the highest score (the maximum).

ratio variable A variable that meets the criteria for an interval variable but also has a meaningful zero point.

raw score Data point that has not yet been transformed or analyzed.

regression to the mean The tendency of scores that are particularly high or low to drift toward the mean over time.

reliability The consistency of a measure.

replication The duplication of scientific results, ideally in a different context or with a sample that has different characteristics.

research hypothesis A statement that postulates that there is a difference between populations, or sometimes, more specifically, that there is a difference in a certain direction, positive or negative; also called the *alternate hypothesis*.

robust Describes a hypothesis test that produces fairly accurate results even when the data suggest that the population might not meet some of the assumptions.

S

sample A set of observations drawn from the population of interest that, it is hoped, share the same characteristics as the population of interest.

scale variable A variable that meets the criteria for an interval variable or a ratio variiable.

scatterplot A graph that depicts the relation between two scale variables. The values of each variable are marked along the two axes and a mark is made to indicate the intersection of the two scores for each participant. The mark will be above the individual's score on the x-axis and across from the score on the y-axis.

simple linear regression A statistical tool that enables us to predict an individual's score on a dependent variable from his or her score on one independent variable.

single-sample _t_ test A hypothesis test in which we compare data from one sample to a population for which we know the mean but not the standard deviation.

skewed distribution A distribution in which one of the tails of the distribution is pulled away from the center.

slope In a regression equation, the amount that _Y_ is predicted to increase for an increase of 1 in _X_.

source table A table that presents the important calculations and final results of an ANOVA in a consistent and easy-to-read format.

Spearman rank-order correlation coefficient A nonparametric statistic that quantifies the association between two ordinal variables.

standard deviation The square root of the average of the squared deviations from the mean; it is the typical amount that the scores in a sample vary, or deviate, from the mean.

standard error The standard deviation of a distribution of means.

standard error of the estimate A statistic indicating the typical distance between a regression line and the actual data points.

standard normal distribution A normal distribution of _z_ scores.

standardization A process that converts individual scores from different normal distributions to a shared normal distribution with a known mean, standard deviation, and percentiles.

standardized regression coefficient A standardized version of the slope in a regression equation; the predicted change in the dependent variable in terms of standard deviations for a 1–standard deviation increase in the independent variable; also called the _beta weight_.

statistic A number based on a sample taken from a population; it is usually symbolized by a Latin letter.

statistically significant Describes a finding for which we have rejected the null hypothesis because the pattern in the data differs from what we would expect by chance.

statistical power A measure of our ability to reject the null hypothesis given that the null hypothesis is false.

success In reference to probability, the outcome for which we're trying to determine the probability.

sum of squares The sum of the squared deviations from the mean for each score. Symbolized as _SS_.

T

_t_ statistic A statistic that indicates the distance of a sample mean from a population mean in terms of the standard error.

time plot or **time series plot** A graph that plots a scale variable on the y-axis as it changes over an increment of time (e.g., second, day, century) labeled on the x-axis.

trial In reference to probability, each occasion that a given procedure is carried out.

two-tailed test A hypothesis test in which the research hypothesis does not indicate a direction of mean difference or change in the dependent variable but merely indicates that there will be a mean difference.

two-way ANOVA A hypothesis test that includes two nominal independent variables, regardless of their numbers of levels, and a scale dependent variable.

Tukey _HSD_ test A widely used post-hoc test that determines the differences between means in terms of standard error; the _HSD_ is compared to a critical value; sometimes called the _q test_.

Type I error The result when we reject the null hypothesis, but the null hypothesis is correct.

Type II error The result when we fail to reject the null hypothesis but the null hypothesis is false.

U

unimodal Describes a distribution that has one mode, or most common score.

V

validity The extent to which a test actually measures what it was intended to measure.

variability A numerical way of describing how much spread there is in a distribution.

variable Any observation of a physical, attitudinal, or behavioral characteristic that can take on different values.

variance The average of the squared deviations from the mean.

volunteer sample A special kind of convenience sample in which participants actively choose to participate in a study; also called a _self-selected sample_.

W

within-groups ANOVA A hypothesis test in which there are more than two samples and each sample is composed of the same participants; also called a _repeated measures ANOVA_.

within-groups research design An experimental design in which the different levels of the independent variable are experienced by all participants in the study; also called a _repeated-measures design_.

within-groups variance An estimate of the population variance based on the differences within each of the three (or more) sample distributions.

Z

_z_ score The number of standard deviations a particular score is from the mean.

_z_ distribution A normal distribution of standardized scores.

_z_ test A hypothesis test in which we compare data from one sample to a population for which we know the mean and the standard deviation.

REFERENCES

Alter, A. L., Oppenheimer, D. M. (2006a). From a fixation on sports to an exploration of mechanism: The past, present, and future of hot hand research. *Thinking & Reasoning, 12,* 431–444.

Alter, A., & Oppenheimer, D. (2006b). Predicting short-term stock fluctuations by using processing fluency. *Proceedings of the National Academy of Sciences of the United States of America, 103,* 9369–9372.

American Academy of Physician Assistants. (2005). Income reported by PAs who graduated in 2004. *American Academy of Physician Assistants.* Retrieved November 20, 2006, from http://www.aapa.org/research/05newgrad-income.pdf

American Psychological Association (APA). (2010). *Publication manual of the American Psychological Association* (6th ed.). Washington, DC: Author.

Archibold, R. C. (1998, February 18). Just because the grades are up, are Princeton students smarter? *New York Times.* Retrieved November 14, 2006, from http://www.nytimes.com

Aron, A., & Aron, E. N. (2002). *Statistics for psychology* (3rd ed.). Upper Saddle River, NJ: Pearson Education.

Azim, E., Mobbs, D., Jo, B., Menon, V., & Reiss, A. L. (2005). Sex differences in brain activation elicited by humor. *Proceedings of the National Academy of Sciences, 102,* 16496–16501. Retrieved February 10, 2006, from http://www.pnas.org/cgi/doi /10.1073/pnas.0408456102

Bailey, D. G., & Dresser, G. K. (2004). Natural products and adverse drug interactions. *Canadian Medical Association Journal, 170,* 1531–1532.

Banks, J., Marmot, M., Oldfield, Z., & Smith, J. P. (2006). Disease and disadvantage in the United States and England. *Journal of the American Medical Association, 295,* 2037–2045.

Bardwell, W. A., Ensign, W. Y., & Mills, P. J. (2005). Negative mood endures after completion of high-altitude military training. *Annals of Behavioral Medicine, 29,* 64–69.

Behenam, M., & Pooya, O. (2006). Factors affecting patients cooperation during orthodontic treatment. *The Orthodontic CYBERJournal.* Retrieved on November 21, 2006, from http://www.oc-j.com/nov06/cooperation.htm

Bellosta, S., Paoletti, R., & Corsini, A. (2004). Safety of statins: Focus on clinical pharmacokinetics and drug interactions. *Circulation, 109,* III-50–III-57.

Benbow, C. P., & Stanley, J. C. (1980). Sex differences in math ability: Fact or artifact? *Science, 210,* 1262–1264.

Berger, J., & Fitzsimons, G. (2008). Dogs on the street, pumas on your feet: How cues in the environment influence product evaluation and choice. *Journal of Marketing Research, XLV,* 1–14.

Bernstein, P. L. (1996). *Against the gods: The remarkable story of risk.* New York: Wiley.

Boone, D. E. (1992). WAIS–R scatter with psychiatric inpatients: I. Intrasubtest scatter. *Psychological Reports, 71,* 483–487.

Borsari, B., & Carey, K. B. (2005). Two brief alcohol interventions for mandated college students. *Psychology of Addictive Behaviors, 19,* 296–302.

Box, J. (1978). *R. A. Fisher: The life of a scientist.* New York: Wiley.

Brinn, D. (2006, June 25). Israeli "clown therapy" boosts fertility treatment birthrate. *Health.* Retrieved April 6, 2007, from http://www.Israel21c.org

Buekens, P., Xiong, X., & Harville, E. (2006). Hurricanes and pregnancy. *Birth, 33,* 91–93.

Canadian Institute for Health Information (CIHI). (2005). More patients receiving transplants than 10 years ago, despite stagnant organ donation rate. Retrieved July 15, 2005, from http://secure .cihi.ca/cihiweb/dispPage.jsp?cw_page=media_ 13apr2005_e

Cancer Research UK. (2003). *Cancer deaths in the UK.* Retrieved June 15, 2005, from http://info.cancerresearchuk.org/ cancer-stats/mortality/cancerdeaths/

Centers for Disease Control (CDC). (2004). *Americans slightly taller, much heavier than four decades ago.* Retrieved May 26, 2005, from http://www.cdc.gov/nchs/pressroom/ 04news/americans.htm

Cohen, J. (1988). *Statistical power analysis for the behavioral sciences* (2nd ed.). Hillsdale, NJ: Erlbaum.

Cohen, J. (1990). Things I have learned (so far). *American Psychologist, 45,* 1304–1312.

Cohen, J. (1992). A power primer. *Psychological Bulletin, 112,* 155–159.

Cohen, J. (1994). The earth is round ($p < .05$). *American Psychologist, 49,* 997–1003.

Cooper, M. J., Gulen, H., & Ovtchinnikov, A. V. (2007). *Corporate political contributions and stock returns.* Available at SSRN: http:// ssrn.com/abstract-940790.

Corsi, A., & Ashenfelter, O. (2001, April). *Wine quality: Experts' ratings and weather determinants* [Electronic version]. Poster session presented at the annual meeting of the European Association of Agricultural Economists, Zaragoza, Spain.

Creighton, C. (1965). *History of epidemics in Britain* (Vol. 2). London: Cassell.

Cunliffe, S. (1976). Interaction. *Journal of the Royal Statistical Society, A, 139,* 1–19.

Czerwinski, M., Smith, G., Regan, T., Meyers, B., Robertson, G., & Starkweather, G. (2003). Toward characterizing the productivity benefits of very large displays. In M. Rauterberg et al (Eds.), *Human-computer interaction- INTERACT '03* (pp. 9–16). IOS Press.

Darlin, D. (2006, July 1). Air fare made easy (or easier). *New York Times.* Retrieved July 1, 2006, from http://www.nytimes.com

DeBroff, B. M., & Pahk, P. J. (2003). The ability of periorbitally applied antiglare products to improve contrast sensitivity in conditions of sunlight exposure. *Archives of Ophthalmology, 121,* 997–1001.

Delucchi, K. L. (1983). The use and misuse of chi square: Lewis and Burke revisited. *Psychological Bulletin, 94,* 166–176.

Dijksterhuis, A., Bos, M. W., Nordgren, L. F., & van Baaren, R. B. (2006). On making the right choice: The deliberation-without-attention effect. *Science, 311,* 1005–1007.

Ditto, P. H., & Lopez, D. L. (1992). Motivated skepticism: Use of differential decision criteria for preferred and nonpreferred conclusions. *Journal of Personality and Social Psychology, 63,* 568–584.

Dubner, S. J., & Levitt, S. D. (2006a, May 7). A star is made: The birth-month soccer anomaly. *New York Times.* Retrieved May 7, 2006, from http://www.nytimes.com

Dubner, S. J., & Levitt, S. D. (2006b, November 5). The way we live now: Freakonomics; The price of climate change. *New York Times,* Retrieved March 7, 2007, from http://www. nytimes.com

Ellison, N. B., Steinfeld, C., & Lampe, C. (2007). The benefits of facebook "friends:" Social capital and college students' use of online social network sites. Journal of Computer-Mediated Communication, 12, http://jcmc.indiana.edu/vol12/issue4/ellison.html.

Engle-Friedman, M., Riela, S., Golan, R., Ventuneac, A. M., Davis, C. M., Jefferson, A. D., & Major, D. (2003). The effect of sleep loss on next day effort. *Journal of Sleep Research, 12,* 113–124.

Erdfelder, E., Faul, F., & Buchner, A. (1996). GPOWER: A general power analysis program. *Behavior Research Methods, Instruments, and Computers, 28,* 1–11.

Facebook.com (2009). Retrieved from http://www.facebook.com/press/info.php?statistics on August 20, 2009.

Fallows, J. (1999). Booze you can use: Getting the best beer for your money. *Slate* online magazine. http://www.slate.com/33771/

Farecast.com (2007). Farecast launches new tools to help savvy travelers catch elusive price drops this summer. Retrieved from http://www.bing.com/travel/about/press/releases/2007-05-15.do on August 20, 2009.

Forsyth, D. R., & Kerr, N. A. (1999, August). *Are adaptive illusions adaptive?* Poster presented at the annual meeting of the American Psychological Association, Boston, MA.

Forsyth, D. R., Lawrence, N. K., Burnette, J. L., & Baumeister, R. F. (2007). Attempting to improve the academic performance of struggling college students by bolstering their self-esteem: An intervention that backfired. *Journal of Social and Clinical Psychology, 26,* 447–459.

Frazier, T. W., & Edmonds, C. L. (2002). Curriculum predictors of performance on the Major Field Test in Psychology II. *Journal of Instructional Psychology, 29,* 29–32.

Friendly, M. (2009). Gallery of data visualization. Retrieved July 21, 2005, from http://www.math.yorku.ca/SCS/Gallery/

Geier, A. B., Rozin, P., & Doros, G. (2006). Unit bias: A new heuristic that helps explain the effect of portion size on food intake. *Psychological Science, 17,* 521–525.

Georgiou, C. C., Betts, N. M., Hoerr, S. L., Keim, K., Peters, P. K., Stewart, B., & Voichick, J. (1997). Among young adults, college students and graduates practiced more healthful habits and made more healthful food choices than did nonstudents. *Journal of the American Dietetic Association, 97,* 754–759.

Gilovich, T. (1991). *How we know what isn't so: The fallibility of human reason in everyday life.* New York: Free Press.

Gilovich, T., & Medvec, V. H. (1995). The experience of regret: What, when, and why. *Psychological Review, 102,* 379–395.

Gilovich, T., Vallone, R., & Tversky, A. (1985). The hot hand in basketball: On the misperception of random sequences. *Cognitive Psychology, 17,* 295–314.

Gimbarzevsky, B. (1995). Canadian homicide trends 1961–1994. Retrieved July 6, 2005, from http://teapot.usask.ca/cdn-firearms /Gimbarzevsky/homicide.html

Gossett, W. S. (1908). The probable error of a mean. *Biometrics, 6,* 1–24.

Gossett, W. S. (1942). *"Student's" collected papers* (E. S. Pearson, J. Wishart, Eds.). Cambridge, UK: Cambridge University Press.

Grimberg, A., Kutikov, J. K., & Cucchiara, A. J. (2005). Sex differences in patients referred for evaluation of poor growth. *Journal of Pediatrics, 146,* 212–216.

Hatchett, G. T. (2003). Does psychopathology predict counseling duration? *Psychological Reports, 93,* 175–185.

Hays, W. L. (1994). *Statistics* (5th ed.). Fort Worth, TX: Harcourt Brace College Publishers.

Headquarters Counseling Center. (2005). Myths and facts about suicide. Retrieved February 12, 2007, from http://www .hqcc.lawrence.ks.us/suicide_prevention/myths_facts.html

Healy, J. (1990). *Endangered minds: Why our children don't think.* New York: Simon and Schuster.

Healey, J. R. (2006, October 13). Driving the hard (top, that is) way. *USA Today,* p. 1B.

Heyman, J., & Ariely, D. (2004). Effort for payment. *Psychological Science, 15,* 787–793.

Hockenbury, D. H., & Hockenbury, S. E. (2003). *Psychology* (3rd ed.). New York: Worth.

Holiday, A. (2007). Perceptions of depression based on etiology and gender. Unpublished manuscript.

Hollon, S. D., Thase, M. E., & Markowitz, J. C. (2002). Treatment and prevention of depression. *Psychological Science in the Public Interest, 3,* 39–77.

Holm-Denoma, J. M., Joiner, T. E., Vohs, K. D., & Heatherton, T. F. (2008). The "freshman fifteen" (the "freshman five" actually): Predictors and possible explanations. *Health Psychology, 27,* s3–s9.

Howard, K. I., Moras, K., Brill, P. L., Martinovich, Z., & Lutz, W. (1996). Efficacy, effectiveness, and patient progress. *American Psychologist, 51,* 1059–1064.

Hugenberg, K., Miller, J., & Claypool, H. (2007). Categorization and individuation in the cross-race recognition deficit: Toward a solution to an insidious problem. *Journal of Experimental Social Psychology, 43,* 334–340.

Hull, H. R., Radley, D., Dinger, M. K., & Fields, D. A. (2006). The effect of the Thanksgiving holiday on weight gain. *Nutrition Journal, 21,* 29.

Hyde, J. S., Fennema, E., & Lamon, S. J. (1990). Gender differences in mathematics performance: A meta-analysis. *Psychological Bulletin, 107,* 139–155.

Hyde, J. S. (2005). The gender similarities hypothesis. *American Psychologist, 60,* 581–592.

IMD International. (2001). Competitiveness rankings as of April 2001. Retrieved on June 29, 2006, from http://www .photius.com/wfb1999/rankings/competitiveness.html

Indiana University Media Relations. (2006). It's no joke: IU study finds *The Daily Show* with Jon Stewart to be as substantive as network news. Retrieved December 10, 2006, from http://newsinfo.iu.edu/news/page/normal/4159.html

Irwin, M. L., Tworoger, S. S., Yasui, Y., Rajan, B., McVarish, L., LaCroix, K., et al. (2004). Influence of demographic, physiologic, and psychosocial variables on adherence to a yearlong moderate-intensity exercise trial in postmenopausal women. *Preventive Medicine, 39,* 1080–1086.

Jacob, J. E., & Eccles, J. (1982). Science and the media: Benbow and Stanley revisited. Report funded by the National Institute of Education, Washington, D.C. ERIC # ED235925.

Jacob, J. E., & Eccles, J. (1986). Social forces shape math attitudes and performance. *Signs, 11,* 367–380.

Johnson, W. B., Koch, C., Fallow, G. O., & Huwe, J. M. (2000). Prevalence of mentoring in clinical versus experimental doctoral programs: Survey findings, implications, and recommendations. *Psychotherapy: Theory, Research, Practice, Training, 37,* 325–334.

Joireman, J., Sprott, D. E., & Spangenberg, E. R. (2005). Fiscal responsibility and the consideration of future consequences. *Personality and Individual Differences, 39,* 1159–1168.

Kida, T. (2006). *Don't believe everything you think.* Amherst, NY: Prometheus Books.

Killeen, P. B. (2005). An alternative to null-hypothesis significance tests. *Psychological Science, 16,* 345–353.

Koehler, J. J., & Conley, C. A. (2003). The "hot hand" myth in professional basketball. *Journal of Sport & Exercise Psychology, 25,* 253–259.

Konner, J., Risser, F., & Wattenberg, B. (2001). Television's performance on Election Night 2000: A report for CNN. Retrieved November 25, 2008, from http://www.cnn.com/2001/ALLPOLI-TICS/stories/02/02/cnn.report/cnn.pdf

Krugman, P. (2006, May 5). Our sick society. *New York Times.* Retrieved May 5, 2006, from http://www.nytimes.com

Kuck, V. J., Buckner, J. P., Marzabadi, C. H., & Nolan, S. A. (2007). A review and study on graduate training and academic hiring of chemists. *Journal of Chemical Education, 84,* 277–284.

Landrum, E. (2005). Core terms in undergraduate statistics. *Teaching of Psychology, 32,* 249–251.

Levitt, S. D., & Dubner, S. J. (2005). *Freakonomics: A rogue economist explores the hidden side of everything.* New York: Morrow.

Lloyd, C. (2006, December 14). Saved, or sacrificed? *Salon.com.* Retrieved February 26, 2007, from http://www.salon.com/mwt /broadsheet/2006/12/14/selection/index.html

Lucas, M. E. S., Deen, J. L., von Seidlein, L., Wang, X., Ampuero, J., Puri, M., et al. (2005). Effectiveness of mass oral cholera vaccination in Beira, Mozambique. *New England Journal of Medicine, 352,* 757–767.

Mark, G., Gonzalez, V. M., & Harris, J. (2005, April). No task left behind? Examining the nature of fragmented work. *Proceedings of the Association for Computing Machinery Conference on Human Factors in Computing Systems* (ACM CHI 2005), Portland, OR, 321–330. New York: ACM Press.

Matlin, M. W., & Kalat, J. W. (2001). Demystifying the GRE psychology test: A brief guide for students. *Eye on Psi Chi, 5,* 22–25. Retrieved January 7, 2006, from http://www.psichi.org/ pubs/articles/article_66.asp

McCollum, J. F., & Bryant, J. (2003). Pacing in children's television programming. *Mass Communication and Society, 6,* 115–136.

Mecklenburg, S. H., Malpass, R. S., & Ebbesen, E. (2006, March 17). Report to the legislature of the State of Illinois: The Illinois Pilot Program on Sequential Double-Blind Identification Procedures. Retrieved April 19, 2006, from http://eyewitness.utep.edu

Micceri, T. (1989). The unicorn, the normal curve, and other improbable creatures. *Psychological Bulletin, 105,* 156–166.

Mitchell, P. (1999). Grapefruit juice found to cause havoc with drug uptake. *Lancet, 353,* 1355.

Murphy, K. R., & Myors, B. (2004). *Statistical power analysis: A simple and general model for traditional and modern hypothesis tests.* Mahwah, NJ: Erlbaum.

Myers, D. G., & Diener, E. (1995). Who is happy? *Psychological Science, 6,* 10–19.

Nail, P. R., Harton, H. C., & Decker, B. P. (2003). Political orientation and modern versus aversive racism: Tests of Dovidio and Gaertner's (1998) integrated model. *Journal of Personality and Social Psychology, 84,* 754–770.

National Center for Health Statistics. (2000). *National Health and Nutrition Examination Survey, CDC growth charts: United States.* Retrieved January 6, 2006, from http://www.cdc.gov/nchs/about/ major/nhanes/growthcharts/charts.htm

Neuman, W. (2005, June 7). In Manhattan, apartments still selling at record highs. *New York Times,* p. 6.

Newell, C. E., Rosenfeld, P., & Culbertson, A. L. (1995). Sexual harassment experiences and equal opportunity perceptions of Navy women. *Sex Roles, 32,* 159–168.

Newman, A. (2006, November 11). Missed the train? Lost a wallet? Maybe it was all Mercury's fault. *New York Times,* p. B3.

Newton, R. R., & Rudestam, K. E. (1999). *Your statistical consultant: Answers to your data analysis questions.* Thousand Oaks, CA: Sage.

Noel, J., Forsyth, D. R., & Kelley, K. (1987). Improving the performance of failing students by overcoming their self-serving attributional biases. *Basic and Applied Social Psychology, 8,* 151–162.

Nolan, S. A., Flynn, C., & Garber, J. (2003). Prospective relations between rejection and depression in young adolescents. *Journal of Personality and Social Psychology, 85,* 745–755.

Oberst, U., Charles, C., & Chamarro, A. (2005). Influence of gender and age in aggressive dream content of Spanish children and adolescents. *Dreaming, 15,* 170–177.

Ogbu, J. U. (1986). The consequences of the American caste system. In U. Neisser (Ed.), *The school achievement of minority children: New perspectives* (pp. 19–56). Hillsdale, NJ: Erlbaum.

Petrocelli, J. V. (2003). Factor validation of the Consideration of Future Consequences Scale: Evidence for a shorter version. *Journal of Social Psychology, 143,* 405–413.

Popkin, S. J., & Woodley, W. (2002). *Hope VI Panel Study.* Urban Institute: Washington, D.C.

Postman, N. (1985). *Amusing ourselves to death.* New York: Penguin Books.

Press, E. (2006, December 3). Do immigrants make us safer? *New York Times Magazine,* pp. 20–24.

Public vs. private schools [Editorial]. (2006, July 19). *New York Times.* Retrieved July 19, 2006, from http://www. nytimes.com

Rajecki, D. W., Lauer, J. B., & Metzner, B. S. (1998). Early graduate school plans: Uninformed expectations. *Journal of College Student Development, 39,* 629–632.

Ratner, R. K., & Miller, D. T. (2001). The norm of self-interest and its effects on social action. *Journal of Personality and Social Psychology, 81,* 5–16.

Raz, A., Fan, J., & Posner, M. I. (2005). Hypnotic suggestion reduces conflict in the human brain. *Proceedings of the National Academy of Sciences, 102,* 9978–9983.

Redelmeier, D. A., & Tversky, A. (1996). On the belief that arthritis pain is related to the weather. *Proceedings of the National Academy of Sciences, 93,* 2895–2896.

Richards, S. E. (2006, March 22). Women silent on abortion on NYT op-ed page. *Salon.com.* Retrieved March 22, 2006, from http://www.salon.com.

Rockwell, P. (2006, June 23). Send in the clowns: No joke: "Medical clowning" seems to help women conceive. *Salon.com.* Retrieved June 25, 2006, from http://www.salon.com

Roberts, P. M. (2003). Performance of Canadian adults on the Graded Naming Test. *Aphasiology, 17,* 933–946.

Roberts, S. B., & Mayer, J. (2000). Holiday weight gain: Fact or fiction? *Nutrition Review, 58,* 378–379.

Ruby, C. (2006). *Coming to America: An examination of the factors that influence international students' graduate school choices.* Draft of dissertation.

Ruhm, C. J. (2000). Are recessions good for your health? *Quarterly Journal of Economics, 115,* 617–650.

Ruhm, C. J. (2006). *Healthy living in hard times* (NBEB Working Paper No. 9468). Cambridge, MA: National Bureau of Economic Research. Retrieved May 30, 2006, from http://www.nber.org/papers/w9468

Ryan, C. (2006, June 21). "Therapeutic clowning" boosts IVF. *BBC News.* Retrieved June 25, 2006, from http://news.bbc.co.uk

Saad, L. (2008, December 26). Obama, Hillary Clinton share "most admired" billing. *Gallup Polls.* Retrieved December 30, 2008, from http://www.gallup.com/poll/113572/Obama-Hillary-Clinton-Share-Most-Admired-Billing.aspx

Salsburg, D. (2001). *The lady tasting tea: How statistics revolutionized science in the twentieth century.* New York: W. H. Freeman.

Sandberg, D. E., Bukowski, W. M., Fung, C. M., & Noll, R. B. (2004). Height and social adjustment: Are extremes a cause for concern and action? *Pediatrics, 114,* 744–750.

Schackman, B. R., Gebo, K. A., Walensky, R. P., Losina, E., Muccio, T., Sax, P. E., et al. (2006). The lifetime cost of current human immunodeficiency virus care in the United States. *Medical Care, 44,* 990–997.

Schmidt, F. L. (1996). Statistical significance testing and cumulative knowledge in psychology: Implications for training of researchers. *Psychological Methods, 1,* 115–129.

Schmidt, M. E., & Vandewater, E. A. (2008). Media and attention, cognition, and school achievement. *Future of Children, 18,* 39–61.

Seymour, C. (2006). Listen while you run. *Runner's World.* Retrieved May 24, 2006, from http://msn.runnersworld.com

Sherman, J. D., Honegger, S. D., & McGivern, J. L. (2003). *Comparative indicators of education in the United States and other G-8 countries: 2002,* NCES 2003-026. Washington, D.C.: U.S. Department of Education, National Center for Health Statistics, http://scsvt.org/resource/global_ed_ compare2002.pdf

Skurnik, I., Yoon, C., Park, D. C., & Schwarz, N. (2005). How warnings about false claims become recommendations. *Journal of Consumer Research, 31,* 713–724.

Smillie, B. (1997, December 18). Japan's fast-paced cartoons prompt question of safety. *The Tuscaloosa News,* p. D3.

Smith, T. W., & Kim, S. (2006). National pride in cross-national and temporal perspective. *International Journal of Public Opinion Research, 18,* 127–136.

Spencer, S. J., Steele, C. M., & Quinn, D. M. (1999). Stereotype threat and women's math performance. *Journal of Experimental Social Psychology, 35,* 1–28.

Stampone, E. (1993). Effects of gender of rater and a woman's hair length on the perceived likelihood of being sexually harassed. The 46th Annual Undergraduate Psychology Conference, Mount Holyoke College, MA.

Steele, J. P., & Pinto, J. N. (2006). Influence of leader trust on policy agreement. *Psi Chi Journal of Undergraduate Research, 11,* 21–26.

Steinman, G. (2006). Mechanisms of twinning: VII. Effect of diet and heredity on human twinning rate. *Journal of Reproductive Medicine, 51,* 405–410.

Stigler, S. M. (1999). *Statistics on the table: The history of statistical concepts and methods.* Cambridge, MA: Harvard University Press.

Strathman, A., Gleicher, F., Boninger, D. S., & Edwards, C. S. (1994). The consideration of future consequences: Weighing immediate and distant outcomes of behavior. *Journal of Personality and Social Psychology, 66,* 742–752.

Suicide Prevention Action Network. (2004). National Strategy for Suicide Prevention Benchmark Survey. Retrieved July 7, 2005, from http://www.spanusa.org.pdf/NSSP_Benchmark_ Survey_Results.pdf

Talarico, J. M., & Rubin, D. C. (2003). Confidence, not consistency, characterizes flashbulb memories. *Psychological Science, 14,* 455–461.

Taylor, G. M., & Ste. Marie, D. M. (2001). Eating disorders symptoms in Canadian female pair and dance figure skaters. *International Journal of Sports Psychology, 32,* 21–28.

the polling company, inc. (2006). Oprah named top choice for meetings we'd love to have, says Citrix GoToMeeting poll. Retrieved April 10, 2006, from http://www.pollingcompany.com/viewPage.asp?pid=134

Tierney, J. (2008a). Health halo can hide the calories. *New York Times.* Retrieved December 7, 2008, from http://www.nytimes.com/2008/12/02/science/02tier.html

Tierney, J. (2008b). The perils of "healthy" food. *New York Times.* Retrieved December 7, 2008, from http://tierneylab.blogs.nytimes.com/

Tucker, K. L., Morita, K., Qiao, N., Hannan, M. T., Cupples, A., & Kiel, D. P. (2006). Colas, but not other carbonated beverages, are associated with low bone mineral density in older women: The Framingham Osteoporosis Study. *American Journal of Clinical Nutrition, 84,* 936–942.

Tufte, E. R. (1997). *Visual explanations.* Cheshire, CT: Graphics Press.

Tufte, E. R. (2005). *Visual explanations* (2nd ed.) (original work published 1997). Cheshire, CT: Graphics Press.

Tufte, E. R. (2006). *The visual display of quantitative information* (2nd ed.) (original work published 2001). Cheshire, CT: Graphics Press.

Twenge, J. (2006). *Generation me: Why today's young Americans are more confident, assertive, entitled—and more miserable than ever before.* New York: Free Press.

Twenge, J., & Campbell, W. K. (2001). Age and birth cohort differences in self-esteem: A cross-temporal meta-analysis. *Personality and Social Psychology Review, 5,* 321–344.

Upton, P., & Eiser, C. (2006). School experiences after treatment for a brain tumour. *Child: Care, Health and Development, 32,* 9–17.

Vergin, R. C. (2000). Winning streaks in sports and the misperception of momentum. *Journal of Sports Behavior, 23,* 181–197.

Vinten-Johansen, P., Brody, H., Paneth, N., Rachman, S., & Rip, M. (2003). *Cholera, chloroform, and the science of medicine: A life of John Snow.* New York: Oxford University Press.

Walker, S. (2006). *Fantasyland: A season on baseball's lunatic fringe.* New York: Penguin.

Wansink, B., & van Ittersum, K. (2003). Bottoms up! The influence of elongation and pouring on consumption volume. *Journal of Consumer Research, 30,* 455–463.

Waters, A. (2006, February 24). Eating for credit. *New York Times.* Retrieved February 24, 2006, from http://www.nytimes.com

Weinberg, B. A., Fleisher, B. M., & Hashimoto, M. (2007). *Evaluating methods for evaluating instruction: The case of higher education* (National Bureau of Economic Research Working Paper No. 12844). Cambridge, MA: National Bureau of Economic Research.

White, M. (1997, July 12A). Toy rover sales soar into orbit: Mars landing puts gold shine back into space items. *Arizona Republic,* p. E1.

Wiley, J. (2005). A fair and balanced look at the news: What affects memory for controversial arguments. *Journal of Memory and Language, 53,* 95–109.

Wolff, A. (2002, January 26). Is the SI jinx for real? *Sports Illustrated.*

Wood, J. M., Nezworski, M. T., Lilienfeld, S. O., & Garb, H. N. (Eds.). (2003). *What's wrong with the Rorschach? Science confronts the controversial inkblot test.* San Francisco: Jossey-Bass.

World Health Organization. (2007). Myths and realities in disaster situations. Retrieved February 12, 2007, from http://www.who.int/hac/techguidance/ems/myths/en/index.html

Yanovski, J. A., Yanovski, S. Z., Sovik, K. N., Nouven, T. T., O'Neil, P. M., & Sebring, N. G. A prospective study of holiday weight gain. *New England Journal of Medicine, 23,* 861–867.

FORMULAS

CHAPTER 11 (Chapter 11 formulas continued from inside front cover)

Tukey *HSD* post-hoc test

$$HSD = \frac{(M_1 - M_2)}{s_M}, \text{ for any two sample means}$$

$$s_M = \sqrt{\frac{MS_{within}}{N}}, \text{ if equal sample sizes}$$

$$N' = \frac{N_{groups}}{\Sigma(1/N)}$$

$$s_M = \sqrt{\frac{MS_{within}}{N'}}, \text{ if unequal sample sizes}$$

One-Way Within-Groups ANOVA

$$df_{subjects} = n - 1$$

$$df_{within} = (df_{between})(df_{subjects})$$

$$df_{total} = df_{between} + df_{subjects} + df_{within}$$

$$SS_{subjects} = \Sigma(M_{participant} - GM)^2 \text{ for each score}$$

$$SS_{within} = SS_{total} - SS_{between} - SS_{subjects}$$

$$MS_{subjects} = \frac{SS_{subjects}}{df_{subjects}}$$

$$F_{subjects} = \frac{MS_{subjects}}{MS_{within}}$$

$$R^2 = \frac{SS_{between}}{(SS_{total} - SS_{subjects})}$$

CHAPTER 12

Two-Way Between-Groups ANOVA

$$df_{rows} = N_{rows} - 1$$

$$df_{columns} = N_{columns} - 1$$

$$df_{interaction} = (df_{rows})(df_{columns})$$

$$SS_{total} = \Sigma(X - GM)^2 \text{ for each score}$$

$$SS_{between(rows)} = \Sigma(M_{row} - GM)^2 \text{ for each score}$$

$$SS_{between(columns)} = \Sigma(M_{column} - GM)^2 \text{ for each score}$$

$$SS_{within} = \Sigma(X - M_{cell})^2 \text{ for each score}$$

$$SS_{between(interaction)} = SS_{total} - (SS_{between(rows)} + SS_{between(columns)} + SS_{within})$$

$$R^2_{rows} = \frac{SS_{rows}}{(SS_{total} - SS_{columns} - SS_{interaction})}$$

$$R^2_{columns} = \frac{SS_{columns}}{(SS_{total} - SS_{rows} - SS_{interaction})}$$

$$R^2_{interaction} = \frac{SS_{interaction}}{(SS_{total} - SS_{rows} - SS_{columns})}$$